COMPARATIVE LAW

This innovative, refreshing, and reader-friendly book is aimed at enabling students to familiarise themselves with the challenges and controversies found in comparative law. At present there is no book which clearly explains the contemporary debates and methodological innovations found in modern comparative law. This book fills that gap in teaching at undergraduate level, and for post-graduates will be a starting point for further reading and discussion.

Among the topics covered are: globalisation, legal culture, comparative law and diversity, economic approaches, competition between legal systems, legal families and mixed systems, beyond Europe, convergence and a new *ius commune*, comparative commercial law, comparative family law, the 'common core' and the 'better law' approaches, comparative administrative law, comparative studies in constitutional contexts, comparative law for international criminal justice, judicial comparativism in human rights, comparative law in law reform, comparative law in the courts and a comparative law research project.

The individual chapters can also be read as stand-alone contributions and are written by experts such as Masha Antokolskaia, John Bell, Roger Cotterrell, Sjef van Erp, Nicholas Foster, Patrick Glenn, Andrew Harding, Peter Leyland, Christopher McCrudden, Werner Menski, David Nelken, Anthony Ogus, Esin Örücü, Paul Roberts, Jan Smits and William Twining. Each chapter begins with a description of key concepts and includes questions for discussion and reading lists to aid further study.

Traditional topics of private law, such as contracts, obligations and unjustified enrichment are omitted as they are amply covered in other comparative law books, but developments in other areas of private law, such as family law, are included as being of current interest.

Comparative Law

A Handbook

Edited by

Esin Örücü
and
David Nelken

·HART·
PUBLISHING

OXFORD AND PORTLAND, OREGON
2007

Published in North America (US and Canada) by
Hart Publishing
c/o International Specialized Book Services
920 NE 58th Avenue, Suite 300
Portland, OR 97213-3786
USA
Tel: +1 503 287 3093 or toll-free: (1) 800 944 6190
Fax: +1 503 280 8832
E-mail: orders@isbs.com
Website: www.isbs.com

Hart Publishing, 16C Worcester Place, OX1 2JW
Telephone: +44 (0)1865 517530 Fax: +44 (0)1865 510710
E-mail: mail@hartpub.co.uk
Website: http://www.hartpub.co.uk

British Library Cataloguing in Publication Data
Data Available

ISBN-13: 978-1-84113-596-0 (paperback)

Typeset by Compuscript Ltd, Shannon
Printed and bound in Great Britain by
TJ International Ltd, Padstow, Cornwall

Preface

Comparative law has often been criticised for lacking in theory, Euro-centric, and black-letter-law and private law oriented. The purpose of this Handbook is to familiarise students with both classical and new material, and with the current and controversial issues of comparative law and comparative legal studies. At present, there is no textbook in the English language on contemporary issues of comparative law or comparative legal studies. Traditional introductory books first cover the aims, purposes, uses and methodology of comparative law, after which students are introduced to the major legal systems and prominent 'legal families'. The substantive law dealt with is private law; the traditional area in which comparatists have hitherto worked. Times have changed. Other topics are of crucial importance today.

Our purpose is to fill this gap in comparative law teaching and study. The Handbook is envisaged for use by undergraduates but will also be of use to postgraduate students for whom it will provide starting points for further discussion. At a basic level it will encourage readers to ask questions and at a later stage, when they have covered the essential groundwork, lead them on to question what they have learnt. Students are introduced to each topic through the work of experts in their fields.

Commencing with a general introduction to comparative law and comparative legal studies, and a critical overview with a detailed signalling system binding the book together, the Handbook moves on to contemporary and burgeoning areas of comparative law. This treatment enables the reader to discuss current relevant debates and issues such as convergence/non-convergence, law in context (culture and economics), cultural distinctiveness, globalism versus localism, systems in transition, the use of comparative law by judges and the role of comparative law in law reform activities and harmonisation, public law comparisons in both constitutional law and administrative law, a new common law in human rights, the 'common core' and the 'better law' approaches, comparative criminal law, commercial law and family law, and comparative law looking beyond the Western world.

Other topics such as comparative environmental law, e-commerce, Alternative Dispute Resolution, bio-ethics or food safety could have been included, but choices had to be made. We selected some topics which have been either hitherto neglected or which do not appear in any standard comparative law textbook. Traditional topics of private law, such as contracts, obligations, unjustified enrichment and tort (delict) are deliberately omitted as these have been amply covered in comparative law textbooks. No direct information is given concerning different jurisdictions either. Since a number of books are readily available covering such jurisdictions, it is more appropriate to leave the choice to individual lecturers.

By using this innovative Handbook, which is reader-friendly both in the topics covered and the way the topics are treated, readers will be placed firmly in the contemporary picture. They will be able both to discuss critically the traditional areas and to access current issues presented by experts.

Each chapter starts with a paragraph on key concepts (glossary) and ends with a list of questions for discussion. There are suggestions for further reading attached to each chapter for those who may wish to write essays on a particular topic. There are diagrams and tables wherever necessary. Each chapter highlights website connections. Links to university web pages, course outlines and reading lists, Comparative Law Forums, such as that of the University of Oxford, and electronic journals, such as the *Electronic Journal of Comparative Law*, are included.

The Editors

Contents

List of Contributors

Masha Antokolskaia is Professor of Private Law of the Vrije Universiteit Amsterdam, The Netherlands.
M.V.Antokolskaia@rechten.vu.nl

John Bell is Professor of Law at the University of Cambridge, UK.
Jsb48@cam.ac.uk

Sjep van Erp is Professor of civil law and European private law, Maastricht University; President of the Netherlands Comparative Law Association; Editor-in-Chief of the *Electronic Journal of Comparative Law*; and Deputy-Justice Court of Appeals Hertogenbosch, The Netherlands.
S.vanErp@PR.unimaas.nl

Roger Cotterrell is Anniversary Professor of Legal Theory at Queen Mary, University of London; and a Fellow of the British Academy, UK.
R.B.M.Cotterrell@qmul.ac.uk

Nicholas HD Foster is a lecturer at the School of Law, School of Oriental and African Studies, University of London, UK; and Editor of the *Journal of Comparative Law*.
Nf4@soas.ac.uk

Andrew Harding is Professor of Asia-Pacific Legal Relations at the University of Victoria, BC, Canada.
harding@uvic.ca

Peter Leyland is Professor of Law at London Metropolitan University, UK.
p.Leyland@londonmet.ac.uk

H Patrick Glenn is Peter M Laing Professor of Law, Faculty of Law and Institute of Comparative Law, McGill University, Montreal, Canada.
h.glenn@staff.mcgill.ca

Christopher McCrudden is Professor of Human Rights Law, University of Oxford, UK.
Christopher.mccrudden@law.ox.ac.uk

Werner Menski is Professor of South Asian Laws, School of Law, School of Oriental and African Studies, University of London, UK.
Wm4@soas.ac.uk

David Nelken is Distinguished Professor of Legal Institutions and Social Change at the University of Macerata, Italy; Distinguished Research Professor of Law, University of Wales, Cardiff, UK; and Visiting Professor of Law at the London School of Economics, UK.
Sen4144@iperbole.bologna.it

Anthony Ogus is Professor of Law, University of Manchester, UK; and Research Professor, University of Maastricht, The Netherlands.
Anthony.Ogus@man.ac.uk

Esin Örücü is Professorial Research Fellow and Professor Emerita of Comparative Law, University of Glasgow, UK; Professor Emerita of Comparative Law, Erasmus Universiteit, Rotterdam, The Netherlands; Visiting Professor of Comparative Law at Yeditepe University, Istanbul, Turkey; and Member of the International Academy of Comparative Law.
e.orucu@law.gla.ac.uk

Paul Roberts is Professor of Criminal Jurisprudence in the University of Nottingham School of Law, UK; Editor of the *International Journal of Evidence and Proof*; and Convenor of Nottingham's LLM in International Criminal Justice and Armed Conflict.
Paul.Roberts@nottingham.ac.uk

Jan M Smits is Professor of European Private Law, Maastricht University, The Netherlands.
Jm.Smits@PR.unimaas.nl

William Twining is Quain Professor of Jurisprudence Emeritus, University College London, UK; and Visiting Professor, University of Miami School of Law, USA.
wlt@wtwining.fsnet.co.uk

I

Comparative Law at a Cross-roads

1

Comparative Law and Comparative Legal Studies

DAVID NELKEN

KEY CONCEPTS

Aims of comparative law; First order and second order enquiries; Multidisciplinary and interdisciplinary study; Law in context; Context in law; Similarities and differences; Practices.

I. INTRODUCTION

WHAT IS HAPPENING to comparative law? Not so long ago it could be said that

colleagues are not interested in foreign law; students are ethnocentric boors; the bar consists of monolingual hicks; deans won't finance foreign travel, nobody will take Comparative Law (Örücü 2004: 215).

But, amidst the current processes of borrowing, imitation and imposition of law and increasing global interdependence (both desired and undesired), comparative law is truly coming into its own. There are still scholars who see the main purpose of the subject as ultimately a practical one, for example as a way of encouraging judges to learn about solutions found in other jurisdictions to problems in tort, contract or other legal areas. Similarly, with an eye on the legislator, there are important collective projects looking for a 'common core' of private law, or seeking to promote legal harmonisation in the European Union. On the other hand, other scholars argue that we need to go beyond such traditional pursuits and reach towards what has been called comparative legal studies (Legrand and Munday, 2003). New journals are being founded (for example, in the United Kingdom, the *International Journal of Law in Context* and the *Journal of Comparative Law*), and path-breaking monographs, such as Patrick Glenn's ambitious study of seven different legal traditions (Glenn, 2000/2004), are stimulating interest and controversy.[1] So the subject finds itself at something of a cross-roads. Jaakko Husa puts it this way:

---

[1] For pedagogic reasons we have had to limit the handbook to work published in English. However, it is important to say in a book about comparative law that foreign legal and academic cultures and

as regards the future of the discipline, we seem to have many incompatible directions and goals instead of one. Professional comparative law and academic comparative law are living together in an uneasy relationship buried under the European integration debate (Husa, 2005:1).

The main point of this Handbook is therefore to offer some signposts for students coming to this important and fascinating but also difficult subject. To this end the volume contains discussions of both theory and substantive areas, and the contributors include distinguished legal and social theorists as well as leading specialists in comparative law. A wide variety of theoretical positions are represented, and some of the standpoints which we have not managed to include, such as the 'neo-romantic turn' (Whitman, 2003a), or post-modern theorising (Frankenberg, 2006a), are discussed by other contributors in their chapters, and referred to in this introduction. But we make no pretence to have covered everything,[2] and there is no substitute for reading writers in their own words. As regards substantive topics, we have succeeded in providing coverage not only of traditional private law topics[3] but also of public law matters, including comparative constitutionalism, and of the increasingly important types of transnational legal processes such as international criminal law and human rights law. But illustrations of more social or socio-technical types of problem-oriented law, such as labour law, immigration law, telecommunications law and environmental law, would also have been instructive. There are also no chapters dealing with the growing role of lawyers and other professionals in forging international standards and mediating transnational disputes. On the other hand, no one book could do justice to the full range of recent contributions to this exploding discipline. Indeed, part of the reason for having a review such as this is to unsettle the normal contents of what would be thought appropriate for a handbook of comparative law.

II. AN OVERVIEW OF THE HANDBOOK

The first part of this volume contains introductory chapters by each of the co-editors of the Handbook. In the first chapter I shall try to bring out some of the common themes that are illuminated when the various contributions to the book are put together. After offering a summary of the other chapters, I then seek to

---

traditions all have distinctive contributions which have often not been translated (and are sometimes not easy to translate). In Italy, for example, whilst many of the scholars in the major comparative law 'school' founded by Rudolfo Sacco publish also in English, some of the most brilliant discussions of transnational legal processes are only be found in still untranslated works such as those by Natalino Irti and Maria Rosaria Ferrarese.

[2] The authors were recruited through the excellent networks of Esin Örücü, who conceived the idea for this Handbook.

[3] This is not to deny that studying private law in Europe still has great potential for producing intellectual surprises. Apart from the regular rewriting of the overlapping history of the common and civil law worlds, European scholars are particularly well placed to bring out differences in these contrasting systems which they can get to know in some depth. See, eg Van Hoecke, 2002, or the prolific work of Pierre Legrand.

show their relevance to understanding the relationship between 'comparative law' and 'comparative legal studies'. In a section called 'Going beyond', I discuss the different directions opening up for comparative law, and then go on to comment on what is involved by seeking to add 'context'. I follow this with a consideration of the vexed problem of similarities and differences, and end with a discussion of comparative law in practice. As will be seen, although these issues are considered separately for clarity of exposition they are also closely intertwined with each other. This chapter is probably best read first lightly as a preface, and again, more carefully, as an afterword, once the later chapters have been studied. The questions at the end are intended to assist in generating discussion of the different approaches and topics dealt with in this Handbook as a whole.

The second of our two introductory chapters, entitled 'Developing Comparative Law', is contributed by Esin Örücü. It sets out to provide a brief survey of the 'state of the art' of the discipline similar to that found in the introductory parts of comparative law courses. Örücü highlights the changing nature of comparative law and discusses issues related to 'intra-cultural and cross-cultural comparison', the definition, uses and purposes of comparative law, macro and micro comparisons and other aspects of its methodology. She reflects on the questions 'What to compare?' and 'How to compare? the two starting points of comparative law and reviews functional, factual and 'law in context' approaches. She also offers an outline of recent debates over the role of comparative law, which she sees as encompassing objectives as varied as aiding law reform and policy developments, providing a tool of research to reach a universal theory of law, giving a critical perspective to students, aiding international law practice, facilitating international unification and harmonisation of laws, helping courts to fill gaps in the law and even working towards the furthering of world peace and tolerance.

The second section of the handbook, entitled 'New Directions for Comparative Research', is that which groups together those chapters dealing with some of the theoretical challenges that are currently facing comparative law. The first chapter, 'Globalisation and Comparative Law' by William Twining, provides a vivid picture of what is probably the most significant of these challenges, namely, how to understand the role of law in the trends, processes and interactions which are making different parts of the world more interdependent in so many complex ways. Twining puts forward a forthright manifesto for moving to a broader agenda of comparative legal studies rather than continuing with 'business as usual'. Comparative law, he argues, lacks adequate analytic concepts and reliable data for giving general accounts of law in the world that comprehend the transnationalisation of law and legal relations which, to a greater or lesser extent, by-pass the state. Whilst warning that the term globalisation can be misused, Twining nonetheless recommends a global perspective capable of doing justice to the diversity of forms of normative and legal ordering, such as the Internet, religious diasporas, networks of NGOs, or the many internal and external relations of large corporations that co-exist in the same time-space context. As well as criticising the narrow focus on European private law of much comparative law, the chapter also raises a series of questions about the relationship between comparative law and other research traditions such as that represented by subject area experts or scholars studying the 'bottom-up' activities of counter-hegemonic social movements.

In his chapter called 'Com-paring', Patrick Glenn argues that Western legal theory has been founded on an epistemology of conflict, based on the twin ideas of separation and reification of human groups. As against this he suggests that thinking in terms of legal traditions allows for an epistemology of conciliation based on multivalent logic and the tolerance of diversity. Legal systems are:

> best conceptualised as instantiations of a particular legal tradition. As such, they are conceptually equal to, and on a par with, other legal traditions, which all exist as self-conscious bodies of legal information, sustained over considerable periods of time.

As the source of normative information, traditions do not have clear boundaries but instead overlap. Rather than presuming a radical separation between laws we should look for a 'logic of fuzziness' because in the real world boundaries are never sharp. He suggests that transnational lawyering and international commercial law provide evidence that legal systems are not separate. He also argues that his approach is one well suited to recognising the continuing importance of religious laws and to reminding us of the lost history of the relationship between 'common laws' and local laws.

The chapter on 'Defining and Using Legal Culture' by David Nelken deals with the ways in which the term 'legal culture' is defined by comparatists and employed in their research projects. He focuses in particular on the way this key concept allows us to bring out the interconnections between law, society and culture. After distinguishing between legal and social scientific uses of the term, Nelken comments on criticisms of the idea of legal culture and of the polysemic concept of culture itself. He then examines some of the main difficulties of using this term in explanatory enquiries: What 'units' of legal culture other than national jurisdictions need to be borne in mind? What gives coherence to the different units? Must such units exist for social actors themselves or is it enough for them to be present for the observer? In using culture or legal culture as an explanation how can the risk of circular and tautological arguments be avoided? Nelken ends by considering the possibility of cultural bias in the ways in which we think about legal culture.

In the subsequent chapter, 'Is it so Bad to be Different: Comparative Law and the Appreciation of Diversity', Roger Cotterrell explores the general conceptual issue of looking for similarities and differences between laws and legal systems. He notes that the concern with harmonisation and convergence can be seen as the continuation of a project of seeking underlying universal principles in law, whilst the concern for difference can be linked to the valuing of diversity. He counterpoises functional and cultural approaches to law and argues that it may be unsafe to identify functions without asking whether local values, traditions or sentiments 'differently colour the definition of those functions, the importance attached to them and the tests of their successful fulfilment'. Cotterrell then introduces an analogy between the concern for difference in comparative law and debates about assimilation and multi-culturalism. He ends by praising recent work which takes a broad approach to explaining cross-cultural differences in values.

The contribution from Anthony Ogus is called 'The Economic Approach: Competition between Legal Systems'. Ogus argues that legal frameworks have an enormous impact on economies and the pursuit of economic growth can also help to explain legal developments and the relationship between developments in different legal systems. He suggests that comparative lawyers could find it useful to think in terms of allocative efficiency and to reason in terms of costs and benefits. The chapter seeks to substantiate the following propositions: Common law systems may have features which have been particularly conducive to economic growth; competition between legal systems occurs particularly where there is freedom of choice as to the applicable legal regime; competition between legal systems tends to influence a convergence of legal principles in areas of facilitative law; practising lawyers may be expected to oppose reforms including proposals for convergence of legal systems which will reduce the demand for their services; and, finally, an economic interpretation of 'legal culture' suggests that it is a 'network' which may reduce the costs of communication between those using the legal system, but, on the other hand, its characteristics may also be exploited by practising lawyers to resist competition. Ogus also suggests that 'hybrid' legal systems may benefit from the competition of legal cultures inherent within one jurisdiction. He ends by indicating the features of English common law which may have been particularly favourable to economic growth.

The starting point of chapter eight, 'A General View of Legal Families and of Mixing Systems' by Esin Örücü, is that the current approach to classification of legal systems is too Euro-centric and is too much shaped by thinking only about legal rules, especially those of private law. She argues that all legal systems are overlaps and, to a greater or lesser degree, mixed. Legal systems of places such as Malta, Hong Kong, Malaysia, Thailand and Turkey are given as examples of certain types of mixes. But the author also challenges the view that the classical 'mixed jurisdictions' are the only mixed systems that should be given pride of place. It is important also to study ongoing mixes that result from encounters, overlaps and combinations. These processes account for the birth of legal systems just as 'contamination' accounts for legal change. These assumptions lead the author to challenge the established classification of legal families and suggest that legal systems should rather be seen as lying along a spectrum. A number of theories are put forward to explain the similarities and differences between legal systems such as the 'tree model', the 'wave theory', and 'transposition'. For Örücü, the point of looking for new metaphors is to deconstruct the conventionally labelled pattern of legal systems and to reconstruct them with regard to origins, relationships, overlaps and inter-relationships, and diverse 'fertilisers' such as the social and cultural context, and the 'grafting' and 'pruning' used in their development.

Towards the end of chapter eight Örücü quotes approvingly the assertion by Andrew Harding that the idea of legal families tells us nothing about legal systems except as to their general style and method, and the idea makes no sense whatsoever amid the nomic din of South East Asia.

The same point is well illustrated in Werner Menski's contribution, 'Beyond Europe' (chapter nine). Menski argues that, for historical reasons, Asian, African and other non-Western legal systems are inherently more attuned than Western legal systems to the intellectual and practical challenges of comparative law and legal pluralism. Practitioners and scholars in these places are acutely conscious of the dynamic nature of legal systems as constantly renegotiated entities that can be manipulated in many ways to achieve desired outcomes. They are likewise more aware of the continuing importance of religion and custom even in modern conditions. Menski shows how Hindu law, Islamic law and other legal systems co-exist within a national legal regime, and all contribute to a culture-specific, composite national identity unique to a particular country. He ends by providing an extended description of how the Indian Supreme court was able to bring Muslim personal law into line with the majority law and the secular 'lead model' in India. The way this was achieved, he suggests, may serve as a model for other nations in terms of coping with diversity and difference.

The third and longest section of the Handbook provides illustrations of more substantive discussions of comparative law.[4] Though it includes relatively uncharted topics it begins by re-examining that most mainstream of issues, the degree of actual or ideal convergence of private law in Europe. In his chapter 'Convergence of Private Law in Europe: Towards a new *ius commune?*' Jan Smits asks: Is there a need for unification of private law in Europe? How does it take place? Is it possible? What methods can be used to make private law more uniform? Smits notes that across Europe there are four types of civil code and that these are interpreted differently in all its many different jurisdictions. He comments critically on current processes towards greater harmonisation through international conventions and European Union Directives saying that these do not make a coherent whole, are difficult to monitor and have unpredictable effects. He then asks how it might be possible to do better. As positive reasons for moving towards unification Smits points to the development of the common market and the need for a symbol of European unity. But he also acknowledges that there are virtues in diversity, as this may be a reflection of economic or cultural preferences and can stimulate competition and innovation. He therefore proposes what he calls a 'bottom up' approach to harmonisation, which involves the enhancement of European legal science and education, the drafting of principles of European law and encouraging competition amongst legal systems.

The theme of harmonisation is taken up again in the subsequent chapter 'Comparative Family Law: Moving with the Times?' (chapter eleven) by Masha

---

[4] While such a division is useful for expository purposes we are not proposing that a hard and fast line can or should be drawn between the more theoretical and more substantive parts of the Handbook.

Antokolskaia. Unlike that of Smits, this chapter reflects the conviction that, at least in this field, some form of top-down harmonisation is both necessary, and is already succeeding. Antokolskaia shows us that traditional norms in Western Europe have been undergoing similar transformations due in part to changes in the economy, especially those leading to more women working and the later socialisation of youth, and also due to pressures of political action in favour of women's rights. She details the general trends in family law in Europe in the last decades, such as the acceptance of the right to marry as a fundament human right, the diminishment of marriage impediments, the lowering of the age of capacity to marry, and the granting of equal legal rights to spouses. She also describes the role played in these developments both by the European Court of Human rights and by groups of family law scholars. While acknowledging that differences remain, she argues in favour of comparative lawyers seeking to produce 'better law'-type recommendations to legislators.

Antokolskaia's account of common trends and principles in family law provides evidence against the common claim that family law is particularly unsuited to harmonisation because it is so linked to historical and cultural specificities. In his chapter on 'Comparative Commercial Law: Rules or Context?' (chapter twelve) on the other hand, Nicholas Foster seeks to make the opposite argument. He emphasises the importance of legal culture, which allows us to move beyond what he calls the common 'instrumentalist' view of commercial law that assumes it to be a culturally neutral technical subject. In a wide-ranging chapter he first sets the background to current developments in commercial law in a globalising world. He goes on to stress how historically-shaped differences in attitudes to commerce still affect legal decision-making even in countries which otherwise have a good deal else in common such as France, the UK and Denmark. Foster also discusses the extent to which differences in legal culture prevent the successful transplanting of commercial law, and reminds us that legal agreements and conventions may often be applied differently in practice from place to place. He does concede, however, that

> where the group of people practising and using the law is quite homogenous (as in international financial law), the broader context may not be of great importance.

The two chapters that follow both have to do with public law. In his chapter on 'Administrative Law in a Comparative Context' (chapter thirteen) John Bell offers a careful comparison of English, French and German law so as to explore the differences within and between common law and civil law approaches. He asks: What does each system include within its conception of 'administrative law'? Who is governed by 'administrative law'? In particular, how are the rules of public law separated from those of private law? What powers does 'the administration' have? What procedures does the administration need to adopt when making decisions? Who provides remedies against the administration? What judicial control is exercised over misuse of powers? When is the administration liable for its actions and how is this liability different from that of a private individual? In responding to these questions Bell describes the different but overlapping understandings of the idea of the 'rule of law', discretionary decisions, the liability of the administration, and the difference between explicit or assumed powers. He also offers illustrations of the practical consequences implied by different answers to these questions with respect, for example, to the way the welfare state mission affects the use of government powers or explaining why either nationalised railways or a national health service can be more or less difficult to privatise in different jurisdictions.

The next chapter by Andrew Harding and Peter Leyland, 'Comparative Law in Constitutional Contexts' (chapter fourteen), focuses on comparing constitutions around the world. It begins by pointing out that constitutions, which seem similar in form, can have different functions, and that what is important in comparing constitutions is to see how they are interpreted, lived with and changed over time. The authors make a distinction between constitutions and 'the culture of constitutionalism'; it is the latter, by shaping political behaviour, that makes effective constitutions possible, rather than vice versa. They therefore warn against thinking that good constitutional design can be a substitute for the exercise of political power with integrity and self-imposed restraint. Harding and Leyland set out an analysis of the functions that constitutions are usually intended to perform as regards the definition of institutional powers, and how they establish lines and schemes of accountability. They also offer a short historical account of four different waves of constitution-making, from the American Declaration of Independence to the constitution-making of former communist states. They underline the contribution that comparative lawyers can make to the drafting of international treaties, and argue that the move towards 'world constitutionalism' must embrace the increasingly important role of international organisations.

Harding and Leyland make some reference to the role of constitutional litigation in human rights cases. But the protection of rights is absolutely central to the two subsequent chapters by Paul Roberts and Christopher McCrudden (chapters fifteen and sixteen). In 'Comparative Law for International Criminal Justice' Paul Roberts argues that comparative law has an indispensable contribution to make to the study of this fast-changing subject. He proposes that we think of it in terms of seven concentric circles. These encompass topics that range from the legal rules and procedures that define international crimes to the institutions which implement and develop such rules, and from the role of international tribunals today as compared to the past, to the difference between permanent and ad hoc hybrid tribunals. He suggests that transnational criminal law, broadly conceived, includes scholars' and researchers' contributions to this interdisciplinary project. Roberts then sets out six ways in which comparative law is relevant to the subject as he has charted it. He concludes that

> [w]ith mounting pressures for closer legal co-operation between Member States to combat fraud, illegal immigration, people trafficking, drug smuggling, cross-border arms running, and—above all—international terrorism, the impetus towards integration and harmonisation of Member States' domestic laws is bound to intensify.

McCrudden's chapter, 'Judicial Comparativism and Human rights' (chapter seventeen), also has to do with studying the spread of types of law and legal institutions that inherently transcend borders. If human rights law is essentially universalistic in its purported reach, comparative law can be useful to human rights theorists in showing how far values are in fact universally shared in practice. McCrudden argues that courts play an impressive role in the creation of a common law of human rights. In an effort to clarify the appropriate relationship between human rights interpretation and comparative legal methods, he offers a discussion of how courts analyse human rights, how they think about the role and function of the comparative method, and the continuing debate about the legitimacy of judicial decision-making.

McCrudden points to tensions in the relationship between comparative law and human rights such as the competition between relativism and universalism, functionalism and interpretavism, the need for judicial review and the counter-majoritarian objection. As an illustration of the issues that arise in the use by judges of comparisons in human rights, he offers a detailed account of recent discussions in the United States Supreme Court of the constitutionality of aspects of the death penalty and the criminalisation of sodomy between consenting adults. Describing the different arguments of the Supreme Court justices he concludes that reference to foreign judgments may be more justified in the area of human rights than in many other areas of law because their development can be seen as part of an ongoing conversation that transcends national jurisprudence.

The final chapters all deal squarely with practical aspects of comparative law. In his chapter, 'Comparative Private Law in Practice: The Process of Law Reform' (chapter seventeen), Sjef van Erp offers us valuable insights from the perspective of an academic who is also a practitioner engaged in giving advice in foreign jurisdictions. He stresses above all the need for a pragmatic attitude. A law reform project, he argues, demands a different approach from that of an in-depth academic article. One has to be realistic and recognise that advice given will not always function well in practice or even be applied at all in the receiving country. It helps if the expert really is an expert, if she has socio-cultural, economic and political awareness as well as legal competence, if she comes from a similar legal tradition and if reference can also be made to wider developments such as the working out of common principles of contract law. Personal integrity is vital, so that the advice is seen as objective information rather than reflecting national interest (so it can be useful if one is from a smaller country such as The Netherlands). Conversely, there can be problems if the funder of a project is tempted to interfere, for example when an institution from a common law country funds a civil law expert. Van Erp mentions some of the situations in which comparative lawyers may be asked to provide advice. He suggests that one has to accept that there are times when one has to step back and leave it to the receiving country to make its own political decisions.

The next chapter, Esin Örücü's 'Comparative Law in Practice: The Court and the Legislator' (chapter eighteen) deals with the subject of when references are made to other legal systems, (a question that is also discussed in McCrudden's comments on courts and van Erp's on legislative reform). Örücü argues that even when judges are convinced that applying their own national laws would offend their sense of justice they nonetheless are reluctant to give the impression that they have used foreign law to plug gaps in their own systems. On the basis of research projects studying the citation of foreign judgments in the UK over the last 30 years, the author shows that regular resort to foreign law occurs mainly in cases where foreign law is itself involved in the legal dispute as well as those that involve international conventions and transnational regulations. She explains some of the different ways in which foreign materials may be (and should be) used, and distinguishes between 'functional' and 'ornamental' citations. She ends by explaining some of the outstanding issues facing judges who wish to use foreign materials.

The final chapter, 'A Project: Comparative Law in Action' (chapter nineteen), by the same author, is directed to those who are new to comparative law and who would like to carry out empirical research but are worried by their lack of social scientific qualifications. Örücü's message is that even relatively unsophisticated methods of gathering data represent an essential supplement to relying on court reports and other documents. She first discusses the central role played by questionnaires about real or hypothetical cases in gathering information about foreign law. She then goes on to describe an early interdisciplinary effort to find out about the level of use of European law by Scottish and Dutch lawyers and their attitudes towards using it. The hypothesis of the research project that Dutch lawyers were more likely than Scottish ones to engage in European litigation and that this was linked to their more favourable attitudes to European lawwere both supported. Örücü suggests that even a basic research exercise of this kind could prove its worth as a way of exploring what use lawyers in the new accession countries will likely make of European Union law.

III. GETTING BEYOND

What idea of comparative law emerges from these chapters? Does it have a proper subject-matter, or is it no more than a method? As we would expect, the aims of the subject will shape the way it is conceived. It will vary depending on whether the goal is that of finding out relevant legal rules in another jurisdiction, understanding another society (and, by contrast, one's own society) through its law, searching for commonalities, or showing the difficulty of translating the texts and experience of other people's law. But, as suggested at the outset of this chapter, much current controversy surrounds the priority that comparative law should give to practical tasks. In a recent overview of the subject, which she characterised as enigmatic, Örücü suggested that its identity can best be understood as pulled between two alternatives. One approach treats comparative law as 'an autonomous branch of social science or science of legal knowledge', as 'a high level analytical subject' and 'an end in itself'. The second is more sceptical about comparison as an activity in its own right and more interested in comparing rules and institutions for the practical purposes of adjudication and law reform. (Örücü, 2004; and Nelken, 2006d). These competing perspectives can be loosely linked, as we shall see, to other contrasts such as that between marginal and mainstream work, liberal and critical stances, and modernist and post-modernist epistemologies. It is over this terrain that a territorial war between comparative law and comparative legal studies is being fought.

We can point to examples in this Handbook of both the approaches that Örücü distinguishes. To these we could add a further approach, however, in which comparative law is seen as a 'second-order' type of investigation (an enquiry into the way other people make their enquiries). The point of comparative law is taken to be to make the best sense possible of the comparative work undertaken by other social actors such as judges, legislators, lawyers and others. Arguably, this approach could also help us to bring out the best in the other two approaches by inviting us *to develop theories about other people's practices*, exposing the variation amongst different groups of actors, in different places—and at different times—as they identify the salient features of other people's legal systems. This approach also extends reflexively to analysing the way comparative law evolves as a discipline, as well as the actions and writings of single authors, as these change over time.

This last approach to comparative law should not be assumed to be in competition with the others. In this volume, for example, many of the authors, whatever else they discuss, *also* engage in analyses of how judges or other comparative law scholars carry out their exercises in comparison. There is even, though to a lesser extent, some consideration given to the important question of how different role requirements and social conditions help to condition such exercises. It follows that the readers of these essays will also be doing comparative law when seeking to interpret the approach to comparative enquiry represented by the various contributions to this Handbook.

But where will all this get us? Certainly there is no lack of ambition in claims being made for what it is that comparative law can achieve. And this contrasts strangely with the more modest claims currently being made for their work by the social scientists or humanist scholars, who are seen as the potential allies of those who advocate a move from comparative law to comparative legal studies. The introduction to the Utrecht Congress of the International Academy of Comparative Law in 2006, for example, announced:

[W]e look over the fence of our neighbour in pursuit of the common fate: to identify and grasp the human nature; indeed, to share the human destiny and to unite the human forces.[5]

Many of the authors in this volume also aim high—even if not quite so high. According to Patrick Glenn, 'the com-paring of laws is fundamental in the

---

[5] Opening address at the XVIIIth Congress of the International Academy of Comparative Law, 16–22 July 2006 at Utrecht by Professor Konstantinos Kerameus, President.

process of globalisation and in the pursuit of peaceful relations between peoples'
(Glenn: 93). Likewise, Paul Roberts argues that comparative law can be used to
demonstrate

> that *there is something that can be done* by the international community in response
> to genocide, crimes against humanity and other massive, state-sponsored violations
> of fundamental human rights during civil wars or by tyrannical governments abusing
> their own people. Almost irrespective of the merits and generalisability of the Tribunals'
> activities, the practical enforcement of international criminal law can no longer be dis-
> missed peremptorily, as the fantasy of idealists (Roberts: 346).

According to Harding and Leyland,

> comparative law offers the law student a whole new dimension: from it he can learn to
> respect the special legal cultures of other people, he will understand his own law better,
> he can develop critical standards which might lead to its improvement, and he will learn
> how rules of law are conditioned by social facts and what different forms they can take
> (Harding and Leyland: 332).

As far as their own chapter is specifically concerned, they argue that comparative
study of constitutions can help bring about 'good governance and global justice, [and] go some way towards correcting the often oppressive and sometimes
incompetent behaviour of governments.' The alternative does not bear thinking
about; 'the price of failure is an increased chance of conflict, poverty and fragmentation affecting everyone.' But could we be asking too much of comparative law?
Even Harding and Leyland admit, regarding comparative constitutionalism, that
'this subject has little history, less theory and relatively few pieces of outstanding
literature'. As far as seeking to bring about 'global justice' is concerned, recent
attempts to do so have made it even harder to tell when indifference or interference is the greater evil.

Manifestos apart, the papers actually delivered at the recent Conference in
Utrecht reveal the familiar bias towards more modest policy-oriented type of work.
A few theoretical papers dealt with what is involved in doing comparative law;
some contributions described developments in the law itself, as seen in titles such
as 'pure economic loss' or 'new developments in succession law'. There were a good
number of presentations comparing legal institutions, such as 'the constitutional
guarantees of the judiciary'; 'the civil, criminal and disciplinary liability of judges';
'plea-bargaining, negotiating confessions and consensual resolution of criminal
cases'; 'new experiences of international arbitration with special emphasis on legal
debates between parties from Western Europe and Central and Eastern Europe';
and 'the constitutional referendum'. The large majority of papers, however, focused
on legal-policy issues with cross-national implications: these included 'the digi-
tisation of literary and musical realisations'; 'cross-border mergers in Europe';
'tensions between legal, biological and social conceptions of parentage'; 'legal
limitations on genetic research and the commercialisation of its results'; 'the fight
against organised crime'; the "polluter pays" principle'; 'abusive advertising on the
internet'; 'euthanasia control'; and 'the responsibility of rating agencies'.

There is no doubt that at least some of these topics have to do with serious (even global?) social problems. But it remains uncertain how far comparative law will help us find the 'solution' to such problems any more than domestic law does for similar domestic problems. Not a few of these 'problems' are closely intertwined with otherwise valued features of national or international society rather than being a simple matter of a conflict between the forces of good and evil. And the answers which would find favour in richer, secular Western countries may often not be the same as those that would be acceptable or appropriate in poorer and more religion-centred societies. Most importantly, it cannot be taken for granted that (more) law is always the answer to such problems. At the least we may suspect that the lack of theoretical papers at the conference meant that these issues were not fully addressed.

Can this volume help us do better? Is the way forward to develop a comparative legal studies—so as to be in a better position to fulfil such projects of socio-legal engineering or alternatively learn to reduce our ambitions? Or could there be something lost as well as gained in going in such a direction—not so much because it makes comparative law less 'practical' but because the subject risks losing its sense of coherence? It is fair to say that all the chapters in this handbook do try to go 'beyond' the existing literature so as to move us in new directions and towards new territories. But our authors do not all speak with one voice about this or other matters. Nor did we expect them too. Hence, they do not all recommend going in the same direction. For example, for some, such as Masha Antokolskaia and Nicholas Foster, the way forward involves looking 'beyond' legal rules so as to encompass the background of social and economic trends. For others, the focus of scholarly work must be more to overcome what Esin Örücü refers to as 'the myth of legal centralism' and in general go 'beyond' models based on centralised European systems.

Twining, for instance, proposes that we rethink the state so as to recognise that 'law itself is a huge field of multiple contests, and an internally plural phenomenon'. And Werner Menski argues that his Indian case-study can help us rethink our ideas about law so as to see it as

> interconnected, linked from the macrocosmic spheres of natural law right through to the personal sphere of the socio-legal domain. All along, it also contains elements of the religious and the secular, the social and the psychological, and virtually anything else. The boundaries between what is legal and what is not become really fuzzy (Menski: 194).

Esin Örücü, too, insists on the importance of legal and cultural pluralism and invites us to give attention to 'the mysteries of the interaction of social norms and legal values' (Örücü: 58) and Patrick Glenn writes of *lex mercatoria* 'being legitimated by their classification within a body of commercial normativity which has prevailed and been recognised for centuries'(Glenn: 105).

The authors of the more substantive chapters in the Handbook do not necessarily endorse these or other recommendations put forward in the theoretical part of the Handbook. As compared to the radical proposals to change direction announced in the chapters by Werner Menski and William Twining, for example, both private law and the search for 'better law' remain important concerns for some of our authors. Few of our authors try to de-centre law in favour of examining other sources of social order—and only Menski himself has much to say about religion. On the other hand, the desire that some of our authors have to colonise new territories does involve some stretching of existing disciplines. Roberts speaks of transnational criminal law breaking the boundaries of international criminal law and taking criminology beyond its 'comfort zone'. Twining, too, claims that broadening our conception of comparative law may bring about a reintegration of 'closely related enclaves of enquiry, such as 'law and development', that have become artificially separated. For him an 'adequate account of law today' has to give some attention to the significance of transnational non-governmental organisations (Amnesty International, Greenpeace, the Catholic Church, international women's movements, international trade union organisations), to peoples that are nations without states (the Maoris, the Scots, Gypsies, the native peoples of North America and Australia), to organised crime, liberation movements, multi-national companies, trans-national legal practices, and significant classes such as the vast herds of 'people on the move' (including migrants, refugees and the internally displaced) (Twining: 75).

If comparative law is to meet these and similar challenges it will need to develop or borrow new concepts. In particular this applies to the idea of 'families of law' but also more generally to the many other metaphors on which comparative lawyers often rely in place of developing theory. In studying the variety of forms legal systems can take and the dynamics of their internal and external relationships, it can be difficult not to think in terms of analogies and metaphors. Nor will language allow us to make arguments without using these forms of speech. But metaphors can sometimes mislead—and, in a sense, are bound to mislead. So they should not be taken too seriously. Much of the effort given to discussing 'legal transplants' as if they should be expected to correspond to botanical or medical transplants thus seems wasted (Nelken, 2002). When Anthony Ogus, in chapter seven, ends by comparing different legal cultures to differently sized railway gauges, this comes in as an attempt to illustrate points he has made in other ways; it does not serve as a substitute for argument itself.

To go from classification to theoretical understanding and explanation requires greater engagement with other disciplines. Comparative law cannot do its work alone. But it might be more exact to say that it never did. What is at stake in moving towards comparative legal studies is the possible replacement or supplementation of legal, historical and philosophical scholarship with concepts and methods taken, for example, from economics, political science, sociology,[6] or anthropology (the latter being especially relevant given its central focus on comparison and the problems of understanding 'the other'). Increasingly, business studies, geography, literary theory or psychology are also being brought into play, and the list could go on.

---

[6] I come to the subject from a background in sociology of law.

A number of difficult issues need to be faced in such opening out to other disciplines. How do we know which is the appropriate discipline for our purposes? Is studying law more like doing physics or more like interpreting art or literature? Social scientists are themselves divided as to whether society and culture should be taken as shorthand for a series of forces and variables or as invitations to read events as if they were texts. Post-modernist writers in both law and the social sciences are suspicious of many of the pretensions to explanation of the behavioural social sciences. Are different academic disciplines appropriate for given legal topics? It may seem obvious that economics has an affinity with private law, and that political science will be most relevant to the sphere of administrative and constitutional law, whilst psychology has more to offer for family law. But the process of understanding the differences between family law regimes in different countries also benefits greatly by a consideration of political factors, for example, in explaining the role of religion or the importance of individualism (Bradley, 1996; see also Antokolskaia in chapter eleven).[7] Even so, it is not possible to go in all directions simultaneously. And as Foster notes in his chapter, we are likely to discover that even the discipline we wish to follow is internally riven and therefore find we need to take sides.

A number of our authors do make reference to the possible gains from looking to other disciplines. Thus, Andrew Harding and Peter Leyland argue that 'comparative constitutional law has to take account of political science to the extent that it explains, in part at least, the context in which the constitution operates'. Esin Örücü talks of the value of sociology of law for comparative lawyers. And John Bell, too, at one point of his discussion concedes that 'the answers to such questions require some legal sociology'. Most of the authors included in the substantive part of the handbook do seem interested in at least some form of multidisciplinary collaboration with those working in other disciplines.

But recognising the importance of other disciplines will not necessarily lead to comparative law becoming an *interdisciplinary* pursuit. What is, as Twining puts it, 'an adequate account of the law today' will depend on our aims in producing such an account.

On the basis of the sample represented here, we could say that many comparative law scholars still prefer a division of labour in which their role is more to *evaluate* the implications of contemporary developments for law rather than *explain why* they are taking place. Perhaps as a result of the stress in legal training on prescription rather than description, they tend to have a rather instrumental interest in the wider matters that make up comparative legal studies. Some of the chapters which say most about social trends refer to them mainly as part of an attempt to justify particular legal proposals or solutions. Antokolskaia's description of what has shaped family law allows her to argue that social change

---

[7] Disciplines are not easily demarcated in terms of subject matter. Because they emphasise different matters, using different conceptions, disciplines are above all, 'ways of seeing'. And every way of seeing is also a way of not seeing.

is flowing in a certain direction and so—by some functionalist alchemy of 'is' and 'ought'—must be right. On the other hand, Menski's claim that 'culture-specific legal realism prevailed in Indian law over globalising ideology' encourages him to argue that such general trends should be resisted.

In his chapter, exceptionally, Paul Roberts sets out a broad conception of international criminal law which involves the sort of wide-ranging study of legal and social change proposed by William Twining. His approach here comes closest to that of an interdisciplinary enquiry where the object is to draw on different disciplines in order to get at the various dimensions of a given topic. Admittedly, interdisciplinary work is difficult;[8] few can master a second discipline, never mind a range of disciplines.[9] But with the help of Google Scholar and other Internet search engines, it should at least be possible to keep an eye on leading studies in one or other of these disciplines which are taken to be most relevant. Given the extent of overlap between disciplines, interdisciplinary work may also be easier to do than it is sometimes made to seem.[10] Social scientists who study legal culture may discover, to their surprise, that their work may be considered (also) a contribution to comparative law. With their curiosity aroused they may then start on a course of reading to see whether comparative lawyers have all along been doing sociology of law!

It is understandable that many comparative lawyers will want to stick to what they think they do best, whether this is identified as cross-cultural legal competence, historical scholarship, expertise in given geographical areas, or practical 'savvy'. They are willing to leave other approaches to others, as in the way Basil Markesinis seeks to delimit 'the legal' from matters which are not the proper sphere of the comparative lawyer, or van Erp (in chapter seventeen) recommends leaving 'political questions' to the politicians. But even to achieve a division of labour it is necessary to decide how to circumscribe the study of legal rules and legal institutions from other enquiries. We should not assume that other disciplines will resolve our problems for us. In particular we must beware of the tendency to think that others will provide the answers to our problems without the need to re-frame the questions. Comparative lawyers are likely to be disappointed, for example, if they ask sociologists of law for a 'theory' that can 'predict' the outcome of legal transplants. In addition, other disciplines may themselves be undergoing rapid change, as in the way international law and international relations are currently being transformed by having to deal with the way transnational legal processes are displacing or complicating relations between nation-states (Berman, 2005;

---

[8] Just as not everyone has the experience or desire to be an 'intellectual nomad' like many of its leading writers were (Curran, 1998: 657 at 661).

[9] Some reviews of Legrand and Munday's book on *Comparative Legal Studies* complained that it would be too difficult for many students of comparative law.

[10] It is important to note that interdisciplinary collaboration can take different forms. A discipline such as economics finds itself in symbiosis with law even, or especially when, its techniques are different. Literary theory, on the other hand, offers close parallels to the interpretative task of the judge or the comparatist herself.

Nelken, 2006a). And, in the absence of any overarching intellectual scheme, some issues may just simply fall between disciplines.

Those who favour a restricted role for comparative law cannot afford to take their information or concepts uncritically from elsewhere; they need to see what is at stake in talking about 'legal pluralism' instead of 'hybridity', or the 'diffusion' rather than the 'harmonisation' of law. So this means that they will have to be able to read other disciplines with at least some level of understanding. Glenn, in his chapter, 'Com-paring', for example, is willing to leave it to sociology to discover how law actually 'works'. But at the same time he is cautious about taking its idea of 'culture' arguing that 'the social science disciplines of sociology and anthropology have themselves become victims of the process of reification' (Glenn: 97). As I suggest in my own chapter (chapter five), however, this perception of how the social sciences talk about culture is partial and somewhat outdated, and illustrates the difficulties of practising too rigid a division of labour between legal and social science scholarship. In general, comparative lawyers also need to understand why other scholars do not focus on law in terms of statutes and judicial decisions as such, but seek rather to understand its changing role and significance using terms such as 'regulation', 'discipline', 'governance', 'governmentality', 'legal fields', and 'legal autopoiesis'.

IV. CONTEXTS

Assuming that we do want to make use of social scientific or other insights, how should we do so? The most common move to get 'beyond legal rules' is to argue for placing 'law in its context'. As Nicholas Foster writes,

> a contextual approach leads to a consciousness of difference in the formulation, practice, interpretation and enforcement of the law, [and] a better understanding of law and lawyers from other jurisdictions (Foster: 279–80).

Looking to context is also an invitation to see how law is used and experienced by those to whom it is addressed. As William Twining argues in chapter three,

> in order to understand law in the world today it is more than ever important to penetrate beyond the surface of official legal doctrine to reach the realities of all forms of law as social practices (Twining: 77).

Using this approach, it is claimed, can both help us explain law and—perhaps also reform it.

But what is meant by law's context? How does law relate to 'its context'? How is it best studied? The term context is used by our authors in many ways—and rightly so—because there are indeed many contexts and ways of grasping them. At a minimum, a given legal rule is itself part of a wider context of other related legal rules, and a branch of law is affected by (and affects) other aspects of law. As Foster argues in his chapter this means that commercial law, for example, cannot be treated as a case apart. Even if we were to concede, for argument's sake, that its rules were less influenced by 'culture' than by other branches of law, it nonetheless uses concepts that belong to and draw on a wider set of legal rules and practices. But, in looking for this sort of context, the relevant rules and practices are not limited to those usually studied in legal curricula. It is crucial, as taught by the Legal Realists long ago, to include studies of the 'law in action' if we want to try to explain or predict the actions of legal actors and others using the law. Only with such knowledge can we develop persuasive comparisons of law in the USA and Europe (Kagan, 2001 and 2007), or bring out the importance of 'infra-structural' aspects of dispute resolution which can account for telling differences even within civil law jurisdictions (Blankenburg, 1997).

Roberts speaks of 'the informal "working rules" of their occupational culture, police officers or cooperation between prosecution and defence'. As he explains,

> frontline professionals' decision-making and conduct is typically motivated by 'third-tier' directives, such as police force orders, prosecutorial codes or military training manuals (which are not necessarily publicly available), rather than by primary legal rules or secondary delegated legislation. Sometimes 'policy' is not even written down; occasionally not written down *on purpose*. Unwritten operational policies occupy the shadowlands of informal agreements, institutionalised routines, shared professional understandings, and taken-for-granted cultural assumptions (Roberts: 359).

John Bell likewise tells us that empirical research is required to know what such rights as the right to a hearing, the right to make representations, to be given reasons or to provide access to documents, really amount to in different jurisdictions. Context is the realm of effects, side-effects and lack of effects. Andrew Harding and Peter Leyland warn of the need, when it comes to evaluating the recent trend toward constitution-making, to examine how constitutional provisions are actually put in practice (or, as often, not put into practice). And Foster tells us that any study of the effects of legal transplants must be alert to 'technical incompetence, lack of enforcement, sidelining, adaptation, isolation and refusal'.

Context is seen as relevant both in studying the way law is shaped by other factors and the way it shapes society itself. As Esin Örücü puts it,

> most of the differences that cannot be explained in terms of the legal system can more easily be explained in terms of the societal, political or economic systems. Social systems may determine the content of the corresponding legal systems and vice versa (Glenn: 57).

Regarding the first of these links, Esin Örücü tells us, with respect to what really influences judicial decisions:

> [T]his discovery of the raison d'être for the differences and similarities, also necessitates moving from the domain of pure legal reasoning to that of contextual factors (Örücü: 49).

On the other hand, with respect to the significance of statutory rules and judicial decisions, Masha Antokolskaia emphasises that 'we need to look behind legal categories to see how provisions of family law are actually used'. She illustrates this with evidence of how many divorcing couples ignore the possibility of no-fault divorce provisions if fault-based divorce provides the quicker route. And Werner Menski, too, notes, as a worrying possible side effect of an otherwise admirable decision by the Indian Supreme Court: 'There is also some concern that more women may be killed in India by their ex-husbands in such circumstances'.

But the contextual approach, or at least this way of understanding context, is not without its detractors. Borrowing from developments in the sociology of law and critical legal scholarship in the United States it may be helpful to contrast two different ways of relating law and context (Nelken, 1986). The first—'putting law in context'—uses context to explain the form and effects of law. The second—'finding the context in law'—seeks to show how law helps to construct and communicate the social context. The first of these approaches points to aspects of the wider society that help explain or make sense of law. Those who seek to expose the 'context in law', however, are usually not that interested in showing how law responds to external conditions, or in demonstrating the differences on the ground between legal rules and actual practices. For them law is to be examined as a 'cultural artefact' (Frankenberg, 2006b) which succeeds in giving the impression of legal certainty and rule governedness despite so much evidence to the contrary.

The Handbook, as we have already had occasion to note, is rich in illustrations of the first approach, that of 'putting law in context'. Clues to law are found in wider society. Thus Nicholas Foster points out that the contrasting status of financial careers in France and the UK tells us much about the roles of commercial law in each society. And wider social developments are taken to explain changes in the law. Andrew Harding and Peter Leyland tell us that

> 'since the end of the cold war, however, there has been an enormous increase in democ-ratisation, and although there are still great differences in political systems and cultures, the main objectives of constitutional law have become more broadly similar than previ-ously, due to the dominant international agendas of 'good governance', 'human rights', 'international trade', and 'sustainable development', all of which have had significant impacts on constitutions. In addition, the same process has tended to blur the distinc-tion between the public and private sectors and therefore between constitutional and private law (Harding and Leyland: 324–5).

Likewise, Masha Antokolskaia's chapter (chapter eleven) makes extensive use of back-ground trends so as to explain the recent evolution of family law. As she sees it,

> '[t]he society dominated by traditional values gave way to a pluralistic society, one in which different forms and sets of family values co-exist[ed] alongside each other. Divorce and serial monogamy began to be considered normal. Extramarital sex, non-marital cohabitation, and birth outside wedlock lost their stigmatic character. Same-sex relationships became first decriminalised, then legalised, and then, in some countries, even equated with marriage. Due to the fact that more and more children were born outside marriage, it became increasingly unacceptable for the legal status of these chil-dren to differ from that of children born in a marriage (Antokolskaia: 241).

In addition to movements in ideas and culture, and in part as a factor shaping them, attention is given to larger contexts of social, political and economic change such as population movements, globalisation and so on. Hence Antokolskaia, in seeking to explain 'an attitudinal shift from marriage based on economic necessity and duty to marriage based on affection and free commitment', speaks of the role of women's emancipation and the women's rights movement, as well as increasing female employment and the progress of social welfare which diminished the function of the family as provider of financial means and security. Once we extend our gaze also to cover such disparate international influences, however, it then becomes difficult to speak of law being 'embedded' in a given national or local context (Nelken, 2007). As a good example we could take the Sabine Oxley reforms, which were recently passed in the United States as a response to major financial scandals there such as the collapse of Enron. Similar principles of corporate governance have been quickly adopted in other countries such as Japan, (and also applied to American companies doing business there), while, back in the United States, the complaint that these reforms make American business uncompetitive means that their repeal or amendment is very much on the agenda.

Putting 'law in context' is often allied to a functional approach in which it is assumed that law is there to solve 'social problems' and otherwise meet the social needs of society. Zweigert and Kötz's influential textbook is framed in terms of seeing how different legal systems deal with similar types of challenges in the context of their own societies. As illustrated by Esin Örücü in chapter two,

> if an institution called divorce is under survey in system A, the comparative lawyer looks for an institution in system B performing an equivalent function, that of freeing an individual from an unsatisfactory marital relationship within which he or she does not wish to remain (Örücü: 51).

For example, in the course of explaining the social trends that led to legal change, Masha Antokolskaia argues that once 30 percent of couples in Europe were cohabiting 'something' had to be done to change family law. Werner Menski likewise uses a functionalist type argument to explain why in India it would not be possible to have irretrievable breakdown as a ground for divorce when he remarks that, 'India is not America, and that country cannot afford a scenario in which millions of women and children are suffering as a result of liberalised divorce laws'(Menski: 201).

But while functionalist arguments of this kind often direct us to worthwhile hypotheses for investigation, the approach can also be a source of errors (see also the discussions in chapter two by Esin Örücü and in chapter six by Roger Cotterrell). These weaknesses include slighting the role of historical explanation, confusing purposes with effects, and begging questions about the 'equivalence' of what is being compared. 'Problems' do not just produce 'solutions'; these have to be fought for by competing interests and groups. It is also always important to bear in mind the extent to which 'social problems' are culturally constructed rather than given. To appreciate how problems are constructed requires grasping different mentalities, not presupposing a common instrumentalist viewpoint. We should not assume that societies being compared will necessarily face the same 'problems' and use law in some way to respond to them. We need to realise the extent to which cultures 'socially construct' what they treat as problems, or the need to deal with them by using the law. While there was a time when social science explanation was virtually co-terminous with functionalism, this is an approach that has now been on the retreat for some time. And even comparative lawyers are learning to rely on it less (Graziadei, 2003).

Those comparatists such as Gunter Frankenberg, who choose rather to study the 'context in law', now even speak of 'the functionalist fallacy', complaining that

> the vague concept of function operates like a magic carpet with which the comparatist shuttles from social problems to legal solutions and from one legal system to another—way above the 'enigma of translation' (Frankenberg, 2006b: 445).

For these writers what often should become salient is precisely what we have called the 'second-order' enquiry into how others grasp foreign law. As Frankenberg goes on to say, once the comparatist recognises that law is a way of seeing,

> she will soon discard the fact/law and law-in-the-books/law-in-action distinctions and deal instead with how she represents in her scholarly work the legal representations of local conflicts, contexts and visions (Frankenberg 2006b: 442).

But this does not imply that law is without social 'effects'. In his recent discussion of constitutions, Frankenberg explains that

> 'in the world of signs and symbols the 'sacred texts' are decanonized and placed in the context of the everyday world: Not only cases and norms and juridical writings appear on the radar screen but also ideas and actions of ordinary people, programmatic visions of social movements, group interests etc. Informed by a constitutive theory the comparatist regards constitutions as reflecting *and* shaping the everyday, in particular as reflecting *and* shaping the imagination of political unity and collective identity as well as offering a framework for ideology. Within this perspective it is crucial to view constitutions as not merely and passively sitting 'at the receiving end' and operating like receptacles or reflectors of culture, but to consider that they actively intervene and, under certain circumstances, shape or transform culture (*ibid: 449*).

While there are no worked-through examples of this type of approach in this handbook, Roger Cotterrell, in his theoretical chapter (chapter six), does show sympathy with this sort of enquiry, and both John Bell and Nicholas Foster in their substantive chapters are in different ways attentive to variations in the way different jurisdictions use legal categories. It is fair to say, however, that many mainstream comparative lawyers feel uneasy with this approach and are suspicious of its practical implications (or fear it does not have any). But this is to underestimate its potential. It is interesting, for example, to see how Frankenberg's discussion of constitutions could contribute to the agenda set out by Andrew Harding and Peter Leyland in chapter fourteen. For Frankenberg,

> 'once comparatists move on to the *constitution as culture*, they transgress the borders of an instrumental understanding and begin to grasp the symbolic dimension (*ibid*).

'Most commonly', he says,

> constitutions present variations of theme of self-government and fantasies of a kind of domination where the subjective factor is magically neutralized—within a 'government of laws and not of men'. Comparative constitutional law can tell fascinating stories about how the self is first elevated as popular sovereign and then reduced and fragmented within schemes of representation, delegation and transfer of power away from the collective self, whose consent to being governed is always implied or invoked. And stories about how conflicts between citizens and their governors, and among citizens, are removed from where they arise, the public arenas, and transformed into controversies under constitutional law to be settled by constitutional or supreme courts (*ibid*: 449–50).

In some respects post-modern comparativists have more in common with their mainstream legal colleagues than with practitioners of social science (as is true of critical legal scholars generally)—and this competition may itself explain the resistance they face. For example, true to the comparative lawyer's penchant for classification, Frankenberg, too, seeks to distinguish different types of constitution. He contrasts for instance, the constitution as 'contract' (as in Europe), as 'manifesto' (as in the American Declaration of Independence), as 'program' (eg in socialist regimes), and as 'law' (evoking the imaginary collective). He claims that constitutions variously provide answers to questions of justice, questions of good life, political wisdom and political risk-management, as well as more familiar problems of constitutional validity, amendment and change. His analysis also offers interesting interpretations of the architecture of constitutions, distinguishing levels of rules, and explaining that within and through meta-rules constitutions talk about themselves, and 'establish the narcissism of the small (national) difference': They stress or even exaggerate insignificant details to others which then become of major importance and thus establish the otherness of others. Furthermore, meta-rules are designed to defend a constitution's dignity as 'supreme law' against ordinary law-interpreting (Frankenberg, 2006b: 439 at 457).

On the other hand, Andrew Harding and Peter Leyland are more interested in studying the 'law in context' as they are in undertaking semiotic interpretations of the 'context in law'. Even though there is probably little in Frankenberg's approach with which they would want to disagree, they could justifiably argue that there is no reason why attention should not also be given to social and economic developments and aspects of the law in action (or inaction). Making sense of constitutional texts as vehicles of communication could be misleading if we do not also investigate channels of communication. For example, it is certainly relevant if we discover that copies of the constitution in some countries may be virtually unobtainable, while, in others, such as the new South Africa, it is on sale in every newsagent. Drawing on both approaches could help to explain the recent failure of the referendums on the envisaged European constitution; something which certainly needs to be understood not only as a result of the way those debating the constitution tried (or failed) to communicate certain messages but also in terms of the larger socio-economic context.

Any choice to base our contextual explanations on one time or space rather than another carries implications and is rarely 'innocent'. For example, is the current explosion of incarceration in the United States to be explained in terms of the last 30, or the last 300 years of its history? (Whitman, 2003b; and Nelken, 2006b). The problem, of course, is how to justify the choice of any given context in 'putting law in context'. This is an issue not only for those attracted by a multi- or interdisciplinary agenda for comparative legal studies, but also for second-order approaches to comparative law. An important branch of contemporary social theory inspired by the work of Niklas Luhmann claims that there is a high degree of social differentiation between the legal and other sub-systems that make up modern society (and that this is necessary). In the light of this and other approaches, theorists debate whether there are *intrinsic* limits to how much of its context law can get to see (or express) if it is to reproduce itself successfully (Cotterrell, 1998; and Nelken, 1998).

If such limits exist, all students of comparative legal studies, and not only those who seek to launch critical or 'pessimistic' attacks on the mainstream, may have to take them into account when they seek to shape the working logics of legally-oriented actors. Such approaches suggest that the task of comparative law might consist in studying social and cultural variation in how *legal actors* frame their context. For example, as we have seen, Anthony Ogus claims that law in common-law countries is closer to the demands that come from society than it is in civil law countries. This may also be reflected in the way law is conceived and taught in different places. In the Anglo-American world the battle for 'law in context' in legal education is considered to have been won (as seen in the expression 'we are all Realists now'). But this is less true of Continental Europe and many other places. Thus the question about how (and how far) legal actors are interested in incorporating information about social context into their decision-making can itself be made the subject of comparative investigation.

V. SIMILARITIES AND DIFFERENCES

As in any comparative exercise, with comparative law the study of similarities and differences is the heart of the endeavour. However, in this field the descriptive question of whether law is similar or different is often subordinated to the prescriptive issue of whether or not it *should* be made more similar (and how this should be achieved). In this Handbook Masha Antokolskaia describes—but also applauds—the emergence of more similar regimes of family law across Europe. And Jan Smits offers a new approach to how such harmonisation in private law can be achieved. But other comparatists seek to defend the virtues of diversity. They claim that the functionalist approach is itself part of an agenda of sameness and a fear of 'the other' (see Roger Cotterrell's contrast in chapter six between the functional and cultural approaches).

The defenders of diversity worry that the pressures of globalisation are leading towards the homogenisation of legal rules and the uniformisation of valuably distinctive ways of conceiving of law. Amongst our contributors, Patrick Glenn reminds us of his thesis that there are seven important, if overlapping, legal traditions. And Werner Menski asks:

> To what extent do we accept that Hindu law, Chinese law, Islamic laws and the myriad of African laws have a future in this globalising world? Will there be a universal concept of law?

He fears that this can succeed 'only at the expense of enlarging the non-cultural domain'. Others, such as Pierre Legrand (discussed in Roger Cotterrell's chapter) provide brilliant and repeated criticism of the harmonisation of national laws being decreed or encouraged by the European Union. This 'contrarian challenge' rejects the attempt to bring together common and civil law traditions on the basis that such different ways of thinking about law cannot be, and therefore should not be, overcome. But both sides to this debate can overplay their hands (Nottage, 2004). The advocates of harmonisation do not deal satisfactorily with the likelihood of their projects producing new differences. And those who claim that difference should be taken as a presupposition do not explain why their concern for difference is restricted to only certain levels or types of difference (Nelken, 2003b). Werner Menski, for example, seems to be happy with the effort to achieve greater harmonisation *within* India, provided that this is brought about in ways that show skill and tact in respecting other local legal orders.

It is immensely valuable to explore unfamiliar legal sensibilities and legal worlds, even if this is a journey without end. However, for some purposes, instead of taking a position *a priori* in favour of similarity or difference, it may be more productive to ask why we expect to find one or the other. It can be instructive to find *differences* in legally-oriented practices when comparing *similar* societies—as where we find large differences in resort to litigation in societies which are otherwise said to be similar socio-economically and culturally (Blankenburg, 1997). But it can be as valuable to find *similarities* in law in societies which are in other respects very *different*. Obviously, these expectations should be based not only on common sense but also informed by the state of the art in relevant scholarly research. Too many studies continue to try to persuade us that the Japanese do after all make use of law, even though this point is by now well-established.

The same applies when it comes to the prospects for legal transfers. It is easier to imagine borrowing and learning from places which are similar and face similar problems. But, *pace* the transplant metaphor, some societies make the effort to borrow from legal systems which are different to them, hoping in this way to become more like them. The same applies to learning from other societies. In chapter nine Werner Menski makes much of the differences between Indian and Western conceptions of law and society, saying, for example, that in India there is an emphasis on

> economic responsibilities between members of social groups and families, and also across gender boundaries. Such methods clash with Western-led assumptions about state centricity, individual autonomy and rights-based approaches. Beyond Europe, however, the notion that one's rights depend on other people's duties remains a strong legal foundation (Menski: 193).

But, on the other hand, he also claims that despite (or because of) these differences the West has much to learn from the way family law was harmonised in India.

Typically, however, comparative lawyers tend to focus on subtle differences between places which are rather similar, showing us for example, that branches of law such as contract, tort and crime can have different boundaries in different places. The ever-present difficulties in such comparisons of knowing exactly when like is like, become the very point of the exercise. In his contribution to the handbook, for example, John Bell asks what is meant by administrative law, and how discretion is defined and structured in Germany, France and UK. After examining ideas concerning the rule of law, he says:

> The divergence in uses of the terminology and the absence of an exact equivalent in the different languages provides much potential for confusion. All the same, these different terms convey some common liberal messages—that the administration is not free to act as it deems to be right in terms of efficiency or to achieve political goals (Bell: 301).

For him, the advantage of comparison is that it allows us to see how similar dilemmas play themselves out in different contexts. He explains that the values of protection of subjects, accountability and efficiency may cut in different directions with different jurisdictions giving different weight to these principles.[11] But he also suggests that in each of these societies the protection of fundamental rights can be trumped by considerations of national security and public order.

Comparison presupposes some similarity. Claims of irreducible difference are seen as bordering on relativism and (therefore?) implausible. Christopher McCrudden asks:

> '[W]hat, exactly, do we mean by 'torture'? When, exactly, is 'discrimination' invidious? ... When the principle comes to be applied, the appearance of commonality disappears, and human rights are exposed as culturally relative, deeply contingent on local politics and values. (McCrudden: 372–3)

This has to be resisted because comparison would be pointless—'a different principle would be being applied (McCrudden: 373).

It is true that some societies are described or may describe themselves as exceptional. Even Esin Örücü has talked of 'extraordinary places'. But it is hard to sustain the case that any given place is 'ordinary'. The United States has a strong claim to be exceptional in its degree of adversarial legalism (Kagan, 2001; Nelken, 2003a) or its level of incarceration rates. Japan has long seen itself as different; Scandinavians see their laws as somewhat exceptional in the European context. Some commentators on law and politics in Italy worry about the 'normality' of their way of doing things, and so on.

How are we to find out in what ways places are different? Our results can only be as good as the reliability of our methods allows. It is certainly not enough to rely on law in the books, some effort must be made to talk to those in touch with the 'law in action' (see Esin Örücü's chapter nineteen). Andrew Harding and Peter Leyland rightly recommend that we engage in dialogue with foreign

---

[11] Those following a more culturalist approach might object that we cannot be sure that these societies do share these common dilemmas, or even how far the idea of having to trade-off amongst different values is common across different societies.

scholars, officials and politicians. But we should not take it for granted that people in other societies always know the answers to our questions about the differences between our ways and theirs. For some purposes outsiders may see more than insiders. What is more, the role—the requirements of our informants, including whether they are practitioners or experts, can vary from society to society: We may need to make allowance for the possibility that in many societies political engagements and commitments mean that those we rely on are more interested in presenting a good face, or pursuing the goals of a given political project, than they are in providing a disinterested description of their system (Nelken, 2000).

If we are to compare successfully, we are also in need of reasonably clear concepts which can be used to guide research. The debate over the concept of legal culture—a possible substitute for the tired idea of families of law[12]—provides a good illustration of the difficulties in finding and working with such concepts. Whilst few doubt that there is some connection between law and culture there is little agreement on how to determine this. Menski for example tells us that 'law is culture-specific and immensely diverse', but van Erp insists that judges from different legal cultures often have a lot in common on account of their role-requirements and social backgrounds (an argument also deployed by Basil Markesinis against those who think legal epistemologies are very different). This term is discussed at some length in David Nelken's chapter, but also makes its appearance in many of the other chapters of this handbook, such as those by Roger Cotterrell, Anthony Ogus, Nicholas Foster, Patrick Glenn and Masha Antokolskaia.

A series of issues need to be faced in using the concept of legal culture. An often-raised problem is the danger of treating culture as fixed or impervious to outside influences (see Patrick Glenn, in chapter four). Culture and legal culture should rather be seen as something that changes and is changeable, and is shaped both by the past and oriented towards the future (Nelken, 1995). In his contribution, John Bell notes that German administrative law is less willing than that in France or the United Kingdom to accept that certain powers belong inherently to government in the absence of special authorisation. He links this to that country's recent experience of dictatorial government.[13] Legal culture, like other aspects of culture, may also rest on an imaginary past and invented traditions. Likewise, law imposed by others quite recently may nonetheless be felt as authentically indigenous (Jettinghoff, 2001).

The units of legal culture range from supranational categories such as 'Asian values' or 'European legal culture' through more familiar national legal

---

[12] Our contributors suggest other pretenders to this role such as, for Patrick Glenn, 'legal traditions' or, for Esin Örücü, the 'tree' metaphor.

[13] Interestingly, a similar historical explanation is used by Lacey and Zedner, 1998, to explain the distrust in Germany of relying on communal and informal justice because of memories of the misuse of informers in the Nazi regime.

cultures, down to regional, local, organisational and professional ones. As shown in William Twining's discussion of the diffusion of law, it is especially important to be open to transnational legal processes and the so-called 'third cultures' not rooted in the state. The increasing need to examine legal culture beyond national boundaries is seen most obviously in the contributions to this Handbook that deal with international criminal law and human rights law. But the chapters on private, public and family law make much the same point. John Bell, for instance, notes that ideas for new ways of running the public sector frequently come from the Organisation for Economic Cooperation and Development, and that ideas for common standards of administrative law are developed by the Council of Europe or the European Union. Masha Antokolskaia describes the development of family law as a collective international project. Legal cultures are thus overlapping and inter-related and may come together in unexpected ways. The method of law-making by Directive of the Commission of the European Union is closer to civil than it is to common law traditions, but much of the substance of such laws has to with common law influenced ideas of liberalism and the free market.

For purposes of explanation we will often also need to distinguish what we mean by culture from other factors such as social structure or group interests. Most authors in fact counterpoise culture—as something bound up with the creation and sharing of symbolic meaning—to more instrumental aspects of social life. But, in chapter seven, Anthony Ogus, whilst starting from a classical definition of legal culture as 'a shared way of thinking and acting', then goes on to offer an economic interpretation of the term. He suggests that 'it is a "network" that may reduce the costs of communication between those using the legal system', but adds that these same characteristics mean that it may also 'be exploited by practising lawyers to resist competition'. Free market competition between legal cultures, in his view, provides the opportunity for the economic interests of law consumers to prevail over the special interests of the law providers.

The issue of legal culture is also crucial to what is one of the most interesting (if serendipitous) contrasts that emerge from the contributions to this collection taken as a whole. It is conventional wisdom, even for sophisticated commentators, that family law is one of those branches of law which is most linked to culture and therefore least easy to copy. By contrast, commercial law is seen as the least 'cultural' type of law and hence that which is easiest to transfer or borrow. This is explained in terms of the relative intimacy and privacy of the relationships or 'communities' being regulated by each type of law (Roger Cotterrell 2006). Yet, surprisingly, the relevant contributions to our Handbook seem to go against these assumptions. Masha Antokolskaia does not tell us a story about the distinctiveness of national family law regimes throughout Europe (though such a story could no doubt be told). On the contrary, she seeks to persuade us that reaching a high degree of consensus in this area of legal regulation is both necessary and possible.

By contrast, Nicholas Foster devotes much of his chapter (chapter twelve) to showing that commercial law also reflects and helps shape local culture. He rejects the assumption, as he summarises it, that

> [c]ommerce, though, is not 'close to peoples' lives', and is therefore not affected by cultural attitudes. Business people everywhere just wants to make money. So commercial law is not affected by culture either, it is just lawyer's law, a mere instrument (Foster: 267).[14]

He argues instead that commerce is in fact 'close to peoples' lives', because it relates to such 'rules of the game of economic struggle' as the distribution of property among social groups, the concentration of power in society, the 'set of prior choices about the role of the state and the private sector in responding to change' and the morality of interactions between people. Therefore it is affected by cultural attitudes. Business people everywhere may just want to make money, but they are still people who function in a culturally determined mentality. Since commercial law concerns the facilitation and regulation of commerce, it too may be affected by cultural attitudes (so long as the law reflects those attitudes)'. Foster claims as a result that

> 'variations in commercial law which reflect those differences are not mere accidents, and will be difficult to change effectively. In particular it may be difficult to change them so as to make the law uniform across various types of society (Foster: 278).

These unusual claims go together with different ways of employing comparative law in argument. Masha Antokolskaia thinks that she can best show the relevance of comparison for family law by describing what has emerged *in common* as a result of convergence of ways of living and thinking. Foster, on the other hand, uses comparative evidence of difference to prove that commercial law is (also) culturally shaped. But we should be careful not to be too carried away by these emphases. It is one thing to show that certain values in family law are widely shared or that commercial law is *also* cultural. It is another to sustain the view that commercial law is *more* culturally rooted than family law. Much more research would be needed to document such an unlikely proposition.

Will difference survive? It is often said that there are forces, linked to globalisation, which are leading to greater convergence in law across the board. Our contributors are cautious about this, and William Twining is almost tempted to ban the use of the word globalisation. Andrew Harding and Peter Leyland offer a balanced assessment:

> while certain contemporary global trends do in fact encourage elements of convergence, and there is plenty of evidence of this taking place, it does not follow that constitutions will all eventually look the same.

For them,

> strong divergences do remain in the implementation of human rights principles and other constitutional features. Moreover, globalisation has within it tendencies which are both conducive and non-conducive to the promotion of constitutional government (Harding and Leyland: 333).

---

[14] But, as Anthony Ogus argues, culture can also be used instrumentally.

We should remember that globalisation can bring about difference as well as similarity. The development of the international economy often uses, emphasises or exacerbates differences in the places which produce goods and services even as it spreads homogenous appetites for such goods.

Convergence can also be pursued as part of a deliberate political project such as harmonisation of law in the European Union. Because this is something in which comparative lawyers play an important part it has led to heated debate about whether harmonisation leads to the sacrifice of diversity and whether this is something to be resisted. Is difference in culture and legal culture itself a value, as with the maintenance of biodiversity? What about objectionable differences? When is 'culturalism' progressive? These are questions to which it is difficult to find conclusive responses. Esin Örücü argues in favour of providing similar answers across the world in cases such as those dealing with workers and others who have contracted diseases from exposure to asbestos (Örücü, 2005). In this way we meet the threat that multi-national companies will otherwise forum-shop or move where worker security is least protected. The same, she thinks, should apply to liability for defective products. What of the granting of rights to illegitimate children? Masha Antokolskaia would say yes. But these three examples give some illustration of the need to decide where to draw the line.

In his chapter (chapter six) Roger Cotterrell sees the attempt to identify 'better law' as part of the old search for universal principles. By contrast, he offers a careful argument in favour of diversity. Cotterrell asks us to draw an analogy between valuing differences in legal arrangements and the celebration of difference in critical race theory and some forms of feminism. It could be said, on the other hand, that the analogy begs the question. Even if sometimes respecting difference can help defend weaker groups from enforced assimilation, in other circumstances insisting on similarity can be useful in warding off ethnic nationalism. Unfortunately, minorities themselves can often be intolerant of other minorities or deviants in their midst. Paradoxically, the European Union has been trying for some time to impose respect for difference across Europe and uses this as a key measure to decide on the eligibility for membership of candidate nations. So here we have a project of harmonisation designed to produce more toleration of difference. (Who said life was simple?)

The perception and evaluation of difference is highly contingent on the observer's starting point. American authors tend to assume that 'external legal culture' (the demands and pressure-group politics of civil society) is what moves the law. But this may itself reflect how law is shaped in the USA rather than representing a more general truth. John Bell's starting questions in examining administrative law cross-culturally presuppose that they are salient in each of the jurisdictions considered, something that his enviable inside knowledge of more than one jurisdiction allows him to assert.[15] However, when he comments that on the continent

---

[15] But Bell's discussion of the relationship between proportionality and reasonableness can be usefully contrasted with Legrand's recent argument that the terms belong within different worlds of thought (Legrand, 2006).

some expansion of judicial review is motivated more by concerns of 'social solidarity' than holding administrations 'responsible', we may begin to wonder if the British jurist is showing through just a little. Likewise, when Masha Antokolskaia tell us that the trend towards the 'de-ideologisation of marriage' shows the 'recognition that law is unable to regulate feelings and moral sentiments' we may wonder whether this is a mere description or at least as much the expression of a particular ideology.

This overlap between objects of study and ways of thinking about it reminds us once again that comparative law can be pursued as both a first or second-order enquiry. As part of a first-order enquiry what judges do and say will be treated as evidence of legal culture. But a central part of their role is itself that of identifying their and other peoples' legal culture. As Christopher McCrudden points out, differences in how this role is understood can lead to considerable national variations in when they consider it appropriate to refer to judicial decisions handed down in other societies. Changes in the aims of comparative law over time also affect the significance of searching for similarities and difference. Goldstein and Marcus, in their classic work in the 1970s on criminal justice decision-making in the United States and Europe (Goldstein and Marcus, 1977), thought it essential to show that European practices were *less* different than was being claimed by other comparatists. They argued that because the Europeans also faced, but were unable to resolve, *similar* dilemmas of low-visibility decision-making to those faced in the United States, there was therefore little to be learned from them.[16] Nowadays, on the other hand, demonstrating similarity is used to provide useful justification for harmonisation: while those who wish to resist the relevance of comparisons tend to point to unbridgeable *differences* so as to support their cause.

VI. PRACTICES

We are now ready to return to Esin Örücü's distinction between those who see comparative law as an end in itself and those who advocate its use as a tool for various practical purposes. Many comparative lawyers express a certain impatience with merely theoretical enquiries. The sensible comparative lawyer, we are told, knows when and where to stop theorising (Palmer, 2004). Lawyers and other users of the law expect no less. As Patrick Glenn tells us in his chapter (chapter four),

> the transnational commercial world is one of free-flowing normative information where the question is never what the best possible rule is (which would be an impractical enquiry) but which solution is preferable to other solutions (Glenn: 100).

Should it be comparative law's goal to be as useful as possible? On the one hand, for some people comparative law can never be practical enough. Students can be amongst its most demanding critics. Nicholas Foster mentions one 'belligerent enquirer' who questioned the value of learning about other peoples' laws and

---

[16] For a recent study which takes their work further, see Hodgson, 2005.

never came back to learn more, probably assuming that if it ever became necessary to work on a case which had to be heard in a foreign jurisdiction he could just rely on a local lawyer.[17] Law may be practical in some respects and not others. Anthony Ogus argues that the common law is inherently more practically useful as compared to civil law because the administration of justice is relatively decentralised and thus removed from 'the heavy hand of government'. In this way law 'accepts, indeed reinforces, what individuals and firms want and protects expectations by rending the desired outcomes legally enforceable' (Ogus: 161). As scholars working in the broader area of comparative legal studies have shown, however, when it comes to providing remedies for tort and other harms the methods of the common law have their own severe drawbacks and there is much to be said in favour of state-organised regulation by bureaucrats and experts (Kagan, 2003).

Many of the post-modernist critics of the mainstream, on the other hand, see the use of comparison for instrumental purposes as what needs to be fought against. For van Erp (in chapter seventeen) such 'post-modern theory is trumped by practice' because of our everyday experience of the import and export of legal ideas and institutions. But of course everything depends on one's evaluation of what is achieved by such efforts at legal transfers. In any case it is clear that even post-modernists do not maintain a sharp separation between theory and practice. Although Pierre Legrand is scathing about the practical concerns of some comparative lawyers (Legrand, 2006), his 'contrarian challenge' (as discussed in chapter six by Roger Cotterrell), is linked to a mission to protect diversity as much as it is to theoretical enquiry for its own sake.[18]

The arguments of the post-modernists should not be identified with that of all proponents of comparative legal studies (they form only one of its strands).[19] Those who engage in multi- or interdisciplinary empirical enquiries not only agree on the need to offer practical benefits, they often argue that only their more 'realistic' approach will bring us to any destination worth reaching. For them, it is only by employing the resources of other disciplines that we can produce reliable findings. It can make all the difference to understanding other people's legal rules and institutions (never mind borrowing from them or seeking to harmonise them) to discover that the time taken on average for civil cases in Europe can be from 1 to 8 years. The same applies when we come

---

[17] As I told one belligerent enquirer, even for his pragmatic purposes it would still be useful to know something about how long court cases would take, judges' behaviour and, not least, lawyers' training, in the jurisdiction concerned.

[18] He also does not hesitate to enrol Teubner (see Teubner, 2001) in support of his arguments about the difficulties of transplanting law, despite the gulf between their theoretical approaches.

[19] A common mistake is to assume that an interpretative approach to social life, one that attempts to understand the meaning of actions or texts rather than 'explain' them using the cause and effect language of the hard sciences, is somehow post-modernist (Peters and Schwenke, 2000). On the contrary, such an approach is central to much of the best 'modern' empirical work in the social sciences. Still less does an interpretative approach have to go together with the alleged relativism attributed to the post-modernists (a relativism, if it existed, that would be difficult to reconcile with their strongly held political positions).

to recognise that high-sounding values can work out differently in practice in ways that contrast with the story law tells about itself. The 'due process' type of procedural guarantees of the criminal processes do not necessarily stand in opposition to 'crime control' priorities. Empirical research suggests that they typically serve to facilitate 'crime control' (McBarnett, 1981).[20]

These wider aspects of legal process are invariably indices of more profound features concerning the role and rule of law. Court delays are not just a sign of inefficiency but (also) of well-established and well-defended forms of social ordering outside state law (Nelken, 2004). By contrast, expeditiousness in legal proceedings, especially on the criminal side, may be an indication that those with power and money are hardly ever likely to be subject to the rigours of the law. The contribution of comparative legal studies should not be limited—as it is some-times—to advising lawyers or politicians whether a particular institution or law will 'work' or has worked. It can also help uncover the different values pursued by different legal systems. Only careful comparison using interviews and other research methods can help to decide what values a system is actually trying to pursue, and the likely competing internal views about this (Nelken, 2006c).

Comparative law may be used for various purposes and we should not neces-sarily expect to find these all to be compatible. Most obviously, seeking to copy best practices from elsewhere is certainly different from showing the ineliminabil-ity of difference. The aims canvassed by the contributors to this volume are not limited to mainstream exercises in harmonising private law, discovering commo-nalities or agreeing on 'better law'. Indeed, when they discuss existing projects in private law they tend to be somewhat critical of them.[21] Even Jan Smits devotes his chapter on the topic of harmonisation to finding a way to avoid this being imposed from the top-down. Nicholas Foster tells us that the conventional idea that private law is easily harmonised because it represents no more than 'lawyers' law' is much exaggerated because the relevant lawyers and wider legal culture may well vary from place to place. The chapter by Anthony Ogus (chapter seven) could be used to make the same point, though he looks to competition between systems to exploit and perhaps overcome these differences.

It is important, our authors argue, not to engage in exercises of harmonisation without finding out as much as possible about the legal systems being compared. As Paul Roberts puts it,

> Comparative inquiry might ascertain not only points of convergence in national crimi-nal laws, suggestive of international 'best practice' in criminalisation, but also distinctive domestic innovations potentially worthy of emulation at the international level.

---

[20] It is still appropriate to mandate principles and seek to hold authorities to them even if they will try to get round them where they think it necessary. But, as Goldstein and Marcus (1977) rightly insisted, only an account of a system which includes information about the likelihood of such depar-tures is useful for comparative purposes.

[21] Masha Antokolskaia is an exception, but she is dealing with schemes to develop better law rather than harmonisation as such.

Similar legal concepts can mean different things in different contexts. The lesson for human rights lawyers is that they ignore the different institutional contexts in which interpretation takes place and the different power relations in these jurisdictions at their peril.

Learning from elsewhere is important for purposes of co-operation in dealing with common problems. As Roberts explains:

> If international norms are partly derived from the legislation, jurisprudence and legal commentary produced by a diversity of national legal cultures and traditions,

then

> working knowledge of these domestic origins must surely be advantageous for any government lawyer or judge attempting to interpret international legal instruments (Roberts: 356).

But, again, to be really useful such enquiries must be well informed about actual practice. If this is attained then,

> local variations in occupational culture virtually guarantee that comparative under-standing will be a significant operational asset in coordinating transborder co-operation and international policing networks. Similar considerations apply to international co-operation between prosecutors, defence lawyers, judges, penal administrators, and military personnel, and in every sphere of informal operational policy-making and mutual judicial assistance (Roberts: 360).

Most of the comparative law and other literature about transferring law focuses on exports to countries of the developing world and/or former communist regimes. Sjef van Erp, writing as someone engaged in such transfers, tells us that typical situations are those where a state wants to change its law to reduce 'transaction costs of different legal regimes, to help organise economic change over', or to come into line with the legal practices of a political or economic grouping that the state in question wishes to join.

It is less common to find examples of learning that go in the opposite direction, where we try to learn from what is called 'the South' (Santos, 2002; and Santos and Rodriguez, 2005).

In his chapter (chapter nine), however, Werner Menski sets out to show us that the West has something to learn from India. After describing some difficult challenges that the legislature and courts have had to deal with in family law, he tells us that,

> [w]hile emphasising modern-looking individual property rights, also of women, the post-modern Indian state also re-employs traditional concepts of interlinkedness, specifically traditional family obligations, as a social welfare mechanism. This dual strategy also protects the state from expectations that it should be directly responsible for social welfare (Menski: 210–11).

He concludes:

> Post-modern India, therefore, seems to have found an exciting solution to the conundrum of legal uniformity which may be a suitable model for many countries … it employed carefully planned minor surgeries over a long period of time, leaving the body of personal status laws intact (Menski: 203).

On the other hand what is to be learnt from practices elsewhere, in the North or in the South, is rarely self-evident. Menski tells us that the Supreme Court decision that he so admires 'was done almost secretly, in record time, and there has been hardly any debate of this important development so far'. It could well be argued that this detracts from the achievement. We could also ask how far this decision (which had been delayed for many years) was only made possible by the fortuitous post-9/11 political climate.

What is or should be our criterion of success in deciding what has been achieved in the course of any alleged transfer of legal practices or ideas? As Esin Örücü explains,

> neither can 'success' be defined from a single standpoint. Pre-determined economic, social, cultural, religious or ideological ends are all factors by which success is measured. Efficiency, internalisation, cultural shift, and the actual use of the new legal structures can all be criteria for measurement' (Örücü: 178; see also Nelken, 2001).

Success is not only a matter of means but also of ends. For Sjef van Erp the means are technical ones: problems of language; the skills of interpreters; the methods for gaining credibility and inducing changes in mentalities. But means can also sometimes be ends in themselves. As Patrick Glenn argues in his chapter (chapter four), comparison must itself be carried out in a way that is respectful of difference. A key question is how to encourage cultures to draw on those aspects of their own traditions which are more in line with universalistic aspirations (Al-Naim, 1991/1996). This applies not only between, but even within, legal cultures, especially where there are obviously competing normative orders. As Werner Menski argues, an important part of the strategy used by the Indian Supreme Court to defeat attempts by members of the Muslim minority to get around women-friendly legal decisions was to appeal to the obligation in the Koran to maintain divorced wives.

Questions about practice are ones that are well suited to an approach which treats comparative law as a second-order enquiry into the practical task of comparing laws. We need to bear in mind who is doing the comparison, and we need to ask who is their imagined audience—for example, judges, lawyers, policymakers or scholars. Finally, and not least, attention needs to be given to the intended beneficiaries, whether they be businessmen, consumers, victims of crime or war, social movements, parties to an actual or possible court case, or those involved in lobbying legislatures or regulatory agencies. Some comparative scholars hope that their work will be of interest for as many groups as possible; others feel the need to respond to the question: 'Who's side are you on?'

What is considered sufficient understanding of other people's law will therefore depend on what that understanding is for. A legislator has one role, the judge or the lawyer another, and the ethnographer yet another (though each can try to use the other's knowledge for their own purposes). With respect to lawyers, Christopher McCrudden tells us that

> Lawyers in the human rights context use comparison to legitimate their argument that a particular interpretation of an existing human rights norm should be adopted, or as part of the process of generating further norms (McCrudden: 376).

It is always instructive to locate the actors behind given comparative projects and the way they draw on and create their 'symbolic capital' (Dezalay and Garth, 1996). The processes of competition between legal systems described by Anthony Ogus and others do not simply measure the response of a 'market' of rational individuals seeking their self-interest. Lawyers are involved in 'selling packages' or giving advice in the setting up of offices. American lawyers, many of them students of distinguished comparatists in the United States, helped develop strategies by which common law would become the law of choice for business in the European Union. In Latin America, economists and lawyers trained in the United States vie for high office.

It is a matter of some controversy how far judges' comparisons are or should be linked to what is needed to resolve single disputes or whether they form part of a search for something more transcendent. For Esin Örücü,

> comparativism must be at the heart of all judicial activity if law is to embody principles that are universal rather than purely domestic or even 'European'.

But Christopher McCrudden has quite a different view. For him, the way judges do comparisons is extremely patchy, and insofar as they look for universal principles this is part of the problem not the solution, As he says:

> [n]ot only is the methodology weak (cherry picking, weak evidence, overly formalistic assessment of what the law is), but several of these functions of comparison tend towards the older universalistic tendencies of comparative law scholarship that are now viewed critically by many modern comparative law scholars (McCrudden: 376).

But he also admits that, as far as judges are concerned, 'incompletely theorised agreements' are all you can have, and all you should want.

Both Christopher McCrudden's description in his chapter (chapter sixteen) of the work of US Supreme Court judges and Esin Örücü's statistical investigation of English and Scottish judges (in chapter eighteen) show that even leading judges are reluctant to use foreign decisions as authorities and that judges' references to other jurisdictions are often, in their words, no more than 'ornamental', 'decorative' or 'rhetorical'. Discussing the same cases as McCrudden, Pierre Legrand has recently stigmatised the way judges use comparative materials as 'comparison-lite' (Legrand, 2006). But how far this is something to be criticised, and how we criticise it, depends on how we (and the judges) interpret the institutional and constitutional role requirements of judges. In developing their own legal traditions they are certainly subject to more constraints than free-wheeling policy-makers or legal scholars. In some cases it could be that judges may even need to make their references to other systems appear to be no more than ornamental, even when they are actually taking them as models.

What of the practices of comparative law scholars themselves? When John Bell talks of 'successful' comparison he means that the scholars concerned have provided persuasive interpretations according to the professional standards of technical skill in interpreting law, and crafting policy recommendations. Comparative law scholars may also be more or less committed to larger projects. In the Indian context, Werner Menski talks of what he calls Anglo-Saxons and other harmonis-ers. Masha Antokolskaia describes and praises the role of comparative lawyers in permanent networks of national experts to advise on matters of family law. The alleged purpose of such projects should not always be taken at face value. Those who try to provide restatements of law may, intentionally or otherwise, be chang-ing it, and the search for common principles may be a disguised way to move to 'better laws'—or vice versa.

Scholarly claims can have effects in the world of legal and political practice even when they rest on false or weak premises. Whatever harmonisers of law assert, it is unclear how far consumers really are put off making purchases in foreign juris-dictions because of the difficulties of bringing court cases in a foreign court.[22] More to the point, even if reducing transaction costs may benefit producers and consumers, the extension of the neo-liberal market place may add to the costs to be paid by others such as workers. Criticising the mainstream approach, Werner Menski argues that

> the Euro-centric perspective that privileged the state (legocentrism) and territoriality (nationalist concerns) is not only quite parochial, but an idiom based on lost memory which does not lead towards a globally acceptable method of understanding law and its many pluralities, mixed manifestations, and commonalities (Menski: 198).

Moreover, he adds:

> This kind of monocultural myopic thinking leads, however, directly to African and other despots, who appear to be top-ranking students of legocentric axioms, and corrupt regimes anywhere in the world (Menski: 194).

For Menski,

> comparative lawyers must learn to harmonise local influences with emerging global patterns of thought, avoiding the current mental cul de sacs that dismiss local cultures as obstacles to the implementation of international laws and globally uniform human rights principles. In the age of localised globalisation, a new phase of diversity-conscious identity construction has become necessary (Menski: 210).

Legrand, for his part, attacks what he sees as the 'totalitarian rationality which privileges regulation, technological standardisation of law and the kind of epi-grammatic answers from foreign laws' (Legrand, 2006). For better or worse, standardised ways of thinking can be talked (or written) into existence as terms like 'economic loss', or 'discretion', which help create a meta-language and meta-perception of legal problems.

As an academic discipline comparative law is itself also a practice. As David Kennedy has shown in many of his writings, the subject has been characterised over time by a series of intellectual 'moves' which exemplify the way individual

---

[22] Goode, 2003 alleges that there is no empirical evidence that shows this to be true. But, more recently, Hondius, 2004 has claimed that there is indeed such evidence.

scholars pursue their agenda. The absence of open discussion of politics by many of the current generation of comparative lawyers can itself be seen as a political position (Kennedy, 2003). The issues discussed in this introduction—'getting beyond', placing in context, and finding similarities and differences—may all be seen in these terms. Masha Antokolskaia's invocation of 'trends', as we have noted, mobilises teleological certainty in the face of what might otherwise be seen as contingent value choices being made by politically-engaged social actors. Some of the developments towards safeguarding individual choice that she sees as crystal-lising what should be considered as better law in Europe are highly controversial as viewed by many in Catholic Italy. She herself recognises that social trends are only half the picture when she describes the European Court of Human Rights as involved in a 'dynamic interpretation' of the European Convention on Human Rights regarding divorce, the rights of extra-marital children, and the right of transsexuals to marry.

As we have seen, many critics claim that mainstream work is dominated by the desire to produce similarity (as a poor simulacrum of universality) rather than to appreciate differences. However, classifying a 'move' as more concerned to safe-guard difference or more to encourage similarity will rarely be sufficient in itself to resolve the politics of given choices. Interestingly, Christopher McCrudden points out in chapter sixteen what he calls a 'tension' between the practice of comparative law and the practice of human rights lawyers. While the former are often focused on significant differences, the latter have a universalistic perspective and mission. But this is not reported by Paul Roberts in his account of the devel-opment of international criminal law. Renaming 'female circumcision' as 'female genital mutilation' is part of an effort to introduce a more universal language so as to reduce the power of local culture (Merry, 2006). On the other hand, talk-ing up the importance of 'culture' can discourage efforts to change things for the better whether it is treated as part of a general trend affecting all modern societ-ies (Zedner, 2002), or used to explain why some countries will always lag behind (Krygier, 1997). Either way, insofar as they have power to help shape events schol-ars too must reflect on their responsibilities.

QUESTIONS FOR DISCUSSION

1. Contrast the theoretical and substantive chapters in this collection. Are some theoretical ideas used more in some substantive areas than others? Why?
2. Are some chapters more contextual than others? Are there good reasons for this?
3. Imagine that you had to rewrite one of the substantive chapters by focus-ing on the issue of legal tradition or legal culture or hybridity. How might the focus of the chapter change? What other data would you need to create or draw on?

4. Do the chapters on given legal topics show full awareness of the methods and findings of those studying other topics? Are the same issues necessarily relevant? What links could you suggest between the substantive chapters?
5. What is the difference between putting the 'law in context' and seeking the 'context in law'?
6. What are 'first-order' and 'second-order' approaches to comparative law? Is this distinction helpful?
7. Do Anthony Ogus and Nicholas Foster agree about the way commercial law evolves?
8. Is the search for 'better law', described in Masha Antokolskaia's chapter on family law, the fulfilment of the overlapping traditions that Patrick Glenn is calling for—or is it its antithesis?
9. What similarities and differences can you detect in the way John Bell, on the one hand, and Andrew Harding and Peter Leyland, on the other, approach the comparative study of public law?
10. Do Paul Roberts and Christopher McCrudden see the spread of human rights in the same way?
11. Are Esin Örücü and Werner Menski making the same points about mixed and hybrid legal systems?
12. Does harmonisation of law have the same implications and the same justifications in the areas of commercial law, family law and human rights law?
13. What practical implications would you draw from each of the substantive chapters in this Handbook?
14. Who are the main audiences targeted by the various contributions to the Handbook? (How far is Anthony Ogus thinking mainly of lawyers, John Bell, of judges, Masha Antokolskaia and Sjef van Erp, of legislators, and so on?) Whom do you think the authors have in mind as the ultimate beneficiaries of their comparisons?
15. Do you think comparative law is the same as comparative legal studies? If not, what are the arguments for and against going more in the latter direction? What would it involve?

BIBLIOGRAPHY AND FURTHER READING

An-Naim, A (1991/1996) *Toward an Islamic Reformation: Civil Liberties, Human Rights, and International Law* (New York, Syracuse University Press).

Berman, PS (2005) 'From International Law to Law and Globalization' 43 *Columbia Journal of Transnational Law* 485.

Blankenburg, E (1997) 'Civil Litigation rates as indicators of legal culture' in D Nelken (ed), *Comparing Legal Cultures* (Aldershot, Dartmouth) 41.

Bradley, D (1996) *Family law and Political Culture* (London, Sweet and Maxwell).

Cotterrell, R (1998) 'Why Must Legal Ideas Be Interpreted Sociologically?' 25 *Journal of Law and Society* 171.

—— (2006) 'Comparative law and Legal Culture' in R Zimmerman and M Reimann (eds), *Oxford Handbook of Comparative Law* (Oxford, Oxford University Press).

Curran, VG (1998) 'Cultural Immersion, Difference and Categories in US Comparative Law' 46 *American Journal of Comparative Law* 657.

De Sousa Santos, B (2002) 2nd edn *Toward a New Legal Common Sense: Law Globalization, and Emancipation* (London, Butterworths).

De Sousa Santos, B and Rodríguez-Garavito, CA (eds) (2005) *Law and Globalization From Below: Towards a Cosmopolitan Legality* (Cambridge, Cambridge University Press).

Dezalay, Y and Garth, B (1996) *Dealing in Virtue* (Chicago, University of Chicago Press).

Frankenberg, G (2006a) 'How to Do Projects with Comparative Law: Notes of an Expedition to the Common Core' 6(2) *Global Jurist Advances* art 1 http://www.bepress.com/gj/advances/vol6/iss2/art1

—— (2006b) 'Comparing Constitutions: Ideas, Ideals, and Ideology: Toward a Layered Narrative' vol 4 *International Journal of Constitutional Law* 439.

Glenn, HP (2000/2004) *Legal Traditions of the World* (Oxford, Oxford University Press).

Goldstein, A and Marcus, M (1977) 'The Myth of Judicial Supervision in Three Inquisitorial Systems: France, Italy and Germany' 87 *Yale Law Journal* 240.

Goode, R (2003) 'Contract and Commercial law: The Limits of Harmonization' (Maastricht 'Wiarda chair' inaugural lecture, METRO).

Graziadei, M (2003) 'The Functionalist Heritage' in P Legrand and R Munday (eds), *Comparative Legal Studies, Traditions and Transitions* (Cambridge, Cambridge University Press) 100.

Hodgson, J (2005) *French Criminal Justice* (Oxford, Hart Publishing).

Hondius, E (2004) 'The Protection of the Weak party in a Harmonised European Contract law: a Synthesis' 27 *Journal of Consumer Policy* 245.

Husa, J (October 2005) Review Article of E Örücü *The Enigma of Comparative Law: Variations on a Theme for the Twenty-First Century* 9.3 *Electronic Journal of Comparative Law* <http://www.ejcl.org/93/review93.html>.

Kagan, RA (2001) *Adversarial Legalism: The Anmerican Way of Law* (Cambridge, MA, Harvard University Press).

—— (2007) 'American and European Ways of Law: Six Entrenched Differences' in V Gessner and D Nelken (eds), *European Ways of Law* (Oxford, Hart Publishing).

Kennedy, D (2003) 'The Method and the Politics' in P Legrand and R Munday (eds), *Comparative Legal Studies: Traditions and Transitions* (Cambridge, Cambridge University Press) 345.

Krygier, M (1997) 'Is there Constitutionalism after Communism? Institutional Optimism, Cultural Pessimism and the Rule of Law' 26 *International Journal of the Sociology of Law* 17.

Lacey, N and Zedner, L (1998) 'Community in German Criminal Justice: a Significant Absence?' 7 *Social Legal Studies* 7.

Legrand, P (2006) 'Comparative Legal Studies and the matter of Authenticity' 1 *Journal of Comparative Law* 365.

Legrand, P and Munday, R (2003) *Comparative Legal Studies: Traditions and Transitions* (Cambridge, Cambridge University Press).

McBarnet, D (1981) *Law, the State and the Construction of Justice* (London, Macmillan).

Merry, S (2006) *Human Rights and Gender Violence* (Chicago, University of Chicago Press).

Nelken, D (1986) 'Criminal Law and Criminal Justice: Some Notes on their Irrelation' in ID Denis (ed), *Criminal Law and Justice* (London, Sweet and Maxwell).

—— (1995) 'Disclosing/Invoking Legal Culture' (in D Nelken (ed) special issue 'Legal Culture, Diversity and Globalisation') 4:4 *Social and Legal Studies* 435.

—— (1998) 'Blinding Insights: The Limits of a Reflexive Sociology of Law' 25 *Journal of Law and Society* 407.

—— (ed) (2000) *Contrasting Criminal Justice* (Aldershot, Ashgate).

—— (2001) 'The Meaning of Success in Transnational Legal Transfers' 19 *Windsor Yearbook of Access to Justice* 349.

—— (2002) 'Legal Transplants and Beyond: Of Disciplines and Metaphors' in A Harding and E Örücü (eds), *Comparative Law for the 21st Century*, (The Hague, Kluwer Law International).

—— (2003a) 'Beyond Compare? Criticising the American Way of Law', *Law and Social Inquiry* 28.3 181.

—— (2003b) 'Comparatists and Transferability' in P Legrand and R Munday (eds), *Comparative Legal Studies: Traditions and Transitions* (Cambridge, Cambridge University Press).

—— (2004) 'Using the concept of legal culture' 29 *Australian Journal of Legal Philosophy* 1.

—— (2006a) 'Signalling Conformity: Changing Norms in Japan and China' 27 *Michigan Journal of International Law* 933.

—— (2006b) 'Patterns of Punishment' 69 *Modern Law Review* 262.

—— (2006c) 'Italian Juvenile Justice: Tolerance, Leniency or Indulgence?' *Youth Justice* 2006 (6) 107.

—— (2006d) Review Article of E Örücü *The Enigma of Comparative Law: Variations on a Theme for the Twenty-First Centrury*, 26 *Legal Studies* 129.

—— (2007) 'Theorising the Embeddedness of Punishment' in D Melossi, M Sozzo and R Sparks (eds), *Travels of the Criminal Question: Cultural Embeddedness and Diffusion* (Oxford, Hart Publishing).

Nelken, D and Fesst, J (2001) *Adapting Legal Cultures* (Oxford, Hart Publishing).

Nottage, L (2004) 'Convergence, Divergence, and the Middle Way in Unifying or Harmonising Private Law' 1 *Annual of German and European Law* 166.

Örücü, E (2004) *The Enigma of Comparative Law: Variations on a Theme for the Twenty-First Century* (The Hague, Martinus Nijhoff).

Palmer, V (2004) 'From Lerotholi to Lando: Some Examples of Comparative Law Methodology' 4 *Global Jurist Frontiers* Issue 2.

Peters, A and Schwenke, H (2000) 'Comparative Law beyond Postmodernism' 49 *Internationall and Comparative Law Quarterly 801*.

Teubner, G (1998) 'Legal Irritants: Good faith in British Law or How Unifying Law Ends up in New Divergences' 61 *Modern Law Review* 11.

Van Hoecke, M (2002) 'Deep-level Comparative Law', *European University Institute working paper* 2002/13.

Whitman, J (2003a) 'The Neo-Romantic Turn' in P Legrand and R Munday (eds), *Comparative Legal Studies* (Cambridge, Cambridge University Press).

—— (2003b) *Harsh Justice* (Oxford, Oxford University Press).

Zedner, L (2002) 'Dangers of Dystopia in Penal Theory', *Oxford Journal of Legal Studies* 341.

Zweigert, K and Kötz, H (1998) 3rd edn *An Introduction to Comparative Law* (Oxford, Oxford University Press).

2

Developing Comparative Law

ESİN ÖRÜCÜ

KEY CONCEPTS

Comparative law, Comparative legal studies, Comparability, Purposes of comparative law, Common core, Methodology of comparative law, Normative inquiry, *Tertium comparitionis*, Presumption of similarity, *De lege ferenda* studies, 'Functional equivalence', The 'factual approach', 'Law in context', Legal families, Legal culture, Legal tradition, Macro comparison—micro comparison

I. PRELIMINARIES

THIS CHAPTER CONSIDERS the traditional topics dealt with in the introductory part of comparative law classes such as the definition, uses and purposes of comparative law, its place in harmonisation and its methodology. It indicates the changing nature of comparative law, the process of comparison and problems connected to intra-cultural and cross-cultural comparisons.

During the past decade we have witnessed increasing interest in all forms of comparative law, international law and transnational law. The character, quality and quantity of work have increased and changed, but the basic problems have remained the same. There is no one definition of what comparative law and comparative method are. While there is now less concern with 'justifying the practical utility of comparative law', 'making its subject matter manageable' and 'avoiding superficiality' (Twining, 2000b: 51), the emphasis has shifted to regarding comparative law as 'a big tent, encompassing lots of different types of scholarship' (Kennedy, 2002: 345).

Comparative law, as we know it today, can be regarded as a child of the 19th century that has reached adolescence in the 20th.[1] During this period, the subject seems to have given comparative lawyers total freedom and provided them with the seemingly endless pastime of discussing its true meaning, historical development, dangers, virtues, scope, functions, aims and purposes, uses and misuses, and the method.

---

[1] The history of comparative law is not to be discussed in this work, but see Zweigert and Kötz, 1998, and the bibliography provided there, at 48–62.

In the 21st century comparative law will reach maturity. Though our century has been heralded as 'the age of comparative law', amazingly, it is still open to question whether comparative law is indeed an independent discipline at all (Samuel, 1998; Gordley, 1998). Not only have comparative lawyers been called upon to re-think their subject (Markesinis, 1990), but it has also been suggested that the best path for comparative law to secure its future is to penetrate other subjects.

Objectives as varied as aiding law reform and policy development, providing a tool of research to reach a universal theory of law, giving a critical perspective to students and an aid to international law practice, facilitating international unification and harmonisation of laws, helping courts to fill gaps in the law and even working towards the furthering of world peace and tolerance have been attributed to comparative law. These objectives can be grouped as practical, sociological, political and pedagogical.

In addition, we see such terms as 'traditional comparative law', 'mainstream comparative law', 'conventional comparative law', 'critical comparative law', and 'post-modern comparative law' being used.

One thing is certain: there is a growing interest in comparative law. There are a number of new journals with 'Comparative Law' in their titles; the number of articles with a comparative element published in these journals has quadrupled within the past 10 years (see Monateri, 1998). It has become indispensable for all doctoral researchers, judges and legislators to consult foreign material as a matter of routine.

> For a long time it looked as though comparative law was a matter for academic research, difficult and, surely, very interesting, beautiful to know something about, but not immediately relevant to the daily life of the law. Over the last ten or fifteen years the legal climate seems to be changing. This evolution may be influenced by the process of European integration; it may also result from the fact that we are living closer together (the 'global village' situation); it may finally be an autonomous process, occasioned by the lawyer's search for fresh perspectives, in particular when completely new legal problems are to be solved (Koopmans, 1996: 545).

Although Harold Gutteridge once observed that, 'the essential problem is not: What is comparative law? The question of real importance is: What is its purpose?' (Gutteridge, 1949/1974: 5), most works on comparative law start with the question: 'What is comparative law?' and then attempt to define it. One rather circular, vague and open-ended definition tells us for instance that 'the words suggest an intellectual activity with law as its object and comparison as its process' (Zweigert and Kötz, 1998: 2).

Comparative law, sometimes referred to as an 'incomplete theme', is the juxtaposing, contrasting and comparing of legal systems or parts thereof with the aim of finding similarities and differences. However, the definition can be much wider than that: Comparative law is a science of knowledge with its own separate sphere; an independent science, producing theoretical distillate. Comparative law can be regarded as the 'critical method of legal science'.

Indeed comparative law is a very broad field and the fruits of comparative study can be put to many uses. Yet, it cannot be justified by its uses or objectives alone. As Rodolfo Sacco points out,

> the use to which scientific ideas are put effects neither the definition of a science nor the validity of its conclusions (Sacco, 1991a).

We know that the everyday process of thinking involves the making of a series of comparisons, that is, a process of contrasting and comparing, juxtaposing the unknown and the known, and we comprehend the phenomena around us by observing differences and similarities:

> Just as the qualities of a yellow, its hue, brilliance and tone are perceived and sharpened most truly by placing it first on or beside another yellow and secondly by placing it in contrast to purple, so we explore the world around us (Örücü, 1986: 57).

So, we see that comparison is involved in all methods of scholarly investigation, 'whose purpose is the discovery of sameness and difference' (Hall, 1963: 20). It is also in this way that we understand the legal world around us.

Looking at the world of law and the environment in which it lives, comparative law can provide knowledge about 'law as rules', 'law in context' and 'law as culture', thus enabling us to have comprehensive and in-depth knowledge of the legal phenomena and their interactions in society. Comparative law draws from the pool of models to illustrate the general points it is making. Like legal theory, legal history and legal sociology, it brings additional perspectives, although it is said that 'traditional comparative law' has failed by paying insufficient attention to context and ignoring the context of ideas (Ewald, 1995). Traditional legal doctrine engages in comparative law through the 'law as rules' approach. This bears the prejudices of positivism and of national legal cultures. It is important to regard comparative law 'as an indispensable international component of a "*culture juridique*"' (Zweigert and Kötz, 1998: 54). Comparative law gives us a tool of communication.

It has also been said that comparative law 'has by common consent the somewhat unusual characteristic that it does not exist' (Kahn-Freund, 1966: 40–1), and that comparative law is not another branch of law; it certainly is not independent of the subject area it is investigating. As Harold Gutteridge observed:

> The process of comparing rules of law taken from different systems does not result in the formulation of any independent rules ... Not only are there no 'comparative' rules of law but there are no transactions or relationships which can be described as comparative (Gutteridge, 1949: 1).

In this view one could at best talk of a comparative family law, a comparative constitutional law or a comparative contract law. Here the comparison is not the central element of the comparative work, the focus being on fields of law that are inquired into comparatively for specific purposes such as law reform, harmonisation or offering solutions to problems of domestic law. There must always be specificity and purpose in comparative law research. One should, in fact, talk of 'applied' comparative law.

William Twining puts forward three reasons for questioning the idea that 'comparative law is an autonomous discipline or sub-discipline'. According to him, the first reason is that such an idea is philosophically dubious; the second that since all legal scholarship involves comparison, 'it is misleading, indeed dangerous' to set comparative law apart; and the third that comparative law has no defined subject-matter (Twining, 2000a: 45).

It has been said that comparative law is simply a method of looking at law. As a technique, comparative law is used to collect information on foreign law—an entire legal system, an institution or a rule—to juxtapose and contrast the findings and make comparisons, that is, to identify similarities and differences. The purposes or objectives of this method are what give comparative law meaning. As a facilitative method, comparative law could be applied to domestic problems or transactions across international boundaries. In this sense it has close connections with international private law.

But for the academic comparative lawyer the prime function of comparative law, sometimes called 'scholarly comparative law', is to provide access to legal knowledge which can be used not only for the purposes of law reform, or as a research tool, or to promote international understanding, but to fulfil its essential task of furthering the universal knowledge and understanding of the phenomenon of law. A succinct view formulated by Richard Tur summarises the ultimate position:

> The unity of general jurisprudence and comparative law consists in the unity of form and content; they are essential moments of legal knowledge, different sides of the same coin. General jurisprudence without comparative law is empty and formal: comparative law without general jurisprudence is blind and non-discriminating. General jurisprudence with comparative law is real and actual: comparative law with general jurisprudence is selective and clear-sighted (Tur, 1977: 238 at 249).

CM Campbell wrote:

> The term 'comparative law' can mean so much or so little that it is only by examining particular methods, aims, approaches and the consequent utilisation that we can glean from 'comparative law' substance and purpose (Campbell, 1966).

In addition to the question: 'What is comparative law?', a second concern is with the name of the subject itself. This concern is voiced mostly in the English-speaking world. Is the term comparative law appropriate? It has been said that the term 'comparative law' is misleading in the English version of the name. In some other languages, as translated, the subject is either called 'Comparison of Laws' or 'Legal Comparison' (*Rechtsvergleichung*, *Rechtsverkelijking*) or 'Law Compared' or 'Compared Law' (*droit comparé*). For some, 'Legal Comparison', as used in Germany, may be the most appropriate term to be used here, since 'Legal Comparison' indicates clearly that there is no interest in the extrinsic factors in the comparisons to be undertaken, which should remain normative. Others today find the terms 'comparative analysis of law' or 'comparative study of law' more suitable. However, it has also been stated that,

[b]ecause law is not only a reference but is the very field of our study, the traditional term of comparative law is fully justified and suitably reflects the field of our scholarly endeavours (Karameus, 2001: 859 at 867).

Not only law, but comparison, are the central elements.

Though the more recently coined and widely used title 'Comparative Legal Studies', has a confusing aspect in that it indicates studies beyond the law as conventionally understood, this has a generality beyond the normative approach dominant among black-letter-law comparatists, and implies a wider approach to law. In a recent work, for example, carrying the title 'Comparative Legal Studies: Traditions and Transitions', it is stated that the term 'Comparative Legal Studies' in the title was chosen deliberately to avoid 'this academic quagmire' (Munday, 2002: 20).

II. METHODOLOGY OF COMPARATIVE LAW

This part considers the methodology, language and problems of comparative law. 'Functional equivalence' and some problems connected to it are discussed and the issue of 'context' is introduced.

The first concern is what is meant by comparability. Is an element of similarity necessary for comparability? What is the so-called 'meaningful' comparison? We have seen that the term 'comparative law' itself is by no means free from ambiguity; the factor of 'comparability' is even less so.

The fact that any one thing can be compared with any other thing has not prevented wide and varied discussion of the concept of 'comparability' by comparative lawyers. The discussion hails from the common belief that 'things to be compared must be comparable', and usually revolves around the words 'like' and 'similar'. It is stressed that 'like must be compared with like' and '*similia similibus*'—these being two well-established maxims of comparative law. What is 'like' in law? How 'like' do things have to be to be 'comparable'? May we not compare diverse legal systems, legal institutions or legal rules and come to the conclusion that they are not 'like'?

Can we not, for example, compare a divorce case with an eviction case if our intention is to find out how courts deal with cases in general and to develop an understanding of how long cases take in court or how decisions are written? Could we not compare, for instance, an English statute on taxation, town and country planning or matrimonial causes with three pieces of German legislation on entirely different topics if we were trying to establish how such documents are prepared and how long or detailed they are, in order to develop an understanding of such a source of law? The examples could be infinite (see Bogdan, 1994: 58).

It is claimed that 'comparison is possible only if the instances are comparable and the results interpretable'.[2] It is further claimed that, 'comparisons can be

---

[2] Merryman, 1974: 92, and also in Merryman, 1999: 489, where he discusses Zelditch's views on comparability, referring to Zelditch, 'Intelligible Comparisons' in Vallier (ed), *Comparative Methods in Sociology* (1971) at 267–307.

useful only if the legal institutions under investigation are naturally or function-ally comparable'. Comparative law is said to be a comparison of 'comparable' legal institutions or of the solutions to 'comparable' legal problems in different systems (Zweigert and Kötz, 1998: 34). Is the approach we want to take today one that says that only 'similar' things could be compared? In many languages the word 'comparable' 'can also mean "approximately similar" or "not too different"' (Bogdan, 1994). Thus to talk of 'comparability' may evoke an intellectual activity of juxtaposing somewhat similar systems, institutions or rules.

Comparative law scholars use the term *tertium comparationis*, a common comparative denominator which could be the third unit besides the two legal *comparanda*, that is, the elements to be compared—the *comparatum* and the *comparandum*. Here, comparability is seen to depend on the presence of common elements that render juridical phenomena 'meaningfully comparable'. What the comparative lawyer looks at as *tertium comparationis* could the 'common func-tion' between institutions and rules, the 'common goal' they set out to achieve, the 'problem', the 'factual situations' they are created to solve or the solutions offered.

Another concern is which methods can and should be used by comparative lawyers. Is there a standard comparative law methodology? Apart from regarding comparison itself as a method, the problems of comparative legal methodology are very varied and have been discussed in different ways by many comparative lawyers.[3] 'Functional equivalence' and the 'problem-oriented' approach, 'model-building' and 'common core' studies, the 'factual' approach and 'method in action' are just some approaches to the question: 'How to compare?' put forward in the last century. 'How to compare now' is actually the title of an article by Pierre Legrand, one of the more controversial comparatists of our times (Legrand, 1996; Legrand, 1999: 1).

'Comparison' clearly is a method used in all fields of study, be they social sci-ences or natural sciences, such as governance, economics, linguistics, architecture and so on. 'It is a way of looking, it is a mode of approaching material, a method in the process of cognition' (Örücü, 1986: 57). In this sense 'comparative method' is an empirical, descriptive research design using 'comparison' as a technique to cognise. However, when the term 'comparative' is included in the name of a sub-division of a field such as comparative architecture, comparative linguistics or comparative law, it denotes an area of study and in that context, the word 'comparative' in the title no longer depicts only a method, but an independent branch of that science. The subject, then, develops its own methods. Comparative law is more closely related to social sciences, from where it borrowed its methods, than to 'pure' normative inquiry, which seems to characterise other types of legal research.

Although comparative law research is open ended—the methodology being dictated by the strategy of the comparative lawyer—and there is no standard

---

[3] See Roberts, 1972; and see also a number of chapters in Legrand and Munday (eds), 2003.

methodology, the possibility of comparison is dependent upon the existence and availability of data. Data can best be obtained by employing social science methodology. The first stage, the inquiry, is also related to concept building, where concepts that are neither so broad as to be meaningless nor too narrow to cover more than one instance, have to be devised. Umbrella concepts may have to be created.

The classical technique of legal methodology of reading texts of all kinds and hoping for insight has serious limitations for collecting data to serve comparative inquiry adequately. Unless there is collaboration between legal and social science researchers, comparative law falls short of its function, not only as a way of enhancing understanding and knowledge of law in context, but also as a source of models and of empirical information and knowledge.

Following the inquiry, a comparative lawyer is expected to describe, juxtapose, identify similarities and differences and then venture into the field of explanation. It is here that hypotheses are needed and it is here that real comparison starts. This explanation, this discovery of the raison d'être for the differences and similarities, also necessitates moving from the domain of pure legal reasoning to that of contextual factors.

Black-letter-law oriented traditional comparative law research is normative, structural, institutional and positivistic. The empirical school suggests that the appropriate method should begin with the facts rather than hypotheses, and end in description. This is said to be a realistic approach, since the present-day lawyer is well equipped to use this method.

Explanation of the differences and similarities identified is an accounting for these findings. It is at this stage that context becomes indispensable for understanding. John Merryman says that 'the explanatory approach represents one attempt to choose error over confusion' (Merryman, 1974: 100). An explanation of findings, of exceptional and typical cases, an accounting for differences and similarities, is thus not just a necessary step in comparative research but is its essence. Some of the hypotheses may also serve as explanations, but for some findings new explanations have to be found. When the comparative law researcher examines these explanations in order to understand why the legal systems have produced the institutions they have, the explanations may not be legal ones, and the texts themselves will show the differences but not offer explanations. Yet explanation is not the final step in a piece of comparative research. Findings must be verified and confirmed, and only then is the work deemed to be complete. This is the theory-testing stage for the tentative hypotheses.

Creative comparative law research may also be interested in suggesting 'core concepts' and point the way to 'ideal systems', or at least to the 'better law' approach. William Twining has remarked that comparative lawyers are concerned 'with description, analysis and explanation, rather than evaluation and prescription' (Twining, 2000a; Twining, 2000b: 34). In relation to the search for 'better law', there is scope for evaluation and prescription. However, the legitimacy of this activity remains questionable.

We must remember that a comparative lawyer faces a number of additional problems. These include the choice of systems, appreciation of cross-cultural systems, language, terminology, translations, both participant and non-participant observer effect, access to material beyond the legal, the absurdity of explanations offered, the reliability of secondary sources, the existence of historical accidents and anachronism of predictions.

In order to fulfil the requirements of scholarly comparative research, both similarities and differences must be considered, keeping in mind, however, that the purpose is not to search particularly for similarity or difference but to observe what is actually there. When there is similarity, this cannot be ignored just because the researcher is keen to follow the 'contrarian challenge', nor can a difference be glossed over because some other policy consideration such as European integration or globalisation dictates that only similarities should be highlighted.

When the comparison is of legal rules, provisions and institutions only, the comparative lawyer starts with rules whose functions are equivalent and collects relevant data that lead to a succinct description. Here, contrasting is the first step of comparing. As suggested by the empirical school, the method begins with the facts, 'the problem', and ends in description. Similarities and differences brought to light by this contrasting and comparing are then identified.

If for instance, a comparative lawyer were asked, say, by the English Law Commission, to look into 'do-it-yourself divorces' in the laws of the Member States of the European Union with a view to facilitating divorce in England, all she would have to do is report on the different schemes, describe them, and identify the differences and similarities between them and also between them and the domestic law. She would not evaluate the findings, this being the task of the Law Commission and to be determined in keeping with the policy decisions made there. In such cases, the comparative lawyer is purely a facilitator, a lawyer looking at laws comparatively. It is for others to build with these bricks. She would not enter the arena of prescription of a 'better law' consequent to an evaluation.

Blueprints have been suggested that could be employed in comparative law research. For example, Peter de Cruz suggests an eight-step method: an outline plan of action identifying the problem; identifying the foreign jurisdiction and the parent legal family; deciding on primary sources of law that will be relevant; gathering and assembling the relevant material (and here he offers a normative checklist); organising the material in accordance with headings; tentatively mapping out the possible answers to the problem (here bearing cultural differences in mind); critically analysing the legal principles according to their intrinsic meaning; and finally, setting out the conclusions within a comparative framework with caveats if necessary (de Cruz, 1999: 235–239).

It is time now to look at 'functional equivalence' and its problems, and at other approaches. At the level of micro-comparison, it has been widely argued that the true basis of comparative law is functional equivalence. According to Michele Graziadei, functionalism represents two distinct currents: the 'functionalist method' which is 'one of the best-known working tools in comparative legal studies', and 'functionalism' in the sense 'that law responds to society's needs' (Graziadei, 2003: 100).[4] Though the 'functionalist method' is not 'the sole or even the dominant approach' in comparative law research, and is being challenged today, it has gained new life 'under the flag' of 'common core studies' in Europe.

When 'law' is regarded as a body of rules only and comparison at the microlevel is directed at these rules, then the functional approach is useful, since a body of rules is created for the purpose of solving human problems, most of which are shared. Thus, in the context of the European Union for example, where comparative law is a driving force and has a decisive role in the harmonisation process, the 'functional comparative analysis method' provides the potential for convergence of both the legal systems and the legal methods of the Member States, leading to gradual and eventual legal integration. In this, to build on similarities is desirable.

In fact the one effective method in comparative law research in relation to European 'common core' projects, is functionalism. This comes from the universalist approach to human needs. Social problems are universal; laws respond to these needs in various ways but the end results are comparable; hence, a 'concrete problem' is the starting block. 'It is possible to compare the incomparable provided that the focus is on the same facts' (Graziadei, 2003: 105); hence the 'factual approach'. If facts are not the same there is no comparability. In the universalist approach the similarity of solutions is paramount. If this were not so there would be no place for comparisons. Functional inquiry also suits the utilitarian approach to comparative law. So, comparative lawyers should seek out institutions that have the same role, that is, those which have functional comparability or solve the same problem, that is, similarity of solutions. Konrad Zweigert and Hein Kötz regard this issue as finite and say:

> the basic methodological principle of all comparative law is that of functionality ... Incomparables cannot be usefully compared and in law the only things which are comparable are those which fulfil the same function (Zweigert and Kötz, 1998: 34).

The question is: 'Which institution in system B performs an equivalent function to the one under survey in system A?' From the answer to this question, the concept of 'functional equivalence' emerges. For example, if an institution called divorce is under survey in system A, the comparative lawyer looks for an institution in system B performing an equivalent function; that of freeing an individual from an unsatisfactory marital relationship within which he or she does not wish to remain. Again, if the institution of 'solicitor' is under survey in Scotland, the comparative private lawyer looks for an institution performing an equivalent function—that of preparing documents for litigation, dealing with

---

[4] See also, for a useful discussion of functionalism with a capital (F) and a small (f), Twining, 2003: 213–17 and 238–43.

non-contentious matters, representing the client, and so on—in another system, for example, The Netherlands.

An alternative to the functional-institutional approach, or a variation of it, is the problem-solving, the sociological approach. This problem-solving basis seeks an answer to the question: 'How is a specific social or legal problem encountered both in society A and society B resolved by their respective (legal or other) systems?' In other words, 'What legal or other institutions have developed to cope with it?' This approach, similar to the 'functionalist' approach, springs from the belief that similar problems have similar solutions across legal systems, though reached by different routes. For example, how is the problem of supporting a wife who would otherwise be destitute after the termination of marriage, resolved in societies A and B? Again, how is an individual represented in court in Scotland and The Netherlands respectively? This matter may be tackled differently and handled by different bodies in the two societies. In this connection it is said that, 'the fact that the problem is one and the same warrants the comparability'.[5]

However, the functional-institutional approach does not solve the issue of comparability as between a Western legal system and a religious system or a developing legal system. In addition, if a problem arises in one legal system but has no counterpart in another, this approach faces another dilemma. Legal systems pertaining to societies that are socio-culturally and legal-culturally different from each other can also be compared even if for the purpose of establishing diversity, and in this case the functional-institutional approach cannot be the basis. The functional-institutional approach has also been challenged as not working between capitalist and socialist legal systems, in spite of the fact that the very basic human needs are universal. There are other fundamental criticisms of this approach on grounds such as the limited number of subject areas that can be compared by using this method and the fact that many areas of law are left out of the scope of comparison since they are regarded as 'not lending themselves to comparison', determined as they are by specific histories, ethical values, political ideologies, cultural differences or religious beliefs. Not only that, but the question of whether each rule or each institution has only one function—'one institution or rule with many functions'—has not been satisfactorily addressed. In addition, although law can be seen as 'a body of rules', it is much wider than that.

It would be odd to allow comparative law research but one methodology, 'functional inquiry', which has only a technical perspective. Therefore, although employing 'functional equivalence' as a tool of comparability at the micro-level for specific projects is appropriate, comparatists opt for a multiplicity of approaches, compare differents and contexts, and extend comparison beyond functionally equivalent rules.

---

[5] Schmitthoff, 1939: 96, where he refers to M Salomon's work, *Grundlegung zur Rechtsphilosophie* (1925).

In fact, recently, many other bases have been presented as being more appropriate. As Michele Graziadei notes:

> no one could have foreseen the plurality of methods which are currently being practised when comparative law was thought to be a method in itself (Graziadei, 2003: 101; and Husa, 2003).

'Comparison' itself could be viewed as the method but this would be reductivist since there are indeed a number of methodological options. Most of these are contextual approaches such as analysis of existing rules and institutions in 'historical context', 'economic context', 'political context' or in 'social or cultural context'. Some of these approaches are now dubbed as post-modernist, intermingled with legal realism. However, the functional method was built to do away with 'the local dimensions' of rules and to reduce the rules to their operative description 'freed from the context' of their own systems; whereas, the contextual approaches specifically stress the 'local dimension'.

In any case, even the so-called functionally equivalent institutions are what they are because they reflect the structure of the legal and social system within which they exist. Thus, legal, social, cultural, economic, religious and political backgrounds cannot be neglected. Indeed, in the explanation of results this background is vital. Legal systems and legal institutions in countries socio-culturally and legal-culturally different from one another must be comparable for a comparative lawyer who wants to leave the shores of Euro-centrisism and to investigate 'localisms' in our 'globalising' world.

III. THE PURPOSES OF COMPARATIVE LAW RESEARCH

We have also seen that there is not one simple answer to the question: What is the purpose of carrying out comparative legal research? A distinction has to be drawn between scholarly activities and the activities of the legislatures, the practitioners of the law and the judiciary. In other words, as there is no one identifiable method, there is no one identifiable purpose, there is a multiplicity of purposes. Comparative law research has moved in a number of distinct directions. If one surveys the bulk of work undertaken to date the following objectives are clear: law reform and policy development by the legislature, aid to the international practice of law, international harmonisation and unification, common core research, and a gap-filling device in law courts. The findings of comparative lawyers can be utilised for any of these. There are also other purposes such as 'giving students perspective', 'being a tool of research to reach a universal theory of law' and 'aiding world peace'.

Let us now consider some of these purposes. First, let us start with the general purpose.

Comparative law research is undertaken to improve and consolidate knowledge of the law and understanding of the law in context. As mentioned in the previous discussion on the nature of comparative law, this branch of legal science gives us insight into law and legal texture as no other branch can. We understand the legal world around us by juxtaposing the unknown to the known. The aim is to sharpen awareness and cognition of the legal, social and cultural environments in which we live. This is best done not just by discovering resemblances between the 'similar' or even similarities between the 'different', but more fundamentally by finding and explaining similarities between the 'different', and differences and divergences between the 'similar'. Comparative law thrives on differences (see, eg Legrand, 2003: 240). Scholarly comparative law research, by increasing detailed understanding of legal phenomena points towards diverse systems; the more diverse the systems, the more rewarding the findings.

The aim is not to create one law for the whole world. Neither is it utopian— to form a dictionary of legal terms in all languages. Far from it. The aim is to dis-cover and understand differences between legal systems and legal institutions and explain the reasons for these in order to enhance knowledge and, at the same time, to discover similarities between different and diverse legal systems and find explana-tions for these.

As early as 1938 it was said by Harold Gutteridge that

> [t]he isolation of legal thought in national watertight compartments has always seemed to me to be one of the factors which is most prolific in producing that frame of mind which leads to a spirit of national egotism. We have much to learn from one another in legal as well as other departments of human activities, and it is, in a sense, a reproach to the lawyers of all nations that they have been unable, up to the present, to arrive at the free interchange of knowledge and ideas which has been attained in other branches of learning (Gutteridge, 1938: 401 at 410).

Let us look now at the second general purpose: the grouping of legal systems. This objective can even be the starting line of all comparative law activity. Legal systems, legal cultures and legal traditions are classified for the purpose of comparison. In recent years, as legal systems shift even more quickly, there have been many developments in this area.[6] Where scholarly comparative law research is also concerned in tracing relationships, legal systems historically related by colonisation, imposition and borrowing, and systems related in other ways must be studied. In order to understand the changes that take place dur-ing the moving of institutions, the emphasis must be placed on the institutions that have moved.

Thirdly, comparative law serves the purpose of broadening the mind of the law student and helps in the development of tolerance. In this context, the most valuable course to be offered to undergraduates is not comparative family law, comparative contract law, comparative civil procedure or even comparative pri-vate law or comparative public law, but an autonomous general comparative law course providing the breadth necessary for the development of critical minds. One very important role of comparative law studies is to put an objective distance

[6] See ch 8.

between the student and her own legal system and to encourage that critical questioning mind in assessing domestic law.

Another purpose that can justify the use of comparative law research is in legislative law reform, when the comparative lawyer works *de lege ferenda,* in which case to aid the legislature, comparative law research can provide a pool of models from which to choose. The purpose will dictate the choice of models: legal systems preferably in socio-cultural and legal-cultural affinity, systems which share the same problem and systems which deal with the same problem in different ways, better ways or more efficient ways, from whose solutions the reformer can learn and derive answers.

Fifthly, comparative law research can also provide a tool of interpretation for judges by making them aware of foreign solutions to similar problems when there are none at home. In other words, it acts as a gap-filling device, *de lege lata.* Judges may have to refer to foreign law out of necessity when the case they are dealing with involves a foreign element, such as where private international law rules apply or cases involve the application of, for example, European Directives or Regulations, where a knowledge of cases from Luxembourg is required or the decisions of the courts of other Member States related to that instrument must be looked at. Recently there has been increasing interest in comparative law among the judiciary; an active search for a universal language.[7] It may soon become possible to talk of a 'common law or a *ius commune* of human rights' for instance.[8] This 'common law' is now being developed by domestic judges in conversation with judges from other jurisdictions and from the European Court of Human Rights. This search for 'commonality' can be seen as connected to 'common core' research, comparative law being geared towards discovering 'common cores', and further, creating 'better law'.

Yet another area where comparative law is of use is in the drawing up of international conventions and agreements. The terminology to be used in international documents must be distilled from the laws of the legal systems of the target audience. Additionally, comparative law is indispensable in the interpretation of international instruments. Comparative lawyers' work is essential in discovering the 'general principles of law recognised by civilised nations' or by 'member states', and in determining the customary rules of public international law.

A seventh purpose is the use of comparative law research in the harmonisation of law. The activity envisaged might either be harmonisation only or unification with prior harmonisation. Here the choice of the legal systems and subjects to be comparatively researched is pre-determined by political considerations. Systems to be studied will be those whose laws will be harmonised or unified. The comparative law researcher's work is to provide ideas for the necessary changes to the legal systems or institutions to be harmonised, to smooth the process or suggest

---

[7] See chs 16 and 18 of this Handbook.
[8] See contributions in Örücü (ed), 2003. See also see ch 16 of this Handbook.

the creation of a model law or a unified law. A thorough knowledge of all the systems involved in the process is required before an approximation is suggested. More problems will be encountered if the two or more systems involved are socio-culturally and/or legal-culturally diverse.

We see today that in the context of the European Union, a number of Commissions are working on projects to produce 'General European Principles' in a number of fields. Most of these are 'common core' based principles. General principles could be drafted 'with a low level modernity and innovation using the common core methodology', or such principles could be drafted 'based upon the highest standard or modernity ... using the "better law" method' (Antokolskaia, 2003: 160). Though harmonisation suggests that the new rules should be 'derived from existing laws rather than invented by the drafters', in practice what is done is to 'make use of a rule that is common for all or most of the relevant jurisdictions', or a rule selected 'that represents a minority or even one jurisdiction' (*ibid*).

Obviously the 'common core' approach is the easiest to use, as it makes justification more straightforward by restating what represents the majority. However, as one tries to move closer to the majority of the jurisdictions, the value of the exercise may diminish. Also, gathering the rules that achieve the same end may prove to be difficult in practice. Even when a 'common core' is found, this may not correspond to a 'satisfactory' solution. Another problem concerns similar legal concepts that conceal fundamentally different understandings. Therefore a move towards the 'better law' approach may become attractive.

However, in the selection of the 'better law', justification of the choice made can be taxing as it is difficult to decide what is 'modernity' and what is 'progressive'. Also the 'better law' approach entails a comparative evaluation of all the legal systems or legal solutions involved. This could prove to be impossible. Inevitably by making choices, drafters take up positions and express value judgements. Even if a quantitative measurement were possible, the 'data' relied on would not answer the question: 'Why?' It may have to be admitted that

> no objective criteria can be found in order to justify the choice as to why the drafters consider the rule they have selected to be the 'better' one (Antokolskaia, 2003: 181).

Especially in areas politically and ideologically coloured, justification would have to be subjective 'depending on the conviction of the drafters' (*ibid*). When courts adopt this approach in search of commonality, then the same considerations must be faced. It is also difficult to secure total agreement on the necessity and desirability of the 'better law' in all localisms involved.

IV. UNITS OF COMPARISON: MACRO-COMPARISON AND MICRO-COMPARISON

'What is to be to compared?' is usually dealt with at two levels: the macro-comparative and the micro-comparative. These levels are complementary, since the second presupposes the first. Let us consider these respectively.

Comparability at the level of macro-comparison, or macro-comparability, materialises at the level of legal systems. Therefore, the definition of a legal system may be the first task to tackle. For one comparative lawyer, John Merryman, a legal system means

> the complex of legal institutions, actors and processes in the context of a legal culture and the secondary legal rules (Merryman, 1974: 101).

Furthermore, a legal system

> has a vocabulary used to express concepts, its rules are arranged into categories, it has techniques for expressing rules and interpreting them, it is linked to a view of the social order itself which determines the way in which the law is applied and shapes the very function of law in that society (David and Brierley, 1985: 193).

Although it is difficult to assess how far any legal system is linked to a specific social order, it can be said that laws are imbedded in political and social cultures. It is essential, for the purpose of later attempts at explaining differences and similarities encountered in the legal systems under comparison, that the notion of a system as a macro-unit combines the legal system with the societal, cultural, political and economic systems. Most of the differences that cannot be explained in terms of the legal system can more easily be explained in terms of the societal, political or economic systems. Social systems may determine the content of the corresponding legal systems and vice versa. The same could be said of the economic systems.

At the level of macro-comparison, many comparative lawyers argue that the comparison must extend to the same evolutionary stage of different legal systems under comparison. For example, Harold Gutteridge understands from 'compare like with like', that 'concepts, rules or institutions under comparison must relate to the same stage of legal, political and economic development' (Gutteridge, 1949: 73). This means that at the macro-level, the legal systems under comparison should be at the same stage of development, economic, social and legal.

However, it could be argued that at the macro-level, 'comparability' may be relative to the interests and the purpose of the comparative lawyer and that it is the aims of the specific comparative study that should determine the choice of legal systems to be compared. Whether the preferred systems have reached the same degree of development, legal or otherwise, may be a secondary consideration (Kamba, 1976: 494 at 507–8). Nor need one carry out comparative research only in groups of legal systems with broadly shared attributes. Even if one were to think the reverse, history shows otherwise, and the overlapping and mixed systems expand the scope of the comparative field to legal systems grouped in different ways and at different levels of development.[9]

Ideally, macro-comparison and micro-comparison should merge, since the micro-comparative topic must be placed within the entire legal system. Hence,

---

[9] See ch 8.

the macro-comparative unit, that is, the totality of the legal system in context, is the frame within which all is contained and evaluated. Within the context of a supra-legal system, such as the European Union for example, the comparative lawyer has an even wider frame within which to evaluate her findings. From such analysis it is possible to venture into suggesting common denominators, be they at the level of the lowest, the average or the highest. 'Common core' studies also can be pursued after such exploration.

Traditionally, as stated, at the macro-level, comparative law has been concerned with comparing 'the legal systems of different nations'. This is the starting point for writers such as René David and John Brierley, and Konrad Zweigert and Hein Kötz. William Twining indicates that 'mainstream' comparative law has two approaches. At the macro-level, the approach is what he calls the very broad 'Grands Systèmes' approach, and at the micro-level, the 'Country and Western' tradition, concentrating on some aspects of private law (Twining, 2000a: 32).

Today, logic necessitates moving the focus from legal system and legal family to legal culture or legal tradition.[10] What a legal culture is may be more difficult to determine than determining what a legal system is, however. It has been said that

> the center of gravity of legal development lies not in legislation, nor in jurisdic science, nor in judicial decisions, but in society itself (Ehrlich, 1912/1939: xv).

This observation takes us into the mysteries of the interaction of social norms and legal rules. For instance, Henry Ehrmann looks at legal culture as a link and says that

> the attitudes, beliefs, and emotions of the operators as well as of the users (and victims) of the legal system have much to do with the way in which it functions (Ehrmann, 1976: 9).

Is it this link that should be studied? Are comparative lawyers then to look into what is called by Henry Ehrmann 'legal culture', but by John Merryman, 'legal tradition', the two definitions given being the same? Then we see Patrick Glenn, who challenges the very notion of culture and insists on the word 'tradition', the term 'tradition' taking on a different meaning (the presence of the past) from that used by John Merryman (see Glenn, 2000).

So, how do comparative lawyers align themselves? In a broader approach, the comparative lawyer must understand the relationship between legal systems, legal cultures and legal traditions as well as find rules that are not necessarily within the formal framework of the legal system but are held by the people to be valid. Both the 'bottom-up' and the 'top-down' models of law must be understood and appreciated. In addition, her approach must be broad and inclusive.

This broad approach to comparative law would certainly move us away from 'legal systems' and the 'law as rules' attitude, as law cannot be understood or re-presented unless it is regarded within broad historical, political, socio-economic and psychological contexts. For John Merryman for instance, a legal system is

---

[10] See chs 5 and 6.

'an operating set of legal institutions, procedures and rules', legal systems being frequently classified into groups or families (Merryman, 1985: 1). He hastens to add, however, that being grouped together does not suggest that the legal systems within a group 'have identical legal institutions, processes and rules'. In fact 'there is great diversity among them'(*ibid*). That they are grouped together signifies that they have something else in common. This 'something else' is what distinguishes them from legal systems differently classified; this is legal tradition which relates the legal system to the 'culture of which it is a partial expression ... and puts the legal system into cultural perspective' (Merryman, 1985: 2). A legal tradition is:

> a set of deeply rooted, historically conditioned attitudes about the nature of law, about the role of law in the society and the polity, about the proper organisation and operation of a legal system, and about the way law is or should be made, applied, studied, perfected, and taught (*ibid*).

Indeed, many contemporary comparative lawyers abide by his definition. For instance, John Bell gives his definition of legal culture as

> a specific way in which values, practices, and concepts are integrated into the operation of legal institutions and the interpretation of legal texts (Bell, 1995: 70).

He thus presents 'legal culture' as a configuration of values, concepts, practices and institutions through which individuals interpret and apply legal norms; legal culture being rooted in general culture. Mark van Hoecke and Mark Warrington go on to say that 'understanding law implies a knowledge and an understanding of the social practice of its legal community' (van Hoecke and Warrington, 1998: 495 at 498), which presupposes an understanding of the general culture of that society, since the legal community is embedded in that society. Therefore, to distinguish legal systems one must locate them and their cultures 'within the broader context of the societal culture to which they belong' *(ibid)*. These cannot be understood by merely comparing rules, legal institutions or even processes. It must be remembered though that culture is never a homogenous whole—neither is the law.

Where should we go to look for legal culture and, how should we investigate it?[11] Comparative lawyers see the need for such understanding and yet require the help of others such as economists, political scientists, sociologists and psychologists in order to grasp true meanings, even when looking at their own legal system. They find it difficult to answer whether differences between legal systems can be explained by 'national character'. Further, can legal cultures faithfully mirror national character and overall culture? Can two legal cultures be more alike but the overall cultures more divergent? Is national character the effect or the cause of differences?

The above shows us two things. The first is that we cannot talk of legal systems as the sole units of macro-comparative inquiry. The second is that there is no clear-cut definition of legal culture and legal tradition or any obvious reasons for preferring one concept to the other.

---

[11] See ch 5 in this Handbook.

A narrower approach regards comparative law as being involved only in the 'top-down' model, that is, the legal system as laid down by the formal law-maker, and elaborated upon by the appropriate high courts. Accordingly, comparative lawyers rely on normative inquiry. Thus, legal systems, together with the legal families in which they sit, are treated as the starting points of macro comparison. A legal system is made up of a set of inter-related parts, each with a specific function. The comparative lawyer analyses the working of these parts. However, Konrad Zweigert and Hein Kötz state that in studying legal systems, we should 'grasp their legal styles' (Zweigert and Kötz, 1998: 67). Yet, the concept of 'legal style' does not go beyond history, mode of thought, institutions and legal sources. The 'last factor' ideology is often discarded today as all five factors need not be used cumulatively. The comparative lawyer finds, describes, juxtaposes and identifies the differences and similarities between statutes, judicial decisions and related material, but often ignores context when it is not of a legal nature. What we have here is a technical perspective, shared with traditional legal doctrine applicable to domestic law.

In Europe, most comparisons are limited to civil law/common law. Interest in other regions of the world, unless seen as extensions of the two families by comparative lawyers, is satisfied by regionalists or anthropologists but not comparative lawyers. As Rodolfo Sacco puts it:

> If one asks what students of comparative law compare, the most obvious answer would be, 'the rules of different legal systems' (Sacco, 1991a: 21).

What, then, is meant by a 'rule'? This question must be addressed at the micro-comparative level. The traditional approach is of a positivist: statutory rules, that is, law as created by the state, case law and pertinent legal documents. Yet, in the context of 'legal pluralism', law goes far beyond the so-called 'official law', and extends to multi-layers of systems. Thus, today, 'law' spans the range of positive law and then moves to non-state law, rules, custom and tradition. What is a comparative lawyer to look at? As seen above, a broad approach to comparative law moves us away from legal systems as macro-units of inquiry and the 'law as rules' approach. The question 'What is law?' must be approached in the same manner.

At the micro-comparative level therefore, comparative law presupposes the existence of rules and legal institutions, and their plurality, but statutory rules alone cannot be the object of comparative inquiry. The first step is to regard judicial decisions as law. Even a monolithic legal system built on a Kelsenian hierarchy may regard both statutory law and judicial law as part of the legal system. Thus, judicial precedents must be considered by the comparative lawyer. In addition, the decisions of lower courts and not only those of the highest courts must be referred to. It is also commonplace today to talk of 'state legal pluralism', a weak version of normative legal pluralism.[12]

---

[12] See, for a discussion of 'weak' and 'strong' versions of legal pluralism, Griffith, 1986.

That said, it must be added that this is not the whole picture. Rodolfo Sacco, for instance, is on a quest to discover the 'formants' of the law and therefore refutes the existence of a 'single rule' and, looking at the 'living law', sees many elements in the search for 'one rule'. Having stated that one needs to recognise the diversity of the 'legal formants', he says that

> within a given legal system with multiple 'legal formants' there is no guarantee that they will be in harmony rather than in conflict (Sacco, 1991b: 343 at 384–5).

The legal formants cited by him are constitutional and legislative rules, case law, operational rules and scholarly writings, although no list is compiled to include all possible 'legal formants'. Rodolfo Sacco goes so far as to say that some 'legal formants' are 'explicitly formulated' and others are not. He calls these 'crypto-types', representing 'non-verbalized' rules and 'implied patterns' (*ibid*). We may ask ourselves: 'What about "formants" other than the legal'? These are also to be taken into account. The comparative lawyer must look at all the elements at work in a given legal system in context. She must remember that rules, institutions and processes must be studied in context and that 'legal formants' themselves develop under the influence of 'contextual formants', such as ideology and religion.

'Official rules' are only one type of rules. Law however, is made at a number of 'layers'. For instance, according to Boaventura de Sousa Santos's broad conception of law,

> modern societies are regulated by a plurality of legal orders, interrelated and socially distributed in the social field in different ways', rather than 'being ordered by a single legal system (Santos, 2002: 89).

This is the idea of legal pluralism, indicating that 'more than one legal system operates in a single political unit', that is, 'non-state law' has equal place with 'official law'. However, he also observes that 'the better choice is to regard this phenomena as given and speak of 'a plurality of legal orders' rather than 'legal pluralism' (*ibid*). He also introduces the concept of 'interlegality' to capture the complex relationships of superimposition, interpenetration and mixing between legal orders and semi-autonomous legal fields. Whenever possible, comparative law studies should extend to norms of non-state law, folk law and customary law, remembering that the law is global, national and local.

In the narrower approach, law is seen as a creation of the nation state. As we have seen at the macro-level, the units of inquiry are the legal systems, and law is what is laid down by formal law-makers and elaborated upon by the appropriate high courts. Normative inquiry is not involved in empirical field studies to find out how things actually are, but confines itself to the study of law in the books. However, if the primary sources of law include court decisions, these are also included in the inquiry. Thus, a degree of 'law in action' is present here too.

Moreover, there is no special way of dealing with foreign law. Whether one is investigating the rules of foreign law or of domestic law makes no difference. Since the comparative process starts with the juxtaposition of the unknown to the known, the rules of the domestic system must be studied first and then 'functional equivalents' sought. In this view, the core of research in micro-comparisons is the 'law as rules' approach. This narrow approach regards comparative law as a practical pursuit not a theoretical one. Most of the comparatists involved here also happen to be private law comparatists.

V. CONCLUDING REMARKS

There are comparative lawyers who see comparative law as a science with its own separate sphere. Others call comparative law merely a method of study and research or even a technique. Some regard it both as a comparative method and a comparative science of law, or see in comparative law more than one of these aspects. It is immediately obvious that those who see comparative law as a method only do not tell us what that method is, leaving this issue unanswered or very vaguely covered, and those who think or feel that comparative law must be more than a mere method do not seem to agree on what this subject-matter is. We have seen that the answers to the questions: 'What to compare?' and 'How to compare?', for example, can be extremely varied. Are we then to conclude that comparative law will depend entirely on what is to be compared and that the purpose of the comparison, and the purpose for which comparative law is studied or taught, will determine the form which the study or instruction should take? Is this a satisfactory position to assume?

It is not fanciful to predict that the 21st century will be 'the age of comparative law' (see Örücü, 2002). There is decidedly a renewed and growing interest in the subject. Academic study, law reform, policy development, research and teaching, international practice of law and law courts all avail themselves of it, in various ways. There are practical, sociological, political and pedagogical objectives in the above activities.

Though the prime objective is the provision of wider access to legal knowledge, comparative law research has a number of practical purposes. There is a place for the generalist comparative lawyer with a curious mind who is fascinated by legal phenomena shaped by extra-legal factors, by movements of the law and the tuning that has to take place to make these movements successful in the new surroundings, and with an interest in theoretical aspects of the subject. However, the comparative lawyer working for a specific purpose may be satisfied by simply seeking answers to problems either at the legislative or judicial level in foreign jurisdictions. It may even be that these two positions may be held by the very same comparative lawyer who at times works for the furtherance of knowledge satisfying the social science objective of comparative law as well as for her own interest, and at times, for example, as a *General Rapporteur* for one of the topics in the four-yearly Comparative Law Congresses, setting out lengthy specific questionnaires for the *National Rapporteurs* to answer and then drawing the threads together in the preparation of her *General Rapport* in that specific topic, or using the 'functional equivalence' or the 'factual approach' in one of the European 'common core' projects.

QUESTIONS FOR DISCUSSION

1. What is comparative law? What are its purposes?
2. What are the subject's particular aims, approaches, methods and how is it used?
3. What trends do we observe today in comparative law studies?
4. What do we mean by 'the identity of the function of the norm'?
5. Why does one engage in comparative law studies? What is the role of comparative law related to academic studies, legal research, legislation and law reform? What is its role in the judicial process, in the filling of gaps, in law-making and interpretation? What is the value of comparison as a source of law? How can comparative law be utilised in harmonisation and unification?
6. Is there one correct method to apply?
7. What is meant by a macro-unit and micro-unit of inquiry?
8. Differentiate between a legal system, a legal culture and a legal tradition.

BIBLIOGRAPHY AND FURTHER READING

Ancel, M (1971) *Utilité et methodes du droit comparé* (Neuchatel, Editions Ides et Calendes).

Antokolskaia, M (2003) 'The "Better Law" Approach and the Harmonisation of Family Law' in K Boele-Woelki (ed), *Perspectives for the Unification and Harmonisation of Family Law in Europe* (Answerp–Oxford–New York, Intersentia).

Bell, JS (1995) 'English Law and French Law—Not So Different?' 48 *Current Legal Problems* (Oxford, Oxford University Press) 63.

Bogdan, M (1994), Comparative Law (Göteborg, Kluwer Tano).

Campbell, CM (1966) 'Comparative Law: Its Current Definition' *Juridical Review* 151.

David, R and Brierley, JEC (1985) *Major Legal Systems in the World Today* 3rd edn (London, Stevens and Sons).

de Cruz, P (1999) *Comparative Law in a changing world*, 2nd edn (London, Cavendish Publishing Limited).

Ehrlich, E (1912/1939) *Fundamental Principles of the Sociology of Law* (trans) WL Moll (Cambridge, MA, Harvard University Press).

Ehrmann, HW (1976) *Comparative Legal Cultures* (New Jersey, Prentice Hall).

Ewald, W (1995) 'Comparative Jurisprudence (1): What Was It Like to Try a Rat?' 143 *Pennsylvania Law Review* 1889.

Glenn, HP (2000) *Legal Traditions of the World* (Oxford, Oxford University Press).

Gordley, J (1998) 'Is Comparative Law a Distinct Discipline?' 46 *American Journal of Comparative Law* 607.

Graziadei, M (2003) 'The Functionalist Heritage' in P Legrand and R Munday (eds), *Comparative Legal Studies: Traditions and Transitions* (Cambridge, Cambridge University Press).

Griffith, J (1986) 'What is Legal Pluralism?' 24 *Journal of Legal Pluralism* 1.

Gutteridge, HC (1938) 'The comparative aspects of legal terminology' 12 *Tulane Law Review* 401.

—— (1949/1974) *Comparative Law*, 2nd edn (London, Cambridge University Press); reprint (London, Wildy & Sons).

Hall, J (1963) *Comparative Law and Social Theory* (Louisiana, Louisiana State University Press).

Harding, A and Örücü, E (eds) (2002) *Comparative Law in the 21st Century* (London, Kluwer Academic Publishers).

Husa, J (2003) 'Farewell to Functionalism or Methodological Tolerance?' 67 *Rabels Zeitschrift für auslandisches und internationales Privatrrecht* 446.

Kahn-Freund, O (1966) 'Comparative Law as an Academic Subject' 82 *Law Quarterly Review* 40.

Kamba, WJ (1976) 'Comparative Law: A Theoretical Framework' 23 *International and Comparative Law Quarterly* 494.

Karameus, KD (2001) 'Comparative Law and Comparative Lawyers: Opening Remarks' 75 *Tulane Law Review* 859.

Kennedy, D (2002) 'The methods and the politics' in P Legrand and R Munday (eds), *Comparative Legal Studies: Traditions and Transitions* (Cambridge, Cambridge University Press).

Koopmans, T (1996) 'Comparative Law and the Courts' 45 *International and Comparative Law Quarterly* 545.

Legrand, P (1996) 'How to compare now' 16 *Legal Studies* 232.

—— (1999) *Fragments of Law-as-Culture* (Deventer, WEJ Tjeenk Willink).

—— (2003) 'The same and the different' in P Legrand and R Munday (eds), *Comparative Legal Studies: Traditions and Transitions* (Cambridge, Cambridge University Press).

Legrand, P and Munday, R (eds) (2003) *Comparative Legal Studies: Traditions and Transitions* (Cambridge, Cambridge University Press).

Markesinis, B (1990), 'Comparative law—A Subject in Search of an Audience' 21 *Hastings International and Comparative Law Review* 825.

Merryman, JH (1974) 'Comparative Law and Scientific Explanation' in JN Hazard and WJ Wagner (eds), *Law in the U.S.A. in Social and Technical Revolution* (Brussels, Bruyland).

—— (1985) *The Civil Law Tradition: An Introduction to the legal Systems of Western Europe and Latin America*, 2nd edn (California, Stanford University Press).

—— (1999) *The Loneliness of the Comparative Lawyer* (The Hague–London–Boston, Kluwer Law International).

Monateri, PG (1998) 'Everybody's Talking': The Future of Comparative Law' 21 *Hastings International and Comparative Law Review* 825.

Munday, R (2002) 'Accounting for an Encounter' in P Legrand and R Munday (eds), *Comparative Legal Studies: Traditions and Transitions* (Cambridge, Cambridge University Press).

Örücü, E (1986) 'Method and object of comparative law' in HW Blom and RJ de Folter (eds), *Methode en Object in de rechtswetenschappen* (Zwolle, WEJ Tjeenk Willink).

—— (1999/2000) *Critical Comparative Law: Considering Paradoxes for Legal Systems in Transition* (Deventer, Kluwer Law International); and 4 *Electronic Journal of Comparative Law* 2.

—— (2002) '*Unde Venit, Quo Tendit* Comparative Law?' in A Harding and E Örücü (eds), *Comparative Law in the 21st Century* (London, Kluwer Academic Publishers).

—— (ed) (2003) *Judicial Comparativism in Human Rights Cases,* 22 United Kingdom Comparative Law Series (London, UK National Committee for Comparative Law/British Institute of International and Comparative Law).

—— (2005) *The Enigma of Comparative Law: Variations on a Theme for the Twenty-First Century* (Leiden–Boston, Martinus Nijhoff).

Peters, A and Schwenke, H (2000) 'Comparative Law Beyond Post-modernism' 49 *International and Comparative Law Quarterly* 800.

Roberts, GK (1972) *What is Comparative Politics?* (Essex, Macmillan).

Sacco, R (1991a) 'Legal Formants: A Dynamic Approach to Comparative law (Installment I of II)' 39 *American Journal of Comparative Law* 1.

—— (1991b) 'Legal Formants: A Dynamic Approach to Comparative Law (Installment II of II) 39 *American Journal of Comparative Law* 343.

Samuel, G (1998) 'Comparative Law and Jurisprudence' 47 *International and Comparative Law Quarterly* 817.

Schmitthoff, M (1939) 'The Science of Comparative Law' 7 *Cambridge Law Journal* 94.

Santos, de Sousa B (2002) *Toward a New Legal Common Sense*, 2nd edn (London, Butterworths).

Tur, RHS (1977) 'The Dialectic of General Jurisprudence and Comparative Law' *Juridical Review* 238.

Twining, T (2000a) *Globalisation and Legal Theory* (London, Butterworths).

—— (2000b) 'Comparative Law and Legal Theory: the Country and Western Tradition' in ID Edge (ed), *Comparative Law in Global Perspective* (New York, Transnational Publishers).

—— (2003) 'A Post-Westphalian Conception of Law' 37 *Law and Society Review* 199.

van Hoecke, M and Warrington, M (1998) 'Legal Cultures and Legal Paradigms: Towards a New Model for Comparative Law' 47 *International and Comparative Law Quarterly* 495.

Zweigert, K and Kötz, H (1998) *An Introduction to Comparative Law*, 3rd edn (trans) T Weir (Oxford, Clarendon Press).

Useful Websites

Comparative Law Methodology and Sources, Lee Peoples@2005

Electronic Journal of Comparative Law (for example for volume 9:2)

http://www/ejcl.org/92/issue92/art92-1.html

http://kub.nl/ejc192/art92-1.html

Oxford University Comparative Law Forum

http://ouclf.iuscomp.org/articles

II

New Directions for Comparative Law

3

Globalisation and Comparative Law *

WILLIAM TWINING

KEY CONCEPTS

Globalisation; Interdependence; G-words; A global perspective; Levels of relations; Levels of ordering; The Westphalian Duo; Non-state law; Normative
and legal pluralism; Total pictures; Spatial metaphors; Boundaries; Changing
significance of boundaries; Ideal types; The *Grands Systèmes* approach; The
Country and Western Tradition; Legal families; Ethnocentrism; Comparative
common law; Diffusion of law; Law as institutionalised social practice.

I. GLOBALISATION

THE IDEA OF 'globalisation' has been in fashion since the late 1980s. It
has stimulated a massive, excited, and somewhat repetitive literature.[1]
Ironically, that literature is quite narrow in that it focuses on a limited
range of issues. This is especially the case where 'globalisation' is restricted to economic matters and is associated with extreme laissez faire ideology and increasing
American and western hegemony. In this narrow sense of economic globalisation,
the term has highly controversial, largely negative associations, as is illustrated
by the 'Anti-Globalisation Movement'. In this chapter, I shall use the term more
broadly to refer to those trends, processes and interactions which are making the
world more interdependent in many complex ways, in respect of ecology, communications, cultures, language, politics, disease, and so on, not just the alleged
development of a single world economy.

---

* This chapter is a condensation and synthesis of themes developed at length in several papers
(for which see full details in the bibliography at the end of this chapter), especially Twining, 2000a
Globalisation and Legal Theory: chs 2, 6 and 7; Twining, 2000b 'Comparative Law and Legal Theory:
The Country and Western Tradition' : 21–76; Twining, 1999 Globalization and Comparative Law;
Twining, 2005a 'General Jurisprudence' (World Congress on Philosophy of Law and Social Philosophy,
Granada); Twining, 2005b 'Diffusion of Law: A Global Perspective'; and Twining, 2006a 'Diffusion of
Law and Globalization Discourse'.

[1] Two of the best introductions are still Featherstone, 1990 and Featherstone, Lash and Robertson,
1995. On law, see Likosky, 2002.

Anthony Giddens characterises the processes as

> the intensification of world-wide social relations which link distant localities in such a way that local happenings are shaped by events occurring many miles away and vice versa (Giddens, 1990a: 64; cf Giddens 1990b: chapter 16).

Even in this broader usage, 'globalisation' is surrounded by controversy and relates to a quite narrow band of issues that are genuinely world-wide.

I teach a course called 'Globalisation and Law'. I encourage students to adopt a global perspective; to think in terms of humankind and our planet as a whole; and to try to construct total pictures of law in the world and to ponder the difficulties involved. However, at the start of the course I ban the unjustified use of 'g-words' from the classroom—'global', 'globalisation', 'globalising' and other forms of globa-babble and globa-hype.

I do this for several reasons. The first is obvious: not only is the term ambiguous, but the currency of 'g-talk' is debased. It too often involves exaggerated, misleading, meaningless, superficial, ethno-centric, or just plain false statements about processes and phenomena that are better discussed in less hyperbolic terms (see Twining, 2001). This is clearly illustrated in loose talk about global law, global governance, global law firms, and global lawyers. There is a standard joke that makes the main point: it might be pedantic to cavil at talk of a World Cup at soccer; it is stretching things to talk of a World Cup at cricket involving 16 countries; but talk of a World Series at baseball is just hype.[2]

The second reason is especially important for lawyers: there is a tendency in the literature on globalisation to move from the very local or the national straight to the global, leaving out all intermediate levels. It is also tempting to assume that different levels of relations and of ordering are neatly nested in a hierarchy of concentric circles ranging from the very local, through sub-state, regional, continental, North/South, global, and beyond to outer space. However, the picture is much more complicated than that: it includes empires, spheres of influence, alliances, coalitions, religious diasporas, networks, trade routes, migration flows, and social movements. It also includes 'sub-worlds' such as the common law world, the Arab world, the Islamic world and Christendom, as well as special groupings of power such as the G7, the G8, NATO, OPEC, the European Union, the Commonwealth, the Catholic Church, multi-national corporations, crime syndicates, cartels, social movements, and non-governmental organisations and networks. All of these cut across any simple vertical hierarchy and overlap and interact with each other in complex ways.

These complexities are reflected in the diversity of forms of normative and legal ordering. Nearly all mainstream Western legal theory and legal scholarship in the 20th century focused on the domestic law of municipal legal systems, sometimes

---

[2] In fact, the American 'World Series' at baseball took its name from a newspaper, *The New York World*, but few people recall that fact. Recently, a baseball competition involving 16 countries was inaugurated in the United States. It was called the 'World Classic', thereby doubling the hype.

extending to public international law in the narrow sense of law governing relations between states ('The Westphalian Duo') (Buchanan, 2000).[3] But if one views law from a global perspective, both geographically and historically, focusing solely on the municipal law of nation states (and classical public international law) this leaves out too much that should be the proper concern of legal scholarship. A reasonably inclusive cosmopolitan discipline of law needs to encompass all levels of relations and of ordering, relations between these levels, and all important forms of law including supra-state (eg international, regional) and non-state law (eg religious law, transnational law, chthonic law, ie tradition/custom) and various forms of 'soft law' (see Appendix I).[4] A picture of law in the world that focuses only on the municipal law of nation states and public international law would be much too narrow for many purposes. For example, it is difficult to justify omitting Islamic law or other major traditions of religious law from such a picture. Yet, to include only those examples of religious law or custom officially recognised by sovereign states (state legal pluralism) would be seriously misleading.[5] To try to subsume European Union law, *lex mercatoria*, international commercial arbitration or all examples of 'human rights law' under public international law similarly stretches that concept to breaking point.[6]

It is especially important for lawyers to be sensitive to the significance of boundaries, borders, jurisdictions, treaty relations, and legal traditions. These messy overlapping patterns make mapping law in the world difficult. They place ideas of normative and legal pluralism at the centre of understanding law from a global perspective. That is to say, we have to acknowledge that normative and legal orders can co-exist in the same time-space context. That, in turn, greatly complicates the tasks of comparative law.

A third reason for lawyers to be sceptical of 'g-talk' in relation to law is our collective ignorance of other traditions and cultures. The Anglo-American, and more broadly the Western, intellectual traditions in law have tended to be quite parochial and inward-looking. Most legal scholarship is particular and most legal concepts are culture-bound. So on the whole we lack adequate analytic concepts

---

[3] Hart, Rawls, Kelsen, Dworkin, and Raz are all examples of this perspective. The main exceptions have been legal anthropologists and other scholars who have emphasised the importance of legal pluralism and non-state law.

[4] On the conceptual difficulties of constructing a conception of law that is broad enough to include important forms of 'non-state law', but not so broad as to include all social institutions and rules, see Tamanaha, 2001, discussed in Twining, 2003.

[5] It is hardly controversial to say that to recognise Islamic or other religious law only insofar as it is recognised by sovereign states involves crude distortion. It would also be odd to accept the idea of a Jewish, Islamic or Gypsy legal tradition, but to refuse to talk about Jewish and Islamic or Gypsy law as 'law'—but that is a corollary of thinking in terms of law as a system of rules.

[6] A theory of state law such as Hart's provides an inadequate theoretical framework for grounding our discipline as it becomes more cosmopolitan and more concerned with multiple levels of legal relations and legal ordering. Hart's concept of state law cannot easily fit European Union law, contemporary public international law, religious law, canon law, medieval and modern *lex mercatoria*, let alone other forms of traditional and customary law that are candidates for our attention as legal scholars and jurists.

and reliable data for giving general accounts of law in the world that include and transcend different legal traditions and cultures. One of the main tasks of comparative law is to make us aware of legal systems other than our own; in future comparative law must extend this de-parochialising role to reducing our ignorance of non-Western legal cultures and traditions.

Even with these crude geographical categorisations, and even without reference to history, a ban on 'g-words' sends a simple message of complexity. It also emphasises the point that in regard to the complex processes that are making people, groups and peoples more interdependent, much of the transnationalisation of law and legal relations is taking place at sub-global levels. Furthermore, there are also local and transnational relations and processes that to a greater or lesser extent bypass the state, such as the Internet, religious diasporas, networks of NGOs, many of the internal and external relations of large corporations, and so on.

Terms like 'global' have their uses. However, in a given context, when confronted with a word such as 'global', 'globalism', 'globalisation', or 'globalising', it is sensible to ask: Is it precise (genuinely referring to all humankind or the world as a whole)? Is it exaggerated (eg a substitute for 'transnational' or 'widespread')? Is it misleading (obscuring levels of law in between the genuinely global and the quite local)? Is it superficially global (like Holiday Inns or the Internet)? Or is it ethnocentric (projecting one's own culture onto the whole world)?

The purpose of this ban on 'g-words' is not to suggest that the processes that are loosely subsumed under 'globalisation' are unimportant. To be sure a single world economy, the global eco-system, and a world atlas can be useful constructs in some contexts. There are genuinely world-wide issues such as climate control, nuclear proliferation, global justice and world poverty. Despite the pitfalls, there are good reasons for thinking globally. But too often 'g-words' are loosely extended to cover topics that belong to one or more less extensive spheres of ordering. It is inappropriate to treat as 'global' issues concerning competition and monopoly within the European Union, or debates within Islam on banking or the status of women, or anti-corruption measures in Eastern Europe, yet they should be of as much concern to us today as genuinely global issues.

There are two exceptions to my ban on 'g-words'. First, a student may employ a 'g-word' provided she can justify its use in that particular context and show that it is being used with clarity and precision. Secondly, I encourage students to adopt *a global perspective* as a starting-point for considering particular topics. This is quite different from talking about 'global law' or 'global lawyers'. It does not involve making any strong assumptions about uniformities. Nor does it need to be reductionist. Indeed, it can reinforce the message of complexity. A global perspective involves looking at the world and humankind as a whole and setting accounts of particular phenomena in the context of broad geographical pictures and long historical time-frames. Constructing 'total pictures' is an important aspect of contextual thinking. The world *is* becoming more interdependent and one needs to adopt a global perspective to understand these processes in relation to law. Our world still has relatively finite boundaries in a way that societies and nation states, increasingly, do not.

Thinking in terms of total pictures is mainly useful for setting a context for more particular studies. Grand synthesising theories, such as Patrick Glenn's account of legal traditions, or organising theories, such as Brian Tamanaha's attempt to construct a broad and inclusive general concept of law, also have their uses (Glenn, 2004; Tamanaha, 2001). They are examples of the synthesising function of legal theory. There may even be value in trying to construct a historical atlas of law in the world as a whole—although my own efforts in this direction have done little more than illustrate some of the obstacles in the way of such an enterprise. Among these are the multiplicity of levels of human relations and ordering, the problems of individuating normative and legal orders, the complexity and the variety of the phenomena that are the subject-matters of our discipline, and the relatively undeveloped state of the stock of concepts and data that would be needed to produce such an overview.[7] Adopting a global perspective also helps to map the extent of our collective ignorance of other legal traditions. However, even if our discipline becomes genuinely cosmopolitan, the great bulk of its attention will inevitably be focused on particular inquiries.

There is a danger of thinking too much in geographical terms (Westbrook, 2006). It is important to recognise that talk of maps and levels of law is a spatial metaphor that is not always appropriate. Gordon Woodman has argued that state law is typically defined in terms of relatively determinate territory, but many laws and legal orders are not.[8] In the standard situation of legal pluralism, 'in which a population observes more than one body of law', there may not be settled 'choice of law' rules, the population may be dispersed, membership of the population may be ambiguous, there may be variations and inconsistencies within a single 'system' or body of law, and an individual may observe different laws for different purposes, even in relation to a single transaction or relationship.[9] This is especially the case with personal and religious laws. The point is well taken. However, if we conceive of law as a form of institutionalised social practice and if we are concerned with the law in action, then we are dealing with actual behaviour, which does take place at particular times in particular places. For example, if we agree that *shari'a* travels with every devout Muslim, a good map of Islamic diasporas can at least give a general indication of where Islamic law is likely to exist at a given time as an institutionalised social practice (Freeman-Grenville and Munro-Hay, 2002).[10] We need to guard against overusing spatial metaphors, but there is still scope for legal geography (see eg Blomley, 1994; Economides, 1996; and Holder and Harrison, 2003).

---

[7] See Twining, 2000a: ch 6—'Mapping Law'.

[8] Woodman, 2003 'Why There Can be no Map of Law'. The practice of relating laws to countries, societies, fields, or localities is, he suggests, a hangover from 'legal centralism', which treats state law as the paradigm.

[9] Woodman (*ibid*) illustrates these points by reference to the Luo on the Kenya/Tanzania border.

[10] On Islamic law in England as a form of custom that has both slowly influenced English municipal law and developed as a form of anglicised custom (*angerezi shar'iat*), see Pearl and Menski, 1998, especially ch 3.

The literature on 'globalisation' is extensive and often controversial. In addition to ideological disagreements, there are debates about such matters as the continuing significance of sovereignty, about the relative importance of the nation-state as an actor on the world stage, whether we are heading for a clash of civilisations, and whether human rights are 'counter hegemonic'.[11] There are, however, some relatively clear themes that are directly relevant to this chapter.

First, it is widely agreed that the processes of globalisation are not new; in many respects they antedate the rise of the modern nation state and can be traced back at least to the 16th century.[12] What has changed recently is the pace and complexity of the processes, especially in such areas as communications.

Secondly, there has been a good deal of self-criticism within disciplines about the extent to which they have over-emphasised the importance of boundaries and have treated societies, states and tribes as self-contained, de-contextualised units. For example, in the mid-1980s several distinguished anthropologists admitted to having erred in treating small-scale societies in which they had done their fieldwork as if they were timeless, self-contained units, isolated from the outside world. Their fault had been that they had ignored the wider contexts of time and space. They reaffirmed the idea that the core focus of anthropology must still be small societies and communities, but in future the study of the local must be seen in the context of history and of ever-widening geographical spheres—relations with neighbours, colonial boundaries, Western colonisation generally, and the world economy (see Collier and Starr, 1989). Similarly, Anthony Giddens and others have criticised orthodox sociology for giving far too much weight to the idea of 'society' as a bounded system (Giddens, 1990).[13] Again, moral philosophers have been criticised for failing to face up to the ethical implications of interdependence. Nowhere is this more apparent than in the criticisms of the treatment of international relations in John Rawls's theory of justice and its assumption that any theory of justice today can treat a society as a 'hypothetically closed and self-sufficient' unit.[14] The general theme is clear across disciplines: the processes of globalisation are fundamentally changing the

---

[11] See eg, Baxi, 2006 (arguing, inter alia, that human rights discourse is in danger of being hijacked by a market-friendly, trade-related paradigm of human rights favouring big business interests); and Santos, 2002 (viewing the world as an arena for a long-term struggle between 'hegemonic' and 'counter-hegemonic' forces).

[12] Halliday states: 'One can indeed argue that far from the "international" arising from the national, and from a gradual expansion of links between discrete entities, the real process has been the other way around: the history of the modern system is both of the internationalisation and the breakdown of pre-existing flows of peoples, religion, trade into separate entities: the precondition for the formation of the modern nation-state was the development of an international economy and culture within which these distinct states then coalesced.' (Halliday, 1994: 2; cf. 20).

[13] Tamanaha, goes so far as to say that 'society' is no longer a useful concept for the sociology of law and substitutes the more flexible 'social arena' (Tamanaha, 2001: 206–8).

[14] Rawls, 1993:41 at 44, criticised by Pogge, 1989, cf Twining, 2000a: 69–75. Rawls did not significantly change his position on this in his book, *The Law of Peoples* (Rawls, 1999), criticised (inter alios) by A Buchanan (Buchanan, 2000).

significance of national and societal boundaries and generally, but not inevitably, making them less important.

A third theme from the interdisciplinary literature on globalisation is the variety of significant actors who are relevant to analysis of patterns of legal relations in the modern world (see eg Alston, 2005). Despite disagreements about the relative importance of particular kinds of actor and their long-term prospects—for example, about the long-term political significance of multi-national corporations, the United Nations and small states—it seems reasonable to proceed on a number of assumptions. First, nation states will continue to be among the most powerful kind of actors for a long time to come, and that some major powers will be more equal than others; conversely, anything approaching world government is not likely to be on the agenda for the foreseeable future. Secondly, in analysing law in the contemporary world, it is not enough to focus on the traditional small cast of actors: sovereign states, official international organisations, and individuals. Can one, for example, give an adequate account of law today which does not give some attention to the significance of transnational, non-governmental organisations (Amnesty International, Greenpeace, the Catholic Church, international women's movements, international trade union organisations), to peoples that are nations without states (the Maoris, Gypsies, the native peoples of North America and Australia), to organised crime, liberation movements, multi-national companies, transnational law firms, and to significant classes such as the vast herds of 'people on the move' (including migrants, refugees and the internally displaced)?[15]

II. IMPLICATIONS FOR THE STUDY OF LAW AND COMPARATIVE LAW

Western Traditions of Academic Law

What are the implications of globalisation for the discipline of law in general and for the sub-discipline of comparative law? If one adopts a global perspective and a long time scale, at the risk of over-simplification, one can discern some general tendencies and biases in Western academic legal culture that are in the process of coming under sustained challenge in the context of 'globalisation'. In crude form, these can be expressed as a series of assumptions that are constituent propositions of an ideal type:

   (a) That law consists of two principal kinds of ordering: municipal state law and public international law (classically conceived as ordering the relations between states) ('the Westphalian duo');

   (b) That nation-states, societies, and legal systems are very largely closed, self-contained entities that can be studied in isolation;

---

[15] The sharp distinction between international refugees and internally displaced persons (an even more numerous category) is rapidly breaking down (Deng, 1993).

(c)   That modern law and modern jurisprudence are secular, and now largely independent of their historical-cultural roots in the Judaeo-Christian traditions;

(d)   That modern state law is primarily rational-bureaucratic and instrumental—performing certain functions and serving as a means for achieving particular social ends (Tamanaha, 2006);

(e)   That law is best understood through 'top-down' perspectives (rulers, officials, legislators, elites) with the points of view of users, consumers, victims and other subjects being at best marginal;

(f)   That the main subject-matters of the discipline of law are ideas and norms rather than the empirical study of social facts;

(g)   That modern state law is almost exclusively a Northern (European/Anglo-American) creation, diffused through most of the world via colonialism, imperialism, trade, and latter-day post-colonial influences;

(h)   That the study of non-Western legal traditions is a marginal and unimportant part of Western academic law;

(i)   That the fundamental values underlying modern law are universal, although the philosophical foundations are diverse.

Of course, all of these general propositions are crude indications of tendencies, subject to many exceptions; none has gone unchallenged within the Western legal tradition; and issues surrounding nearly all of them constitute a high proportion of the contested agenda of modern Western jurisprudence. However, at a general level this bald 'ideal type' highlights some crucial points at which such ideas and assumptions are being increasingly challenged. For example it has been contended that:

(a)   from a global perspective a reasonably inclusive picture of law in the world would encompass various forms of non-state law, especially different kinds of religious and customary law that fall outside the 'Westphalian duo';

(b)   sharp territorial boundaries and ideas of exclusive state sovereignty are under regular challenge;

(c)   we may be living in 'a secular age' in the West, but much of the rest of the world is experiencing a religious revival;[16]

(d)   while nearly all members of the United Nations and many international and transnational organisations are institutionalised in accordance with some model of bureaucracy, large parts of the world's population live in societies and communities that are differently organised;

(e)   'top-down' perspectives are being more persistently challenged by bottom-up perspectives that range from Holmes' Bad Man, to user theory, to various forms of post-colonial subaltern perspectives (Nader, 1984; Tamanaha, 2001: 239–40; Twining, 2000a: chapter 5; and Baxi, 2006: xxii);

---

[16] Misztal and Shup, 1992. On Islam, see Moosa, 2000; On Christianity, see Jenkins, 2002; on the Yoruba religion, see Abimbola and Abimbola, to be published 2007.

(f) in order to understand law in the world today it is more than ever important to penetrate beyond the surface of official legal doctrine to reach the realities of all forms of law as social practices (Twining (2007) forthcoming);

(g) until the mid-20th century imperialism and colonialism were probably the main, but not the only, engines of diffusion of law, but in the post-colonial era the processes of diffusion are more varied and there is a growing realisation that diffusion of law does not necessarily lead to harmonisation or unification of laws (eg Twining, 2005b; Legrand, 1997);

(h) the study of non-Western religious and other legal traditions is increasingly important (eg Glenn, 2004) and our juristic canon needs to be extended to include 'southern' jurists (Twining, 2006c);

(i) the world today is characterised by a diversity of deep-rooted, perhaps incommensurable, belief systems; and one of the main challenges facing the human race in a situation of increasing interdependence is how to construct institutions and processes that promote co-existence and co-operation between peoples with very different cosmologies and values. Insofar as belief pluralism is a fact, it is foolish to hope for achieving a consensus on values by imposition, persuasion or rational dialogue (Hampshire, 1989).

Viewed from a global perspective, during the 20th century and before, Western academic legal culture has tended to be state-oriented, secular, positivist, 'top-down', North-centric, unempirical, and universalist in respect of morals. In short, it has been rather parochial in respect of focus, audience, sources, and perspectives.[17] Of course, it is hardly surprising that the main focus of the Anglo-American tradition of academic law has been on detailed particular study of the concepts and doctrine of local municipal law of particular jurisdictions, such as England and Wales, or of countries, such as the United States or Australia. More broadly, the main Western traditions of legal scholarship have concentrated very largely on domestic law of modern nation states.

Again, viewed from a global perspective, Western comparative law has shared many of the tendencies of the institutionalised discipline of law. To be sure, within our tradition, the subject has had a de-parochialising role. In some respects it has served as a Ministry of Foreign Affairs, establishing contacts and developing relations with legal scholarship from other countries and cultures. But it has not fostered sustained relations between many countries. With two major exceptions, the study of Roman law and the *Grands Systèmes* approach, nearly all comparative law has been concerned with the study and comparison of modern foreign state legal systems within the Western legal tradition. By and large it has not succeeded in reducing our collective ignorance of most of the major legal traditions.

---

[17] On different forms of parochialism see Twining, 2000a: 128–9.

Two Traditions of Western Comparative Law

Comparative legal studies have a long and complex history. But modern comparative law did not become institutionalised or attain critical mass until after the Second World War in the common law world, somewhat earlier in continental Europe. Standard secondary writings about comparative law distinguish between two main approaches: macro-comparative studies exemplified by the *Grands Systèmes* approach of René David and others, and micro-comparative studies, which are usually depicted as approximating to an ideal type that I have mischievously called 'the Country and Western Tradition' (Twining, 2000b). The distinction is recognised not to be sharp, for macro- and micro-studies are interdependent, but this is a convenient way of labelling two rather different kinds of enterprise strongly influenced by a particular conception of academic law at a formative period in their history.

After the Second World War there developed the practice in some European countries of presenting overviews of '*Les Grands Systèmes de droit contemporain*'. This led to some modest textbooks (David and Brierley, 1968/1985; Arminjon, Nolde and Wolff, 1950–51; Zweigert and Kötz, 1971) and to the revival of a long-running and unsatisfactory debate about how major systems, traditions, or families of law should be classified. It is not necessary here to repeat the details of this debate, but it may be useful to consider the least unsatisfactory of these attempts. Konrad Zweigert and Hein Kötz's *An Introduction to Comparative Law* was, for a generation, the leading student textbook on the subject. Rejecting single criteria such as race, ideology, geographical location, stages of economic development, or relations of economic production, they focused on the 'styles of legal thought' of contemporary living legal systems and suggested multiple criteria for classifying them into families:

> (1) its historical background and development; (2) its predominant and characteristic mode of thought in legal matters; (3) especially distinctive legal institutions; (4) the kind of legal sources it acknowledges and the way it handles them; (5) its ideology. (Zweigert and Kötz, 1998: 69–75).

These multiple criteria led them to adopt a seven-fold classification of 'legal families' (ie groups of legal systems) as follows:

> (1) Romanistic family; (2) Germanic family; (3) Nordic family; (4) Common law family; (5) Socialist family; (6) Far Eastern systems; (7) Islamic systems; (8) Hindu law (*ibid*).

Although this scheme has attracted a lot of criticism, it was probably adequate for an introductory student text and it had the merit of identifying some of the main difficulties underlying this problem of classification. For present purposes, it is enough to identify two main weaknesses: First, the eight categories do not refer to species of a single genus: the first five 'families' refer to state legal systems (but some have historic roots preceding the rise of the nation state); the sixth is more a rag-bag than a family, joined together only by geographical location; the seventh and eighth open the way for recognition of non-state law, for Zweigert and Kötz recognised that it would be a distortion to limit their account of Islamic law to Islamic states or even to those aspects recognised as a source of law in plural state legal systems. But this meant a shift of meaning of 'system' from existing state legal system to a system of thought. However, the label 'system' is dropped in respect of Hindu law, perhaps because there is no modern Hindu state. Analytically, this scheme is more like a muddle than a systemic classification, but, of course, that may not matter if not much depends on the classification anyway.

A second criticism of Zweigert and Kötz's approach is that by focussing on contemporary 'living' systems, they downplay the importance of history. The best hope for developing a coherent overview of law in the world, it has been suggested, is to adopt an historical perspective. This is the approach adopted by Patrick Glenn in his path-breaking book, *Legal Traditions of the World* (Glenn, 2004).

Anglo-American commentators have generally been dismissive of the *Grands Systèmes* tradition: the more outspoken ones, such as Alan Watson, have criticised it as too broad and superficial to deserve the name of scholarship (Watson, 1974: chapter 1). The majority have voted with their feet by concentrating on micro-comparative work. I believe that such dismissiveness was mistaken. It is admirable to give novice law students a broad overview of their field, not least because it can help them to set more particular studies in a broad geographical and historical context. It can also provide them with an initial framework for organising their understandings of law. An elementary Cook's Tour need not be intellectually ambitious or even particularly rigorous, but laying a sound theoretical foundation for the study of law needs to aim higher. If the main objective of the discipline of law is to advance knowledge and understanding of its subject-matter, then surely one aspect of this must be the aspiration to build up an accurate and sophisticated total picture (or series of pictures) of law in the world.

During the 1990s, partly in response to the challenges of globalisation, a number of jurists have attempted to construct broad overviews of law in the world that are quite different from the *Grands Systèmes* approach. Three in particular deserve mention. First, Boaventura de Sousa Santos (Santos, 1995; 2002) advanced a bold interpretation of law in a globalising era in terms of an emerging struggle between 'hegemonic' forces (mainly associated with capitalism) and 'counter-hegemonic' forces (exemplified by human rights, some social movements and the World Social Forum). From the perspective of world history, Patrick Glenn interprets the heritage of law in terms of continuously interacting traditions that are sufficiently different and sufficiently stable to underpin a vision of 'sustainable diversity' (Glenn, 2004). Glenn's concept of tradition, though controversial, is more sophisticated and more coherent than attempts to paint a picture in terms of families of legal systems or legal cultures and it avoids the narrowing assumptions of the 'Country and Western Tradition'. Brian Tamanaha has sought to construct a broad conception of law as the basis for a positivist, socio-legal general jurisprudence (Tamanaha, 2001). Although Tamanaha's specific criterion of identification of law[18] has been criticised, his systematic deconstruction and filleting of Hart's concept of state law opens the way for a broadened and more coherent conception of law as an organising concept within the tradition of legal positivism. I have commented at length on each of these three important works en route to developing a rather different conception of general jurisprudence as an activity that might provide some useful theoretical underpinnings for a genuinely cosmopolitan discipline of law.[19]

Micro-comparative Studies: The 'Country and Western Tradition'

Let us now turn to micro-comparative studies. In taking stock of modern comparative law scholarship it is important to distinguish between the vast heritage of particular studies of foreign and comparative law that have been published since the Second World War and the way the field has been conceptualised in general terms by its more influential figures. The former is rich and very diverse; the latter is remarkably monolithic. It is my contention that the praxis of comparative law is much richer and more diverse than the predominant theory allows.

From the accounts of leading comparatists, especially in the formative period after the Second World War until about 1990, we can construct an ideal type of a conception of mainstream comparative law with the following characteristics:

(i)   The primary subject-matter is the positive laws and 'official' legal systems of nation states (*municipal legal systems*);

(ii)   It focuses almost exclusively on *Western capitalist societies* in Europe and the United States, with little or no detailed consideration of 'the East' (former and surviving socialist countries, including China), the 'South' (poorer countries), Latin America, and richer countries of the Pacific Basin.[20]

(iii) It is concerned mainly with the similarities and differences between *common law and civil law*, as exemplified by '*parent*' traditions or systems, notably France and Germany for civil law, and England and the United States for common law;

(iv)   It focuses almost entirely on *legal doctrine*;

---

[18] '*Law is whatever people identify and treat through their social practices as "law" (or "droit" or "recht" etc.)*' (Tamanaha, 2001: 166–71, 194).

[19] Twining, 2005a. On Santos, see Twining, 2000a: ch 8; on Glenn, see Twining 2005c; and on Tamanaha, see Twining, 2003. Unlike Tamanaha, I am not convinced of the value of constructing a general definition of law outside any particular context, but in the context of constructing total pictures of law in the world, I use variations on the following formulation: law as a form of institutionalised social practice is oriented towards ordering relations between subjects at different levels of relations and of ordering. This is quite close to MacCormick, 2007.

[20] During the period of the Cold War, a major exception was Soviet or Socialist law, which was treated as belonging to 'Comparative Law' in a way in which African, Indian, Islamic and Hindu law were not.

(v)   It focuses in practice largely on *private law*, especially the law of obliga-
         tions, which is often treated as representing 'the core' of a legal system or
         tradition;

(vi)   The concern is with *description and analysis* rather than evaluation and
         prescription, except that one of the main uses of 'legislative comparative
         law' is typically claimed to be the lessons to be learned from foreign solu-
         tions to 'shared problems'—a claim that is theoretically problematic.

This set of propositions is not a 'paradigm', nor is it intended as a caricature
of actual practice. Rather it is an ideal type to which most explicit secondary accounts of the nature and scope of comparative law and many implicit
assumptions in the discourse approximate more or less closely. I suggest that
this is a fair reconstruction of a recognisable set of ideas that have influenced the
development of Western comparative law since the Second World War. Insofar
as this is correct, it is relevant to make a number of points in relation to it.

First, between about 1945 and 1990 this set of assumptions was very influential in respect of the conceptualisation of the sub-discipline and its institutionali-
sation in journals, textbooks, courses, projects, and above all, ways of thought. It
is still influential today. Just to take two examples. Most historical surveys of the
field, including that of Konrad Zweigert and Hein Kötz, do not include Western
scholars of the stature of Duncan Derrett on Hindu Law, Joseph Schacht and
Norman Anderson on Islamic law and Antony Allott and James Read on African
law, even when they deal with these fields as part of macro-comparative law.
Hardly any non-Western scholars feature in these histories. Perhaps even more
remarkable is the fact that internal critics of the tradition, such as William Ewald,
Pierre Legrand, Basil Markesenis, and—perhaps less clearly—Alan Watson by
and large do not challenge the main assumptions. Ewald, for example, in his
fascinating philosophical critique of the tradition ('What was it like to try a
rat?'), assumes throughout that comparative law is concerned with analysis of
doctrine (especially private law) of 'parent' common law and civil law systems
(Ewald, 1995).

Thus insofar as it has been influential, the model has served to exclude from
the *concept* of 'comparative law' vast tracts of work, including the specialised
study by Western scholars of non-Western law, studies of foreign law that were
not explicitly comparative,[21] and cross-jurisdictional studies within the common law world—what may be termed comparative common law (Twining,
2000a: 145–8). This exclusive concept did not prevent scholarly work from
being undertaken; in recent years comparative legal studies have diversified

---

[21] Comparatists sometimes insist on a quite sharp distinction between foreign and comparative
law. This distinction is not sustainable for several reasons. Comparison covers a variety of activities
and foreignness is a relative matter. At a theoretical level nearly all description involves comparison,
which can be more or less implicit or explicit. We make loose comparisons in everyday life, explicitly
or implicitly, using analogies, models, metaphors, ideal types and a variety of other devices. So, too,
do comparatists.

in many directions—look, for example, at the contents of the leading journals—but its conceptualisation may have marginalised some areas of work and held back theoretical development.

The 'Country and Western' model is restricted in respect of each of its elements: municipal law of Western nation states; doctrine, especially private law; and contrasts between so-called 'parent' civil and common law systems as the central focus. Each of these elements can be challenged as narrow. In some contexts such narrowing had pragmatic justifications: ie manageability, relevance to other subjects in the curriculum, academic respectability, and sharpness of focus. The comparative study of the French, German, and English law of obligations, for example, has attained a very high degree of sophistication and specificity. But the price has been a heavy one. Apart from the exclusions already mentioned, the label 'comparative law' has been appropriated by practitioners and critics of one particular tradition in ways that artificially isolate it from very similar work, especially in respect of shared problems of methodology. The result is that much of the secondary literature about comparative law as a field is narrowly focused, overlooks some examples of best practice, and underestimates the richness, diversity and unevenness of transnational and cosmopolitan legal studies. It neither draws on nor illuminates these neglected areas.

The 'Country and Western' model is now out of date, but it has not been replaced by any coherent theory or theories. This is not to suggest that one should replace one reductionist theory by another, but rather that central issues relating to scope, method, comparability, explicit and implicit comparison and the relationship to other enquiries need to be addressed rigorously.

This critique of the 'Country and Western' model should not be taken as an all-out attack. Indeed, I think that it is a heritage to be valued and built on. First, there were good reasons for narrowing the focus, especially at the pioneering stage. This pragmatically motivated ideal type usefully guided development of a fragile new subject in a potentially hostile environment at a particular stage of its development. In England the pioneers such as H Gutteridge, FH Lawson and CJ Hamson had to emphasise the relevance, the respectability and the practical value of their field as part of their struggle for acceptance in the academy. Basil Markesenis, building on them, plays on similar themes in arguing for a more central place for comparative law in our legal culture (Markesinis, 1997). Secondly, as I have already noted, there were benefits as well as costs, not least in the quality of some of the work done within the 'Country and Western' framework. We should not just dismiss this part of our heritage. In my view, work done within the 'Country and Western Tradition' stands to comparative law as classical music stands to music: It is the best we have.

However, the model no longer fits what is being done in the name of comparative law, let alone work that has been excluded from the label. From a global perspective, the 'Country and Western' model has four main weaknesses: it is narrowly conceived; it has been artificially isolated from cognate fields; it is out of date; and it is under-theorised. What is lacking is a coherent view of the enterprise and above all sustained discussion of shared issues of comparability, method, levels and objectives across a broader range of enquiries. One result of this is that those who do comparative work—that is, most of us—do not get sufficient help and guidance from theory by way of synthesis, conceptual clarification, middle-order theorising, critical evaluation of assumptions and presuppositions and so on. In short, the jobs of jurisprudence are not being adequately performed for comparative or cosmopolitan legal studies. So the time is ripe for a quite radical rethink, not least in the light of globalisation and the need for a revived general jurisprudence.

A Naive Model of Diffusion

Some implications of adopting a global perspective and a broadened conception of law are illustrated by the topic of diffusion of law—sometimes referred to as reception, transplants, or transposition. Diffusion (under different labels) has been the subject of much attention, notably in long-running debates between Alan Watson and a number of leading scholars, including Otto Kahn-Freund, Lawrence Friedman, Pierre Legrand, and Esin Örücü. However, nearly all of these debates have focused on the diffusion of state law. Adopting a genuinely global perspective radically alters the landscape of diffusion, not only, or even mainly, by extending the ambit to include non-state law.

From some of my own early attempts to give an account of 'reception', I have constructed 'a naive model of reception' that has 12 elements, none of which are necessary and some of which are not even characteristic of most processes of diffusion.[22] The assumptions of the model can be briefly restated as follows:

> [A] *bipolar* relationship between *two countries* involving a *direct one-way* transfer of *legal rules or institutions* through the agency of *governments* involving *formal enactment or adoption* at a particular moment of time (*a reception date*) *without major change* ... [I]t is commonly assumed that the standard case involves *transfer from an advanced (parent) civil or common law system to a less developed one*, in order to bring about *technological change* ('to modernise') by *filling in gaps or replacing* prior local law (Twining, 2005b: 2–3).

Each of these assumptions can be shown not to be a necessary element of the processes of diffusion of law and several are almost certainly not typical. For example, governments are not the only, or even the main agents of diffusion; the pathways of diffusion are often indirect and influences are reciprocal; imported law rarely fills a vacuum or wholly replaces prior local law; and cross-level diffusion can be as significant as the more familiar horizontal (eg country-to-country) diffusion.[23]

---

[22] The model is introduced and discussed in Twining, 2005b.
[23] For further examples, see Twining, 2005b.

If we view this model as an ideal type of accounts of reception/transplantation in the legal literature, we find that some of the deviations are recognised by some commentators, but overall some such model is widely assumed to represent a paradigm case.[24] Appendix II illustrates just some of the possible variants/deviations from each element in the model. This is just one example of how adopting a global perspective can radically alter perceptions of a topic.

III. CONCLUSION

As the discipline of law is becoming more cosmopolitan in response to the processes loosely labelled 'globalisation', so comparative law as a sub-discipline has been moving from a relatively marginal role, dealing with foreign relations, to a much more central role at the hub of the subject. Serious comparative work is extremely difficult and, in the view of scholars like Max Rheinstein, requires a long apprenticeship—perhaps a minimum of 10 years (Rheinstein, 1968).[25] However, today nearly all legal studies are cosmopolitan in that legal scholars, and indeed law students, regularly have to use sources, materials and ideas developed in more than one jurisdiction and increasingly in more than one legal culture. In that sense, we are all comparatists now and we need help from more experienced scholars, especially in respect of methodology. We need to be equipped with at least the rudiments of coping with such material. So comparative method needs to be treated as a central element of 'legal method'.

Broadening our conception of comparative law may bring about a reintegration of closely related enclaves of enquiry that have become artificially separated. I find it bizarre that most standard accounts of the history of 'comparative law' make virtually no mention of 'law and development', or 'comparative human rights' or of the fields for which the School of Oriental and African Studies has been almost solely responsible in Britain, such as Islamic, Hindu, African, Indian, Chinese and, more recently, Buddhist law (Huxley, 1997). Apart from the intellectual gains, such a reintegration would further the practical cause of persuading colleagues that these fields should be treated as part of the mainstream rather than as exotic out-posts in our discipline.

Adopting a global perspective shows up some of the limitations of what is in many respects a rich tradition of Western comparative law. It should also alert us to the extent of our collective ignorance and warn against unfounded, often ethnocentric, generalisation about matters legal. Such a perspective reminds us of the diversity and complexity of legal phenomena, but it is mainly useful in setting

---

[24] A striking exception is Patrick Glenn, who seems to treat none of these features as necessary or even characteristic of the processes of interaction between legal traditions. (Glenn, 2004, *passim*, discussed in Twining, 2005c).

[25] Because it is so difficult, few comparatists indulge in explicit comparison in the sense of careful sustained analysis of similarities and differences between discrete, comparable phenomena. But, as Charles Taylor reminds us, nearly all description and interpretation involves at least implicit comparison, 'Comparison, History, Truth' (Taylor, 1995).

a broad context for more particular studies. Most of the processes of 'globalisation' occur at sub-global levels. Even in an interdependent world, the comparative study of law needs to focus mainly on detailed particulars that are local, practical, and embedded in specific cultural contexts.

APPENDIX I

Levels of Law[26]

If law is conceived of as a form of social practice concerned with ordering relations between subjects or persons (human, legal, unincorporated and otherwise) at a variety of levels of relations and of ordering, not just relations within a single nation state or society, one way of characterising such levels is essentially geographical:

- *global* (as with some environmental issues, a possible *ius humanitatis*) (eg mineral rights on the moon) and, by extension, space law;
- *international* (in the classic sense of relations between sovereign states and more broadly relations governed, eg by human rights or refugee law or international criminal law);
- *regional* (eg the European Union, European Convention on Human Rights, and the Organisation of African Unity);
- *transnational* (eg Islamic, Hindu, Jewish law, Gypsy law, transnational arbitration, a putative *lex mercatoria,* Internet law and, more controversially, the internal governance of multi-national corporations, the Catholic Church, or institutions of organised crime);
- *inter-communal* (as in relations between religious communities, Christian Churches, or different ethnic groups);
- *territorial state* (including the legal systems of nation states, and sub-national jurisdictions, such as Florida, Greenland, Quebec, Northern Ireland, and Zanzibar);
- *sub-state* (eg subordinate legislation, such as bye-laws of the Borough of Camden) or religious law officially recognised for limited purposes in a plural legal system; and
- *non-state* (including laws of subordinated peoples, such as native North Americans, Maoris, Gypsies, or illegal legal orders such as Santos's Pasagarda law, the Southern People's Liberation Army's legal regime in Southern Sudan, and the 'Common Law Movement' of militias in the United States) Which of these should be classified as 'law' or 'legal' is essentially contested within legal theory and also depends on the context and purposes of the discourse.

[26] Adapted from Twining, 2000a:139. Recent studies of Gypsy law have been pioneered by Walter Weyrauch. See especially, Weyrauch and Bell, 1993 and *Symposium on Gypsy Law* (Romaniya) 45(2) *AJCL* (Spring, 1997). The Southern Peoples' Liberation Army operated a system of courts dealing with both civil and criminal cases in areas which they occupied in the civil war in the Southern Sudan (Kuol, 1997). On the Common Law Movement, see Koniak, 1996 and 1997.

APPENDIX II

Diffusion of Law: A Standard Case and Some Variants[27]

	Standard Case	Some Variants
a. Source-destination	Bipolar: single exporter to single importer	Single exporter to multiple destinations. Single importer from multiple sources. Multiple sources to multiple destinations etc.
b. Levels	Municipal legal system-municipal legal system	Cross-level transfers. Horizontal transfers at other levels (eg regional, sub-state, non-state transnational)
c. Pathways	Direct one-way transfer	Complex paths. Reciprocal influence. Re-export
d. Formal / informal	Formal enactment or adoption	Informal, semi-formal or mixed
e. Objects	Legal rules and concepts; Institutions	Any legal phenomena or ideas, including ideology, theories, personnel, 'mentality', methods, structures, practices (official, private practitioners', educational etc), literary genres, documentary forms, symbols, rituals etc etc.
f. Agency	Government-government	Commercial and other non-governmental organisations. Armies. Individuals and groups: eg colonists, merchants, missionaries, slaves, refugees, believers etc who 'bring their law with them'. Writers, teachers, activists, lobbyists etc.
g. Timing	One or more specific reception dates	Continuing, typically lengthy process
h. Power and prestige	Parent civil or common law >> less developed	Reciprocal interaction
i. Change in object	Unchanged Minor adjustments	'No transportation without transformation'
j. Relation to pre-existing law	Blank slate. Fill vacuum or gaps. Replace entirely.	Struggle, resistance. Layering. Assimilation. Surface law

(continued on next page)

[27] From Twining, 2005b: 16.

continued

	Standard Case	Some Variants
k. Technical/ideological/ cultural	Technical	Ideology, culture, technology
l. Impact	'It works'	Performance measures. Empirical research. Monitoring. Enforcement

QUESTIONS FOR DISCUSSION

1. Why should we be suspicious of such phrases as 'global law', 'global law-yers', 'a global law school'? Can you think of any genuine examples of any of these categories?

2. In what ways are the processes of globalisation changing the significance of national boundaries?

3. 'Most processes of "globalisation" take place at sub-global levels.' Do you agree? Give examples.

4. What kinds of legal orders would you include in a reasonably comprehensive map (or series of maps) of law in the world? What kinds of institutionalised normative orders could you reasonably exclude?

5. 'Western academic legal culture has tended to be state-oriented, secular, positivist, "top down", North-centric, unempirical, and universalist in respect of morals.' To what extent has your legal education to date fitted this description?

6. This chapter includes three 'ideal types' of approaches to academic law—in respect of Western academic legal culture generally: the 'Country and Western Tradition' of comparative law, and a naïve model of diffusion of law. Are these unfair caricatures of scholarly legal practices?

7. 'We are all comparatists now'. Discuss.

8. Is it true that we are approaching a time when we will live in 'a border-less world', experience 'the end of sovereignty', and live under a World Government? Or are these ideas just 'hype'?

BIBLIOGRAPHY AND FURTHER READING

Abimbola, W and Abimbola, K (to be published 2007) *Orisa: Yoruba Religion and Culture in Africa and the Diaspora* (Birmingham, Iroko Academic Publishers).

Alston, P (ed) (2005) *Non-state Actors and Human Rights* (Oxford, Oxford University Press).

Arminjon, P, Nolde, B and Wolff, M (1950–51) *Traité de droit Comparé* (Paris, Librairie Générale de Droit et de Jurisprudence).

Baxi, U (2006) *The Future of Human Rights*, 2nd edn (New Delhi, Oxford University Press).

Blomley, N (1994) *Law, Space and the Geographies of Power* (New York, Guilford Press).

Buchanan, A (2000) 'Rawls' Law of Peoples: Rules for a Vanished Westphalian World' 110 *Ethics* 697.

Collier, J and Starr, J (eds) (1989) *History and Power in the Study of Law* (Ithaca, Cornell University Press).

David, R and Brierley, JEC (1968, 1985) *Major Legal Systems in the World Today*, 1st edn; 3rd edn (London, Stevens and Sons).

David, R (1964/1992) *Les grands systèmes du droit contemporain*, 1st edn; 10th edn by C Jauffret-Spinosi (Paris, Dalloz).

de Cruz, P (1995) *Comparative Law in a Changing World*, 2nd edn (London, Cavendish Publishing Ltd).

Deng, FM (1993) *Protecting the Disposessed: A Challenge to the International Community* (Washington, DC, Brookings).

Derrett, JDM (1968) *Religion, Law and State in India* (New York, Free Press).

Economides, K (1996) 'Law and Geography: New Frontiers' in P Thomas (ed), *Legal Frontiers* (Aldershot, Dartmouth).

Ewald, W (1995) 'Comparative Jurisprudence (I): What Was It Like To Try a Rat?' 143 *University of Pennsylvania Law Review* 1889.

Featherstone, M (ed) (1990) *Global Culture: Nationalism, Globalization and Modernity* (London, Sage).

Featherstone, M, Lash, S and Robertson, R (eds) (1995) *Global Modernities* (London, Sage).

Freeman-Grenville, GSP and Munro-Hay, SC (2002) *Historical Atlas of Islam* (New York, Continuum).

Giddens, A (1990) *The Consequences of Modernity* (Cambridge, Polity Press).

—— (1990a) *Sociology* (Cambridge, Polity Press).

Glenn, HP (2000/2004) *Legal Traditions of the World*, 2nd edn (Oxford, Oxford University Press).

Gutteridge, H (1946) *Comparative Law* (Cambridge, Cambridge University Press).

Halliday, F (1994) *Rethinking International Relations* (Basingstoke, Macmillan).

Hampshire, S (1989) *Innocence and Experience* (Cambridge, MA, Harvard University Press).

Holder, J and Harrison, C (eds) (2003) *Law and Geography*. (Oxford, Oxford University Press).

Huxley, A (1997) 'Golden Yoke, Silken Tent' 106 *Yale Law Journal* 1885.

Jenkins, P (2002) *The Next Christendom: the rise of global Christianity* (Oxford, Oxford University Press).

Koniak, S (1996) 'When Law Risks Madness' 8 *Cardozo Studies in Law and Literature* 65.

—— (1997) 'The Chosen People in our Wilderness' 95 *Michigan Law Review* 1761.

Kuol, MA (1997) *Administrative Justice in the (SPLA/M) Liberated Areas: Court Cases in War-Torn Southern Sudan* (Oxford, Refugee Studies Programme).

Legrand, P (1995) 'Comparative Legal Studies and Commitment to Theory' 58 *Modern Law Review* 262.

—— (1997) 'The Impossibility of Legal Transplants' 4 *Maastricht Journal of European and Comparative Law* 111.

Likosky, M (ed) (2002) *Transnational Legal Processes* (London, Butterworths).

MacCormick, DN (2007) *Institutions of Law* (Oxford, Oxford University Press).

Markesenis, B (1997) *Foreign Law: Comparative Methodology* (Oxford, Hart Publishing).

Misztal, B and Shup, A (eds) (1992) *Religion and Politics in Comparative Perspective: revival of religious fundamentalism in East and West* (Westport, CT, Praeger).

Moosa, E (ed) (2000) *Revival and Reform in Islam*. (Boston, MA, One World).

Nader, L (1984) 'A User Theory of Law' 38 *Southwestern Law Journal* 951.

Örücü, E (2004) *The Enigma of Comparative Law: Variations on a Theme for the Twenty-First Century* (Leiden, Martinus Nijhoff).

Pearl, D and Menski, W (1998) *Muslim Family Law*, 3rd edn (London, Sweet and Maxwell).

Pogge, T (1989) *Realizing Rawls* (Ithaca, NY, Cornell University Press).

Rawls, J (1993) 'The Law of Peoples' in S Shute and S Hurley (eds), *On Human Rights* (Oxford Amnesty Lectures, New York, Basic Books).

—— (1999) *The Law of Peoples* (Cambridge, MA, Harvard University Press).

Santos, B de Sousa (1995/2002) *Toward a New Legal Common Sense*, 2nd edn (London, Butterworths).

Rheinstein, M (1968) 'Comparative Law—Its Functions, Methods and Usages' 22 *Arkansas Law Review* 415.

Schlesinger, RB (1950/1988/1998) *Comparative Law: cases, text, materials*, 1st edn and 5th edn (Mineola, NY, Foundation Press); 6th edn by H Baade, P Herzog, and EM Wise).

Symposium on Gypsy Law (Romaniya) 45 *Am. Jo. Comp. L* No. 2 (Spring, 1997).

Tamanaha, B (2001) *A General Jurisprudence of Law and Society* (Oxford, Oxford University Press).

—— (2006) *Law as a Means to an End* (New York, Cambridge University Press).

Taylor, C (1995) 'Comparison, History, Truth' in C Taylor, *Philosophical Arguments* (Cambridge, MA, Harvard University Press).

Twining, W (1999) Globalization and Comparative Law 6 *Maastricht Journal of Comparative and European Law* 217.

—— (2000a) *Globalisation and Legal Theory* (London, Butterworths).

—— (2000b) 'Comparative Law and Legal Theory: The Country and Western Tradition' (School of Oriental and African Studies Law Dept 50th anniversary lectures) in ID Edge (ed), *Comparative Law In Global Perspective* (Ardsley, NY, Transnational Publishers).

—— (2001) 'A Cosmopolitan Discipline? Some Implications of "Globalisation" for Legal Education' 8 *International Journal of the Legal Profession* 23.

—— (2003) 'A Post-Westphalian Conception of Law' 37 *Law and Society Review* 199.

—— (2005a) 'General Jurisprudence' (World Congress on Philosophy of Law and Social Philosophy, Granada) in M Escamilla and M Saavedra (eds), *Law and Justice in Global Society* (IVR 2005, Seville) 609 (Spanish version, 563).

—— (2005b) 'Diffusion of Law: A Global Perspective' 49 *Journal of Legal Pluralism* 1.

—— (2005c) 'Glenn on Tradition: An Overview' 1 *Journal of Comparative Law* 107.

—— (2006a) "Diffusion of Law and Globalization Discourse" 47 *Harvard International Law Journal* 507.

—— (2006b) *Rethinking Evidence*, 2nd edn (Cambridge, Cambridge University Press).

—— (2006c) 'Human Rights: Southern Voices' 11 *Review of Constitutional Studies* 203.

Watson, A (1974/1993) *Legal Transplants: an approach to comparative law*, 1st Edn (Edinburgh, Scottish Academic Press); 2nd edn (University of Georgia Press).

Westbrook, D (2006) 'Theorizing the Diffusion of Law' 47 *Harvard International Law Journal* 489.

Weyrauch, WO and Bell, MA (1993) 'Autonomous Lawmaking: The Case of the "Gypsies"' 103 *Yale Law Journal* 323.

Woodman, G (2003) 'Why There Can be no Map of Law' in Rajendra Pradhan (ed) *Legal Pluralism and Unofficial Law in Social, Political, and Economic Development* 383 (XIIIth International Congress of Commission on Folk Law and Legal Pluralism, Kathmandu).

Zweigert, K and Kötz, H (1971/1987/1998) *An Introduction to Comparative Law* (1st edn in German); 2nd edn, 3rd edn (trans) T Weir, Oxford University Press.

4

Com-paring

H PATRICK GLENN

KEY CONCEPTS

Comparison; Epistemology of conflict; Epistemology of conciliation; Binary logic; Multivalent logic; Separation; Reification; Legal system; Culture; Common law; Legal tradition.

I. INTRODUCTION

WHY WAS COMPARATIVE law a distinct, marginal and boring discipline for the 19th and 20th centuries? It was distinct because it was constructed as separate from law itself, and as something which followed it (like the cigarette after sex, in the old movies). It was marginal because people are more interested in the real action than in that which follows it. It was boring for all of the above. Yet there appear to be symptoms (this book is one of them) of a major change in attitude towards the comparing of laws and towards the people who should be doing the comparing. This is linked to what is said to be a decline in the normative authority of states, so large forces appear to be at work, and we appear obliged to think more extensively about what comparison is, what concepts are used in comparing (or in refusing to compare) laws, and why it matters. The first problem is the idea of comparing.

Most of us think we know what comparing is. It involves determining whether two things or concepts or laws are similar or different. That's it. There the two are, similar or different. What can we do now to fill up the rest of the hour, or day, or year? Comparison here is empirical in character, inert, the way foreign law is often taught in many courses entitled 'comparative law', in which the effort appears to be one of understanding what the foreign law somehow *is*, with very little or no place for discussion of why it might be the way it appears to be, and what consequences that might have for the law we have already learned in other courses (but which is not on the exam for this one). Comparison here has all of the characteristics which it has been given by the intellectual constructions of the last two centuries (including those of legal education) and since that is all that comparison appears to be, then comparative law had to be (even more) distinct, marginal and boring.

This is not necessarily the way comparison has to be, however, and many of the lawyers of the world have understood this. Where does the word come from? It is not a construction of recent, 'modern' thought. It comes (you have already guessed) from Latin, and is a composite of two words: 'com', a version of 'cum' or 'with'; and 'pare' or peer. So com-paring is bringing together with a peer, with that which is prima facie equal for purposes of consideration. There is nothing in the word, moreover, that suggests that the result of the process is somehow terminal, in ensuing uniformity, or ensuing disastrous conflict. Com-paring thus would involve bringing together, and keeping together, of equals, which are presumed to endure, throughout and beyond the process of com-paring. Some have spoken of convivencia[1] or living together in harmony and in a way respectful of difference, which is usually far from boring, as you know if you have ever lived with someone different (and almost everyone is). Com-paring thus involves an enduring *process* of peaceful co-existence (in spite of difference, in spite of potential conflict), in a way which ensures not uniformity but ongoing diversity.

Living with different people in a spirit of mutual respect is not a distinct, marginal and boring process. Many would say it is the greatest challenge there is, particularly in times of so-called 'globalisation'. So what happened to the underlying idea of com-paring, to turn it from an essential and vital idea into a non-essential one? This is a very large question, involving some very large intellectual constructions, some having their origins in law itself, others lying outside of law but having enormous influence within it. But if large forces are at work in today's world, then large questions have to be asked. We are interested in how the idea of non-com-paring, or of rejecting equals, or of separation, came to prevail over ideas of com-paring. Where does the idea come from that people, or concepts, or things, can be kept apart, and that the idea of com-paring is simply a banal one of noting their separate characteristics? What are the legal and intellectual equivalents of the Berlin wall (now down, so it can happen) and the Israel-Palestine wall (now going up)? These walls are meant to eliminate contact, but in themselves do nothing to eliminate underlying ideas of conflict, and may even be seen as the final and most visible elements in a long process of separation or refusal of convivencia. So separation seems related to conflict and we are perhaps therefore looking for intellectual constructions, or an epistemology, of conflict or separation, as opposed to an epistemology of conciliation or com-paring. How do we *think* about human relations and the relations between laws, and what are the basic ideas we use in this process?

---

[1] Note the lack of italics, a typographical device of separation meant to signal formally that which is considered foreign. Yet languages have always been entirely open to one another, as English received a layer of French following the Norman Conquest, as a means of enrichment and not replacement (will/testament, ask/demand, wish/desire, room/chamber, start/commence, bit/morsel, etc), as to which see Bragg, 2004: 58–9.

II. AN EPISTEMOLOGY OF CONFLICT

It might be thought that if two groups are separated from one another, the separation itself will prevent conflict. There is an old English adage 'Love your neighbour, yet pull not down your hedge' and a poet, Robert Frost, had his neighbour famously saying 'good fences make good neighbours' while himself wondering:

> *Why* do they make good neighbours? ......
> Before I built a wall I'd ask to know
> what I was walling in or walling out.

Some say rather that 'bad neighbours make good fences'. There could, though, be a good—or at least arguable—case for both fences and private property. Yet this does not seem conclusive for larger questions of the relations between peoples and their laws. Their separation means there is necessarily no convivencia, no peaceful intermingling of equals and no need for each to understand the other. They would rather exist as separate blocks, whose relations in case of contact could only be conflictual, each attempting to displace the other. Non-com-paring thus would result from a logic of separation, as well as a construction of opposing collective identities, or reification of human groups into distinct and irreconcilable entities, in a way that would be hostile to the process of com-paring.

The Logic of Separation

Much time is spent in law schools in teaching people to 'think like a lawyer', though there is usually little explanation of what this means. If one looks at the way law is usually taught, however, thinking like a lawyer would involve rigorous intellectual constructions, where conclusions follow irresistibly from prior premises or givens. Being a lawyer would involve being logical and consistent, as well as being unflappable, cool and elegant in execution. The cool part would involve personal characteristics, the logical part would be simply ... logic; here applied to human affairs as opposed to maths or the physical sciences. This is at least how things are often made to appear.

Logic, however, does not admit of a single or simple definition. The most famous definition was that of Aristotle, who early on formulated what has ever since been known as the rule of the excluded middle, sometimes (slightly) re-formulated as the law of non-contradiction (which thus requires consistency). What does the law of the excluded middle tell us? It involves what otherwise would appear to be an extraordinarily depressing proposition for lawyers and others involved in dispute resolution, that there is no middle ground between opposing concepts. If you take A and its negation, not-A, they each exclude one another and together exclude all the ground which might exist between them. The opposition is total, and so you must choose between them, A *or* not-A. Asserting at the same time A *and* not-A would be asserting a contradiction, not being logical (in the Aristotelian sense). It would be asserting that opposites can co-exist and that their co-existence implies a middle ground between them. Early on we are taught, however, of the excluded middle as an irrefutable fact of life. You cannot have your cake and eat it too, though you might as a child have wondered, rightly, why not.

Ideas of radical separation are here made to appear inherent in the nature of (correct) human thought. Consistency would be found in following a logic of separation, though it is never explained why A and not-A are taken as radically separate from one another, as opposed to being the simple ends of a continuum running between them, where there is more middle ground than anything else. This latter view would represent another type of logic, which of course has its own logic, not of separation but of gradation, and which consists of challenging the underlying (but never justified) assumption of Aristotelian logic, that of separation. It is now known in English, perhaps unfortunately, as 'fuzzy logic', but it should be understood not as a logic which is imprecise (it is very precise indeed), but as a logic of fuzziness.[2] The fuzziness is that of the real world, where boundaries are never sharp (in spite of what our limited means of physical perception tell us) and where the physical sciences now recognise the possibility of infinite gradations of measurement. Fuzzy logic (or multivalent logic as it is sometimes called—admitting many values) admits the complexity and imprecision (lack of separation) of the real world and attempts to expand our base of information so we can comprehend it. Com-paring would be necessarily multivalent, in bringing together and keeping together very different people and very different laws, with no necessity of choosing definitively between them. It implies an ever-present, included middle.

The logic of separation is profoundly implanted, however, in intellectual and popular life (remember the cake) and in ways of thinking about laws, peoples and underlying values. One manifestation is found in the idea of 'incommensurability', by which is meant not (simply) that two ideas or concepts are incompatible with one another (A *or* not-A again, which is bad enough), but that it is simply not possible to comprehend A *and* not-A and their relations with one another. They would be incapable of common measure (hence incommensurable) and thus incapable of mutual understanding. The popular version is that of not being able to compare apples and oranges, an outrageously false proposition but repeated endlessly by people who consider themselves rational. The original idea of incommensurability would have come from mathematics, where the Greeks found that some geometrical lengths could not be measured with whole numbers or integers (which is all they then worked with), but has now been extended to moral philosophy (eg, friends are incommensurable with money) and law (Soviet law would have been incommensurable with bourgeois, western law;

---

[2] For references, see Glenn, 2004a: 350–52, and for how the legal traditions of the world are all built on notions of multivalent, as opposed to Aristotelian, or bivalent, logic, see below.

even the common law, though bourgeois, would be incommensurable with the civil law). The notion of incommensurability is derived from Aristotelian ideas of separation and logic, and is incompatible with multivalent forms of logic, where A and not-A would be simple elements (though at the extremities) of a continuum of meaning. It may be said that Chicago is incommensurable with the number nine, but how do we even make such an assertion if we have not made some (preliminary) evaluation of them both? The com-paring need be done not with a numerical or other measure common and external to both of them (a so-called tertium comparationis), but in terms of the characteristics which each possesses, or does not possess. Chicago is thus spatially-defined, whereas the number nine is not; Chicago has freight-yards, but the number nine does not. This may not be very helpful information, but if com-paring is possible here can it really be excluded elsewhere, notably in law?

One major field of law, however, where there might just as well be profound incommensurability, is the field of legal education. Since the 11th or 12th centuries, when law schools were begun in Europe, in both England and on the continent, only one law has been taught. There is here a 'primordial' idea of there being only one true legal model, the ius unum. In Oxford and Cambridge, and in the great Universities of the continent, that law, known as the ius commune, was a then-current adaptation of still older Roman law, which in its (Aristotelian) rationality was seen as an effective means of combating the unwritten or local laws which were such an obstacle to centralised church and state authority. Why was a single, intellectualised law taught, which in almost all cases had little or nothing to do with the lives of people (which were governed by feudal and customary law)? The Holy Roman Empire had much to do with it on the continent, since emperors prefer uniformity—their uniformity—and the Church was not opposed since the Empire was, after all, Holy. It has been written lately that there was a great fear of 'contamination' from the teaching of other forms of normativity (Thunis, 2004: 6). When the reaction against this enforced uniformity of high-level instruction came about, as it inevitably did, another law, the law of the state, came to be taught, not in addition to the ius commune, but in its place. So the idea of a *ius unum*, uncontaminated, continued to prevail into the present century; a constant theme of over a millennium's duration, of separating laws and teaching only one of them—that considered fit to be taught—in pure form. This allowed, moreover, demonstration of the (Aristotelian) logic of the only law allowed to be taught. Comparative law could exist in this intellectual environment, strongly influenced even today by imperial and canonical ideas, only as a distinct, marginal and boring topic, if it was allowed at all.

Mention of the church of course brings to mind another famous separation of the western world, that between church and state. There are relatively few jurisdictions which actually have a constitutional principle of separation of church and state, but the idea of a separation between an earthly city and the city of God is built into christian thinking ('Give unto Caesar …', etc), so most people in western jurisdictions actually think there is a constitutional principle of separation even when their own country (say, England or Canada) has no such principle. Still, the principle of separation would be the main reason for thinking of some jurisdictions as 'secular', even though such jurisdictions appear as very christian to much of the rest of the world, because of their 'secularity'. Where there is a clear constitutional principle of separation of church and state, as in the United States of America, the separation has clearly not given rise to an absence of conflict, though much of the litigation now turns on what a separation of church and state could possibly mean, where many people live religious lives. Separation has not been possible, and litigation over it has itself become a means of conciliation.

These underlying ideas of separation, profoundly rooted in ways of thought and institutional structures, have had a profound effect on the possibility of com-paring. Where comparative law has existed it may be seen as almost miraculous, so the fact that it has been distinct, marginal and boring becomes much less severe a judgement than it may have initially appeared. Yet there have been other major obstacles to com-paring, mostly in the form of an amazing tendency to objectify or reify human groupings, such that they appear almost certain to be constantly colliding with one another. War is the obvious example, but we are now finding ways of colliding, and killing, short of actually declaring war.

The Process of Reification

In the (beautiful) Indian dance of Kuchi-pudi, from the village of that name, all is done with mime, largely through movements of hands and eyes. The mime for conflict is two hands clenched into fists, not striking one another but simply pushing one another for the same space. There is no convivencia of large, dense objects. The mime for conciliation is again two hands, this time with the fingers outstretched towards those of the other hand, and the fingers of both hands becoming interlaced as the two hands are brought together. The hands here are not reified into fists, but allowed to exist as many points of contact and even cohesion, though the two hands remain readily identifiable. This form of dance was not meant as just another form of rap, but as a means of teaching important things in a non-literate society, such that conflict could be largely avoided through notions of mutual support and understanding. This type of teaching, however, is abandoned with the contemporary process of social reification.

The most obvious form of social reification is found in the contemporary state or national legal system. Contemporary states have claimed to be the exclusive source of law on their territories, though this has been compared with Baron Münchhausen pulling himself out of the swamp by his own hair. For much of the 19th and 20th centuries, however, legal theory accepted and developed the idea of a national legal system. A national legal system, according to leading explanations, could be seen as a simple, positive fact, based on the reality of obedience to it (at least where this existed, which is less and less frequent in the world, with notions of failed or failing states). The system need not, therefore, be normatively justified, but could be simply explained, notably by Herbert Hart in terms of primary rules of conduct and secondary rules which would allow for change and articulation of the primary rules (Hart, 1994). Why was the national legal system an obstacle to com-paring? Because each legal system was incompatible with every other legal system, and each legal system could tolerate only laws valid according to its own secondary rules. This is quite consistent with general systems theory, which directs our attention to the interaction of the elements of the system within the cadre of the boundaries fixed by the system. There is therefore no need for com-paring of different laws, since there could be none, on the same territory. Moreover, since a legal system existed as simple fact, it could have nothing normative to say about whether it should leave room, say, for the law of a religious minority or for the law of an international tribunal of some kind (unless it formally enacted such a rule). So the separation of legal systems from one another was largely complete, at least in legal theory. The result was a notion of conflict of laws (the heart of the major discipline of private international law) according to which any transborder activity could be conceived only in terms of conflict, triggering a choice-of-law rule based largely on geographic contacts. The worst manifestation of this highly conflictual and non-com-parative view of the relations of laws is found in the present law of some continental jurisdictions, which says that rules of private international law are of obligatory application by the court. Accordingly, every transborder case requires an initial decision on what law is applicable to it, without even any enquiry as to whether there is a real difference or conflict between the laws. Here, reification of the system creates enormous trouble and expense, the justification of which appears more and more impossible in current circumstances of communication and trade. Should there really be a presumption of conflict amongst the laws of the European Union?

The formal nature of state law and the state legal system is now being challenged by many developments of a transnational character, but there have been challenges also by the valuable work of many sociologists, who have been able to determine whether state law, in particular circumstances, works or does not work. This is highly salutary and involves a type of comparison between formal texts and the situation on the ground. Sociology and anthropology of law are open to much more information than are legal systems, and so much can be expected of them in terms of meaningful comparison of laws. Much has also been delivered. Yet a major caveat is in order, to the extent that the social science disciplines of sociology and anthropology have themselves become victims of the process of reification, notably in the development of the idea of culture. Everyone talks about culture these days, though no-one knows what it really is. There have been hundreds of definitions offered, none in any way successful. This is not, however, the problem for com-paring. The problem is that the notion of culture has itself been reified, in spite of its ambiguity, and attached to particular groups of people as a defining element of them. In the 19th and 20th centuries there were many definitions of culture which sounded very close to definitions of legal systems, in terms of their being a 'complex whole', a 'total system', or even a 'totality' (see Glenn, 2007: 7). Since a culture had to be internally consistent to be recognisable as a culture, diversity within one's own culture became inherently problematical, and diversity within other cultures (of which less was necessarily known) became essentially inconceivable. This is now known as essentialism, and is criticised, yet it was inevitable, given the large and homogenising concept of culture which was deployed. The same method of reification has been used by the US political scientist Samuel Huntington in speaking of a 'clash of civilizations', in which civilisations are defined as 'entities', such that com-paring is impossible and the only relations that can possibly exist are conflictual in character (Huntington, 1996: 28, 41 and 43).[3]

The 19th and 20th century concepts of culture are now recognised as major liabilities by many sociologists and anthropologists and major efforts of re-conceptualisation are taking place. The notion of the 'multi-cultural' (many conflicting entities) is now being sought to be replaced by a notion of the 'inter-cultural' which would be more compatible with com-paring. This involves, however, re-educating the general public, which now thinks in terms of culture wars, so it is impossible to predict the effect of present efforts of refinement.[4] There is, moreover, an underlying conceptual problem of whether it is even possible to retain a notion of culture which would not be seen as a 'complex whole' or as a 'totality'. This is what culture has been, and if it is not that, then it may well dissolve into its component parts, whatever they may be.[5] Stay tuned.

The reification process has thus manifested itself in terms of systems, cultures, civilisations, and further even in terms of 'mentalités'. These have all been boundary-tracing endeavours which both homogenise (within) and differentiate (without), in a way incompatible with com-paring or convivencia. The situation is not as bleak, however, as this discussion indicates. Theory, which has been the object of the discussion, often does not control the world, and theory tends to become dated as the world moves on, as it is rapidly doing. There is room for discussion of another type of epistemology.

III. AN EPISTEMOLOGY OF CONCILIATION

To find an epistemology of conciliation it appears, from all of the efforts of separation we have seen, that we must look elsewhere, and notably away from legal and social theory of the major western jurisdictions. If you are already

---

[3] See also (*ibid*: 21): 'We know who we are only when we know who we are not and often only when we know whom we are against' and (*ibid*: 42): 'A civilization is a "totality"'. Huntington's book was translated into German with the title *Kampf der Kulturen*.

[4] For the notion of a 'culturally unitary group ... tied to "its" territory' as 'difficult to shake because ... so deeply ingrained in the modern consciousness', see Berman, 2005:485 at 513, with refs; but for concept of culture being 'misused' as weapon in cultural wars, see Nelken, 2001: 26.

[5] For this process of dissolution, see Cotterell, 2004: 1 at 9 'the concept of culture should be broken down into distinct components and its vagueness and indeterminacy thereby reduced'.

well-versed in such theory, and inclined to defend it, please withhold judgement for a bit, as an immediate exercise of com-paring. There may be things worth knowing about out there, and you may even run into them in your future, fantastic, galactic legal practice. Where has an epistemology of conciliation developed amongst lawyers, allowing for widespread and active processes of com-paring?

A Multivalent Logic of Legal Practice

Can practice be possible without high theory, notably of the legal system? Well, a major and important book has just been written about Jewish law, which would have existed for a least a couple of millenia without any western-style theory (though it would have something called faith to help it along) (Rynhold, 2005). Here there would be a 'Priority of Practice' which would take precedence over a 'Priority of Theory', and the practice would be highly specific, alive to individual particularities and nuances (think of the common law, perhaps even today), such that ideas of boundaries or general systems somehow fade away in the challenge of the immediate case. Cases would be decided in comparing them with other cases, with no closureof information or general boundaries impeding the process. There would be here something similar to the way in which the unwritten law of chthonic or native peoples would have been recognised by Crown negotiators in North America, not through their imposition of categories of theory but through having 'simply listened' to what they were being told. Wittgenstein would have approved of the process, having criticised the 'craving for generality' and argued for understanding a general term only through the practical activity of using it in various circumstances.[6]

So practice may actually be more conducive to com-paring than either legal or social theory of the last centuries. Are there any other indications of this? There may well be in the emerging process of practising law in a transnational manner. Something is going on here, though it does not appear to be reflected in any theoretical work, anywhere. What is happening is that legal practitioners are beginning to enjoy a vantage point above and beyond that of state law. Since legal practice was highly local for much of legal history, knowledge of foreign law was very hard to come by. Experts had to be called upon, and there was (is) that continental rule that if a case has any foreign element it is immediately whisked away from the practitioners while a court decides what law is applicable to it and foreign content of the law can then be officially obtained (usually through a university or government research institute). Not much com-paring could go on, and not much place was left for a 'priority of practice' or principle of mutual recognition.

---

[6] For the combination of Wittgenstein and aboriginal negotiations, themselves based on a principle of 'mutual recognition' and therefore of com-paring, see Tully, 1995: 105–19.

Today, however, law firms exist in transnational form (true or linked partnerships) and are able to sit in judgement upon, choosing, state law, both for choice of jurisdiction and for choice of substantive law.[7] Lawyers also sit on arbitration panels, largely prohibited by state law in the 19th century, and may call upon many models of state law in reaching their decision. They also sit on arbitration panels in free-trade dispute-resolution processes, even engaging in comparative debates on whether national, public (administrative) law rules have been violated and according to what criteria. They seek 'best practices', and the transnational commercial world is one of free-flowing normative information where the question is never what the best possible rule is (which would be an impractical enquiry), but which solution is preferable to other solutions.

Comparative legal practice is not limited, however, to the corner offices of the large transnational firms. Given the level of population mobility in the world, family law practice has become transnational and comparative in character, and courts in all jurisdictions are occupying themselves with the reconciliation of state norms and those of non-western legal traditions.[8] The same phenomenon is evident in what was previously seen as internal commercial practice (eg, the 'islamic mortgage', or bond).[9] Even in criminal law that which is, unfortunately, known as the 'cultural' defence has emerged, in the form of reliance on specific principles or rules of non-western traditions as a means of defence against criminal charges; defences which are usually rejected except to the extent they may bear on the mental element of the crime—and hence they must be considered at least for this purpose (Renteln, 2004). Nor is the practice of comparison limited to the private, practising, professions. Judges are now actively engaged in consideration of extra-national (even 'foreign') law and even in matters of public law. In the 1970s Otto Kahn-Freund spoke of the latter in particular as a misuse of comparative law (since it related to local structures of power) (Kahn-Freund, 1974), but now judges engage in round-table discussions of how and why to engage in the process.[10] Difficult human rights cases in particular appear to call for consideration of (comparable) other cases. The United States Supreme Court is now actively debating the extent to which it should engage in citation of foreign cases in interpretation of the United States Constitution. To the extent it does so it would be returning to an open position which prevailed in the 18th and 19th centuries, before notions of national systems and closure began to take effect.

---

[7] For the process, see Glenn, 2001 (and also on new mobility of lawyers, and the need for comparison of different ethical rules).

[8] For recent United States practice, see Estin, 2004: notably 540 at 541–2 (US judges developing multi-cultural family law, making 'space for traditions to flourish').

[9] In the United States, see Shepherd, 2000.

[10] Roundtable, 2005. For the House of Lords in England relying extensively on civilian and Anglo-American common law authority, see *Fairchild v Glenhaven Funeral Services Ltd* [2003] 1 AC 32 (HL).

These transnational forms of practice and com-paring may appear disparate and even incoherent, particularly in the face of an epistemology of conflict and the logic of separation and reification, discussed above. They represent, however, an epistemology of conciliation which is as coherent and justifiable as its opposite. It may even be articulated in long-standing legal concepts which predate the idea of the national legal system and which have continued to be operative even during the period of legal nationalism. The most important of these long-standing legal concepts is that of common law. Most lawyers today think of common law as the legal tradition developed by the courts of England, subsequently transported to many parts of the world. Coincidentally, there would have been another common law in the form of the ius commune, discussed above in relation to legal education, which would have differed fundamentally from the common law in being based on Roman law and being essentially doctrinal in character as opposed to judge-made. This view of common law does not fully reflect, however, the widespread character of the notion of common law in European and world legal history. There was also a French common law ('droit commun'), a Spanish common law ('*derecho commún*'), a German common law ('gemeine Recht') and so on (Glenn, 2005). What was common to all of these common laws, including 'the' common law and 'the' ius commune, was that they co-existed alongside non-common , particular laws (as with the local customs of England), and law which was common had to be designated as such to distinguish it from the law which was not. The English common law was thus known as common law not because it was case law, which had nothing to do with its name, but because it was capable of application (though not necessarily applied) throughout an entire territory, in contrast to the local laws that were limited to particular territories. Whether the English, French, German or Spanish common law actually did apply, in a given case, was the result of a process of reconciliation of the claims of the common and particular laws. It resulted from com-paring the two, and it was generally accepted that common laws would yield to local particularity where the local law claimed its own application with sufficient vigour. Still today, local custom prevails over the common law (of England) when it is proven according to satisfactory standards.

Did these common laws survive the period of legal nationalism, the process of codification on the continent and the development in the 19th century of stare decisis in the common law? The usual response to this question is negative, since national legal systems in Europe were seen as abolishing sources of law other than those of state authority. This is the logic of separation and reification at work and it has been very influential. Consider the nature, however, of these common laws and their territorial application. They were not limited to the territory of a particular nation state in Europe. Indeed, these states were not even recognisable (well, England perhaps, because of the shoreline) in the 15th century when their law began to be exported abroad in the process of colonialism. The common laws of England, France and Spain, notably, became the common laws of empires, potentially applicable far beyond the mère patrie. They were not always applied, and the legal history of colonialism is very similar to the expansion of the common laws within their original territories. The common laws yielded to local particularity when local particularity so required (though criminal law had its own requirements). In this they remained true to their character as common laws, and the process of their application was the same process of reconciliation and comparison. In the Commonwealth, the test for the application of English (common) law was its 'suitability', and this involved an extensive, com-parative exercise with English and local law being brought together as equals and interrogated on their claims and suitability for application. The English law did not always win; indeed it often lost. Quebec law is what it is today because the common law, then still in the form of writs, could not displace the written, substantive law of French origin that was already in place.

Lawyers in the colonised world (almost all of the world), thus engaged in an active process of reconciliation of law from the 15th century. Did this change with the advent of the idea of the national legal system? Did the European states which gave rise to common laws succeed in abolishing them wherever they had taken root in the world? This was impossible, since nation states are sovereign (so it is taught) only on their own territory. The result has been an ongoing process all over the world, of consultation of both local law and the relevant common law (English, French, Spanish, German, Dutch, etc) in the decision-making process in individual cases and certainly also in any legislative processes. This massive phenomenon of the ongoing influence of common laws in the world, and the comparative process which it implies, has been completely by-passed (necessarily so) by theories of national legal systems and exclusivity of national laws. State laws, however—including those of the states having originated common laws—exist today within a broad cadre of ongoing common law which can always be called upon as a means of remedying the deficiencies of local law, in the historical manner of common laws. Commonwealth lawyers know this well, and the *Oxford University Commonwealth Law Journal* is the latest manifestation of the phenomenon, but the process is replicated in much of the rest of the world as well. The notion of common law thus provides, and has provided for centuries, an ongoing justification for the process of com-paring and reconciliation of laws. There is a further conceptual instrument available for this purposes, however, in the concept of legal tradition.

Legal Traditions

The notion of tradition has been the object of great vilification in the western world. Edward Shils concluded that it was not only the tradition of the ancien régime which the 'enlightenment' sought to eliminate, but the concept of tradition itself (Shils, 1981: 6). This would leave the field free to contemporary rationality, to modernity, and then to post-modernity. This is still how the popular, western world largely conceives of itself, but there are now indications of growing, theoretical recognition that the western tradition is one of many, and that there is need for reconciliation of them all. The western tradition is one which calls itself modernity. It is a tradition which denies its historical past and valorises present rationality, but there is no escaping the historical past of that which has led to notions of modernity and the valorisation of present rationality. Most other people of the world do not think this way, and it took many millennia for western people to come to think this way, so we are essentially dealing with highly developed bodies of normative information, of long standing, which tell us how to live and how to solve our disputes.

Tradition, including legal tradition, is thus best thought of as a body of 'highly self-conscious' information (Philips and Schochet, 2004: ix), necessarily normative in character because of its long duration, which would constitute the essential subject-matter of today's 'information society'. The 'new orality' of the electronic world, for example, would thus be providing new vitality to oral traditions of previously limited geographical reach. It is true that much of the information that the world generates is simply noise, but the operation of the techniques of tradition, in effecting the necessary capture and transmission of the information of the tradition, eventually eliminates the noise and makes the past readable, and understandable, for those of the present.

As a long-standing body of normative information, tradition has also been castigated in western thought as inherently conservative in character. It is that which must be struggled against, in the name of many desirable reforms. This is a very particularised and inaccurate view of the real force of tradition. It is particularised because it derives from the European struggle against the ancien régime, a tradition well-worthy of being overthrown in many of its characteristics (social classes, privilege, corruption, etc). It is inaccurate because the tradition was overthrown not on the basis simply of present rationality, whatever that might be, but because the reformers of the enlightenment justified their conduct by appealing to sources of rationality recognised to have originated with the Greeks. Hence we have the word 'revolution', which involves a return, or re-volving to an original, earlier position. In astronomy, this meant for Copernicus[11] the return of a planet or moon to the point of origin of its orbit. In revolutionary politics it meant resort to an alternative tradition of rationality as a means of reform. The word 'revolution' thus acknowledges the ancienneté of the rationalist tradition, as well as the disruptive and legitimising force of alternate traditions.

How can the concept of tradition, however, faced with the silent fact of large and dense legal systems, contribute to a process of reconciliation and convivencia? From within a legal system the view is limited, since the system is exclusive, irreconcilable with other laws, and conflictual in character. Tradition, however, would allow you to step outside of the system, still remaining within (traditional) law, and require it to justify itself, to provide the means of com-paring and grounds for reconciliation. How is this so? There are three avenues to explore. They all have the effect of surrounding legal systems and requiring them to justify themselves.

---

[11] Copernicus, *De Revolutionibus*, 1543.

The first avenue is through the history, and even pre-history, of legal systems themselves. Positive legal thought grounds legal systems on contemporary social facts of obedience (Herbert Hart) or efficiency in operation (the view of the Austrian jurist Hans Kelsen). But, one may well ask, where did these ideas come from? In philosophy, the idea of a 'fact' is now questioned, as it is in legal traditions other than western ones, so it can be demonstrated that the standard definitions of a legal system are historically grounded.[12] Legal systems would not be grounded on what positivists say they are grounded on, since that is a definition internal to the systemic manner of thought. Legal systems would rather be grounded on the thought, or tradition, which enabled positivist legal theorists to reach these conclusions. Legal systems are thus best conceptualised themselves as instantiations of a particular legal tradition. As such, they are conceptually equal to, and on a par with, other legal traditions, which all exist as self-conscious bodies of legal information, sustained over considerable periods of time. So one can stand outside western legal systems, as a western lawyer, but still stand within law, by placing oneself within a western legal tradition, and even a western tradition of positive law and legal systems (now cognisant of its traditional character). There would thus be underlying common law (and we are back to it here), or ius publicum universale, as it used to be ambitiously called, justifying the range of distinct states which emerged in Europe and the world. This tradition is not dumb; it speaks to the need and justification for legal systems, and is capable both of recognising their weaknesses, their need for reinforcement, and degrees of effectiveness in their implementation. Western legal tradition is normative; it speaks to questions which legal systems, as purported facts, are unable to speak to. This is why Article 6 of the Treaty of the European Union speaks of Europe's 'common constitutional traditions', since it is necessary to resort to such underlying common tradition as a means of critiquing, com-paring, and going beyond, the national systems of Europe.

The second avenue of exploration is through the juxtaposition of the national legal system with other legal traditions within the national territory. This cannot be done by legal theorists posing abstract questions, and probably cannot be done at all by theorists of national legal systems. There is a large and important empirical requirement, which is that of a population which adheres to non-state normativity, and an equally important procedural requirement of accessibility to formal institutions of adjudication on the part of this population. These requirements are now met in many of the jurisdictions where the idea of a legal system has been

---

[12] Putnam, 2002: 3 and 63: 'the terms one uses even in description in history and sociology and the other social sciences are invariably ethically coloured'; and for the history, or tradition of the concept of 'fact' see Shapiro, 1994: 245; and Shapiro, 2000: 3, 9, 11, 60, 107 and 110 (the notion of fact in medieval common law procedure was drawn from romano-canonical tradition and then adopted by other disciplines, though 'fact' in law was only an issue placed before a jury, either fictional or real, and came to be an 'established truth' only under the influence, notably, of Bacon, Hobbes, and contemporary scientific thought).

well received, such that the concept of an exclusive system is now challenged from within. Once this happens, once it is recognised that there is challenge by lawyers, raising justiciable issues, to the exclusivity of the system, the system can be made to respond, to argue back, and even to yield to other forms of normativity which thus come to be recognised as law. In Canada, until the 1970s, the Canadian government rejected negotiation of claims of aboriginal or chthonic peoples as being too 'vague' for legal recognition (a very systemic view). This position changed once the Supreme Court recognised the justiciability of these claims.[13] A tradition of unwritten law was thus recognised as a legal tradition; and as a legal tradition it required a response from the state legal system, now more clearly recognisable as an alternative tradition and no longer as a large, silent, and immovable object. In Australia as well, the lex non scripta of the Australian aborigines is now explicitly designated as 'traditional law'. The concept of tradition is thus a roomy one. It encompasses many different types of law, including that of the state. And since tradition is defined in terms of information, the information of each tradition is accessible to the others, so the possibilities of dialogue and conciliation are enhanced.

The concept of tradition thus allows a better understanding of state law, and a better understanding of other laws which may be raised within its territory. Tradition is also the best explanation of much transnational law (a third avenue of exploration), which exists in diverse and variable form, but in all instances as normative information, the force of which increases to the extent that it is recognised as a traditional source of law. This is why very sophisticated and contemporary forms of international commercial legal practice are designated as lex mercatoria. They would be legitimated by their classification within a body of commercial normativity that has prevailed and been recognised for centuries. Tradition is also the only conceptual means of recognition of religious laws (without doing violence to revelation) which consider themselves incompatible with western notions of system or culture.

As normative information, tradition simply goes with the flow. There are no inherent boundaries to tradition, as is the case with systems, though particular traditions such as that of the nation state may construct boundaries for themselves. Traditions function according to multivalent forms of logic and tolerate diversity (see Glenn, 2007). They have large and roomy middle grounds. The tradition of the Anglo-American and Commonwealth common law is a good example of this, existing as it does in various, often contradictory forms throughout the world while maintaining a recognisable identity as a common law. Traditions thus do not conflict and compete for space (though nothing prevents people from doing so), but rather influence, through a process of com-paring. It has been said recently that the concept of tradition has become, in the last quarter of a century, the 'dominant paradigm' in understanding the world's laws, and that this is so

---

[13] *Calder v British Columbia* [1973] SCR 313, 34 DLR (3d) 145.

because the concept of tradition would look 'beyond ... legal systems and families as static and isolated entities' (Reimann, 2002.:677; and see Merryman, 1985; Glendon, Gordon and Osakwe, 1994; Zimmermann, 1996; and Glenn, 2004a). Traditions thus allow for convivencia, and the study of legal traditions and their ongoing relations with one another should therefore not be a distinct, marginal and boring process, but an integrated, vital and challenging part of what is known as globalisation.

QUESTIONS FOR DISCUSSION

1. Why would the notion of exclusive state law have developed in the particular circumstances of Europe and nowhere else in the world? Why does this question challenge positivist explanations of legal systems?
2. Would tradition be too vague in its definition of law to allow legal practice to continue? Would it be the case that a particular tradition, such as that of a legal system, would allow for formal identification of law where this was thought necessary? To what extent do you think legal practice, as practice, is systemic in character?
3. Is the reason why different legal traditions are not taught because most law professors don't know anything about them? Why would this be so? Is it a justification?
4. To what extent is the study of different legal traditions encumbered by problems of language? Is it necessary to learn about a law in its original language? Can a law exist and be effectively applied only in unilingual form? What is the linguistic history of 'the' common law?
5. If account must increasingly be taken in the world of different legal traditions, will this be an obstacle to development and commercial efficiency? If so, is this a good thing or a bad thing?
6. Why is the discipline of private international law not compatible with a process of com-paring of laws?
7. Why is a comparative law process of classifying the different laws of the world into different legal families (civil law, common law, islamic law, etc) not compatible with a process of com-paring of laws?
8. Why is a course in comparative law not compatible with a generalised process of com-paring of laws? Is public international law part of the solution or part of the problem?
9. How can an argument be made (it is now being made) that, say, the common law is more efficient than the civil law? What criteria of comparison could be used? Is there such an entity as the common law or the civil law (as opposed to particular manifestations of them) the efficiency of which can be judged in the abstract?
10. Why do legal exchange programmes not involve any com-paring of laws?

BIBLIOGRAPHY AND FURTHER READING

Berman, PS (2005) 'From International Law to Law and Globalization' 43 *Columbia Journal of Transnational Law* 485.

Bragg, M (2004) *The Adventure of English* (London, Hodder & Stoughton).

Cotterell, R (2004) 'Law in Culture' 17 *Ratio Juris* 1.

Canivet, G, Andenas, M and Fairgrieve, D (2004) *Comparative Law before the Courts* (London, British Institute of International and Comparative Law).

Drobnig, U and van Erp, S (eds) (1999) *The Use of Comparative Law by Courts* (The Hague–London–Boston, Kluwer Law International).

Estin, A (2004) 'Embracing Tradition: Pluralism in American Family Law' 63 *Maryland Law Review* 540.

Glendon, MA, Gordon M and Osakwe, C (1994) *Comparative Legal Traditions* (St Paul, West Publishing).

Glenn, HP (2001) 'On Removing the Boundaries: Comparative Law and Legal Practice' 75 *Tulane Law Review* 977.

—— (2004) 'Legal Cultures and Legal Traditions' in M Van Hoeck (ed), *Epistemology and Methodology of Comparative Law* (Oxford, Hart Publishing).

—— (2005) *On Common Laws* (Oxford, Oxford University Press).

—— (2007) *Legal Traditions of the World*, 3rd edn (Oxford, Oxford University Press).

Hart, HLA (1994) *The Concept of Law*, 2nd edn (Oxford, Clarendon Press).

Huntington, S (1996) *The Clash of Civilizations and the Remaking of World Order* (New York, Simon & Schuster).

Husa, J (2004) 'Classification of Legal Families Today: Is it Time for a Memorial Hymn?' *Revue internationale de droit comparé* 13.

Kahn-Freund, O (1974) 'On Uses and Misuses of Comparative Law' 37 *Modern Law Review* 1.

Kosko, B (1993) *Fuzzy Thinking: the New Science of Fuzzy Logic* (New York, Hyperion).

Legrand, P and Munday, R (eds) (2003) *Comparative Legal Studies: Traditions and Transitions* (Cambridge, Cambridge University Press).

Mattei, U (1997) *Comparative Law and Economics* (Ann Arbor, IL, University of Michigan Press).

Merryman, JH (1985) *The Civil Law Tradition*, 2nd edn (Stanford, Stanford University Press).

Nelken, D (2001) 'Towards a Sociology of Legal Adaptation' in D Nelken and J Feest *Adapting Legal Cultures* (Oxford, Hart Publishing).

Nelken, D and Feest, J (eds) (2001) *Adapting Legal Cultures* (Oxford, Hart Publishing).

Örücü, E (2004) *The Enigma of Comparative Law*, (Leiden and Boston, Martinus Nijhoff).

Philips, MS and Schochet, G (2004) 'Preface' in MS Philips and G Schochet (eds), *Questions of Tradition* (Toronto/Buffalo/London, University of Toronto Press).

Putnam, H (2002) *The Collapse of the Fact/Value Dichotomy* (Cambridge, MA, Harvard University Press).

Reimann, M (1996) 'The End of Comparative Law as an Autonomous Subject' 11 *Tulane European and Civil Law Forum* 49.

—— (2002) 'The Progress and Failure of Comparative Law in the Second Half of the 20th Century' 50 *American Journal of Comparative Law* 671.

Renteln, AD (2004) *The Cultural Defense* (New York, Oxford University Press).

Roundtable, (2005) 'Comparative Constitutionalism in Practice' 3 *International Journal of Constitutional Law* 543.

Rynhold, D (2005) *Two Models of Jewish Philosophy: Justifying One's Practices* (Oxford, Oxford University Press).

Shapiro, B (1994) 'The Concept 'Fact': Legal Origins and Cultural Diffusion' 26 *Albion* 1, reprinted in D Sugarman (ed), (1996) *Law in History: Histories of Law and Society*, vol II (New York, New York University Press).

—— (2000) *A Culture of Fact: England, 1550–1720* (Ithaca (NY)–London, Cornell University Press).

Shepherd, R (2000) 'Islamic finance is a growing niche' *National Law Journal* A22.

Shils, E (1981) *Tradition* (Chicago, IL, University of Chicago Press).Slaughter, A-M (2004) *A New World Order* (Princeton, Princeton University Press).

Sugarman, D (ed) (1996) *Law in History: Histories of Law and Society*, vol II (New York, New York University Press).

Thunis, X (2004) 'L'empire de la comparaison' in FR van der Mensbrugghe (ed), *L'utilisation de la méthode comparative en droit européen* (Namur, Presses universitaires de Namur).

Tully, J (1995) *Strange Multiplicity: Constitutionalism in an age of Diversity* (Cambridge, Cambridge University Press).

Van Hoeck, M (ed) (2004) *Epistemology and Methodology of Comparative Law* (Oxford, Hart Publishing).

Zimmermann, R (1996) *The Law of Obligations: Roman Foundations of the Civilian Tradition* (Oxford, Clarendon Press).

5

Defining and Using the Concept of Legal Culture

DAVID NELKEN

KEY CONCEPTS

Internal legal culture; External legal culture; Coherence; Units; Explanation and interpretation; Circular argument; Relational legal culture; Reflexivity.

I. INTRODUCTION

T HE TERM LEGAL culture is both widely used and as regularly criticised in academic works which try to bring together socio-legal studies and comparative law. One author who had previously named his book *Dutch Legal Culture* has preferred to replace it with the less question-begging 'Dutch law in action' (Blankenberg and Bruinsma, 1995; and Bruinsma, 2000). Even Lawrence Friedman, responsible for introducing the concept into the sociology of law, has recently described it as 'an abstraction and a slippery one', and now says that he is not sure he would want to reinvent it (Friedman, 2006). Yet the term, like the word culture itself, seems to be one that we cannot do without. As a recent World Bank study reported: [1]

> Legal culture is often considered as a given feature of the local environment to which proposed legal reform projects must adapt; many argue that legal and judicial reform programs must be tailored to fit local legal culture or they will fail. Other times, the prevailing legal culture itself may be the object of reform, rather than merely a constraint. Thus, understanding the arguments related to the concept of legal culture will become increasingly important for aspiring legal reformers. Does the legal system not work well because people distrust the courts, or do people distrust the courts because the legal

[1] World Bank:
Http://72.14.221.104/search? q=cache:YebgTjDewqAJ:www1.
worldbank.org/publicsector/legal/ruleoflawandevelopment

system doesn't work well? Is the introduction of a new contract law unlikely to have an effect because the business culture prefers informal deals with family and friends, or does the preference for informal dealing exist only because no one has yet passed an efficient contract law? These sorts of problems are not easy to resolve, especially because the causality clearly runs in both directions, and the interactions between beliefs and actions are extraordinarily complex.

As this use of the term suggests, the promise of the concept of the legal culture for many comparative lawyers is the part it can play in specific efforts at socio-legal engineering stimulated by the current round of legal transplantation. But it is relevant more generally to any enquiry in comparative law that seeks to explore similarities and differences in legal practices and legal worlds. How far are legal systems trying to do the same thing (and how could we tell)? What are the deeper sources of rules and procedures? What, if anything, sets the limits of variation within and between given systems? Unlike the tired categories of 'families of law', a focus on legal culture directs us to examine the interconnections between law, society and culture as they are manifested also in the 'law in action' and the 'living law'.

The best work using the idea of legal culture typically starts from some puzzle about the relationship between the role and the rule of law within given societies.[2] Why do the United Kingdom and Denmark complain most about the imposition of European Union law but then turn out to be the countries which have the best records of obedience? Why does The Netherlands, otherwise so similar, have such a low litigation rate compared to neighbouring Germany? Why in the United States and the United Kingdom does it often take a sex scandal to create official interest in doing something about corruption, whereas in Latin countries it takes a major corruption scandal to excite interest in marital unfaithfulness!? Why have constitutional courts managed to consolidate themselves in some post-communist societies but not in others—and why are they emerging now in East Asia? Why are the higher courts in Latin American countries such as Chile or Columbia currently seeking to guarantee minimum social security rights despite the 'formalistic legal culture' that is alleged to characterise their role? How does this connect, if at all, with the neo-liberal policies being pursued on the advice of the Chicago-educated technocrats in government?

On the other hand, the concept of legal culture will be of little assistance to us in investigating these and other similar questions if we cannot achieve some degree of agreement on what it means and how it should be used. Hence the task of this chapter. I shall first discuss debates about legal culture and consider some of the alternative terms on offer. I shall then go on to examine some of the difficulties in using the concept. I shall consider in particular how to demarcate

---

[2] There is insufficent space to provide references to the many case studies relevant to the theme of legal culture. For examples, see Blankenburg, 1997 and Ginsburg, 2003.

units of legal culture, how to imagine what gives them their coherence, and how to avoid the problem of circular argument when using the term in explanations of legally-related behaviour.

II. DEFINING LEGAL CULTURE

What is the point in calling a particular pattern of behaviour, opinions or ideas an instance of legal culture, and what follows from this? As with descriptions such as 'legal system' or 'legal process', many of those who adopt the term do so at a minimum so as to alert prospective readers (or librarians) to expect their work to include some discussion of the behaviour or ideas of legal professions or courts in a given place or time. The term also suggests, explicitly or implicitly, the existence of some larger historically or geographically defined entity that gives law some commonalities (see, eg Gessner, Hoeland and Varga, 1996; and Varga, 1992). If we are to develop legal culture as a 'term of art' we will need to think more carefully about what exactly we are talking about. Taken generally, the terms 'law' and 'culture' when brought together cover a large range of possible permutations of law in culture or culture in law (Fizpatrick, 2005). These meanings can include law seen as a cultural artefact, rather than merely as a form of social engineering (Kahn, 1999); law as it becomes present in every-day life experience, or as filtered through the media (Sarat and Kearns, 1993; Sarat and Kearns, 1998), or even the significance of law in accommodating cultural defences or protecting cultural treasures (Cotterrell, 2004). In one common use (outside of English language jurisdictions) the term signifies the aspiration towards the 'culture *of* legality', the nearest, though not perfect equivalent, to which in English is 'the rule of law'. This meaning is particularly common in those jurisdictions, or parts of jurisdictions (for example in the former Soviet Union, Latin America or the south of Italy) where state rules are systematically avoided or evaded. In such cases talk of 'legal culture' is intended to underline the normative goal of getting 'legality' into the culture of everyday social and political life, so as to re-orient the behaviour of such populations towards (state) law.

As this shows, legal culture is a term that can be used prescriptively as well as descriptively. What is meant by the 'legal' in the term legal culture? Legal and social scientific answers may not be the same. Both law and culture are words whose interpretation and definition have illocutionary effects ('this is the law', 'that behaviour is inconsistent with our culture'). Likewise the term legal culture can be used by judges or others within the legal system or the culture so as to make claims about what is, or is not, consonant with a given body of law, practices or ideals. This use, prescriptive even as it purports to be descriptive, helps 'make' the facts it purports to describe or explain. So, one interesting way, especially for jurists (Rebuffa and Blankenburg, 1992) to study legal culture would be as an attempt to understand such actors' attempts to describe, ascribe, or produce coherence in the course of their decision-making.[3] As argued by Jeremy Webber,

> [t]he concept of culture is not so much a way of identifying highly specified and tightly bounded units of analysis, than, as a heuristic device for suggesting how individual decision-making is conditioned by the language of normative discussion, the set of historical reference points, the range of solutions proposed in the past, the institutional norms taken for granted, given a particular context of repeated social interaction. The integrity of cultural explanations does not depend upon the "units" being exclusive, fully autonomous, or strictly bounded. Rather, it depends upon there being sufficient density of interaction to generate distinctive terms of evaluation and debate. When there is that density, any examination of decision-making in that context will want to take account of those terms (Webber, 2004: 32).

On the other hand, the classical starting point for those aiming to use the term for explanatory purposes is the work of Lawrence Friedman. Friedman first introduced his version of the concept in the late 1960s, modelling it on the idea of political culture seen as the key to understanding voting patterns and other factors which shape political systems. He still chooses to define it as

> what people think about law, lawyers and the legal order, it means ideas, attitudes, opinions and expectations with regard to the legal system (Friedman 2006: 189).

In more elaborated discussions, however, he helpfully distinguishes 'internal' legal culture—which acknowledges the special role in the law of judges and other legal professionals and scholars—from what he calls 'external' legal culture which refers especially to those individuals or groups who bring pressure to bear on the law to produce social change. Friedman has argued that internal legal culture as a factor in explaining socio-legal change has tended to be exaggerated, usually by those who have an investment in doing so. He prefers to concentrate on the importance of external legal culture, for example giving attention to increasing public demand for legal remedies—what he calls the drive to 'Total Justice' (Friedman, 1985; Friedman, 1990)—as the predominant force for producing legal and social change.

Friedman has no monopoly over the definition of legal culture. For example, Erhard Blankenburg (a leading European sociologist of law) defines legal culture to include four components: law in the books; law in action as channelled by the institutional infrastructure; patterns of legally relevant behaviour; and legal consciousness, particularly, a distinctive attitude toward the law among legal professionals (Blankenburg and Bruinsma, 1995). In the United States, on the other hand, most socio-legal scholars following on from Friedman have placed their main focus on exploring the legal consciousness of those subject to the law. In

---

[3] Philosophers of law have sought to understand the activities of the various legal professionals and jurists who bear the responsibility of (re)producing such purported coherence, by making reference to the 'rule of recognition' or to the ideal of 'law as integrity', but the sort of coherence at issue for them is, above all, normative consistency.

adapting Friedman's approach for comparative enquiries, a broad definition that best alerts us to the range of possibly different features of foreign systems may be helpful. As I have proposed,

> [l]egal culture, in its most general sense, should be seen as one way of describing relatively stable patterns of legally-oriented social behaviour and attitudes. The identifying elements of legal culture range from facts about institutions such as the number and role of lawyers or the ways judges are appointed and controlled, to various forms of behaviour such as litigation or prison rates, and, at the other extreme, more nebulous aspects of ideas, values, aspirations and mentalities. Like culture itself, legal culture is about who we are, not just what we do (Nelken, 2004: 1).

Debates around legal culture may be confusing because authors can disagree not only over the question of what is true of a given legal culture (which should presuppose agreement about what they mean by the term itself), but also about how best to think about and study legal culture as such. An important example of the first kind of disagreement (involving both inside observers and outside commentators) is the variety of answers offered to the question of why the Japanese, despite living in the world's second most successful economy, make relatively little use of the courts. In the 1950s it was conventional to adopt 'harmony culture' explanations, which treated Japan's legal culture as an expression of the influence of Confucian shaped-culture that emphasised harmonious and hierarchical relationships. But by the 1970s and 1980s this approach had fallen out of favour relative to more structural explanations that argued that the limited numbers of legal professionals and courts represented institutional barriers maintained by government bureaucracies and business elites, to protect their corporatist agreements from the unpredictability of court interventions. Discussion continues, with some authors suggesting that Japan sometimes makes more use of courts than other places (Feldman, 1997; Feldman, 2001; Feldman, 2006), and others arguing that Japan offers an example of non-legally obsessed communitarianism that has special merits (Nottage, 2006).

Are litigation rates the key to understanding legal culture? Some contributors to the Japanese debate questioned this (Hamilton and Sanders, 1992). But they are central to the work of Blankenburg (Blankenburg, 2003). In one of his best known studies he set out to explain the much lower use of courts in The Netherlands as compared to adjoining parts of West Germany, two places which otherwise had so much in common (Blankenburg, 1997). The answer provided by Blankenburg was that these rates depended less on what people want from law than on the availability of other institutional possibilities for dealing with their disputes and claims. The Netherlands, he argued, possessed a much wider range of 'infrastructural' avenues for disposing of cases in ways that did not require court litigation as compared to Germany. In opposition to Friedman, Blankenburg stresses the importance of the 'supply' rather than the 'demand' for law. He claims that his 'natural experiment' showed the overriding explanatory role that should be attributed to institutional 'infrastructures'. He concluded, perhaps over-confidently 'there is no legal culture outside existing legal institutions': the influence of 'folk' or general cultural mentalities may therefore be safely ignored.

III. THE QUESTION OF CULTURE

For some writers however, the issue is not just what is true of a given legal culture, or even whether it is more shaped by demand or supply, but whether the term is one worth holding on to at all. The objections have to do with the use of the term 'culture' in legal culture. What is involved in describing a given set of ideas and behaviour as 'culture'? For many critics culture has too wide a variety of meanings for it to be a serviceable concept. Is culture a determining source of behaviour or only a 'tool kit' that can be drawn on selectively? Which option is intended can make all the difference to what is being claimed in using the term. Though the term has become increasingly important in many disciplines, strangely, anthropologists, who originally developed the term, have found its common meanings less and less illuminating for the purpose of explanation (Kuper, 1999).

'Over the last two decades', writes Sally Merry,

> anthropology has elaborated a conception of culture as unbounded, contested, and connected to relations of power. It does not consist only of beliefs and values but also practices, habits, and common-sensical ways of doing things. The contemporary anthropological understanding of culture envisions a far more fluid, contested, and changing set of values and practices than that provided by the idea of culture as tradition. Culture is the product of historical influences rather than evolutionary change. Its boundaries are fluid, meanings are contested, and meaning is produced by institutional arrangements and political economy. Culture is marked by hybridity and creolization rather than uniformity or consistency. Local systems are analysed in the context of national and transnational processes and are understood as the result of particular historical trajectories. This is a more dynamic, agentic, and historicised way of understanding culture (Merry, 2003: 55 at 69).

Certainly, great care must be taken in employing any concept which makes reference to culture. We shall need to avoid reifying national or other stereotypes, and recognise that much that goes under the name of culture is no more than 'imagined communities' or 'invented traditions'. It is easy to fall into the opposed vices of 'Occidentalism' or 'Orientalism', making other cultures seem either necessarily similar or intrinsically 'other' (Cain, 2000). If culture is, to a large extent, a matter of struggle and disagreement, the purported uniformity, coherence or stability of given national or other cultures will often be no more than a rhetorical claim projected by outside observers or manipulated by elements within the culture concerned. Any assumption that long-standing historical patterns cannot be altered can be 'dystopic' and may block possible reforms (Krygier, 1997). Legal culture, like all culture, is a product of the contingencies of history and is always undergoing change (Nelken, 1995). For our purposes it can be salutary to recall the rapid transformations in attitudes towards 'law and order' in the short period that elapsed from Weimar to Hitlerian Germany. But, on the other hand, we should note that Merry herself still uses the term. Even invented traditions may of course be real in their effects. Whilst talk of 'culture wars' is often exaggerated, it would be equally mistaken to assume that cultural differences do not exist—of all kinds and at many levels—or deny that some of these may indeed clash.

Critics of legal culture see it as inevitably carrying the inconsistent or misleading referents that come with the term culture. Patrick Glenn reminds us that cultures should not be treated as 'super organic', or 'substantive, bounded entities', but rather seen as 'shreds and patches remaking themselves' (Glenn, 2004). But, whilst legal actors do (perhaps must?) work with some such ideas of culture as normative pre-suppositions, few sociologists of law actually make such assumptions. At this time of export and import of legal institutions and ideas it would be implausible indeed to see cultures as closed and self-referential. Friedman, on the contrary, argues that law is necessarily converging, and has written about the development of global culture (Friedman, 1994), again, if anything, underestimating the continuing importance of national boundaries, or the persistence of alternative ways of dealing with poten-tially law related troubles (see, eg Engel, 2005). But it is a fair criticism of Friedman's approach to legal culture to say that it does not seem to have been influenced by the 'interpretive turn' in the social sciences. He seems unconcerned as Glenn puts it, that 'culture may be an effect of our descriptions, not its precondition'. The need to treat attempts to interpret culture as part of the object itself is certainly one key way in which notions of culture have changed since Friedman borrowed his term from discussions of political culture.

Those who think that there is no way of avoiding the pit-falls if we talk of cul-ture, suggest that it would be better to use other terms than legal culture to do the same job. There is no shortage of such alternatives: these include living law, the law in action; epistemes, mentalities, and formants; legal traditions, legal ideology, legal fields, legal or regulatory styles, and even path dependency. Insofar as the underlying issue is what (if anything) holds a legal and social system together, a challenge to the whole 'law and society' paradigm comes from Niklas Luhmann's autopoiesis theory (see, eg Teubner, 1998; and Nelken, 2001). Those who prefer other terms will point to their virtues as compared to legal culture (and say less about their own drawbacks). Patrick Glenn, himself an advocate of the term legal tradition, argues that it is more natural to speak of non-traditional behaviour and innovation than to make the same point when using the term culture. Talking about traditions, he adds, suggests overlap rather than closure because within a given tradition there is always a range of creative possibilities. The very existence of a tradition is necessarily a result of persuasive argument and interpretation. For Glenn, because tradition is a matter of 'information' it is hard to reify it as some-thing 'beyond us'. He also suggests that all societies have a notion of tradition, but not all use the term culture. As against this, however, others might argue that tradition can also be a confusing term, and it has often been said to be one that tends too easily to distract attention from questions of power and interest.

The choice between terms will also be influenced by wider theoretical assumptions about the role of law in society. Roger Cotterrell, who favours legal ideology, claims that such a term offers us a focus on the ideas of legal professionals and jurists and their influence over popular consciousness. One of the main questions that interests him is how law succeeds in being at the same time both fragmented and abstract; how it pretends to be a gapless system while filling in the gaps. For Cotterrell this provides us with a well-defined topic suitable for empirical investigation. But of course it is only one such topic. As opposed to Friedman's interest in the permeability of law to social demands, the concept of ideology draws our attention to the way rules and values of law resist modification and thrive on their inconsistencies. As this suggests, there is no easy way to choose a priori which concept to employ. What is important is to be clear what we mean by whatever term we adopt, and why we think that it, rather than an alternative concept, could best serve the purpose of our particular enquiry (rather than fall into the error of thinking that 'when you have a hammer, everything is a nail'). Those preferring the terms 'legal tradition' and 'legal ideology' might find, for example, that these were not necessarily well suited to explaining why countries differ in their levels of court delay (Nelken, 2004; and Nelken, 2006a). Or, more exactly, they would need to think about what aspects of the problem their terms might be less likely to illuminate as compared to a more open-ended focus on legal culture.

IV. USING THE CONCEPT OF LEGAL CULTURE

As this suggests, the value of this or any other concept for comparative enquiry can also be clarified by seeking to use it in empirical enquiries. As social scientists say, this requires that the concept be 'operationalised'. The difficulties here are well posed in Roger Cotterrell's influential, highly critical, observations on Friedman's use of the term.[4] As he notes, Friedman used legal culture in a variety of ways raging from the culture of the individual to that of whole societies. In his work legal culture becomes, 'an immense, multi-textured overlay of levels and regions of culture, varying in content, scope, and influence and in their relation to the institutions, practices and knowledge of state legal systems' (Cotterrell, 1997). For Cotterrell this makes it implausible to use legal culture in explanatory enquiries. In theory, he says, such a variety of level of super- and sub-national units could provide a rich terrain for inquiry. But he nonetheless rejects the idea that legal culture can be reflected in 'diversity and levels' whilst also having a 'unity'. For him,

> if legal culture refers to so many levels and regions of culture (with the scope of each of these ultimately indeterminate because of the indeterminacy of the scope of the idea of legal culture itself) the problem of specifying how to use the concept as a theoretical component in comparative sociology for law remains (Cotterrell, 1997).

---

[4] Cotterrell, 1997. Friedman's reply to Cotterrell is Friedman, 1997. Cotterrell, 2006 is less damning.

Other commentators have also questioned its role in explanation (Kenny, 1996). These objections are well taken. What needs more consideration, however, is how far, as I would argue, these problems point more to the complexities of what needs to be explained than to the inaproriateness of this conceptual tool.

Demarcating the Unit

Take first the theoretical problem of trying to delineate 'the unit' of legal culture.[5] Most books and articles on legal culture identify this with the boundaries of national jurisdictions. They write of French criminal justice (Hodgson, 2006), the Japanese way of justice (Johnson, 2002), and (for two editions) Dutch legal culture etc.[6] Likewise, leading scholars currently debate the specificity or even the 'exceptionalism' of the United States' type of legal procedure (see, eg Garapon and Papadopoulos, 2003) by showing its high level of 'adversarial legalism' (Kagan, 2001) or severity of its punishments (Whitman 2003). But books about legal culture do not have to take the same starting point as those which describe a system's 'law in the books'. In comparative law, studies using the notion of families of law make uneasy compromises between taking for granted the importance of differences between systems of common and civil law, or other such contrasts, and also seeking to acknowledge national variations. Thus The Netherlands and Italy are both members of the civil law world. But any similarities this may give rise to in legal culture are dwarfed by the greater similarities between England and Wales and The Netherlands in their pragmatic approach to law or openness to public opinion. Legal culture is also not necessarily uniform (organisationally and meaningfully) across different branches of law (see Bell, 2002). Lawyers specialising in some subjects may have less in common with other lawyers outside their field than they have with those abroad.

Patterns of legal culture can and must also be sought both at a more micro- as well as at a more macro-level than the nation state. At the sub-national level there can be as much variation as between different areas of a nation state (and groups within it) as there is between one state and another, and this is all the more likely when we study less industrialised and/or less consolidated states. More than this, at this level it will often be of interest to study differences in the 'local legal culture' of the local court, the prosecutor's office, or the lawyer's consulting room. As important, there is also increasing need to consider those processes that transcend the nation state. The past regular transfers of legal institutions and ideas make it often misleading to argue that legal culture is embedded in its current national context (Nelken, 2006b; Nelken, 2006c). Much domestic law in Europe in the 19th

---

[5] The term 'unit' is not intended to carry any specific theoretical implications. It should not be limited to legally-defined jurisdictions or branches of law. It would be interesting, for example, to theorise such units as 'structures of relation' or 'fields of action'. This also has implications for the issue of coherence discussed in the next part.

[6] This is also true of most of the chapters in this Handbook.

century, such as the law of copyright, was mainly invented as a response to its existence elsewhere (Sherman, 1997). Some of the laws and legal institutions that people think of as most typically their own are the result of imitation, imposition or borrowing. Thus there are 'Dutch' disputing mechanisms which are in fact a result of German imposition during the occupation, and which have been abandoned in Germany itself (Jettinghof, 2001).

The adoption of dissimilar legal models is common where the legal transfer is imposed by third parties as part of a colonial project and/or is insisted on as a condition of trade, aid, alliance or diplomatic recognition. It has also often been sponsored by elites concerned to 'modernise' their society or otherwise bring it into the wider family of 'advanced' nations. Japan and Turkey are the most obvious examples. In these cases imported or imposed law is designed to change existing contexts rather than reflect them.[7] Likewise, the hope in many cases of current transplants is that law may be a means of resolving current problems by transforming the existing society into one more like the source of such borrowed law. In what is almost a species of sympathetic magic, borrowed law is sometimes deemed capable of bringing about the same conditions of a flourishing economy or a healthy civil society that are found in the social context from which the borrowed law has been taken. In Eastern Europe legal transfer becomes part of the effort to become (or to be seen to be) more democratic, or more economically successful. Turkey, with its eye on accession to the European Union, tries to make its laws appear (even) more secular. Those who study these transfers, on the other hand, question their potential for producing change in the absence of the surrounding context from which they were taken, and emphasise how far such innovations are likely to be (re)shaped by the prevailing norms and ideas in the places will be applied and interpreted.[8]

Current developments leading to the increasing globalisation of markets and communications mean that the role of super-national entities, organisations and networks goes well beyond cases of simple legal transfers (Heyderbrand, 2001). The boundaries of the nation state as a unit are regularly traversed as transnational public and semi-public networks substitute, to an increasing extent, for national governments in building a 'real new world order' (Slaughter, 1997). The language of transplants is not well suited to studying new forms of norm-making, dispute-channelling and regulation such as the growth of the *lex mercatoria*, the use of 'soft law' or other non-binding agreements and persuasive practices by international regulators, nor the use of their power to enforce private orders by

---

[7] Thus, South Africa modeled its new constitution on the best that Western regimes had to offer rather than on constitutional arrangements found in its nearer neighbours in Africa.

[8] Nelken, 2003. Commenting on the introduction of United States-style business governance in Japan, John Ohnesorge argues that,

the proper functioning of that institutional framework depends upon what are, in essence, cultural norms, expectations and practices. Truly adopting US-style corporate governance thus becomes a matter of importing US business and professional culture more generally (Ohnesorge, 2006).

multinational companies. The use of *lex mercatoria*, for example, is said to 'break the frame' of national jurisdiction. The multiple orders that grow up produce what Santos calls 'interlegality', a term that describes 'a highly dynamic process' where different legal spaces are 'nonsychronic' and result in 'uneven and unstable combinations of legal codes (codes in a semiotic sense)' (Santos, 1995: 473).

Lawyers and accountants also play an increasing role as entrepreneurs of new forms of dispute prevention and settlement (Dezalay and Garth, 1996), mainly, if not entirely, so as to service the increasingly important international business community. In turn, the opportunities for such activity transform the legal profession(s). The importance of private actors has also altered as a result of the growth of multinational and international production networks, new technology, and changes in work patterns. Rule-formulation and settlement increasingly takes place within new agencies of transnational governance, such as North Atlantic Trade Association (NAFTA), the Organization of Economic Cooperation and Development (OECD), and the World Trade Organisation. Legal fields are increasingly internationalised, even if this process does not affect all fields to the same extent and varies by different areas of legal and social regulation. All this means that it makes less and less sense to think of 'domestic' norms as forming part of distinct national jurisdictions that then interact with transnational norms. As important, for those seeking to mark the limits of culture, it becomes ever more difficult to set boundaries to our imaginations and expectations: 'we inhabit' it is argued, a 'de-territorialised world'. We can participate via the media in communities of others with whom we have no geographical proximity or common history. Hence,

> all totalising accounts of society, tradition and culture are exclusionary and enact a social violence by suppressing contingent and continually emergent differences (Coombe, 2000: 21–40).

Instead, we must face the 'challenges of transnationalism and the politics of global capitalism or multiple overlapping and conflicting "juridiscapes"' (*ibid*). At the same time, however, even networks are themselves shaped by different contexts. As Merry suggests, to keep track of these transnational flows we need to find ways to study 'placeless phenomena in a place' (Merry, 2005: 44).

In advance of empirical investigation it would therefore be rash to assume any necessary 'fit' between law and its environing national society or culture. But claims about the decline of the nation state can no doubt be taken too far. Given the way it often sets boundaries of jurisdiction, politics, and language, the nation state will often serve as a relevant starting point for comparing legal culture. Where law is deliberately used as a unifying state-building device, practices focusing on law may have even more in common than general culture does. The state will also often be the main or only source of relevant statistics of such matters as litigation or incarceration rates. Beyond law, there is some empirical basis for claimed differences in national traits in the way people relate to each other (Hofstedte, 1980). Such different, historically conditioned (but therefore also changing) sensibilities may persist over quite long periods.[9] And even apparently unconnected branches of law may in fact manifest remarkable levels of cultural similarity within a given society. As James Whitman has claimed recently, in replying to criticisms of his culturalist approach to penal law,

> the pattern that we see in comparative punishment is also the pattern we see in many other areas of the law. Indeed, I would claim it as a virtue of my book that it shows that punishment law cannot be understood in isolation from the rest of the legal culture. For example, American workplace harassment law differs from German and French workplace harassment law in very much the same way. The same is true of comparative privacy law ... just as it is true of the law of hate speech and everyday civility ... I think these studies carry cumulative weight (Whitman, 2006: 389 at 392).

THE NATURE OF COHERENCE

On the other hand, it would certainly be wrong to limit our enquiry to the nation state. As we have seen, we also need to apply the term 'legal culture' to a variety of different units, each of which is changing and in a relationship of mutual interaction with the others. These units shape social life in a variety of ways, for example through organisational routines and professional socialisation (at both sub-national, national, international and transnational levels). Culture is sedimented both in historical memories and traditions as well as in more general, relatively taken-for-granted, types of practices, attitudes, expectations and ways of thinking. Cotterrell is right to remind us that these units may not add up to a 'unity'—except from the point of view of those whose job it is to try to show them to be coherent. But, rather than serving to show the concept to be otiose, this may be taken to testify to the intricacies of lived legal culture with its mix of overlapping and potentially competing elements (a complexity also encountered by those comparative lawyers who focus on societies with plural legal orders).

How do we show that these units serve as the source of cultural patterns of ideas and behaviour? What is involved may be captured in any one or more of the following claims:

(1) that there is some intrinsic link between the elements that make up the unit;

(2) that the connection exists insofar as participants talk about it 'as if' it exists; or

(3) that the supposed coherence is one imposed on units by the observer and commentator, for example through processes of classifications or the construction of 'ideal types'.

For many purposes these three forms of coherence may need to be carefully distinguished. Certainly, all students of culture know how important it is to take

---

[9] But careful historical research is needed to avoid confusing short-term and long-term trends.

seriously what participants think they are trying to do—since this is what gives meaning and purpose to their actions. But this has to be balanced against the need for analytic distance. Often, claims about legal culture will need to rely on data or findings about comparative patterns that may be unknown to the participants themselves. The insider does not know, and cannot know everything that the observer would consider relevant to her comparative enquiry.

For example, even well-informed people living in India think that the courts are slow because the country has such a relatively high rate of litigation. But they are wrong (Galanter and Krishnan, 2003). Americans, as well as many others, are convinced that US tort system regularly produces excessive and undeserved awards, but it turns out that, in large part, this impression is manufactured by the media (Haltom and McCaan, 2004). More generally, those societies where legal professionals express least concern for what Anglo-American writers since Roscoe Pound have called the 'gap' or gulf between the 'law in books' and 'law in action', may not be those where the gap is least problematic but those where the gap is overwhelming.

On the other hand, there are also difficulties in drawing boundaries when discussing processes which seek to draw boundaries. How far are we finding, how far only imposing, cultural coherence? Certainly, these three types of coherence may also have effects on each other, when participants, including legal actors or observers, make claims about the existence of cultural patterns which then help bring them into existence. The coherence of any given pattern of legal culture may be something ascribed to the unit itself or else be something that relates more to the relationship of one unit to other units. Table 1 offers some illustrations of such variations of coherence patterns that could be relevant for comparative enquiry.

The first type of coherence (set out in cell 1) concerns the elements that are hypothesised to hold together units of internal or external legal culture. The most common kind of claim here has to do with the alleged coherence of a given internal legal culture or part of it. An example would be Damaska's well-known attempt to show the contrasting 'affinities' between the rules of criminal procedure in common law as compared to civil law countries (Damaska, 1986). With respect to external legal culture, on the other hand, we could note Friedman's invitation to think about the shape of expectations towards law held by different groups,

Table 1. Varieties of coherence in units of legal culture

Internal Coherence	External Coherence
(1) That which holds together given units of internal or external legal culture	(3) The relationship between legal culture and general culture
(2) Legal culture in relation to political culture/economic culture, etc in the same unit	(4) Given units of legal cultures as compared to others

in different times and places. But we could also include Cotterrell's proposal that we presuppose 'ideal types' of community which have different propensities to structure their relationships in terms of law (Cotterrell, 2001). The second kind of internal coherence (cell 2), on the other hand, invites attention to variability in the connections between legal culture and other aspects of culture such as political culture or economic culture (Brants and Field, 2000). As we have already seen in Damaska's argument, many commentators have suggested that in civil law, 'strong state' systems, law tends to be more linked to politics, whilst in common law systems it is more linked to the market. For this reason the privatisation encouraged by neo-liberalism and the de-coupling of law from politics associated with globalisation has been more of a 'shock' for the civilian world.

The third type of coherence (cell (3)) concerns the relationship between, on the one hand, legal ideas and, on the other, practices and ideas in the wider society. For example, it can be instructive to examine what there is in common between what are considered appropriate methods of truth-finding within and 'outside' of legal institutions (Chase, 2005). Are the same methods of persuasion found in law and other forms of enquiry? 'Legal' and 'scientific' forms of truth telling may be symbiotic because they use somewhat different approaches to truth finding. It is often assumed that the direction of influence is mainly from culture in general to legal culture in particular. But those who argue for so-called constitutive theories of 'law in society' would see things also working the other way round. It is law, or at least different forms of ordering practices, which help shape common behaviours and ideas (Calavita, 2001). Societies may also differ in the extent to which they encourage similarities in legal and wider cultural practices. An insistence on 'formalism' in legal matters may often go together with the presupposition that there is or should be less formalism in the 'life world' of ordinary social interaction.

The last type of coherence (cell (4)) refers to the traditional type of legal or socio-legal attempt to compare larger legal cultures as relatively independent units (often national ones). Scholars adopt a variety of ways to carry out such comparisons. Emphasis may be placed more on behaviour or on values. Freek Bruinsma, for example, as we have seen, is no longer happy to assume the existence of Dutch legal culture as an objective matter that reflects differences in practices shaped by institutional 'infrastructures'. He now argues that the specificities of legal culture lie in social valuations; Dutch legal culture, as compared to other legal cultures, is best understood if we consider the typically pragmatic way the Dutch handle issues such as drugs, prostitution and euthanasia (Bruinsma, 1998). As we have noted, we do not necessarily have to assume that the links we are describing are somehow intrinsic to the object being described. If the focus is on 'perceived' or even 'invented' and 'imagined' unities, research may then seek to show how such perceived or imagined differences themselves help to reproduce the boundaries of culture.

The Problem of Circular Argument

Even if we try to be clear about the unit that we wish to explore, and take care to specify the coherence that gives it its unity, we still have to face a further major hurdle in using the term legal culture for the purposes of explanation. As Roger Cotterrell and many others have objected, we need to avoid falling into the trap of 'essentialism' or 'culturalism', whereby circular arguments are simply assumed to show that cultural values cause a given response to events. Question: Why do they use law that way in Japan? Answer: Because that is their (legal) culture. Or, to put the point another way, when we talk about American or Japanese legal culture are we already offering some sort of explanation of behaviour or only indicating that which needs to be explained? Is legal culture the name of the question or the answer?

While this issue is a serious one, it should not be exaggerated. It is above all mainly relevant for those with an interest in prediction who hope to develop (positivist) social science explanations showing how variables produce outcomes. What legal factors correlate with economic growth? Which conditions are likely to determine whether this transplant takes or not? But not all scholars want to use the term for this purpose. Many comparative lawyers will be at least as interested in classification, mapping and description. How should we make sense of legal pluralism (Harding, 2001)? How should the phenomenon of 'soft law' be categorised (Heyderbrand, 2007)? What is there in common between current transnational legal processes (Nelken, 2006d)? More importantly, a central part of their work has to do with the type of understanding that can only be reached through interpretation (see eg Legrand, 1997). What does this legal institution, procedure or idea mean? What, if anything, is it trying to achieve? It could even be argued that by formulating their questions in this way scholars are more likely to be in tune with the many post-positivist schools of social science and cultural theorising that have endorsed the so-called 'interpretative turn' away from earlier mainstream ways of pursuing behavioural science.

Whereas the positivist approach would seek to throw light on legal culture by seeking to assign causal priority between competing hypothetical variables, so as to explain variation in levels and types of legally related behaviour, the interpretative approach, on the other hand, would be more interested in providing 'thick descriptions' (Geertz, 1973) of law as 'local knowledge' (Geertz, 1983). It would see its task as doing its best faithfully to translate another system's ideas of justice and fairness so as to make proper sense of its web of significance. It asks about the different nuances as between the terms 'rule of law', '*Rechtsstaat*', or '*Stato di diritto*' or the meanings of 'community' in different societies (Zedner, 1995). It seeks to understand why litigation is seen as essentially democratic in the United States, but as anti-democratic in France (Cohen-Tanugi, 1996/1985). In this search for holistic meaning, any insistence, for example, on distinguishing the 'demand' for law from the 'supply' of law, is likely to obscure more than it reveals and could lead to mistaken practical conclusions (Nelken, 1997). Arguably, if there are differences in the significance attached to official law and legal institutions in Germany and in The Netherlands, then even if Germany had the same alternative routes to litigation that are present in The Netherlands they could well end up producing even more work for lawyers and courts.

For the interpretative approach, concepts both reflect and constitute culture; as in the changes undergone by the meaning of 'contract' in a society where the individual is seen as necessarily embodied in wider relationships (Winn, 1994), or the way that the Japanese ideogram for the new concept of 'rights' came to settle on a sign associated with 'self interest' rather than morality (Feldman, 1997). In order to test its hypotheses the positivist approach is obliged to develop a socio-legal 'Esperanto' which abstracts from the language used by members of different cultures, preferring, for example, to talk of 'decision-making' rather than 'discretion'. The rival strategy, concerned precisely with grasping linguistic subtleties and 'cultural packaging', would ask whether and when the term 'discretion' is used in different legal cultures and what implications the word carries (Nelken, 2002). Not least, the interpretative approach is quick to recognise the reflexivity of (legal) culture as 'an enormous interplay of interpretations in and about a culture' (J Friedman, 1994), and thus appreciate that the scholar may also be a (bit) player in the processes of legal culture that she seeks to understand.

This said, rather than treating these approaches as necessarily in competition, explanation and interpretation will often be pursued as two complementary parts of the search for understanding culture (Nelken, 1994). Many, probably most, social scientists do still use terms like legal culture with explanatory intent. Friedman himself recommends the term as helpful in enquiries into why people use or do not use law, for instance why women do or do not turn for help to the police in Italy or France, or why Italian drivers are less likely than the English to wear seat belts. So, any effort to encourage a dialogue between comparative lawyers and social scientists must face the issue of circular argument head on. As Roger Cotterrell rightly noted, special difficulties here arise from the fact that Friedman applied the term not only to such variables but also to the units produced by such variables. While he treats legal culture as a cause of what he calls 'legal dynamics', he also uses it to describe the results of such causes—writing, for example, about the traits of a variety of large aggregates such as 'American culture', 'Latin American legal culture' (Friedman and Perdomo, 2003), 'modern legal culture', and even 'global legal culture'. Although what he means by legal culture when speaking of these aggregates does have a lot to do with people's expectations of the law, the 'traits' he indicates as characterising modern legal culture are not only about such expectations; they also describe the results of such expectations.

To avoid confusion it would be best to distinguish between talking about legal culture as a variable having to do with attitudes, opinions and behaviour towards the law, and speaking about it as an aggregate (what Glenn calls 'a holistic signifier'). For added clarity, legal culture as a variable describing attitudes etc towards law could perhaps be re-labelled 'legal consciousness', as in Table 2 below. Nonetheless, it would be a fallacy to assume that variables always explain, or that aggregates never do. The difference between legal culture as a variable and as an aggregate can often be slippery. We tend to think of aggregates as large, often national, units of legal culture, but all variables could also be seen for some purposes as aggregates. For example, attitudes to law, which Friedman treats mainly as a variable, could, where appropriate, be dis-aggregated into the different elements that make them up. This is even true at the level of the individual, where a person's 'attitude' could be taken to represent the sum of opinions tested in a survey instrument. Conversely, aggregates can also 'explain'. Even large aggregates, such as American legal culture, become variables when they act on or influence something else. Thus, as Table 2 below indicates, legal culture as variable and as aggregate serves both in making explanations, and a means of representing matters which themselves need to be explained. The key here is to recognise that the term legal culture may be used in a variety of different kinds of explanations.

As indicated by Table 2, Friedman's interest in legal culture as the term for why people turn to law can be examined as a topic that can serve both as an explanation and as something that needs to be explained (cells (1) and (2)). Friedman's approach tended to merge the question of understanding people's demands on and expectations of the law with a range of somewhat different questions such as how law changed to meet the new needs created by technological change, or how powerful groups were able to bring pressure on law to shape it to suit their ends. But micro-social qualitative studies in sociology of law in the United States over the past 20 years have been especially concerned to probe the role of legality for different social actors as it emerges from their narratives about their lived experiences. They have tried not to assume that law is or should be a priority in everyday life and have sought to tease out its often contradictory role in people's lives. Quantitative survey research has also shown that people distinguish between confidence in the technical efficiency of legal remedies and their views about its social legitimacy (Toharia, 2003). More recently there have been calls to reconsider the way macro-social factors shape the way law is presented to consciousness (Silbey, 2005; Garcia-Villegas, 2006).

Table 2. Explanations using the concept of legal culture

	Legal Consciousness	Legal Culture
As Explanation	(1) Feelings about the law and the choice to use law as one factor which shapes the legal system	(3) The influence exerted by given patterns of attitudes etc.
As Needing Explanation	(2) Why people choose to use or not to use the law	(4) Why given units of legal culture have different patterns

The other two cells (3) and (4) have to do with legal culture seen holistically as both a tool of explanation and as something to be explained. Difficult theoretical issues that arise in using legal culture for these types of explanatory enquiry revolve around the question of how to mark off 'the cultural' from other types of motivation or aspects of collective life. Is culture something to be related to and contrasted with other aspects of society, for example, legal rules, institutional resources or social structure? Or does its influence work through these? Should the term culture be reserved for irrational, or at least value-based action, rather than purely instrumental social action? If not, how else can we draw a line between culturally shaped behaviour and all other behaviour? In general, how far should (legal) culture be treated as a residual explanation of individual or collective action, to be resorted to only after other social, economic or political factors or reasons have been exhausted?

It is important to notice that cell (3), where the effort is to show how legal culture influences individual or group behaviour within a given society or unit, is the one in which the dangers of circular or tautological arguments are greatest. But there are plausible arguments for asserting such influence. These can range along a continuum in which, at one extreme, the term describes the consequences of giving allegiance to highly dramatised common values, and, at the other, culture refers to the implications of taking certain things for granted. Of especial interest in the current historical period is the phenomenon of what we might call 'relational legal culture', ie the extent to which attitudes and behaviour in one legal culture are influenced by information (or alleged information) about what is happening in legal cultures elsewhere. For example, there is evidence that when 'league tables' of legally-relevant behaviour such as incarceration rates are published, countries try to come into line so as not to be too distant from the norm or average of other countries. In a multitude of transnational economic, health, criminal justice, human rights and other initiatives, governmental and non-governmental agencies, networks of regulators and others exert pressure to change through processes of signalling and monitoring conformity (Nelken, 2006d). One of the most pressing tasks of the comparative sociologist of law is to try and capture how far in actual practice what is described as globalisation represents the attempted imposition of one particular legal culture, in particular the Anglo-American model (Ferrarese, 2001). For Friedman, we are rather seeing a convergence towards the individualistic type of legal culture suited to the socio-economic challenges of 'modernity' (Friedman, 1994).

Where legal culture is that which needs to be explained rather than that which does the explaining (cell (4)) the risk of circular argument is less (but we still may find ourselves tempted to use one feature of legal culture to 'explain' another feature). On the other hand, this sort of enquiry risks becoming unwieldy and inconclusive. Almost everything about a society (or other unit) can turn out to be relevant to explaining why its legal culture, or even just one aspect of it, differs from another's. Why does Italy, for example, have such long court delays? The answer involves looking at a long list of factors. In the first place there are the relevant laws, especially those to do with civil and criminal procedure. In addition, the role of the European Court of Human Rights is crucial in creating pressure for the Italian legal system to come into line. There is also the management and organisation (or lack of organisation) of the courts and legal profession, claims about the supply of law not keeping pace with the demand, economic interests, political priorities etc (Nelken, 2004). It can prove surprisingly difficult to decide which of these factors is crucial (especially as the relevant facts can be elusive). For example, comparative statistics suggest that Italy, too, has a comparatively low rate of litigation despite the continual complaint about court overload (Blankenburg, 2003). Interpretations of these facts can be even more controversial. Do economic interests such as those represented by small businessmen gain from the current situation, or are they its chief victims? If the latter, why don't they put more pressure on the politicians to do something?

V. CONCLUSION: THE NEED FOR REFLEXIVITY

In this chapter we have discussed some the meanings of legal culture as well as some of the benefits and problems of using this term in enquiries in comparative law. It should now be easier to appreciate why simply reframing questions about legal transfers or legal engineering in terms of the compatibility or potential resistance of local legal culture will rarely, if ever, provide conclusive answers about what should be done. (But arguably this is also true of any other attempt to apply ideas in the world of practice.) We could add that legal culture as a term of art has not been developed mainly by comparative lawyers. Insofar as its roots lie in the social sciences, the comparative lawyer will have to ask herself how far, in using this term, she 'buys into' any larger set of theoretical ideas about law and society and related methodological protocols. Friedman uses the concept in the context of an input-output model of social systems and a pluralist view of power. But the sense of legal culture would certainly change if marshalled within competing approaches such as those of Marx, Foucault, Bourdieu—or Luhmann. In addition, our understanding of the meaning of legal culture will need to change as scholarly ideas of culture change.

The main advantage of thinking about law in the same breath as culture is that it alerts us to cultural variation in how law is thought about and its ascribed and actual role in social life. For example, amidst all the effort to reform the efficiency of legal institutions in developing countries, few have stopped to consider that in many societies (and in all societies in at least some contexts) official law is mainly experienced as a source of unpredictability that threatens to disrupt everyday normative patterns and agreements. But we also need to learn about our own cultural common-sense. If Friedman thinks that external legal culture is what really gives law its shape, whereas civil law scholars tend to assume that its dynamics must be located more in internal legal culture, this may be in part at least a reflection of differences in expectations about legal culture in the common law and civil law world. Likewise, for those coming from the Anglo-American world it is too easy to take for granted a 'pragmatic-instrumentalist approach' to law; the idea that law is designed to achieve something (which means we struggle to make sense of the many ritual and expressive aspects of legal institutions and procedures even in our own society). When we find that foreign institutions do not perform as we expect them to we may be too quick to describe their claims as myths (Goldstein and Marcus, 1977)—rather than recognising that in some respects nothing can be as important as a myth (Langbein and Weinreb, 1978; and Nelken, 2002). The possibility that we are working with an ethno-centric idea of legal culture is all the more likely as we range more widely in the world's cultures (Chiba, 1989).

QUESTIONS FOR DISCUSSION

1. How would you define the term 'legal culture'? How does your definition relate to competing terms such as 'legal tradition' and 'legal ideology?' How would you decide which was the appropriate term to use?
2. Can legal culture be used as an explanatory concept? How?
3. Does it still make sense to talk of national legal cultures at a time of increasing transnational legal processes?
4. Imagine that you have been asked to act as a consultant for a World Bank project designed to make courts in a third world country more accessible and efficient for local and international users. What type of local and international social, economic and political factors would be relevant to your consultancy? How, if at all, could the effort to understand the local legal culture be useful?
5. Consider the following two claims:
   (1) The concept of legal culture is an essential tool for the comparative lawyer in making sense of current transnational legal processes.
   (2) The concept of legal culture has too many meanings to be useful to comparative lawyers.

What arguments could you find in support of each of these statements?

BIBLIOGRAPHY AND FURTHER READING

Barron, G (2005) *The World Bank and Rule of Law Reforms* London School of Economics Working Papers December 2005 ISSN 1470–2320.

Bell, JS (2002) *French Legal Cultures* (Cambridge, Cambridge University Press).

Blankenburg, E (1997) 'Civil Litigation Rates as Indicators for Legal Culture' in D Nelken (ed), *Comparing Legal Cultures.*

—— (2003) 'Judicial systems in Western Europe: Comparative indicators of legal professionals, courts, litigation and budgets' in EG Jensen and TC Heller (eds), *Beyond Common Knowledge: Empirical Approaches to the Rule of Law* (Stanford, Stanford University Press).

Blankenburg, E and Bruinsma, F (1995) *Dutch Legal Culture*, 2nd edn (Deventer–Boston, Kluwer Law International).

Brants, C and Field, S (2000) 'Legal Culture, Political Cultures and Procedural Traditions: Towards a Comparative Interpretation of Covert and Proactive Policing in England and Wales and the Netherlands' in D Nelken (ed), *Contrasting Criminal Justice* (Aldershot, Ashgate).

Bruinsma, F (1998) 'Dutch Internal Legal Culture' in J Brand and D Strempel (eds), *Soziologie des Rechts. Festschrift Erhard Blankenburg* (Baden-Baden, Nomos Verlagsgesellschaft).

—— (2000) *Dutch Law in Action* (Nijmegen, Ars Aqui Libre).

Cain, M (2000) 'Orientalism, Occidentalism and the Sociology of Crime' 40 *British Journal of Criminology* 239.

Calavita, K (2001) 'Blue Jeans, Rape, and the "De-Constitutive" Power of Law' 35 *Law and Society Review* 89.

Chase, A (2005) *Law, Culture, and Ritual: Disputing Systems in Cultural Context* (New York, New York University Press).

Chiba, M (1989) *Legal Pluralism: Toward a General Theory of Law Through Japanese Legal Culture* (Tokyo, Tokai University Press).

Cohen-Tanugi, L (1996/1985) 'The Law without the State' in V Gessner, A Hoeland and C Varga (eds), *European Legal Cultures* (Aldershot, Dartmouth).

Coombe, RJ (2000) 'Contingent Articulations: a Critical Studies of Law' in A Sarat and T Kearns (eds), *Law in the Domains of Culture*.

Cotterrell, R (1997) 'The concept of Legal culture' in D Nelken (ed), *Comparing Legal Cultures*.

—— (2001) 'Is There a Logic of Legal Transplants?' in D Nelken and J Feest (eds), *Adapting Legal Cultures* (Oxford, Hart Publishing).

—— (2004) 'Law in Culture' 17 *Ratio Juris* 1.

—— (2006) *Law, Culture and Society: Legal Ideas in the Mirror of Social Theory* (Aldershot, Ashgate).

Damaska, MR (1986) *The Faces of Justice and State Authority* (New Haven, CT, Yale University Press).

Dezalay, Y and Garth, B (1996) *Dealing in Virtue* (Oxford, Oxford University Press).

Engel, D (2005) 'Injury Narratives: Globalization, Ghosts, Religion, and Tort Law in Thailand' 30: 3 *Law & Social Inquiry* 469.

Feldman, E (1997) 'Patients' Rights, Citizen Movements and Japanese Legal Culture' in D Nelken (ed), *Comparing Legal Cultures*.

—— (2001) 'Blood Justice, Courts, Conflict and Compensation in Japan, France and the United States' in 34 *Law and Society Review* 651.

—— (2006) 'The Tuna Court: Law and Norms in the World's Premier Fish Market' 94 *California Law Rev* 1.

Ferrarese, MR (2001) *Le istituzioni della globalizzazione* (Bologna, Il Mulino).

Fitzpatrick P (2005) 'The damned word' Culture and Its (In)compatibility with Law' 1 *Law, Culture and the Humanities* 2.

Freeman, M (2006) (ed) *Law and Sociology* (Oxford, Oxford, University Press).

Friedman, J (1994) *Cultural Identity and Global Process* (London, Sage).

Friedman, LM (1985) *Total Justice* (New York, Russell Sage).

—— (1990) *The Republic of Choice: Law, Society and Culture* (Cambridge, MA, Harvard University Press).

—— (1994) 'Is there a Modern Legal Culture?' *Ratio Juris* 117.

—— (1997) 'The Concept of Legal Culture: A Reply' in D Nelken (ed), *Comparing Legal Cultures*.

—— (2006) 'The Place of Legal Culture in the Sociology of Law' in M Freeman (ed), *Law and Sociology* (Oxford, Oxford University Press).

Friedman, LM and Perdomo, P (eds) (2003) *Legal Culture in the Age of Globalization: Latin America and Latin Europe* (Stanford, Stanford University Press).

Galanter, M and Krishnan, JK (2003) 'Debased Informalism: *Lok adalats* and legal rights in modern India' in EG Jensen and TC Heller (eds), *Beyond Common Knowledge: Empirical Approaches to the Rule of Law.*

Garapon, A and Papadopoulos, I (2003) *Juger en Amérique et en France* (Paris, Odile Jacob).

García-Villegas, M (2006) 'Comparative Sociology of Law: Legal Fields, Legal Scholarships, and Social Sciences in Europe and the United States' 31 *Law & Social Inquiry* 343.

Geertz, C (1973) 'Thick Description: Towards an Interpretive Theory of Culture' in C Geertz *The Interpretation of Culture* (London, Fontana).

—— (1983) *Local Knowledge: Further Essays in Interpretive Anthropology* (New York, Basic Books).

Gessner, V, Hoeland, A and Varga, C (eds) (1996) *European Legal Cultures* (Aldershot, Dartmouth).

Ginsburg, T (2003) *Judicial Review in New Democracies* (Cambridge, Cambridge University Press).

Glenn, HP (2004) 'Legal Cultures and Legal Traditions' in M van Hoeck (ed), *Epistemology and Methodology of Comparative Law* (Oxford, Hart Publishing).

Goldstein, A and Marcus, M (1977) 'The Myth of Judicial Supervision in Three "Inquisitorial" Systems: France, Italy, and Germany' *Yale Law Journal* 240.

Haltom, W and McCaan, M (2004) *Distorting the Law* (Chicago, IL, Chicago University Press).

Hamilton, V and Sanders, J (1992). *Everyday Justice: Responsibility and the Individual in Japan and the United States* (New Haven, CT, Yale University Press).

Harding, A (2001) 'Comparative Law and Legal Transplantation in South East Asia' in D Nelken and J Feest, (eds), *Adapting Legal Cultures.*

Heyderbrand, W (2001) 'From Globalization of Law to Law Under Globalization' in D Nelken and J Feest (eds), *Adapting Legal Cultures.*

—— (2007) 'Globalization and the Rise of Procedural Informalism in Europe and America' in V Gessner and D Nelken (eds), *European Ways of Law* (Oxford, Hart Publishing).

Hodgson, J (2006) *French Criminal Justice* (Oxford, Hart Publishing).

Hofstede, G (1980) *Culture's Consequences: International Differences in Work Related Values,* (Beverly Hills, CA, Sage).

Jensen, EG and Heller, TC (eds) (2003) *Beyond Common Knowledge: Empirical Approaches to the Rule of Law* (Stanford, Stanford University Press).

Jettinghoff, A (2001) 'State Formation and Legal Change: On the Impact of International Politics' in D Nelken and J Feest (eds), *Adapting Legal Culture.*

Johnson, D (2002) *The Japanese way of Justice* (Oxford, Oxford University Press).

Kagan, R (2001) *Adversarial Legalism: The American Way of Law* (Cambridge MA, Harvard University Press).

Kahn, P (1999) *The Cultural Study of Law: Reconstructing legal scholarship* (Chicago, IL, Chicago University Press).

Kenney, S (1996) 6: 9 *Law and Politics Book Review* 122.

Krygier, M (1997) 'Is There Constitutionalism After Communism? Institutional Optimism, Cultural Pessimism, and the Rule of Law' 26, 4, *International Journal of Sociology* 1996–1997, 17.

Kuper, A (1999) *Culture: The Anthropologists Account* (Cambridge, MA, Harvard University Press).

Langbein, JH and Weinreb, LL (1978) 'Continental Criminal Procedure: "Myth" and Reality' *Yale Law Journal* 1549.

Legrand P (1997) *Fragments on Law as Culture* (Nijmegen, Ars Aqui).

Legrand, P and Munday, R (eds) (2003) *Comparative Legal Studies: Traditions and Transition* (Cambridge, Cambridge University Press).

Likosky, MB (ed) (2002) *Transnational Legal Processes* (Cambridge, Cambridge University Press).

Merry, SE (2003) 'Human Rights Law and the Demonization of Culture (And Anthropology Along the Way)' 26:1 *Polar: Political and Legal Anthropology Review* 55.

—— (2005) *Human Rights and Gender Violence: Translating International Law into Local Justice*, (Chicago, IL, Chicago University Press).

Nelken, D (1994) 'Whom can you Trust?' in D Nelken (ed), *The Futures of Criminology* (London, Sage).

—— (1995) 'Understanding/ Invoking Legal Culture' in D Nelken (ed) special issue on Legal Culture, Diversity and Globalization 4 *Social and Legal Studies* 435.

—— (1997) 'Puzzling out Legal Culture' in D Nelken (ed), *Comparing Legal Cultures* (Aldershot, Dartmouth).

—— (2001) 'Beyond the Metaphor of Legal Transplants?: Consequences of Autopoietic Theory for the Study of Cross-Cultural Legal Adaptation' in J Priban and D Nelken (eds), *Law's New boundaries: The Consequences of Legal Autopoiesis* (Aldershot, Dartmouth).

—— (2002) 'Comparing Criminal Justice' in *The Oxford Handbook of Criminology*, 3rd edn (Oxford, Oxford University Press).

—— (2003) 'Comparativists and Transferability' in P Legrand and R Munday (eds), *Comparative Legal Studies: Traditions and Transition.*

—— (2004) 'Using the Concept of Legal Culture' *Australian Journal of Legal Philosophy* 1.

—— (2006a) 'Rethinking Legal Culture' in M Freeman (ed), *Law and Sociology* 200.

—— (2006b) 'Il Radicamento Della Penalità' in A Febbrajo, A La Spina and M Raiteri (eds), *Cultura Giuridica e Politiche Pubbliche* (Milan, Giuffre Editore).

—— (2006c) 'Patterns of Punishment' 69 *Modern Law Review* 262.

—— (2006d) 'Signalling Conformity: Legal Change in China and Japan' 27 *Michigan Journal of International Law* 933.

Nottage, LR, 'Translating Tanase: Challenging Paradigms of Japanese Law and Society' (May 27, 2006). Sydney Law School Research Paper No. 07/17 Available at SSRN: http://ssrn.com/abstract=921932.

Ohnesorge, JKM (2006) 'Politics, Ideology, and Legal System Reform in Northeast Asia' in C Antons and V Gessner (eds), *Globalisation and Resistance: Law Reform in Asia since the Financial Crisis* (Oxford, Hart Publishing).

Rebuffa, G and Blankenburg, E (1993) 'Culture Juridique' in A Arnaud (ed), *Dictionnaire encyplopédique de théorie et de sociologie du droit* (Paris, LGDJ).

Santos, De Sousa B (1995) *Towards a New Common Sense.* (London, Routledge).

Sarat, A and Kearns, TR (eds) (1993) *Law in Everyday Life* (Ann Abor, Michigan University Press).

—— (eds) (1998) *Law in the Domains of Culture* (Ann Abor, Michigan University Press).

Scheuerman, WE (1999) 'Globalization and the Fate of Law' in D Dyzenhaus (ed), *Recrafting the Rule of Law: The Limits of Legal Order,* (Boston, John Hopkins Press).

Sherman, B (1997) 'Remembering and Forgetting: The Birth of Modern Copyright Law' in Nelken, D (ed), *Comparative Legal Cultures* (Aldershot, Dartmouth).

Silbey, S (2001) 'Legal culture and consciousness' in *International Encyclopedia of the Social and Behavioral Sciences,* (Amsterdam, Elsevier Science).

—— (2005) 'After legal consciousness' 1 *Annual Review of Law and Social Science* 323.

Silbey, S and Ewick, P (1998) *The Common Place of the Law: Stories from Everyday Life* (Chicago, IL, Chicago University Press).

Slaughter, A-M (1997) 'The Real New World Order' *Foreign Affairs* September, 183.

Snyder, F (1999) 'Governing Economic Globalisation: Global Legal Pluralism and European Law' 5 *European Law Journal* 334.

Teubner, G (1997) 'Global Bukowina: Legal Pluralism in the World Society' in G Teubner (ed), *Global Law without a State* (Aldershot, Dartmouth).

—— (1998) 'Legal Irritants: Good Faith in British Law or How Unifying Law Ends up in New Divergences' 61 *Modern Law Review* 11.

Toharia, J (2003) 'Evaluating systems of justice through public opinion: Why? What? Who? How? and What for?' in Jensen and Heller (eds) *Beyond Common Knowledge: Empirical Approaches to the Rule of Law* (Stanford, Stanford University Press).

Varga, C (1992) *Comparative Legal Cultures* (Aldershot, Dartmouth).

Webber, J (2004) 'Culture, Legal Culture, and Legal Reasoning: A Comment on Nelken' in *Australian Journal of Legal Philosophy* 25.

Winn, JK 'Relational Practices and the Marginalization of Law: Informal Practices of Small Businesses in Taiwan' (1994) 28 *Law and Society Review* 193–23.

Whitman, JQ (2003) *Harsh Justice* (Oxford, Oxford University Press).

—— (2005) 'Response to Garland' 7(4) *Punishment and Society* 389.

Zedner, L (1995) 'In Pursuit of the Vernacular: Comparing Law and Order Discourse in Britain and Germany' in D Nelken (ed), *Comparing Legal Cultures.*

6

Is it so Bad to be Different? Comparative Law and the Appreciation of Diversity

ROGER COTTERRELL*

KEY CONCEPTS

Similarity and difference between laws and legal systems as foci of comparative law; Harmonisation and unification of law as dominant concerns of comparative lawyers; Analogies in comparative law with debates about assimilation and multiculturalism; The importance of respect for the distinctiveness of legal cultures; European legal convergence, its cultural supports and its critics; Legrand's 'contrarian challenge' to the mainstream of comparative law; Cultural diversity and the new jurisprudence of difference; Methods and problems of cultural comparison in comparative law; The comparative study of fundamental legal values; Whitman on American 'liberty' and European 'dignity'; The challenge of cross-cultural observation and understanding.

I. UNITY FROM LEGAL DIVERSITY

I s IT so *bad* to be different? Is it undesirable that laws apparently regulating the same matters differ from one legal system to another, perhaps permitting things in one system, while prohibiting them in another? Does it matter that styles of legal thought, or traditions of legal practice, may vary greatly, so that lawyers in one legal system have great difficulty understanding how lawyers in another think and how legal decisions are made and justified? Legal sociologists have shown that there are also strikingly different popular ideas in different countries about the purposes of law and what is to be expected from it (see eg Nelken, 2003). At least since the time of the ancient Greeks, realistic commentators have seen legal diversity as inevitable. 'The things which are just by virtue of convention and expediency are like measures', wrote Aristotle, 'for wine and corn measures are not everywhere equal, but larger in wholesale and smaller in retail

* I am grateful to David Nelken for comments on this chapter.

markets. Similarly, the things which are just not by nature but by human enactment are not everywhere the same' (Aristotle: 7).

Yet there have always been scholars who have sought more from law than is
represented by this diversity. Aristotle sensed that, alongside the differing laws of
different jurisdictions, there might be a natural justice that 'everywhere has the
same force and does not exist by people thinking this or that' (*ibid*). Later, over
the centuries, philosophers postulated the existence of a 'natural law', more fundamental than enacted law; a law given by 'nature'—the natural order of the world,
or perhaps human nature—and thus superior to (and underpinning the authority
of) the contingent, man-made laws of different nations. They asked how far law
could really be worthy of respect if it had nothing universal about it.

What kind of knowledge is law if that knowledge is true (valid) in one town
but invalid in another, a few miles away across the border? Similarly, what kind
of moral force can law have if here it says one thing about right and wrong, and
there it says something else (perhaps the opposite)? Thus, *epistemological* arguments favour a search for unifying foundations of law (ie arguments focused on
worries about law's status as a philosophically secure form of knowledge), and
moral arguments operate too (suggesting that if law is to have moral worth it must
depend on more than the contingencies of where political borders lie). Equally,
political arguments have long encouraged some kind of universalist ambition for
law: maybe political misunderstandings between states could be reduced if agreement on legal principles (perhaps governing the actions of states themselves)
could be achieved.

The search for unifying foundations of national laws in natural law was always
controversial insofar as it depended purely on philosophical speculation. As
modern comparative law emerged in the 19th century, when empirical scientific
methods were increasingly favoured as a foundation of knowledge, debates about
law's universality took new forms, grounded in the study of specific legal systems. The philosophers' aim of finding a natural law to inspire the improvement
of man-made law, justify its existence or provide its moral censor, was largely
superseded. Its place was taken by the comparatists' aim of studying foreign
legal systems and improving law by harmonisation (creating rules to harmonise
relationships between legal systems) or unification (producing uniform rules
applicable across national boundaries in place of divergent national rules). Yet
comparative law, seeking 'grand similarities' behind national 'differences in detail'
still held to the ambition to 'deepen our belief in the existence of a unitary sense
of justice' (Zweigert and Kötz, 1998: 3). One might say that the torch of legal
universality passed from philosophers to lawyers, and from theory to practice.
Instead of speculating on human nature as a basis for a universal, morally imperative law, comparatists aimed at practical legal reform in fields where reconciling
differences between legal systems seemed a real possibility.

This agenda of harmonising or unifying law has dominated much of
comparative law since the beginning of the 20th century and given it a solid,
if multi-faceted legitimacy. Some comparatists seeking to reconcile differences

between legal systems might see themselves as connected to generations of philosophers pursuing the ideals of natural law.[1] They might also think of themselves as linked with the pioneers (often themselves influenced by natural law thinking) of an international law to promote peace between nations.[2] But, above all, they could see themselves as facilitating everyday legal communication—especially on economic matters[3]—between advanced nations of the modern world. An important means of doing so could be by harmonising private (especially contract and commercial) law between continental European civil law systems,[4] and perhaps later (as today in the European Union) between civil law and common law approaches. This harmonisation work would simplify legal transactions and reduce cost, delay and legal uncertainty in commerce.

But it might be asked whether old aspirations (for example, of the natural lawyers) to understand the deepest roots of law in the human condition have been lost as modern comparatists have become diligent selectors or drafters of uniform laws. Comparative lawyers realised that it was important to study the diversity of laws and not just assume some ultimate unifying authority for them in 'nature'. But did comparatists fail to take the roots of that diversity sufficiently seriously? Powerful attacks on natural law thinking in the 18th and 19th centuries came from scholars who argued that law must be studied in relation to the cultures in which it develops (Stein, 1980). Natural law thinking failed to appreciate that law is rooted less in a universal human condition than in the specific conditions of different cultures. Hence differences between laws and legal systems may not be just matters of contingency; they may express profound characteristics of the cultures that produce them. This cultural awareness failed, however, to become a dominant influence in comparative law.

Some writers see a main reason for this failure in the pervasive influence of legal positivism (Legrand, 2005: 631 at 643; Legrand, 2003: 242, 277; and Ewald, 1995: 1889 at 1982–3). Treating law as 'posited'—enacted or declared by human law-makers in official processes—legal positivism marginalises law's links to other things not officially posited in this way. So, ultimate values (such as liberty, human dignity or equality) are not in the foreground of positivist legal analysis. Nor are matters of tradition (accumulated historical experience, custom, collective memories) or emotional bases of law (such as elements of national sentiment or patriotism). Analysis is of rules, rather than of the values they may imply, traditions they may embody, or sentiments that may surround them.

Legal positivism tends rather to view law as *instrumental*; a tool of government (ie policy-driven law), or private interests (ie in the form of contracts, property

---

[1] See Del Vecchio, 1969: 31–7, exploring philosophical bases of comparative law.
[2] Compare Lepaulle, 1922: 838 at 857: 'divergences in laws cause other divergences that generate … misunderstandings and conflicts among nations which end with blood and desolation'.
[3] *Cf* Édouard Lambert's view that, 'the essential mission of comparative law is one of economic peacemaking, the realisation of an international economic entente' (Jamin, 2002: 701 at 715).
[4] *Ibid*: 701 at 716.

entitlements, etc). Law appears as a means of pursuing projects and regulating deals—changing the world in big or small ways. And much contemporary comparative legal scholarship also sees law mainly in these terms. Legal positivism may be a necessary part of Western lawyers' professionalism, but it sees law as little more than clusters of rules, to be juristically organised and refined to fit them for their purpose. In comparative law, this refining is often a search for the most appropriate precept from the rule-books of various legal systems.

Given the importance of a predominantly instrumental view of rules, it seems unsurprising that positivist comparative law should define its own rationale in instrumental terms, guided by the practical tasks that law is required to serve. In fact, the idea of purpose or *function* has provided the primary modern basis for legal comparison. The search for the most efficient rule to serve a given social or economic function has been the primary technique for unifying law in comparative legal studies. But is functional efficiency everything? And can functions be identified without asking whether in different legal systems, local values, traditions or sentiments may differently colour the definition of those functions, the importance attached to them and the tests of their successful fulfilment? In short, can we talk about similarity and difference in laws and their functions without talking about culture?

II. AN ANALOGY: ASSIMILATION AND MULTICULTURALISM

It might be helpful to put comparative law to one side for a moment and think about everyday life. Is it so bad to be different, or to be *thought* to be different? Sometimes, clearly yes: one might be misunderstood, patronised, discriminated against or bullied. Practical definitions of similarity and difference are adopted by majority populations or powerful groups. They are used to label others (minorities, the less powerful) and to make assumptions about them that fit the labellers' preconceptions, rather than the experience of the labelled. If people are singled out as different, life may be easier for them if they try to be *less* different by assimilating to the dominant norm, trying to hide the things that make them seem different. But this may be impossible. Even limited efforts may be counterproductive in the assimilators' lives, denying a part of who they are. In any case, these deliberate changes may be inadequate—criteria of difference can always be revised, the goal posts can be moved.

Anyway, why should anyone be required to attempt such a self-denying transformation? Will communication be made easier by an attempt to become 'the same'? Those people who want to communicate will seek to do so across difference (and may see difference as enriching the experience). For effective communication there will need to be sincere efforts on both sides to translate the experience of each in terms that the other can understand. There will also need to be a serious wish on both sides to appreciate the other's experience and viewpoints and there will need to be mutual respect for the autonomy and dignity of others (both those considered different and those seen as similar) as human beings. Where these conditions are sustained over time, communication may become rich, with perceptions of difference being part of the richness. But those not wishing to communicate may use the impossible demand for assimilation (that the different become the same) to control or silence minorities or to victimise the powerless.

An entirely reasonable stance (for those who feel strong enough, individually or collectively) is to refuse demands or temptations to assimilate, even to the extent that assimilation is possible. Instead, one might legitimately demand to be treated with respect in one's difference, as long as one is prepared to give equal respect to the difference of others. Indeed, it might be suggested that the idea of difference could be replaced with that of individuality or distinctiveness. Why should difference not be accepted and welcomed—re-interpreted in terms of facets of individual experience or distinctive character? The claim might be that productive integration requires not assimilation, but mutual acceptance and mutual learning about the other, in a framework of universal respect for human dignity and autonomy.

How does this relate to comparative law? Is the process of unifying law between different legal systems anything like a process of assimilation between different people? Certainly, parallels can be drawn and they help to clarify what is at stake in recent demands that comparative law should shift focus from seeking legal similarity (via harmonisation or unification) towards appreciating the virtues of legal diversity. Indeed, some comparatists have invoked ideas reminiscent of those that feature in debates about multiculturalism and assimilation. They have demanded respect in comparative legal studies for distinctive *cultures*, including legal cultures, in a way that parallels demands for respect for individual or group identity in the face of calls to assimilate to majority norms.

Some comparatists today, reflecting ideas of earlier jurists and historians (Whitman, 2003a: 315–26), emphasise that law's identity is inseparable from its culture. They insist that a legal culture's integrity and identity should be respected against calls for legal harmonisation. Correspondingly, an ethnic minority group might demand that its cultural integrity and collective identity, its special subjective experience, be respected against calls for 'difference' to be erased or reduced (for example, calls for its distinctive traditions, norms or beliefs to be abandoned where they differ significantly from those of the majority). The demand for respect for difference—whether applied to legal cultures or minority populations—often appeals to arguments that cultural richness is lost by reducing diversity, that imposing uniformity is morally illegitimate, and that homogenisation (removal of difference) is impossible and attempting it will produce confusion, disruption and disorder.

Perhaps most fundamental, in relation to all these debates, is the question of relative power. The main problem for those who suffer from the way the labels 'similar' or 'different' are used is their *lack of control* over the use of these labels. For example, how far two people, X and Y, resemble or differ from each other is a matter of the perceptions of both X and Y, negotiated between them. But if X has greater power than Y to define what counts as similarity or difference, to determine its significance and control its consequences, X may effectively decree how and with what effects Y is treated as the same or different. This is what produces the main resentments surrounding invocations, denials or criticisms of difference. Y wishes to have equal control of the defining process—to be a subject asserting difference or similarity, not merely a differentiated or assimilated object. The language of similarity and difference should belong to *both* X and Y.

Is this a no less fundamental complaint with regard to the relations of legal systems, or legal cultures? Some are far more powerful or influential than others; they may define what is normal, optimal or most appropriate in law. When other, less powerful legal systems or legal cultures are defined in their degrees of difference or similarity by the more powerful ones, the more powerful may ultimately determine the fate (the independence and integrity) of the less powerful. To defend one's own right to assert difference, to demand that one's own subjective experience in one's own (legal) culture be respected and valued, not removed or subjected to assimilation (harmonisation or unification), becomes, in such circumstances, obviously a form of resistance to power. It is an effort to gain access to the vocabulary of difference *for one's own purposes*, rather than accepting the definitions and purposes of the stronger party. In a legal context, what is meant here is resistance to the imposition of legal ideas, styles or purposes by economically, militarily or politically stronger nations or groups of nations.

When matters are expressed in this way one can see a direct analogy between— and sometimes a similar level of emotional investment in—the politics of multiculturalism and the politics of difference (between legal cultures) in comparative law.

III. LEGRAND AND EUROPEAN PRIVATE LAW

Emotional investment is clearly present in the writings of Pierre Legrand, the most outspoken and passionate current advocate of the need to appreciate difference in comparative law. Legrand uses words like 'repression', 'oppression', 'totalitarianism' and 'violence' in talking about the orthodox practices and attitudes of comparatists, as he sees them. Comparative lawyers, he says,

> must purposely privilege the identification of differences across the laws they compare lest they fail to address singularity with authenticity (Legrand, 2001: 1033 at 1049).

Insofar as they fail to do this (which is often),

> comparative legal studies, because of the totalitarianism and the oppression inherent to a strategy of sameness and assimilation, is a practice of violence (Legrand, 2005: 631 at 706).

Legrand's attacks have focused mainly on the most sustained international harmonisation enterprise in contemporary comparative law—the effort to develop a common European private law. He sees this project as a reckless denial of legitimate difference between the legal systems of Europe. Its most ambitious aspect is the (tentative and controversial) idea of creating a European code of private law (Legrand, 1997). Legrand has criticised, in the harshest terms, the kinds of thinking that inspire work preparing the way for such a code. More broadly, he claims that despite the long-term harmonisation efforts of comparatists in international committees and permanent study groups, as well as the impetus from European Union Directives in many legal fields, European legal systems are not converging in either regulatory practice or juristic outlook (Legrand, 1996). They remain separated by differences of legal culture—above all, in his view, by profound cultural incompatibilities between English common law and continental European civil law.

For Legrand, the 'ambition of a European concordantia is (and must be) a chimera.' (*ibid*: 52 at 81). Harmonisation of European private law is 'impossible' and 'wishful thinking' (Legrand, 2001: 1033 at 1037, 1039 and 1043) because civil law and common law approaches in Europe are 'irrevocably irreconcilable', representing different *mentalités*—ie cultural outlooks or worldviews (Legrand, 2006: 13 at 30, 31). Their ways of reasoning with, practising and developing law, and their attitudes to legal sources and professional traditions are fundamentally different. A civil lawyer and a common lawyer cannot think like each other when it comes to understanding the most profound assumptions of their respective legal traditions. Of course (one assumes), they can learn much from each other but (Legrand insists) they cannot substitute their most basic professional formations.

We might want to stop at this point and ask: If cultures can present this irreconcilable difference when set against each other, what are their boundaries (how are cultural similarity and difference determined)? and what are the specific components of cultures that set up these formidable barriers to assimilation or harmonisation? We might turn to the multiculturalism analogy again and note that *individuals* can certainly cross cultures and can see themselves as inhabiting several cultures. They can, in some circumstances, leave cultures and join new ones, or move in and out of cultural environments. Indeed, they might find their cultural identity a very complex, shifting, negotiable, even sometimes indeterminate matter.

Thus, immediately, the issue of what culture is presents itself. Actually it is a cluster of issues. What are the components of culture and how are they to be separated and structured? What is the nature of cultural experience? How are cultures to be identified by those who inhabit them as well as by those who observe them as outsiders? These are hardly new questions and have been much discussed in, for example, the literature of anthropology, where culture has long been a central concept. In relation to law, one might ask: What cultural boundaries exist and which really matter? For Legrand, a civil law/common law cultural boundary is fundamental, legal cultural variations in the civil law world being apparently much less problematic. While he offers few reasons for his view that *this* cultural divide is crucial, rather than others, there is no doubt that in the formative period of modern comparative law, many comparatists on the European continent saw

English common law as profoundly alien to the Romanist traditions that shaped a significantly shared European civil law outlook.

Whether this legal cultural divide remains as significant as Legrand claims is, however, much disputed. Ole Lando, drawing directly on his extensive experience as a leading figure in the Commission on European Contract Law over more than two decades, and in other harmonisation projects, sees shared values and a 'common attitude' among lawyers from different European countries (including Britain) as the key to success in reaching agreement on uniform law.

> Several factors have caused this common attitude. The similar economic and political structure of the [EU] Member States is one. Another is their common cultural heritage. All Europeans share the Christian ethic, and have been influenced by Roman law and the great moralists. The milieu in which both judges and law professors are raised and live is also a factor. Most of the guardians and preachers of our law and justice grew up in well-to-do bourgeois homes with moral traditions. In Europe, the middle class has been the guardian of ethics, and so have the parents of the judges and professors ... Thus, the legal values of the European brotherhood of lawyers are very similar (Lando, 1999: 20, at 21–22).

These views are hardly uncontroversial, but the idea of a European legal elite with a common culture of its own that facilitates negotiation to achieve harmonisation is a familiar one; very much a self-image of comparative lawyers seeking legal similarity. 'To a considerable degree,' the influential comparatist Alan Watson claims, 'the lawmakers of one society share the same legal culture with the lawmakers of other societies' (Watson, 1983: 1121 at 1157). Again, then, the question as regards culture is: Which cultures count most? Is a common culture of transnational juristic elites (if such a culture exists) the dominant one, even if it may differ from cultural environments of everyday legal practice and popular legal experience in different national systems?

Lando's approach, like that of many comparatists, presupposes functionalism. Recalling harmonisation discussions in which he participated, he notes that

> the participants would consider how the courts of their own country had or would have reacted to a case, and they often found that although the rules were different, the courts had or would have reached the same results. The consensus was greater than one would have expected when one compared the legal rules and techniques of the various countries (Lando, 1999: 20).

Functional analysis emphasising common problems to be solved is seen as a route to consensus, by-passing conceptual differences and differences of legal style.

Legrand, like other cultural comparatists, has attacked what he sees as the poverty of functional analysis (Legrand, 2005), but European legal harmonisation is mainly driven by a desire to ensure that law serves agreed (largely economic) functions in Europe as efficiently as possible. Something like Lando's assumptions about a shared legal professional culture (reinforced by a common European culture: see, eg Wieacker, 1990) operate to fuel general optimism about harmonisation. Thus, the divide between common law and civil law approaches is often presented as no more than a minor bump in the road for the harmonisation steamroller to roll over. Nevertheless, Legrand is right to note that striking misunderstandings still exist about the nature of common law among some civil lawyers engaged in harmonisation. Even as sophisticated a German jurist as Reinhard Zimmermann writes of 'the casuistic nature of the English law, with its bizarre traditionality, or with its peculiar interlocking of common law and equity' (Zimmermann, 1996: 576 at 587), and others mistake common law's careful empiricism and pragmatism—with its deliberate distrust of theory and of large-scale conceptualisation—for evidence of its primitive condition.

But why insist on the 'impossibility' of harmonising European law when this harmonisation seems to be well under way? Legrand's answer is that harmonising rules is very far from achieving a unification of legal understandings and practices. The same rule interpreted in two different national legal cultures will actually mean something different in each of them. So, legal harmonisation is illusory. There might be standardisation of the letter of the rules but there will not be harmonisation of their meaning as law.

> Since the legal is also cultural, 'uniformity', in the sense of a commonality across laws, is a promise that law is simply ontologically incapable of fulfilling (Legrand, 2001: 1033 at 1047).

In support, Legrand often cites Gunther Teubner's well-known argument (Teubner, 1998) that unpredictable consequences will follow from the introduction, as a consequence of a European Directive, of the concept of good faith in English contract law (eg Legrand, 2006: 13 at 26; Legrand, 2003: 293 and 303). Teubner sees no reason to suppose that good faith will mean the same thing in English law as in, say, German law, once the economic conditions of commerce and contracting in the two countries are taken into account:

> [T]he question is not so much if British contract doctrine will reject or integrate good faith. Rather, it is what kind of transformations of meaning will the term undergo, how will its role differ, once it is reconstructed anew under British law? (Teubner, 1998: 11 at 12).

In fact,

> it is inconceivable that British good faith will be the same as *Treu und Glauben* German style which has developed in a rather special historical and cultural constellation (*ibid*: at 20).

The meaning of law depends on how a legal discourse reacts to its specific environment.

Teubner's arguments certainly help Legrand by showing that a general appeal by comparatists to common functions served by different laws in different systems may gloss over complex historical conditions, colouring the way law's functions are understood. Law's relations to economy, polity and 'diverse fragments of society' may vary ('from loose coupling to tight interwovenness') in different countries (*ibid*: at 18). But it is very important to note that Teubner rejects any unified notion of culture as an analytical tool, or even as a rhetorical device for criticising legal harmonisation. Instead, he draws on a sophisticated social theory (developed by the sociologist Niklas Luhmann) that breaks down everything that Legrand would understand as culture into an interplay of more of less distinct social systems of communication.

In the present context, two conclusions should be drawn from Teubner's complex arguments. First (supporting Legrand), there are strong grounds for saying that functional analysis alone is inadequate as a method for comparatist harmonisers—too many unanalysed assumptions stand behind the idea that common functions of law can be found to unite legal systems. But, secondly (against Legrand), it remains doubtful whether a concept of culture as such can be operationalised to explain why meanings of law may differ between legal systems even when legal rules seem the same. Perhaps the *portmanteau* concept of culture needs breaking down into defined, analysable elements, so that it might become possible to understand, more precisely, how different aspects of culture colour law's meanings, or indeed supply them.

IV. HARMONISATION'S MORAL DEFICIT?

Whether or not harmonisation is 'impossible', Legrand sees much wrong with even attempting it. It is 'politically complicitous, inherently oppressive, and fundamentally antihumanistic'; it 'sings oh-so-sweetly to Power', to the narrow demands of commerce, capital and the forces of globalisation:

> I find it unlikely that the European civil code will prove socially progressive and not pander to market-oriented 'law-and-economics' dogmas (Legrand, 2006: 13 at 27).

European harmonisation serves 'instrumentalism, and managerialism' (*ibid*: at 28) and 'operates in a deracinating world of faceless markets' (Legrand, 2001: 1033 at 1048). Through it, the cult of efficiency will rule everything and drive forward economic liberalisation in Europe—an anti-humanistic development because it ignores other values, other important aspects of culture and human flourishing. In opposition to it, Legrand sets an ideal of fostering 'the respect due the variety of lived experiences' (*ibid*).

Clearly, the focus of attack has shifted here—but without any major change of tone—from claims about the technical problems of harmonisation to much broader moral and political arguments. Behind everything are claims about the nature of communication through law. Legrand seems to see, on one side, instrumental technically-oriented communication, narrow in aims and cultural reference, and thus impoverished to an extent that may make it hardly meaningful communication at all: 'a promise [of understanding] that law is simply ontologically incapable of fulfilling' (Legrand 2001:1033 at 1047). On the other side is the elusive but essential ideal of cultural communication—an opening up to an awareness of the 'other' (especially the other's law) which involves a difficult, sustained effort of sensitivity. In preferring this latter kind of communication,

Legrand shifts to moralistic language. It is 'bad faith' (*ibid*: at 1043) to fail to recognise difference and to try to sweep it aside by assuming (or engineering) similarity; and there is a duty of 'justice', owed to culture itself, to leave it as rich as before, not to impoverish it (Legrand, 2006: 13 at 36).

At the same time, Legrand asserts, the mundane claim that transaction costs will be lowered through harmonisation is a 'cheap fiction' (*ibid*: at 27). Even instrumentalism requires moral honesty and should not be pursued through sleight of hand. If economic efficiency were (misguidedly) to be accepted as an adequate reason for trying to remove legal differences in Europe, no one has yet proved that harmonisation will promote this efficiency. Legrand is surely right to make this last point. It is striking that although efficiency claims are frequently made in favour of harmonisation, little or no empirical research is cited to support them. Leading harmonisers feel the need only to say that

> we consider it to be a safe assumption, supported by anecdotal evidence, that significant cost factors are involved and that these costs factors are operative in practically all sectors of the market economy (Von Bar, Lando and Swann, 2002: 183 at 198–9).

These matters, it seems, do not need empirical demonstration.

Harmonisation, for Legrand, is intellectually authoritarian: a 'cultural totalitarianism' (Legrand, 2006: 13 at 27). What seems to be meant is that experience, in all its complexity and richness, is reduced by this process to fit a grid of legal rules. A European code of private law, 'as a form of law, will contain what would otherwise overflow: experience' (*ibid*: at 21). Law should express what people think, feel and encounter in everyday social relations, but uniform positive rules abstracted from context (which are what harmonisation promotes) will deny this connection of law to life. For Legrand, English common law in Europe risks becoming a sacrifice offered to the gods of positivist-functionalist harmonisation, so that it will be 'encrypted into the language of the grid' (*ibid*: at 19), its life (as accumulated historical experience and a style of juristic working that reflects that experience) drained away in the process.

A final problem links these claims as to why harmonisation *should* not be attempted with the earlier claim that it *cannot* actually be achieved. Because, as Teubner suggests, harmonised law will mean different things in different legal systems, its precise effects are, for Legrand, dangerously unpredictable, risking legal 'chaos' for the common law system as it becomes 'de-embedded' (*ibid*: at 33). There will be

> disintegrative consequences either in terms of broken linkages across various fields of local law or fractured connections between law and other disciplines (Legrand, 2001: 1033 at 1042).

Legrand envisages lawyers in Britain being put in a kind of limbo between Europeanised positive law and a local common law culture at odds with it. Because, for him, the link between law and culture is so fundamental, a severing (or major disruption) of it will not only impoverish positive law and make its meaning uncertain, but will put lawyers in a very undesirable situation—serving a law that has lost its roots, and therefore becoming, themselves, functionaries without roots in their own culture; morally unanchored technicians.

How should we take stock of these moral-political criticisms of harmonisation, and the claim that European legal difference is to be celebrated and protected? We can note, firstly, that the cultural critique is far from being the only kind of criticism levelled at European legal harmonisation. Arguments around the value implications of harmonisation, the efficiency claims made for it, its relevance to European integration, its disruptive effects on national laws, the legal powers available to pursue it and the best methods for achieving it have been developed in a huge literature.[5] Alongside such an array of issues, the sometimes monotonous insistence on cultural difference in Legrand's 'contrarian challenge' can seem a rather limited standpoint from which to approach the complex problems of legal unity or diversity in Europe. Indeed, comparatists' debates, however framed, about legal similarity and difference might seem a narrow perspective from which to view what are ultimately profound conflicts over different *economic and social visions* of Europe. Brief mentions of 'economic liberalism' and 'faceless markets' are not enough to link discussion of the rights and wrongs of legal harmonisation to larger, far more fundamental themes about the effects of globalisation and the power-play of international relations in European transformation (see, eg Van der Pijl, 2006).

It might even be said that, although European legal harmonisation has been (largely because of Legrand's work) a main focus for recent demands for comparatists to appreciate legal difference, it is actually one of the *weakest* fronts on which to fight for a re-orientation of comparative law. So much activity is now aimed at creating new European law that the demand for comparatists to privilege European cultural (in this context especially national) differences may seem a Canute-like stance in the face of a tide of legal change. And, very significantly, the invocation of culture works here for *harmonisation* as well as against it. Claims, noted earlier, about a common European culture and about the cultural unity of legal elites can easily be set against claims of cultural diversity in Europe. Again, it can be argued that, perhaps by contrast with some other legal and social fields, the private law relationships where harmonisation is sought do not reflect major European cultural differences. So, familiar issues reappear. What bits of culture matter most, and how? Whose culture counts most? Can cultural similarities be assumed for some problems or tasks of legal regulation but not for others? How are distinctions within culture to be drawn and understood?

In general, the task of making the appreciation of legal difference as prominent in comparative law as the search for legal similarity is very difficult. In a climate where lawyers and legal scholars are expected to be (and generally wish to see

---

[5] For summaries of the issues see, eg Wilhelmsson, 2002; Weatherill, 2004; and Hesselink, 2004.

themselves as) 'useful', the practical benefits of reducing legal differences may seem self-evident (even if evidence to prove the efficiency payoff is not necessarily sought). The appreciation of difference, however, is usually justified in much broader humanistic terms—the arguments are, as has been seen, mainly moral ones. They must, in many instances, be set against deep-rooted juristic convictions; in particular, the positivist approach to law that is second-nature to most modern lawyers, and the functionalist outlook often assumed in legal policy debates.

V. THE LEGAL VISIBILITY OF CULTURAL DIFFERENCE

Yet the moral imperative to appreciate difference will not go away. For all its difficulties there is something of immense importance in it. Positivism and functionalism—the default positions for legal inquiry, the easy-ways-out for avoiding entanglement with culture—have allowed modern comparative law to marginalise the broadest humanistic aspirations of comparatists and to discard, as impractical or lacking in analytical rigour, the inheritance of philosophical, historical and sociological ideas present at the birth of modern comparative law in the decades leading up to the start of the 20th century (Cotterrell, 2006a: chapter 8).

Must practicality and efficiency trump humanistic appreciation of individuality and difference? We need to return again to the multiculturalism analogy. Assimilation (a single cultural outlook) rather than multiculturalism (an ongoing, sometimes difficult conversation between cultures) might seem to be a way to avoid friction—to achieve *efficiency*, in a sense—in social arrangements. But the social 'efficiency' might be superficial. Where it is the result of coercion by more powerful groups to change the cultural practices of weaker ones, it may produce resentment. If the weaker groups eventually gain strength they may react against it with unforeseeable consequences. And often, as noted earlier, to become culturally the same is impossible. These problems affect the search for unity in law, insofar as law expresses or reflects culture. What has prevented arguments about culture from getting a fair hearing in modern legal inquiry has been the dominance of the positivist view that law can be understood without specific reference to culture.

For various reasons this analytical separation of law from culture is breaking down in important respects in many Western societies. Cultural differentiation has been brought sharply to the attention of legal elites even in the United States, where the viability of cultural assimilation was long assumed.[6] American critical race theory (CRT), created by lawyers belonging to—and seeing themselves, in some respects, as speaking for—ethnic minority groups, has demanded a hearing in debates on the nature and effects of law. As a 'minority critique' of dominant legal ideas, CRT has forced itself on the attention of American legal elites. It

---

[6] On debates around this policy, see Wacker, 1979; and on the survival or revival of assimilationism, see Jacoby, 1994, and Alba and Nee, 2003.

has contributed to the growth of a 'jurisprudence of difference' (see Cotterrell: 2003: chapter 8), which no longer views law's regulated population as culturally uniform and sees new agendas for law as it confronts difference. Some American comparatists have sensed both a challenge and an opportunity for comparative legal studies in this situation (Demleitner, 1999; and Curran, 1998). Lawyers have long understood the virtues of assuming similarity—treating all as equal before the law and recognising no special statuses derived from cultural particularities. But the new jurisprudence of difference emphasises the fact that law applies differently to different groups in the same population. These groups may also seek different things from law, asking that it recognise cultural conditions specific to them.

This situation ultimately poses great dilemmas. The demand to appreciate difference through law comes not just from minority populations pressing claims on law, but from jurists re-examining the normative unity of law: that is, its integrity as a coherent set of rules underpinned by common values, shared traditions, convergent projects and uniform sentiments. Does law really have this unity? What is in issue here is *cultural* unity. Rules may cohere in juristic analysis but not in the meanings they have for the various cultural populations subject to them. Here, raised in a new, different context, is Legrand's basic question of law's *meaning*, with its answer dependent on cultural context.

In contemporary Britain, which has been characterised explicitly in recent decades as a multicultural society (not one seeking assimilation of minorities to a consciously fostered uniform culture), the issues go further. It is not just a matter of law being seen from different cultural standpoints, but of demands, in some contexts, for a recognition of *differential law*—law that can express cultural difference (for example, the distinctive practices associated with particular religious beliefs or ethnic traditions). The idea of a kind of legal pluralism (a situation in which different laws might apply to different cultural groups, at least to a limited extent) has been mooted, and even seen as reflected in practice (Shah, 2005).

What has this to do with comparative law? As long as comparative law is assumed to be concerned only with relations of laws between different nation states the answer may be: very little. But comparatists have long addressed the question of how far legal uniformity is possible between population groups having different legal traditions, values and expectations. That these groups have been largely identified as *national* populations might even be a relatively inessential detail of the comparatists' general project. The European private law focus, discussed earlier, may not be wholly satisfactory for debating general approaches to legal similarity and difference, but it at least illustrates that comparative law has a role in analysing the development of law *within* a legal system (in this case, that of the European Union) as well as between national systems. Equally, since comparatists have long been familiar with different degrees of power, influence or prestige operating between the legal systems they compare, there should be no particular difficulty in recognising an interaction of more or less powerful, influential or prestigious bodies of law derived from different cultural sources in the same political society. For example, among British Muslims, an unofficial 'living law' reflecting Islamic traditions (*angrezi shari'at*) now exists alongside official state law as a significant form of normative regulation in certain contexts (Pearl and Menski, 1998: chapter 3; and Menski, 2001).

Thus, what started out in this chapter as an analogy between debates on multi-culturalism and debates in comparative law becomes, in these circumstances, no longer just an analogy but rather a range of contexts for considering *the same set of problems* focused on negotiating legal similarity and legal difference.

The idea that comparative law's main concerns are with seeking similarity (unification, harmonisation) seems narrow and increasingly out of touch with changing legal experience, when law is required to recognise changing popula-tions, diverse cultures in nation states, and new issues about the relations between law, religion and tradition. Law is faced with representing or managing difference in legal *aspirations* no less than with promoting similarity in legal experience. Questions about national sentiment and diversity of cultural allegiances are also becoming legally significant (as matters bearing on law's practical claims to authority) in a far more obvious way than in past decades. In a culturally complex world, allegiances (to law as to most other embodiments of authority) become complex and multiple. Yet, as we noted earlier in discussing conditions of multi-culturalism, something is needed to hold the diverse elements together. To address these newly pressing issues about law and culture, comparative law must adjust its gaze. Like other legal studies it needs to abandon its attachment to an exclusive focus on the nation state. The great virtue of an emphasis on cultural difference is that it points towards a far richer comparative law, aware of the way the world is changing beyond (and more profoundly than) the transnational extension of economic networks and the ever quickening pace of world commerce.

How is this richer comparative law to be realised? Legrand's own insistence that comparatists should privilege difference is certainly not limited to his attacks on the harmonisation of European law. But where he goes beyond this focus (Legrand, 2005) his statements about what comparative law should be doing, and why, become vague. The 'contrarian challenge' sometimes seems to come down to a general exhortation to respect the other and to study law with the aid of history, philosophy and sociology. This is important but does not take us far. The reason, I think, for the lack of specificity is a reluctance to explore exactly where a focus on cultural difference in law leads.

Ultimately it must lead to the study of culture itself, with all the problems that entails. Indeed, where culture has become a focus for critical legal theory (espe-cially in American critical race theory) it is significant that lines between legal and social analysis tend to blur. The need to assert cultural difference in all its complex manifestations is so pressing for critical race theorists that legal aspects are some-times reduced to just one aspect—a specific, limited expression—of diffuse but pervasive social experience (see, eg Delgado and Stefancic, 2000). For comparatists, however, the reason for invoking culture is likely to be to understand differences specifically in *juristic* practice and experience. For Legrand, the essential cultural difference is even narrower, namely, a difference between common law and civil law juristic practice. The appeal to culture seems to be reduced to a restatement of comparatists' familiar distinctions between legal styles or 'families' of law. It is left to legal sociologists to point out the sheer complexity of exploring how modern legal and cultural experience inter-relate in practice, and how culture in its many aspects shapes legal understandings (Nelken, 2005; and Nelken, 2003).

VI. HOW CAN WE STUDY CULTURAL DIFFERENCE IN LAW?

This is not to suggest that when lawyers recognise cultural difference they invariably stop short of considering the broadest horizons that this recognition opens up. Sometimes, attempts to study foreign law raise such profound challenges of cultural 'otherness', that scholars of this law become 'area' specialists, immersing themselves fully in the cultural matrix of a particular area of the world (for example, China, India or South East Asia) and trying to explore this matrix 'from inside' so as to assign meaning to its legal aspects as these are understood within it. But this entails that these scholars often do not see themselves as comparatists, since their exploration of law *within* culture has largely taken the place of interpreting law across cultures (Huxley, 2002: 5). Comparative legal study, however, involves not giving up on the possibility of translating experience across cultural difference. There has to be a way of appreciating (interpreting and understanding) difference; not merely observing strangeness.

Here the task seems much harder than that of seeking similarity by harmonising law. Harmonisers assume that a common framework of understanding is available and that their task is to find and use this. The task of the difference-focused comparatists, however, is somehow to understand without such a common framework, without assimilating the unfamiliar to the familiar. Cultural comparatists write of the 'impossibility of perfect comparison' since each 'cultural context is unique to some extent' (Curran, 1998: 43 at 45, 49). However, the aim is communication and empathy; a matter of understanding the experience, sentiments and beliefs of the other (Ewald, 1995: 1889 at 1941–2). For Legrand, appreciating difference involves 'thick or deep understanding' (Legrand, 2003: 280, 289, 297). For the American comparatist Vivian Curran it entails imaginative 'immersion' in the foreign cultural context (Curran, 1998). But these formulations do not clarify the preconditions and limits of these strategies, or how to distinguish good comparisons from poor ones.

We have seen that reliance on the concept of culture itself adds further difficulties. Culture tends to be treated as a unity rather than analysed into distinct components, which might have some structured relation to each other (see Archer, 1985) and be more manageable entities for comparison. Nevertheless, culturally-focused comparative law opens up exciting possibilities if ways can be found to break down culture into components that can be compared in their relations to law and if the methodological difficulties are always kept in mind, so that comparatists are modest in their claims to be able to understand 'the other' and the other's law. The findings of cultural comparative law will always be provisional, partial and contested—yet they may still be enlightening and thought-provoking, perhaps not just for the researcher's 'home' audience, but even for the foreigners whose law is being studied.

Some ambitious recent work by an American comparatist illustrates the kind of enlightenment that might be hoped for, as well as the difficulties discussed above. James Whitman, in a series of major articles, has studied profound differences between United States law and continental European law in terms of what he sees as contrasting cultural values underlying significant parts of this law. Because he focuses on fundamental values—primarily 'liberty' in the American case and (human) 'dignity' in the European context—he implicitly breaks down the idea of culture, taking one set of elements from it for consideration. I have argued elsewhere that culture (for the purposes of legal inquiry) is made up of distinct elements that can be roughly summarised as shared ultimate values or beliefs, common traditions and experiences, collective sentiments, and common or convergent (primarily economic) projects (Cotterrell, 2006a). What is important is to distinguish the components of culture analytically and to explore their ramifications when they are expressed in or addressed by law. Whitman's approach might, then, be promising in avoiding generalised appeals to culture and concentrating on the element of values; asking what meaning is given to these values in different contexts and how they are expressed in positive law.

Whitman's starting point is a regret expressed by some American legal scholars about the difficulties of introducing European-style 'hate speech' legislation in the United States to criminalise the use of calculatedly insulting or inflammatory words. In America, he explains, the legal value of freedom of speech trumps most efforts to control hate speech. A main reason, for Whitman, is that the United States lacks a 'culture of dignity', found notably in Germany and France, which has underpinned controls on hate speech in these and other European countries.

In a 120-page essay (Whitman, 2000) he explores the sources and effects of this culture of dignity, finding its origins in old conceptions of social hierarchy and of the protection of aristocratic honour, for example through duelling. These conceptions gave rise to penal laws (still existing in Germany) to protect individuals from insult and affront to their dignity. Legal provisions that once protected aristocratic honour and ensured due deference were gradually transformed by a process of social 'levelling-up' into laws protecting the honour and dignity of every citizen from insult. In France, dignitary law, as Whitman calls it, has atrophied as a distinct form but the culture of dignity remains strong, expressed in forms of civility notably different from those typical in the United States. Thus Whitman's argument—developed through an elaborate presentation of relevant law and social norms—is that European ideas of human dignity, fundamental to continental legal culture, are traceable to old European conceptions of social hierarchy. The United States lacks any such legal emphasis on individual dignity because its social and legal history is different. Lacking a tradition of aristocracy, it also lacks a legal concept of human dignity.

In other writings Whitman has continued to emphasise a sharp contrast between American and continental European legal cultures. He notes, for example, that attitudes to privacy differ greatly between the United States and continental Europe. Americans and Europeans care deeply about privacy, as their law shows, but in different ways. Compared to French and German law, American law provides relatively little commercial privacy (for example, as regards credit ratings) but treats the privacy of the home as sacrosanct (in Europe wire-tapping has been much less of a legal issue than in the United States). The American focus is overwhelmingly on privacy against the state and on the protection of commercial interests. American law recognises a 'right of publicity', essentially to control the commercial exploitation of one's image and related matters. In continental European systems, law gives rights to control the use of one's image on the grounds of protection of human dignity. It is an aspect of personal dignity and autonomy to have a legal right to choose whether and how one's image is used. In the United States the right to free speech (often, in practice, exercised by the mass media and other commercial interests) invariably triumphs over claims of human dignity but, in continental Europe, the former is always balanced against the latter through the assertion of rights to 'dignity', 'honour' or 'personality' (Whitman, 2004: 1151 at 1197). In summary:

> Europeans are consistently more drawn to problems touching on public dignity, while Americans are consistently more drawn to problems touching on the depredations of the state (*ibid*: at 1163).[7]

In a brief discussion it is impossible to represent the detailed legal analysis that accompanies Whitman's arguments about American and continental European legal cultures.[8] What is important here is to note how ambitious these arguments are. They range over large areas of positive law and do not confine themselves within orthodox juristic fields. Positivist comparatists might scorn such wide generalisations about legal cultural difference (despite the considerable legal doctrinal detail offered) as well as about categories such as 'dignitary law' that are not juristically recognised in the legal systems studied. Again, it might be asked what the scope of Whitman's arguments is intended to be: for example, how much of the legal idea of human dignity he considers to be traceable specifically to old norms of social honour (Neuman, 2003). The cultural and legal canvasses on which he paints are obviously vast.

---

[7] On contrasts between legal values of 'liberty' in the United States and of 'dignity' in Germany, see also Eberle, 2002.

[8] See also Friedman and Whitman, 2003, arguing that the legal concept of sexual harassment, imported from American law, is being transformed in some continental European countries into a more general concept of 'moral harassment' centred on protection of employees' dignity in the workplace.

There is a more fundamental problem, however. How far can Whitman, as a cultural 'outsider', understand the European legal culture(s) he studies? Europeans may well recognise the sources of important elements of their legal culture in old ideas of social hierarchy, yet see a fundamental distinction between the old law of insult and more pervasive modern ideas of human dignity. They may trace the latter much more directly, for example, to reactions to the experience of war and destruction in 20th century Europe. Again, there may be debate about Whitman's understanding of civility. When he talks of European ideas of civility as based on a 'levelling up' of requirements of respect and honour he sees 'some vision of hierarchical superiority' surviving in them (Whitman, 2000: 1279 at 1331).

> Respect has, at its heart, something to do with superiority and inferiority' (*ibid*: at 1332) and the promise of dignity is for 'most people, most of the time ... a promise that they will be regarded as better than somebody else (Whitman, 2003b: 265).

Thus, he sees something false in European civility. An

> outward show of respect ... a realm of form and not of inner conviction, a realm of purely ritual self-abasement' rather than 'the sincere acknowledgement of the equality of others. (Whitman, 2000: 1279 at 1291).

By contrast, American manners focus on the latter. They represent, for Whitman, a 'levelling down' to a basic social equality reflected in informality and directness in social contacts.

As cultural observation this is surely interesting but matters could be seen differently. A European view might be that, in essence, civility is not about social equality or inequality at all. It is about treating the other as a fellow human being with whom it is necessary to co-exist and who must therefore be shown respect simply to avoid friction and ease the processes of social interaction. European civility does not *need* to be characterised (as in Whitman's account) as somehow false. In fact, ostensibly respectful treatment is unlikely to be viewed as civility if perceived to be false. But neither is it an affirmation of social position. It is possible to have civility between social unequals (and this is culturally valued) no less than between equals. It may be important for civility to be *neutral* as regards social status.

Perhaps, indeed, Whitman's interpretation reflects his own American cultural heritage of (presumed) social equality and what he himself characterises as American incomprehension of European ideas of civility. More fundamentally, following his own arguments about a contrast between American and European cultural values, European understandings of civility may be coloured by a sense of human dignity as a value, while American understandings of civility may be coloured by a corresponding sense of liberty and of the social equality (of opportunity) needed to enjoy it.

I raise these very speculative matters only to illustrate that comparative studies of fundamental legal values (as, probably, of other aspects of culture in relation to law) can never be conclusive, but only suggestive. Clearly there can be no standpoint outside culture from which to pursue comparative legal studies. But this insurmountable problem does not destroy the interest or significance of studies of legal culture. They may contribute to the intercultural conversation that leading cultural comparatists advocate. Unless done with immense sensitivity and a real desire for empathy, these studies may provoke irritation, or worse, from those who see the foreign culture under scrutiny as their own. And there can be no way of escaping the imprecision of the concept of culture itself. For all these reasons cultural comparative law is likely to be enduringly risky. It will not measure up to the protocols of rigour that positivist legal analysis demands. It may seem impractical and unfocused in its objectives when set alongside some of the business-like efforts of comparatist harmonisers, but the potential of cultural studies of legal difference for allowing a bolder spirit of curiosity to flourish in comparative law might be some considerable consolation. These studies might be seen as vehicles through which comparatists can take on again the mantle of humanist scholars analysing law as a rich cultural creation. If we can no longer believe in the promises of a universal natural law rooted in human nature and experience, it might be possible to believe in the possibility and validity of a study, through comparative law, of the infinitely rich varieties of human experience and their specifically legal expressions.

QUESTIONS FOR DISCUSSION

1. Has comparative law been more interested in 'seeking similarity' between laws and legal systems, or in 'appreciating difference' between them? What factors have inclined it towards one or other of these emphases?
2. Why does Legrand think that harmonisation of laws in Europe cannot be achieved? Is it, as he claims, wrong even to try to work towards this harmonisation?
3. How should comparative lawyers understand the concept of culture? What aspects of culture are most significant in affecting legal development?
4. How useful is the analogy between debates about multiculturalism and debates in comparative law about the merits of harmonisation of laws?
5. How far is it possible for people—including comparative lawyers—to understand a culture different from their own? What methods should they use in trying to do so?
6. Is it a worthwhile general aim today to try to reduce differences between legal systems, legal styles or legal cultures?
7. Is the study of fundamental legal values a potentially fruitful approach in comparative law?

BIBLIOGRAPHY AND FURTHER READING

Alba, R and Nee, V (2003) *Remaking the American Mainstream: Assimilation and Contemporary Immigration* (Cambridge, MA, Harvard University Press).
Archer, MS (1985) 'The Myth of Cultural Integration' 36 *British Journal of Sociology* 333.

Aristotle, *Nicomachean Ethics* bk V.

Cotterrell, R (2003) *The Politics of Jurisprudence: A Critical Introduction to Legal Philosophy*, 2nd edn (Oxford, Oxford University Press).

—— (2006a) *Law, Culture and Society: Legal Ideas in the Mirror of Social Theory* (Aldershot, Ashgate).

—— (2006b) 'Comparative Law and Legal Culture' in R Zimmermann and M Reimann (eds), *Oxford Handbook of Comparative Law* (Oxford, Oxford University Press).

Curran, VG (1998) 'Cultural Immersion, Difference and Categories in US Comparative Law' 46 *American Journal of Comparative Law* 43.

Del Vecchio, G (1969) 'The Unity of the Human Mind as a Basis for Comparative Legal Study' in RA Newman (ed), *Man and Nature: Selected Essays of Giorgio Del Vecchio* (Notre Dame, University of Notre Dame Press).

Delgado, R and Stefancic, J (eds) (2000) *Critical Race Theory: The Cutting Edge*, 2nd edn (Philadelphia, PA, Temple University Press).

Demleitner, NV (1999) 'Combating Legal Ethnocentrism: Comparative Law Sets Boundaries' 31 *Arizona State Law Journal* 737.

Eberle, EJ (2002) *Dignity and Liberty: Constitutional Visions in Germany and the United States* (Westport, CT, Praeger).

Ewald, W (1995) 'Comparative Jurisprudence (I): What Was It Like to Try a Rat?' 143 *University of Pennsylvania Law Review* 1889.

Friedman, GS and Whitman, JQ (2003) 'The European Transformation of Harassment Law: Discrimination versus Dignity' 9 *Columbia Journal of European Law* 241.

Hesselink, MW (2004) 'The European Commission's Action Plan: Towards a More Coherent European Contract Law?' 12 *European Review of Private Law* 397.

Huxley, A (2002) 'Introduction' in A Huxley (ed), *Religion, Law and Tradition: Comparative Studies in Religious Law* (London, Routledge-Curzon).

Jacoby, R (1994) 'The Myth of Multiculturalism' 208 *New Left Review* (1st series) 121.

Jamin, C (2002) 'Saleilles' and Lambert's Old Dream Revisited' 50 *American Journal of Comparative Law* 701.

Stein, P (1980) *Legal Evolution: The Story of an Idea* (Cambridge, Cambridge University Press).

Lando, O (1999) 'Optional or Mandatory Europeanisation of Contract Law' in S Feiden and CU Schmid (eds), *Evolutionary Perspectives and Projects on Harmonisation of Private Law in the EU*, EUI Working Paper LAW 99/7 (Florence, European University Institute).

Legrand, P (1996) 'European Legal Systems are not Converging' 45 *International and Comparative Law Quarterly* 52.

—— (1997) 'Against a European Civil Code' 60 *Modern Law Review* 44.

—— (2001) 'The Return of the Repressed: Moving Comparative Legal Studies Beyond Pleasure' 75 *Tulane Law Review* 1033.

—— (2003) 'The Same and the Different' in P Legrand and R Munday (eds), *Comparative Legal Studies: Traditions and Transitions* (Cambridge, Cambridge University Press).

—— (2005) 'Paradoxically, Derrida: For a Comparative Legal Studies' 27 *Cardozo Law Review* 631.

—— (2006) 'Antivonbar' 1 *Journal of Comparative Law* 13.

Lepaulle, P (1922) 'The Function of Comparative Law' 35 *Harvard Law Review* 838.

Menski, WF (2001) 'Muslim Law in Britain' 62 *Journal of Asian and African Studies* 127.

Neuman, G (2003) 'On Fascist Honour and Human Dignity: A Sceptical Response' in C Joerges and NS Ghaleigh (eds), *Darker Legacies of Law in Europe: The Shadow of National Socialism over Europe and its Legal Traditions* (Oxford, Hart Publishing).

Nelken, D (2003) 'Beyond Compare? Criticising "The American Way of Law"' 28 *Law and Social Inquiry* 799.

—— (2005) 'Doing Research in Comparative Criminal Justice' in R Banakar and M Travers (eds), *Theory and Method in Socio-Legal Research* (Oxford, Hart Publishing).

Pearl, D and Menski, W (1998) *Muslim Family Law*, 3rd edn (London, Sweet and Maxwell).

Shah, P (2005) *Legal Pluralism in Conflict: Coping with Cultural Diversity in Law* (London, Glasshouse).

Teubner, G (1998) 'Legal Irritants: Good Faith in British Law or How Unifying Law Ends Up in New Divergences' 61 *Modern Law Review* 11.

Van der Pijl, K (2006) 'Lockean Europe?' 37 *New Left Review* (2nd series) 9.

Von Bar, C, Lando, O and Swann, S (2002) 'Communication on European Contract Law: Joint Response of the Commission on European Contract Law and the Study Group on a European Civil Code' 10 *European Review of Private Law* 183.

Wacker, AF (1979) 'Assimilation and Cultural Pluralism in American Social Thought' 40 *Phylon* 325.

Watson, A (1983) 'Legal Change: Sources of Law and Legal Culture' 131 *University of Pennsylvania Law Review* 1121.

Weatherill, S (2004) 'Why Object to the Harmonisation of Private Law by the EC?' 12 *European Review of Private Law* 633.

Whitman, JQ (2000) 'Enforcing Civility and Respect: Three Societies' 109 *Yale Law Journal* 1279.

—— (2003a) 'The Neo-Romantic Turn' in P Legrand and R Munday (eds), *Comparative Legal Studies: Traditions and Transitions* (Cambridge, Cambridge University Press).

—— (2003b) 'On Nazi "Honour" and the New European "Dignity"' in C Joerges and NS Ghaleigh (eds), *Darker Legacies of Law in Europe: The Shadow of National Socialism over Europe and its Legal Traditions* (Oxford, Hart Publishing).

—— (2004) 'Two Western Cultures of Privacy: Dignity versus Liberty' 113 *Yale Law Journal* 1151.

Wieacker, F (1990) 'Foundations of European Legal Culture' 38 *American Journal of Comparative Law* 1.

Wilhelmsson, T (2002) 'The Legal, the Cultural and the Political—Conclusions from Different Perspectives on Harmonisation of European Contract Law' *European Review of Business Law* 541.

Zimmermann, R (1996) 'Savigny's Legacy: Legal History, Comparative Law and the Emergence of a European Legal Science' 112 *Law Quarterly Review* 576.

Zweigert, K and Kötz, H (1998) *An Introduction to Comparative Law*, 3rd edn (trans) T Weir (Oxford, Clarendon Press).

7

The Economic Approach: Competition between Legal Systems

ANTHONY OGUS

KEY CONCEPTS

Efficient and efficiency; Competition between legal systems; Heterogeneous demand for law; Homogeneous demand for law; Artificial product differentiation; Network.

I. INTRODUCTION: ECONOMICS AND LAW

THE STARTING POINT for this chapter is the obvious fact that the legal framework has an enormous impact on the economy, national and global. Economic historians have demonstrated how some of the key characteristics of a legal system have helped to facilitate and sustain economic growth. From this, the intriguing possibility arises that the causal link between the law and the economy can be traced in the *opposite* direction: if certain types of law facilitate economic growth, then perhaps the pursuit of economic growth can help to explain legal developments. If this causal connection can plausibly be established, then understanding the economic functions of law can make a major contribution to comparative law, for example, by explaining why, in some areas, convergences between legal systems occur.

Economists use the word 'efficient' to indicate arrangements and processes which maximise economic welfare.[1] In tracing the possibility that the law in different jurisdictions is driven, or at least influenced, by a concern to reach efficient outcomes, we should distinguish between the two principal instruments for legal development: legislation and case-law. And we ought also to recognise that in both forms of law-making, the economic goal will have to compete with other goals, for example a desire to redress or control outcomes which are regarded as unfair or

---

[1] More particularly 'allocatively efficient', which applies to maximising welfare in a given society, to be distinguished from 'productively efficient', which means maximising output for a given individual or firm. See Ogus, 2006: 26–7.

unjust—these goals are sometimes referred to collectively as 'distributional justice'. Now, of course, the importance to be attributed to efficiency, relative to distributional justice, may well vary not only between legislature and judges but also between different jurisdictions. That would mean that, politically or ideologically, it is considered desirable in certain jurisdictions to sacrifice some economic growth to achieve greater fairness in society. For example, it might be the case that the history of civil law systems reveals a greater readiness to protect consumers against traders than that of common law systems.

Nevertheless, it is not always easy to identify the extent to which the law-making process adopts or reflects particular goals. First, law-makers (politicians and judges) are not always explicit about their aims and objectives. Secondly, even if they are explicit, the statement of goals may disguise the true intent. Indeed, an important economic theory (known as 'public choice') suggests that much legislation has little to do with general goals such as efficiency or distributional justice; rather it serves to advance the interests of those groups who are most successful in lobbying politicians. In such cases, there may be insufficient transparency to detect the private interest motivation.

We should note also the possibility that the law might evolve spontaneously towards efficiency, without this being the conscious aim of law-makers. The political-economist Hayek famously argued that customary law, as developed particularly in common law jurisdictions, has this spontaneous effect because judges seek in general to match the law to the expectations of citizens (von Hayek, 1973–79). Other evolutionary theorists have, in a similar vein, argued that the processes of litigation lead to the same outcome because litigants will tend, in general, to appeal against inefficient rules, rather than efficient rules, and thus, over time, efficient rules will survive better than inefficient rules: the 'efficiency of the common law theory' (Priest, 1977).

II. THE LAW AND ECONOMIC GROWTH

Some early writers on political economy perceived the importance of law for economic welfare. Hobbes, for example, recognised that if entrepreneurs lacked confidence in the coercive power of the state to enforce contracts, they would not enter into trade; and Adam Smith recognised that 'a tolerable administration of justice' was an important condition to carry a state to 'the highest degree of opulence' (Smith, 1980: 322). More from an historical and sociological perspective, Max Weber found that economic development was a consequence of formal and 'rational' legal systems.

In modern times, there has been much focus on how adherence to the 'rule of law' facilitates economic development. Although the 'rule of law' has been given a variety of meanings, it must clearly be distinguished from 'rule by law', which implies mainly that law is used as an instrument of governmental power and perhaps also for resolving disputes. As linked to the familiar concept of 'law and order', a system so characterised may be one subservient to tyrannical and arbitrary government and may not be conducive to trade and commerce. The 'rule of law' which has been shown to facilitate economic growth (Keefer and Knack, 1997) tends to have the following features:

- rules published and thus knowable in advance
- mechanisms ensuring the application of rules without discrimination
- binding decisions by an independent judiciary
- (a minimum) recognition of basic human rights
- compliance by the government and its officials with relevant rules

What then of private law? What features have had a particularly strong impact on the economy? In comparing economic development in different European countries, economic historians have found an explanation in the ability of the private law framework to generate effective incentives for creative and productive activity. This meant in particular the extent to which contract law could generate mutual trust in commercial transactions and to which property rights could ensure an adequate return on investment.

Now since all legal systems, however primitive, have some set of contractual and property rights, the crucial question is how well they are able to adapt to changing conditions. This is a matter not only of the capacity of the system to broaden its parameters to embrace, for example, intellectual property; it is also a question of doing so at relatively low cost. Put succinctly, the benefits arising from legal instruments must exceed the costs of using them.

Take, first, the benefits of legal developments responding to technological or other changes. When agricultural land was used mainly to support the local community, a system of common ownership was unproblematic. But with the growth of markets and the need to specialise, advantages were to be secured from the enclosure of the land and the amalgamation of smaller units. Property law, which inhibited enclosure or insisted on the physical division of land for inheritance purposes, would thus hinder economic growth. Then, in response to technological development, industry became more dependent on large-scale capital investment and organisations. No doubt, existing systems of property and contract rights could be applied, but the key to success lay in devices for reducing the costs of applying appropriate legal instruments. The legal system required mechanisms which could, at low cost, finance transactions (eg negotiable instruments), spread risk (insurance) and, most importantly, underpin legal organisations by arrangements which, while generating a sufficient return for entrepreneurs, would ensure the effective monitoring of inputs to the profit-making enterprise (limited liability corporations).

The extent to which, in a particular jurisdiction, these developments may have occurred faster or slower depended on a variety of factors related to legal culture and the law-making process. For comparative lawyers the intriguing questions arise whether the common law or the Romano-Germanic systems have been, in this regard, more or less successful, and what characteristics of the legal culture have had an important impact on economic growth.

It has, for a long time, been recognised that the English common law, through its development of banking and insurance, the joint-stock company and patent law, was conducive to the economic developments that became known as the 'industrial revolution'. Studies also suggest that countries adopting legal institutions from within the common law tradition have experienced, in more recent times, faster growth than those countries drawing on the civil law tradition.

If these generalisations are accepted, what characteristics of the common law culture might provide the explanation? At a very general level, it should be noted that civil law countries have been more identified with government intervention in the market than common law countries. Of course, to a large extent, this reflects political ideology, but the determinants of political ideology and legal culture might not be that far apart. Take the following hallmarks of traditional common law culture:

- non-career judges
- greater use of juries and non-professional judges
- greater reliance on customary law and precedent
- less reliance on legislation and codification
- oral rather than written processes

Most of them are consistent with the idea that the administration of justice should be decentralised and thus further removed from the heavy hand of government, which can so often constrain economic development.

III. COMPETITION BETWEEN NATIONAL LEGAL SYSTEMS

The economic perspective has, in recent times, generated important insights into the relationship between legal developments in different jurisdictions through the idea of there being some degree of competition between legal systems. The idea is relatively simple and is drawn from the way that markets for ordinary products and services operate. If suppliers of (say) teddy bears have to compete with one another, consumers can choose by reference to how each supplier's combination of price and quality meets their preferences. Provided that information about the available options is readily available, this should lead to the production of what consumers want at lowest cost. In a sense, and to a certain degree, a democratic system of government functions in this way: political parties compete by offering different programmes to match what the voting population may desire.

It might seem strange to think in terms of legal subjects (individuals and firms) having a choice between different legal orders: the legislature in any one jurisdiction normally has the monopoly of law-making powers. Nevertheless, there may be some limited competition between that legislature and the courts and also between different court systems with overlapping jurisdictions, such as famously occurred between the common law and chancery courts before the 19th century. Once we introduce transactions involving more than one jurisdiction, the issue of competition between legal sources becomes less artificial and, with the increased mobility of enterprises and the globalisation of markets of modern times, it has become quite significant.

Take, first, the decisions of large firms where to site their business. Subject to their freedom to do so, they will want to establish in the jurisdiction which best meets their preferences, regarding the security of their employees and assets, and those aspects of local conditions which best enhance their profit-making capacity. A number of different considerations are involved, amongst which may feature the legal system, and the costs which the local law imposes on their business. For their part, governments are also interested in attracting large firms to their jurisdiction because that is likely to generate more employment as well as increased tax revenue.

Secondly, to some extent, the principles of private international law enable firms and individuals to select a legal system to govern their transaction or business, even though the connection with the jurisdiction may not be very strong. The freedom, subject to public policy constraints, of parties to an international contract to choose the law to apply to the contract constitutes the classic example. There is, indeed, a long tradition of foreigners selecting English law to govern their contract and submitting to the jurisdiction of the English courts even where the transaction has no particular connection with the UK. So too, if only to a lesser extent, corporations may be 'registered' in a jurisdiction, and therefore be subject to its law, even if the firm has no major physical presence there: in the United States the State of Delaware famously attracts a large number of firms to its corporate law regime.

Clearly there are also advantages to the local legal profession in having its legal system adopted in this way. It will normally lead to more work for them and therefore an increased income. Moreover, because of their technical legal expertise, relevant members of those professions are likely to be able to influence local law-makers to adapt law to meet the preferences of those who will create more business for them.

To observe this process of competition in practice, take the case of *Trendex Trading Corporation v Central Bank of Nigeria.*[2] A Nigerian bank was sued for defaulting on a commercial letter of credit. It invoked the principle of sovereign immunity because of its close connection to the Nigerian government. A majority of the Court of Appeal held that even if the bank were to be regarded as a department of government it could not claim immunity in respect of a purely commercial transaction. This ruling followed judicial developments in Belgium, Germany, The Netherlands and the United States, rather than a long line of English authorities. Recognising the importance of the decision for those adopting English law in contracts, Lord Denning, MR observed [1977] QB at 556:

> Whenever a change is made, someone some time has to make the first move. One country alone may start the process. Others may follow. At first a trickle, then a stream, last a flood. England should not be left behind on the bank … 'We must take the current when it serves, or lose our ventures': Julius Caesar, Act IV, sc. III.

---

[2] *Trendex Trading Corporation v Central Bank of Nigeria* [1977] QB 529 (CA).

Note, too, that even without the possibility of physical mobility or the operation of choice of law clauses, a comparison of domestic law with its foreign counterpart may show that local industry is legally disadvantaged relative to its international competitors. For example, if the industry has to comply with stringent regulation governing the safety of its products or services, its costs will be higher and therefore so also will be its prices. Representatives from that industry then might apply pressure to politicians within the jurisdiction to alleviate the burden.

In summary, some degree of competition between national legal systems can be envisaged when those who are the subject of law—firms and individuals—have an effective choice as to the legal regimes which should govern their affairs. To this may be added a further proposition: the more the legal subjects are engaged in transboundary activities, the more likely that they will have an effective choice of legal regime. In the case of a sale of goods between parties within a single jurisdiction, it may be theoretically possible for them to select the law of another jurisdiction to govern their transaction, but it is very unlikely they will do so, given that they will both normally incur higher costs in nominating a foreign jurisdiction. In an international sale of goods, by hypothesis, there is no single jurisdiction which unites the two parties in this way. It follows, too, that there are areas of law that are less likely to deal with transboundary activity—such as land law—and in relation to which, therefore, there will be less competition between jurisdictions.

IV. CONSEQUENCES OF COMPETITION: DIVERGENCE AND CONVERGENCE

What consequences are likely to flow from competition between legal systems? Will there be (as Lord Denning's observation suggests) a convergence of legal principles by means of imitation and transplants? Or will differences remain and perhaps even increase? To answer these questions, we need to have regard to two key factors: the area of law concerned; and possible barriers to transplants and convergence.

Provided that there is a democratic basis to, or inspiration for, law-making, legal developments occurring in a particular jurisdiction are likely to reflect preferences, values and generally-held opinions in that jurisdiction. In some areas of law, the preferences, values and opinions are going to differ sharply between jurisdictions even though they may be close both geographically and in economic development. For example, a jurisdiction (say) in Southern Europe, which is influenced by the Roman Catholic church is unlikely to share the same set of values regarding family relationships and therefore family law as (say) a jurisdiction in northern Europe where the influence of religion on legal policy-making is much smaller. Nor, from the United Kingdom, do we have to travel very far to find a jurisdiction, namely France, which offers a far more generous set of laws governing the compensation of road accident victims; and that difference must reflect a divergence in social values.

Now, competition may exert some pressure on national law-makers even in areas such as these. Single sex couples may be attracted to living and working in countries where there relationship is to some degree formalised; and there is even an argument that tourism may be boosted by laws more favourable to less common lifestyles (Brown, 1996: 271–4). More generous road accident compensation provision leads to higher transport costs for industry in France, compared to England, and may result in competitive pressure from that source. Nevertheless, these competitive forces, if they exist at all, are unlikely to be significant relative to the strength of opinion that underpins the legal differences. Putting this another way, and using the language of economics, the demand for the law governing these areas is 'heterogeneous'. Note, too, that the law governing such areas tends to be interventionist law, that is, law which imposes outcomes, according to the public policy adopted. In summary, competition among suppliers of interventionist law, reflecting heterogeneous demand, is unlikely to result in a convergence of legal principles.

In contrast, law can also be facilitative, that is, rather than imposing policy determined outcomes, it accepts—indeed reinforces—what individuals and firms want and protects expectations by rending the desired outcomes legally enforceable. The classic example of facilitative law is contract, but parts of company law and property law also fit into this category. The demand for facilitative law is predominantly homogenous, rather than heterogeneous: that is, the preference of those wishing to invoke the law is unlikely to vary significantly across jurisdictional boundaries. Those making contracts in Greece or Portugal basically have the same desire as their equivalents in Britain or Sweden, that the consensually approved outcome should be reached at minimum cost. The qualification 'at minimum cost' is important, because if one legal system provides the legal means of achieving the desired outcome at a significantly higher cost than another legal system and the parties are free to choose the latter to govern their contract, then they will be motivated to do so. If other contracting parties have the same perception and act in the same way, the jurisdiction with the higher set of costs will lose legal business and the law-makers there will be under pressure from legal practitioners to reform the law.

To give an example, suppose that a seller in Jurisdiction A enters into a contract with a buyer from Jurisdiction B. In the event of a serious breach, both parties would prefer that the party not in breach would be able to terminate the contract without a formal judicial decision to that effect. Suppose that Jurisdiction A permits such unilateral termination, but in Jurisdiction B termination normally requires a judicial decision. Subject to other considerations, it is in the interests of the parties to select Jurisdiction A in their choice of law clause. If there is a reduced demand for the more costly rule in Jurisdiction B, competition between the two legal systems will generate pressure for the formalistic approach in Jurisdiction B to be abandoned, and in consequence there will be some convergence between the two legal systems.

The *Trendex Trading* case, described above, is an example of English courts being under competitive pressure to change the law in favour of an approach adopted abroad. Another interesting area of convergence is that of the trust. In comparison with civil law equivalents, the Anglo-American trust concept has proved to be a very cost-efficient device for certain types of financial transactions, and civilian systems have been under pressure, at the very least, to recognise the existence of the concept under the rules of private international law and, in some cases, to assimilate the device. As an Italian jurist has observed: the 'trust has obtained an easy and well-deserved victory in the competition in the market of legal doctrines' (Mattei, 1994: 10).

To summarise: competition between legal systems may be expected to influence legal developments, but not necessarily towards convergence. In areas of law which are predominantly 'interventionist', with rules inspired by public-policy imposing outcomes, there are likely to be differences in public policy values in different jurisdictions and legal rules may thus continue to diverge. Where, on the other hand, the law is predominantly 'facilitative', allowing firms and individuals to determine their own preferred outcomes, some degree of convergence may be anticipated, on the assumption that pressure will be exerted for legal rules which enable those preferred outcomes to be reached at lowest legal cost.

V. TRANSPLANTS AND OBSTACLES TO CONVERGENCE

Convergence, whether or not resulting from competition, normally takes place by one jurisdiction imitating rules or concepts of another jurisdiction, what are sometimes referred to as 'legal transplants'. There has been much discussion in the mainstream comparative law literature on the difficulties of transplanting from one legal culture to another (notably, Kahn-Freund, 1974; and Legrand, 1996). In this part, I wish to explore why there may be economic reasons for such difficulties, and that entails returning to the question whether legal practitioners within a particular jurisdiction will be motivated to support, or rather to oppose legal transplants. The question is important because the legal profession plays a very important role in influencing law-makers on what law reform is, or is not, desirable.

We may start by recognising that practising lawyers can benefit from an increased demand for their services when their legal system is adopted by legal subjects either migrating to the jurisdiction or adopting it under choice of law principles. That might suggest a strategy of facilitating competition between legal systems and supporting reform measures which, as in the *Trendex Trading* example, reduce legal costs in order to attract more legal business. On the other hand, practising lawyers will wish to retain the business emanating from legal subjects already located in the jurisdiction. If competition between legal systems means that the loss of such business exceeds potential gains from 'immigrant' legal business, then legal practitioners will oppose measures which facilitate the competition. For an example, take the continental European approach to choice of law governing a company's existence and internal affairs. Traditionally, this has been dominated by the 'real seat' doctrine, whereby the applicable law is that of the jurisdiction in which the firm's administration is physically situated. This doctrine inhibits freedom in the choice of law, which, as we have seen, has had such an impact in the United States, enabling many corporations to establish legally in Delaware. There is some evidence (Carney, 1997) that a change to the European approach was resisted by the French authorities on the ground that, if greater freedom were to be conferred in where firms could incorporate, chartering business in France would be lost to competing jurisdictions.

Resistance to the international harmonisation of law by practising lawyers from a particular jurisdiction may, indeed, indicate that in the 'market for law' a significant number of those (mainly firms) requiring a legal framework for their activities have a preference for the distinctive set of rules emanating from that jurisdiction. In 1981 the Law Society of England and Wales opposed the Vienna Convention on Contracts for the International Sale of Goods on the ground, inter alia, that it would result in a diminished role for English law within the international trade arena (Lee, 1993: 132).

There is, nevertheless, a possibility that the profit motivation of lawyers who benefit from the demand for legal work in a particular jurisdiction can lead them to exaggerate the peculiarities of the law in that jurisdiction, in order to resist competition from those practising in other jurisdictions. Economists use the expression 'artificial product differentiation' to describe a situation in which a supplier draws attention to unreal or irrelevant differences between a product supplied and those otherwise available in the market, in order to secure a monopolistic position and make enhanced profits. Lawyers everywhere tend to use jargon and procedures which distance them from other professional activities (such as accounting), thereby rendering the content of the law more abstruse than it needs to be and, in consequence, inflating the demand for their services. By parity of reasoning, it is possible to argue that lawyers will be tempted to emphasise the characteristics of their own legal system that are not easily grasped by lawyers from other jurisdictions, in order to create a barrier to competition from those lawyers (Ogus, 2002). And that will, of course, lead them to oppose proposals for harmonising the law that would deprive them of these advantages. When, therefore, comparative lawyers refer to the incompatibility of certain legal cultures that constitute major obstacles to harmonisation, these may be phenomena which exist, which are enhanced by human design, and which have an economic explanation.

VI. LEGAL CULTURE: A NETWORK LIKE THE RAILWAYS?

When the railways were developed in Europe in the 19th century, there was not originally a single system, but a number of different systems scattered geographically, each of them with its own set of technical specifications, notably as regards the distance between the rails. And this diversity led to some degree of competition, in particular between 'narrow-gauge' and 'broad-gauge' railways. As the amount of travel increased and intercommunication between the systems reduced costs, so a struggle for which would be the dominant system emerged, initially within national boundaries and subsequently internationally. Eventually, a single set of specifications was adopted for most of Europe so that, for example, the same rolling stock could be used for a journey between Paris and Istanbul.

Railways constitute what economists call a 'network'. This is a technical system providing links for users of services, such that the greater the number that use it, the greater the value for all of them. (Another example is the fax system. I would be stupid to purchase a fax machine unless many of the people I wish to communicate with also have one; and the more they use it, the more all of us will benefit). As the system becomes more and more popular, so demand tips in its favour, rendering competition by alternative systems less and less effective. Eventually, the system may become so dominant that it acquires monopolistic power, at least for some time, until technological advance generates other possibilities (think of DVDs eventually challenging video systems).

We can think of legal cultures in a similar way. Consider how a legal 'system' emerges. Within any society there will be some individuals or institutions responsible for resolving disputes and perhaps some others responsible for the formulating of rules to deal with such disputes. A particular set of linguistic, conceptual and procedural devices will become conventional for these purposes, and their regular use will reduce the costs of reaching decisions in individual cases. Although within a given society there may be a number of different networks of language, concepts and procedures, as with railways, the attractiveness of one set will enable it to achieve dominance. The greater the number of transactions and disputes adopting a particular set, the higher the expectation that in future other transactions and other disputes will also adopt it. Some competition may continue to exist for some time (think of the rivalry historically in England between the common law and equity), but at least rules will develop for co-ordinating them.

Within a jurisdiction, the monopolistic power of the dominant legal culture is likely to be enhanced by the efforts of legal practitioners, for the profit motive described above (Part V), to reinforce differences with other systems. But what about transactions and other legal relationships that transcend jurisdictional boundaries? We have already seen (Part III above) how parties involved in these are likely, if they have freedom of choice of law to govern the issue, to select the legal system which minimises their costs. That phenomenon might well have the effect of destabilising the (for domestic practising lawyers) profit-generating peculiarities of the legal cultures relevant to the issues involved, because those peculiarities are likely to render adoption of the law from that jurisdiction more costly.

The conclusion to be drawn from this is that those areas of law (for example, sale of goods) which frequently govern interjurisdictional transactions and relationships are likely to be far less marked by distinctive legal cultures than those areas of law (for example, land law) only rarely involved in such trans-actions and relationships. And the analogy with railways is again pertinent. Ordinary railway systems in continental Europe frequently cross national boundaries, and an international set of technical standards superseded national standards. However, urban underground railway systems have, by and large, preserved their own sets of specifications.

VII. HYBRID LEGAL SYSTEMS

In the last part we considered jurisdictions in which there is a single dominant legal culture. We come, finally, to jurisdictions where this is not the case and which comparative lawyers refer to as 'hybrid', 'mixed' or 'pluralistic', because the legal system has absorbed two or more legal cultures. These include juris-dictions (for example in Africa) where one legal culture has been imposed by a colonial power, but where it must 'compete' with a native legal culture. Also, jurisdictions whose legal systems reflect the different legal cultures of succes-sive occupations, for example, Quebec (French and English) and South Africa (Roman-Dutch and English). A third category covers jurisdictions, for example Japan and Turkey, which experienced industrialisation relatively late and which needed to import legal cultures to provide a more sophisticated legal frame-work than native law could supply: indeed, there was some degree of competi-tion between, for example, French and German law, to provide this framework (Örücü, 1999: 80–117).

In considering how hybrid legal systems evolve in the face of competition among legal orders, it is possible to make generalisations which apply to all three categories. So, for example, importing transplants from other legal systems may be assumed to be easier than for jurisdictions of a single dominant legal culture because the existing system is already sufficiently flexible to accommodate differ-ent cultures. We might also expect that in hybrid jurisdictions, legal practitioners will be less able to exploit legal-cultural characteristics in the manner envisaged above in Part V, because some degree of internal competition between the legal cultures will reduce the monopolistic power of the profession to engage in exces-sive jargon and complexities. However, for this to be the case, the competition between the cultures must be real, and not merely hypothetical. Take the cases of Japan and Turkey. The fact that the domestic law-makers could choose between the foreign models did not necessarily mean that the selection would be made by reference to the lowest cost criteria. The selection process could, for example, be heavily influenced by professional groups who had a financial interest in one of the foreign legal cultures, perhaps because they had received training within that tradition. Nevertheless, commercial interests, keen to invest in the jurisdiction, might also apply pressure and that might override the profit-seeking efforts of practising lawyers.

VIII. CONCLUSIONS

The analysis in this chapter can lead to the following conclusions:

- Law is important for economic growth and the goal of economic growth can help to explain legal developments, so also the relationship between developments in different legal systems;
- Common law systems may have features which have been particularly conducive to economic growth;
- Competition between legal systems occurs particularly where there is freedom of choice as to the applicable legal regime;
- Competition between legal systems tends to influence a convergence of legal principles in areas of facilitative law;
- Practising lawyers may be expected to oppose reforms, including proposals for convergence of legal systems, that will reduce the demand for their services;
- An economic interpretation of 'legal culture' suggests that it is a 'network' which may reduce the costs of communication between those using the legal system, but its characteristics may be exploited by practising lawyers to resist competition;
- 'Hybrid' legal systems can benefit from the competition of legal cultures inherent within the jurisdiction.

QUESTIONS FOR DISCUSSION

1. In what ways can law stimulate economic growth?
2. What distinguishing features of the common law and civil law legal traditions might either stimulate, or rather inhibit, economic growth?
3. To what extent, and in what circumstances, is there competition between national legal orders?
4. When is competition between national legal orders likely to lead to a convergence of principles and when to a divergence?
5. How and when might practising lawyers benefit from a convergence of legal principles or from a divergence?
6. In what ways can a legal culture inhibit competition for legal services?
7. Are 'hybrid' legal systems likely to be more or less conducive to competition for legal services than legal systems with a single dominant legal culture?

BIBLIOGRAPHY AND FURTHER READING

Brown, JG (1996) 'Competitive Federalism and Legislative Incentives to Recognize Same-Sex Marriage in the USA' in W Bratton, S Picciotti and C Scott (eds), *International Regulatory Competition and Coordination: Perspectives on Economic Regulation in Europe and the United States* (Oxford, Oxford University Press).

Carney, W (1997) 'The Political Economy of Competition for Corporate Charters' 26 *Journal of Legal Studies* 303.

Eggertsson, T (1990) *Economic Behaviour and Institutions* (Cambridge, Cambridge University Press).

Farber, DA and Frickey, PP (1991) *Law and Public Choice: A Critical Introduction* (Chicago, IL, University of Chicago Press).

Glaeser, E and Shleifer, A (2002) 'Legal Origins' 117 *Quarterly Journal of Economics* 1193.

Kahn-Freund, O (1974) 'On Uses and Misuses of Comparative Law' 37 *Modern Law Review* 1.

Keefer, P and Knack, S (1997) 'Why Don't Poor Countries Catch Up? A Cross-National Test of Institutional Explanation' 35 *Economic Inquiry* 590.

La Porta, R, Lopez-de-Silanes, F, Shleifer, A and Vishny, R (1999) 'The Quality of Government' 15 *Journal of Law, Economics and Organization* 222.

Lee, RG (1993) 'UN Convention on Sale of Goods: OK for the UK?' *Journal of Business Law* 131.

Legrand, P (1996) 'European Legal Systems are not Converging' 45 *International and Comparative Law Quarterly* 52.

Mahoney, P (2001) 'The Common Law and Economic Growth: Hayek Might Be Right' 30 *Journal of Legal Studies* 503.

Mattei, U (1994) 'Efficiency in Legal Transplants: An Essay in Comparative Law and Economics' 14 *International Review of Law and Economics* 3.

—— (1996) *Comparative Law and Economics* (Ann Arbor, MI, University of Michigan Press) ch 4.

North, DC and Thomas, RP (1973) *The Rise of the Western World: A New Economic History* (Cambridge, Cambridge University Press).

Ogus, A (1999) 'Competition between National Legal Systems: A Contribution of Economic Analysis to Comparative Law' 48 *International and Comparative Law Quarterly* 405.

—— (2002) 'The Economic Base of Legal Culture: Networks and Monopolization' 22 *Oxford Journal of Legal Studies* 419

—— (2006) *Costs and Cautionary Tales: Economic Insights for the Law* (Oxford, Hart Publishing).

Örücü, E (1999) *Critical Comparative Law: Considering Paradoxes for Legal Systems in Transition* (Nederlandse Vereniging Voor Rechtsvergelijking).

Priest, GL (1977) 'The Common Law Process and the Selection of Efficient Rules' 6 *Journal of Legal Studies* 65.

Roth, W-H (2003) 'From Centros to Ueberseering: Free Movement of Companies, Private International Law, and Community Law' 52 *International and Comparative Law Quarterly* 177.

Smith, A (1980) in WPD Wightman and JC Bryce (eds), *Essays on Philosophical Subjects* (Oxford, Clarendon Press).

von Hayek, F (1973–79) *Law, Legislation and Liberty* (London, Routledge).

8

A General View of 'Legal Families' and of 'Mixing Systems'*

ESİN ÖRÜCÜ

KEY CONCEPTS

Legal family; Family tree; Tree model; Wave theory; Diffusion; Transposition; Mix; Mixed system; Mixedness; Encounter; Overlap; Combination; Underlay; Overlay; Cross-fertilisation.

I. INTRODUCTION

ONE OF THE conventional tasks of comparative law has been the placing of legal systems in legal families for taxonomic purposes and ease of organisation, although

the idea of a 'legal family' does not correspond to a biological reality; it is no more than a didactic device (David and Brierley, 1985: 21).

However, biological and linguistic taxonomies have been used in classification as organising devices. The practice has been to study legal systems that best represent large groups and then make generalisations based on concepts such as originality, derivation and common elements.[1] Similarities and relationships serve as the bases for classification. The interest in classifications is confined to general characteristics, substance, sources and structure. The essence does not lie in diversity of rules in a given topic, nor in external criteria and context, only in the affinities being considered.

Today, what is needed is an entirely fresh approach within which legal systems can be classified according to parentage, constituent elements and the resulting

---

* This chapter hails from Örücü, 2004b ('Family Trees for Legal Systems: Towards a Contemporary Approach'): 359–75 as well as Örücü, 2004a: ch 10:3.

[1] For a summary of some past efforts at classification see Zweigert and Kötz, 1998: 63–7. See also Bogdan, 1994: 82–91.

blend, and then be re-grouped on the principle of predominance.[2] Although parts of the new landscape may resemble the old, the whole will look very different.

Existing classifications rely on private law, are Euro-centric and therefore heavily weighted towards the civil law and the common law families. Moreover, fixed classifications can have only a limited life-span as legal systems may shift from one cluster towards another, so that the placing of a legal system in the legal families framework may have to be re-thought from time to time (Zweigert and Kötz, 1998: 66). New families may appear. For example, it has been suggested that an 'African legal family' is emerging (*ibid*); and interest in 'mixed jurisdictions' is now increasing, such jurisdictions being seen as members of a so-called 'third family'.[3]

René David talked of 'constant elements' (David and Brierley, 1985: 17–20) and Konrad Zweigert and Hein Kötz proposed using 'legal styles' to discover shared distinctive elements between legal systems (Zweigert and Kötz, 1998: 67–8). However, they also pointed out that

> as the example of 'hybrid' systems shows, any division of the legal world into families, or groups is a rough and ready device (*ibid*: 72).

We are also warned:

> The suitability of any classification will depend upon whether the perspective is world-wide or regional, or whether attention is given to public, private or criminal law (David and Brierley, 1985: 21 and Bogdan, 1994: 85).

Yet in Europe today in search of a 'new *ius commune*', it is commonplace not only to talk of civil law and common law families, but to treat them as if they are the only two monolithic entities. Such an approach is inadequate.

In short: traditional classifications, mostly based on the 'law as rules' approach differ as to whether they simplify or multiply the number of legal families, in how they place various legal families in their schemes, and consider official law and the 'top-down' models exclusively. It might be said that the groupings are all 'legally structured', and 'structure-specific'. An entirely culture-specific approach may not be conclusive, but the relationship between legal and social systems must be given due weight. This indicates the importance of sociology of law to comparative lawyers together with a multi-disciplinary approach.

It is apparent that the 'legal families' division based on the 'law as rules' approach is collapsing. Other approaches are being put forward. One such suggestion, presented as being less biased, is the 'cultural families' division based on the 'law as culture' approach. On this basis four broad cultures have been distinguished: the African, the Asian, the Islamic and Western (that is, cultures with European roots—Europe, America and Oceania) (van Hoecke and Warrington, 1998: 495 at 502).

---

[2] This chapter hails from my 'Family Trees for Legal Systems: Towards a Contemporary Approach' Chapter 18 in van Hoecke (ed) 2004b, 359–375 as well as Örücü, 2004a, Chapter 10:3.
[3] Note the launching of the World Society of Mixed Jurisdiction Jurists in New Orleans (November 2002), and see Palmer, 2001.

Adam Podgorecki places legal systems in ten groups: based on official and intuitive law; based on different types of legitimacy; adequate, guiding and restrictive; monolithic and pluralist; oppressive (including punitive) and tolerant (including liberal); based on state and less formal types of conflict resolutions; self-generated and imposed; accessible and inaccessible; based on religious attitudes of the population; and those rooted in capitalist and communist social reality (Podgorecki, 1985: 3).

Another approach, giving prominence to yet another context, is the 'law and economics' approach. Here we see how Ugo Mattei tries to draw the taxonomy away from the so-called Euro-centric axis to present a new map for the world's legal systems. This classification is based on the rule of professional law, the rule of political law and the rule of traditional law, these three forming a triangle on the apices of which all legal systems can be placed (Mattei, 1997).

Andrew Harding, whose main interest is in South East Asia, categorically tells us that all Eurocentric comparatists fall into the 'legal families trap'. According to him,

[l]egal families tell us nothing about legal systems except as to their general style and method, and the idea makes no sense whatsoever amid the nomic din of South East Asia (Harding, 2002: 36 at 51).

All the above indicates that scholars fail to agree on whether the notion of families is basic and scientific, or theoretically and descriptively useless. Those who use the concept do not even agree on the criteria for classification and groupings.

The discussion might also consider whether there is an emerging 'European legal family', but this would be yet another monolithic approach, a new creation ignoring developments both within and outside Europe.

Recently there has been increasing interest in mixed, or hybrid systems. Vernon Palmer calls 'mixed jurisdictions' the 'third family' (Palmer, 2001)— the first and the second being for him, civil law and common law; and Jan Smits has published a monograph entitled 'The Making of European Private Law: Towards a Ius Commune Europaeum as a Mixed Legal System' (Smits, 2002). To talk of a new family with the name 'mixed jurisdictions', however, would not be satisfactory, as clearly, not all 'mixes' can be pooled together and not all the existing members of such a family would have the same or similar ingredients. It would be extremely difficult to place, for example, Quebec and Algeria—both mixed systems—into one family. The simple mixes, the complex mixes, as well as the dual systems and systems adhering to legal pluralism cannot be lumped together (see Örücü, 1996).

II. ENCOUNTER, OVERLAP AND COMBINATION

Pier Guiseppe Monateri has suggested 'contamination' as the basis for understanding the world of legal systems:

[T]he actual legal world is more to be seen as a world of 'contaminations' than a world split up into different families (Monateri, 1998: 83 at 107).

He claims that this idea is neither new nor linked to globalisation since 'practically every system, even in antiquity has grown through "contaminations"'(*ibid*), the practice of borrowing having always been the normal path of development. In his view, the

> widespread cross-diffusion of French and German patterns within Civil law, and the overcoming of American models at the present, shape a similar legal landscape all across the world, with a wilderness of local variants (*ibid*).

It is true that a comparative lawyer can detect cross-pollination and 'horizontal transfers' between systems at all times.

Surely what is necessary today is a re-assessment of individual legal systems according to the old and new overlaps, combinations and blends, and of how the existing constituent elements have mingled and are mingling with new elements entering them. I propose a scheme that regards all legal systems as mixed and overlapping, overtly or covertly, and groups them according to the proportionate mixture of the ingredients. To do this, it is essential to look at the constituent elements in each legal system and to re-group legal systems on a much larger scale according to the predominance of the ingredient sources from whence each system is formed. The starting point is appreciation of the fact that all legal systems are overlaps, combinations and mixes to varying degrees.

Thus, some continental systems, such as the Dutch, are combinations of Roman, French, German and indigenous laws, and some are combinations of Canon, Roman, French, Austrian and German Laws and *ius commune*, such as the Italian. Indeed, all European systems can be better approached as overlaps. Then there are other combinations such as common law, religious law and indigenous customary laws, as in countries such as India and Pakistan; and French, Socialist, Islamic and indigenous customary tribal laws, as in Algeria. In fact, French law, German law and common law are themselves all outcomes of overlaps of various ingredients. English law is becoming more and more an overlap of common law, various civilian systems and European law. Indeed, classical English common law itself was an overlap of Roman law, civilian ideas, canon law, equity and domestic common law.[4] In this approach the underlays and the overlays must be carefully distinguished, because layers may also shift their positions. For example, in Hong Kong, until 1990, English common law was the overlay, with Chinese customary law the underlay, but now, common law is becoming an underlay alongside Chinese customary law, both under a growing overlay of modern Chinese law.

This approach would particularly help the classification of systems such as those of Malaysia, Singapore, Burma and Thailand. In fact, the whole of South East Asia would be better served by this approach. In this way, off-shoots and sub-groups can be more clearly seen and catered for. For example, since the end of

---

[4] For contributions from Islamic and Talmudic laws into common law, see the literature mentioned by Glenn, 2001 133 at 141–2. See also Glenn, 2005.

the 19th century, Thailand, which was never a colony, has had in its modern texture a real mixture of sources such as English law, German law, French law, Swiss law, Japanese law and American law. These sit alongside historic sources which have been in existence since 1283: rules from indigenous culture and tradition, customary laws and Hindu jurisprudence are still to be found in some modern enactments. In addition, Thai codes were originally drafted in English and French and subsequently translated into Thai. So, where could this legal system be placed in the traditional classification of legal families?

The same question can be posed for Malaysia, where first there was the 'native' law of the aboriginal inhabitants which is still today regarded as positive law by courts. Then came layers of transplanted law: *adat* law (a number of Malay customs); Hindu and Buddhist laws; Islamic law; Chinese law; Thai law; the English common law tradition coloured by Anglo-Indian codes and the United States model. There are further influences in South East Asia: French, Dutch, German, Swiss, Portuguese and Spanish Civilian traditions; American, Japanese and Soviet laws (Harding, 2002: 36 at 42–3). The region

> has an abundance of legal traditions, practically all of them having been 'received' or 'transplanted' in one sense or another, and encompassing all of the world's major legal world views and systems ... except perhaps for African law and Eskimo law (*ibid*: 36 at 47).

Which of the commonly used classifications deal with these?

Of special interest are four kinds of encounters between legal systems, legal cultures and socio-cultures: (see Örücü, 1995) those between systems of socio- and legal-cultural similarity; those between systems of socio-cultural similarity but legal-cultural differene; those between systems of socio-cultural difference but legal-cultural similarity; and those between systems of both socio- and legal-cultural difference. These encounters lead to overlaps, interrelationships, mixed and mixing systems and systems in transition. Law can be approached as the product of a process of transposition. The concept 'transposition', as in music, helps to highlight the crucial importance of the internal tuners who adjust the mix, adapting it to the new instrument (see Örücü, 2002).

Considering legal systems as overlaps, combinations, marriages and off-spring leads to terminology such as fertilisation, pollination, grafting, intertwining, osmosis and pruning, which paves the way to an understanding of developments in our day.

In linguistics, the 'tree model' of language development reflects an evolutionary approach and is the one generally used to explain ramification and divergence. The 'wave theory', on the other hand, showing that changes can spread like waves over a wide area, can also handle the equally important forces of convergence,[5] as can 'diffusion' (Twining, 2004). However, similarities do not always arise from

---

[5] See, for an analysis of these theories, Renfrew, 1987, especially 105 at 244–8.

genetic relationships, neither does resemblance necessarily indicate common origin. There can be 'horizontal transfers' between adjacent systems. 'Horizontal transfer' can also explain why a borrowed concept or institution does not always exactly retain its original meaning. Areas nearest or adjacent to the initial change will change first and may even give up their own peculiarities. Subsequent re-groupings may come about on the 'wave model' mentioned above. Thus, convergence can occur between concepts or systems that were originally very different. It flows from the foregoing that a wave need not start from a fixed centre either. Developments can take place in steps with no one locale as the prime innovating centre. It is not necessary to depict one as the donor and the other the recipient. In this perspective, there is no one localised homeland but 'cumulative mutuality'. Interaction is the essence. The 'tree model' and the 'wave model' can be used together to explain developments; so can the 'knock-on-effect'. This combined approach indicates a way forward for an understanding of how legal systems function, change and develop.

Civil law and common law would appear near to, but not necessarily at the prime innovating center. It is of course, possible to go right back to the laws of Hammurabi and to Greek laws before even considering Roman law—the ingredients of which possibly included elements of Hindu law through Egyptian and Greek channels—as the starting point of civil law.

When one looks at legal cultures and traditions, one sees that civil law and common law are but two of the ancestors, others being, according to one divide for instance, Chthonic, Talmudic, Islamic, Hindu, and Asian (Glenn, 2000). Even then, Patrick Glenn says:

> In looking at (only) seven legal traditions of the world, it has been impossible to avoid the existence of other recognisable legal traditions. Some might say the other legal traditions are minor ones, which complement or oppose the traditions which have been examined. This may or may not be accurate, since there are no well established criteria for distinguishing major from minor traditions ... If the traditions in law which have been examined here ... appear presently as the major ones of the world, it may be that this is only a conclusion of first impression, and that there are other legal traditions ... which are still more profound and which await investigation, and recognition, as being of primary importance (Glenn, 2000: 318–19).

So we see that combinations have taken place between systems and sub-systems of different origins. It may be difficult to determine with exactitude the degrees of hybridity when there is much overlap, cross-fertilisation, reciprocal influence, fusion, infusion, grafting and the like. The simple conclusion is that there are no pure systems in the legal world and that there are various degrees of hybridity arising from different levels and layers of crossing and intertwining between the roots and branches of adjacent 'family trees'.

Some of the off-spring showing overt signs of their different legal-cultural, racial, ethnic and religious origins, have already been grouped as 'mixed jurisdictions', and treated as *numerus clausus*. However, there are many overt and covert mixtures that are the off-spring of the same or of other combinations.

Even within the continent of Europe, one can see complicated crosses such as those in Malta (Ganado, 1996), where legal history began with the Phoenician settlement and continued with the Roman conquest bringing the *Corpus Iuris*. Then the Normans invaded and brought feudal law as applied in Spain, Naples and Sicily. The invasion of the Moors had direct influence on the Maltese language. The sovereignty of the Knights of St. John recognised local usage and issued declarations of private law drawing on laws of other countries, mostly Italian. Then came the French with their Napoleonic laws. Finally, the British brought the common law. So here in Malta we see a good example of an eclectic criminal code drafted under a strong Italian influence but with pervasive English and Scottish impact, and a commercial code largely based on the French, with maritime law following English law. The 1873 Civil Code is predominantly based on the French and Italian codes and also on the Municipal Code de Rohan, the Civil Code of Louisiana and the Austrian Civil Code. Canon law applies in the realm of family law where there is also the influence of English law, German law, Italian law and French law. Constitutional law is mainly British. The official languages are Maltese and English. The ingredients work cumulatively and interactively.

There are, of course, even more extreme and unexpected crosses. Sometimes, seeds are scattered even more widely. For example, Turkey is a cross between Swiss, German, Italian, French and Roman laws, a covert Islamic law and local customary law, as well as more recently, European law and American law. This was brought about as a result of grafting, pruning, tuning and intertwining by an elite concerned with changing not only the law and legal culture but the people themselves and the way of life from the traditional to the modern, by the introduction of radical social reform laws to accompany the forging of a new legal system by receptions from abroad (see Örücü, 2006).

It is possible to say that European law today reflects combinations between common law—such as Irish, English and American laws—and civil law in its many varieties—such as German, French, Dutch and Danish laws—as well as the laws of mixed jurisdictions, such as Scottish law, all with their own diverse historic ingredients. An enlarged Europe will have even more to accommodate, as it will have to engage with socialist law and legal culture and other varieties of the civilian tradition. The status of Islamic law and its impact in Europe is now an important subject of study. As people are on the move in Europe, so are legal systems.

One can no longer concentrate solely on what are regarded classically as the great 'parent' systems (Zweigert and Kötz, 1998: 41).

The 'family trees' approach I proposed (Örücü, 2004a; and Örücü, 2004b) is initially deconstructive and critical. After deconstruction, the aim is to reconstruct a more reliable map of the legal systems of the world.[6] Distinctiveness cannot be

---

[6] The question still remains, however, whether this approach could go far enough to embrace legal pluralism and all layers of law such as the global, international, regional, transnational, intercommunal, territorial, state, sub-state and non-state, in the mapping. See Twining, 2000: 136–41.

ignored, and even when comparative law is used as an instrument of integration in Europe, one must be aware of the virtues in 'distinction' and 'diversity'. Whereas in classical classifications only 'similarity' mattered, in the 'family trees' approach 'distinctiveness' matters as well as similarity. The relevant degrees of distinction and similarity decide on the place of a legal system. The 'family trees' project rests on the assumption of fluidity.

In this attempt at re-aligning legal systems and placing them on their genealogical trees, we must consider transpositions, reciprocal influences and cross-fertilisation, both horizontally and vertically. Transpositions tell us much about the development of the law and allow us to understand cultural and legal navigation as well as the role of tuning in legal development.

Legal systems have always looked to each other for law reform. The legal systems of today, most of which are in transition, need models that are socio-culturally and/or legal-culturally different from their own. History tells us that when legal systems of diverse socio- and/or legal-cultures meet, the diverse elements co-exist side by side in the resultant legal system (Örücü, 1995; and Örücü, 2002).

Some of the terms employed for analysis of movements today are 'seepage', 'contaminant', 'irritant', 'underlay', 'overlay', 'cross-fertilisation', 'incremental reception', 'competing systems', 'hyphenated' legal systems, 'layered law', 'chance', 'choice', 'prestige', 'efficiency', 'elite' and 'historical accident'. Any one of these terms may be appropriate for the analysis of a specific move and for the explanation of a specific growth.

In the past many shoots sprouted on the family trees through impositions and colonial contact. Indeed, the English common law has been likened by Lord Denning to an 'oak tree' which grows only in English soil and if this tree were to be planted elsewhere, it would need to be severely pruned.[7]

Today we do not live in a period of imposition or solely in a period of voluntary reception. It is a time of imposed reception—a seemingly voluntary activity of import under circumstances in which the exporters hold all the cards. In this market, the exporter packages and labels his model as the one to be preferred over others. Such imposed receptions are frequently seen in the Central and East European states, and within the context of European integration. While the continental civilian systems are trying to impose civilian type codes on the English common law, the English common law is introducing the system of judge-made law to them. Whatever the means, the end result will be more transposition, more intertwining and more new shoots.

Past receptions from civil law and Roman law into English law for instance, have been called 'sporadic receptions' or 'injections', with 'civil law based reasoning filtering into common law' (Ibbetson, 1998: 224 at 228) ensuring that

---

[7] Denning LJ (as he then was) in *Nyali Ltd. v Attorney General* [1955] 1 All ER, 646 (CA) at 653. This case and opinion is also quoted by Mubirumusoke, 1978:131 at 154.

English law was constantly enriched. However, any rules based on Roman law or the later *ius commune* 'were immediately cut off from their roots', and 'assimilated into the specifically English framework, and given life outside their original context'. The resultant new law 'did not remain in dialogue with the old law from which it derived', and 'once the borrowings are cut off from their roots they cease to be part of the same culture' as they grow in the new soil. Therefore, the influences were not systematic and the solutions did not remain the same. Nevertheless, these affected the growth of the tree. Today, European law is regarded by many as an 'irritant' or a 'contaminant' of the common law. Again, the results will become apparent in the manner of the tree's growth.

To sum up: as comparative lawyers, our main work now is to deconstruct the conventionally labelled pattern of legal systems and to reconstruct them with regard to origins, relationships, overlaps and interrelationships, and diverse 'fertilisers' such as the social and cultural context, and the 'grafting' and 'pruning' used in their development. In this way the comparative lawyer can draw up family trees, leaving ample space for newly forming growths.

III. MIXING SYSTEMS

The conclusion, then, is that all legal systems are mixed. There are no exceptions. Only the ways of mixing and the character of the ensuing mixtures are different. The level of combination and therefore the extent of the mix varies (see Reid, 2003). The word 'mixed' is now much more frequently used and has acquired many different meanings: a 'combination of various legal sources'; a 'combination of more than one body of law within one nation, restricted to an area or to a culture'; 'the existence of different bodies of law applicable within the whole territory of a country'; and 'legal systems that have never had a single dominant culture'.

It has been pointed out that 'mixed', as in 'mixed jurisdictions', implies a historic fact, a reality and a 'local jurisdiction', whereas the emphasis should be on 'experiences in encounters' and therefore, the 'encounter' and the ensuing dynamic exchange should be highlighted (Kasirer, 2003: 481 at 488). Patrick Glenn, who analyses the encounters between the various common laws of the world—which he calls 'relational laws'—sees 'mixed systems' for instance, as places of confluence of these common laws which he regards as in 'ongoing interdependence'; places where we see an unsuccessful 'process of exclusive appropriation of one of the common laws'. However, he also foresees a decline in the significance of the notion of the historically designated 'mixed jurisdictions' 'with the increase in importance in the world of overlapping laws' today (Glenn, 2005: 119).

Instances of mixing are complicated. They may be overt or covert, structured or unstructured, complex or simple, blended or unblended, and are often difficult to define. When talking of 'mixed legal systems', the importance of the 'ongoing mixing' of legal systems must also be considered. In ongoing states of 'mix', a wide knowledge is required to fully analyse this phenomenon, since many systems are shifting and in transition, and new types of mixes are constantly coming into being.

The new 'mixes' are like cake mixes, where the outcome is not precisely known until the cake is fully cooked. There is always the chance of the cake being spoilt by under or over-cooking. Moreover, whether the final taste of the cake retains the taste of the individual ingredients, whether the cake tastes 'right' in the mouth and whether the recipe is a good one cannot be determined until the cake is eaten. However, in legal mixes the degree of success cannot be measured as easily. Neither can 'success' be defined from a single standpoint. Pre-determined economic, social, cultural, religious or ideological ends are all factors by which success is measured. Efficiency, internalisation, cultural shift, and the actual use of the new legal structures can all be criteria for measurement.

It has already been said that all systems are in fact separate and distinct. All differ in the way they have been formed, as their histories show. All have elements from different sources. Systems also differ in the way the legal elite react to their mix, handle it and tune the incoming legal elements to mould them into a legal system. In addition, systems differ as to how the mix is sustained, nurtured or killed (see du Plessis, 1998). In all these senses each system is unique. However, as well as having features that are unique, each has features shared with others and features common to all. This enables us to study mixed systems both separately and together.

In addition, a study of a legal system 50 years ago and again today may reveal considerable changes in its structure, context and conceptual infill, and also in the attitude of lawyers, academics and people to it and its 'mix'.

Sometimes 'mixedness' can be the manifestation of a transition, sometimes it can be a final outcome of the process. When 'mixedness' is the end result and is there to stay, this state of 'mixedness' justifies applying the term 'mixed jurisdiction' to the legal system. It must be recognised that mixed systems share their 'mixedness' to a higher or lower degree with these other mixed systems called 'mixed jurisdictions'. 'Mixedness' is usually a result of historical accident and accidents can lead to unexpected outcomes along unexpected paths. Thus, mixed systems can be viewed along a spectrum. As a general observation, one can start with simple mixes[8] where the blend is mainly between two Western traditions—the civilian and the common law. This blend is as to content and substance, and not necessarily as to structure, although some of these systems have codified their civil laws, such as that of Louisiana, and some have not, such as that of Scotland. Today, at the substantive level, all legal systems are mixed, whether we regard them as mixed legal systems or not.

Scotland for instance, designated as a classical 'mixed jurisdiction', has one of these simple mixed systems, a system 'mixed' only at the substantive level. Its

---

[8] See, for an analysis of mixed systems, Örücü, 1995 and Örücü, 1996.

history is unusual. The path of the migration of law from different sources into Scots Law was seepage, imitation, inspiration, voluntary reception and imposed reception. The starting point was Scots customary law, which was then overlaid by Anglo-Norman law, canon law, Roman law and European civil law, and later in modern times by English law. Further, the system now has to absorb European Community law and European human rights law.

The Scottish mix did not 'result from the imposition of the Common Law upon a Civilian system by a colonial power, as in Louisiana or South Africa', but rather from the close cultural and political ties with the jurisdictions of both traditions 'at different stages of its history' (Reid, 2001). Thus the Scottish legal system can be regarded as being a system 'mixed from the very beginning' (Sellar, 2000), while Scottish jurists created the 'mix' by selecting 'the best' of the ingredients from various sources. However, the exact balance between the elements of this 'mix' in modern Scots law has long been, and still is, the subject of constant controversy at home and abroad.

Since, through cross-fertilisation and horizontal transfers, all legal systems within the European Union will eventually mix to some degree, a study of legal systems already mixed can provide valuable lessons for these mixing systems, and therefore the study of how they work is fruitful. In fact, mixed legal systems have always been the 'laboratories' of comparative lawyers, their 'vantage point' (Kasirer, 2003). Now they have gained a special place in the process of European integration. Jan Smits, for example, says that mixed legal systems will provide 'inspiration' and that the experiences of South Africa, Scotland, Quebec and Louisiana are consequently of great importance for the future developments of European private law (Smits, 2001: 9; and Smits, 1999: 25 at 35).

The existence of 'mixed legal systems', the creation of new mixes, and the present process of mixing may prove to be problematic for those who adhere to the definitive role of the cultural context. Unless one starts from the premise that 'mixedness is itself the culture', there is no easy way forward. Even if one does start from that premise, one has to probe into the generation of the 'mixedness'. This is related to 'horizontal transfer', the possibility of which in turn is refuted by those who state that 'legal transplants are impossible' (Legrand, 1997; and Legrand, 2001). So we can end in an impasse.

Obviously the mixed legal systems that attract attention in the European integration process are the simple ones, the 'mixing bowl' type,[9] with only a limited number of ingredients. For seekers of a new *ius commune*, one of the obstacles is that the ingredients to be blended or interlocked come from two different legal cultures—the common law and the civil law—and this, notwithstanding the variety that exists among the systems that belong to the so-called civil law tradition.

We must not limit our view of the world of 'mixing' to the confines of the European Union or the Western world, however. When looked through the lens

---

[9] See, for the coining and explanation of such terminology, Örücü, 1995; and Örücü, 1996.

of history, we see that many of the mixes of the past were formed by strong movements of transmigration of legal institutions and ideas, mostly in the form of impositions, and of divergent linguistic, communal or religious traditions. Legal systems are constantly mixing, blending, melting, and then solidifying into new shapes as they cool down, while transposition and tuning take their effect. There will always be new movements, new transposition and further tuning. As noted earlier, law is the outcome of a series of transpositions and legal systems are born out of overlaps.

Yet, as a consequence of transmigration of law, problems do arise. Systems that are mixing are evolving, are in transition, are inter-related or are in the process of becoming mixed systems. Special attention must be paid to legal-cultural convergence and non-convergence that may come about as a result of legal import, and to any ensuing socio-cultural non-convergence. In this context, cultural pluralism, the clash of diverse cultures, and the consequences for the importing legal system are of particular contemporary interest, and legal pluralism is another significant concern.

As has already been observed, mixed systems can be visualised as lying along a spectrum. At the far end of the spectrum is the position where transposition has not worked and the official legal system has 'curdled' and is dysfunctional, as is the case in Burkina Faso and Micronesia (see Tamanaha, 2001: xi–xii). At the other extreme is the position where the transmigration works smoothly, because of extensive similarities in structure, substance and culture and fine 'tuning' such as in The Netherlands. Between these extremes lies a range of places. The composition of each depends on conditions such as the size of the transmigration, the characteristics of the legal movement, the degree of success of transpositions and 'tuning', the element of 'force' or 'choice' inherent in the move and the social culture of the new environment.

At times, elements from socio-culturally similar and legal-culturally different legal systems come together forming 'mixed jurisdictions' of the already mentioned 'simple' kind, which I call 'mixing bowls', the ingredients being still in the process of blending but in need of further processing if a 'purée' is to be produced. An example of this type is Scotland as seen above. Next come the 'complex' mixed systems, where the elements are both socio-culturally and legal-culturally different. I have called this type the 'Italian salad bowl', where, although the salad dressing covers the salad, it is easy to detect the individual ingredients clearly through the side of the glass bowl. A good example of this is Algeria. Then there is what I call the 'English salad plate', the ingredients sitting separately, far apart on a flat plate with a blob of mayonnaise at the side into which the different ingredients can be dipped before consumption. Examples of this are the Sudan and Zimbabwe, which lie towards the far end of the spectrum. The examples become more extreme along the path, ending in 'curdling', with a dysfunctional legal system, as already mentioned.[10]

---

[10] For a picture of this spectrum see Örücü, 1995; and Örücü, 1996.

The more complex mixes might appear in places where the legal system or the law is based on, or heavily determined by, religion or belief, but they could also be in places where unexpected events are happening. Examples of this are: Hong Kong, where in its relationship with China there is talk of 'one country two systems'; Hungary, where there was a civilian tradition with no civil code, a socialist era with some freedom for the civilian tradition to live on and where there is now a new era of transformation; and Turkey, where the dominant elite had a 'vision' which entailed changing not only the legal culture but also the socio-culture by employing foreign legal models leading to the erasure of the indigenous ones, followed by a 'limping marriage' with the European Union. Transmigration of laws might take place between legal systems of both legal and socio-cultural diversity, creating either legal pluralism, a mixed jurisdiction or hybrid system, or unexpected results under pressure from an *'élite dominante'*. Sometimes there are overlaps between these meanings, and a place could have a 'complex' system in any or in all these senses. These systems obviously defy the traditional theory of 'legal families', classical paradigms being totally inadequate.

However, as ever, an evolutionary dynamism emerges and systems go their own way. There can never be sameness. Concepts or institutions coming into different environments begin to change and internal 'contamination' occurs. Here the 'wave theory' of linguistics already referred to, which shows how change spreads like waves over a whole area and which can handle both resemblance and difference, may aid our understanding.

When the Euro-centric spectacles are removed, the comparative lawyer immediately sees that indigenous laws rarely consist of single homogenous systems. Many indigenous legal orders and social orders can live side by side. To find, understand and re-present this law can be extremely difficult, especially when some of it is unwritten and some written but imperfectly translated. For example, in many Asian systems Western law was added to the religious laws of Hinduism, Buddhism, Confucianism and Islam, which themselves co-existed prior to colonisation. The mixture was also complicated by the fact that not all laws were applicable to all peoples, different parts of the population being classified as 'foreign Orientals', 'assimilated Asians', 'Europeans', 'non-natives' or 'natives'. The resultant mixture continues to give rise to problems in countries such as Indonesia, Taiwan and Malaysia even today. The comparative lawyer must understand the relationship between these layers of systems in order to depict such systems in transition today.

In summary, transmigration of law has followed the paths of colonisation, re-settlement, occupation, expansion, and inter-relationship. The methods of these migrations were imposition, reception, imposed reception, co-ordinated parallel development, infiltration, imitation, and variations and combinations of these. The consequences have been the birth of systems in transition and mixing, mixed jurisdictions, inter-related systems, evolving systems, layered-law, hyphenated legal systems, harmonisation, unification and standardisation. There are conceptual implications in all this.

Reciprocal influences must be examined in new ways, since the emphasis, the consequences and the means are different to those of the past. Most obvious 'reciprocal influence' today is in Europe within the European Union, but transpositions from the Western legal traditions to the Central and East European legal systems are of greater importance. Beyond Europe, other cross-fertilisations are taking place. One such is that between China and Hong Kong. The consequences are the birth of a 'new genre of *mixité*', more 'complex' mixes, the blurring of the demarcation lines between the generally accepted classifications of legal families, and the emergence of new clashes between legal cultures themselves, or legal cultures and socio-cultures. The means are apparently voluntary reception rather than colonisation and imposition as in the past, though imposed receptions are more prominent in some instances.

Many legal systems are experiencing fundamental upheaval, some re-shaping themselves in social, economic and legal terms, with the help of outside models chosen from competing systems. They are systems in transition. Some, living within certain regions or groupings, are fundamentally affected by reciprocal influences. Some others are swayed by globalisation. Comparative lawyers must approach this new world with improved tools.

As seen above, it has been suggested by Vernon Palmer that we should be talking of a new 'third legal family' alongside the common law and the civil law families with the name 'mixed jurisdictions', to include a number of historically determined mixes which he regards as sharing certain characteristics. These systems, Palmer says, 'are built upon dual foundations of common-law and civil-law materials'—that is, there is a 'specificity of the mixture'; the mix is obvious to both insiders and outsiders—that is, 'obvious to an ordinary observer'; and the private-law sphere has 'the outward appearance of a "pure" civil-law system', whereas the public law sphere 'will appear to be typically Anglo-American'—that is, there is a 'structural allocation of content'. According to him, these 'are the lowest common denominators of a mixed jurisdiction' (Palmer, 2001: 7–9; and Palmer 2006: 467–8).

The concept of 'mixed jurisdictions' is used by Vernon Palmer in a narrow and conventional sense, which considers only co-existing and commingling between the civil law and the common law—that is 'simple' mixes—and talks of a 'closed family' of 15 members, with seven of them studied in his work.[11] His entry 'Mixed Jurisdictions' in the *Elgar Encyclopedia of Comparative Law*, starts with a summary of his views.

> 'Mixed jurisdictions' as they are classically called, make up roughly 15 political entities, of which 11 are independent countries. Most (excluding Scotland and Israel) of these

---

[11] These are Israel, Louisiana, the Philippines, Puerto Rico, Québec, the Republic of South Africa and Scotland. One could take issue even with some of these systems which have also other ingredients, such as Israel. Zimmermann says that Palmer uses the term 'mixed legal systems' in a restricted, technical sense (Zimmermann, 2004: 3).

are the former colonial possessions of France, the Netherlands or Spain which were subsequently transferred to Great Britain or the United States (Palmer, 2006: 467).

This is only a partial answer, as clearly not all 'mixes' can be pooled together and not all the existing members of such a family would have the same or similar ingredients. It would be difficult for example, to place Scotland, Quebec, Hong Kong, Thailand and Algeria—all mixed systems—into one family. Simple mixes, complex mixes, and dual systems and systems adhering to legal pluralism cannot be all grouped together.[12] Even if we were to accept that Palmer's 15 individual legal systems share certain characteristics to justify placing them together and to give this conglomeration the status of a 'third family of mixed jurisdictions', what of contemporary mixing systems and systems in transition? How would these be grouped and analysed? Palmer's attempt does not solve the problems of understanding and analysing the world we live in today.

One other approach is that offered by Anthony Ogus, who looks at mixed or 'hybrid' systems through the lenses of a 'law and economics' scholar and places them into three categories (Ogus, 2001). In his first group are those systems 'where a culture was imposed by a colonialist power, but where a native culture persisted to some degree'. In this category the native culture 'competes' with the imposed culture. He gives many African countries as examples. 'Countries which have experienced successive colonialist or other occupation' fall into his second category. Here, each successive foreign culture has had a major impact on the legal culture and competes with the others. The examples he chooses for this category are Quebec, Louisiana and South Africa. Countries

> which experienced industrial and commercial development relatively late and where rulers recognised the need to look elsewhere for more sophisticated legal input than the domestic legal system could provide (Ogus, 2001: 36).

form his third category, his examples being Japan, Turkey and Greece. Ogus says that in this category 'there were effectively "tenders" from several major legal cultures to supply the necessary set of specifications'. East European States using Western models for law reform are also regarded as falling into this category, though 'in somewhat different circumstances' (ibid).

Anthony Ogus offers some predictions for the future. He is of the opinion that the three categories share characteristics that separate them from legal systems

---

[12] A number of examples follow:

- mixed systems with civil law and common law: Botswana, Cyprus, Malta, Mauritius, Seychelles;
- mixed systems with civil law and customary law: Burundi, Burkina Faso, Ethiopia, Mali, South Korea, Japan;
- mixed systems with civil law and Muslim law: Algeria, Egypt, Syria, Tunisia, Brunei;
- mixed systems with civil law, common law and customary law: Cameroun, Sri Lanka, Vanuata, Zimbabwe;
- mixed systems with civil law, common law and Muslim law: Iran, Jordan, Somalia, Yemen;
- mixed systems with civil law, Muslim law and customary law: Djibouti, Eritrea, Indonesia.

with one dominant culture. The expected outcome is that mixed systems will be 'more efficient, and adapt more readily to changing external variables, than those with a single dominant culture', though much depends on how the competition works. Of course, there is always the possibility that optimal selections may not be made from between the different 'tenders'. The 'rents' to be enjoyed by a particular foreign legal system may be too attractive for domestic lawyers trained in that system to resist. Despite such problems however, from the 'law and economics' point of view, the future is quite bright for mixed systems. They should, 'unless obstructed by private interest groups allied to a particular culture, adapt more readily to efficient legal reform' (*ibid*: at 36–7). Comparative lawyers need to consider what contribution does a 'law and economics' approach have in assessing 'mixed systems' over and above other approaches.

We should ask ourselves whether the examples referred to in this chapter could be better understood using the approaches suggested by Anthony Ogus or Vernon Palmer.

One of our examples was Malta, which has now joined the European Union. What kind of new mixing can we expect? How is it possible to fit this mixture into any of the suggested categories?

Another example was Thailand, which was never a colony. Its modern texture has been formed from many sources and the legal system of today still grapples with problems of translation and connotation. How, then, are we to categorise Thailand?

Turkey, yet another example, was placed by Anthony Ogus in his third category. It might fit there. But does that aid our understanding of the system as it works? Further still, can his predictions for future success apply here? Turkey is now trying to assimilate many European Community Directives and the '*acquis communautaire*' in the hope of joining the European Union. One of the conditions is the 'improvement of the legal system' and further 'modernisation' of the law, 'modernisation' being understood to mean further elimination of 'traditional values'. What does the future hold for this mixture?

Although not 'mixed jurisdictions' in Vernon Palmer's sense, the three examples above are certainly 'mixed' and 'mixing' systems, the various elements from different sources being woven into the tapestry of their laws.

IV. CONCLUDING REMARKS

All legal systems are born of different parentage, from marriages between systems and sub-systems of such. Some parents cohabited, some had life-long and some passing relationships. It is difficult to determine the exact level of hybridity in each legal system. What is clear, however, is that combinations of disparate legal and social cultures give birth to mixed systems. Later formations of such systems are by horizontal transfer. Overlap, cross-fertilisation, reciprocal influence, fusion, infusion, grafting and the like are all responsible for the coming into being of mixed and mixing systems, all forever in flux, as are all legal systems. As is now widely acknowledged, there are indeed no pure systems in the legal world and various degrees of hybridity arise from various degrees, levels and layers of crossing and intertwining.

It is obviously easier to handle such legal systems when there are clear signs of their different legal cultural, racial, ethnic and religious origins. Some of these systems have already been grouped as 'mixed jurisdictions' and are treated as *numerus clausus* as noted. However, as has also been pointed out, there are many other overt mixes with different origins. More important still, there are also covert mixtures, the results of the same or of other combinations. It is the covert and the ongoing mixes that really tease the comparative lawyer.

It follows from the foregoing that awareness that law is not static, that it moves and changes and that legal systems today are at a crossroads, is essential. Irrespective of whether the future holds confluence or divergence for legal systems, one thing is certain: more and more systems will be mixed and mixing, be they in Europe, in South East Asia or the Middle East. In line with these developments, comparative law research itself is at a cross-roads, and the new turning point is to study this process of 'mixedness' in order to facilitate an understanding of current and future patterns of legal development. It is the study of this 'mixedness' that can illuminate the path towards the comprehension of the interaction of law and culture.

QUESTIONS FOR DISCUSSION

1. Are the suggested terms 'transposition' and 'tuning' the most appropriate terms for movements of law? Explain with examples.
2. Should the 'transplant theory' be re-considered? If yes, how?
3. Can 'mixed systems' be analysed in general terms? Can there be a satisfactory definition of a 'mixed system'? Discuss.
4. How is the existence of mixed systems to be reconciled with the classical classifications of legal families?
5. Discuss various outcomes of movements between systems.
6. Palmer regards mixed jurisdictions as a new 'third family'. Assess this view.
7. Are there shared characteristics of mixed jurisdictions? If yes, what are these characteristics?
8. Should mixed legal systems be studied more as experiences in encounters, 'meeting points' or 'points of contact' rather than as jurisdictions?
9. Do mixed systems represent cross-cultural dialogue?
10. Analyse 'mixed' as a historical reality and 'mixing' as an ongoing flux.
11. What questions arise when the system of laws of one country is taken over by another? What chances are there that the new law will be adjusted to the home environment and what are the risks that it will be rejected?
13. Which of the classifications and criteria used to group legal systems into legal families do you find most helpful?

BIBLIOGRAPHY AND FURTHER READING

Bogdan, M (1994) *Comparative Law* (Göteborg, Kluwer Tano).

David, R and Brierley, JEC (1985) *Major Legal Systems in the World Today, An Introduction to the Comparative Study of Law,* 3rd edn (London, Stevens and Sons).

du Plessis, J (1998) 'The promises and pitfalls of mixed legal systems: The South African and Scottish Experiences' 3 *Stellenbosch Law Review* 338.

Eörsi, G (1973) 'On the Problem of the Division of Legal Systems' in M Rotondi (ed), *Inchieste di diritto comparato 2. Buts et méthodes du droit comparé* (New York, Padova).

—— (1977) 'Convergence in Civil law?' in Szabo and Péteri (eds), *A Socialist Approach to Comparative Law* (Budapest, Leyden).

Friedman, LM (1994) 'Is There a Modern Legal Culture?' 7 *Ratio Juris* 117.

Ganado, M (1996) 'Malta: A Microcosm of International Influences' in E Örücü, E Attwooll and S Coyle (eds), *Studies in Legal Systems: Mixed and Mixing* (London, Kluwer Law International).

Glenn, HP (2000) *Legal Traditions of the World* (Oxford, Oxford University Press).

—— (2001) 'Are Legal Traditions Incommensurable?' 49 *American Journal of Comparative Law* 133.

—— (2005) *On Common Laws* (Oxford, Oxford University Press).

Harding, A (2002) 'Global Doctrine and Local Knowledge: Law in South East Asia' 51 *International and Comparative Law Quarterly* 36.

Husa, J (2004) 'Classification of the Legal Families Today' *Révue internationale de droit comparé* 12.

Ibbetson, DJ (1998) 'A Reply to Professor Zimmermann' in TG Watkin (ed), *The Europeanisation of Law,* UK Comparative Law Series 18 (London, UK National Committee for Comparative Law).

Kasirer, N (2003) 'Legal Education as *Métissage*' 78 *Tulane Law Review* 481.

Legrand, P (1997) 'The Impossibility of "Legal Transplants"' 4 *Maastricht Journal of European and Comparative Law* 111.

—— (2001) 'What "Legal Transplant"?' in D Nelken and J Feest (eds), *Adapting Legal Cultures* (Oxford, Hart Publishing).

Malmström, A (1969) 'The System of Legal Systems, Notes on the Classification in Comparative Law' 13 *Scandinavian Studies in. Law* 127.

Mattei, U (1997) 'Three Patterns of Law: Taxonomy and Change in the World's Legal Systems' XLV *American Journal of Comparative Law* 1.

Monateri, PG (1998) 'The "Weak" Law: Contaminations and Legal Cultures' in *Italian National Reports to the XVth International Congress of Comparative Law,* Bristol (Milan, Giuffrè Editore).

Mubirumusoke, C (1978) 'Application of the Received Law of Torts in East Africa and the Problem of Transplanting Legal Norms' in TW Bechtler (ed), *Law in a Social Context (Liber Amicorum Honouring Professor Lon L Fuller)* (Deventer, Kluwer Law International).

Ogus, A (2001) 'The Contribution of Economic Analysis of Law to Legal Transplants' in JM Smits (ed), *The Contribution of Mixed Systems to European Private Law* (Groningen, Intersentia).

Örücü, E (1995) 'A Theoretical Framework For Transfrontier Mobility of Law' in R Jagtenberg, E Örücü and A de Roo (eds), *Transfrontier Mobility of Law* (The Hague, Kluwer Law International).

—— (1996) 'Mixed and Mixing Systems: A Conceptual Search' in E Örücü, E Attwooll and S Coyle (eds), *Studies in Legal Systems: Mixed and Mixing* (London, Kluwer Law International).

—— (2002) 'Law as Transposition' 51 *International and Comparative Law Quarterly* 205.

—— (2004a) *The Enigma of Comparative Law—Variations on a Theme for the Twenty-First Century* (Leiden, Martinus Nijhoff).

—— (2004b) 'Family Trees for Legal Systems: Towards a Contemporary Approach' in M van Hoecke (ed), *Epistemology and Methodology of Comparative Law* (Oxford, Hart Publishing).

—— (2006) 'A Synthetic and Hyphenated Legal System: The Turkish Experience' 1 *Journal of Comparative Law* 27.

Palmer, VV (2001) *Mixed Jurisdictions Worldwide: The Third Legal Family* (Cambridge, Cambridge University Press).

—— (2006) 'Mixed Jurisdictions' in JM Smits (ed), *Elgar Encyclopedia of Comparative Law* (Cheltenham, UK–Northampton, MA, Edward Elgar).

Podgorecki, A (1985) 'Social Systems and Legal Systems—Criteria for Classification' in A Podgorecki, CJ Whelan and D Khosla (eds), *Legal Systems and Social Systems* (London, Croom Helm).

Reid, KGC (2003) 'The Idea of Mixed Legal Systems' 78 *Tulane Law Reveiew* 5.

Reid, E (2001) 'Comparative Law: Perspective from a Mixed Jurisdiction' in *HLS Cahier Nr 2 Methodology and its application* (Groningen, Facilitair Bedrijf), 49.

Renfrew, C (1987) *Archeology and Language: The Puzzle of Indo-European Origins* (London, Jonathan Cape).

Sellar, WDH (2004) 'Scots law—mixed from the very beginning? A tale of two receptions' 4 *Edinburgh Law Review* 3.

Smits, JM (1998) 'A European Private Law as a Mixed Legal System 5 *Maastricht Journal of European and Comparative Law* 328.

—— (1999) 'How to Take the Road Untravelled? European Private Law in the Making: A Review Essay' 6 *Maastricht Journal of European and Comparative Law* 25.

—— (ed) (2001) *The Contribution of Mixed Legal Systems to European Private Law* (Groningen, Intersentia).

—— (2002) *The Making of European Private Law: Towards a Ius Commune Europaeum as a Mixed Legal System* (Maastricht, Metro).

Tamanaha, B (2001) *General Jurisprudence of Law and Society* (New York, Oxford University Press).

Twining, W (2000) *Globalisation and Legal Theory* (London, Butterworths).

—— (2004) 'Diffusion of Law: A Global Perspective' 49 *Journal of Legal Pluralism* 1.

van Hoecke, M and Warrington, M (1998) 'Legal Cultures and Legal Paradigms: Towards a New Model for Comparative Law' 47 *International and Comparative Law Quarterly* 495.

Zimmermann, R (2004) 'Double Cross: Comparing Scots and South African Law' in R Zimmermann, D Visser and K Reid (eds), *Mixed Legal Systems in Comparative Perspective* (Oxford, Oxford University Press).

Zweigert, K and Kötz, H (1998) *An Introduction to Comparative Law*, 3rd edn (trans) T Weir (Oxford, Clarendon Press).

9

Beyond Europe

WERNER MENSKI

KEY CONCEPTS

Globalisation; Harmonisation; Indian law; Legal families; Legal uniformity, Muslim law in India, Post-divorce maintenance; Transplants; Uniform Civil Code.

I. INTRODUCTION

I N THIS CHAPTER, I explore the stony yet immensely fertile field of comparative law beyond Europe and argue that, largely for historical reasons, Asian, African and other non-Western legal systems seem inherently more attuned than Western legal systems and scholars to the intellectual and practical challenges of comparative law and legal pluralism. Non-Western legal systems appear deeply aware of the mixed nature of all laws, and have been acutely conscious of the dynamic nature of legal systems as constantly negotiated entities that can be manipulated in many ways to achieve desired outcomes (Menski, 2006a). While non-Western legal systems and concepts have been systematically belittled over the past centuries, a side effect of globalisation and of post-modernity is a notable current resurgence of acknowledgment that legal systems beyond Europe need to be studied in their own right and have a legitimate place on the global tree of law (see Örücü, 2004). At the same time, this complex process of post-modern and largely post-colonial re-thinking remains shackled by 'white' colonial presuppositions.

Practical pressures and enhanced historical awareness have propelled some modern legal systems beyond Europe (about which we generally know far too little) to construct plurality-conscious models of handling legal diversity and conflicting concepts. This happens in hotly contested environments, sidetracked by politically motivated assaults of 'modernists' as well as 'traditionalists', in a spirit of implied commitment to what universalist scholarship tends to call 'human rights', but which manifests itself as situation-specific 'justice' or 'equity'. Since such legal developments beyond Europe retain deep respect for the internal plurality of traditional rule systems and processes, they are easily misconstrued as commitments to traditionalism. This has led to anguished inconclusive debates about whether there are legitimate value systems underlying different human rights conceptualisations across various legal cultures (Renteln, 2004). The critical question, then, becomes, at a global level, whose values we accept as conducive to justice.

At the same time, the necessarily hybrid legal constructs in Asia, Africa and other regions of the South have been achieved without giving up the vision of harmonisation as practically advantageous in a global world and in modern nation states. Of much interest to comparative lawyers, pluralism and legal uniformity appear everywhere beyond Europe in multiple contests. After some contextualisation, this chapter provides two Indian case studies of plurality-conscious legal constructs, demonstrating how Hindu law, Islamic law and other legal systems can co-exist within a national legal regime and can all contribute to a culture-specific, composite national identity unique to a particular country. This may serve as a model for other nations in terms of coping with diversity and difference, not only outside Europe. It is also a lesson in how to 'do' comparative law beyond Europe.

II. THE CONTEXT OF THE FIELD

Having accepted an impossible brief, I start with the comment that law beyond the Bosporus and Gibraltar, and similarly beyond the Mexican border, is still little known among most Western scholars, who tend to have outdated perceptions of what laws the people of these Southern regions actually follow. These are the vast majority of today's world population, mainly brown and black people, with their own laws, partly transplanted from the North, but by no means just inferior copies of Western legal systems.[1] Legal scholarship world-wide has not yet overcome centuries of Euro-centric legal study assuming that Enlightenment and legal theory were produced—and are owned—by the West. As a result, one finds the odd admission that legal scholarship on a global level may learn something from Asia and Africa, but it is not clear what such knowledge can contribute to existing legal theory. Where does that leave the voices of Asian, African, Oceanic and South American laws and lawyers? How are we going to make sense of such laws, and can we, indeed, learn from them? Where do we start, and how far can we get? Anyone working in this field seems to be classified as a 'comparative lawyer', but perhaps all law should be perceived as comparative law (Twining, 2000: 255).

---

[1] As a specialist on South Asian laws, emphasising the critical role of Hindu law and Muslim legal concepts in the sub-continent, rather than just common law influences, I often encounter surprise and opposition. On Hindu law, see Menski, 2003. On South Asian Muslim law, see Pearl and Menski, 1998. On common law influences, see Galanter, 1989. Exaggerated claims that colonial influences virtually wiped out indigenous knowledge are found in Cohn, 1997. More balanced is Benton, 2002.

Looking around, we find the term 'comparative law' contested, with scholars quibbling over minute details, rather than working on the 'big picture'.[2] Comparative law is not yet a mature entity and is only just beginning to shake off colonial hubris and the 'white' supremacist presuppositions that went with it (see David and Brierley, 1985; and Zweigert and Kötz, 1998). Prized new studies of the many different legal traditions of the world have pushed the boundaries of the field in interesting, much discussed directions (Glenn, 2000/2004).[3] Assessments of comparative law have been critical (eg Legrand, 1996), but there is widespread agreement that we are at a new cross-roads, enjoying rejuvenation and exciting times for comparative lawyers (see Harding and Örücü, 2002). In the advertising blurb for the Elgar Encyclopedia of Comparative Law (Smits, 2006), Alan Watson, doyen of the 'transplant theorists' and long-standing critic of comparative law, writes:

> Comparative law is moving swiftly from a long infancy to teenage maturity, and Jan Smits provides the essential tonic … I agree with many of the arguments and disagree with others. This is the nature of healthy adolescence (Watson, 1974/1993).

These new wise words of an old man are subtle confirmation that jurisprudence, or legal theory (if you prefer that term) and comparative law are intensely political, and remain quite personal.[4] Legal scholarship often links closely to the instrumentalist uses of law as a tool to implement reforms and to make dreams come true. Legal philosophers are like a small army of armchair revolutionaries, often using the stones from the fertile field of comparative law as weapons. Legal theory accounts for much brain-washing in legal education and also underpins much illegality in legal practice, as Hans Kelsen found when the Pakistanis applied his brilliant legal theory to justify military dictatorships.[5]

Legal theorists have largely tended to ignore the social dimensions of law, but there are (and have always been since Montesquieu and other early great minds) notable exceptions (see Cotterrell, 1989; and Cotterrell, 2006). Law as experienced by 'little people', akin to Ehrlich's 'living law' (Ehrlich, 1936), has not received sufficient attention. The socio-legal dimension remains undervalued all around the world.[6] Attempts to critique Euro-centric positivism through showing the limits of law remain insufficiently received (Hinz, 2006). Polite critical voices from the East receive equally subtle acknowledgment, but little more, it seems (Chiba, 1986; Chiba, 1989). Law as a globally known concept is actually built on un-agreed

---

[2] Annelise Riles notes 'ubiquitous angst about the disciplinary identity of comparative law today' (Riles (ed), 2001: 3). Andrew Harding and Esin Örücü note the growing popularity of comparative law, but highlight that 'it is also fraught with internal contradiction, uncertainty, and a sense of mid-life crisis' (Harding and Örücü, 2002: xii).

[3] For a set of critical reviews, see (2006) 1.1 *The Journal of Comparative Law* 100. Glenn, 2005, introduces 'common laws' as a globally present form of interactional law.

[4] Riles, 2001 contains excellent case studies.

[5] Kelsen, 1970 was famously interpreted by Pakistani judges to legitimise military rule in *State v Dosso*, PLD 1958 SC 533.

[6] For a vigorous critique of Indian legal scholarship in this respect, see Baxi, 1982; and Baxi, 1986.

and thus constantly shifting and negotiated foundations, marked by an endless internal plurality that many legal scholars find irritating and deeply frustrating.[7] Legal pluralism, another unruly adolescent in the extended joint family of legal studies, struggles to find acceptance in mainstream legal scholarship,[8] but miniscule progress may be recorded over time. There is much justification for a sustained critique of comparative law as a willing handmaiden for various imperialistic agenda (Menski, 2006a: 46–50).

Students of comparative law need to be aware of such troublesome issues on a global level and will have to make up their own minds about which arguments they accept and which they would tend to oppose. Can we really have one law for the whole world? (Menski, 2006a: 3–24) Do we assume that secular legal approaches can eventually get rid of the influence of religion on law? Can state law fully abolish and override 'religion' and 'tradition' by declaring that they are not law? (See Carroll, 1997: 97 at 105) Can customary laws, one of the basic foundations of legal traditions, really become entirely irrelevant in legal modernity? Do state-made laws actually create new forms of custom, and what sense do we make of the argument that customs are at the same time old and new? (Bennett, 2004) Can state law, at the stroke of a pen, introduce a new legal system?[9] More specifically for the present discussion, is there room in the world's joint family of law for the many legal systems of Asia and Africa that are undoubtedly 'mixed', beyond recognising that they are hybrids and often contain elements of Western laws? What about frequently unacknowledged non-Western elements? To what extent do we accept that Hindu law, Chinese law, Islamic laws and the myriad of African laws have a future in this globalising world? Will there be a universal concept of law? And what, then, would this look like?

Such big questions indicate that there will never be universal agreement on what we mean by law. Presently, much existing scholarship is still not willing to acknowledge this and to accept that people in Asia and Africa, and elsewhere in the erstwhile 'Third World' have their own laws and claim ownership of their own ways of dealing with legal matters. We are often still just looking for traces of European transplants, and proudly clutch evidence of perceived success without examining how such positive results are achieved in socio-legal reality. Not only in Asia and Africa do reported cases and official documents not give a faithful picture of the totality of law in a particular nation.[10]

---

[7] For details see Menski, 2006a, introduction and ch 1.

[8] From pioneers like Hooker, 1975, and Moore, 1978, it has been a long way to current applied studies like Shah, 2005, focusing on the contested position of non-European legal traditions in today's Western legal systems. See also Shah and Menski (eds), 2006.

[9] Communist China tried this in Art 1 of the Marriage Law of the People's Republic of China 1950 by abolishing the feudal marriage system and putting into effect the new democratic marriage system.

[10] An example of treating restitution of conjugal rights as a barbaric remedy, is found in *Sareetha v Venkata Subbaiah* AIR 1983 AP 356, while *Harvinder Kaur v Harmandil Singh* AIR 1984 Del 66 took the opposite view. The Indian Supreme Court in *Saroj Rani v Sudarshan Kumar* AIR 1984 SC 1562 found in favour of maintaining the family, and against the 'bull-in-the-china-shop' effect of individualism.

Asian and African debates about the direction of legal reform today often take place prominently within the wider context of globalisation and the many assumptions that this term carries with it (see Held, McGrew, Goldblatt and Perraton, 1999; and Robertson, 2003), as well as now in the context of international debates about human rights and good governance with a focus on constructing a world legal order. The tainted heritage of comparative law in this respect is well known (Harding and Örücü, 2002: vii–viii; Menski, 2006a: 38–45), and only partly overcome. Post-colonial legal, political and military realities do not reassure new nations that they have the right to develop as they see fit. However, we should not waste precious space here by simply criticising various inadequate approaches. Rather, the present chapter provides constructive examples—case studies that readers may pursue in more depth—of how today's laws beyond Europe actually work in practice. It is a fact that non-European laws are more self-consciously plural than European laws and tend to recognise value pluralism. They prefer community-based processes of dispute resolution, tend to privilege tort over crime, with resultant compensation regimes,[11] and tend (not only because they are resource-starved 'developing countries') to emphasise economic responsibilities between members of social groups and families, and also across gender boundaries. Such methods clash with Western-led assumptions about state centricity, individual autonomy and rights-based approaches. Beyond Europe, however, the notion that one's rights depend on other people's duties remains a strong legal foundation.

When we approach comparative legal studies in a culture-sensitive way, as practical comparative lawyers, we need (or are developing in the process) expertise in particular national legal systems or in specific legal traditions of the world.[12] Few law students in the world are required to venture into this field of legal studies.[13] It remains extremely difficult to approach legal traditions or non-Western national laws, since this requires much cultural knowledge, insight into chthonic traditions and value systems that are not our own, and use of technical terms from languages that may not even have words for 'law'.[14] Going down that route, we are bound to realise that 'law' is culture-specific and immensely diverse. Recent scholarship on legal theory suggests that ultimately we are maybe just fussing over different values, bringing us back to basic debates about natural law, expressed earlier in Rudolph Stammler's concept of 'good law',[15] or Masaji Chiba's

---

[11] Eg, in relation to the Islamic 'blood money' (*diyat*).

[12] A good example of the latter approach is Glenn, 2000/2004.

[13] On a model of good practice, see Menski, 2006a: 66–81.

[14] Thus in Sanskrit, the classical language of Indic traditions, *rita* ('macrocosmic order') and *dharma* ('microcosmic order'), the duty of every individual to do the right thing at all times, cannot simply be translated as 'law'.

[15] The German jurist Rudolf Stammler (1856–1938) proposed a theory of 'natural law with a changing content', which holds that 'while the ideal of justice is absolute, its application must vary with time, place and circumstance' and depends heavily on moral attitudes. For further details see Stone, 1965: 167–81.

'legal postulates',[16] while Emmanuel Melissaris now speaks of 'value pluralism' (Melissaris, 2004). Law is, of course, also intimately linked to 'power' in all kinds of forms, and to economics, giving rise to perennial complaints about corruption and lack of accountability and transparency.

The recognition that law itself is a huge field of multiple contests, and an internally plural phenomenon, was long suppressed in dominant and largely idealistic Western legal thought that simplistically privileged the state as a maker of rules and came out, ultimately, as 'legal centralism', the claim that the state alone was the maker of laws. That this myopic modernist vision is difficult to maintain in real life is becoming more evident in world-wide legal practice,[17] and is acknowledged in recent theoretical writing (Örücü, 2004: 42). Lego-centric domination was earlier savagely criticised by John Griffiths (Griffiths, 1986), supported since by many others, but our thought patterns continue to associate law primarily with the state. It seems difficult to unlearn such mental maps, since they creep into the subconscious and influence our daily language—we may not even notice (see Menski, 2006a : 79–80). It remains, of course, tempting, anywhere in the world, to simply assume or claim (especially on the part of those in power) that positivism is the foundation of law. This kind of mono-cultural myopic thinking leads, however, directly to African and other despots, who appear to be top-ranking students of lego-centric axioms, and corrupt regimes anywhere in the world.

III. INTERLINKEDNESS AS A FOUNDATION FOR 'MIXING' LAWS

Beyond Europe, there is a long-standing, immensely rich awareness that 'law' is first of all a culturally embedded phenomenon and is specific to particular people who are interlinked at many levels. This does not mean that one gives up on law reform, but a typical non-Western state would probably be a 'soft state', allowing much room for non-state law. Beyond Europe, 'law' is not normally perceived as a separate entity that can be manipulated without repercussions in lots of other areas. It is interconnected, linked from the macrocosmic spheres of natural law right through to the personal sphere of the socio-legal domain. All along, it also contains elements of the religious and the secular, the social and the psychological, and virtually anything else. The boundaries between what is legal and what is not become really fuzzy, leading to irritated comments by legal scholars (see Tamanaha, 1993; and Tamanaha, 2001). Since this fuzzy interlinkedness is explicitly recognised in Asian and African perceptions of 'law' and their current diasporic manifestations all over the world, there seems no need for insiders to

---

[16] Chiba writes: 'A *legal postulate* is a … value system specifically connected with a particular official or unofficial law … It may consist of established legal ideas such as natural law, justice, equity … sacred truths and precepts … social and cultural postulates' (Chiba, 1986: 6).

[17] An interesting example from the United Kingdom is *Chief Adjudication Officer v Bath* [2000] 1 FLR 8 (CA), where English law had to recognise, ultimately, that an unregistered Sikh marriage could still be treated as legally valid.

discuss this in so many words, with the result that outsiders often do not notice that the European approach, to the effect that 'law' is just 'law', does not really make sense in such cultural contexts. Many meaningful silences need to be studied when we analyse law beyond Europe.

Law is therefore not just about rulers and their codified rule systems, but about a plurality of voices and values, and thus negotiations of difference and diversity at many different levels, and at all times. The book of law is never closed. Any form of law, even God-given Islamic law, is philosophically and practically perceived and applied as inherently dynamic and interactive.[18] It is not just a given static entity that cannot be negotiated in particular social contexts. Beyond Europe, states and their people are almost always deeply attuned to the constant need for skilled legal navigation at all times.[19]

As a result, most legal systems outside Europe continue to cultivate personal law systems, or personal status law, where at least family law and matters of succession and property (but often much else) are governed by different rules and processes for different groups of people. Often, but not always, the determinative criterion is 'religion', as in the Ottoman *millet* system (see Yılmaz, 2005). In the personal laws of India today, the internally plural systems of Hindu law, Muslim law, Christian law, Parsi law, Jewish law and, importantly, a secular option co-exist side by side. Apart from 'religion', the criterion for distinction is often social and ultimately 'ethnic', leaving room for social groups with different identities to develop their own ways of doing things. That this leads to limitless plurality 'on the ground' troubles only fundamentalists, among whom one must count those who still dream of global legal uniformity.

Others, concerned to bring some sort of legal order into this limitless mess, often in the context of nation building, focus more on harmonisation and uniformisation. But such top-down strategies often face fierce accusations of neo-imperialist designs and post-colonial civilising missions, especially if the modernising forces are driven or supported by a dominant majority or by foreign donor agencies. For, whose value systems should prevail in such a harmonised legal entity? How does one construct national legal uniformity in a state composed of many different people without overlooking or victimising certain interest groups and disregarding certain types of law? In this context, there are huge concerns, often in relation to Islamic countries, about minority protection and freedom of religion. As in comparative law, if in comparative religion one does not respect that 'the other' should have a voice and a claim to legitimacy, there are bound to be what we now call human rights abuses, and there will be terrorism and war.[20]

---

[18] See Menski, 2006a: ch 5. Current soul searching and violence among Muslims is centrally concerned with this particular dilemma. For a good discussion see Ramadan, 2005.

[19] For example in Iranian law, the traditional Shi'a 'temporary marriage' (*mut'a*) has today taken the shape of an engagement-like arrangement, allowing young couples to move in public without being harassed by the morality police.

[20] In Sri Lanka, much of the vicious conflict between dominant Buddhists and the Tamil Hindu minority concerns the right of minorities to recognition as an integral different element of the nation state. No proper balance has been found so far.

Beyond Europe, there is much heartburn over the boundaries of 'general law' and 'personal law', with encroachments from either side jealously watched and harshly critiqued.[21] Protagonists of national legal uniformity (who are often also ardent visionaries of globally uniform law) are quick to condemn aberrations from the path of uniformisation, but one finds also exciting examples of official laws explicitly taking account of local customary norms, building them into new national legal systems.[22] In some countries, for example Thailand, earlier exposure to European laws that did not necessarily produce appropriate results leads now to a re-indigenisation.[23] Next door Malaysia maintains the bipolar vision of co-existence of local Muslims with their internally plural *Shari'at* law and 'others' (Chinese, Hindus, Christians and others) covered by a secular legal system without sufficient recognition of specific cultural roots, though it does not work satisfactorily (Aun, 1999; and Teik, 2003). Other countries in the region struggle to find an appropriate balance between national visions and local plural realities. Where interaction between and within different legal systems is not recognised, there are bound to be problems over minority rights and justice for certain groups of people (see eg Kooistra, 2001; and Dillon, 2001).[24]

Beyond Europe, the legal families concept makes even less sense than it does from a Euro-centric perspective. The realisation that law is not simply a matter of state-centric positivism strikes students of Asian and African legal history the moment they start looking at ancient systems of law in which the state seems peripheral. The entirely Euro-centric, rough taxonomic models privileging common law and civil law have led to a carving up of the earlier colonial realms into common law and civil law spheres of influence as two monolithic entities (see David and Brierley, 1985; Zweigert and Kötz, 1998; and de Cruz, 1999). In Africa, the application of this rationale allows for Anglophone, Francophone and Lusophone classifications, which are still not enough to cover the immense pluralities of the 'dark continent'.[25]

In traditional non-European legal systems, we find many different factors influencing how a legal tradition develops over time. In ancient Hindu law (Menski, 2006a: chapter four), but not only there,[26] the state seems for a long time virtually absent as law-maker. Later ruler figures (the *rājā* as king, but equally as head of

---

[21] For a strong critique of the encroachment of local custom on criminal law in India, see Dhagamwar, 2003: 1483–92.

[22] Good case studies would be the Republic of South Africa and Namibia, on which see Hinz (ed), 2006). In Namibia, the Traditional Authorities Act, 2000 and the Community Courts Act, 2003 give explicit recognition to local customary courts. In India, the deliberate retention of customary forms of Hindu divorce under s 29(2) of the Hindu Marriage Act, 1955 allows customary patterns of divorce to co-exist with statutory forms under s 13 of the same Act, leading to remarkable confusions in private international law.

[23] I have heard this referred to as 'Thaiification'. On Thai law, see Harding, 2001.

[24] One could also look in more detail at Tibetans in China.

[25] See the various entries under 'Law' in Middleton (ed), 1997, vol 2, 526–59. For a sharp critique of the treatment of African customary laws, see Ramose, 2006: 351–74.

[26] On ancient Chinese law, see Bodde and Morris, 1967; and van der Sprenkel, 1977.

household) appear as servants of a higher cosmic order rather than powerful legal entities in their own right. No holder of legal power is really perceived as totally autonomous.[27] There is always the dimension of interlinkedness with other and higher entities, the latter not just religious, but also in a secular sense, precisely because the underlying methodology of interlinking everything permits no clearly definable boundaries between what is religious and what is not.

So the ancient Chinese Emperor held the Mandate of Heaven, as long as he could keep control of his realm, but also risked being legitimately removed if things went wrong in his Empire. The basic structure of traditional Chinese law and its institutions shows an intricate linkage of state, society and values, manifest ultimately as 'confucianisation of the law' (see Menski, 2006a: ch 7). Confucianist idealistic principles of self-controlled order and adherence to a sense of duty and performance of proper conduct (*li*) were combined with more realistic statist legalism that privileged formal state law (*fa*) and deterrent and deliberately cruel punishments (*hsing*). This pattern of underlying cultural presuppositions about whether individuals are good or bad, equal or different, and whether they can be educated through punishments or not, is roughly matched in other traditional legal systems, reflecting vigorous early debates about such universal questions virtually everywhere in Asia and Africa.

Such alertness to difference, and sensitivity to the interlinkedness of law with other concepts, led to forms of traditional governance in which traditional rulers were (and are) limited in their range of activities, responsibilities and authority,[28] often heading a 'soft state'. A Hindu ruler, for example, was always in theory (and thus largely in practice, because he could be legitimately killed if he ignored such concepts) subject to a higher order, embedded in a pattern of natural law, as were Islamic, African and ancient Chinese rulers in their own culture-specific ways. Experienced field scholars have perceptively written of the ideal of an equilibrium and, even for Africa, highlighted the 'relative emphasis on imperium, tradition and divine revelation' (Kuper and Kuper, 1965: 17).[29] Such interlinkages were not appreciated by early Western scholars and were actually denied by Max Weber and others (Rheinstein, 1954; and Weber, 1968).

Significantly, such ancient culture-specific understandings of good governance are reflected in modern methods of governance in some countries, shown below in detail for India. Culture-specific forms of natural law and plural normative order are omnipresent and impact on methods of dispute settlement, which never rely just on one source of law, but strongly recognise the need to negotiate conflicting perspectives. The result is a conscious search for agreeable compromises, not a winner-take-all approach of the adversarial model.

---

[27] But for early Islamic law, and particularly the much-criticised Umayyads as God's representatives on earth, see Hallaq, 1997; and Hallaq, 2001.

[28] T Bennett refers to popular maxims to the effect that 'a chief is a chief by the people', (Bennett, 2004: 4). On African kings, see also Ramose, 2006: 351–74.

[29] This matches my triangular model of state, society and values: see Menski, 2006a: 185–9.

Seen from this comparative perspective, recent comparative law scholarship subtly indicates that maybe the Euro-centric perspective that privileged the state (lego-centrism) and territoriality (nationalist concerns) is not only quite parochial (Twining, 2000: 3), but an idiom based on lost memory which does not lead towards a globally acceptable method of understanding law and its many pluralities, mixed manifestations, and commonalities (Glenn, 2005). Below I now present two case studies from Indian law to illustrate the cultivated complexity of laws beyond Europe and our current difficulties in making sense of new developments in such plurality-conscious legal systems.

IV. THE INDIAN UNIFORM CIVIL CODE: HARMONISED PERSONAL LAWS RATHER THAN UNIFORMITY

India became independent from Britain at midnight on 14/15 August 1947, while Pakistan was carved out of that same colonial Empire at the same midnight hour as a state explicitly for Muslims.[30] The Republic of India then laboured with its composite past and the new challenges of the globalising 20th century to develop, eventually, new models of plurality-conscious reconstruction which are today highly instructive for comparative lawyers.

India started from a basic position of secularism, which in its specific Indian meaning implies a non-discrimination guarantee to all non-Hindu minorities that they would also have a legitimate place and a voice in this new state, despite there being a Hindu majority of more than 80%.[31] Built on such deliberately 'mixed' foundations, and a conscious renunciation of power by the 'religious' majority, India has over the past 50+ years managed to remain a stable democracy,[32] to the surprise of many observers (Menski, 1995: 561–5). Meanwhile, it has quietly restructured its entire legal system to remain in harmony with this plurality-conscious national vision, which has been in need of adjustment over time. The subtlety of this process only partially explains why there is so little debate.

The key challenge is whether a young nation state, with now well over a billion people, can aim to have a legal system that is nationally the same for all citizens.[33] India swiftly created a Constitution by 1950, much amended by now, and has a huge array of colonially-grounded general laws that apply to all citizens, and often

---

[30] Initially split between West and East Pakistan, by 1971 the Bengalis of East Pakistan had had enough of West Pakistani colonialism and created the new state of Bangladesh. Since the late 1970s, Pakistan has gradually re-inforced its vision of an Islamic Republic, which fails to give due recognition to minority laws, the concerns of women, and different faiths (even sects among Muslims) in the country.

[31] Specifically on secularism, see Madan, 1987, and Madan (ed), 1994. More broadly, see Larson (ed), 2001.

[32] On the Indian Emergency of 1975–77 as a shock therapy and cathartic experience, see Menski, 2006a: 259–73.

[33] A challenge also faced by other large countries, eg China, Brazil, Indonesia and the rainbow nation of South Africa.

to all persons in India. The best example of such laws remains the Indian Penal Code of 1860, still applied today all over the sub-continent. Another important law, discussed below, is the restructured Criminal Procedure Code of 1973, originally of 1898. Such laws apply to all citizens alike, at least in theory (see Menski, 1996: xxv-liv).[34]

The challenge of legal uniformity arises particularly in family laws, where the personal law system has been retained, while the vision of a uniform civil code appeared on the horizon immediately after independence and made its first official appearance as a programme for development in Article 44, a Directive Principle of State Policy in the Indian Constitution of 1950:

> 44.   Uniform civil code for the citizens
> The state shall endeavour to secure for the citizens a uniform civil code throughout the territory of India.

Article 44 must be read within the wider agenda of secular post-colonial nation building, seeking equality for all citizens, as guaranteed in the Fundamental Rights, especially Article 14.[35] This aim was built on the assumption that law reform happens through secular codification, despite Nehru's realisation that ultimately people themselves would have to change their ways of doing things (Sagade, 1981: 27–35).

India's ambition to promulgate a uniform civil code is not just an Indian problem, therefore, but concerns a universal predicament for lawyers and legal systems. Torn between legal uniformity and normative plurality, with innumerable local and regional diversities of cultures, customs, religions and therefore of laws, the new nation's desire for nationally uniform legal regulation was strong in the 1950s, and uniformity continues to be an important vision. But achieving justice through total equality seems rather difficult when one is faced with many continuing diversities which are simply not going to disappear because of legal intervention. This raises the question whether difference and plurality are actually as problematic as is often made out by Euro-centric legal scholarship. Beyond Europe, readier recognition of difference reflects cautious acceptance of the multiple realities of human life. If a good law is perceived to be about a 'good life', it is an ancient truth (to which India can lay much claim because of its ancient Sanskrit literature) that this can manifest itself in quite different ways. India, it seems, has re-learnt important lessons about such issues since the 1950s. To see this simply as re-traditionalisation or even evidence of fundamentalist nationalism would not do justice to the complexity of the issues encountered by India in its post-colonial efforts to find its national identity as a composite entity.

---

[34] A country with 300+ million people living below the poverty line can hardly claim that its basic fundamental rights are a fact for all citizens.

[35] While Art 14 guarantees equality before the law and equal protection of the laws to all persons in India, Arts 15 and 16 permit the state to make special provisions particularly for women, children and historically disadvantaged classes, thus reflecting awareness that equality is not a socio-legal reality and remains a long-term goal.

The idea that a developed law should appear in codified form had been implanted in the minds of Indian scholars at least since Sir Henry Maine's *Ancient Law* in 1861. Such evolutionist thinking has remained strong but is much criticised today (see Sack and Aleck, 1992: xviii–xix). In independent India, from the start, it was not an option that the Hindu majority of the new state should impose its law on all other citizens. Indian law could not be just Hindu law, it had to be 'secular'. Hence arose the deeply flawed modernist vision that a new, culturally neutral law should be constructed through a uniform civil code. But which law is culturally neutral?

Notably, Indian legal reform efforts focused initially on an older secular colonial legal model, which needed updating. The resulting Special Marriage Act, 1954 allowed any Indian to marry and divorce according to a state-controlled legal regime of secular rules, irrespective of religious affiliation, with rules following European statist models. Thus, marriages were only legally valid if registered before a state official. Grounds for divorce, which involved a court hearing, copied English-style legal rules into Indian law and were warmly welcomed at the time. This law was thought to be particularly attractive for people entering mixed marriages, and was the proper law under which a foreigner would marry an Indian spouse. However, the 1954 Act never became popular in India and leads a peripheral existence. It is today beginning to be criticised as outdated, inter alia because (reflecting the spirit of the 1950s) its rules, even today, insist on parental consent to marriage (Champappilly, 2006: 149).[36]

Wide-ranging reform efforts focused around the same time on the modernisation of Hindu personal law, sparking off huge debates. Most controversial were the formal abolition of polygamy for Hindus and the introduction of divorce on fault grounds, with significant consequences for female property rights, maintenance and access to children. There is no room for details here (see Derrett, 1970; Derrett, 1978; Menski 2001; and Menski 1998), but the next part focuses specifically on divorced Indian women's right to maintenance from the ex-husband.

Since the secular approach was pervasive after independence, Hindu chauvinism appears to have been kept in check from the start by the secularity-focused leadership under Nehru, which also ensured that the Sikhs, Buddhists and Jainas were in unifying efforts subsumed under Hindu law.[37] Subsequent family law reforms continued the 1950s trend of copying Western legal developments, and especially the important Marriage Laws (Amendment) Act, 1976 further harmonised the Special Marriage Act, 1954 and the Hindu Marriage Act, 1955.

But since the early 1980s, statutory reforms to Hindu law have basically ended and the focus has shifted to the courts, while particularly feminist efforts to

---

[36] He notes that the 1954 Act 'is now obsolete. It has not travelled with the time'.

[37] This caused some vigorous protest, reflected in numerous court cases. Particularly, the Sikhs felt the reforms gave women excessive property rights. On the more docile reaction of Jainas, see Menski, 2006b: 417–35.

engineer further statutory changes have created much debate and some recent results.[38] Meanwhile, there has been increasing judicial recognition that the Western-inspired Hindu divorce reforms might not, after all, be an ideal model (see Derrett, 1978; and Menski, 2001: chapter two). India rejected 'irretrievable breakdown' as a formal ground for divorce among Hindus,[39] and since the late 1980s courts have been refusing more divorce decrees to men and women, saying in effect that India is not America, and that the country cannot afford a scenario in which millions of women and children are suffering as a result of liberalised divorce laws (see Menski, 2001: 130–3). This growing social welfare concern gave rise to determined judicial and legislative activism since the late 1970s in relation to post-divorce maintenance, an issue debated in the next part.

Regarding the vision of a uniform civil code on marriage and divorce, India appeared to make no progress. However, after the liberalising 1976 reforms of Hindu divorce law, the tiny Parsi community of India agreed in 1988 to reform its colonial family law;[40] clearly an attempt to preserve their ethnic identity within Indian legal structures. This now left only the Muslims, Jews and Christians of India outside the nascent uniform statutory framework. The Jews of India were by now too depleted in numbers to take action (see Katz, 2000), and still seem to wait for the uniform civil code to materialise. The Muslims of India, as always, resented any pressure to have their personal laws codified by the state and, despite admission of crisis (see Mahmood, 1986), opposed suggestions that their *shari'at* law could be statutorily regulated. However, Indian Muslim *shari'at* law permits fairly easy divorce, favouring the husband's extra-judicial *talaq*.

The Christians of India, comprising many different sects and churches, were held back through opposition by their conservative religious leadership to a more liberal divorce regime. Christian divorce law therefore eventually stuck out as imprisoning spouses in unhappy marriages. Until recently, particularly a Christian wife was virtually chained into a marriage for ever, while her co-citizens of other religions could seek divorce. Under the Constitution of India and its equality provisions, here was clearly a case for relief through a uniform civil code.

But this was not an easy process. Amazing things happened during the 1990s when the High Court of Kerala, a southern state with more than 20% Christian population, dared to rewrite section 10 of the colonial Indian Divorce Act, 1869 to permit divorce among Christians in Kerala on the basis of simple cruelty.[41] Such deliberately provocative judicial activism, a significant development in Indian law with wide repercussions worth studying (see Ahuja, 1997; Menski, Alam and Raza, 2000; and Sathe, 2002) gave strong signals to Parliament that it ought to bring

---

[38] See the Hindu Succession (Amendment) Act, 2005, following a series of earlier local Acts, mainly in Southern states.

[39] See particularly *V Bhagat v (Mrs) D Bhagat* AIR 1994 SC 710.

[40] The Parsi Marriage and Divorce (Amendment) Act, 1988 amended the 1936 Act, thus bringing it in line with Hindu law and the secular rules of the Special Marriage Act, 1954.

[41] *Mary Sonia Zachariah v Union of India*, 1995(1) Kerala Law Times 644.

the hopelessly outdated Christian divorce law into line with the majority law and secular concepts under the 1954 Act. The 1869 Act had been promulgated at a time when divorce was granted only in the most exceptional circumstances, facing 'religious' opposition from the Churches.

But nothing further happened for a long time after 1995, and several Supreme Court judges found it necessary, even beyond 2001, to issue strongly worded calls, in certain strategically important cases, about the desirability of a uniform civil code.[42] Such cases caused catchy headlines in the press, but they were becoming rarer, while some older academics still propagated legal uniformity as a desirable aim for India today (Kumar, 2003).

Meanwhile, India's Parliament was evidently waiting for the right time to reclaim the initiative in law making. It is probably no coincidence that on 24 September 2001, just two weeks after 9/11,[43] the purportedly slumbering colossus of the Indian legislative machinery suddenly sprang into action, passing the Indian Divorce (Amendment) Act, 2001. This finally brought Indian Christian divorce law broadly into line with India's other divorce laws, providing 10 grounds for dissolution of Christian marriages, plus an additional ground for the wife if she could prove that 'the husband has, also since the solemnisation of the marriage, been guilty of rape, sodomy or bestiality'. After enormously tortuous lobbying and many setbacks, this Act finally almost completes the jigsaw puzzle of Indian legal uniformity: Another personal law system of India was now brought into line with the majority law and the secular 'lead model'. This was done almost secretly, in record time, and there has been hardly any debate of this important development so far.

Why this remarkable silence? Apart from the Jews, Indian Muslims are now the only community not formally covered by the gradually emerging uniformised personal law system of India in relation to marriage and divorce. But it makes perhaps little difference whether a personal law is formally codified or not. What matters are the substantive provisions, and these are in fact similar for Indian Muslim law, despite the absence of codification. So, India now basically has a uniform civil code without admitting it!

But the original vision of a uniform civil code, as a new common code shared by all citizens, has simply not been realised and, I believe, will never materialise.[44]

---

[42] Concern about abuse of conversions to Islam and polygamy appears in *Sarla Mudgal v Union of India*, AIR 1995 SC 1531. Several later cases did not fully support the uniform civil code: see *Ahmedabad Women Action Group (AWAG) v Union of India*, AIR 1997 SC 3614; and *Pannalal Bansilal Pitti v. State of AP*, AIR 1996 SC 1023. The judges in *Lily Thomas v Union of India*, AIR 2000 SC 1650 almost apologised for *Sarla Mudgal* and, while finding a uniform law highly desirable, cautioned against premature action, warning that it might be 'counter-productive to unity and integrity of the nation' (at 1669). The most recent judicial endorsement of a uniform civil code is found in *John Vallamattom v Union of India*, 2003(3) Kerala Law Times 66 (SC), where VN Khare, CJ stated (at 80): 'A common civil code will help the cause of national integration by removing the contradictions based on ideologies'. Oddly, this was about two years *after* the reforms of 2001, discussed below.

[43] And, most notably, only two days after *Danial Latifi v Union of India*, 2001(7) SCC 740 had been decided, in the same sitting as the Criminal Procedure Code (Amendment) Act, 2001 (see below).

[44] AN Allott anticipated earlier that this was 'no more than a distant mirage' (Allott, 1980: 216).

Instead we see, more than 50 years later, how Indian family law has made skilful use of a different model of legal uniformity, which the original law-makers perhaps did not perceive as a viable option, but which represents legal realism in India today.[45] What has happened under our very noses, then, but even most Indians have not noticed (let alone the outside world), is that virtually all the various Indian personal laws have been uniformised along similar lines without losing their status as separate personal laws. This is the revised culture-specific Indian model of a uniform civil code, equity rather than equality, harmonised personal status laws without going as far as introducing a newly codified uniform civil code as originally envisaged.

Post-modern India, therefore, seems to have found an exciting solution to the conundrum of legal uniformity which may be a suitable model for many countries in the world and may require a revision of legal theory (Menski, 2006c: 13–28). The Indian experience shows that achieving greater legal uniformity does not necessarily require dangerous radical surgery through introduction of a strictly uniform code of family law for all citizens. Rather, India employed carefully planned minor surgeries over a long period of time, leaving the body of personal status laws intact. The result is more than cosmetic surgery, however. The various Indian personal laws now look more like each other than ever, but they are still identifiable as Hindu, Muslim, Parsi, and Christian law, by title and substance. They respect ethnic and religious identities without giving up on major national reform agenda, in this case seeking to achieve a more gender-equitable divorce regime.

Despite the impression of a refusal to submit to law reforms, this also goes for Muslim law in India, which retains its uncodified form and respects the apparent reluctance of Muslim leaders and spokespersons to contemplate legal reform. In substance, but not in form, Indian Muslim law now differs little from the other, codified personal laws. This leads to the politically tricky question whether some reforms in this field have actually been made in Hindu-dominated secular India by adjusting the laws in this field to traditional Muslim legal norms.

Whatever the answer to this somewhat provocative suggestion, Indian law has certainly not been static over the last 50 years, but the subtle movements—often highly politicised and perceived as dangerous for communal harmony in a pluralistic state dominated by Hindus and Hindu concepts—have had a deeper silent agenda which has not been abandoned despite communal riots, multiple accusations of fundamentalism, and much politicised commentary by academics, who often place their own agenda above the national interest. India has now virtually reached its aim of having a uniform personal law for all Indians in the fields of marriage and divorce. Since 2001, the result has not been a formally uniform legal provision, but much greater substantive equality than before. The fact that

---

[45] The possibility of this particular model (which was then not favoured) was clearly indicated in Dhagamwar, 1989: 67.

this remarkable achievement, by 2001, had hardly been commented on is largely due to the nature of scholarly politics. As the next part demonstrates, some signal events in Indian law (specifically the *Shah Bano* case) have almost entered global consciousness. This raises another uncomfortable question: Why is there such selective reception of non-European laws in the West?

The answer, I suggest, lies not only in global scholarly agenda, but in the fact that India's determined restructuring into a harmonised concurrent system of personal laws by 2001 does not fit with modernist perceptions of what law reform beyond Europe should look like. India has refused to adopt the uniformising, Western-inspired 1950s modernist agenda and has constructed its own culture-specific model—actually a typically Asian model—taking account of the fact that its people adhere to different legal systems while sharing a territorial framework.[46] Significantly, though, the recent developments are not only a defeat for dreamy universalism or Euro-centric modernism, but also an equally serious defeat for Hindu fundamentalism, which appears to be another major reason why in India itself there has been such widespread embarrassed silence over the 2001 reforms.

Some further explanations are required on the last point. Conscious of being a vast majority, many Hindus had all along wanted all Indians to follow basic principles of Hindu law under the guise of a uniform civil code. More radical elements among Hindu nationalists (the so-called *hindutva* brigades) expected the end of Muslim law in India as a result of the uniform civil code, and thus advocated uniformisation through creeping hinduisation of the entire Indian legal system. During the recent period of governance by a central Indian government composed mainly of Hindu nationalists, the enormity of this Hindu nationalist project struck many more observers, but certainly not enough legal scholars. The uniform civil code project as a tool of *hindutva* would have been deeply unacceptable to the plurality-conscious secularists of India, who clearly prevailed. It would have been disastrous for India as a nation, too.

Since the overriding policy and vision of secularism has always restrained Indian hinduisation and has asserted itself successfully in the context of the uniform civil code, India now has to continue negotiating different concurrent personal laws, and will, in my view, indefinitely retain that system. I see no other acceptable route for a huge nation composed of so many different kinds of people. Plurality consciousness in the garb of Indian secularism (with its special meaning, clearly too little understood) has rescued the nation from the blood-stained dark alleys of communalist excess. Here, then, comparative lawyers find strong evidence that national laws beyond Europe may take a quite different form even in their most developed manifestations, not following the state-centric uniformising territorial paradigms of Western jurisdictions. Beyond Europe, mixed legal systems clearly create different shoots on the global tree of law.

---

[46] This also illustrates, as U Baxi emphasises, that '[t]he local, not the global ... remains the crucial site of struggle for the enunciation, implementation, enjoyment, and exercise of human rights' (Baxi, 2002: 89).

V. THE *SHAH BANO* BANDWAGON: THE MYTH OF INDIAN
POST-DIVORCE MAINTENANCE LAW

Culture-specific legal realism prevailed in Indian law over globalising ideology
also in another, closely related field. It demonstrates even more than the previous
example how Western scholars and their non-Western followers can easily misun-
derstand and misrepresent non-European legal developments that do not fit their
own political and intellectual agenda. The result may be a totally distorted image
of socio-legal reality and even of legal facts, as the present scenario shows.

The Shah Bano bandwagon started rolling slowly, even prior to the case
itself, when explicit concerns about the predicament of divorced wives in India
were imported—significantly by Indira Gandhi[47]—into the revised Criminal
Procedure Code, 1973, which in section 125(1) now defined a 'wife' as including
a divorced wife. This itself is a remarkable pro-women achievement, with tricky
consequences for Indian men, as we shall see. Thus, important social welfare
considerations were introduced, by a combination of legislative alertness and
eventual judicial activism, to help protect Indian divorced wives from vagrancy
and utter destitution. Because the 1973 Code applies to all Indians, it now became
possible for Muslim wives to petition for maintenance beyond the traditional
iddat period of roughly three months,[48] and to ask for life-long maintenance.[49]
Well before the famous *Shah Bano* case of 1985,[50] the Indian Supreme Court had
already established by 1979 that a Muslim ex-husband would only be exempt
from further responsibility for his ex-wife if the provisions he had made were
sufficient for her 'to keep body and soul together'.[51]

By the time Shah Bano's husband engineered his case to get around such
women-friendly social welfare arguments of Indian law, the battlefield was set,
and the key facts are almost stereotypical: After almost 40 years of marriage and
several children, an elderly Muslim woman was divorced by her lawyer husband
who wanted to enjoy life with a younger woman. He claimed that giving his old
former wife the stipulated *iddat* money and the *haq mahr*[52]—together just a few
hundred rupees—fulfilled his legal obligations towards her, relying on traditional
Muslim law to exempt himself from any further liability towards his ex-wife.
The Shah Bano bandwagon really started rolling when she eventually obtained a
verdict from the Supreme Court,[53] holding that her ex-husband had a legal

---

[47] On Indira Gandhi as 'Mother India' and a modern 'traditional' ruler, see Menski, 2006a: 264–6
and Menski, 2003: 258–9.

[48] The *iddat* comprises three menstrual periods and is primarily designed to ascertain paternity of a
child in the womb. During this period, the Muslim husband must maintain the wife.

[49] Earlier, a Muslim husband faced with a claim for maintenance from his wife could simply have
divorced her by *talaq*, ending her status as a 'wife'.

[50] *Mohd. Ahmed Khan v Shah Bano*, AIR 1985 SC 945.

[51] *Bai Tahira v Ali Hussain Chothia*, AIR 1979 SC 362.

[52] The *mahr* or *mehr* is the dower promised by the Muslim husband to the wife at the time of the
marriage. For details, see Pearl and Menski, 1998: 190–201.

[53] *Mohd Ahmed Khan v Shah Bano*, AIR 1985 SC 945.

obligation to maintain her until death (remarriage not being a realistic option) under section 125 of the 1973 Code as well as under traditional *shari'at* law.[54] Even under the Qur'anic provisions, so the Supreme Court said, there was an obligation on divorcing Muslim husbands to be good and generous to a former wife.

Instantly a storm broke loose among Indian Muslims, with riots and vigorous protests which highlighted the difficult relationship between Indian Muslims and the state. The young Prime Minister at the time, Rajeev Gandhi, took remedial action by resorting to rapid codification. Acceding to the demands for a separate Act for Muslims on post-divorce maintenance, Gandhi upset the proponents of a uniform civil code and was universally perceived to cave in to Muslim pressures by swiftly promulgating a special Act called the Muslim Women (Protection of Rights on Divorce) Act, 1986. Despite murmurs of disapproval, there were no riots on the street: the legislative ploy had worked, since everyone was happy to believe that divorcing Indian Muslim men now had no further legal responsibility for their ex-wives after the *iddat* period.[55] Secular activists were disgusted and the *Shah Bano* bandwagon rolled faster.

Despite its pro-women name, this Act was thus believed to be designed to exonerate Muslim ex-husbands from the obligations imposed by the *Shah Bano* case and section 125 of the 1973 Act. The 1986 Act, portrayed as 'a terrible blunder all around',[56] was immediately challenged in numerous constitutional petitions by secularists and modernists,[57] but the Indian Supreme Court sat on these important cases for almost 15 years. We know today that this was deliberate judicial passivism, while outside observers simply saw further evidence that Indian law was inefficient and suffered from extraordinary delays in litigation. There was, however, a higher purpose behind this long judicial silence, which only recent findings have uncovered.[58]

Meanwhile, all around the world, after the 1986 Act, modernist scholars of various hues had climbed onto the *Shah Bano* bandwagon and loudly deplored the backwardness of Indian law, which had allegedly let down Indian Muslim women (see Rajan, 1999; and Jaising: 2005: 7–8, 17–18). *Shah Bano* became a global symbol for the unacceptability of non-Western laws in the modern world and signified India's stubborn patriarchal backwardness. The world was appalled: Journalists joined the chorus, claiming that India had not only abandoned modernity and legal uniformity, but had let down its Indian Muslim women so badly that they would be driven onto the streets and into destitution. India had given in to Muslim fundamentalism. Hardly anybody cared to ask whether it was in line

---

[54] Part of the problem was that five Hindu judges were interpreting the Qur'an.

[55] This is reflected in virtually all serious publications: see, eg Weiss, 1995: 341 at -343, which suggests that the 1986 Act 'revoked Muslim women's rights to maintenance granted under the state's civil laws'.

[56] Mehta, 1994: 98.

[57] The recollections of Baxi, 2002: 82 sharply bring out the conflict of laws scenario.

[58] The evidence is found in Agnes, 2001: 91–2, where she reports that arguments in the Danial Latifi case 'were concluded in August/September 2000 and the judgment is reserved till date'.

with Islamic principles to simply abandon Muslim ex-wives to destitution and prostitution. The dominant tenor was that Muslim men had been given exceptional privileges by the modern Indian state and had got away, once again, on the basis of religious exemption. The contested image of the Indian state was further sullied by such scholarly and publicity-seeking outbursts, which continue today. Even the most respected legal scholars of India, 'modern traditional' positivists at heart, seemed to rely on such political gossip, which created serious misinformation (see Sathe, 2002: 19).

Fortunately for India and for Indian Muslim women, this is not the whole truth. While the cacophony of devastating criticism of Indian law-making drowned the voices of reason for a long time, calm straightforward statutory interpretation in a spirit of legal realism found it hard to gain eventual acceptance in this highly politicised cauldron of anger, contempt and suspicion. The full story is not told in a few words, but ended as a damp squib on 22 September 2001, when the Supreme Court of India finally delivered its verdict in the constitutional petitions of 1986.[59] Remarkably, just two weeks after 9/11, having waited for 15 years, the Indian Supreme Court merely reiterated the familiar legal position that making reasonable distinctions between citizens on the basis of certain criteria—in this case religion—would not be unconstitutional in itself. Muslims in India (this was the message) had a right to be different and to be heard as part of the nation. However, they also had the same basic constitutional obligations as other citizens, so that the terms of their existence were determined ultimately by state law, not by higher communal or religious authority. Indian state law, then, clearly did not give in to Muslim demands, but met them half way: 'You may have a separate law as a matter of Muslim personal status, but you are bound, as everyone else, by shared national criteria and, in this case, specific concerns over social welfare for ex-wives'. At the end of the day, so the Supreme Court's message went, Indian Muslim husbands who wished to divorce retained a legal responsibility under Indian state law (as well as a moral obligation under *shari'at*) for the future welfare of their former wives. In India, these obligations would have to be met within a tight time frame, namely within the *iddat* period, to protect the ex-wife from destitution. Similar legal obligations are shared by all other Indian ex-husbands under section 125 of the Criminal Procedure Code of 1973, which had sparked off the controversy in the first place. Demanding a separate Muslim Act was thus not a viable escape route for Muslim ex-husbands.

No riots followed this skilfully crafted judgment, which avoided explicit reference to the desirability of a uniform civil code. Rather, there was stunned silence, not surprising since the decision in *Danial Latifi* represented another defeat for legal modernism, and was therefore not welcome for positivism-focused legal

---

[59] *Danial Latifi v Union of India*, 2001(7) SCC 740.

scholars. Once again, post-colonial post-modern Indian law was able to respect the traditional plurality of personal status laws while maintaining an equitable uniform system of rule, and protecting women's rights as well.

To analyse this scenario in more depth, one needs to be aware that earlier the stipulated upper financial limit for the ex-husband's support under section 125 of the Criminal Procedure Code, 1973 extended only to 500 rupees, reflecting concerns about vagrancy of near-destitute ex-wives. The Muslim Women (Protection of Rights on Divorce) Act, 1986 contained no such stipulated upper limit, skilfully following the *shari'at* principle that the particular circumstances of husband and wife need to be considered from case to case. That the 1986 Act had not in fact taken away the rights of divorced Muslim wives was gradually confirmed by an increasing number of High Court cases, since well before 1988.[60] It emerged that section 3(1)(a) of the 1986 Act, interpreted progressively, not only required a Muslim ex-husband to maintain his ex-wife during the *iddat* period (which any decent Muslim should do anyway), but he also had to make provisions for the time after the *iddat* period, and should do so during the *iddat* period.[61] In other words, if a Muslim divorced wife reaches the end of her *iddat* period and the husband has not maintained her and has not made reasonable provisions for her future welfare (which might include arranging a remarriage for her) the ex-wife can go to court once the *iddat* finishes and can claim both entitlements.

There is a 1990 case in which a rich Muslim woman claimed more money from her millionaire husband and succeeded.[62] Muslims were thus potentially worse off than all other Indian ex-husbands. The growing body of High Court cases re-assured the faraway Delhi law-makers (who appear to have been watching this carefully) and the Indian Supreme Court (which cautiously maintained a studied silence), that the climate was eventually beginning to be right for further steps in securing better and more equitable financial protection to all Indian ex-wives. That appropriate moment, it appears, came just two days after the *Danial Latifi* decision, on 24 September 2001, when the Indian Parliament removed the 500 rupees limit for all Indian ex-husbands by passing the Code of Criminal Procedure (Amendment) Act, 2001. Notably, this small but highly significant Act restored legal uniformity across the board in financial terms, while maintaining the separate Muslim law enactment.

There seems to be no explanation of legislative intent. Whether this is purposeful silence, legislation by stealth, or a new strategy to reinstate a higher level of

[60] Important decisions are *Arab Ahemadhia Abdullah v Arab Bail Mohmuna Saiyadbhai*, AIR 1988 Guj. 141; *Ali v Sufaira*, 1988(2) Kerala Law Times 94; and a large number of cases in the Kerala High Court and in other courts. There are only a few High Court decisions that absolved Muslim husbands from further responsibility.

[61] The relevant portion in s 3(1)(a) reads that a divorced Muslim woman shall be entitled to 'a reasonable and fair provision and maintenance to be made and paid to her within the *iddat* period by her former husband'.

[62] Significantly, again from Kerala, see *Ahammed v Aysha*, 1990(1) Kerala Law Times 172.

legal uniformity is not clarified, but this Act achieves three important things at once. First, it simply removes the earlier ceiling of 500 rupees in section 125(1) for all Indians, which now seems to encourage litigation by wives and other needy relatives also in middle class scenarios, opening up attractive new avenues for legal business. Secondly, the Act introduced a new proviso to strengthen rights to interim maintenance, *pendente lite*; crucial in Indian conditions of widespread poverty. Thirdly, and closely linked, the amendment promised speedy disposal of cases, as far as possible within 60 days from the filing of the petition. The Indian state evidently means business here, yet people will need time learning to use (and rebalance) this new law, and there will be much resistance. This partly symbolic legislation is likely to have a deep impact on future negotiation of gender relations in Indian law and society. In India's official maintenance law for women after divorce, legal harmonisation was successfully reinstated after the 1986 Muslim personal law detour—a textbook example of an activist and progressive personal law enactment, ultimately designed to strengthen legal uniformity, national cohesion and women's rights.

While this new social welfare law awaits implementation, there are early indications of severe difficulties for most Indian ex-wives in claiming their legal entitlements, including Muslim ex-wives claiming under the 1986 Act.[63] But comparative lawyers, aware that law anywhere in the world has crucial symbolic functions and that these are highly significant in legal systems beyond Europe, should not become too pessimistic: laws everywhere are there to be negotiated in a spirit of plurality-consciousness (Menski, 2006a: 612). That the Indian state so clearly supports the claims of divorced wives from all communities speaks volumes about the awareness of inside players behind such law reforms, the seriousness of the problems faced by many Indian ex-wives, and the role of judicial alertness.

Evidently, the Indian legal developments on post-divorce maintenance closely match the uniform civil code strategies discussed above. Both confirm that substance is more important to the Indian state than form and that legal plurality is not a problem in itself. Developing such plurality-conscious legal arrangements, India has gone well beyond simply protecting the most vulnerable sections of society from vagrancy.

VI. CONCLUSIONS: TOWARDS LEGAL HARMONISATION
WITHIN PERSONAL LAW SYSTEMS

What lessons about laws beyond Europe does this contain for comparative lawyers? The Asian and African experience, exemplified here by India, indicates that all countries, in light of their own culture-specific legal histories and resultant diversities, have to construct legal systems that suit their specific people. There is

---

[63] See the excellent work by Vatuk, 2001: 226–48.

no 'law of the world'; no one model that every state could follow. Beyond Europe, there will always be a vast array of mixed legal systems, from which the 'identity postulate' of any given country needs to be constructed as a kind of ethnic entity,[64] indeed akin to Stammler's 'right law' (Stone, 1965: 167–81).

In these mixed legal systems, local cultural elements are evidently going to remain critical ingredients. In a state like India, these are bound to be Indic, even Hindu, but they will never be exclusively in control. Academic writing, afraid of nationalist fundamentalism, may deny and oppose the influence of Hindu and other personal laws, privileging state-made 'secular' laws over the culturally-anchored laws of the people, but in global comparative law this reflects wishful thinking rather than rational analysis.[65] Not only beyond Europe, comparative lawyers must learn to harmonise local influences with emerging global patterns of thought, avoiding the current mental cul de sacs that dismiss local cultures as obstacles to the implementation of international laws and globally uniform human rights principles. In the age of localised globalisation, a new phase of diversity-conscious identity construction has become necessary, but many scholars from outside Europe, too, find it hard to overcome the Euro-centric domination of legal thinking.

The Indian case studies demonstrate how the tensions between legal uniformity and respect for difference can be (and need to be) carefully negotiated over time to achieve gradually a more justice-sensitive approach that takes account of all stakeholders, especially structurally disadvantaged people like women and children. While blind modernisation was always treated with some caution in India, from about 1988 onwards Indian judges (and probably also Parliament) re-thought the andro-centric strategies of dealing with family conflicts in a wider social welfare context, recognising that most women, living within a patriarchal system, remain disadvantaged in access to resources. Having made repeated symbolic moves to improve the property rights of Indian Hindu and Christian women,[66] the Indian state sees no contradiction in pursuing individualising strategies while also reminding those with privileged access to family resources (mostly men) of their duties towards other family members. Looking specifically at the facts and circumstances of each case—an ancient prominent strategy of legal systems beyond Europe—Indian courts are now more attuned to alleviating the negative effects of patriarchy. While emphasising modern-looking individual property rights, also of women, the post-modern Indian state also re-employs traditional concepts of interlinkedness, specifically traditional family obligations,

---

[64] On the concept of 'identity postulate of a legal culture', see Chiba. He explains that

'[i]t guides a people in choosing how to reformulate the whole structure of their law, including, among others, the combination of indigenous law and transplanted law, in order to maintain their accommodation to changing circumstances' (Chiba, 1989: 180).

[65] An instructive recent example of such supposedly rational Indian legal writing, inspired from Canada, is Sagade, 2005.

[66] Most recently in the Hindu Succession (Amendment) Act, 2005.

as a social welfare mechanism. This dual strategy also protects the state from expectations that it should be directly responsible for social welfare.

This gendered dialectic of rights and duties is more clearly visible now, and shows that India pursues both individual autonomy and reinforcement of collective responsibility to bring better justice within reach for all citizens. The signals are indeed confusing and contradictory. While men can often afford better lawyers and continue to hold unfair advantages as controllers of most resources, in post-modern India they are now again held primarily liable for the welfare of needy family members. This kind of moral responsibility has increasingly been turned into a legal obligation by the quiet activism and occasional deliberate passivism of the Indian judiciary. Indian men, irrespective of religion and personal laws, might now feel that they are all in the same perilous boat: Getting married under Indian law now means taking on serious responsibilities for women and children—potentially for life—whether the marriage lasts or not. As demonstrated, the agenda of uniformising nation building and support for traditional family life have been conflated in unexpected ways, leading to latent perceptions of the oppression of men (see Mahmood, 1986; and Kusum, 1993).

Thus, accepting patriarchy as a fact, which is hardly a difficult task for Indian lawmakers—(though it hurts the feelings of many activists), has become a newly invigorated *Grundnorm* for Indian law today. Post-modern constitutional *dharma* in India, hardly new, feeds again on traditional joint family models (see Menski, 2001). Individualised European welfare models are known, but widely perceived as unsustainable. It is not readily acknowledged that Western laws have not overcome patriarchy and gender discrimination either, and have only managed to remove some glaring discriminations. The realistic post-modern Indian strategies of gendered re-negotiation are far too slow for many impatient activists (Sagade, 2005), and are widely perceived as oppressive (Jaising, 2005).

In this wider context, we see a gradual shift away from the initial vision of a nationally uniform civil code towards a system in which supposedly indigenous values—here the ancient Indic notion of relative justice or equity (*nyāya*)—reassert themselves, now as gender-sensitive re-alignment of responsibilities of Indian family members to each other. As indicated, comparable processes of re-invention of tradition are observable in many legal systems beyond Europe. India's new social welfare orientation has clearly relegated the political football of the uniform civil code to a minor position on the league table of agenda. Through *Danial Latifi*, the Indian state de-prioritised the 'modern' principle of formal legal uniformity in favour of securing 'traditional' equitable legal entitlements. India's judges, secular gate-keepers of the welfare system, firmly cajoled Muslim sharks back into the Indian net of social welfare arrangements. This net of national law does not have escape holes, but different sections. Thus, it becomes clear that Indian Muslims can keep their personal laws, but cannot wriggle out of social welfare obligations that apply uniformly to all Indians.

The Indian state thereby acknowledges the need to avoid, as far as possible, that millions of women, children and now, increasingly, old people become destitute, without being able to offer direct help. In most nations beyond Europe, this is a huge issue. The number of welfare claimants under any category would be enormous. Fiscal prudence, as much as a desire to protect women, children and senior citizens, demands a different approach to social welfare from that stipulated by Western-style state-driven modernity; a lesson that prosperous European nations are painfully learning at present when they have to scale back. Developing countries like India seek to avoid such problems by not even promising their citizens state welfare as part of the social contract.

Despite the prominence of Western-dominated positivist legal indoctrination, many Indian judges have become post-modern Indic realists, probably the hard way. There are accounts of judges choking over their breakfast while reading reports of atrocities committed by the state and its agents.[67] One prominent retired Indian judge recounts how his sensitivities for justice were sharpened by suffering abuses himself (Iyer, 2004: 29).

The almost stunned reception of *Danial Latifi*, two weeks after 9/11, swiftly cleared the road for an alert government to further smooth the path towards greater harmonisation of India's personal status law and a deepening of social welfare commitments. This demonstrates how global events may influence local laws. While critical matters of social welfare have moved centre-stage, the case for the introduction of a uniform civil code in India has now become less and less convincing,[68] especially since the personal law system demonstrates that it can take care of the pressures of potential inequality through a process of gradual harmonisation of all Indian personal laws. Thus, as we saw, India has actually achieved the equivalent of a uniform civil code, but in a different shape than envisaged earlier. Meanwhile legal debates lag seriously behind the actual law, with its situation-specific justice of *dharma, nyāya and shari'at* in their idealistic secularised reconfiguration, which is always going to remain culture-specific.

The challenge now is to make these existing personal laws work better within the protective framework of a general Constitution and wider international norms. This is a central legal task everywhere beyond Europe, by no means unique to Indian law: it is in fact a global legal challenge. The lessons that India has begun to draw from its new scenario of sophisticated plurality will be of much relevance to comparative legal scholarship worldwide.[69]

---

[67] This may lead to *suo motu* petitions, as in the case of a widow aged 80 deprived of pension rights: *Ram Pyari v Union of India*, AIR 1988 Raj. 124.

[68] Significantly, Rajeev Dhavan points out that the uniform civil code agenda 'grows out of a nineteenth-century dream to codify all laws in the manner of the later Justinian of Roman law or of the Napoleonic Code' and 'has now been trivialized into becoming a tragic farce' (Dhavan, 2001: 317).

[69] Recognition that the world is more like India than the United States is reflected in Larson, 2001: 345.

QUESTIONS FOR DISCUSSION

1. To what extent could it be argued that non-Western legal systems are more attuned to pluralism than Western legal systems?
2. What, if anything, can the study of comparative law from an Asian/African angle contribute to global legal theory?
3. Why does the 'legal families' concept not make much sense beyond Europe?
4. Discuss, with examples, the concept of 'interlinkedness' as a central feature of laws beyond Europe.
5. 'Non-European informal methods of dispute settlement might resemble healing rituals rather than legal processes, but they are just as powerful as formal legal mechanisms'.
    Discuss with examples.
6. 'Laws beyond Europe demonstrate that, while recognition of difference and plurality is hardly unproblematic, it does not need to be perceived as a problem that prevents thinking about creative solutions'.
    Discuss with examples.
7. Is law ever culturally neutral?
8. To what extent is legal uniformity a value in itself?
9. Looking at the example of Indian laws, how realistic is it to assume that an ex-husband should maintain his ex-wife until she dies or remarries?

BIBLIOGRAPHY AND FURTHER READING

Agnes, F (2001) *Judgment Call. An Insight into Muslim Women's Rights to Maintenance* (Mumbai, Majlis).
Ahuja, S (1997) *People, Law and Justice. Casebook on Public Interest Litigation*, vols 1 & 2 (London, Sangam Books).
Allott, AN (1980) *The Limits of Law* (London, Butterworths).
Aun, WM (1999) *The Malaysian Legal System*, 2nd edn (Kuala Lumpur, Longman).
Baxi, U (1982) *The Crisis of the Indian Legal System* (New Delhi, Vikas).
—— (1986) *Towards a Sociology of Indian Law* (New Delhi, Satvahan).
—— (2002) *The Future of Human Rights* (New Delhi, Oxford University Press).
Bennett, T (2004) *Customary Law in South Africa* (Lansdowne, Juta and Co).
Benton, L (2002) *Law and Colonial Cultures. Legal Regimes in World History, 1400–1900* (Cambridge, Cambridge University Press).
Bodde, D and Morris, C (1967) *Law in Imperial China* (Cambridge, MA, Harvard University Press).
Carroll, L (1997) 'Muslim Women and "Islamic Divorce" in England' 17.1 *Journal of Muslim Minority Affairs* 97.
Champappilly, S (2006) *Muslim Law. An Analysis of the Judgments Rendered by Justice VR. Krishna Iyer* (Cochin, Southern Law Publishers).
Chiba, M (ed) (1986) *Asian Indigenous Law in Interaction with Received Law* (London and New York, KPI).

—— (1989) *Legal Pluralism: Towards a General Theory Through Japanese Legal Culture* (Tokyo, Tokai University Press).

Cohn, BS (1997) *Colonialism and its Forms of Knowledge: The British in India* (New Delhi, Oxford University Press).

Cotterrell R (1989/2003) *The Politics of Jurisprudence. A Critical Introduction to Legal Philosophy*, 1st edn (London and Edinburgh, Butterworths); 2nd edn (London, LexisNexis).

—— (ed) (2006) *Law in Social Theory* (Aldershot, Ashgate).

David, R and Brierley, JEC (1985) *Major Legal Systems in the World Today*, 3rd edn (London, Stevens and Sons).

Derrett, JDM (1957) *Hindu Law Past and Present* (Calcutta, A Mukherjee & Co).

—— (1970) *A Critique of Modern Hindu Law* (Bombay, NM Tripathi).

—— (1978) *The Death of a Marriage Law* (New Delhi, Vikas).

Dhagamwar, V (1989) *Towards the Uniform Civil Code* (Bombay, NM Tripathi).

—— (12 April 2003) 'Invasion of Criminal Law by Religion, Custom and Family Law' *Economic and Political Weekly* 1483.

Dhavan, R (2001) 'The Road to Xanadu: India's Quest for Secularism' in GJ Larson (ed), *Religion and Personal Law in Secular India. A Call to Judgment* (Bloomington and Indianapolis, Indiana University Press).

Dillon, M (2001) *Religious Minorities and China* (London, Minority Rights Group).

Ehrlich, E (1936) *Fundamental Principles of the Sociology of Law* (Cambridge, MA, Harvard University Press).

Galanter, M (1989) *Law and Society in Modern India* (New Delhi, Oxford University Press).

Glenn, HP (2000/2004) *Legal Traditions of the World: Sustainable Diversity in Law* (Oxford, Oxford University Press).

—— (2005) *On Common Laws* (Oxford, Oxford University Press).

Griffiths, J (1986) 'What is Legal Pluralism?' 24 *Journal of Legal Pluralism and Unofficial Law* 1.

Harding, A (2001) 'May There be Virtue: "New Asian Constitutionalism in Thailand"' 3 *Australian Journal of Law* 24.

Harding, A and Örücü, E (eds) (2002) *Comparative Law in the 21st Century* (London, Kluwer Academic Publishers).

Hallaq, W (1997) *A History of Islamic Legal Theories: An Introduction to Sunni Usul Al-fiqh* (Cambridge, Cambridge University Press).

—— (2001) *Authority, Continuity and Change in Islamic Law* (Cambridge, Cambridge University Press).

Held, D, McGrew, A, Goldblatt, D and Perraton, J (1999) *Global Transformations. Politics, Economics and Culture* (Cambridge, Polity Press).

Hinz, MO (ed) (2006) *The Shade of New Leaves. Governance in Traditional Authority: A Southern African Perspective* (Berlin, LIT Verlag).

—— (17 January 2006) 'Beyond the Limits of Law'. The First Antony Allott Memorial Lecture, held at the School of Oriental and African Studies, University of London.

Hooker, MB (1975) *Legal Pluralism. An Introduction to Colonial and Neo-colonial Laws* (Oxford, Clarendon Press).

Iyer, VR Krishna (2004) *Leaves From My Personal Life* (New Delhi, Gyan).

Jaising, I (ed) (2005) *Men's Laws, Women's Lives. A Constitutional Perspective on Religion, Common Law and Culture in South Asia* (New Delhi, Women Unlimited).

Katz, N (2000) *Who Are the Jews of India?* (Berkeley, CA, University of California Press).

Kelsen, H (1970) *Pure Theory of Law* (trans) from the 2nd rev. German ed. (Berkeley, CA, University of California Press).

Kooistra, M (2001) *Indonesia: Regional Conflicts and State Terror* (London, Minority Rights Group).

Kumar, V (2003) 'Uniform Civil Code Revisited: A Juridical Analysis of John Vallamattom' 45:3–4 *Journal of the Indian Law Institute* 315.

Kuper, H and Kuper, L (eds) (1965) *African Law: Adaptation and Development* (Berkeley, CA, University of California Press).

Kusum, (1993) *Harassed Husbands* (New Delhi, Regency).

Larson, GJ (ed) (2001) *Religion and Personal Law in Secular India. A Call to Judgment* (Bloomington and Indianapolis, Indiana University Press).

Legrand, P (1996) 'How to Compare Now' 16.2 *Legal Studies* 232.

Madan TN (1987) 'Secularism in its Place' 46 *Journal of Asian Studies* 747.

—— (ed) (1994) *Religion in India*, 2nd enl. edn (Oxford, Oxford University Press).

Mahmood, T (1986) *Personal Laws in Crisis* (New Delhi, Metropolitan).

Mehta, V (1994) *Rajiv Gandhi and Rama's Kingdom* (New Haven and London, Yale University Press).

Melissaris, E (2004) 'The More the Merrier? A New Take on Legal Pluralism' 13.1 *Social and Legal Studies* 57.

Menski, W (1995) 'Hinduism' in SM Lipset (ed), *The Encyclopedia of Democracy* (Washington DC–London, Congressional Quarterly Inc and Routledge).

—— (1996) 'Introduction: The Democratisation of Justice in India' in G Singh, *Law of Consumer Protection in India. Justice Within Reach* (New Delhi, Deep & Deep).

—— (2001) *Modern Indian Family Law* (Richmond, Curzon)

—— (2003) *Hindu Law. Beyond Tradition and Modernity* (New Delhi, Oxford University Press).

—— (2006a) *Comparative Law in a Global Context. The Legal Systems of Asia and Africa*, 2nd edn (Cambridge, Cambridge University Press).

—— (2006b) 'Jaina Law as an Unofficial Legal System' in P Fluegel (ed), *Disputes and Dialogues: Studies in Jaina History and Culture* (London, Routledge-Curzon).

—— (2006c) 'Rethinking Legal Theory in Light of South-North Migration' in P Shah and W Menski (eds), *Migration, Diasporas and Legal Systems in Europe* (London, Cavendish Publishing Ltd).

Menski, W, Alam, RA and Raza, MK (2000) *Public Interest Litigation in Pakistan* (Karachi–London, Pakistan Law House and Platinium).

Middleton J (ed) (1997) *Encyclopedia of Africa South of the Sahara* (New York, Charles Scribner's Sons).

Moore, SF (1978) *Law as Process: An Anthropological Approach* (London, Routledge & Kegan Paul).

Örücü, E (2004) *Enigma of Comparative Law—Variations on a Theme for the Twenty-First Century* (Leiden, Martinus Nijhoff).

Pearl, D and Menski, W (1998) *Muslim Family Law*, 3rd edn (London, Sweet and Maxwell).

Rajan, RS (ed) (1999) *Signposts: Gender Issues in Post-Independence India* (New Delhi, Kali for Women).

Ramadan, T (2005) *Western Muslims and the Future of Islam* (Oxford, Oxford University Press).

Ramose, MB (2006) 'The King as Memory and Symbol of African Customary Law' in MO Hinz (ed), *The Shade of New Leaves. Governance in Traditional Authority: A Southern African Perspective* (Berlin, LIT Verlag).

Renteln, A (2004) *Cultural Defense* (New Delhi, Oxford University Press).

Rheinstein, M (ed) (1954) *Max Weber on Law in Economy and Society* (Cambridge, MA, Harvard University Press).

Riles, A (ed) (2001) *Rethinking the Masters of Comparative Law* (Oxford, Hart Publishing).

Robertson, R (2003) *The Three Waves of Globalization: A History of a Developing Global Consciousness* (Nova Scotia, London and New York, Fernwood Publishing and Zed Books).

Sack, P and Aleck, J (eds) (1992) *Law and Anthropology* (Aldershot, Dartmouth).

Sagade, J (1981) 'Law and Social Reforms in Rural India with Special Reference to Child Marriages' 1 *Supreme Court Journal*, Journal section 27.

—— (2005) *Child Marriage in India: Socio-legal and Human Rights Dimensions* (New Delhi, Oxford University Press).

Sathe, SP (2002) *Judicial Activism in India: Transgressing Borders and Enforcing Limits* (New Delhi, Oxford University Press).

Shah, P (2005) *Legal Pluralism in Conflict: Coping with Cultural Diversity in Law* (London, Glass House Press).

Shah, P and Menski, W (eds) (2006) *Migration, Diasporas and Legal Systems in Europe* (London–New York, Routledge-Cavendish).

Smits, JM (ed) (2006) *Encyclopedia of Comparative Law* (Cheltenham, Edward Elgar).

Stone, J (1965) *Human Law and Human Justice* (Stanford, Stanford University Press) 167.

Tamanaha, BZ (1993) 'The Folly of the "Social Scientific" Concept of Legal Pluralism' 20.2 *Journal of Law and Society* 192.

—— (2001) *A General Jurisprudence of Law and Society* (Oxford, Oxford University Press).

Teik, K Boo (2003) *Beyond Mahathir: Malaysian Politics and Discontents* (London, Zed Books).

Twining, W (2000) *Globalisation and Legal Theory* (London, Butterworths).

van der Sprenkel, S (1977) *Legal Institutions in Manchu China. A Sociological Analysis.* Reprint (London, Athlone Press).

Vatuk, S (2001)'Where Will She Go? What Will She Do? Paternalism Toward Women in the Administration of Muslim Personal Law in Contemporary India' in Larson, GJ (ed), *Religion and Personal Law in Secular India. A Call to Judgment* (Bloomington–Indianapolis, Indiana University Press).

Watson, A (1974/1993) *Legal Transplants. An Approach to Comparative Law*, 1st edn (Edinburgh, Scottish Academic Press); 2nd edn (Athens, GA, University of Georgia Press).

Weber, M (1968) *The Religion of China: Confucianism and Taoism* (New York, Free Press and Collier-Macmillan).

Weiss, AM (1995) 'Women and Social Reform: Social Reform in South Asia' in JL Esposito (ed), *The Oxford Encyclopedia of the Modern Islamic World* (New York, Oxford University Press).

Yılmaz, I (2005) *Muslim Laws, Politics and Society in Modern Nation States. Dynamic Legal Pluralisms in England, Turkey and Pakistan* (Aldershot, Ashgate).

Zweigert, K and Kötz, H (1998) *An Introduction to Comparative Law*, 3rd edn (trans) T Weir (Oxford, Clarendon Press).

III

New Territories for Comparative Law

10

Convergence of Private Law in Europe: Towards a New Ius Commune?

JAN M SMITS

KEY CONCEPTS

European private law: *Ius commune;* Unification and harmonisation.

I. INTRODUCTION

T HE EMERGENCE OF a common private law for Europe is a topical issue. Over the last two decades we have seen much debate on the question to what extent the European Union is in need of a uniform private law and what this law should look like. The symbolic starting point of this debate is often seen as the 1989 resolution of the European Parliament in which it called for the elaboration of a European civil code.[1] Since then, many books and journal articles have been devoted to the future of private law in Europe and it is certainly no exaggeration to say that out of this debate a whole new scholarly discipline of 'European private law' has emerged with its own journals,[2] annual conferences and university chairs. This discipline looks at questions related to the convergence of the laws of contract, tort and property as well as of family law. Often, these questions are referred to as the *ius commune*-debate, referring to that period of time (mainly the 17th and 18th century) in which a true common law did exist in continental Europe, even though the present time can hardly be compared with the cultural and legal climate to that time, in which all lawyers—at least in large parts of the European continent—used the same legal language (that of Roman law) and were all part of one unified culture.

---

[1] Resolution A2–157/89. This call was repeated in 1994 (A3–00329/94) and 2001 (C5–0571/2001). Cf. resolution A6–0055/2006.

[2] Among these are the *Zeitschrift für Europäisches Privatrecht* (ZEuP, established 1993); *European Review of Private Law* (ERPL, 1993); *Maastricht Journal of European and Comparative Law* (MJ, 1994); and *Europa e Diritto Privato* (1998).

The aim of this contribution is to discuss several of the questions which the emergence of a European private law raises; not to give definitive answers but to provide the reader with the tools necessary to answer them for him or herself. First (Part II below), attention is paid to the *need* for convergence of private law: What are the reasons usually given for harmonising or unifying private law and are these reasons in any way convincing? Secondly, the question is raised how convergence of private law takes place at present. Thus, unification by treaties and harmonisation through Directives are discussed below in Part III, together with the far-ranging idea of creating a European civil code. A third question (Part IV below) is whether convergence of private law is at all possible. Some have argued that the differences among the 28 private law systems we have in Europe (27 national systems and Scots law) are too large to come to any real convergence. This is an important argument which deserves to be mentioned here. Finally, various other methods to reach (further) convergence of private law in Europe will be considered. Should the European Union continue with the present harmonisation process by issuing European directives or should other methods (also) be used to reach more convergence of law? For instance, such wide-ranging pleas have been made for promoting a European legal science and education and for convergence of law through competition of legal systems. These and other methods are discussed in Part V below.

Before embarking upon our venture, one remark on terminology seems apt. Often, the terms convergence, unification, harmonisation and legal integration are used interchangeably to describe the process of the coming together of the national private laws of the Member States of the European Union. In this sense, these are 'utterly flexible and indeterminate' terms (Boodman, 1991). However, it seems useful to reserve the term harmonisation for the specific method of legal convergence through European Directives. This leaves diversity as to the form and means used in place, only harmonising the end result to be achieved by the Member States (*cf* Article 249 of the EC Treaty[3]). On the other hand, I will use the term unification for the process that may lead to uniform law (such as in the case of treaty law). This uniform law presupposes that national legal systems completely disappear and that a new, uniform, law is applied in a uniform way across all of Europe—a result that, as we will see, is hardly ever reachable.

II. THE NEED FOR CONVERGENCE

Diversity of Private Law in Europe

Any contribution on the unification of private law should start with acknowledging that the European Union's private law is at present immensely diverse. One can identify four groups of private law regimes within the European Union on

---

[3] Treaty Establishing the European Community (Consolidated version), [2006] OJ C 321.

the basis of common history, the sources of law recognised and the predominant mode of legal thought. The first group consists of the common law systems of England and Ireland, with their emphasis on judge-made law and the central authority of the English House of Lords and the Irish Supreme Court respectively. Cyprus (a British colony until 1960) also belongs to this group. The second group consists of the traditional civil law countries, characterised by a central role for a national civil code, but also by a highest court whose decisions are in practice often just as important as the code provisions. Among these countries, one can distinguish between those that have a code that is to a greater or lesser extent still based on the Code Napoleon (France, Belgium, Luxemburg, Spain, Portugal, Italy and Malta) and those that have a code that is based more on the German model (Austria, Germany, Greece and The Netherlands).

A third group is formed by the Scandinavian Member States (Denmark, Sweden and Finland). They not only share a common history, but also have several common statutes, such as a common statute on sale of moveable goods and a common contract law Act. Finally, there is the large group of countries that entered the European Union in 2004, almost all of which have a new or at least recently revised civil code (Poland, the Czech Republic, Slovakia, Hungary, Estonia, Lithuania, Latvia and Slovenia). The way in which these new or revised codes are applied and interpreted by the national courts cannot be compared to the way in which this is done in traditional civil law countries. Generally speaking, the mode of interpretation is much more literal.

It should also be noted that within these four groups there can be considerable differences in substance. Even such basic topics as formation of contract, damages in tort and transfer of property are often treated differently depending on the jurisdiction involved. And where the substance is the same, the judicial style and way of reasoning may still differ.

The First Motive for Convergence: the Internal Market

What should one think of these differences? Sometimes, it is seen as a goal in itself to get rid of legal diversity: differences between European countries are to be avoided because differences are *bad*. Why should it be that title to a moveable object be transferred with the contract of sale in Belgium, but upon delivery in The Netherlands? And why should the victim of a traffic accident be protected less in Portugal than in France? This line of reasoning, which does not even address the adverse effects of diversity, does not seem very convincing. There have to be other, *real*, motives for unification.

The development of the common market is usually seen to be the most impor-tant motive for convergence of private law within the European Union. Articles 2 and 3 of the EC Treaty make it clear that 'the approximation of the laws of the Member States to the extent required for the functioning of the common mar-ket' may be pursued. This implies that in so far as national private law stands in the way of this common market, the European Union is competent to take measures.

It is worthwhile to look in somewhat more detail at this relationship between the common market and private law. How is it, exactly, that divergence of private law may distort the functioning of the European economy? The reasoning of the European legislator becomes clear from the following passage from the preamble to Council Directive 93/13/EEC on Unfair Terms in Consumer Contracts:[4]

> [T]he laws of the Member States relating to the terms of contract between the seller of goods or supplier of services, on the one hand, and the consumer of them, on the other hand, show many disparities, with the result that the national markets for the sale of goods and services to consumers differ from each other and that distortions of competition may arise amongst the sellers and suppliers, notably when they sell and supply in other Member States.

It is thus the creation of similar European conditions for the *seller* (or otherwise professionally acting party) that is decisive for the European Union: if legal regimes differ too much, competition among sellers from various European countries will be distorted. It is this basis of Article 3 (elaborated in Article 95 of the EC Treaty) on which most European Directives with relevance for private law are based. This so-called *acquis communautaire* consists of almost 20 Directives on the core of private law.[5] Most of them deal with specific contracts such as consumer sale, time-share, package travel, consumer credit, financial transactions and distance marketing, others regulate, for example, products liability, electronic commerce and unfair contract practices. There are no Directives on family law and the law of immoveable property for the simple reason that these topics are probably not covered by Article 95.

An interesting question is whether the argument of the European Commission is completely convincing: Does harmonisation of private law really promote the internal market? This is an important issue because, in its 'Tobacco judgment' of 2000,[6] the European Court of Justice (ECJ) held that a measure based on Article 95 of the EC Treaty must *genuinely* have as its object the improvement of the conditions for the functioning of the internal market. The mere finding of disparities between national rules and 'the abstract risk' of distortions of competition is not enough: these must be real or at least probable. If this condition is not met, the ECJ can strike down the measure taken.

To the European Commission, the question has a clear answer. For consumers and small and medium-sized enterprises in particular, not knowing other private law regimes may be a disincentive to undertaking cross-border transactions. This may lead some suppliers of goods and services to refrain from offering to consumers in other countries, while others will enter into business but then suffer from

---

[4] [1993] OJ L 095/29.

[5] There are various text editions of these Directives available. See, eg Radley-Gardner, Beale, Zimmerman and Schulze, 2003; and Smits, Hardy, Hesen and Kornet, 2006.

[6] Case C–376/98 *Germany v European Parliament and Council* [2000] ECR I–8419 (**ECJ**).

high transaction costs.[7] This way of reasoning is, however, not entirely satisfactory. In itself it is true that concluding a transfrontier contract is more costly than concluding a contract in one's own country, but it is an open question whether harmonisation of private law will reduce these costs substantially. It is likely that in this respect not only other parts of the law (such as tax law and procedural law) are more important, but it is also to be recognised that the costs of transfrontier contracting are primarily caused by *de facto* barriers such as different languages, cultural differences and distances (Smits, 2006b; and Vogenauer and Weatherill, 2006). Also for consumers, such barriers seem to be more important than differences in private law.

The Second Motive for Convergence: a European Civil Code as a Symbol of one European Identity

Another motive for unification of private law is in the desire to create a European identity: one Europe requires one private law (Alpa, 2000). In the same way that the 19th century national codifications were a means to create a national identity distinct from the identity of other peoples, a European civil code would be the symbol of one Europe and of solidarity among the Member States (mentioned in Article 2 of the EC Treaty). This motive is closely connected to the very reason for the founding of the European Communities. In the aftermath of World War II, the desire to bury the hatchet once and for all among European countries and get rid of national differences that might serve as a new reason for conflict, was an essential part of this.

The identity argument does not seem very strong. It is often remarked that the core of the European identity does not lie in uniformity but in cherishing the European plurality of languages, cultures and law. What is more, even the official motto of the European Union is 'united in diversity'. One only needs to point at the example of the United States to realise that one national identity does not necessarily imply a uniform law: every American state has its own private law. It also seems likely that for example, a common foreign policy is much more a token of European unity than a common law (*cf* Wilhelmsson, 2002).

III. A EUROPEAN PRIVATE LAW THROUGH IMPOSITION: INTERNATIONAL CONVENTIONS, EUROPEAN DIRECTIVES AND THE IDEA OF A EUROPEAN CIVIL CODE

Unification through International Conventions

The traditional method of achieving uniformity, ie through binding treaties between different countries, has not been very successful in the field of private law. The reason is obvious: A treaty can only come into being with the agreement of the contracting states and will only enter into force after approval by the states

---

[7] See, eg Communication from the European Commission to the European Parliament and the Council: A More Coherent Contract Law: An Action Plan, COM (2003) 68 final, OJ EC 2003, C 63/01.

in which the treaty is to apply. Experience shows that reaching such uniformity is particularly difficult in the area of private law. And if agreement *is* reached, the treaty is often either based too strongly on one legal system or has, by way of compromise, escaped into vague formulations, leaving the treaty with little unifying effect in practice.

Private law conventions include treaties on bills of exchange and cheque law, leasing, factoring, letters of credit, liability for nuclear damages and oil pollution and transportation law. The best-known example is the United Nations Convention on Contracts for the International Sale of Goods 1980 (CISG)[8] that provides substantive rules for transfrontier and commercial sale of moveable goods. This convention is now ratified by almost 70 countries. One of the main problems with the CISG, however, is that its provisions are rather abstract and consequently leave much discretion to national courts in interpreting the convention. This also illustrates a more general problem with unification through conventions. They usually do not provide for a highest court that can take the lead in interpreting the treaty, thus leaving real unification ineffective.

There is still a third problem with conventions, at least from the viewpoint of legal convergence in Europe. This is that it is open for states to decide whether to become a party to the treaty or not. Thus, the CISG was not ratified by the United Kingdom and Portugal. Of course, this can also be seen as an advantage because where the convention *is* ratified, it is passed through national parliaments and is thus democratically more legitimate than, for example, European Directives or Regulations. It is precisely for this reason that some argue that instruments unifying private law should first pass through national parliaments also in order to gain sufficient democratic legitimacy.

Harmonisation through European Directives

Until now the most widely used method of achieving a higher degree of uniformity between the private laws of the European Union has been through European Directives. Directives are binding as to the result to be achieved, but leave form and methods of implementation to the Member States (Article 249 EC Treaty). Thus, harmonisation leads to a 'law of uniform results', whereby the rules that achieve these results are national in character. This has the obvious advantage that a Member State can decide for itself how to fit a new Directive into the national legal system's structure and terminology. The reverse side of this is that it is sometimes difficult for the European Union institutions to monitor to what extent a Member State has implemented the Directive in a proper way. Another problem with Directives is that the duty to implement European law can lead to *Fremdkörper* (foreign bodies) inside the national legal system. A well-known example of this is the introduction of a requirement of good faith in consumer contracts in English law. This has been

---

[8] Final Act, U.N. Doc. A/CONF.97/18 (1980).

criticised by Teubner as forming a 'legal irritant' (Teubner, 1998), not leading to harmonised law *and* endangering the unity of the private law system.

The present *acquis*, as outlined above, has not generally been met with enthusiasm. It has been characterised as being fragmentary, arbitrary, inconsistent and ineffective. It is fragmentary because it only covers certain topics, a 'Brussels brick here and there' (Remien, 1996: 8 at 11). For example, in the field of contract law only some specific contracts are covered and of these contracts only specific aspects are dealt with (such as the duty to inform the consumer about the qualities of the object sold). This is worrying for continental lawyers, as their ideal of a comprehensive and consistent civil code is being disrupted by law of European origin. It was precisely this fragmentation that prompted the European Parliament's call for a European civil code. The *acquis* is also quite arbitrary in the sense that it is unclear why some types of contracts are being covered and others are not. Why is it that package travel and consumer sale are addressed, but not the regular insurance contract? If the European legislator believes in harmonisation to remedy defects in the functioning of the common market, there is much more to be addressed than previously. Thirdly, the *acquis* is inconsistent. Often time periods for revocation differ without good reason (from seven calendar days in case of door-to-door sales, seven working days for distance contracts and 10 calendar days for timeshare, to 14 calendar days for distance marketing of financial services). Finally, the *acquis* is not very effective. Almost all directives in the field of private law aim at minimum harmonisation, meaning that Member States can establish more stringent provisions to protect consumers. The effect of this is that companies are still being confronted with divergent legislation and may still be deterred from doing business elsewhere. Minimum harmonisation may thus not be suited to create the desired level playing field for European business.

These problems were decisive in leading the European Commission to start a debate about the future of European contract law.[9] It is likely that this will lead to a so-called 'common frame of reference' (CFR) in the field of contract law, which is, after all, the most important part of the present *acquis*. This CFR will provide three types of provisions. First, it will consist of definitions of legal terms like 'contract' and 'damages' so that we know how these should be interpreted in a 'European' way. Secondly, the CFR is to contain fundamental principles (such as freedom of contract, binding force and good faith). The most important part of the CFR, however, will consist of model rules of contract law, drawing on the present *acquis* and the 'best solutions' found in the Member States' legal orders. This CFR will serve as a 'tool box' for the European legislator:[10] where it finds this appropriate it can make

---

[9] Communications from the European Commission to the European Parliament and the Council on European Contract Law, COM (2001) 398 final, OJ EC 2001, C 255/1; A More Coherent Contract Law: An Action Plan, COM (2003) 68 final, OJ EC 2003, C 63/01; European Contract Law and the Revision of the *Acquis*: the Way Forward, COM (2004) 651 final.

[10] Communication from the European Commission to the European Parliament and the Council: 'European Contract Law and the Revision of the *acquis*: The Way Forward' COM (2004) 651 final, Annex 1.

use of the CFR to draft directives or review the existing *acquis*. In addition to this, the ECJ and national courts could also use the CFR as a source of inspiration.

One can express doubts about the usefulness of the CFR as long as it is only a non-binding instrument. We have to wait and see whether it will really be used to re-draft the present Directives that are often a compromise of the various views in the Council of Ministers. It is also hard to see how the CFR can deal with the above problems of the *acquis* being fragmentary, arbitrary and only offering minimum harmonisation. It probably takes a more active European legislator to deal with these problems. This raises a fundamental question: Could the disadvantages of the current centralist methods of unification not be avoided if the European Union were to take more decisive action and introduced a European civil code?

The Idea of a European Civil Code

Traditionally, civil codes, as we find these on the European continent, aim at a systematic, coherent, complete and national codification of private law. Most of the continental codes were introduced as part of a desire to create a national identity for the countries involved. They cannot, in any way, be compared to the 'codes' that we know in the common law world, such as the Uniform Commercial Code (UCC) and the American compilations of separate statutes. Civil law codes are the alpha and omega of civil law reasoning, even though there are many statutes on private law outside of the codes and even though the courts have an essential role in interpreting the codes and in creating new law.

It is quite obvious that a European civil code cannot be like a national code in this civil law way. Two differences immediately spring to mind. First, a European code as a systematised and complete whole presupposes a European system of private law (Jansen, 2006: 253). Such a system does not exist yet. What is more, the view that law should be put into a comprehensive code is not adhered to by common lawyers. It seems rather arrogant to think that the civil law approach of codifying law would also appeal both to the English and the Irish. Below (Part IV below), we will see that this is an important argument against the view that convergence of law is possible by imposing rules on the European Member States. Secondly, if a European civil code were to be created, it could only be successful if also a European court were also put into place to control its interpretation. It is unlikely that the most effective way of doing this—that is, by giving this European court the competence to decide concrete cases that have passed through the national judiciary—would be accepted by countries such as France or the United Kingdom.

There is yet another reason why introducing a civil code for the European Union[11] would be problematic. Article 95 of the EC Treaty may provide a sufficient basis for the regulation of contract law (see above), but certainly not for

---

[11] See, in more detail, Smits, 2002: 28 *ff.*

other parts of the law one usually finds in national codes (think of family law, property law and tort law). In addition to this argument, one wonders if it is wise to base the far going step of introducing a European civil code into the EC Treaty. A separate treaty would probably be a better option because this would allow national parliaments to decide on the introduction of the code. It has already been argued by some authors[12] that, in drafting the CFR, it is wrong to follow a merely technical approach. Instead of fully discussing the political decisions that are to be made—like to what extent a European code should enhance 'social justice' and protect weaker parties—the focus is now on the *drafting* of rules.

All this leaves little doubt about the chances of introducing for Europe a civil code as known in the civil law tradition. However, types of codes other than the traditional ones are more feasible. Two possibilities spring into mind. One is to create a model code that can be chosen by the Member States if they so desire. This is the model of the American UCC. It has the clear advantage that no competence in the EC Treaty is needed. The decision is taken at the national level. Moreover, not every state would have to opt for ('opt in') the code and if it did, it could amend the code as it wished. The other possibility is to have the relevant actors (such as contracting parties) elect a European set of rules to exist *next* to the national ones. Such an 'optional instrument' was proposed by the European Commission in its 2004 Communication. However, in both scenarios private law will continue to suffer from an inevitable fragmentation.

Unification by Imposing Law

Looking over these attempts to create a more convergent private law in a centralist way (through the classic methods of unification and harmonisation), the result is not encouraging for those who have set their hopes on European and State institutions. But there is still another important argument that needs to be taken into account in this debate: Is it at all possible to have convergence of private law? We have already seen that this was denied by Gunther Teubner for the principle of good faith. In the next part, we will see that Pierre Legrand makes a more extreme claim about the possibility of unifying law.

IV. IS CONVERGENCE OF LAW AT ALL POSSIBLE?

Once one has established that there is sufficient reason for the unification of private law, another question calls for attention: If a European private law is put into place, will it lead to *real* convergence? This is denied by some, including the Canadian scholar Pierre Legrand, who eloquently argued that a European civil code, or any other attempt at unifying European private law, is not feasible

---

[12] Study Group on Social Justice in European Private Law, 'Social Justice in European Contract Law: a Manifesto' (2004) 10 *European Law Journal* 653 *ff.*

because of cultural differences among the various European countries and in particular between the civil law and common law tradition.

Legrand takes as a starting point that merely drafting uniform *rules* does not result in uniform *law*. To him, law is much more than just rules. The meaning of a particular rule in a particular cultural and national context can only be established after studying that context. And this context, the legal *mentalité*, differs between the various countries. Legrand claims that these differences are even unbridgeable in the case of continental civil law and English common law. Epistemologically, the common law reasons inductively with an emphasis on facts and related case law, while in the civil law systematisation is of crucial importance. Whilst the *civilian* lawyer tries to rationalise judgments and statutes into a logical system, the Anglo-American lawyer has an aversion to formal rules and makes a conscious choice for driving out and even fighting continental civil law influence. This choice stems from cultural differences: an English child is already a *common-law lawyer in being*, claims Legrand, long before it ever knows that it wants to be a lawyer.

This view has far-reaching consequences for the convergence debate. It implies that any attempt at harmonisation of civil law and common law is doomed to failure. The Englishman will continue to look at European measures as a common lawyer, and the Frenchman as a *civilian* lawyer. To the former, law is an *ars judicandi*, for the latter a *scientia iuris*. Moreover, in Legrand's view the whole idea of a European codification is arrogant because it imposes on common lawyers the supposedly superior world view of civilian legal doctrine. The truth is, claims Legrand, that they each offer fundamentally different accounts of reality. This leads Legrand to conclude that 'legal systems ... have not been converging, are not converging and will not be converging'(Legrand, 1996: 52 at 61–2; and Legrand, 1997).

Legrand's argument is to be taken seriously. Even though it has radical implications and was severely attacked as being, *inter alia* 'pessimistic', 'destructive', 'anti-European' and 'esoteric',[13] no one will deny that superficial similarities among legal systems do not reveal anything about underlying differences in legal culture. This point is well formulated by Esin Örücü:

> We can predict ... that if, for example, codes were moved into the common law, they would soon become glossed by judicial decisions, exceptions would creep in and the general principles therein would lose their significance altogether. Again, if the style of decisions in the common law were inserted into the civilian legal culture, within a short period of time they would start getting shorter and less comprehensible; facts would become blurred; reference to past decisions would be replaced by reference to statutory provisions and so on (Örücü, 1987).

This is both a very practical and a highly convincing view on the European convergence process. It makes clear that law and society are closely interrelated and

---

[13] Legrand himself sums these up, and other, qualifications of his own work by others (Legrand, 2006).

texts will always be interpreted in the legal culture in which they are applied. There may come a time when this legal culture is entirely European, but this time has not yet come. In this sense, Legrand is right to say that European legal systems 'have not been converging' and 'are not converging.' To hold that they also 'will not be converging' is a more problematic statement because this we cannot predict: legal culture can change.

This critical view of the European convergence process points to other than centralist methods towards a common private law for Europe. If we agree that *imposition* of a uniform text will not lead to uniform *law*, we should look for methods that allow the element of national legal culture to play a role in deciding whether uniformity is needed or not. Only such *soft* methods of convergence allow us to find out when legal culture stands in the way of unification. After all, the premise is that if unification is not left to the Member States or to European institutions but to the actors that are directly touched by legal unification, they will decide to what extent they are in need of uniform law. Bottom-up methods of unification make this possible.

V. HOW TO ACHIEVE FURTHER CONVERGENCE? THE BOTTOM-UP APPROACH

Introduction

In this part, the various non-centralist methods that can be used to reach further convergence of private law are discussed. Such 'voluntary creation' can take different forms. First, the role of legal education and legal scholarship is discussed. Then, attention is paid to the method of drafting principles of European private law. Finally, we will look at competition of legal systems.

European Legal Science and Education

The first method to be discussed here is the creation of a European private law by legal science and legal education. Its adherents draw inspiration from the times before the national codifications of private law in the 19th century. They point out that the *ius commune* tradition, as based on the Justinian codification of Roman law, provided a common European background to the local variations of law in Europe for a long time. Just as the *ius commune* of the 17th and 18th centuries was a legal system primarily made at the Universities, a new *ius commune* should find its origin there as well. Paul Koschaker (1879–1951) therefore started his famous book on the history of Roman law in Europe with the sentence: 'there is no legal discipline that is more European than private law'(Koschaker, 1947). It implies that students can be raised in a European legal fashion and practitioners could benefit from the comparative legal material made available to them by scholars. Thus, it is by 'reception' that in the end a *ius commune europaeum* will emerge.

Of course, it takes European handbooks to be written and national courts and legislators being able to look for solutions abroad, but if such revival of the European legal tradition (and therefore a *denationalisation* of law) takes place, it opens the door towards a new *ius commune*. Reinhard Zimmermann, one of the best known proponents of this view, puts it like this:

> [T]he essential prerequisite for a truly European private law would appear to be the emergence of an 'organically progressive' legal science, which would have to transcend the national boundaries and to revitalise a common tradition (Zimmermann, 1997: 293).

This is an appealing view that will probably continue to inspire legal scholarship in the following decades. But there are two things we should be aware of in evaluating the importance of legal scholarship and education for the Europeanisation process.

First, it should not be forgotten that for this new European legal scholarship to be effective it should differ in one important aspect from the old *ius commune*. The old *ius commune* was to a very large extent a European continental tradition only. English law was but part of it to a limited extent. Zimmermann is right in stating that in England also Roman law was taught at the universities of Oxford and Cambridge and was sometimes applied by courts, but this should not lead us away from the fact that the *ius commune* tradition was far more influential on the European continent (Zimmermann, 2004: 21 *ff*). A new European legal science should be just as much formed by English scholars as by *civilians*—and there is no doubt that this is what will happen.

Secondly, we should once more emphasise that the old *ius commune* was primarily a scholarly tradition. It did not mean that there was uniformity in legal practice. Just as Roman law could only incrementally influence legal practice, a new European legal science will only be received very slowly in national legal practice. In this respect, one must not forget that in most continental countries there have been two centuries of separate development of national law. In all European universities, the study of national law is still far more important than the study of a European common core. This cannot be changed in one or two decades—if ever.

But apart from these two remarks, the importance of a Europeanisation of legal science and education cannot be over emphasised. It is the necessary 'flanking measure' (van Gerven, 2002: 405 *ff*) for any harmonisation or unification: the denationalisation of private law must necessarily go hand in hand with an internationalisation of legal education and research. Legal scholars are always glad to add that it is the only way to forego Rudolph Von Jhering's famous statement of 1852 that legal science had been degraded to 'Landesjurisprudenz' and that this was a situation unworthy for a true science (von Jhering, 1924: 15).

In the context of this chapter, it is only possible to point at some initiatives to develop European curricula and research projects. The number of law faculties offering fully developed bachelors degrees in European or comparative law can still be counted on the fingers of one hand, but there are not many European universities left where no attention is paid to the comparative aspect at all. Besides, it will never be the case that all European law students will attend a 'European' law school. This is also the experience in the United States. Only the 'national law schools' train their students in American law and their graduates form only a small percentage of the total number of American law graduates (Reimann, 1996). It is the law of the state that is taught in most law schools. If one adds to this the often major differences in the educational system of the European Member States, as well as linguistic differences, one cannot be too optimistic.

On the other hand legal scholarship has Europeanised enormously since the 1990s. Apart from many new law journals and books devoted to the study of European private law, several big research projects have been initiated. They illustrate the various approaches one can adopt in doing this type of research. Thus, within the so-called Trento common core project, inspired by the work of Rudolf Schlesinger on formation of contract in the 1960s (Schlesinger, 1968), a large group of scholars, mostly from European countries, have united to seek the common core of European private law. Their approach is to draft fictitious cases and see how these cases are solved in the various European jurisdictions. They thus do not 'wish to push in the direction of uniformity' but only want to *describe* how the law differs. This is also the case with the Casebooks for the Common Law of Europe, a project inspired by the example of American casebooks. Here too, the aim is 'to help uncover the common roots of the different legal systems ... not to strangle ... diversity'.[14] Unlike the Trento project, these casebooks contain cases actually decided in Europe's main jurisdictions. Casebooks on tort law, contract law and unjust enrichment have already been published. Another large project directed at educating PhD students in a European way is the Maastricht based *Ius Commune* Research School. Finally, mention must be made of the so-called European Civil Code project, led by the Osnabrück professor Christian Von Bar. Its aim is to draft provisions that could become part of a European civil code.

Again, the example of the United States shows that we should be aware of the fact that the influence of these writings on national legal practice may be very little. In the United States, the most popular academic products are casebooks, but they hardly play a role in legal practice (Reimann, 1996). But perhaps, the climate in Europe is different: the '*Ius Commune* Casebook on Tort Law', for example, has already been cited at least twice by the House of Lords.[15]

Drafting Principles of European Private Law

Another well-known method consists in drafting 'principles' of European private law. The best-known set of European principles is that formed by the *Principles of European Contract Law* (PECL), first published in 1995.[16] They were followed

---

[14] Foreword to van Gerven, Larouche, Lever, Von Bar and Viney (eds), 1998 *Casebook—Tort Law: Scope of Protection* (Oxford, Hart Publishing – out of print): v.

[15] *McFarlane v Tayside Health Board* [2000] 2 AC 59 (HL); *Fairchild v Glenhaven Funeral Services Ltd* [2002] 3 WLR 89 (HL).

[16] All the principles mentioned can be found in Smits, Hardy, Hesen and Kornet, 2006. Another set of contract law principles, based on the Italian Codice Civile, is provided by Gandolfi, 2001.

by *Principles of European Trust Law* (1999), *European Insolvency Law* (2003) and *European Tort Law* (2005). Within the European Civil Code-project, principles on tort law, special contracts and restitution are being drafted, and work on *Principles of European Family Law* is well under way. Unlike what the word 'principles' would suggest, these sets often contain very detailed rules after the model of civil code provisions. The drafters usually try to codify either the common core of European legal systems or a 'progressive' solution which they find to be the best rule for the European Union. It is important to emphasise that these principles are not drafted by the EU itself, but are private initiatives mainly by legal academics. This does not preclude the European Commission from closely following and sometimes even co-financing the drafting process.

There is little doubt that the idea of drafting principles of private law is based on the American experience with the so-called 'restatements' of law. Since 1923, the American Law Institute has tried to make the law of the 50 American private law jurisdictions more intelligible by issuing such restatements. Still, there is a difference: American law is presumed to form one common law—despite diversity among the States—that only needs to be described, while the drafters of the European principles have to make what are sometimes difficult choices between different solutions. But both the restatements and the sets of principles should have persuasive authority: they can inform parties, courts and legislators because of their inherent quality.

It may be useful to illustrate the functions of European principles by reference to the PECL. The drafters themselves describe three functions (Lando and Beale, 2000: xxiii and Article 1:101). First, contracting parties can expressly adopt the PECL as the law applicable to their contract. A choice for such a 'neutral' set of rules can be useful where parties cannot reach agreement about an applicable national law. However, at present this choice is problematic because it is not certain that Article 3 of the EC Convention on the Law Applicable to Contractual Obligations 1980[17] (the Rome Convention) allows a choice for other than a *national* legal system. This implies that national mandatory law will remain applicable. It is also doubtful whether parties will find the PECL *precise* enough, with its rather abstract provisions, and in the absence of extensive case law on how to interpret these.

A second function of the PECL is that they can serve as a model for legislators and as a tool for courts. Thus, the Unidroit Principles of International and Commercial Contracts of 1994, in content very similar to the PECL, were used as a model for parts of the new Civil Code of the Russian Federation and the new Chinese Contract Code. Likewise, courts can interpret their own law or the CISG in the light of the PECL.

Finally, the PECL can be a tool for the institutions of the European Union itself when making contracts with third parties or when drafting new legislation.

---

[17] Convention on the Law Applicable to Contractual Obligations (Rome 1980) (80/934/EEC)

It is, for example, likely that the CFR (Part III above) will closely resemble the PECL. In the same vein, the ECJ could profit from the principles of European tort law. Article 288 of the EC Treaty states that the liability of the Community institutions and its civil servants exists 'in accordance with the general principles common to the laws of the Member States'. Without scholarly work on what these principles are, the ECJ will have a tough job in deciding a case on this provision.

How should these projects to draft principles be assessed? We should keep two things in mind. The first is that representing the law through general principles is typically a civil law way of looking at the law. The phrase by Oliver Wendell Holmes (1841–1935) that 'general propositions do not decide concrete cases'[18] has more than a grain of truth in it, even for civil law jurisdictions. In a national legal system, drafting principles is fruitful because there is an underlying morality that all national legal actors know of. To make use of principles at the European level is more problematic, at least as long as a European morality is missing. Again, an example is provided by the principle of good faith. Article 1:201 of the PECL unconditionally states that 'each party must act in accordance with good faith and fair dealing'. What this principle means when deciding an individual case very much depends on the national system in which it is applied. In France, it may mean something else than in Germany, let alone in England.[19] In this sense, European principles can only offer a skeleton, leaving out the 'flesh and blood' that national systems offer.

Second, it is likely that there are diverse views on what are the right and 'fair' principles for the European Union.[20] Thus, one uniform principle can probably not take into account the diversity of different socio-economic constellations within Europe, unless it is a very abstract one. This is also what the Privy Council accepted for the British Commonwealth when it stressed that the strength of the common law tradition is that it is able to adapt itself to the differing circumstances of the different countries.[21]

It is for this reason that I believe the main aim of drafting European principles should not be found in their practical functions, or in being a precursor to imposed law, but elsewhere. It is first and foremost the role they can fulfill in legal education and research that makes them worth drafting. They can be a language of communication among students and scholars from different countries, a *tertium comparationis*. And in this function in particular, the PECL and Unidroit Principles have already been very successful: they are used at many universities as teaching material, not primarily to study a future European law but to better understand one's own legal system.

---

[18] *Lochner v New York* 198 US 45 (1905).

[19] *Cf Walford v Miles* [1992] 2 AC 128 (HL) at 138.

[20] Walzer, 1983: 8 'There is no single set of primary or basic goods conceivable across all moral and material worlds—or, any such set would have to be conceived in terms so abstract that they would be of little use in thinking about particular distributions'.

[21] *Invercargill City Council v. Hamlin* [1996] 2 WLR 367.

Competition of Legal Systems

Above we have seen several reasons why attempts to unify private law may not be successful: there may not be sufficient basis for it in the EC Treaty, it may lead to a fragmented and incoherent law, and national legal culture may prevent convergence from taking place. But there are also positive arguments in favour of legal diversity. One of these arguments was originally put forward by the American scholar Charles Tiebout (1924-1968). Tiebout describes the needs of firms and consumers in terms of differing preferences (Tiebout, 1956). If there is diversity of law, it means that legal systems can compete with each other to satisfy these preferences: consumers and firms can choose the legal system which, in their view, best protects their interests, provided they can leave a jurisdiction which they do not like ('vote with their feet'). Introducing uniform law would reduce this exit-opportunity and lead to less preferences being satisfied.

Apart from this advantage of satisfying as many preferences as possible, there is still another benefit of diversity of law. It makes it easier to make innovation in the law. Looking at other countries' solutions to legal problems shows whether these solutions function or not. In this way, states can be regarded as 'experimenting laboratories'. The well-known American judge Louis Brandeis (1856–1941) once wrote:[22]

> It is one of the happy incidents of the federal system that a single courageous State may, if its citizens choose, serve as a laboratory and try novel social and economic experiments without risk to the rest of the country.

Experience elsewhere can be an enlightening or a frightening example. Thus, recognition of gay marriage by The Netherlands in 2002 has been an example to other countries. Recognition of this type of marriage would most probably not have been possible in case European family law would have been harmonised by the European Union.

It is important to see that, in this view, diversity of law is not seen as a coincidence but as a reflection of diverging preferences: the role of eg good faith is different in England than in Italy because of, perhaps unconscious, diverging views on what is just. Often this argument is related to Friedrich Carl Von Savigny, who emphasised the 'organic link' between the law and the people (Von Savigny, 1814: 78). But one need not endorse this 'Historical School' perspective to admit that it is wrong to impose one uniform preference on all: those for whom the law exists should decide which rules serve their interests best.

An important question is whether this competition among legal systems could also contribute to unification of law. In fact it could do so in two different ways. First, if everyone would be able to move to the jurisdiction they prefer, practically, it would mean that there would be only one law applied. But it is likely that long before this exit-process would be finished, something else would happen. This is

---

[22] Brandeis, J in *New State Ice Co. v Liebmann* 285 US 262 at 268.

the second way in which competition contributes to uniform law: if too many people were likely to leave, national governments would be stimulated to make their jurisdiction more attractive by offering the same or a more attractive law as the other country. This is also one of the main objections[23] to allowing full competition of legal systems: it may lead to the famous 'race to the bottom'—a level of law that is the lowest of all the jurisdictions among the competitors. Yet, as often as this fear for 'social dumping' is expressed, there is as yet little empirical evidence to support it (Barnard, 2000). More importantly, full competition among legal systems does not seem to be desirable. It is precisely the purpose of minimum harmonisation to allow the 'race' only to take place within certain restrictions. Sometimes, the law has to be mandatory if it is to offer protection to weaker parties.

As long as this minimum level is guaranteed, regulatory competition provides an important method of convergence because the need for unification is primarily determined by legal practice itself and is not imposed from above. This still leaves open the question what such competition should look like. Two remarks have to be made.

First, it should be clear that competition does not necessarily imply that citizens or firms really move *physically* from one jurisdiction to another. It is also possible that they choose another legal system while physically staying in their country of origin. In the field of company law, the European Court of Justice has already paved the way for a free movement of companies.[24] They can establish the firm in their country of choice while still doing business in their place of residence. If they prefer the English limited company as a more suitable means for their company than the Dutch 'BV' or the German 'GmbH', they are free to choose it. Within the limits of Article 3 of the Rome Convention, this is also possible in the field of contract law.

Theoretically, one could even think of a variant in which not so much an entire legal system is chosen as the applicable law but *specific rules* are. This 'free movement of legal rules' allows the transfer of rules from one country to another on a 'market of legal culture'. (Mattei, 1997; and Smits, 1998). There is abundant evidence for such 'legal transplants' leading the legal historian Alan Watson to conclude that most legal change is the result of borrowing law from elsewhere (Watson, 1974: 94). Thus, in the 19th century, contract law rules, such as those on offer and aceptance, were exported from Germany to the common law world, while at the present time many Anglo-American institutions like trust, franchising and lease are being borrowed by countries on the European continent. Of course, it would be wrong to think that law can travel through time and place without any fundamental change in meaning, but it is certainly true that these transplants do contribute to a more uniform law.

---

[23] There are other objections as well: see Smits, 2006a.
[24] Case C–212/97 *Centros Ltd v Ehrvervs—og Selskabsstryelsen* [1999] ECR I–1459 (ECJ).

Secondly, competition only works if there is sufficient information available about other legal systems. Often, this is not the case: a Dutch party may not know the intricacies of German law or English law, let alone Polish or Czech law. This is different in the United States, where there is plenty of information available on more than 50 jurisdictions and where all this information is in one language. Within the European Union, comparative lawyers thus have an important role to fulfill in unveiling information about foreign law. Moreover, the legislator can try to promote competition by creating an 'optional legal system'. Such a '28th system' (in view of the presence of Scots law besides the 27 state legal systems, not a completely justified term) was in fact proposed by the European Commission in its Communication of 2004.[25] It could, for example, be chosen by contracting parties if they felt it served their interests better than a national jurisdiction. The advantage of such a 26th system is that it could be made available in all languages of the European Union and be made as transparent as possible. Once such an attractive system were put into place, one could see whether parties would choose it or not. In this way, creating an optional system is an experimental way of establishing the need for uniform law: if legal culture prohibited the choice of other laws than one's own, it would become apparent automatically.

VI CONCLUSION: AN ORGANIC DEVELOPMENT OF LAW, OR NOT?

The above can be summarised in six points:

(1)   With 26 different jurisdictions, the present private law of the countries of the European Union is very diverse. This diversity provokes four different questions. First, is there a need for unification of private law in Europe? Secondly, how does convergence take place at present? Thirdly, is convergence of law at all possible? Fourthly, what are the best methods for moving towards a more uniform private law?

(2)   There are usually two motives given for unification of private law: the development of the European common market (Articles 2 and 3 of the EC Treaty) and the need for a symbol of a European identity. However, it is questionable whether these arguments—if they are accepted—justify replacement of national private law by a uniform law of European origin: they need to be weighed against the arguments in favour of diversity. These arguments are that legal diversity allows different (national) preferences to be satisfied and allows innovations in the law.

(3)   Traditionally, convergence of private law takes place through unification (by international conventions) and harmonisation (through European Directives). Each of these methods has its problems. Harmonisation through Directives is the most advanced in the field of contract law, but

---

[25]   See n 10 above. See also the First Annual Progress Report on European Contract Law and the *Acquis* Review, COM (2005) 456 final.

this *acquis* suffers from being fragmentary, arbitrary, inconsistent and ineffective. It is an open question whether the newly proposed Common Frame of Reference (CFR) will remedy these deficiencies.

(4) There is a recurrent call for a European civil code. Although such a code could deal with most of the problems associated with the present methods of convergence, there are also a number of objections to it. One is that the idea of a code as a systematic and complete codification (and a European court to interpret it) is alien to common lawyers. Another objection is that there is no basis for a comprehensive civil code in the EC Treaty.

(5) The possibility of unifying European private law is denied by Pierre Legrand. He argues that there are unbridgeable epistemological differences between the civil law and the common law tradition, rendering convergence of law impossible. This argument prompts the need for a 'bottom-up' approach towards convergence: If unification is not left to the European institutions but to the national actors that are directly touched by it, they will decide to what extent they are in need of uniform law.

(6) Three bottom-up approaches towards convergence are: the enhancement of European legal science and education; the drafting of principles of European private law; and allowing competition of legal systems. Each of these *soft* methods has its merits and problems. The problems can partly be overcome by an active approach by the European legislator setting minimum standards to protect weaker parties and creating optional legal regimes.

The gist of the above is that, as long as we are uncertain about the need for uniform law and do not know whether national legal culture stands in the way of its imposition, a 'bottom-up' approach towards unification is to be preferred. In my view, only this approach can reveal to what extent national private law is resistant to unification. It does not mean the European legislator should sit still: it can very well promote competition of legal systems by creating an optional regime and by setting minimum standards. Likewise, the drafting of principles and enhancing of European legal education and scholarship are vital as flanking measures. But in the context of this book, the fact that the author adopts this 'organic' view of the convergence process is not important, as the reader will also find the arguments for the opposite view in the above. This is what makes the discipline of European private law such a fascinating topic for debate: many views on the future of private law in Europe can be argued for.

QUESTIONS FOR DISCUSSION

1. List three problems with unification by way of international conventions. To what extent do these problems also persist with respect to harmonisation through European Directives?

2. How do you weigh the arguments in favour of and against a uniform European private law? Is it in this respect useful to differentiate between various areas of the law (contracts, torts, property and family law)?

3. In the 1997 volume of the Modern Law Review, there is an article by Pierre Legrand entitled 'Against a European Civil Code' (Legrand, 1997). In this contribution, he applies his line of thinking discussed above to the idea of introducing a civil code for Europe. Do you agree with this line of thought?

4. Competition of legal systems seems to be a promising method for allowing convergence without at the same time endangering national legal culture. Can you also identify objections to this method? Can these be overcome?

BIBLIOGRAPHY AND FURTHER READING

Alpa, G (2000) 'European Community Resolutions and the Codification of Private Law' *European Review of Private Law* 333.

Barnard, C (2000) 'Social dumping and the race to the bottom: some lessons for the European Union from Delaware' 25 *European Law Review* 57.

Boodman, M (1991) 'The Myth of Harmonization of Laws' 39 *American Journal of Comparative Law* 699.

Collins, H (1995) 'European Private Law and the Cultural Identity of States' 3 *European Review of Private Law* 353.

Gandolfi, G (ed) (2001) *Code européen des contrats* (Milano, Giuffre Editore).

Grundmann, S and Stuyck, J (eds) (2002) *An Academic Green Paper on European Contract Law* (The Hague, Kluwer Law International).

Hartkamp, AS, M. Hesselink, E. Hondius, C. Joustra, E. du Perron and M. Veldman, (eds) (2004) *Towards a European Civil Code*, 3rd edn (Nijmegen and The Hague: Ars Aequi Libri).

Hesselink, MW (2001) *The New European Legal Culture* (Deventer, Kluwer).

—— (2002) *The New European Private Law* (The Hague: Kluwer Law International).

Jansen, N (2006) 'European Civil Code' in JM Smits (ed), *Elgar Encyclopedia of Comparative Law* (Cheltenham, Edward Elgar).

Koschaker, P (1947) *Europa und das römische Recht* (Munich, Beck).

Lando, O and Beale, H (eds) (2000) *Principles of European Contract Law*, Parts I and II (The Hague, Kluwer Law International).

Legrand, P (1996) 'European Legal Systems Are Not Converging' 45 *International and Comparative Law Quarterly* 52.

—— (1997) 'Against a European Civil Code' 60 *Modern Law Review* 44.

—— (2006) 'Antivonbar' 1 *Journal of Comparative Law* 37.

Örücü, E (1987) 'An Exercise on the Internal Logic of Legal Systems' 7 *Legal Studies* 318.

—— (2004) *The Enigma of Comparative Law: Variations on a Theme for the Twenty-First Century* (Leiden, Martinus Nijhoff).

Mattei, U (1997) *Comparative Law and Economics* (Ann Arbor, MI, University of Michigan Press).

—— (2003) *The European Codification Process: Cut and Paste* (The Hague, Kluwer Law International).

Radley-Gardner, O, Beale, H, Zimmermann, R and Schulze, R (2003) *Fundamental texts on European Private Law* (Oxford, Hart Publishing).

Reimann, M (1996) 'American Private Law and European Legal Unification—Can the United States be a Model?' 3 *Maastricht Journal of European and Comparative Law* 217.

Remien, O (1996) 'Über den Stil des Europaischen Privatrechts' 60 *RabelsZeitschrift* 8.

Schmid, CU (2001) 'Legitimacy Conditions for a European Civil Code' 7 *Maastricht Journal of European and Comparative Law* 25.

Schlesinger, RB (ed) (1968) *Formation of Contracts: a study on the common core of legal systems* (Dobbs Ferry, Oceana).

Smits, JM (1998) 'A European Private Law as a Mixed Legal System' 5 *Maastricht Journal of European and Comparative Law* 328.

—— (2002) *The Making of European Private Law* (Antwerp-Oxford: Intersentia).

—— (2006a) 'European Private Law: a Plea for a Spontaneous Legal Order' in DM Curtin, JM Smits, A Klip and JA McCahery (eds), *European Integration and Law* (Antwerp-Oxford, Intersentia)

—— (2006b) *The Need for a European Contract Law* (Groningen, Europa Law Publishing)

Smits, JM, Hardy, R, Hesen, G and Kornet, N (eds) (2006) *European Private Law* (Nijmegen, Ars Aequi Libri).

Teubner, G (1998) 'Legal Irritants: Good Faith in British Law or How Unifying Law Ends Up in New Divergences' 61 *Modern Law Review* 11.

Tiebout, C (1956) 'A pure theory of local expenditures' 64 *Journal of Political Economy* 416.

Van Caenegem, RC (2002) *European Law in the Past and the Future* (Cambridge, Cambridge University Press).

Van Gerven, W (2002) 'Codifying European Private Law: Top Down *and* Bottom Up' in S Grundmann and J Stuyck (eds), *An Academic Green Paper on European Contract Law* (The Hague, Kluwer Law International).

Vogenauer, S and Weatherill, S (eds) (2006) *The Harmonisation of European Contract Law* (Oxford, Oxford University Press).

Von Jhering, R (1924) *Geist des römischen Rechts*, vol 1, 8th edn (Leipzig).

Von Savigny, FC (1814) *Vom Beruf unserer Zeit für Gesetzgebung und Rechtswissenschaft* (Heidelberg).

Walzer, M (1983) *Spheres of Justice: a Defense of Pluralism and Equality* (New York, Basic Books).

Watson, A (1974) *Legal Transplants* (Edinburgh, Green).

Wilhelmsson, T (2002) 'The Legal, the Cultural and the Political—Conclusions from Different Perspectives on Harmonisation of European Contract Law' *European Business Law Review* 546.

Zimmermann, R (1997) 'The Civil Law in European Codes', in DL Carey-Miller and R Zimmermann (eds), *The Civilian Tradition and Scots Law* (Berlin).

—— (2004) 'Roman Law and the Harmonisation of Private Law in Europe' in AS Hartkamp, M Hesselink, E Hondius, C Joustra, E du Perron and M Veldman (eds), *Towards a European Civil Code*, 3rd edn (Nijmegen, Ars Aequi Libri).

Principles of European Contract Law (PECL):
http://frontpage.cbs.dk/law/commission_on_european_contract_law

Unidroit Principles of International Commercial Contracts:
http://www.unidroit.org/english/principles/contracts/main.htm

Principles of European Tort Law:
http://www.egtl.org/Principles/index.htm

The Common Core of European Private Law ('Trento-project'):
http://www.jus.unitn.it/dsg/common-core

European Commission's website on European Contract Law:
http://ec.europa.eu/comm/consumers/cons_int/safe_shop/fair_bus_pract/cont_law/
   index_en.htm

Study Group on a European Civil Code:
http://www.sgecc.net

Ius Commune Casebooks for the Common Law of Europe:
http://www.law.kuleuven.be/casebook/index.php

11

Comparative Family Law: Moving with the Times?

MASHA ANTOKOLSKAIA

KEY CONCEPTS

Marriage; Capacity to marry; Equality of spouses; Same-sex marriage; Grounds of divorce; Irretrievable breakdown of marriage; Cohabitation outside marriage; Registered partnership; Harmonisation of family law.

I. INTRODUCTION

T HE PRESENT FAMILY law in Europe is to a large extent the product of the radical transformations that commenced in the 1960s and 1970s. As result of these changes, by the end of the millennium the monopoly of the traditional family based on marriage as a life-long union, which seemed to have been so universal and everlasting, had gone—a situation that is considered almost as self-evident today as it has been unthinkable for centuries. The society dominated by traditional values gave way to a pluralistic society, one in which different forms and sets of family values co-exist alongside each other. Divorce and serial monogamy began to be considered normal. In this general atmosphere of tolerance, men and women became more and more free to choose between marriage or some other form of personal relationship. Extra-marital sex, non-marital cohabitation, and birth outside wedlock lost their stigmatic character. Same-sex relationships became first decriminalised, then legalised, and then, in some countries, even equated with marriage. Due to the fact that more and more children were born outside marriage, it became increasingly unacceptable for the legal status of these children to differ from that of children born within a marriage. Thus, eventually illegitimate children were granted a truly equal place alongside their legitimate brothers and sisters. The women's rights movement managed to overcome the centuries-long dominance of the man within the family.

Another important aspect of the contemporary picture of family law in Europe is the influence of the human rights instruments. By far the most important among these instruments is the 1950 European Convention of Human Rights and Fundamental Freedoms. The European Court of Human Rights (ECtHR) has both been accused and praised for deriving 'a whole code of family law'[1] from its Article 8, which initially contained no more than the negative obligation on the part of the state to refrain from arbitrary interference in the family. In developing the concept of family rights, the ECtHR had to use the so-called 'dynamic interpretation' of the Convention. Because the text of all three Articles relating to family rights—Articles 8 (the protection of family life), 12 (the right to marry and to found a family) and 14 (the prohibition of discrimination)—did not always provide relief, the Court, in deciding cases, had to involve factors which were external to the Convention, and considered that 'the Convention must be interpreted in the light of present-day conditions'.[2] Since the political mandate of the Court was indubitable only within the margins of the Convention, it needed an additional source of authority every time it employed an extensive or even contra-legal interpretation of the original provisions. In seeking such authorisation, the ECtHR generally referred to the consensus or the 'common European standard' among the Contracting States. One of the vehicles that balanced the need for a gradual extension of the protection of family rights and the self-restraint of the Court's power was the doctrine of 'margin of appreciation'. Because the scope of protection of family rights under the Convention has been developed by the Court on an unsystematic case-by-case basis, the level of protection that is actually attained in various fields of family law is also quite uneven. As the following examples will show, it varies from the lowest common denominator in respect of the right of divorce, to a high degree of protection with regard to the equality of marital and extramarital children and the right to marry on the part of post-operative transsexuals.

II. THE LAW OF MARRIAGE

A New Concept of Marriage

Since the 1960s, marriage has undergone important transformations. The importance of the procreative function of marriage diminished as marriage ceased to be the only union through which children were bestowed full legal rights in respect of the parents and their families (Willekens, 1997: 69). The relationship between the spouses evolved from the inferior position of the wife to spouses' equality. Due to women's emancipation, increasing female employment and the progress of social welfare, the function of the family as provider of financial means and security also diminished. This development contributed to an attitudinal shift from marriage based on economic necessity and duty, to marriage based on affection and free commitment. The modus of marriage generally

---

[1] *Marckx v Belgium* Series A no 13 (1979) 2 EHRR 330 (Sir Gerald Fitzmaurice, dissenting).
[2] *Ibid.*, para 41.

evolved from life-long monogamy to serial monogamy. This evolution of the concept of marriage is reflected, after some delay, in the European human rights law. The initial variant of the Convention for the Protection of Human Rights and Fundamental Freedoms of 1950 was based upon the traditional concept of marriage as a heterosexual, male-dominated union. Article 12 of the European Union Charter of Fundamental Rights, and the identical provision of Article II–69 of the rejected European Union Constitution slightly modernised this concept by making the right to create a family independent of the right to marry. The main tendencies in regard of marriage during the last half of the 20th century in every European country were the secularisation and de-ideologisation of marriage law, the acceptance of the right to marry as a fundament human right, the diminishing of marriage impediments, the lowering of the age of capacity to marry, and the granting of equal legal rights to spouses.

General Tendencies in the Law of Marriage

De-ideologisation of the Law of Marriage

The present state of affairs is that the actual level of de-ideologisation of marriage is still quite different throughout Europe. Two opposing tendencies with regard to the de-ideologisation of marriage law are apparent in Europe throughout the period under discussion. On the one hand, the avoidance of ideological declarations both in the definition of marriage and during the civil marriage ceremony can be considered as one of the general trends of marriage law. On the other hand, many European countries (eg England and Wales) are quite reluctant to strip marriage law completely of its traditional ideological *décor*.

In Western European countries the tendency towards the de-ideologisation of marriage comes down to stressing the contractual nature of marriage and the release of marriage law from religious influence. In the Eastern European countries the same tendency is apparent, but here it is rather a reaction to communist marriage ideology. In both cases the de-ideologisation tendency reflects the growing awareness that the law is unable to regulate feelings and moral convictions. It is for these reasons that many countries have chosen to avoid declarative rules that cannot be enforced and at best can only provide some educational effect. Another incentive to avoid ethical declarations has to do with the difficulty of finding shared ethical values with regard to marriage in a modern pluralistic society. The best example of such an attitude is the Swedish 'neutrality policy' formulated during the preparation of legislative reform of 1973 (Agell, 1998: 127–9). This policy was based on two fundamental choices—respect of ideological pluralism and the non-privileged legal treatment of marriage as compared to unmarried cohabitation. According to the neutrality policy,

> the legislation on marriage should not contain laws of specified, ethical nature, since ethical viewpoints could vary and couples should be allowed to develop their relationship within their own individual assumptions and values (*ibid*: 127).

The tendency towards de-ideologisation is also overtly manifest in Dutch marriage law, which deliberately avoids dealing with ethical and religious aspects of marriage and limits itself to regulation of its practical civil aspects. The same applies to Russian law. In similar fashion, Swedish law deliberately allows spouses to avoid vows for life.

At the same time, many European countries continue to preserve the traditional ideological message of the law of marriage. In spite of the secularisation and liberalisation of marriage law during the 1960s and '70s, in conservative circles marriage retains a symbolic ethical and ideological meaning, inherited from the past. This appreciation is still an appealing argument for retaining the vows for life and the duty of fidelity as part of the marriage ceremony. Of course in a time of widespread divorce, a promise of commitment for life is more an expression of intent than the reflection of a future reality.[3]

Secularisation of the Law of Marriage

The secularisation of marriage law has gone so far that presently there is no European state that does not provide for the civil registration of marriage. It is here, however, that the 'common core' ends. Europe continues to be divided into countries with obligatory civil marriage and those with a two-tier system of civil and religious marriage.

A majority of European jurisdictions, eg the Czech Republic, Denmark, England and Wales, Finland, Greece, Croatia, Iceland, Ireland, Italy, Latvia, Lithuania, Malta, Norway, Northern Ireland, Poland, Portugal, Scotland and Sweden, provide for a dual system of civil and religious marriage. Such a solution could be characterised as half-hearted secularisation, but it could also be attributed to respect for pluralism and religious tolerance. The latter interpretation is reinforced by the presence of countries with the most liberal family law, e.g. the Scandinavian countries, among the countries with a dual system of marriage celebration. Two tendencies, perhaps at first glance contradictory, can be traced with respect to the development of the dual system of marriage registration in Europe. On the one hand, predominantly Catholic countries, like Malta and Spain, have democratised the choice between civil and religious marriages. On the other hand, in Latvia, Lithuania, Poland, the Czech Republic and Croatia, where the compulsory civil registration of marriage was associated with the militant atheism of the Soviet domination, alternative religious celebration of marriage was introduced in the framework of the post-communist restoration of democracy (Kaserauskas, 2004: 322). The two aforementioned tendencies complement each other in the way that they provide individuals with free choice with regard to the form of the celebration of their marriage.

---

[3] For instance, in the English literature it is suggested that the life-long character of marriage can now only be interpreted to mean that 'the marriage must last for life unless it is previously terminated by a decree or some other act of dissolution' (Lowe and Douglas, 2007: 41).

A minority of European jurisdictions, ie Austria, Belgium, Bulgaria, Estonia, France, Germany, Luxemburg, Moldova, The Netherlands, Russia and Turkey, recognise only civil marriage as a legal marriage. Some, while refusing religious marriage's civil consequences, do not prohibit its celebration prior to civil registration. Others, eg France, Belgium, Luxemburg, Switzerland, The Netherlands, Germany, Austria and Turkey, are more strict and do prohibit the celebration of religious marriage prior to civil celebration. All of these countries adhere to a strict separation of church and state and consider that, as the religious celebration of marriage is allowed prior or subsequent to civil marriage, religious freedom is sufficiently safeguarded without the attribution of legal consequences to such celebration.

Capacity to Marry

After the 1960s, national laws on capacity to marry became increasingly devoid of remnants of religious concepts of marriage and related legal restrictions. The right to marry assumed the status of a fundamental human right in 1950, when it was incorporated into Article 12 of the European Convention of Human Rights. However, neither Article 12 nor the case law of the European Court of Human Rights or later international human rights instruments, like Article 9 of the non-binding European Union Charter and the corresponding Article II–69 of the rejected European Union Constitution, present the right to marry as an absolute and unconditional right. The determination of restrictions to the right to marry is left to the national laws of the Member States (van Grunderbeeck, 2003: 201 *ff*). This capacity on the part of the national states is rather broad, albeit not unrestricted. Thus, the national states are not allowed to implement restrictions affecting the fundamental essence of the right to marry. Such violation of a right to marry is, however, not easily acknowledged. As a result, the international human rights instruments did not initiate any developments in this area, but rather codified the common core that had already been achieved through the progressive development of the substantive laws of the national states.

The laws governing the age of marriage display a similar tendency towards coupling the age of marriage to the age of majority. This development is clearly supported by the lowering of the age of majority as part of the overall emancipation of youth after the 1960s. At present the great majority of European countries have coupled the age of marriage to the age of majority which is set at 18 years. In only a few countries (eg the United Kingdom) the general age of marriage is still below the age of majority. A second tendency that can be observed is a trend towards equating the age of marriage for both sexes and lifting the minimum age of marriage. This transformation has to do with the later socialisation of the youth in industrialised countries and the equalisation of the social roles of men and women. It has also been held that differing ages of marriage for males and females falls within the scope of unjustified discrimination on the ground of sex, prohibited by the international human rights instruments.

There is also a clear tendency to diminish the number of marriage impediments that are based on consanguinity and affinity. A marriage between descendents and ascendants is prohibited all over Europe. The same applies to a marriage between brothers and sisters.[4] Some countries have limited the number of impediments to these closest blood-relatives.[5] However, the majority of European countries provide for a more extensive list of impediments based on consanguinity and affinity. These prohibitions are often mitigated by the possibility to seek dispensation.

Transsexual Marriage

As was already mentioned, the traditional requirement that the marriage partners must be of opposite sexes has become a matter of a sharp discord. Many European countries on their own initiative have hesitantly granted transsexuals the right to marry. The issue of transsexual marriage remained nonetheless controversial. The process of piecemeal recognition of the rights of transsexuals to marriage was brought to an end through the intervention of the European Court of Human Rights. The matter has more than once been a subject of scrutiny by the ECtHR,[6] but only in 2002, in the case of *Goodwin v United Kingdom*[7] did the ECtHR finally acknowledge that the refusal to provide legal recognition to the new gender of post-operative transsexuals violates both Article 8 and Article 12 of the Convention. In this landmark decision the ECtHR, in spite of the continuing absence of consensus among the European countries, withdrew the issue of the legal recognition of post-operative transsexuals from the scope of the Contracting States' margin of appreciation and imposed on them the obligation to grant transsexuals the right to marry. The significance of this decision can hardly be overestimated. It has already had,[8] and will continue to have, an indefectible impact on the marriage laws of all European countries.

Of course, the marriage of persons of the same sex remains a highly controversial issue of capacity to marriage. With the ECtHR's abandonment of the traditional notion that procreation is an indispensable characteristic of marriage,[9] one of

---

[4] Only Sweden has made marriage of half-brothers and sisters possible upon dispensation; see Bradley, 1996: 67.

[5] Eg Austria, Germany, The Netherlands, Norway, Russia and Sweden.

[6] In *Rees v United Kingdom* Series A no 106 (1986); *Cossey v United Kingdom* Series A no 184 (1990); *X, Y and Z v United Kingdom* (1997) 24 EHRR 143; and *Sheffield and Horsham v United Kingdom* (1998) 27 EHRR 163.

[7] *Goodwin v United Kingdom* (App no 28957/95) (2002) 35 EHRR 18.

[8] For instance, the law of England and Wales has been changed according to this decision. The Gender Recognition Act 2004 (which came into force on 4 April 2005) allows post-operative transsexuals to marry in their acquired gender.

[9] The court observed that 'Article 12 secures the fundamental right of a man and woman to marry and to found a family. The second aspect is not however a condition of the first and the inability of any couple to conceive or parent a child cannot be regarded as *per se* removing their right to enjoy the first limb of this provision.' *Goodwin v United Kingdom* (App no 28957/95) (2002) 35 EHRR para 98.

the most important arguments against same-sex marriage seems to have been removed. Also, the definition of the right to marry in Article 9 of the European Union Charter and Article II–69 of the rejected European Union Constitution contains some alterations, compared to the corresponding Article 12 of the Convention. In contrast to Article 12, the Charter does not use the words 'men and women' in respect to this right. However, the Explanatory note reveals that

> this Article neither prohibits nor imposes the granting of the status of marriage to unions between people of the same sex. This right is thus similar to that afforded by the Convention, but its scope may be wider when national legislation so provides.

At the moment the majority of European jurisdictions, with the exception of The Netherlands, Belgium and Spain, are reluctant to open up marriage for same-sex couples. However, there are indications that Sweden and Denmark are likely to join these three countries in the near future. At the same time, the proliferation of same-sex marriage has also provoked a counter-reaction. Thus, in December 2005, Latvia introduced no less than a constitutional ban on same-sex marriage.

Equalisation of the Rights of Spouses

In the 1970s–1980s, all Western European countries embraced formal legal equality between the spouses, which had already been introduced in Russia and Scandinavia in the 1920s and in West Germany and the Eastern European countries after the Second World War. By the end of the 20th century, spousal equality, save for some remnants in the field of the law of names, had been achieved in every European country.

III. LAW ON DIVORCE

Advance of No-Fault Divorce

The law on divorce was deeply affected by the transformations of the 1960s–1970s. The most important change was that divorce lost its social stigma and is no longer seen as deviant behaviour. The period after the 1960s is characterised by important liberalisation of divorce—and in Ireland, Portugal, Spain and Italy—by its (re)-introduction. The transformation of divorce law underwent in this period a major qualitative change. Before this time, the steady liberalisation of divorce law amounted, for the most part, to a 'steady accumulation of specific grounds', largely accomplished by adding 'new specific matrimonial offences and conditions' to already existing ones (Phillips, 1988: 563). In the 1960s the main event of liberalisation became the introduction and the advance of no-fault divorce.

England and Wales

In England the 1969 divorce reform reflected a compromise between the proponents and opponents of liberalisation of divorce. The new Law formally introduced a single ground for divorce: the irretrievable breakdown of marriage. However, this breakdown could be proven only upon the existence of certain circumstances (Lee, 1974: 73). As a result 'the practical proposals to implement this new principle [irretrievable breakdown] were as conservative as the idea itself was radical' (Stone, 1990: 307). Three of the 'circumstances' were the same old fault grounds that were accepted before: adultery, cruelty (which was now called 'unreasonable behaviour') and desertion. In addition there were no-fault 'circumstances': two years of separation followed by an application for divorce by mutual consent; and five years of separation followed by an unilateral application, contested by the other spouse (*ibid*). The state control of divorce was reinforced by the introduction of a hardship clause. In 1996 a long-debated attempt to introduce no-fault divorce based on a period of separation for reflection failed. The Family Law Act 1996, which provided for no-fault divorce, did not come fully into effect.[10]

Germany

In Germany the fault grounds were abolished during the 1976 divorce reform and irretrievable breakdown became the sole ground for divorce. In the case of divorce by agreement, the breakdown was presumed if the spouses had been separated for at least one year. It has been suggested in German literature that the real purpose for this one-year delay was 'to serve the scruples of those who disapprove of divorce by mutual consent', which remained highly controversial, as undermining the stability of marriage (Giesen, 1973). If the spouses had lived apart for three years, this constituted an irrefutable presumption of marital breakdown. However, a hardship clause allowed the court to postpone the dissolution of a marriage in exceptional circumstances (Gottwald, Schwab and Büttner, 2001: 59).

France

When divorce reform was first contemplated in France in the 1970s, French society appeared to be highly politically divided upon the issue. The spirit of the French Revolution

> was flourishing in some of the learned writings, and the divorce proposals of the socialist and communist parties were seeking to eliminate fault divorce completely and replace it with divorce for objective grounds (Glendon, 1976).

The opponents of liberalisation of divorce opposed these ideas and the general public was hopelessly split (*ibid*). As a result, the French divorce law provided for a mixed system: *divorce à la carte* (*ibid*), retaining the fault-based divorce, alongside divorce by mutual consent and divorce on the ground of the irretrievable

---

[10] In 2001 the Government announced its decision to repeal it (Lord Chancellor's Department, *Divorce Law Reform—Government Proposes to Repeal Part II of the Family Law Act 1996* (LCD, 2001)). For the history and context of the Act see: Cretney, Masson and Bailey-Harris, 2002: 304–8.

breakdown of a marriage (to be proven by a six year separation). An attempt to introduce no-fault divorce in France failed in 2004. After almost five years of debate about the future of French divorce law, fault was retained. The new French divorce law of 2004[11] maintained the plurality of grounds of divorce. The main changes brought about by the new law were in the modifications of the particular grounds. Divorce upon mutual consent has been greatly simplified and de-formalised. Divorce upon unilateral request on the basis of the irretrievable breakdown of marriage after six years of separation was changed into unilateral divorce on the basis of the irretrievable breakdown of marriage after a two-year separation (Fulchiron, 2005: 245–7). Divorce based upon fault has been retained because of the conviction that it still 'meets the needs of the majority of French people' (Fulchiron, Ferré-André and Gouttenoire, 2004: 184).

Sweden

Rather out of pace with the rest of Europe, Sweden took a radical step in the liberalisation of divorce law by introducing divorce on demand. In the mid-1960s a 'new radicalism' had come to dominate Swedish politics. The Swedish minister of justice laid down in a directive for the experts appointed to prepare the new legislation that 'legislation should not under any circumstances force a person to continue to live under a marriage from which he wishes to free himself'.[12] The concept of fault was also to disappear entirely from Swedish divorce law. The resulting Law of 1973[13] provides that in the case of unilateral divorce or when the spouses have minor children, a divorce is to be automatically granted after a six-month period of reflection without any inquiry into the reasons for the divorce. If both spouses agree to divorce and no minor children are involved, a divorce has to be granted immediately. The Swedish system openly left behind the concept of irretrievable breakdown and started to speak of divorce in terms of an entitlement and a right (Bradley, 1996: 71–2).

Re-introduction of Divorce in Italy, Portugal, Spain and Ireland

Alongside the introduction of no-fault divorce in the countries with a more or less long-standing divorce tradition, no-fault divorce was adopted by some countries that previously had no divorce at all. In Italy, Portugal (for the Catholics) and Spain, divorce, based upon both fault and non-fault divorce, was re-introduced respectively in 1970, 1977 and 1981. In contrast, Ireland instantly embraced the principle of irretrievable breakdown of marriage in its Law of 1996.

---

[11] Law 2004–439 of 16 May 2004 came into force on 1 January 2005.
[12] Abstract of protocol in justice department matters (1971), 233–234.
[13] Entered into force on 1 January 1974 and is still applicable. In 1987 the rules on divorce were incorporated in the new Marriage Code. See Jänterä-Jareborg, 2003: 3.

Beyond the Fault/no-Fault Dichotomy

The advance of no-fault divorce throughout Western Europe evoked the idea that Europe is moving towards a spontaneous harmonisation of family law.[14] However, as the turn of millennium approached, the no-fault movement gradually lost most of its vigour. Attempts to get rid of the fault grounds failed in England and Wales in 1996, in France in 2005, and in Belgium in 2007.[15] Two Eastern European countries, Latvia and Lithuania, have recently re-introduced fault grounds in their divorce law. This retroactive movement is consonant with the situation in regard to covenant marriages in the United States.[16]

The introduction of no-fault divorce on the ground of irretrievable breakdown of marriage was such a change compared to the fault-based divorce sanction, that there was a strong temptation to see the map of European divorce law mainly in the light of the fault/no-fault dichotomy. However, with the passage of time it appeared that the reality is much more complicated. As long as many countries allowed divorce *exclusively* on the ground of fault, this analysis had its merits; in such a situation the 'innocent' spouse had no other option but to opt for an accusatorial procedure, while the 'guilty' spouse had no option at all except to purchase or coerce the co-operation of the 'innocent' party. Since nowadays not a single European country retains fault-based divorce as the sole ground (Martiny, 2003), the situation has utterly changed. The invocation of fault is now only one option among many, often providing the fastest route to divorce. Thus, although the retention of fault grounds still has its (often symbolic) meaning, it no longer says a great deal about the character of the divorce law of a particular country, and the abolition of such grounds does not automatically mean that divorce becomes any easier. The unsuccessful attempt to remove fault grounds in England and Wales provides a good example. The current law offers the spouses the possibility to obtain a fault-based divorce within four to six months,[17] whereas the repealed provisions of the Family Law Act 1996 made it impossible to obtain a divorce decree before a one-year period of 'reflection' had elapsed, which was to be extended by six months, even for consenting spouses if they had children. In addition, although the Act removed the need to prove a reason for the breakdown of the marriage,

---

[14] K Neumayer even spoke of 'entering into the period which is marked by a kind of *ius commune*' (Neumayer, 1978: 1). In a similar vein see also Pintens and Vanwinckelen, 2001: 16; and Phillips, 1988: 570.

[15] The Belgian divorce is changed by Law of 12 April 2007. This law is proclaimed that irretrievable breakdown of marriage and the mutual consent to be the only two grounds for divorce. However the breakdown can be established upon the proof of specific 'circumstances'. Culpable behaviour is maintained among such circumstances.

[16] Three American States: Louisiana (in 1991); Arizona (in 1999); and Arkansas (in 2001), have retreated from no-fault divorce by adopting legislation allowing a couple at the time of marriage to sign a 'covenant marriage' agreement, stating that they voluntarily restrict the grounds for possible future divorce to fault grounds: see Maxwell, 2003: 263–4.

[17] *Fourth Annual Report of Advisory Board in Family Law* (2000–01), para 3.5 (cited in Maxwell (2003): 299, n 95).

the new system insisted that the couple should settle ancillary matters beforehand, which may be much more difficult than proving any fault (Hale, 1997: 9).

What is Hidden Behind the Concept of the Irretrievable Breakdown of Marriage?

The recent survey of current divorce law in Europe provided by the Commission on European Family Law (CEFL) National Reports,[18] reveals a phenomenon, which, paraphrasing Zweigert and Kötz, could be called 'functional disequivalence' (Zweigert and Kötz, 1998: 36 *ff*). It is easy to see that, confusingly enough, under one and the same designation of 'irretrievable breakdown' virtually every type of divorce can be hidden[19]; from fault-based (England and Wales, Scotland, Greece and partly also Poland and Bulgaria) to divorce by consent (The Netherlands, Russia). If we look beyond these labels, we can roughly distinguish five more or less pure functional types of divorce grounds: fault-based grounds, irretrievable breakdown in the narrow sense of this term, divorce on the ground of separation for a stated period of time, divorce by consent and divorce on demand.

In theory, fault-based divorce presupposes a court enquiry into a matrimonial offence, but the strictness of this inquiry has been watered down over the course of time. For instance, in England and Wales, the so-called 'special procedure' under which undefended divorces are granted without any court hearing resembles more an administrative divorce than the old-fashioned divorce trials. That, combined with the possibility of obtaining a divorce immediately, sometimes makes fault-based divorce attractive even for consenting spouses.

Divorce based upon irretrievable breakdown in the narrow sense is granted upon a subjective criterion alone—if the court is convinced that the marriage cannot be saved (as in Bulgaria, the Czech Republic, The Netherlands, Poland, Hungary etc.)—or upon a subjective as well as an objective criterion, such as a certain period of separation (four years in Ireland, three years in Austria etc). In the jurisdictions that prescribe the subjective criterion alone, the court inquiry is nearly a dead letter in non-contested cases; however, in contested cases it may be quite intrusive, especially in countries like Bulgaria and Poland where allocation of the fault is required. In the jurisdictions that combine subjective (convincing the court or other competent authority) and objective (period of separation) criteria, proving the breakdown is twice as difficult, because even after the stated period of separation has expired the court can refuse a divorce if it is not convinced that the marriage has irretrievably broken down.

---

[18] See Jänterä-Jareborg, 2003; and Boele-Woelki, Braat and Sumner, 2003. The National Reports are further referred to by the name of the reporter and the reported country.

[19] This is apparent from the CEFL National Reports. See Martiny, 2003: 537–40.

Many jurisdictions where divorce is to be granted after the simple expiry of the stated period of separation call this an irrefutable presumption of the irretrievable breakdown of a marriage, but others consider it a separate ground (Norway). In both cases, however, a divorce is granted automatically and without further inquiry. The accessibility of divorce basically depends on the length of the separation period. These periods vary quite significantly: six years in Austria; two years with consent and five years without consent in England and Wales; four years in Switzerland and Greece; three years in Italy and Portugal; two years in Germany and France; and one year in Denmark, Norway and Iceland. As in most of the jurisdictions these periods are rather lengthy, this form of divorce is less attractive if a shorter route is available to the spouses.

Divorce by consent is covered in some jurisdictions under the designation of irretrievable breakdown, and constitutes an irrefutable presumption thereof (eg Austria, Czech Republic, Denmark, Germany, The Netherlands, England and Wales, Russia, Scotland). In other countries consent is presented as a separate ground (Belgium, Bulgaria, France, Greece and Portugal). In both cases the court with competent authority grants divorce automatically and without inquiry into the reasons for divorce if the spouses are agreed. However, most of the states still consider divorce by consent to be a dangerous diminishment of state control of divorce. The multiple restrictions of the right to divorce by consent often make it a less attractive and speedy form of divorce. Only Dutch and Russian law *de facto* allow for divorce on the ground of simple consent without any further restrictions. In some countries the marriage must be of a certain duration: three years in Bulgaria, two years in Belgium, one year in the Czech Republic and Greece. Other countries allow consensual divorce only after a certain period of separation: two years in England and Wales; one year in Scotland and in Germany; and six months in Denmark, the Czech Republic and Iceland. In most countries (Austria, Belgium, Bulgaria, Greece, Germany, Hungary, Denmark and Portugal) an agreement to divorce alone is not sufficient and the spouses are required to reach an agreement on ancillary matters as well. This list of restrictions reveals that most of these countries are still reluctant to recognise the autonomous decisions of the spouses alone as a sufficient ground for divorce. The state, in one way or another, has to protect spouses from their own ill-considered decisions.

Divorce on demand, when each of the spouses is simply considered to be entitled to divorce irrespective of the objections of the other spouse, is explicitly recognised in Sweden, Finland and Spain, and indirectly in Russia. This is, beyond doubt, the easiest form of divorce; fully respecting the autonomous decisions of the spouses (or at least of one of them) and accepting that the state is not capable of keeping a marriage intact against the will of even one of the spouses. The only state intervention in this kind of divorce is a short waiting period of six months for contested divorces or divorces with minor children in Sweden, the same period for all divorces in Finland, and a possibility of a three-month reconciliation period for contested divorces under Russian law.

Many countries have not just one, but multiple grounds for divorce. In this case especially, consenting spouses have the possibility of a kind of 'ground shopping'. Empirical data seems to suggest that spouses, assisted by their lawyers, are always able to choose the shortest way to divorce just as water will always find its way to the lowest point. [20]

This rough survey illustrates that , in spite of all the optimistic expectations that were derived from the no-fault reforms, no substantial common core has so far emerged. Even if the fault grounds were to completely disappear from the European scene in the foreseeable future, this alone would not significantly increase the scope of the common core.

IV. NON-MARITAL COHABITATION

From the 1960s onwards, Europe witnessed a rapid and unprecedented rise of non-marital cohabitation. At the turn of the millennium, around 30 per cent of all couples under 30 years old in Europe were cohabiting.[21] The legislative response to this major social change was somewhat delayed. In the beginning only few countries chose to acknowledge it with favourable legal policy. A notable exception was Sweden, which in the late 1960s proclaimed a positive attitude towards cohabitees. This became known as the 'neutrality' policy (Sörgjerd, 2005: 343–5), which holds that the law should be 'neutral in relation to the different forms of living together and different moral views' and warns 'not [to] create unnecessary difficulties' for those who decide to create a family without marrying.[22]

However, even after the attitude towards cohabitation became more benevolent, the majority of European countries were reluctant to pass specific regulation with respect to non-marital cohabitation. This reluctance was not the reflection of a conservative attitude alone, but was grounded in objections originating from different sides of the political spectrum. Together these arguments led to the idea that there should be a 'law-free space', an area of deliberate non-regulation. Part of this idea was inspired by the fear that legal regulation of cohabitation would weaken the institution of marriage.[23] Another reason had to do with the concern for personal autonomy (Deech, 1980: 300).[24] It was argued that if cohabitees

---

[20] For instance, in England and Wales 68.6 % are granted upon fault grounds, as this proves to be the shortest route to a divorce: see Lowe, 2003: 103.

[21] The European Union average for all age groups is 8% (Editorial Note, 'The European Picture of Cohabitation' (2001), 168).

[22] Committee Report (SOU 1972: 41), 58.

[23] For a short account, see Forder, 1999: 7. On the undesirability of creating 'two competing systems', see Agell, 2003: 131.

[24] Ruth Deech, for instance, argued that each of the basic ideas of individualism—the dignity of the individual, the autonomy, the privacy and the self-development—had its influence on the legislative non-intervention in the field of cohabitation.

voluntary choose to avoid the legal regulation attributed to marriage, the state should respect this choice and not try to impose another form of legal regulation on them (*ibid*: 300–301). Another ground for the non-regulation policy was the fear that cohabitation regulation modelled on marriage would reinforce traditional gender-role divisions, resulting in women's dependency (O'Donovan, 1984). In addition to this, the multiplicity of different patterns of cohabitation gave rise to the view that it is impossible to design any general rules that are able to cover all those forms (Forder, 1999: 7).

Eventually, the discussion surrounding the regulation of different-sex cohabitation came to be intertwined with same-sex couples' struggle for legal and social recognition (Schrama, 2004: 117). The problems of same-sex couples were, from the outset, rather different from those of heterosexual cohabitees. The main problems of same-sex cohabitees were two-fold: they had no legal protection; and society did not recognise their relationship. Differing from opposite-sex cohabitees, the lack of legal protection for same-sex couples did not result from their own implicit or explicit choice not to marry, but from the legal impossibility of doing so.

First Legislation on Unmarried Cohabitation

Thus, albeit for different reasons, the legal regulation of both opposite- and same-sex cohabitation remained controversial for a long time. The accommodation of heterosexual cohabitation, partly by way of piecemeal adjustments of the existing laws and partly by virtue of judicial activity, started in the 1970s. In 1973 Sweden was the first European country to pass specific legislation on non-marital cohabitation.[25] In 1987 legal protection was extended to same-sex couples. Thus, Sweden also became the first country where same- and opposite-sex cohabitation acquired equal legal protection. The law was applicable to unmarried cohabitees by virtue of *de facto* cohabitation, without a requirement of registration, contract or any other expression of an intent to institutionalise their relationship. The main purpose of the law was to grant a weaker party some minimal protection if the relationship ceased (see Saldeen, 2005: 504)[26]. Therefore, the legal protection was of a rather limited scope and mainly covered only patrimonial relationships and some public law issues.

In 1991 the Joint Household Act (see Sarcevic, 1980: 294),[27] with a significantly more limited scope of protection, was enacted in Norway.

---

[25] The Unmarried Cohabitees Act was enacted in 1973. In 1987, it was replaced by the more comprehensive Cohabitees (Joint Homes) Act.

[26] Before the 1987 Act entered into force, the Law on Homosexual Cohabitees made its provisions equally applicable to same-sex couples.

[27] Act relating to the Joint Residence and Household when a Household Community Ceases to Exist, of 4 July 1991.

It is often forgotten that Yugoslavia and Hungary were also among the countries that pioneered the regulation of non-marital cohabitation. After 1974[28] the codes of Bosnia-Herzegovina, Croatia, and Serbia and Kosovo extended some rules of matrimonial property and maintenance law to durable marriage-like relationships (Mladenovic, Janjic-Komar and Jessel-Holst, 1998: 26). In 1992, the same was done in Macedonia. Slovenia was a case apart among the Yugoslavian autonomies states. In 1976, the Slovenian Marriage and Family Regulation Act completely assimilated durable cohabitation into marriage in almost all personal and property aspects. This example was followed by Serbia in 2005. In Hungary, the statutory regulation of non-marital cohabitation dates from 1977. Initially, both former Yugoslavian autonomies and Hungary regulated only opposite-sex cohabitation. In 1995, the Hungarian Constitutional Court proclaimed the legal definition of cohabitation as an exclusively opposite-sex union to be discriminatory and therefore unconstitutional.[29] The court gave the legislature one year to adjust the law. In 1996, the definition of non-marital cohabitation was amended and made gender-neutral. Thus, same-sex couples came to enjoy the same protection as opposite-sex couples. In 2003, Croatia also extended legal regulation regarding cohabitation to same-sex couples.

Advance of Registered Partnership Legislation

However, up to the mid 1990s the countries referred to above were a mere exception. Only in the last decades of the 20th century was there a clear sea-change. The legal policy surrounding cohabitation generally evolved from tolerance to positive recognition. This shift in attitude was, however, largely confined to the regulation of same-sex cohabitation only. In order to accommodate the needs of same-sex couples many countries introduced the institution of registered partnership. The model of registered partnership that spread across Europe was first introduced in Denmark in 1989. In the following decade, the same model was adopted by the whole of the Nordic region: in Norway in 1993; in Sweden in 1995; in Iceland in 1996; and in Finland in 2001. In 1998, The Netherlands introduced the same model with one significant difference; registered partnership was opened for both same- and different-sex couples. In 2001, Germany followed the Scandinavian example as well, but initially, due to political and constitutional constraints, went significantly less far in the equalisation of registered partnership with marriage. In 2004, a form of registered partnership similar to the Scandinavian model was introduced, among others, in the United Kingdom, and in 2005 in Switzerland.

---

[28] In 1974 the newly adopted Federal Constitution of Yugoslavia placed the jurisdiction of family matters into the hands of the autonomies, which then enacted comprehensive family codes in the next decade.

[29] Decision No 14 of 8 March 1995.

Several countries, such as France, Belgium and the Spanish autonomies chose a model rather different from the registered partnership Scandinavian style. The *Pacte civil de solidarité* (*PACS*) that was adopted in France in 1999, the Belgian regime of statutory cohabitation, and the various laws that were enacted in the Spanish autonomous communities from 1998 onwards, granted only very limited protection, and only for those same- and opposite-sex couples who elected for the prescribed registration.[30]

Apart from same-sex marriage as such, the institution of registered partnership is the most forthright and uncompromising response to same-sex partners' demands for equality and recognition. The introduction of registered partnership actually paved the way for the opening-up of marriage to same-sex couples in some countries. The idea of registered partnership is based on the 'equal but separate' doctrine, which involves granting same-sex couples nearly all the rights of married couples, without giving their union the name of marriage. Such a marriage-like institution is capable of giving same-sex partners adequate legal protection while almost eliminating institutional discrimination and contributing to the further social acceptance of same-sex couples.

V. DELIBERATE HARMONISATION OF FAMILY LAW IN EUROPE

The picture of present day family law in Europe is not complete without mentioning the recent activities aimed at the promotion of the harmonisation of family law in Europe. In the 1990s, the harmonisation of private law in Europe began to receive a good deal of attention. Private initiatives dealing with this subject one way or another had already been evolving at the beginning of the 1980s. Family law was a relative latecomer and played more or less the role of Cinderella within the harmonisation setting. This probably had to do with the alleged unsuitability of family law for harmonisation due to strong cultural and historical constraints. The so-called 'cultural constraints' argument suggests that the family laws of the different European countries are embedded in their unique national cultures and history. This cultural and historical diversity is unbridgeable and therefore family laws do not converge spontaneously and cannot be harmonised deliberately. The cultural constraints argument is verbalised in a nutshell by Wolfram Müller-Freienfels, who wrote a long time ago:

> Family law concepts are especially open to influence by moral, religious, political and psychological factors; family law tends to become introverted because historical, racial, social and religious considerations differ according to country and produce different family law systems (Müller-Freinfels, 1968–69); see also de Oliveira, 2000; and Hohnerlein, 2000–01).

---

[30] With the exception of Catalonian law and the laws of some other Spanish autonomies, which made their cohabitation laws applicable to unmarried opposite-sex couples' *de facto* cohabitation.

Marie-Thérèse Meulders-Klein has even claimed that family law constitutes the hard core of any legal culture (Meulders-Klein, 2003: 109). For this reason the issue of harmonisation of family law long remained on the fringes of the discussion surrounding the harmonisation of private law in general. However, in the late 1990s the attitude towards the harmonisation of family law gradually evolved towards a more positive one (Boele-Woelki, 2002b: 175–7).

As result of this change of attitude, in 2001 the international Commission on European Family Law (CEFL) was established by an international group of prominent scholars.[31] Like all other groups and commissions active in the field of harmonisation of private law, CEFL is a self-appointed group, composed of academics who do not represent their national governments, nor are commissioned by any supranational organisation. CEFL consists of two bodies: the Organising Committee and the Expert Group. The Organising Committee acts as a co-ordinating and organising body.[32] The Expert Group comprises 22 members, including the six members of the Organising Committee. They cover almost all European countries, among which are all the EU Member States and most of the candidate countries, as well as non-associated countries like Norway, Switzerland and Russia.[33]

The objective of the CEFL is to elaborate non-binding *Principles of European Family Law*, which can serve not only as reference works for scholars and students, but also as sources of inspiration and perhaps even as models for national and supra-national legislatures (Boele-Woelki, 2005d; and Örücü, 2005). The first subjects chosen by the Organising Committee for CEFL's activities were the grounds for divorce and the maintenance obligations of former spouses. The reasons for this choice have been extensively elucidated by the chairperson of the CEFL Katharina Boele-Woelki (Boele-Woelki, 2002a: 22–5). Divorce law was selected because of the pan-European convergence tendency that is manifest in the gradual shift from fault-based divorce to divorce based on the irretrievable breakdown of marriage (Pintens and Vanwinckelen, 2001). The *Principles* on divorce were published in 2004 (Boele-Woelki, 2003b). The same year the CEFL started to work on the second field: parental responsibilities. The choice for this subject was, to a large extent, determined by the wealth of the international instruments in this field.[34] The *Principles* on parental responsibility are published in 2007 (Boele-Woelki, 2007). After this the CEFL will start working on the third subject: informal long-term relationships.

The Drafting Methods

The method of comparative research-based drafting adopted by CEFL is the same as that practiced by most other groups engaged in the promotion

---

[31] See http://www.law.uu.nl/priv/cefl > Establishment.
[32] See http://www.law.uu.nl/priv/cefl > Organising Committee.
[33] See http://www.law.uu.nl/priv/cefl > Expert Group.
[34] For more on the reasons for this choice see Boele-Woelki, 2005: 142–4.

of harmonisation of European private law. The first step is to draw up a comprehensive questionnaire. Such questionnaires, drafted from a comparative perspective, aim to cover all the variations within European jurisdictions. On the basis of the questionnaire, the members of the Expert Group deliver National Reports. On the basis of these reports the draft *Principles*, along with comments and a comparative overview are elaborated by the Organising Committee. After thorough discussion of the draft *Principles* by the whole of the CEFL, the final draft is drawn up by the Organising Committee (Boele-Woelki, 2005b: 14–41). While drafting the *Principles* on the basis of the comparative material delivered in the National Reports, two methods are generally used: the so-called 'better law' and 'common core' methods. The 'common core' method involves the elaboration of rules that are common for all or most of the relevant jurisdictions. The 'better law' method involves the selection of a rule that represents a minority or just one jurisdiction, or even the elaboration of a completely new rule by the drafters themselves (Antokolskaia, 2003: 159–83).

In spite of the wealth of literature on the harmonisation of family law[35] and the blooming drafting activities on the part of the CEFL, the harmonisation of family law remains highly controversial and the discussion on its feasibility and desirability is far from being at an end (Martiny, 2004: 307–33). This lack of consensus has led to the situation that while the popularity of the idea of harmonisation of family law has been notably increasing throughout the last decade, resistance to it has not diminished. The opponents of harmonisation keep relying on the cultural and historical constraints as their main contention. The progress of the harmonisation activities only made the debate sharper. The perseverance of the opposition as such is no indication of weakness of the idea of the deliberate harmonisation. Nor does it mean that the CEFL, or indeed the various other groups and commissions in the field of private law in general, have started their work prematurely without awaiting genuine consensus. A general consensus on such a controversial issue will probably never be reached. This means that if harmonisation activities were ever to be started, they could only have started in spite of serious opposition. Whatever the practical impact of the CEFL *Principles* will be, their contribution to the development of comparative family law is undisputable. The National Reports made by the CEFL experts[36] and the comparative overviews not only represent a new methodology of comparative research; working in a permanent network of national experts, they also form a wonderful source of reliable, up-to-date comprehensive information on the national family laws in Europe.

---

[35] For a recent overview see Martiny, 2004: 328–33 and the CEFL website: http://www2.law.uu.nl/priv/cefl/ under the rubric 'publications'.

[36] The integral reports are published on the CEFL website: http://www.law.uu.nl/priv/cefl > working fields 1(Divorce/Maintenance) and 2(Parental Responsibility). The integrated version of the reports are published in Boele-Woelki, Braat and Sumner, 2003 and Boele-Woelki, Braat and Curry-Sumner, 2005.

QUESTIONS FOR DISCUSSION

1. Which general trends can be monitored in the development of family law in Europe during the last 50 years?
2. What are the main tendencies in the development of marriage law in Europe during the last decades?
3. Does the advance of no-fault divorce make divorce laws in Europe more similar?
4. What is the main difference between the problems surrounding the legal regulation of same-sex and different-sex cohabitation?
5. What are the main reasons for the differences in pace and profundity of the modernisation of family law in the various European countries?
6. What is your opinion in regard to the feasibility and desirability of deliberate harmonisation of family law in Europe?

BIBLIOGRAPHY AND FURTHER READING

Agell, A (1998) 'Should and Can Family Law Influence Social behaviour?' in J Eekelaar and T Nhlapo (eds), *The Changing Family: International Perspectives on the Family and Family Law* (Oxford, Hart Publishing).

—— (2003) 'The Legal Status of Same-Sex Couples in Europe—A Critical Analysis' in K Boele-Woelki, A Furchs (eds), *Legal Recognition of Same-Sex Couples in Europe* (Antwerp, Intersentia).

Antokolskaia, M (2003) 'The "Better Law" Approach and the Harmonisation of Family Law' in K Boele-Woelki (ed), *Perspectives for the Unification and Harmonisation of Family Law in Europe*, European Family Law Series No 4, (Antwerp, Intersentia).

—— (2006) *Harmonisation of Family Law in Europe: A Historical Perspective. A Tale of Two Millennia* (Antwerp, Intersentia).

Boele-Woelki, K (2002a) 'Divorce in Europe: Unification of Private International law and Harmonisation of Substantial Law' in H Lemaire and P Vlas (eds), *Met recht verkregen. Liber Amicorum IS Joppe* (Deventer, Kluwer Law International).

—— (2002b) 'Comparative Research-based Drafting of Principles of European Family Law' in M Faure, J Smits and H Scheider (eds), *Towards a European Ius Commune in Legal Education and Research* (Antwerp, Intersentia).

—— (ed) (2003a) *Perspectives for the Unification and Harmonisation of Family Law in Europe* European Family Law Series No 4 (Antwerp, Intersentia).

—— et al (2003b) *Principles of European Family Law Regarding Divorce and Maintenance Between Former Spouses* (Antwerp, Intersentia).

—— (ed) (2005a) *Common Core and Better Law in European Family Law*, European Family Law Series No 10 (Antwerp, Intersentia).

—— (2005b) 'The Working Method of the Commission on European Family Law' in Boele-Woelki, K (ed), *Common Core and Better Law in European Family Law* European Family Law Series No 10 (Antwerp, Intersentia).

—— (2005c) 'Parental Responsibilities—CEFL's Initial Results' in K Boele-Woelki (ed), *Common Core and Better Law in European Family Law*, European Family Law Series No 10 (Antwerp, Intersentia).

—— (2005d) 'The Principles of European family law: its aims and prospects,' 12 *Utrecht Law Review* www.utrechtlawreview.org.

—— et al (2007) *Principles of European Family Law Regarding Parental Responicbilities* (Antwerp, Intersentia).

Boele-Woelki, K, Braat, B and Sumner I (eds) (2003) *European Family Law in Action:* vol I *Grounds for Divorce* and vol II *Maintenance Between Former Spouses* (Antwerp, Intersentia).

Boele-Woelki, K, Braat, B and Curry-Sumner, I (eds) (2005) *European Family Law in Action. Volume III: Parental Responsibilities* (Antwerp, Intersentia).

Boele-Woelki K and Furchs, A (eds) (2003) *Legal Recognition of Same-Sex Couples in Europe* (Antwerp, Intersentia).

Bradley, D (1996) *Family Law and Political Culture. Scandinavian Laws in Comparative Perspective* (London, Sweet & Maxwell).

Cretney, S, Masson, J and Bailey-Harris, R (2002) *Principles of Family Law* (London, Sweet & Maxwell).

Deech, R (1980) 'The Case Against Legal Recognition of Cohabitation' in J Eekelaar and S Katz (eds), *Marriage and Cohabitation in Contemporary Society* (Toronto, Butterworths).

Forder, C (1999) 'Civil Law Aspects of Emerging Forms of Registered Partnerships', paper to the Fifth European Conference on Family Law, *Civil Law Aspects of Emerging Forms of Registered Partnerships. Legally Regulate Forms of Non-Marital Cohabitation and Registered Partnerships* (The Hague, Hague Conference).

de Oliveira, G (2000) 'Een Europees familierecht? Play it again, and again ... Europe!' 12 *FJR* 272.

Fulchiron, H (2005) 'The New French Divorce Law' in A Bainham (ed), *The International Survey of Family Law* (Bristol, Jordan Publishing).

Fulchiron, H, Ferré-André, S and Gouttenoire, A (2004) 'A Pause in the Reform of French Family Law' in A Bainham (ed), *The International Survey of Family Law* (Bristol, Jordan Publishing).

Giesen, D (1973) 'Divorce Reform in Germany' 4 *Family Law Quarterly* 358.

Glendon, MA (1976) 'The French Divorce Reform Law of 1976' 24 *American Journal of Comparative Law* 201.

—— (1989) *The Transformation of Family Law* (Chicago–London, University of Chicago Press).

Gottwald, P Schwab, D and Büttner, E (2001) *Family and Succession Law in Germany* (Munich, Beck).

Hale, B (1997) 'The Family Law Act 1996 – the death of marriage?' in C Bridge (ed), *Family Law Towards the Millennium: Essays for P M Bromley* (Toronto, Butterworths).

Hohnerlein, M (2000–01) 'Konturen eines einheitlichen europäischen Familien- und Kindschaftsrecht—die Rolle der Europäischen Menschenrechtskonvention' 4 *European Legal Forum* 252.

Jänterä-Jareborg, M (2003) *Swedish Report concerning the CEFL Questionnaire on Grounds for Divorce and Maintenance Between Former Spouses*, http://www.law.uu.nl/priv/cefl working field 1(Divorce/Maintenance) > The Reports' Sweden.

Kaserauskas, Š (2004) 'Moving in the Same Direction?' Presentation of Family Law Reforms in Lithuania' in A Bainham (ed), *The International Survey of Family Law* (Bristol, Jordan Publishing).

Lee, B (1974) *Divorce Reform in England* (London, Peter Owen).

Lowe, N (2003) 'National Report for England and Wales' in K, Boele-Woelki, B, Braat and I, Sumner (eds), *European Family Law in Action*: vol I *Grounds for Divorce and* vol II *Maintenance Between Former Spouses* (Antwerp, Intersentia).

Lowe, N and Douglas, G (2007) *Bromley's Family Law*, 10th edn (Oxford–New York, Oxford University Press).

Martiny, D (2003) 'Divorce and Maintenance Between Former Spouses—Initial Results of the Commission on European Family Law', in K Boele-Woelki (ed), *Perspectives for the Unification and Harmonisation of Family Law in Europe*, European Family Law Series No 4 (Antwerp, Intersentia).

—— (2004) 'Is Unification of Family Law Feasible or Even Desirable?' in A Hartkamp, M Hesselink, E Hondius, C Joustra, E du Perron and M Veldman (eds) *Towards a European Civil Code* (Nijmegen, Ars Aequi Libri) and the CEFL website: http://www2.law.uu.nl/priv/cefl under the rubric 'publications'.

Maxwell, N (2003) 'Unification and Harmonisation of Family Law Principles: The United States Experience' in K Boele-Woelki (ed), *Perspectives for the Unification and Harmonisation of Family Law in Europe*, European Family Law Series No 4 (Antwerp, Intersentia).

Mladenovic, M, Janjic-Komar, M and Jessel-Holst, C (1998) 'The Family in Post-Socialist Countries' in MA Glendon (ed), *International Encyclopaedia of Comparative Law* (Dordrecht, Martinus Nijhoff).

Meulders-Klein, MT (2003) 'Towards a European Civil Code of Family Law? Ends and Means' in K Boele-Woelki (ed), *Perspectives for the Unification and Harmonisation of Family Law in Europe*, European Family Law Series No 4 (Antwerp, Intersentia).

Müller-Freienfels, W (1968–69) 'The Unification of Family Law', 16 *American Journal of Comparative Law* 175.

Neumayer, K (1978) 'General Introduction' in A Chloros (ed), *The Reform of Family Law in Europe* (Deventer, Kluwer).

O'Donovan, K (1984) 'Legal Marriage –Who Needs It?' 47 *Modern Law Review* 118.

Örücü, E (2005) 'Viewing the Work in Progress of the Commission on European Family Law' 7 *International Law Forum du droit international* 219.

Pintens, W and Vanwinckelen, C (2001) *Casebook: European Family Law* (Leuven, Leuven University Press).

Phillips, R (1988) *Putting Asunder: A history of divorce in Western Society* (Cambridge, Cambridge University Press).

Saldeen, Å (2005) 'Cohabitation Outside Marriage or Partnership' in A Bainham (ed), *The International Survey of Family Law,* (Bristol, Jordan Publishing).

Sarcevic, P (1980) 'Cohabitation without Formal Marriage in Yugoslavian Law' in J Eekelaar and S Katz (eds), *Marriage and Cohabitation in Contemporary Society* (Toronto, Butterworths).

Schrama, W (2004) *De Niet-huwelijkse samenleving in het Nederlandse en Duitse recht* (Amsterdam, Kluwer Law International).

Sörgjerd, C (2005) 'Neutrality: the Death or the Revival of the Traditional Family' in K Boele-Woelki (ed), *Common Core and Better Law in European Family Law* (Antwerp–Oxford, Intersentia).

Stone, L (1990) *Road to Divorce. England 1530–1987* (Oxford, Oxford University Press).

van Grunderbeeck, D (2003) *Beginselen van personen- en familierecht. Een mensenrechtelijke benadering* (Antwerp, Intersentia).

Willekens, H (1997) 'Explaining Two Hundred Years of Family Law in Western Europe' in H Willekens (ed), *Het gezinsrecht in de sociale wetenshappen* (The Hague, Vuga).
Zweigert, K and Kötz, H (1998) *An Introduction to Comparative Law* (Oxford, Clarendon Press).

Websites

http://www.law.uu.nl/priv/cefl > working fields 1(Divorce/Maintenance) and 2(Parental Responsibility)

12

Comparative Commercial Law: Rules or Context?

NICHOLAS HD FOSTER*

KEY CONCEPTS

Commerce; Commercial law; Instrumentalist view; Contextual approach.

T HIS CHAPTER EXAMINES the reasons for the importance of comparative commercial law, and considers what approach should be taken to its study. Is commercial law purely technical? If so, one need only compare rules. If it is not, then the broader context must be considered, and the topic becomes considerably more complex.

After considering various examples, the chapter concludes that the broader context does affect commercial law and that a contextual approach is necessary. An outline is given of the ways in which the context is relevant, together with an indication of the main characteristics of a contextual approach. It also concludes that comparative commercial law is fundamentally no different from other comparative law topics, and is of general significance for comparative legal studies.

I. GLOBALISATION AND COMPARATIVE COMMERCIAL LAW

The essence of commerce can be found in the Latin words which make it up: *cum* (with) and *merx/merci-* (goods). It is the exchange of assets and services with a view to profit. Commercial law can therefore be defined as the law relating to the facilitation and regulation of commerce.

However, the use of the term varies both across and within legal traditions. *Across* traditions, the common law tendency is to restrict its use to transactions, whereas civilians extend it to institutions, such as companies and partnerships. Civilian[1] usage is followed in this chapter, but the emphasis is on transactions.

---

* Many thanks to Peter Muchlinski and Camilla Baasch Andersen for their comments on this chapter and to Camilla for suggesting some additional wording, as well as stimulating discussions resulting from co-teaching.
[1] 'Civilian law' refers to continental European legal systems and their offshoots. It is used in preference to 'civil', because this word can also mean the sort of law regarded as basic in such systems, such as the law of persons and the law of obligations. 'Civil law' is used only in the latter sense.

Within traditions, the term can cover the law governing all types of transactions, ranging from those taking place between private individuals and consumer transactions to multi-billion dollar contracts. This chapter deals only with the law relevant to business-to-business transactions.

Why study commercial law in a comparative light? Firstly, because comparative commercial law constitutes a useful laboratory for the formulation and testing of general comparative law theories, furnishing numerous intriguing case studies. But most people study it because globalisation has made it important from a practical point of view.

In the period immediately preceding 'globalisation',[2] roughly 1947–1989, the world was very different. It was divided into two ideologically hostile camps, the capitalist and the socialist/communist. Almost everywhere, the state took an active part in the economy, notably through nationalised industries. In socialist/communist regimes, the state owned the means of production and attempted to control all economic activity by means of commands (the command system). Protectionism (the protection of domestic markets and jobs from foreign competition), although substantially less than before the Second World War, was still at a relatively high level in many economies, some of which were effectively closed to the outside world.

From the late 1970s to the early 1990s various decisive events took place. In the People's Republic of China (the PRC), the death of Chairman Mao Zedong in 1976 was followed by the 'Open Door Policy', the progressive opening of the Chinese economy to the outside world. In 1979, Margaret Thatcher was elected Prime Minister of the United Kingdom. Departing from the previous right-wing policy of leaving in place reforms made by socialist predecessors, she initiated a series of unprecedented changes, including the privatisation of large sectors of the economy. In the United States President Ronald Reagan also pursued 'neo-liberal' policies which favoured free markets and private enterprise. The Soviet Union's empire in Eastern Europe collapsed in 1989. In 1991 the Soviet Union was dissolved. The Uruguay Round of the GATT[3] concluded in 1995 with a significant reduction in protectionism and the creation of the World Trade Organisation, which has far more members than the GATT (nearly all the countries in the world, in fact), and a much stronger enforcement system, including effectively compulsory dispute settlement procedures.

Throughout this period great technological advances were made. In particular, information storage, manipulation and diffusion were revolutionised. Examples include the Internet, e-mail, mobile telephones and computerised databases. Calculations can be effected far more quickly than before at a fraction of their former cost as a result of a vast increase in computer calculation power.

---

[2] Or, more accurately, the present period of internationalisation.

[3] The General Agreement on Tariffs and Trade (GATT) is an international agreement the aim of which is to reduce protectionism. It is now administered by the World Trade Organisation. A 'round' is a series of international negotiations aimed at the further reduction of barriers to trade. 'The Uruguay Round' was so named because its first session took place in Punta del Este, Uruguay.

The consequences were profound. The ideological conflict between capitalism and socialism/communism has practically disappeared, a situation famously (and controversially) described by Francis Fukuyama as 'the end of history' (Fukuyama, 1989). Neo-liberal, market-based ideology predominates, albeit with local modifications. The ideal role of governments has become economic encouragement, co-ordination and regulation rather than participation or control (see Salacuse, 1999). Formerly socialist/communist regimes abandoned the command system. They and the mixed capitalist/socialist countries followed Margaret Thatcher's example and largely marketised and privatised their economies. Most states have drastically reduced barriers to trade, foreign investment and foreign participation in their economies, financial markets are much more open, financial flows are far less restricted and, thanks to technological advances, financial transfers are easy and cheap. People are much freer to move from one country to another. International trade and international investment have greatly increased. Business activities have been transferred to developing countries. States compete for foreign business and investment. Multinational corporations have become even more powerful. International business transactions have increased in number and complexity. To put it more generally, we live in a world in which 'the intensification of worldwide social relations ... link distant localities in such a way that local happenings are shaped by events occurring many miles away or vice versa' (Giddens, 1990: 64).

Commerce is an essential part of this new order, and there has been a consequent enormous increase in commercial and associated law-making activity, founded on two generally, if not universally held, assumptions: (1) an efficient legal system which protects property rights and facilitates transactions is essential for commerce; (2) differences in commercial law are inefficient, and they can and should be removed by harmonisation. Like the global marketplace itself, both types of activity tend to be dominated by neo-liberal, market-driven, Anglo-Saxon ideology and Anglo-Saxon concepts of commercial law, a dominance augmented by large multinational law firms, all of which are American or English in origin.

At the same time, we also see 'localisation', 'a re-tribalisation of large swaths of humankind by war and bloodshed.' According to Benjamin Barber, 'The planet is falling precipitantly apart AND coming reluctantly together at the very same moment' (Barber, 1992: 53). Examples include the resurgence of Islam (1979 was also the year the Shah left Iran after the Iranian Revolution), the tragic events of 11 September 2001 and their aftermath and the break-up of the former Yugoslavia.

On the domestic legal level the result is 'the most massive effort that the world has ever known to use state power instrumentally through law' (Seidman and Seidman, 1995: 44). Sometimes voluntarily, sometimes as a result of external pressure, governments rushed to create commercial law systems which facilitate trade and foreign direct investment, always by some form of imitation of, or inspiration from, Western law. On the international level there has been a huge increase in harmonisation activity. Take security law. In 1977 Ulrich Drobnig presented a report to UNCITRAL on possible harmonisation (UNCITRAL, 1977).[4] In 1980 further action in this area was indefinitely postponed because success was considered to be 'in all likelihood unattainable' (UNCITRAL, 1980: para 28). In stark contrast, the list of harmonisation projects since 1994 is too long to set out here, but includes the UNCITRAL draft Legislative Guide on Secured Transactions 2002, the EBRD Model Law on Secured Transactions 1994 and the OAS Model Inter-American Law on Secured Transactions 2002, as well as numerous individual country projects (see Goode, 1998: 47-8).[5] On the other hand, the consequences of localisation include a growth in interest in non-dominant regimes such as Islamic finance, the 'return to the Shari'a'[6] in some Muslim-majority jurisdictions, and a resistance to harmonisation in certain quarters.

The number of people wishing to acquire knowledge in these areas has therefore greatly increased. They come principally from two types of jurisdictions: (1) the legal systems of economically developed countries (the 'Westerners', subdivided into the Anglo-Saxons and the Rest); and (2) legal systems in the course of 'modernisation', some of which experience considerable tension between the various internal and external sources of their law (the 'Modernisers'). Those working on harmonisation of law can be considered as a third group, made up of lawyers from all types of jurisdictions.

In the Western group, the Anglo-Saxons wish to acquire a general understanding of the sort of local law they might encounter in a transaction governed by their law, eg a project finance transaction in which the main contract is governed by English law, but the security contracts are governed by German, Kuwaiti and Indonesian law. The Rest need to understand the Anglo-Saxon law of the main agreements and the way it differs from, and interlocks with, their law. The Modernisers have the same goals as the Rest, but also wish to understand Western law in order to use it better to reform their own law, or to perform the difficult task of defending their legal culture while at the same time accommodating the needs of globalisation. The Harmonisers need to understand each other's law and view their own law from an outsider's perspective in order to produce regimes acceptable to all parties.

How should this expertise be acquired? Most people assume that we should base our approach on what we might call 'the instrumentalist view', which runs something like this. Some human activities are 'close to people's lives' (Kahn-Freund, 1974: 10). Therefore they are affected by the way in which the members of a given society think and feel about things which are important to them, their

---

[4] UNCITRAL: United Nations Commission on International Trade Law.

[5] EBRD: European Bank for Reconstruction and Development; OAS: Organization of American States.

[6] 'Shari'a' is usually, if somewhat misleadingly, translated as 'Islamic law'.

cultural attitudes.[7] It seems logical that these attitudes should affect the law governing such activities.[8] So if we wish to study the law, we need to study the broader context within which the law was formed and operates. This is particularly true if we wish to conduct a comparative study, because we go beyond our own law, the cultural background to which we instinctively understand, to someone else's law, the cultural background to which we cannot attempt to understand without an explicit explanation. Commerce, though, is not 'close to people's lives', and is therefore not affected by cultural attitudes. Business people everywhere just want to make money. So commercial law is not affected by culture either. It is just lawyer's law, a mere instrument (hence 'instrumentalist view') formulated to perform technical functions in a technical field. If we wish to study it, all we need do is study the different rules and compare them. The broader context is irrelevant.

It follows that, if an activity is affected by cultural attitudes, those attitudes will differ from one society to another, and the law governing those activities will differ from one society to another. It will be difficult to change the law so long as the culture remains the same, and in particular it will be difficult to change it so as to make it uniform across various types of society. The converse is also true. If an activity is not affected by cultural attitudes, attitudes towards it will not differ from one society to another. Any variations in the law are mere accidents, and it will not be difficult to change the law in order to make it uniform. If commerce is not affected by cultural attitudes, the latter set of consequences apply to it.[9]

A good example of the instrumentalist view occurred a few years ago during the introduction to an LLM course at the School of Oriental and African Studies, University of London. The author and his colleague explained the contextual methods used, involving a grounding in such matters as comparative law methodology, the relevant legal systems and their history, and the relationship of such matters to commercial law. One student belligerently asked why we did not simply deal with subjects like comparative contract formation, implying that our approach was an impractical waste of valuable time, which could be much better spent on the comparative study of the rules.

---

[7] Culture is a difficult concept. One definition is that it

> consists of patterns, explicit and implicit, of and for behavior acquired and transmitted by symbols, constituting the distinctive achievements of a human group, including their embodiments in artifacts; the essential core of culture consists of traditional (ie historically derived and selected) ideas and especially their attached values; culture systems may, on the one hand, be considered as products of action, on the other as conditioning elements of further action (Kroeber, Kluckhohn and Untereiner, 1983: 1152–3).

'Tradition', preferred by some scholars, is not used herein. This decision was taken solely in order to simplify the arguments, and nothing further should be read into it. On the debates, see chs 3, 4 and 5 above.

[8] This assumption, the 'mirror thesis', is itself controversial. See Tamanaha, 2001 (the idea of reflection is outlined at 1–2; it is challenged in chs 3, 4 and 5). See also Kennedy, 1991.

[9] There are numerous difficulties associated with the words 'uniform' and 'harmonisation'. 'Uniform' is used here in a general, non-technical sense.

Systems and Cultures

In order to find out whether he was right or not, consider the ideas of system and culture as they relate to commercial law.[10]

Working outwards from the bare rules, it is clear that each topic forms a system, a set of interconnected norms, mechanisms and principles which makes a unified whole. The parts of the system are given meaning and effect not just by their content, but also by their relative place within the system. Since each such system is legal, it would be logical to call them 'legal systems', but that term is normally used to denote the entirety of such systems in a given jurisdiction, eg 'the English legal system'. Therefore, for each system below the level of 'legal system' in this sense, we will use the word 'regime' instead. Each regime nests within, overlaps, intersects and intertwines with other regimes. They are all interdependent:

> there are only a few rules that can be understood and applied without reference to other legal rules or concepts (Pistor, 2002: 98).

English security law is a specialist topic within the law of contract. It is also part of financial law, and has strong links to insolvency law. It relies on the general law of contract, property law, etc. Security and contract law both rely on the general principles and approaches of the English legal system as a whole, such as the doctrine of precedent and freedom of contract. But they also have a degree of autonomy, with specialist rules and mechanisms.

All these regimes and legal systems are associated with groups of people, each of which has its legal culture, its

> deeply rooted, historically conditioned attitudes about the nature of [their regime/system], about [its] role ... in the society and the polity, about [its] proper organization and operation ... and about the way [it] is or should be made, applied, studied, perfected, and taught (Merryman, 1985: 2).[11]

There are English and French legal cultures, associated with the English and French legal systems as wholes. English lawyers think, act and emotionally and subconsciously react in a certain way. French lawyers think, act and emotionally and subconsciously react differently. There are also legal cultures associated with regimes such as English commercial law and international financial law. English commercial lawyers think, act and react differently from their colleagues who practise family law. All these cultures overlap and intertwine with others. For example, although recognisably English, English commercial legal culture has features in common with French commercial legal culture.

Since these groups practise, enforce, maintain and develop the law, their legal cultures constitute major influences on it. So much can be regarded as fairly clear.[12]

---

[10] The following discussion deals simplistically with complex issues used as foundational arguments. For fuller treatments, see in particular chs 2, 3, 4 and 5 above.

[11] The original quotation refers to the culture of an entire legal system, the words in square brackets replace the word 'law' in the original.

[12] It should go without saying that other significant influences exist, which may trump legal culture.

Moving outwards once more, to what degree do the regimes and legal systems reflect society generally and its culture?[13] One might expect an interaction between law and society, law reflecting society's culture and needs, society determining the content of the law. Sometimes this is clearly the case. When divorce was socially unacceptable in Western societies, it was legally very difficult to obtain. When cultural attitudes changed, the law changed too. However, the metaphor of 'reflection' must be used carefully, for the degree of reflection may vary considerably according to the circumstances. The law may be out of step with society, reflecting the culture of the past, not the present. One of the functions of legal culture is to maintain the legal system, so it is a necessarily conservative force which tends to keep the regimes and legal systems as they were at the time of their formation, while general culture moves on. In addition, regimes are often not connected to all society, but only to a part of it.

The Development of English and French Commercial Law: A Comparative Historical Sketch

Let us look at how systems and cultures interact in the commercial law context by examining the formation of the English and French regimes.

The two jurisdictions share some common history. When the Western Roman Empire collapsed, trade practically disappeared (Volckart and Mangels, 1999: 435–46). The feudal system which grew out of the ruins of the Empire was based on land. The result was a contempt for commerce among the aristocracy, an attitude bolstered by the Catholic Church, which also held trade in generally low regard. According to St Paul, 'The love of money is the root of all evil' (I Tim 6:10), therefore: 'No profession was more suspect than that of the merchant' (Le Bras, 1963: 574; see also Mallat, 2000: 92). When trade revived, the aristocracy continued to view it in a poor light, even when it had grown greatly in importance, although by the 15th century the theologians had been obliged to concede that trade was acceptable, even if speculation was not.

Attitudes towards finance were even more negative than those towards trade. Not only was money-lending viewed with contempt by the aristocracy, 'usury' was forbidden by the Bible: 'the profession of merchant can scarcely ever be agreeable to God [but the usurer] is the most damnable' (de Roover, 1963: 76).[14] The Church banned first the clergy and then the laity from lending at interest. Some secular laws followed, and in 1311 Pope Clement V declared that secular laws allowing usury were void. When trade grew, so did the need for finance, and the ban on usury was at first evaded, then slowly lifted. By the early 17th century usury had become 'a matter of private conscience' (Visser and Macintosh, 1998: 179, citing Ruston, 1993: 173–4), and the very meaning of the word changed from

---

[13] On 'reflection', see n 8 above.
[14] Citing the canon (Church decree) *Ejiciens Dominus*.

'everything received by a lender over and above the capital lent' (Le Bras, 1963: 564) to 'excessive interest'.

The two jurisdictions then went down different paths. England's success in exploiting the opportunities arising from the New World and the Far East, accessible as a result of advances in maritime technology and navigational knowledge, eventually led to the creation of a trade-based empire. At a later period, technological advances, the Napoleonic wars and the Industrial Revolution combined in a long period of relative political stability to make commerce even more important. It flourished in a general atmosphere of policies favouring private property free from state interference, free markets, private projects and their private financing. A significant mitigation (although not the complete elimination) of the old aristocratic distaste for trade was in evidence, as was a high degree of trust for those involved in business and finance. Much was made, chauvinistically but with a degree of justification in the context of the time, of 'English liberty', the fundamental principle being: 'If it is not forbidden, it is allowed'. Despite being significantly eroded, the basics of these attitudes persist. For example, the City of London owes its continuing status as a major international financial centre to the authorities' liberal attitude towards overseas banks in the 1960s and 70s.

In France, by contrast, although significant, commerce was less important. The contempt for trade had always been stronger and more formalised, reflected in a ban on the participation in trade by nobles and the clergy (Masson, 1786: 121, cited in Kessler, 2003: 518). France lost out in her colonial and commercial ventures in North America and the Far East, lost the Napoleonic wars, and went through a period of political instability, suffering further defeat in the Franco-Prussian war. The collapse of John Law's banking and trading schemes in 1720 made many French people mistrustful of modern financial systems for generations. The economy remained predominantly agricultural for longer than in the United Kingdom, industrialisation took place later. The revolutionaries continued their predecessors' policy of centralising government, and the post-revolutionary economic system was more government-controlled than in England, giving less prominence to market forces (see Dickerson, 2005: 31–2), in an environment in which the starting point was: 'If it is not permitted, it is forbidden'.

Without a reason to be modified, the old attitudes tended to persist, and indications of them can still be seen today. For example, a financial career in the City of London is a symbol, even a caricature, of English middle-class respectability, whereas corresponding caricatures in France are the civil service, engineering, medicine and (private) law.

The two jurisdictions also differed in their commercial legal history. There is a degree of commonality between them, the result of some common ancestry in the *lex mercatoria* (literally 'merchant law', also called 'law merchant'). This is alleged by some to have been an international body of rules, created and applied by the merchants themselves in all Western Europe (often in their own courts) but is thought by others not to have existed in this form, or at all (see, eg, Sachs, 2006). Whatever the truth of the matter, normative phenomena of some sort did exist in various fields, together with doctrinal writing on the subject, and they influenced the law of both jurisdictions.

However, there were also some important differences. In England, the commercial courts of the Middle Ages gradually disappeared. The insertion of commercial law into the common law and its further development were effected by the common law judges. They partially used common law techniques, dealing with problems as they arose in cases, making no formal distinction between it and other parts of the law. This pragmatic approach was of great value in grounding the evolving law in the practice of merchants. Lord Mansfield (Chief Justice 1756–88), the master architect of English commercial law, even went as far as appointing businessmen to his juries and inviting them to dinner to learn about their practices. It seems that the new system was also significantly influenced by Continental ideas on the *lex mercatoria*.[15] The law so developed was a product of the time described above. It had a favourable attitude towards private property rights and free markets, and gave great freedom to business people, pragmatically taking account of and sanctioning their practices whenever possible. The system received statutory support at crucial junctures, notably at the end of the 19th century by the enactment of the Sale of Goods Act 1893, the Partnership Act 1890, the Bills of Exchange Act 1882 and the Marine Insurance Act 1906.

The most striking characteristics of the resulting regime include: (i) its relative autonomy from other areas of law, allowing a marked difference of approach to business-to-business as opposed to business-to-consumer and consumer-to-consumer transactions; (ii) the principle of the encouragement of commerce (it leads, the law follows); (iii) pragmatism, including the encapsulation of experience and the result of creativity in standard documentation (see McKendrick, 2003: chapter 12); (iv) a high degree of party autonomy in contracting, resulting in flexibility and adaptability;[16] (v) considerable scope for creativity by the lawyers (see Cranston, 1997: 218–19); (vi) certainty (once parties are contractually bound, the courts tend to hold them to their bargain, favouring certainty over fairness in the individual case, with minimal protection for the weak or the ignorant—

> The attitude of the old common law judges was that life in the business world is rough and tough and you should not get into it if you do not know what you are doing (Goode, 1992);

(vii) the existence of specialised fields, created by a combination of party autonomy, certainty of contractual obligation and standard form documents; (viii) the fairly efficient and relatively quick resolution of problems, notably through self-help; and (ix) the specialised knowledge and skill of commercial lawyers.

On the negative side, the law is apparently incoherent, 'a collocation of ill-assorted statutes bedded down on an amorphous mass of constantly shifting case

---

[15] The degree to which rules were imported (or existed in a form which could be imported) is disputed. See, eg Volckart and Mangels, 1999 and Cordes, 2005.

[16] See *Kum v Wah Tat Bank Ltd* [1971] 1 Lloyd's Rep 439 at 444 (PC), per Lord Devlin.

law' (Goode, 2004: 1203), and it is therefore inaccessible to anyone other than a specialist. It is relatively inflexible from the statutory point of view, for Parliament deals with commercial law only rarely and reluctantly, a situation which has led our most eminent academic authority to write that: 'our parliamentary machinery is wholly inadequate for modern commerce' (Goode, 2001: 760). The same author has argued that contemporary English commercial law is failing to adapt to modern conditions (*ibid*).

In France, the development of commercial law was, for the most part, separate from the civil law. Growing up initially through trade with England, Flanders, Germany and Italy at the fairs in Brie, Champagne and later Lyons, it drew on various sources, such as the statutory law of the Italian cities, parts of Roman law (adapted for commercial use), collections of customs and case-law, local regulations and Italian doctrinal literature.[17] In contrast to the judge-led developments across the Channel, the system was centralised by government action (one cannot at this stage talk of it being incorporated into French law, as only local laws existed), notably by the creation of commercial courts and two important codifications, the *Ordonnance sur le commerce de terre* of 1673 ('Land Commerce Ordinance') and the *Ordonnance sur la marine* of 1681 ('Marine Ordinance'). However, it must also be said that the Ordinances were based on the experience and input of practitioners.

When the new French legal system was created, the Ordinances formed the basis of commercial law, to which was assigned the role of a set of adjuncts to, and derogations from, the civil law. One consequence of this arrangement is that civil law thinking influences commercial law to some degree. Take the indivisible and land-based principle of property, the principles requiring a high level of contractual certainty, or the restrictive attitude towards transfers of rights. To the common lawyer, the first principle seems too inflexible, the last two over-protective. Indeed, some French colleagues share the common lawyer's feeling. According to a noted company law scholar, the French 'legal system all too often surrounds [business people] with a climate of systematic suspicion' (Guyon, 1990: 948—my translation).

Another result of the subordinate status of commercial law was that less attention was paid to it than to civil law and a less satisfactory product emerged. The Commercial Code was less well drafted, rapidly went out of date and, as further legislation was passed in specialist areas, became more and more irrelevant until its replacement in 2000. Even now, levels of logic, structure and coherence are significantly lower than in civil law. The legal profession was prevented from doing as much to improve the situation as it might have done in England by another consequence of centralisation, the dominance of legislation, resulting in less flexibility and less adaptability.

On the other hand, the extent of the differences should not be exaggerated. Both jurisdictions provide reasonably efficient commercial law regimes, and there

---

[17] This list comes from Hilaire, 1986: 27.

has recently been a degree of convergence.[18] English law modified its *laissez-faire* law of contract, and has recently adopted a more 'social' attitude, evidenced, inter alia, by the legislation providing for automatic interest on late payment of debts (the Late Payment of Commercial Debts (Interest) Act 1998—a measure designed to protect small businesses) and the new administration procedure contained in the Enterprise Act 2002, the main aim of which is to save viable businesses experiencing temporary problems. A new creativity is evident in the French legal profession (Paillusseau, 1997). And the French system is superior in some ways. It is more apparently accessible than English law, especially since the coming into force of the 2000 Commercial Code, which has remedied many of its predecessor's defects, and the legislator plays a more active role than in England, a considerable advantage in the modern age, which often requires detailed statutory regimes.

We can see from this account that the English and French commercial law regimes result from historical processes in which differing attitudes to commerce have produced different results. Those attitudes, which one can, with some justification, call 'cultural', were determined by the broader (economic, social, military, political, philosophical etc) context, as well as by the history and culture of the English and French legal systems.

Specific Examples

Some specific examples may shed some more light on the matter.

Consider the *Centros* case.[19] English law does not require the payment of a minimum amount of capital on formation of a company; Danish law requires payment of a substantial sum. Two Danish resident nationals incorporated Centros Limited in England solely in order to avoid the Danish requirement. The company applied to set up a branch in Denmark, but the application was refused. Centros claimed that the refusal was a denial of its EC law right to freedom of establishment. The Danish government claimed that their law protected 'the interests of [a company's] employees and creditors', so the refusal was justified.[20] The European Court of Justice found in favour of Centros.

The case seems to show the influence of general cultural attitudes on law. In Denmark, the protection of the individual, including creditors, and particularly employees, is considered vital, and companies are seen as having a social, as well as a profit-making, function. This view can be contrasted with that prevalent in

---

[18] But see the World Bank assessment of how easy it is to do business in France, which has caused a considerable stir there. In the 2006 survey, for example, France was ranked overall 35th in the world, the United Kingdom 6th (http://www.doingbusiness.org/).

[19] C–212/97 *Centros Ltd v Erhvervs-og Selskabsstyrelsen* [2000] Ch 446 (ECJ); see, eg, Looijestijn-Clearie, 2000; see also C–167/01 *Kamer van Koophandel en Fabrieken voor Amsterdam v Inspire Art Ltd* [2003] ECR I–10155 (ECJ) and C–208/00 *Überseering BV v Nordic Construction Company Baumanagement GmbH* [2002] ECR I9919 (ECJ).

[20] *Ibid* [2000] Ch 446 at 454, per Advocate General La Pergola.

the United Kingdom, where it is considered more important to encourage business in order to stimulate economic activity, thereby creating jobs in a more fluid employment market, and where companies are seen as no more than mechanisms to make money for shareholders. The Danish general cultural attitude has affected Danish legal culture, so that it has become an article of faith that a company must have a substantial minimum capital in order to provide a reasonable assurance that it will be able to pay its creditors. The attachment to this attitude was so strong that the Danish government expended a considerable amount of resources defending the rule, despite the fact that minimum capital requirements do not in fact provide adequate protection in most cases.

Another example from company law can be found in the People's Republic of China, which had no general company law from the Communist takeover until 1994. As well as being mechanisms for the private concentration and exploitation of capital, joint stock companies are also concentrations of power outside the state. In communist ideology, neither has a place in the polity. Once the enforcement of communist ideology was relaxed, company law was introduced: a clear example of a direct link between general culture and the law.

Moving to transactions, we see sharp cultural contrasts when considering Islamic law. In finance, the foundation of the Western system is interest. Islamic law forbids *riba*, roughly 'illegitimate gain'. The consensus among scholars is that *riba* includes interest. The entire field of Islamic finance law is based on this cultural/religious difference: another clear example of the influence of general culture on law.

Security law provides some striking examples.

— *Numerus clausus.* Commercial law must be able to adapt to changing commercial needs and practices. This can be done by the legislator, but courts may play just as important a role, and they should be allowed to do so. However, French legal culture is obstructive rather than helpful in this regard, because that pillar of civilian mentality, the dominance of legislation, is fixed in security law by means of the *numerus clausus* principle, ie the rule that the list of security mechanisms is closed (exceptions do exist) (Foster, 1997–98: 14).[21]

— *Universal security.* In modern economies, it is considered important to encourage lending. One way of doing this is to allow lenders to take security over all the assets, present and future, of commercial borrowers ('universal security'). In England this is so normal that it is hardly ever discussed. In France, such a grant was for many years viewed as dangerous, because it would allow financiers to abuse the power it gives them (Foster, 2002: 61–2).[22] This attitude was no doubt comprehensible in the Middle Ages when the economy was overwhelmingly rural and borrowers were vulnerable, but to the common lawyer it does not seem to be justified in the 21st century, when many businesses are just as sophisticated

---

[21] But note the 2006 reforms.
[22] See also below on the 'modernisation' of the law in this regard.

as their banks and the non-commercial borrower is protected by consumer and financial services law.

— *Fragmentation.* Efficient security regimes provide general mechanisms which can apply to broad categories of assets, reducing complexity and transaction costs. Civilian regimes, however, are typically fragmented, with one type of statutory regime per type of asset. Attempts have been made in Italy to encourage borrowing by widening the categories of asset which may be given in security. The first attempt, however, shows the degree to which the drafters remain conditioned by their legal culture. The reform consisted of a law on pledging hams (*prosciutti*)... To the common lawyer, this is needlessly specific, therefore expensive and inefficient. The introduction of a new, and general, regime (Article 9 of the United States Uniform Commercial Code (UCC) is a model which has been followed elsewhere) was literally unthinkable. More recently, a 'rotating pledge' (*pegno rotativo*) has been recognised by the courts, but it still falls far short of the flexibility of the English floating charge. The Civil Code, however, contains detailed provisions concerning such rural matters as swarms of bees, trained animals, rabbits and fish.[23]

In the first two instances above, legal culture has frozen the law. In the third, it has, in the view of the common lawyer and some Italian commercial practitioners, stultified its development.

In a related field, the transfer of rights and obligations, very early in its history English law allowed the transfer of rights to payment of money without notice to the debtor. Civilian lawyers still regard such transfers as wrong, even distasteful, to the extent that when the English law position is explained to them some find it so outlandish that they are convinced the lecturer has made a mistake. Once again, the rationale for the attitude, mainly the possibility of 'Nasty Creditor' taking the place of 'Nice Creditor' and enslaving the debtor or sending her to prison for non-payment, disappeared many years ago. Once again, legal culture has frozen the law.

Various useful examples come from an area of particular importance for comparative legal studies, that of 'legal transplants'.[24]

— *Unsuitability.* The 'classic' issue in this area is the potential unsuitability of the transplant for the host jurisdiction. The argument runs that if law is developed in, by and for the context of jurisdiction *A*, then introducing it into the different context of jurisdiction *B* will not lead to the same results in *B* as are produced in *A*. This may not be problematic if the transplanted law still produces useful results, but it is possible that the results will be less good or even non-existent. So if context

---

[23] Pledging hams: Law of 24 July 1985, no 401. The rotating pledge was first recognised by first instance courts in the late 1980s. It was sanctioned by the Court of Cassation judgment of 28 May 1998, no 5264. The references to animals are contained in Arts 924–926 of the Italian Civil Code. Many thanks to Emanuele Bosia for the information.

[24] The transfer of an item of law from one legal system to another: the very term is controversial, hence the inverted commas.

influences commercial law, we should see problems. Take Albania. The law of insolvency was introduced despite the almost total lack of commercial lending and is therefore, for the time being at any rate, irrelevant (Channell, 2005: 5–6).

An intriguing instance in which an (ineffective?) attempt was made to deal with the issue was the introduction of Western company law into Russia. It was realised that 'effective corporate law is context-specific'; that in developed countries it 'evolved in tandem with supporting legal institutions', including, for example, judges skilled in corporate law; that it developed against a certain cultural background; and that introducing United States law into a jurisdiction of 'insider-controlled companies, malfunctioning courts, weak and sometimes corrupt regulators, and poorly developed capital markets' was pointless (Black and Kraakman, 1996: 1914).

Phenomena other than unsuitability also merit consideration in the commercial context. They include technical incompetence, lack of enforcement, sidelining and adaptation, isolation.

— *Technical incompetence.* Since a legal regime is part of the regimes and the legal system in which it is embedded, on a purely technical level it must be properly inserted into the host jurisdiction. For example, when the Ottoman government attempted to import French company law, they failed to enact some essential parts of the French legislation because, according to Chibli Mallat:

> the Ottoman legislator forgot that it was in the French civil code, and not in the commercial code, that the main regulations of commercial companies are to be found (Mallat, 2000: 102).

— *Lack of enforcement* is a common problem. Examples abound. We can cite the example of Albania again:

> Albanian lawyers today often speak proudly of the new system, noting, however, that the new laws are European, not Albanian, and that they are not actually being applied (Channell, 2005: 5).

— *Sidelining* occurs when some item of commercial law is imported, used and enforced but, since it was not developed within the host legal system, never really 'takes', never really puts down roots. So it is not reformed or adapted to current needs, or is reformed without proper care (Pistor, Keinan, Kleinheisterkamp and West, 2002: 840–41).[25]

— We see *adaptation* in the French acceptance of a type of universal security (previously frowned upon as seen above), but 'civilised' before being absorbed into its new environment.[26]

---

[25] Where they identify problems of 'lethargy' and 'erratic change'.

[26] See the new 'gage des stocks' (pledge of stocks), Art L527 of the French Commercial Code.[TS please line space]

— *Isolation* can be regarded as a typical solution of cultural difference in the commercial field, a compromise adaptation to accommodate dominant Anglo-Saxon ideas. An otherwise objectionable commercial legal regime is corralled into a confined space, for use only by the commercial community, protecting the rest of the legal system from contamination. Take the United Arab Emirates. It has a Western-inspired commercial code, largely insulated from the Islamically-grounded civil code, and has recently transplanted English law into the Dubai International Financial Centre, a geographical area set aside as a separate jurisdiction (see Blair and Orchard, 2005). Or take the passing of specific laws in civilian jurisdictions allowing the transfer of rights without notice to the debtor in certain defined, commercial, circumstances (see Foster, 2003–04: 79–80).

Finally, the influence of legal culture on commercial law can also be seen in an area which is quite closely linked to legal transplants, the harmonisation of 'lawyers' law'. Such harmonisation is generally thought to be easily achieved, because it is not cultural. In fact, though, the opposite can be true, because it is very much part of the culture of the lawyers concerned. So if lawyers play a significant role in the process, and they usually do, the influence of legal culture can be considerable. One example is the United Nations Conventions on Contracts for the International Sale of Goods, 1980 (CISG), which is interpreted differently in different legal cultures, despite the very considerable efforts expended in trying to make it uniform (see Baasch Andersen, 2005).

II. COMPARATIVE CULTURE IN COMMERCIAL LAW?[27]

What conclusions can we draw? First, a caveat. The examples were chosen on the basis of the author's knowledge and experience rather than by rigorous scientific method, so it cannot be claimed that they are comprehensive. It is submitted, though, that they are sufficiently numerous and varied to provide reasonably reliable, if admittedly somewhat anecdotal, evidence.

Subject to this, it seems clear that commercial law regimes must be considered as part of a network of regimes.[28] We can therefore say that a local element, the interaction with other local regimes, is relevant. This conclusion alone, however, does not necessarily affect the core of the instrumentalist view. One might argue that such an interaction is a technical legal matter, and that it proves nothing about the significance of the extra-legal context.

It does seem clear, though, that the law can be influenced by historically and culturally conditioned attitudes to commerce, and that these vary from one society to another. We have seen, for instance, that the historical and cultural backgrounds which influenced the development of commercial law in England and France, two neighbouring Western European jurisdictions, were quite different,

---

[27] A phrase coined by Anthony Dicks as the title for the MA course taught by the author.
[28] See the Ottoman and Russian company law examples above.

leading to legal differences. We have seen that Islam regards as sinful something on which the Western world has built its economy, resulting in the development of Islamic finance. And we have seen that divergent views about the role of companies in society prevail in Denmark and the United Kingdom, informing aspects of their company law.

This is not to say that the link between cultural attitudes to commerce and the law is necessarily direct. In certain situations it can be: recall such examples as the lack of company law in the People's Republic of China until 1994, Islamic finance, and some instances of unsuitability and lack of enforcement of legal transplants. But it can also be indirect. We have observed above instances of cultural attitudes to commerce influencing legal culture and the law (the *Centros* case, French security law, the problems of sidelining, adaptation and isolation in legal transplants, and the problems associated with the harmonisation of 'lawyers' law').

In addition, another cultural element, legal culture, must be taken into account. What seems like a purely technical regime to the lay person may have the force of culture for a lawyer working in that field.

So the instrumentalist view is wrong, as was our belligerent enquirer—who, by the way, did not return. Commercial law is historically and culturally conditioned.

Let us return to, and adapt, the formulation of the instrumentalist view. Commerce is in fact 'close to people's lives', because it relates to such 'rules of the game of economic struggle' (Kennedy, 1991: 327) as the distribution of property among social groups, the concentration of power in society, the 'set of prior choices about the role of the state and the private sector in responding to change' (Mahoney, 2001: 504), and the morality of interactions between people. Therefore it is affected by cultural attitudes. Business people everywhere may just want to make money, but they are still people, who function in a culturally determined mentality. Since commercial law concerns the facilitation and regulation of commerce, it, too, may be affected by cultural attitudes (so long as the law reflects those attitudes). So a given commercial law regime may well not be a mere instrument formulated to perform technical functions in a technical field.

It follows that, since cultural attitudes to commerce will differ from one society to another, local variations in commercial law which reflect those differences are not mere accidents, and may be difficult to change effectively. In particular it may be difficult to change them so as to make the law uniform across various types of society, and legal culture may prove to be a strong conservative force in this regard.

It also follows that comparative commercial law can be of considerable value for the advancement of comparative law knowledge and should be treated, by and large, in the same way as other comparative law topics. The subject has its idiosyncrasies, of course, but this is true of all areas. It is not inherently different.

One must be careful, though, not to generalise too broadly or exaggerate and, in addition to the cautious wording of the text above, several caveats should be made. The relationship between cultural attitudes to commerce and commercial law may be remote, complex, unexpected, and difficult to disentangle. For example, law and legal culture may reflect attitudes to commerce prevalent when the law was developed, rather than those prevalent now, with the result that the main obstacle to change is not a general, but a legal, cultural attitude which may be over-ridden (if there is sufficient political will, for example). One can see this in the case of the apparent aversion to universal security in French law, which did not prevent recent reforms allowing security over present and future assets (so long as the latter are adequately specified) and a security over stock. In other words, legal cultural attitudes relating to this regime were not as strong as they appeared, and were not effective as barriers to reform of the law.[29] Furthermore, if the law is a transplant, cultural atti-tudes underlying it may be of little or no relevance to the host society. And in some instances, for example where the group of people practising and using the law is quite homogenous (as in international financial law), the broader context may not be of great importance, and the law can be treated for most purposes as technical.

More generally, nothing herein should be taken as denying that significant commonalities of attitude towards commerce exist among societies, nor that simi-larities in legal results exist among apparently different legal systems. Of course they do. Nor should anything herein be taken as denying that globalising forces have extended and deepened a significant number of such commonalities. Of course they have. But similar is not the same, and appearances can be deceptive.

To recap, using the words of William Allen, a former Chancellor of the Delaware Court of Chancery (writing of corporation law—the principle is the same for commercial law):

> Every general field of law embraces materials from which analysis can unearth the deepest questions that our social life recurringly presents to us. In some fields of law such questions lie near the surface ... Other fields of law ... appear or are more technical, more narrowly 'legal'. In such fields, legal problems may seem less pregnant with potentialities and answers may seem ... less controversial. It is easy in such fields to lose sight of—indeed it may some-times be difficult to ever catch a first glimpse of—*the contestable philosophical or political pre-suppositions that lie at their foundations, buried beneath the legal superstructure.* Corporation law is such a field (Allen, 1993: 1395, emphasis added).

It also follows that the instrumentalist view can only give satisfactory results where there is a close commonality between cultural attitudes to commerce and legal cultures in the relevant societies. Witness the examples above, none of which can be adequately analysed using a solely rule-based approach. If such a close commonality does not exist, the instrumentalist view leads to poor service to clients, ineffective legislation and little used harmonised regimes. On the other hand, a contextual approach leads to numerous benefits: a consciousness of difference in the formulation, practice, interpretation and enforcement of the law;

---

[29] For the new pledge see Art 2333 of the Civil Code; for the new pledge of stock see Art L527 of the Commercial Code. A summary of the new law is set out at http://www.justice.gouv.fr/presse/conf220306.htm. See generally, Le Nabasque and Adelle, 2005. On the other hand, attitudes found in legal culture may also persist, perhaps in a modified form, in general culture, which itself can be influ-enced by legal culture. It is also noteworthy that the 2006 French security law reforms were effected by means of the adaptation of French law, not the wholesale import of, say, Art 9 of the UCC.

a better understanding of law and lawyers from other jurisdictions; an outsider's perspective on your own law; and an appreciation that the difficulties associated with legal transplants, harmonisation and the relationship between law and society have the potential to apply just as much to commercial matters as to any other field. It also leads, one hopes, to better service to clients, more effective legislation and more successful harmonisation, for: 'In order to be efficient, you must avoid being blocked in your own universe' (Garnot, 1995: 351).

How should a contextual study be conducted? Only the briefest of discussions is possible here. Contextual does not mean 'woolly'. Mastery of the legal technicalities is essential, as is a sound understanding of the history, general culture and legal cultures of the jurisdictions concerned and the relationship between them. One must also have a reasonable grasp of the essentials of comparative law methodology, harmonisation theory and legal transplant theory, and do one's best to acquire at least the fundamental notions of other relevant disciplines. The most essential tool, though, is an open and inquiring mind.

The contextual approach has its drawbacks. The acquisition of the necessary knowledge requires much time and effort. Materials may only be available in unfamiliar languages, difficult to find, or both. The factors which one should ideally take into account are so numerous that one cannot be truly systematic, and one may well be superficial. It is easy to make mistakes, including, notably, those induced by subjectivity. Venturing into other, complex, disciplines runs the risk of amateurism, and those disciplines are full of controversies and debates, so clearcut answers are rarely, if ever, provided.[30]

In other words, the contextual approach is a counsel of perfection, an unattainable goal. On the other hand, although the outcomes will necessarily be imperfect, they will be much superior to those derived from the study of rules alone. And the journey towards them will be more interesting—dare one say more fun?

QUESTIONS FOR DISCUSSION

1. Does the literature on legal transplants give commercial lawyers the answers they need to solve the problems they encounter in today's world?
2. You are taking part in the revision of the OECD Principles of Corporate Governance, 2004 (http://www.oecd.org/dataoecd/32/18/31557724.pdf). What comparative law considerations will you need to bear in mind when undertaking this work?
3. 'English commercial law was invented by the judges as a tool for the development and continuation of the British Empire. French commercial law was the poor relation of the Civil Code.' Discuss.
4. Does it really matter that the civilian law relating to the transfer of receivables requires notice to the debtor, given that the legislator has intervened in the most important areas?

---

[30] Much of this paragraph comes from a lecture by Camilla Baasch Andersen.

BIBLIOGRAPHY AND FURTHER READING

Bibliography—Works Cited in the Text

Allen, WT (1993) 'Contracts and Communities in Corporation Law' 50 *Washington and Lee Law Review* 1395.

Baasch Andersen, C (2005) 'The Uniform International Sales Law and the Global Jurisconsultorium' 24 *Journal of Law and Commerce* 159.

Barber, BR (1992) 'Jihad vs McWorld' March *The Atlantic Monthly* 53.

Black, B and Kraakman, R (1996) 'A Self-Enforcing Model of Corporate Law' 109 *Harvard Law Review* 1911.

Blair, M and Orchard, J (2005) 'Legal Issues Arising in the New Dubai International Financial Centre' 20 *Journal of International Banking Law and Regulation* 207.

Channell, W (2005) 'Lessons Not Learned: Problems with Western Aid for Law Reform in Postcommunist Countries' 57 *Democracy and Rule of Law Project* 2005.

Cranston, R (1997) 'Doctrine and Practice in Commercial Law' in D Harris and K Hawkins (eds), *The Human Face of Law: Essays in Honour of Donald Harris* (Oxford, Clarendon Press).

de Roover, R (1963) 'The Scholastic Attitude toward Trade and Entrepreneurship' 1 *Explorations in Entrepreneurial History* (2nd series) 76.

Dickerson, CM (2005) 'Harmonizing Business Laws in Africa: OHADA Calls the Tune' 44 *Columbia Journal of Transnational Law* 17.

Foster, NHD (1997–98) 'Commercial Security over Movables in the UAE: A Comparative Analysis in the Light of English Law, French Law and the Shari'a' in E Cotran and C Mallat (eds), 4 *Yearbook of Islamic and Middle Eastern Law* (The Hague, Kluwer Law International).

—— (2002) 'Transmigration and Transferability of Commercial Law in a Globalised World' in E Örücü and A Harding (eds) *Comparative Law in the 21st Century* Kluwer.

—— (2003–04) 'Owing and Owning in Islamic and Western Law' in E Cotran and M Lau (eds), vol 10 *Yearbook of Islamic and Middle Eastern Law* (Leiden, Brill).

Fukuyama, F (1989) 'The End of History?' Summer *The National Interest* 3.

Garnot, SFR (1995) 'Des juristes au service d'une entreprise industrielle opérant au plan international' 47 *Revue internationale de droit comparé* 345.

Giddens, A (1999) *Runaway World: How Globalisation is Reshaping our Lives* (London, Profile).

Goode, RM (1992) 'The Concept of "Good Faith" in English Law' *Centro di studi e ricerche di diritto comparato e straniero, Roma*, 3, available at: http://soi.cnr.it/~crdcs/crdcs/goode.htm.

—— (1998) 'Security in Cross-Border Transactions' 33 *Texas International Law Journal* 47.

—— (2001) 'Insularity or Leadership? The Role of the United Kingdom in the Harmonisation of Commercial Law' 50 *International and Comparative Law Quarterly* 751.

—— (2004) *Commercial Law*, 3rd Edition (London, Penguin Books).

Guyon, Y (1990) *Droit des affaires: Tome 1: Droit commercial général et sociétés*, 6th edn (Paris, Economica).

Kahn-Freund, O (1974) 'Uses and Misuses of Comparative Law' 37 *Modern Law Review* 1.

Kennedy, D (1991) 'The Stakes of Law, or Hale and Foucault!' 15 *Legal Studies Forum* 327.

Kessler, AD (2003) 'Limited Liability in Context: Lessons from the French Origins of the American Limited Liability Partnership' 32 *Journal of Legal Studies* 511.

Le Bras, G (1963) 'Conceptions of Economy and Society' in MM Postan and E Rich (eds), *Cambridge Economic History of Europe*, vol III: *Economic Organization & Policies in the Middle Ages* (Cambridge, Cambridge University Press).

Le Nabasque, H and Adelle, J-F (2005) 'France: Reform of French Securities Law' 20 *Butterworths Journal of International Banking and Financial Law* 37.

Mahoney, PG (2001) 'The Common Law and Economic Growth: Hayek Might Be Right' 30 *Journal of Legal Studies* 503.

Mallat, C (2000) 'Commercial Law in the Middle East: Between Classical Transactions and Modern Business' 48 *American Journal of Comparative Law* 81.

Masson, P-J (1786) *Instruction sur les affaires contentieuses des négociants, la manière de les prévenir, ou de les suivre dans les tribunaux* (Paris, LeClerc).

McKendrick, E (2003) *Contract Law: Text, Cases and Materials* (Oxford, Oxford University Press).

Merryman, JH (1985) *The Civil Law Tradition: An Introduction to the Legal Systems of Western Europe and Latin America*, 2nd edn (Stanford CA, Stanford University Press).

Paillusseau, J (1997) 'L'enrichissement du droit et de la théorie juridique par la pratique professionnelle (un témoignage)' in *Le droit de l'entreprise dans ses relations externes à la fin du XX° siècle: Mélanges en l'honneur de Claude Champaud* (Paris, Dalloz).

Pistor, K (2002) 'The Standardization of Law and its Effect on Developing Economies' 50 *American Journal of Comparative Law* 97.

Pistor, K, Keinan, Y, Kleinheisterkamp, J and West, MD (2002) 'The Evolution of Corporate Law: A Cross-Country Comparison' 23 *University of Pennsylvania Journal of International Economic Law* 791.

Salacuse, JW (1999) 'From Developing Countries to Emerging Markets: A Changing Role for Law in the Third World' 33 *International Lawyer* 875.

Seidman, A and Seidman, RB (1995) 'Drafting Legislation for Development: Lessons from a Chinese Project' 44 *American Journal of Comparative Law* 1.

UNCITRAL (1977) *Report of the Secretary-General: Study on Security Interests* (A/CN9/131 1977) VIII *UNCITRAL Yearbook* 171.

—— (1980) *Report of the United Nations Commission on International Trade Law on the Work of its Thirteenth Session* (1980) (A/35/17) XI *UNCITRAL Yearbook*, Part One 11.

Visser, WA and Macintosh, A (1998) 'A Short Review of the Historical Critique of Usury' 8 *Accounting, Business & Financial History* 175.

Volckart, O and Mangels, A (1999) 'Are the Roots of the Modern Lex Mercatoria Really Medieval?' 65 *Southern Economic Journal* 427.

Guided Further Reading

In addition to the works cited in the text and listed above, the following may be of interest for the reader wishing to study the subject further.

For an extensive coverage of many of the issues discussed in this chapter, see: Dalhuisen, JH (2004) *Dalhuisen on International Commercial, Finance and Trade Law*, 2nd edn (Oxford, Hart Publishing).

Globalisation

The Historical Background Pre-globalisation:
Gaddis, JL (2005) *The Cold War: A New History* (Harmondsworth, Penguin).
Kopacsi, S (1989) *In the Name of the Working Class* (London, Fontana).

Mazower, M (1998) *Dark Continent: Europe's Twentieth Century* (London, Penguin).
http://en.wikipedia.org/wiki/Communism.
http://en.wikipedia.org/wiki/Communist_state.

The Transformation:
Barber, BR (1992) 'Jihad vs McWorld' March *The Atlantic Monthly* 53.
Fukuyama, F (1989) 'The End of History?' Summer *The National Interest* 3.
Huntington, SP (1993) 'The Clash of Civilizations' 72 *Foreign Affairs* 22.
Stephan, PB (1995) 'The Fall—Understanding the Collapse of the Soviet System' 29 *Suffolk University Law Review* 17.

Globalisation Generally:
Giddens, A (1999) *Runaway World: How Globalisation is Reshaping our Lives* (London, Profile).
Stiglitz, JE (2002) *Globalization and its Discontents* (New York, WW Norton).

Globalisation and Law:
Muchlinski, PT (2003) 'Globalisation and Legal Research' 37 *International Lawyer* 221.
Salacuse, JW (1999) 'From Developing Countries to Emerging Markets: A Changing Role for Law in the Third World' 33 *International Lawyer* 875.
Twining, W (2000) *Globalisation and Legal Theory* (London, Butterworths).

Commercial Law and Economic Development:
de Soto, H (2000) *The Mystery of Capital: Why Capitalism Triumphs in the West and Fails Everywhere Else* (New York, Basic Books).
Hayek, FA (1960) *The Constitution of Liberty* (London, Routledge and Kegan Paul).
Mahoney, PG (2001) 'The Common Law and Economic Growth: Hayek Might Be Right' 30 *Journal of Legal Studies* 503.
Pistor, K (2001) 'The Evolution of Legal Institutions and Economic Regime Change' in J Stiglitz and P Muet (eds), *Governance, Equity and Global Markets* (Oxford, Oxford University Press) (a balanced and comprehensive introduction).

Systems and Cultures

Systems:
Allan, DE (1984) 'Credit and Security: Economic Orders and Legal Regimes' 33 *International Comparative Law Quarterly* 22 (out of date as regards the instances given, but excellent on the importance of context).
Luhmann, N (2004) *Law as a Social System* (Oxford, Oxford University Press).
Pistor, K (2002) 'The Standardization of Law and its Effect on Developing Economies' 50 *American Journal of Comparative Law* 97.
Teubner, G (ed) (1997) *Global Law without a State* (Aldershot, Dartmouth).
von Bertalanffy, L (1968) *General System Theory: Foundations, Development, Applications* (Rev edn, New York, George Braziller).

Business Culture:
Hofstede, G (1997) *Cultures and Organizations: Software of the Mind*, Revised edn (New York, McGraw-Hill).

Legal Culture:
Abel, RL (1994) 'Transnational Law Practice' 44 *Case Western Reserve Law Review* 737 (transnational law firms).

Dezalay, Y (1990) 'The Big Bang and the Law: The Internationalization and Restructuration of the Legal Field Theory' 7 *Culture and Society* 279 (transnational law firms).

Gessner, V (1994) 'Global Legal Interaction and Legal Cultures' 7 *Ratio Juris* 132 (commercial law).

Watson, A (1983) 'Legal Change: Sources of Law and Legal Culture' 131 *University of Pennsylvania Law Review* 1121.

Path Dependence:

David, PA (1985) 'Clio and the Economics of QWERTY' 75 *American Economic Review* 332.

Liebowitz, SJ and Margolis, SE (1990) 'The Fable of the Keys' 33 *Journal of Law and Economics* 1.

Specific Examples Used in the Text

PRC Company Law:

Art, R and Gu, M (1995) 'China Incorporated: The First Corporation Law of the People's Republic of China' 20 *Yale Journal of International Law* 273.

Islamic Finance:

Vogel, FE and Hayes, SL (1998) *Islamic Law and Finance: Religion, Risk and Return* (The Hague, Kluwer Law International).

Security Law:

Wood, PR (2005) *Maps of World Financial Law*, 5th edn (London, Allen & Overy).

Transfer of Rights and Obligations:

Foster, NHD (2003-04) 'Owing and Owning in Islamic and Western Law' in E Cotran and M Lau (eds), vol 10 *Yearbook of Islamic and Middle Eastern Law* (Leiden, Brill).

Legal Transplants:

Twining, W (2004) 'Diffusion of Law: A Global Perspective' 49 *Journal of Legal Pluralism and Unofficial Law* 1.

Unsuitability: Black, B and Kraakman, R (1996) 'A Self-Enforcing Model of Corporate Law' 109 *Harvard Law Review* 1911.

Berkowitz, D, Pistor, K and Richard, JF (2003) 'Economic Development, Legality, and the Transplant Effect' 47 *European Economic Review* 165.

Channell, W (2005) 'Lessons Not Learned: Problems with Western Aid for Law Reform in Postcommunist Countries' 57 *Democracy and Rule of Law Project* 2005; also in 1 *Journal of Comparative Law* 321.

Sidelining: Pistor, K, Keinan, Y, Kleinheisterkamp, J and West, MD (2002) 'The Evolution of Corporate Law: A Cross-Country Comparison' 23 *University of Pennsylvania Journal of International Economic Law* 791.

Adaptation: Seidman, A and Seidman, RB (1995) 'Drafting Legislation for Development: Lessons from a Chinese Project' 44 *American Journal of Comparative Law* 1.

Harmonisation:

Goode, RM (1991) 'Reflections on the Harmonisation of Commercial Law' 1 *Uniform Law Review* 54.

Hobhouse, JS (1990) 'International Conventions and Commercial Law' 106 *Law Quarterly Review* 530.

Stephan, PB (1999) 'The Futility of Unification and Harmonization in International Commercial Law' 39 *Virginia Journal of International Law* 743.

English and French Attitudes to Commerce and Commercial Law

There is no general history of commercial law in English. See the relevant sections of Holdsworth, WS (1924) *A History of English Law*, 3rd edn (London, Methuen). Treatises in continental European languages include Hilaire, J (1986) *Introduction historique au droit commercial* (Paris, Presses universitaires de France), in particular chapters 1 and 2.

General Legal Cultural and Legal History:
Zweigert, K and Kötz, H (1998) *An Introduction to Comparative Law*, 3rd edn (Oxford, Clarendon Press), in particular chapter 6 (The History of French Law) and chapter 14 (The Development of the English Common Law).

Medieval Attitudes:
de Roover, R (1963) 'The Scholastic Attitude toward Trade and Entrepreneurship' 1 *Explorations in Entrepreneurial History (2nd series)* 76.
Le Bras, G (1963) 'Conceptions of Economy and Society' in MM Postan, and E Rich (eds), *Cambridge Economic History of Europe, vol III: Economic Organization & Policies in the Middle Ages* (Cambridge, Cambridge University Press).
Visser, WA and Macintosh, A (1998) 'A Short Review of the Historical Critique of Usury' 8 *Accounting, Business & Financial History* 175.

The Weber Thesis:
Weber, M (1930) *The Protestant Ethic and the Spirit of Capitalism* (London, G Allen & Unwin).

Lex Mercatoria:
The *Chicago Journal of International Law*, Summer 2004 issue, contains a useful collection of articles.
Cordes, A (2005) 'The Search for a Medieval Lex Mercatoria' in V Piergiovanni (ed), *From Lex Mercatoria to Commercial Law* (Berlin, Duncker & Humblot).
Sachs, SE (2006) 'From St Ives to Cyberspace: The Modern Distortion of the Medieval "Law Merchant"' 21 *American University International Law Review* 5.
Sutherland, Stuart L (1934) 'The Law Merchant in England in the Seventeenth and Eighteenth Centuries' in 17 *Transactions of the Royal Historical Society* (4th series) 149.
Volckart, O and Mangels, A (1999) 'Are the Roots of the Modern Lex Mercatoria Really Medieval?' 65 *Southern Economic Journal* 427.

French and English Commercial Law:
Dalhuisen, JH (2004) *Dalhuisen on International Commercial, Finance and Trade Law*, 2nd edn (Oxford, Hart Publishing), chapter 1, especially 1–26.
Goode, RM (2004) *Commercial Law*, 3rd edn (Harmondsworth, Penguin), chapters 1 and 40.
Nouel, P (1996) '"Cartesian Pragmatism": Looking for Common Principles in French and English Law' 24 *International Business Lawyer* 22.
Rouvillois, F (ed) (2005) *Le modèle juridique français: un obstacle au développement économique?* (Paris, Dalloz).

13

Administrative Law in a Comparative Perspective

JOHN BELL

KEY CONCEPTS

Administration; Administrative procedure; Discretionary powers; Duty to give a hearing; Duty to give reasons; Fundamental rights; Incompetence; Judicial Review; Legitimate expectations; Liability of the administration; Misuse of powers; Public body; Public Law and Private Law; Proportionality; Rule of law; Standards of good administration; State; Ultra vires.

I. INTRODUCTION

ADMINISTRATIVE LAW IS about the institutions and powers of the executive branch of government and the controls exercised by law over them. The term 'the administration' has no specific meaning in many legal systems, but it is a convenient label to cover central and local government, as well as the variety of public bodies that may exist.

The main questions for any comparison of legal systems are:

1. What does each system include within its conception of 'administrative law'?
2. Who is governed by 'administrative law'? In particular, how are the rules of public law separated from those of private law?
3. What powers does 'the administration' have?
4. What procedures does the administration have to adopt when making decisions?
5. Who provides remedies against the administration?
6. What judicial control is exercised over misuse of powers?
7. When is the administration liable for its actions and how is this liability different from that of a private individual?

II. WHAT IS ADMINISTRATIVE LAW?

Rules on Powers or Rules on Remedies?

The label 'administrative law' is used in different ways in different legal systems. In continental European traditions, administrative law (*droit administratif, Verwaltungsrecht*)[1] is concerned with the powers and organisation of the executive organs of the state. The common law use of the term 'administrative law' is more synonymous with 'administrative litigation' (*contentieux administrative, Verwaltungsgerichtsbarkeit*), and even in the common law world the topic is often called 'judicial review (of administrative action)'. 'Administrative law' is best used to identify a general body of principles that govern the organisation, powers and procedures of the administration and the rules governing the remedies (judicial or otherwise) available for breaches of those principles. These remedies cover both the judicial review of the exercise of powers and administrative liability.

What is Specific About Administrative Law Rules?

A second area of difficulty in comparison lies in the scope of administrative law. In one important sense, administrative law includes all the rules and principles that apply to the administration. But this usage would be unnecessarily broad. If the distinctive feature of administrative law is the organisation and exercise of public power, then our attention is focused more on aspects that involve the exercise of state authority or the organisation of public services, rather than on everything that a state body might do. There is no particular reason why the ordering of newspapers for the common room of city councillors or liability for an accident caused by the mayor's official car should be governed by rules that are different from those governing similar activities in the lives of ordinary individuals. These situations are typically governed by the general law of the land. 'Administrative law' is therefore best confined to those rules and principles that apply in a distinctive manner to the organisation and actions of the state, its organs and other public bodies. Within the scope of this distinctive law, it is usual to distinguish between rules and principles of general application, and the special rules that apply either to a particular type of public body (eg local authorities) or to a particular sphere of activity (eg housing law or environmental law). This chapter is limited to the general principles of administrative law, and it does not cover special administrative law.

---

[1] This chapter uses mainly English, French and German terminology. Although these are the major European traditions of administrative law, there are important differences between these particular legal systems and those that are closely related to them. When studying the relationship between any two particular legal systems, the reader will have to be aware of possible differences.

III. WHO IS GOVERNED BY 'ADMINISTRATIVE LAW'?:
PUBLIC LAW AND PRIVATE LAW

The general principles of administrative law apply to 'the administration' or the executive branch of government. But the difficulty is that there is usually no single institution which is called 'the administration'. There are a variety of bodies through which governments act or through which public services are delivered. There are government departments, local government, public corporations or agencies. But, in addition, foundations and even private corporations or associations can be closely involved in delivering public services and may be given special powers. So are these also included as bodies regulated by administrative law?

In order to express the difference between the distinctive rules of administrative law and the general rules of law, legal systems typically distinguish between 'public law' and 'private law' to draw the boundary.[2] The distinction between public law and private law is drawn either in terms of *activity*, focusing on the distinctive mission and values of public law, or in terms of the legal form of *institutions*, focusing either on certain organisations through which public power is exercised or services are delivered, or on the courts and tribunals through which redress for administrative wrongdoing is provided.

The French tradition (and that of the countries such as Spain and Italy that are connected to it) adopts an *activity-based distinction* between public and private law. It attributes a distinctive mission to public law. Public law is concerned with the common good, not private advantage, a view articulated by Ulpian (Digest 1.1.1.2) in the 3rd century. The state is given special powers and is authorised to act only if it serves the public good. A good example would be the power of the state to expropriate private property for public utility upon the payment of compensation (Erasmus, 1990). A private person has to buy the property of another, and can only do so when that other person is willing to sell. The state can expropriate, even where the property owner objects. The public good justifies its special position. Another area would be emergency powers, where the state can detain or expel people or requisition their property against their consent in ways that are not permissible to a private individual.[3] In both cases, the state is authorised to restrict the rights of individuals without their consent in order to promote the common good. The 'common good' is traditionally seen as the product of national political decision-making processes. But in more recent times, the emphasis has been on the need for at least some minimum set of requirements that must be satisfied by a state claiming the 'common good' in order to satisfy international standards of human rights protection.

Even this idea of a mission to promote the common good remains difficult to apply. One of the indicators for such a mission can be whether a body has been

---

[2] For an example, see CERAP, *Le contrôle juridictionnel de l'Administration* (Paris, Economica, 1991).

[3] See International Commission of Jurists, *States of Emergency: their Impact on Human Rights* (Geneva 1983).

given powers that exceed those of a private individual (as is clear in the case of expropriation). Where special powers are being exercised, then this needs special regulation. The public interest many not only authorise the state to interfere with the rights of private individuals, but may confer on the state special privileges. This occurs, for example in the provision of public services, where a public provider is exempt from many of the restrictions of competition law in order to enable it to provide a service in the general interest. For example, European Union law has increasingly identified special rules relating to 'services in the general interest'. These two criteria of public law find their expression in the European Union doctrine of 'organ of the state' for the purpose of direct effect. In *Foster v British Gas plc*[4] the European Court of Justice held that a body is treated as an organ of the state, whatever its legal form, if it is providing a public service under the control of the state and has special powers for that purpose that go beyond those which exist in relations between individuals.

Although the distinction between actions undertaken for the common good and those undertaken for private advantage is easy to state, it is hard to apply. In some situations, the administration is only one provider, among many, of social activities, for example sports facilities. If these happen to be run by the community through a local council, rather than by a private company, is there really any special social policy that makes this administrative activity different in character from that of the private sector? (see Flogaitis, 1986: chapter two) If the sports *facility* is run as part of a 'fitness for all' programme at subsidised prices, it is possible to argue that the activity is different in character from a profit-making private leisure club. Different countries operate here in different ways. The English or Dutch traditions would now treat some public services, such as electricity, gas or transport, as essentially private activities with some limited public obligations for which the public pays. By contrast the French tradition would confer on these *activities* a special mission in the service of the public good, and would treat the operators as participating in this mission (Brown and Bell, 1998: 131–4). The practical consequence of the difference in approach is that in France the relationship between the operator of the service and the government is essentially a matter of public law, and public law principles on contracts and liability apply. When exercising the powers conferred on a public service provider, the private operator is exercising public power. In the English tradition, the relationship is essentially of a commercial service provider operating within constraints of the government's supervisory power.

In the German tradition, the distinction between public law and private law is essentially a matter of whether the *institution* has the legal form of a public law organisation or a private law organisation. Different rules govern each category of organisation. The result is that, once an activity is transferred to the private sector, it ceases to be treated as a public law activity. As a result, it makes sense to present the system in terms of the powers of local authorities, schools, the police and so

----

4 Case C–188/89 *Foster v British Gas plc* [1990] ECR I–3313 (ECJ).

on, and to differentiate the way these can behave from the behaviour of private individuals and companies.

A different *institutional* approach relates to the courts which have jurisdiction over issues. The common law approach focuses on a distinction between public law remedies and private law remedies, each of which is provided in a different way. Such a distinction does not clearly focus on the powers which certain bodies must have in the first place, but more on the remedies available when they misbehave. In part, the need for such remedies lies in the issue of standing. Only parties who have rights affected by a private contract or wrong can sue. In public law, a wider group of people are frequently held to have a legitimate interest in a decision, even if no rights of theirs have been affected. [Even then this distinction is not as sharp as between systems that have distinct courts for dealing with the administration and those that deal with private and criminal law matters.] This is discussed in more detail below.

Questions for Discussion

1. What does each system mean by the notion of 'public law' as opposed to private law? How far do the systems apply different rules because of the nature of the activity or simply because of the kind of organisation that is engaged in a particular activity?

2. What is the consequence of declaring an issue to be a matter of public law? Do special rules apply? Does the body undertaking the activity have special powers and responsibilities? Will special remedies apply if something goes wrong?

IV. THE ALLOCATION OF POWERS

Sources

The powers of the administration are derived either because of the character of its activity (*inherent powers*) or because specific powers have been attributed to it by the legislature. French and English laws recognise that certain powers ought to belong inherently to government, even in the absence of specific authorisation. In England, these are typically the prerogative powers of the Crown, eg to make war and sign treaties, to maintain public order, to grant honours and the like. A controversial example in recent times came when the Home Secretary provided weapons to a local police force without the approval of its immediate superior, the local police authority.[5] Although there was no specific power, it was held that this was inherently a power of the Crown to regulate public order. The French Constitutional Council has likewise recognised the power of the government to regulate public order, eg in controlling hunting, even in the absence of specific legislative powers to this effect.[6] In France, certain actions in the field of foreign

---

[5] Eg *R v Home Secretary, ex p Northumbria Police Authority* [1989] QB 26 (CA).
[6] CC decision 87–149L, 20 February 1987, Rec 22. See also Bell, 1992: 288.

affairs, the deployment of armed forces and the grant of honours are recognised powers of the government, often now mentioned in the Constitution (Articles 15, 16 and 30).

A second group of inherent powers are recognised in relation to the organisation of the civil service. In addition, and unlike in England, the French recognise an inherent power to create and operate public services. There is debate whether the organisation of the civil service is a 'prerogative' in the strict sense, because the government appears to be acting no differently from a private business in organising its employees and internal activities. But the special protection typically offered by the law to public employees, and their responsibility to the public service and not just to their political masters, marks civil servants out as distinct.[7]

A third activity that may be seen as inherent is the power to make contracts or to dispose of property. Again, these seem at first sight to be activities that any legal person might undertake. The public interest, however, imposes a distinctive approach to making such transactions—they are undertaken not in the self-interest of the organisation but to serve the public, and there are distinctive requirements of procedure to ensure the even-handed treatment of potential contractors.

Predominantly, the powers in question relate to the functions of the 'night-watchman state'—defence, internal public order, the internal organisation of the government service and contracts. In both England and France, such inherent powers have been largely, but not completely, overtaken by specific legislation. Nonetheless, Article 21 of the French Constitution of 1958 confers inherent powers on the Prime Minister to take measures to implement legislation passed by the Parliament and also grants inherent powers to legislate in areas not specifically identified by Article 34 of the Constitution as falling within the competence of Parliament.

The advantage of inherent powers is that the government can act on new policy in a speedy way. For example, in England, the creation of agencies within the civil service (the so-called 'Next Steps Agencies') to manage the delivery of public services in areas such as social security benefits was achieved without the need for legislation. But the privatisation of nationalised industries and the creation of new public sector organisations, such as NHS trusts, have required legislation. Similarly, French governments can act by decree to re-organise the structures of a public service such as education.

By contrast, German law is more modern in insisting that the administration only has those powers that have been attributed to it. This is a more common principle accepted in Europe that the administration needs to receive specific authorisation from the legislature for its activities. Its concept of the *Gesetzesvorbehalt* (authorisation by law) is contrasted with the idea of inherent powers of the administration found in French law and in the English Crown

---

[7] See CE 28 June 1918, *Heyriès*, Leb 651. See also *Council of Civil Service Unions v Minister for the Civil Service* [1985] AC 374 (HL).

prerogative. Given the history of dictatorships in so many parts of Europe, the reluctance to allow the administration inherent powers is understandable. Article 20 III of the Basic Law provides that officials are subordinated to the law. In addition, as Helmut Maurer states:

> The principle of the rule of law requires that the legal relationships between the state and the citizen should be governed by general legislation, which not only determine administrative actions, but also make them foreseeable and calculable for the citizens (Maurer, 1994: 98).

Naturally, the law cannot prescribe everything, so the German courts have understood the principle as requiring that the *essential* rules are laid down by statute. For example, in the operation of schools, the legislator cannot leave major matters to be decided by school administrations, such as the structure of secondary schools, requirements that pupils re-sit a year that they have not passed, or on sex education.[8]

Questions for Discussion

1. Where are the powers of the administration to be found in the systems you are studying?
2. Does the system adopt the fundamental principle that legislative powers must be authorised by legislation, or does it accept that there are some powers which require no specific authorisation?
3. Do the powers you are considering come from general legislation (eg laws on public procurement) or from specific legislation (eg laws on contracts in local government).

The Conception of 'the State'

The function of the state determines the powers that a particular administration is given. Powers have to be interpreted in the light of the role the state is playing in society. Where there is what is termed the '*nightwatchman* state', the administration has a limited role in society, confined to protecting internal and external order and basic rights of individuals. Through the 19th and 20th centuries, the state took on a much larger role in securing individual well-being. It created collective systems of health care, education, housing and social security. The task of ensuring the basic infrastructure of a modern society has been the role of either local or central government through investment in the network utilities of electricity, gas, post and telecommunications. The *welfare* or *transforming* state had a major role in delivering necessary services and also in achieving economic change by the activities the state undertook. In this latter role, it often sought to control and own

---

[8] See BVerfGE 41, 251; BVerfGE 56, 155; BVerfGE 47, 46 and 194.

the commanding heights of essential industries, such as coal and steel. Since the 1980s, this model of the state has fallen into decline in Western Europe. It has not been thought that the state is good at running industrial activities or even many services in an efficient and cost-effective manner. Utilities have been privatised. The function of the state is increasingly focused on *regulating* the private market to ensure competition and to secure the availability of certain public services, by subsidy if necessary. The deficiencies in the free market are cured not by replacing it, as under nationalisation, but by establishing a framework of regulatory rules to ensure that the market benefits everyone. The place of governmental activity on the spectrum between the models of the welfare state and the regulatory state is determined differently in different countries within Europe, depending both on the political party in power and on the tradition of government activity. In Britain, the National Health Service has been a strongly centralised governmental activity funded by a national insurance scheme. In France and in Germany, the service is funded largely through private insurance, leading to a more fragmented and local pattern of healthcare. The government has less of a role in managing the system than in England. By contrast, the British railway system is much more privatised than that of France or Germany.

In interpreting powers in the nightwatchman state, there is an assumption that the state should interfere as little as possible with individual freedom of action. By contrast, in the welfare or transforming state, there is a need for a more benevolent interpretation of the scope of administrative powers in order to ensure that there is sufficient scope to undertake the necessary action. Thus, in Germany, an explicit power to secure housing was held to include an implied power to provide subsidy to tenants.[9]

The Devolved State

The constitutional attribution of powers between different levels of government is critical. This is most commonly seen in federal countries where there is an explicit division of competence between national and regional governments. In some countries, the principle of subsidiarity governs the relationship between the different levels. This is the case in Germany where the Federation only has competence in a number of specified areas and the Länder have residual competence. Subsidiarity ensures that decisions are left to the local level where possible. Such a principle does not apply to countries that have devolved power from the national level, such as the United Kingdom, Italy and Spain, where residual power lies with the national parliament and government. Even where subsidiarity is a principle relevant to the relationship between national and regional governments, it does not normally apply to the relationship between national and local governments.

---

[9] BVerfGE 6, 282.

The State within Supranational Organisations

The competence of the administration is not only controlled by national legislation, but also by supranational rules, whether in the form of treaties such as the European Convention on Human Rights, or from the European Union. The sources of administrative law will thus not only be national, but supranational. On the whole, the inspiration for adapting national administrative law will come from the rulings of these supranational bodies, either courts or organisations. Thus, ideas for new ways of running the public sector frequently come from the Organisation for Economic Cooperation and Development (www.oecd.org) based in Paris. Ideas for common standards of administrative law are developed by the Council of Europe or the European Union.

V. ADMINISTRATIVE PROCEDURE

Even if institutions of government are often specific to a particular country, standards for administrative procedure often have much in common. The comparative study of administrative procedures is interesting not just for their content, but also for what this topic shows about the sources of administrative law in different jurisdictions. In a number of countries, there are legal codes governing the procedure by which the administration makes decisions, starting in Austria with the General Law on Administrative Procedure of 21 July 1925 and in the United States with the Administrative Law Procedure Act 1946. Other examples include the German *Verwaltungsverfahrensgesetz* of 25 May 1976, the Italian law of administrative procedure of 7 August 1990, and the Dutch general law on administration of 1992. Prior to these statutes, much of the general law was judge-made, though there were specific procedures laid down by statute in relation to specific activities, such as expropriation. In other systems, such as the English common law, that mix of judge-made principles and sector-specific rules still remains the case. In addition to these different national sources, there are broadly conceived transnational standards. Some of these transnational standards are not legally binding, but exercise a general influence over the development of the law in particular countries.[10] Other standards are set by international treaties, such as the European Convention on Human Rights, and are legally binding. Comparative law is interested not only in comparing the different national standards, but also in how national standards meet international standards.

Such procedural obligations are founded not only on ensuring the protection of the subject who is subordinated to the unilateral power of the administration,

---

[10] See Resolution R (77) 31 of the Council of Ministers of the Council of Europe of 28 September 1977, on the protection of the individual in relations with the state. Rights identified in this Resolution included the right of access to administrative documents, the right to legal advice and assistance in preparing a case before the administration, and the right to the reasons for the decision and to information on rights of appeal. All these involve, in some way, the right to defend individual interests against the general interest.

but also on ensuring accountability for its actions to the citizens of the state. Thus the duty to provide reasons not only provides transparency that can enable superiors to exercise control, but also contributes to a better dialogue with citizens. A third reason would be the economy and efficiency of administrative decisions. Simplicity and comprehensibility in procedures may avoid excessive cost and improve the comprehensibility of decisions.

Comparison is undertaken at three levels. The first is a discussion of the general principles of administrative procedure. Some experienced commentators suggest that the diversity of the activities and purposes of administrative action is such that any attempt to develop uniform principles to govern its procedure is bound to fail, either because the duties would be too numerous and burdensome for many situations, or the rules would be so partial and incomplete as to provide inadequate supervision (see Torchia, 1993: 43). For example, the procedures appropriate for making decisions in schools may be inappropriate in dealing with immigration or planning. A single set of procedures for all these cases would be inappropriate. But others consider that there are common standards, grounded in ideas of *fairness* and in the need to simplify procedures for the citizen in her dealings with different facets of the administration.[11] Most of the 'principles of good administration' developed in the European Union or the Council of Europe are focused on these general standards.

A second level of comparison would focus on the procedures of particular administrations or processes. An example would be planning inquiries. Clearly the difficulty here is establishing that the institutional context is sufficiently similar that the procedures followed can be compared in a useful manner.[12] The use of public hearings as part of planning inquiries is different institutionally from the process by which objections to the grant of planning permission are handled in France, where public inquiries are restricted to the development of general plans. As a result, more planning objection cases end up in court in France.

A third level would focus on particular procedural duties. Among the issues debated in recent years is the duty of decision-makers to provide reasons for their decisions and the access of the public to information (Birkinshaw, 2003: chapter six). In this context, it is also useful to understand the effect of the breach of a mandatory procedural requirement. In most systems, this gives rise to the nullity of a decision.

Duty to Give a Hearing

The duty to give a hearing is a basic principle of all administrative law systems, but it is expressed in different ways in different systems. The common law has a principle of natural justice that a person has to be heard before a disciplinary or similar decision

---

[11] See Konijnenbelt, 1993: 64.
[12] See the warning of Loughlin, 1993: 44 at 57 about the importance of institutional context in deciding whether comparison is useful.

is taken against him or her. French-related systems have within the *droits de la défense, le principe du contradictoire*, the right for the person to rebut arguments made against him or her, whether orally or in writing. The broad similarity of the basic principle nevertheless hides some basic assumptions. First, the form of hearing may differ. The common law model of natural justice starts from a judicial archetype of decision-making, based on an oral hearing (hence *audi alterem partem*: 'hear' both sides). The French and German models start from a bureaucratic paradigm where even judicial decisions need not be taken after an oral hearing, so the right is really one to make representations. Secondly, continental European systems are clearer about the kinds of decision that require a hearing to be given to those affected. They distinguish between individual acts—measures affecting specified individuals—such as expropriation, and regulatory acts—measures of general application—such as legislation. Where the measure is individual, then those whose rights are specifically affected can expect to have a hearing. On the other hand, where the measure is of general application, such as a tax on all houses, the persons affected do not have a right to be heard specifically by the decision-maker. This difference is not as well articulated in the common law.

The Duty to Give Reasons/Transparency

At least before the Human Rights Act 1998, the duty to give reasons for decisions was not an established principle of the common law. Judges did not always have to give reasons, so administrators could not be required to do so. It was good practice, but not a legal requirement.[13] By contrast, the principle formed part of French and German administrative law from an early date. The difference between these two approaches is less than might first appear. The English common law did impose the obligation on courts and administrators to given reasons to the Court of Queen's Bench where a decision was challenged by way of case stated or by certiorari. In those cases, the High Court was inspecting the decision, and could expect the inferior court or administration to justify its decision. The problem was to show sufficient doubt about the legality of the decision so as to obtain leave to bring proceedings in the High Court in the first place. By contrast, the continental systems only required limited statements of reasons, often amounting to no more than giving the legal basis of the decision, rather than a justification of the formal reasons.

As a result, all systems have needed the right to reasons to be supplemented by the right of access to administrative documents that may cast light on the context and reasons for the decision. Access to public documents has been a much more recent development in most administrative law systems and it has come through legislation, rather than judicially developed principles. The British Freedom of Information Act 2000 was much later than similar legislation in France or Germany. In Germany this is contained in the Administrative Procedure Law of

---

[13] *R v Home Secretary, ex p Doody* [1994] 1 AC 531 (HL).

1976 and in France, in legislation of 1978. The English legislation has a number of specific categories of documents that are exempt from disclosure. The French and the Germans have general principles. Thus, in Germany the exclusions from disclosure cover the protection of confidential information or business secrecy or where there would be harm to the federal or Länder governments.

Standards of Good Administration

Operationally, the administration must conform to standards of good administration, including efficiency. Standards of good administration are typically laid down as ideals of administrative practice, rather than legal standards. For example, the moves in the 1990s to treat the user of public services as a form of consumer spawned a series of administrative charters, which had no legally binding effect, but which sought to guarantee compensation for failures to meet certain basic standards of public service defined by the administration. In more recent times, the citizen's right to good administration has been enshrined in the *Charter of Fundamental Rights* Article 41 and in Article II-101 of the *European Constitutional Treaty*. A more detailed statement, the Code of Good Administrative Behaviour was voted on by the European Parliament on 6 September 2001. Many such norms, such as the Code, do not have legal value, but act as guiding standards, that may often form a background to the way in which lawyers and ombudsmen identify how the administration ought to behave, and how legal norms ought to be interpreted. A major area of comparison is administrative procedure, discussed below.

Questions for Discussion

1. Do the concepts used in different systems have the same basic meaning in terms of the way in which the administration must conduct itself? Test this out by asking how the rules would apply in certain specific situations.
2. Does it matter whether the rules on procedure are set out in the general principles typically articulated by judicial decisions or are set out in legislation?
3. Does the detailed style of common law statutes actually lead to significant differences in practice compared with the general principles set out in continental European statutes. Freedom of information legislation might be a good example.

VI. INSTITUTIONS PROVIDING LEGAL REDRESS

There are significant differences between countries in the structure of judicial institutions. Most legal systems have specialist administrative courts to hear matters concerning decisions of the administration. Thus the German, French, Italian and Swedish systems all have an administrative court structure that is separate from that of the private law courts. In other systems, such as the English, Scots, Irish, Spanish and Dutch, any special administrative court is a division within the general courts. Judges may specialise in administrative matters, but there is no separate administrative jurisdiction. The advantage of the former approach is that there are courts that are specialist in dealing with administrative law issues, and they can develop a set of principles that recognise the distinctiveness of the control of the administration. In particular, procedures can be simpler than those used in private litigation and judges can adopt a more pro-active role in requiring evidence to be produced by the administration. As a result, the citizen is assisted in assembling the evidence required to sustain a complaint. The disadvantage is that litigants may find it difficult to work out whether a particular matter belongs in the administrative courts or in the private law courts. Even a system that has been in operation for over 200 years, such as that in France, still finds some 30 cases a year of conflicts of jurisdiction between the public and private law courts, that require resolution by a special court, the *Tribunal des Conflits*.

Legal redress may not only be provided by the courts, but also by tribunals. Tribunals are typically staffed by a combination of lawyers and lay experts. Their procedure can be less formal than a court and there may be no need for legal representation. In dealing with small claims to social welfare benefits this may be easier for the litigant and offer greater expertise in the special social problems arising. In France, there are a number of *commissions*, such as that in dealing with refugees. It is often difficult to decide whether such bodies should be designated as courts or not. In European law, professional disciplinary bodies whose decisions are recognised by the state are treated as 'courts'. The balance of cases between courts and tribunals varies a lot between legal systems.

The Swedish system of independent administrative redress through the Ombudsman has been followed by many European states. The ombudsman offers an independent investigation of complaints which requires little evidence gathering by the complainant. The ombudsman takes steps to find out from the administration what happened. This process resolves a large number of disputes. All the same, it typically suffers from the disadvantage that the recommendations resulting from an investigation are not binding on the administration.

The German system requires that an individual seek redress through the administration before bringing a case in the courts. This *Widerspruch* request enables the administration to deal with mistakes before a court case has started. It is normal in the French system also to require that a complainant request that the administration withdraws its decision and can only bring an action where the administration refuses or (commonly) when it fails to respond within a legally specified time. English law achieves something similar through the Pre-Action Protocols in civil procedure.

Questions for Discussion

1. (Where do citizens normally find redress against administrative decisions)—in the courts, through tribunals, or through the Ombudsman? You might look at statistics in annual reports of the courts or the Ombudsman to find out.
2. What are the differences between bringing an action in the administrative courts and bringing an action in the ordinary civil courts? Examine the differences in procedure. Are the differences to the advantage of the citizen making a complaint?

VII. THE JUDICIAL CONTROL OF POWERS

The Basis

In many legal systems, there is no code or statute that authorises the courts to control the legality of administrative action or defines the grounds on which this is done. Accordingly, there is much debate in various countries about the constitutional foundation of judicial review of the administration. For some, it is simply a matter of enforcing the wishes of the legislature. For others, there are more fundamental values that justify a restrictive interpretation of the powers of the administration.

Rule of Law

Although the term 'rule of law' is frequently used to express a fundamental value of any liberal political system, there are different understandings of this idea among different legal systems. Within the common law tradition, the English-language expression 'rule of law' embraces a number of understandings. In some contexts, it merely refers to conformity to law—an administrative act is authorised by a higher norm. In the view of AV Dicey, the rule of law emphasised the absence of privileges for the administration, and, in his view, the subordination of the administration to the ordinary law of the land (Dicey, 1959: chapter twelve).[14] For him, that entailed the subordination of the administration ultimately to the ordinary courts. In modern times, the idea of compliance with human rights has gained strength and was part of the Delhi declaration of the International Commission of Jurists in 1959. The French conception of *l'état de droit* expresses the idea that all public power is limited by the legal rules which it is bound to respect. It offers the control of power through law. The law is administered, especially by the *Conseil d'Etat* as adviser and judge. But such an expression does not contain substantive content, and it certainly does not entail that the ordinary judges have powers over the administration. In French, the English conception is

---

[14] This view he held despite the fact that the Crown at that time enjoyed immunity from actions in the court.

often translated as '*le règne du droit*' in that the law (conceived in the broad sense of legal values) prevails over the administration. The German-language concept of the *Rechtsstaat* has the idea that the administration is given power by the law and is constrained by it.[15] The principle applies to all the administration without immunities. The concept is usually understood to include rights of defence against the administration. The German expansion of this into the '*sozialer Rechtsstaat*' involves a number of substantive rights and social justice. To a great extent, the scope of notions such as 'the rule of law' depends on how far the term is allowed to spread to embrace other constitutional values. The divergence in uses of the terminology and the absence of an exact equivalent in the different languages provides much potential for confusion. All the same, these different terms convey some common liberal messages—that the administration is not free to act as it deems to be right in terms of efficiency or to achieve political goals. The administration has to remain within the constraints laid down by law.

Fundamental Rights

Many constitutions, particularly those drafted since 1945, contain enumerations of fundamental rights. These set out further values that the administration must respect and, in some cases, actively promote. A number of types of comparative study have been undertaken to assess the impact of this process. Some simply set in parallel the impact of a specific human rights instrument on national laws. For example, this has been done in relation to the European Convention on Human Rights and Fundamental Freedoms of 1950. Some studies have simply shown how the Convention has operated at national level. Others, however, have tried to compare the extent of the impact and discuss the reasons for the way it has worked in the different legal systems (eg Gearty, 1997). The concern of such studies is often the outcomes of compliance and an assessment of how far individual legal systems fall short of what the Convention requires. There is less attention to the reasons why national systems absorb such international standards in different ways. The work of Philip Alston (Alston, 1999), however, has been innovative in examining the processes of introducing fundamental values. The use of bills of rights as legal instruments raises issues of how far the enactment of a legal text has an impact on the way in which the legal system works and what is required to ensure that a culture of respect for fundamental values is embedded. Although the answers to such questions require some legal sociology, some clues can be found in the extent to which the legal system has adapted to the new culture of rights. Bills of rights are often copied from other constitutions, so there is scope to study legal transplants in this area and to assess how far the embedding of new ideas depends on the legal professions and traditions of the receiving country.

---

[15] The concept was coined by von Mohl in 1832. See Stolleis, 1992: 173.

Comparison can be undertaken as to how far administrative law reflects certain fundamental values. Many of these values are included in notions of a fair procedure. The influence of fundamental rights is a theme in many general studies of administrative law in Europe (see Schwarze, 1996). Much of the comparison of fundamental rights occurs in the discussion of influences of international treaties on national law and this applies well outside Europe, though many of the issues are similar.

Reviewable and Non-reviewable Decisions

In the past, there were two types of decision that were typically excluded from the purview of judicial review. On the one hand, acts of state were matters of high policy with which judges should not interfere.[16] On the other hand, internal acts within the administration were seen as being on too low a level for judges to be occupied considering them. In line with the requirement of access to legal redress under Article 6 of the European Convention on Human Rights, these limitations have been reduced. While very high-level policies such as a declaration of war or the signature of a treaty do remain excluded, other decisions that would be treated as acts of state, such as the issue of passports, are now subjected to review. More significantly, the exclusion of internal acts of the administration has been almost eradicated. A good example is prison discipline, which used to be treated as merely a matter of the internal regulation of the public service, but is now seen very much as a reviewable matter.[17]

Grounds of Review

The broad grounds of review accepted by most legal systems would cover lack of competence (*ultra vires* in the strict sense) and procedural irregularity, both of which are external to the decision in that the body making it had no power to make it or should have only done so after following certain mandatory procedural steps. On examining the content and justifications given for the decision, it may be apparent that the decision was taken on the basis of an error of law or following a misuse of discretion.

Lack of Competence

As has been noted in the section on powers, the administration has powers either inherently as the executive branch of government or attributed to it by Parliament. Every decision requires a legal basis from one of these sources. Sometimes the administration may try to overstep its powers because it seeks to achieve a policy objective in the short term,[18] in which case, there is no power to take any decision on that subject.

---

[16] See, eg BVerwGE 62, 11 (imprisonment of war criminal Hess).

[17] See CE Ass 17 February 1995, *Marie*, Leb 85. See also *R v Deputy Governor of Parkurst Prison, ex parte Leech* [1992] 1 AC 58 (HL).

[18] See abuse of discretion below.

Procedural Irregularity

Legislation may prescribe a particular procedure for a decision to be taken. For example, the decision on a planning application may require prior notice to neighbours in a prescribed form. Failure to conform may lead to the invalidity of the decision. Where there is no specific prescribed procedure, then the administration will be required to respect general principles of administrative procedure. As has been said, in some countries these are contained in statute, whereas in other countries, such as England or the European Union, the principles are unwritten—the so-called principles of natural justice.

Control over Discretion

Courts do not hear an appeal on the merits of decisions, but they do scrutinise the justifications to see that the legally relevant considerations have been taken into account. A decision that is taken for a different reason would be unlawful as it involves an error of law[19] Countries differ in the intensity with which they scrutinise administrative decisions. In Germany and France, it is normal to distinguish between decisions where there is strict scrutiny of decisions and those where there is a strong deference to the judgement of the executive. The English common law is not usually as explicit in this regard and tends to be less willing to review discretionary decisions.

  Strict scrutiny is applied to decisions that affect fundamental rights. Even where the administration enjoys a wide discretion, a decision that infringes a fundamental right will need a particularly strong justification. For example, German courts struck down a decision to dismiss a policeman which was made on the ground that he breached an order not to marry his pregnant fiancée.[20] The right to marry should not be restrained except for a very serious reason, which did not exist in this case. Equally, a decision to prevent the exercise of freedom of speech can only be restricted where the administration is able to demonstrate an immediate and serious threat to public order.[21] Such considerations have not been as strong in the British tradition, where considerations of national security or public order have often prevailed over the protection of fundamental rights.[22] It might be argued that the British courts have become less reluctant to intervene in administrative decisions, even where national security is at stake, since the enactment of the Human Rights Act 1998.[23]

---

[19] See eg CE 4 July 1924, *Beaugé*, Leb 641 (public order powers cannot be used for financial gain). See also *R v Foreign Secretary, ex parte World Development Movement* [1995] 1 All ER 611(CA) (development aid powers cannot be used to provide counterpart funding for arms sales).
[20] See BVerf GE 14, 21; BVerfGE 30, 29. Similarly unlawful was a decision to expel a foreigner without taking into account that he had married a German national and had a child at school in Germany: BVerfGE 35, 382.
[21] CE 19 May 1933, *Benjamin*, Leb 541.
[22] See *R v Home Secretary, ex parte Brind* [1991] 1 AC 696 (HL); and *R v Home Secretary, ex parte Cheblak* [1991] 2 All ER 319 (CA)
[23] See *A v Home Secretary* [2005] UKHL 71.

By contrast, decisions that involve complex, practical judgements involving competing public interests are only subjected to limited scrutiny. For example, judges in most countries would not consider it appropriate to question decisions on the siting of a nuclear power station, or professional judgements about examination or appraisal or promotions.[24]

The issue for a comparative lawyer is the extent to which particular decisions are subjected to strict or weak scrutiny in the different jurisdictions studied. The traditional English law approach has been to apply a test of *Wednesbury* unreasonableness to decisions where there has been no error of law. This permits the court to quash a decision where it is so unreasonable that no reasonable authority could have come to it.[25] This formulation is more restrictive than the French or European Union test of a 'manifest error in evaluation' which denotes simply a serious error of judgement by the administration. The administration enjoys a margin of appreciation in the application of a legal concept or category, but it must not exceed that margin.

Many of the most successful works in comparative law have limited their focus to these specific grounds of review in different jurisdictions. The purpose of such studies has been to understand the differences between national conceptions of administrative justice. A good example is the notion of 'proportionality'. The term has migrated from German administrative law to become a principle recognised in most jurisdictions. (It began as a principle to control the exercise of police powers that interfered with basic rights, but has come to be applied to a wider range of decisions.) It has three components: a requirement that administrative action be necessary; that it be properly directed to the objective being pursued; and that the burdens imposed on individuals do not seriously outweigh the benefits to the community as a whole (ie they are not 'disproportionate' in a narrow sense). Much comparison has been undertaken with the object of clarifying how far there is a real difference between this (often foreign) concept and longer established concepts used in domestic law, such as *erreur manifeste d'appréciation* or *unreasonableness*. The most successful studies of this kind is by Aldo Sandulli, who examines the way in which the term is used in the different jurisdictions and the extent to which it represents a difference in the scope of review from traditional terms. In his survey of legal developments in the European Union, France, Germany, Italy and the United Kingdom, he notes that all countries accept the principle of preventing the administration making excessive use of its descretionary powers, but they take diverging views on the extent to which judges should impose constraints on the exercise of such powers. National approaches to the control

---

[24] See CE 4 May 1978, *Département de la Savoie*, AJDA 1979, 38; *R v Environment Secretary ex parte Greenpeace* [1994] 4 All ER 352 (QBD); and BVerfGE, 53, 30 on nuclear installations. See CE 9 June 1978, *Lebon*, Leb 245 on career judgements.

[25] *Associated Picture Houses Ltd v Wednesbury Corporation* [1948] 1 KB 223 (HL).

over the administration reflected different views about the scope for judges to limit the freedom of the administration, especially in the field of discretionary power (Sandulli, 1998: 37–134; also see Ellis, 1999). The German approach is more stringent than the English, reflecting a greater role for the courts in controlling the administration. Familiarity with the use of this standard in the exercise of European Union law competences and in applying the European Convention on Human Rights made many countries more receptive to the concept of proportionality. It was difficult to have one standard applied to purely domestic cases and another applied in European cases. All the same, he notes that the concept of 'proportionality' is used with differing degrees of deference depending on whether a court is controlling a legislative action or the action of the administration. Such work requires considerable attention to the detail of the different systems and how particular issues are handled.

Legitimate Expectations

An area of divergence in the terminology used by legal systems occurs with the extent to which they will control the exercise of discretion not to protect fundamental rights, but to protect the legitimate expectations that have grown up as a result of assurances by or actions of the administration in the past. If the administration has been given a discretion, it is in order that it might review the needs of the public interest from time to time and have the flexibility to revise its decisions. At the same time, statements made or past actions through which the administration has already exercised its discretion may give rise to expectations that these will guide its decisions in the future. German law and European Union law use the term 'legitimate expectation' to describe the interest that the citizen has in discretion continuing to be exercised in the way previously announced. But the administration's duty to keep exercising its discretion requires it to reflect on contemporary needs of the public interest. Accordingly, the idea of a legitimate expectation does not prevent the administration reconsidering a decision, but merely requires it to take account of the interest in question before changing the policy and the impact of the new policy on established practices. French law does not use the concept of 'legitimate expectation' in this context, preferring the duty to respect legal certainty (see Schønberg, 2001).

Indeterminate Concepts

The intensity of review to which administrative decisions are subject can be illustrated best by cases involving what the Germans call 'indeterminate concepts', legal terms that are not defined in the empowering legislation. Does the administration have unfettered power to determine the meaning of these concepts? For example, German legislation empowered the administration to prohibit the sale of books and magazines that were 'dangerous to young people'. The authorities considered that the magazine, *Stern*, was dangerous, and it was banned. The decision was annulled on the ground that it interfered disproportionately with the freedom of information of adult readers.[26] The interference with an individual right encouraged the court to apply a test of strict scrutiny and the concept of proportionality in order to protect it.

Works examining the development of common European standards of administrative law typically focus on the grounds of review as illustrating the values by which the administration is meant to abide. These values are then used by the European courts as benchmarks to judge the conduct of a transnational administration such as the European Union (Hartley, 1998: chapter four). In turn, these standards, developed as general principles recognised by the Member States, are then used to judge the actions of particular Member States. There is thus a two-way circulation of ideas.

Abuse of Discretion

However wide a discretionary power, it must be used for the purpose granted by the legislator or for which it exists. If the power is used for an extraneous purpose then that administrative decision is unlawful. An extraneous purpose may well be personal animosity to the citizen affected or it may be some personal gain by the decision-maker.[27] An abuse of discretion may occur where a power is used to achieve an objective in the public interest distinct from that which was envisaged when it was granted.[28]

Questions for Discussion

1. What concepts are used in the systems you are studying to identify the different grounds of review mentioned in this section?
2. How far are the courts in your systems willing to scrutinise the exercise of discretion by the administration? Does this willingness depend on whether fundamental rights are at issue or not?
3. If a term such as 'proportionality' or protection of 'legitimate expectation' is used in your systems, are they used in the same way? If the term is not used, are equivalent terms used or does the difference in terminology reflect a difference in policy?

VIII. LIABILITY OF THE ADMINISTRATION

The liability of the administration provides an example of an area in which the distinctiveness of administrative law will vary from system to system. One focus of

---

[26] BVerwGE 39, 197. See also BVerfGE 83, 30, where the ban on a work of literature was held to be disproportionate; CE 17 April 1985, *Les Editions des Archers*, Leb 100.

[27] See CE 23 July 1909, *Fabrègue* Leb 727; CE 14 March 1934, *Rault*, Leb 337; and *R v Port Talbot BC, ex parte Jones* [1988] 2 All ER 207 (QBD).

[28] Compare *R v Home Secretary, ex parte Fire Brigades Union* [1995] 2 AC 513 (HL).

analysis would be the values and the basis of liability. Some systems have adopted the view that the liability of the administration should be the same as that for private individuals. Typically, a French writer would argue, however, that the specificity of governmental liability is to be found in the balance that has to be struck between protecting the interests of the citizen and preserving the ability of the administration to act in the public interest (eg Guettier, 1993: 97). Some take the view that specific individuals who suffer disproportionately from actions taken in the public interest should be compensated on a very different basis to those harmed by the actions of private individuals. At the same time, the risks taken in the public interest may justify a greater caution in terms of the compensation of harms suffered. A public body undertaking a risky activity should not be deterred by the danger that it will have to compensate those who suffer harm as a result. An example would be police actions taken to deal with a sudden threat to public order. While it is useful to look at the general principles and structures of the liability of the administration, there are advantages in taking particular themes in order to gain focus. Other comparisons have focused on the outcomes in this area, but it is necessary to go beyond examining merely on the results of particular actual or hypothetical cases. Basil Markesinis and his colleagues make this clear through a comparative study of five fact situations in different countries. They set the decision in a legal and socio-economic context to assess its meaning and importance (Markesinis, Auby, Coester-Waltjen and Deakin, 1999: 107). In addition, attention to individual cases needs to go beyond the reasons given by judges in order to analyse them in terms of the underpinning ideas. In particular, there is the question of whether the principles setting out the basis of compensation are the same.

Although concepts may vary somewhat from one system to another, it is useful to talk in terms of five general foundations of a right to compensation from a public authority. The first concept is *fault*. We have a moral responsibility to make good the harm that has been caused by our neglect or wrongdoing. A key issue is how fault is established. In common law systems, fault involves the breach of a duty of care. In other systems, fault simply means a failure by a public authority to conduct itself in a way that can be reasonably expected.[29] Such a standard would be close to the failure of the administration to perform its mission. It is commonly found that the mere breach of a legal norm does not automatically give rise to liability; that the fault of the administration is judged by objective criteria looking at the knowledge of the administration, rather than of the individual administrator; and that liability will arise where there has been a breach of an individual right or a materially protected legal position relative to the administration (a kind of 'legitimate interest'). In the past, many systems have insisted on proof of serious

---

[29] See Principle 1 of the Council of Europe Recommendation R (84) 15 on Public Liability, adopted by the Council on 18 September 1984:

> Reparation should be ensured for damage caused by an act due to a failure of a public authority to conduct itself in a way which can reasonably be expected from it in relation to the injured person.

fault (*faute lourde*) where the administration has a particularly difficult task, such as in policing. But this is declining in most countries.

The second concept is that of *risk*. Even without fault, if a body has created a situation of risk of harm for its own purposes (or for the community which we serve), then there are grounds for holding it responsible. The idea of sharing benefits and burdens is well acknowledged. In economic terms, a body must internalise the costs of the operation, rather than externalising them to other people.

Both of these justifications apply equally to public and private persons. But there is a further set of justifications which apply more specifically to public authorities, and which are acknowledged with greater or lesser clarity in the different systems. Roger Errera explains that equality before public burdens justifies French public law liability, both in areas of fault and risk (Errera, 1986). This is based on Article 13 of the Declaration of the Rights of Man 1789 under which all have to contribute to public expenses, and from which is deduced the principle that no one can be expected to contribute an excessive amount for the public good. German lawyers talk about the idea of special sacrifice (*Sonderopfer*) in such circumstances. Now, this principle is easy to understand where there is a planned risk created for the public benefit, but where there is an unplanned consequence, such as a prisoner on parole committing a bank robbery,[30] then this idea of internalising consequences is less clearly a matter of responsibility. Where there is an expropriation, we are already moving from a notion of liability to social justice. The classic *Couitéas* decision[31] shows a kind of expropriation, where the authorities refused to remove squatters from private land, because this would upset local public order. One person was suffering for the benefit of the community and received compensation on the basis of the liability of public authorities for an inequality before public burdens. But is this really justified by a notion of liability, ie taking responsibility for one's actions and the harm they cause, or is it a matter of social solidarity—that social burdens, however created, should not be unequally borne?

Social solidarity offers an alternative basis for requiring the state to pay compensation to those who suffer injury. The French Constitution proclaims the solidarity of all in the face of national calamities. The moral idea is based on the view that, if we find ourselves as part of a community, that situation of mutual dependence generates duties of solidarity. It could be argued that social solidarity is not an appropriate basis for liability, but rather a principle of social justice that could justify a redistribution of resources based on compassion, rather than entitlement.[32] We are not lone actors, as the private law model of liberty would suggest. Our obligations do not arise simply from our voluntary choice, but also from the social position we occupy. The argument is founded on an idea of

---

[30] CE Sect, 29 April 1987, *Banque populaire de Strasbourg*, AJDA 1987, 488.
[31] CE 30 November 1923, Leb 789.
[32] See Fairgrieve, Andenas and Bell, 2002: xix–xxii and references therein.

social justice. Solidarity with those who suffer provides a special justification for compensating for injuries resulting from industrial and social diseases, but also from major risks in the field of medicine. For example, many countries provide compensation to children who suffer adverse reactions from vaccinations. The mechanisms are often some form of an insurance fund. But the justifications differ between countries. For example, in France compensation was originally justified on the basis that the vaccination was an activity undertaken in the public interest. The risk incurred was a disproportionate burden on a few individuals, and so the community ought to pay. The argument is one of fairness in the apportionment of burdens. The English Vaccine Damage Act 1979 is based more on *compassion*, rather than an argument of social justice. The ability of society to shoulder the burden—its deeper pocket—is more in evidence, rather than a sense that society is benefiting from an activity and so should, in fairness, share the burdens. *Compassion* is a commendable virtue, but not a matter of moral duty. It is a work of superrogation.

A fifth and connected justification is that the state is simply best placed as the *organiser* of compensation. Given its information and resources, it can manage the provision of compensation in the most efficient manner. The issue is well illustrated by the case of technological risks and disasters. After a particular disaster at a chemical plant in Toulouse, a French law was passed in 2003 under which the compensation of victims is secured by a guarantee fund which will pay out if a person does not have appropriate insurance cover. This is an instance of society arranging some form of collective protection against risks which are not obvious to most people, but where the state can be expected to undertake a risk assessment. The privileged position of the state to make provision for a major pollution incident justifies giving the state a responsibility. This is a way of socialising risk not so much out of solidarity as through a process of identifying the best-informed organiser of compensation.

The different justifications in this area relate to different conceptions of the role of *liability law*, as opposed to the *law on compensation*. We can legitimately conceive of an argument that justifies the compensation of the victim without imputing liability to any individual. The court process is appropriate for identifying blame either individual or institutional, and this function is often cathartic for the victims and their families, but this role of the law is often parallel to administrative liability. In France, in the 1980s and 1990s findings of *criminal* liability against public officials provided a strongly expressive mechanism to achieve this end. It has subsequently been much reduced by reforms of criminal liability which impose this on public officials only in cases of clear fault (see Article 121-3 of the *Code pénal*). English public administration tends to use other mechanisms for dealing with blame. Political accountability and administrative responsibility are sufficient. Whereas fault and risk are clear instances of liability, I would argue that the situations of solidarity, compassion and organisation are best seen as instances of publicly-established compensation.

Questions for Discussion

1. On what basis is the administration liable in the systems that you are studying? Is it just liability for fault or for serious fault (recklessness)? Is there liability for risk?
2. Is the administration liable on the same basis as a private individual? In what way does the liability of the administration differ in procedural or substantive terms?
3. How far is compensation sought through the courts and how far are there special compensation schemes for particular kinds of injury or activity? Do these have the same justification as liability through the courts?

BIBLIOGRAPHY AND FURTHER READING

To go further on this subject, the reader is advised to look both at explanations of the administrative laws of relevant jurisdictions and also at comparative discussions.

Bell, J (1992) *French Constitutional Law* (Oxford, Oxford University Press).

Brown, LN and Bell, J (1998) *French Administrative Law*, 5th edn (Oxford, Oxford University Press).

Birkinshaw, P (2003) *European Public Law* (London, Butterworths).

Schwarze, J (ed) (1996) *Administrative Law under European Influence* (London, Nomos).

Ellis, E (ed) (1999) *The Principle of Proportionality in the Laws of Europe* (Oxford, Hart Publishing).

Flogaitis, S (1986) *Administrative law et droit administrative* (Paris, LGDJ).

Fairgrieve, D, Andenas, M and Bell, J (2002) *Tort Liability of Public Authorities in Comparative Perspective* (London, British Institute of International and Comparative Law).

Konijbelt, W (1993) 'The New Dutch Code of General Administrative Law' in L Torchia (ed), *Il procedimento amministrativi: profili comparati* (Padua, CEDAM).

Markesinis, BS, Auby, J-B, Coester-Waltjen, D and Deakin, SF (1999) *Tortious Liability of Statutory Bodies: A Comparative and Economic Analysis of Five English Cases* (Oxford, Hart Publishing).

Sandulli, A (1998) *La proporzionalità dell'azione amministrativà* (Padua, CEDAM).

Schønberg, S (2001) *Legitimate Expectations in Administrative Law* (Oxford, Oxford University Press).

Singh, MP (2001) *German Administrative Law*, 2nd edn (Berlin, Springer).

Thomas, R (2000) *Legitimate Expectations and Proportionality in Administrative Law* (Oxford, Hart Publishing).

FURTHER READING

Alston, P (1999) (ed) *Promoting Human Rights through Bills of Rights* (Oxford, Oxford University Press).

Dicey, AV (1959) *An Introduction to the Law of the Constitution*, 10th edn (London, Macmillan).

Erasmus, GM (ed) (1990) *Compensation for Expropriation* (London, British Institute of International and Comparative Law).

Errera, R (1986) 'The Scope and Meaning of No-Fault Liability in French Administrative Law' *Current Legal Problems* 157.

Gearty, CA (1997) *European Civil Liberties and the European Convention on Human Rights. A Comparative Study* (The Hague, Martinus Nijhoff).

Guettier, C (1993) *La responsabilité administrative* (Paris, LGDJ).

Hartley, TC (1998) *The Foundations of European Community Law*, 4th edn (Oxford, Oxford University Press).

Loughlin, M (1993) 'The Importance of Elsewhere' *Public Law* 44.

Maurer, H (1994) *Allgemeines Verwaltungsrecht*, 9th edn (Munich, Beck).

Stolleis, M (1992) *Geschichte des öffentlichen Rechts in Deutschland* vol II (Munich, Beck).

Torchia, L (1993) *Il procedimento amministrativi: profili comparati* (Padua, CEDAM).

14

Comparative Law in Constitutional Contexts

ANDREW HARDING AND PETER LEYLAND*

KEY CONCEPTS

Administrative law; Autochthonous; Checks and balances; Civil liberties; Comparative politics; Constitution (flexible/rigid); Constitution (codified/ uncodified); Constitution (controlled/uncontrolled); Constitutional accountability; Constitutional amendment; Constitutional conventions; Constitutional court; Constitutional monarchy; Constitutionalism; Contracting state; Devolution; Federal; Good governance; Judicial [or constitutional] supremacy (*Marbury v Madison* principle); Liberal democratic; Local government; Ombudsman; Parliamentary sovereignty; Referendum; Rule of law; Separation of powers; State; Totalitarian; Watchdog bodies.

I. INTRODUCTION

JUST AS THERE are many challenges for constitution-makers, there are many challenges for students of comparative constitutional law in the 21st century. Not only does this subject have little history, less theory and relatively few pieces of outstanding literature, but the problems it now faces—and which are of very great importance to the world at large—are immense and very pressing. At the same time this very situation offers the hope that critique and imagination can, in the age we conceive of as being that of good governance and global justice, go some way towards correcting the often oppressive and sometimes incompetent behaviour of governments. The prize to be won is a major contribution to a happy, fair and stable future for the broad majority of humanity under enlightened government nationally and internationally. The price of failure is an increased chance of conflict, poverty and fragmentation affecting everyone. What this chapter therefore aims to do is to explore the nature and tasks of comparative constitutional law in the contemporary world.

* The authors would like to thank Joana Thackeray, Tom Ginsburg, Mark Sidel, Lucio Pegoraro, Justin Frosini and Ben Berger for their encouragement and helpful comments.

The reformation of comparative law in the last 10 years or so has been remarkable in many ways, not least in its re-awakening of comparative constitutional law (Harding, 2000; Harding, 2002; and Leyland, 2002). It scarcely needs to be argued now, as opposed to a few years ago, that comparing constitutions is a useful and respectable activity. Nonetheless, in this discussion we will rehearse the arguments and circumstances that led to this conclusion. Next, in Part II of the chapter, we ask what constitutions are, and consider what they are for. In Part III attention is directed to reviewing the discipline of comparative constitutional law, with a view to understanding how it relates to comparative law in general, and how it differs from comparative politics. Part IV examines the practice of comparative constitutional law, attempting to answer the question of what practical purposes comparative constitutional law serves, for example in the contexts of constitution-making processes and human rights adjudication. In Part V we inquire further into the question, how we might begin to classify and analyse constitutions. Allowing for the fact that constitutions may appear similar in form but may, in practice, function very differently, is there a framework of analysis that can be applied to organise constitutions according to their principal characteristics? Additionally, to what extent might constitutions be analysed by constructing a series of ideal types against which more detailed comparison can be attempted? While not recommending a particular methodology of comparative constitutionalism, at a practical level, we proceed to identify a set of issues that nearly always have to be addressed by researchers and commentators in this field. In Part VI we discuss some strategies that might be adopted for teaching comparative constitutional law. Finally, in Part VII we set out our conclusions and pose one very important question for the future.

II. WHAT ARE CONSTITUTIONS AND WHAT DO THEY DO?

Before addressing the nature, purposes and methods of comparative constitutional law, we need first to ask: What actually are constitutions and what do they do?

What are Constitutions?

The answer to this question may not be as simple as it appears. According to most formal definitions the constitution of any state embodies a higher form of law antecedent to government.[1] The text of a constitution sets out the institutional framework, particularly how the organs of the state are intended to interrelate with each other and the ways in which power is to be divided between them. In

---

[1] The antecedence of the constitution to government, developed by writers such as Tom Paine in the 18th century and Henry David Thoreau in the 19th century, is now taken for granted in most societies.

addition, the constitution includes a statement of individual and collective rights and sometimes also duties of citizens and/or duties of the state in relation to economic and social questions.[2] In practical terms, there is no difficulty accessing the text of most 'constitutions of the world' on the internet.[3] However, the problem with a definition which prioritises the text is that it provides only a formalistic answer. Such a response underplays the importance of conventions or other informal rules associated with the constitution. More seriously, this approach would appear to deny that any society without a constitutional text has a constitution at all: it would, for example, preclude modern 'constitutional' states such as Israel, New Zealand and the United Kingdom (where the constitution is said to be 'unwritten') from having a constitution at all.

Having said this, for those nations with a formal, codified constitution, in one sense the constitution itself is *always* what is stated in the text. Unless it has been amended, the text attempts to freeze or anchor the particular aspirations which were influential at the moment of its inception and crystallised in it. Obviously, then, the text has special significance because it was drafted with the purpose of entrenching particular principles. It will therefore always be highly relevant to start by examining the text and the implications of the text (Pegoraro, 2001: 115 ff). Indeed, it may be useful to be able to identify and compare the surface structure and characteristics revealed by examining the text, and it may be possible to infer that elements of constitutional design are often related to, or even borrowed from, other constitutions (Henkin and Rosenthal, 1990; Beer, 1992; and Harding, 2004).

As an example of this process, we can compare the constitutions of the United States and Nigeria (Fallon, 2004: Ewelukwa, 1993). Despite having very different histories and traditions there are clear parallels between the two. As well as being relatively large nations in population and size they share obvious constitutional characteristics. For example, they have in common a strict separation of powers with executive power at national level vested in a President elected separately from the legislature. The Supreme Court in each jurisdiction has the last word on constitutional questions, and both constitutions describe systems of symmetrical federalism with the upper house of the national legislature containing an equal number of elected representatives of each of the states. More crucially, however, any comparative analysis exposes significant differences. For instance, the powers of the US Supreme Court were implied under the *Marbury v Madison* principle,[4] and not, as in Nigeria, explicitly stated in the constitution itself.[5] Nigeria has a full statement of individual human rights, based on the European Convention on Human Rights, which are very different in extent and conception from the first

---

[2] Some constitutions, eg the Irish Republic and India, contain extensive 'directive principles of state policy'.

[3] See websites cited below in the Bibliography and Further Reading section.

[4] *Marbury v Madison* 1 Cranch 137 (1803). See Vile, 1976. This case asserted that the courts have the power of judicial review of legislation.

[5] Constitution of the Federal Republic of Nigeria 1999, Art 1.

10 amendments to the United States Constitution.[6] Also, the USA has a secular state, while the Nigerian constitution recognises the special role of Islamic law in its northern states.[7]

There are of course fundamental problems associated with formal definition and comparison at the level of description. If constitutions were mere texts, we would be simply concerned with listing written rules, paying no attention to the various norms that take the form of practices, customs, interpretations, case law, conventions and the ways in which these change over time. interpretive contexts, notably literary, doctrinal, political, economic, social, historical and cultural.

> If it is correct that both constitutional law and constitutional systems depend importantly on popular understandings and the political-social environment, then the work of constitutional law and comparative constitutional law cannot carry forward in intellectual isolation from the work of other disciplines of political science, cultural anthropology, the cognitive sciences, or economics (Jackson and Tushnet, 1999: xviii).

In short, a given constitutional text, although essential to the study of constitutional law, will only describe 'the constitution' in a very limited sense. For example, even where provisions seek to safeguard individual, social or economic rights, the document itself will not prescribe the method for attaining such goals, nor will it address in any detail the crucial normative dimension which was intended to underpin the constitution, and which itself may take on an evolving significance over time.[8] Rather, the text refers the analyst back to the prevailing ideas at the time of drafting or amendment.

It has been asserted that 'the facts are stronger than constitutions' (Duguit, 1970), in the sense that the analyst must address questions associated with practical implementation, peering forwards and looking at the progressive application of the constitution and its associated rules. A crucial distinction may be drawn between the constitution (namely what is stated in the text), and the manner of its implementation, which is explained here in terms of 'constitutionalism'.[9]

Any given constitution may appear to display close textual similarities with another selected example. However, each constitution will invariably acquire and display strong 'autochthonous' characteristics as the constitutional form stretches with its application in response to local conditions, much in the way unyielding leather shoes adapt their shape to accommodate the feet of the wearer. By 'autochthonous' we mean 'home-grown' or 'intimately related to the local context'. It is in fact relatively easy to identify such features of a given constitution, to the extent that one can read a constitution sometimes as an autobiography of the nation.[10]

---

[6] *Ibid*, ch IV.

[7] *Ibid*, Arts 275–2799.

[8] See below for the discussion of the relevance in this context of 'constitutionalism'.

[9] This is further elaborated upon below.

[10] Many provisions of the Constitution of South Africa 1996 and the Constitution of East Timor 2002 (for example, the fundamental rights provisions) may be explained in terms of the need to prevent the recurrence of human rights abuses.

Autochthonous elements may also relate intimately to traditional institutions or religion.[11]

Constitutions then, to conclude, are texts, but are also more than texts. They can include potentially all of the aforementioned issues and their study might involve an understanding of any combination of the above interpretive contexts.

What then do Constitutions actually do?

There are some tasks that all constitutions seek to perform. A constitution will set out the way in which the principal institutions come into being and are to operate, and how their powers are limited. For example, constitutions generally establish the cycle of elections, parliamentary representation, and government formation. And they will normally, although by no means always, lay down the fundamental rights of individuals and groups. In addition, constitutions may have many other facets, including declaring the national ideology and governmental objectives; defining the conditions under which organisations, both state and non-state, as well as the political system itself, are to operate.

It is important to recognise that the power-allocation function, which is central to every constitution, is achieved in different ways. The constitution will provide some kind of separation or balancing of powers between state institutions and bodies. By this we mean that a constitution, to be worth the name, principally has to define the executive, legislative and judicial powers and how they relate to each other. Again we find that a traditional term—the 'separation of powers'—is inadequate. Some constitutions clearly embody 'separate' powers, but others 'fuse' powers, or at least do not completely separate them. The United States Constitution is often cited as a classic example of the former, because it was formulated on the basis of a relatively strict separation of powers, with the President, representing the executive branch, kept distinct from, but accountable to, the legislative branch in the form of Congress, and both branches being accountable to the judiciary. Here, powers were separated in order to provide checks and balances. In France, by contrast, the idea of separation of powers—in its original form at least—was to give analytically different functions to the executive, legislature and the judiciary, so that each function was performed without trespassing on the preserve of the others. In the British, Italian and German Constitutions, however, ministers representing the executive branch are members of their respective Parliaments and—in theory at least—accountable to Parliament. Most constitutions in some important ways provide for the definition of the content of, and the counterbalancing of, the three powers, which is now often linked to the concept of checks and balances rather than simply a strict separation of functions. Furthermore, in

---

[11] Some constitutions make provision for ancient institutions predating the constitution itself, eg the Great Council of Chiefs in Fiji, in the Constitution of Fiji, ch 8.

order to achieve any meaningful separation of powers, independent methods of appointment and funding will need to be linked to any such constitutional provisions. For example, this will be crucial in relation to judicial appointments and appointments to a constitutional court.[12]

Moreover, power-allocation may also be multi-dimensional in that, in systems with strong forms of federal, devolved or regional government,[13] the constitution determines[14] the relationship between the central government structures and those operating at the periphery. It is especially true of many federal constitutions that they deal with very detailed questions of federal-state powers and relations and are therefore complex. More generally we find that some constitutions provide a bare minimum of prescription, while others go into quite laborious detail. It is obviously an advantage of a brief constitution, such as that of the United States, that it hardly ever needs to be amended, and a disadvantage of a longer one, such as that of Malaysia, that it requires frequent amendment.[15] On the other hand a brief constitution is often vaguer and more open to abusive interpretation.[16]

Another conventional answer to the question of what constitutions do is that they provide for the definition of state institutions, and the relationship between the state and the individual. However, this answer is both unexceptional to the point of being unhelpful, and inaccurate to the point of being misleading. In fact constitutions tend to define only *some* institutions of state, and define only *some* aspects of the relationship between the state and the individual. These tasks are completed, usually very imperfectly, by the ordinary law or the practice of government. It has been pointed out that the state as a distinct apparatus of government was only formally recognised as institutionally significant during the period following the French revolution, as a more sophisticated notion of the separation of powers began to develop (Allison, 2000: 48).

The state came to be conceptualised as a distinct apparatus of government performing functions at a step removed from the King or the executive authority, thus giving rise to modern conceptions of the separation of powers. Although setting out institutional arrangements is pivotal to the organisation of the state, constitutions, or the body of laws relating to the state, rarely define the state itself: in fact terms such as 'the people', 'the government', 'the Crown', and 'the executive power' are commonly employed in preference to 'the state'. However, in many nations

---

[12] For the role of constitutional courts, see below.

[13] The United States, Canada, Australia, Germany, Nigeria, Pakistan, Mexico and India are notable examples of symmetrical federalism. Malaysia has an asymmetrical, two-tiered, federal system. The United Kingdom, like Spain and Italy, has (asymmetrical) devolution of powers (to Scotland, Wales and Northern Ireland).

[14] In the United Kingdom, which lacks a codified constitution, devolution was introduced in 1998, following referenda, by means of special Acts of Parliament.

[15] As at January 2006 the Federal Constitution of Malaysia had, since its inception in 1957, been the subject of 48 amending Acts embodying 650 individual amendments.

[16] Eg the Constitution of the Republic Indonesia 1945, especially before amendments were enacted in 1999–2004.

the task of designing effective mechanisms for constitutional accountability has been rendered more complex because the contemporary state has been radically reconfigured as part of a trend towards some type of 'contracting state' (Harlow and Rawlings, 1997: 129). Such an agenda attempts to reduce the size of the state apparatus, including the civil service, federal, regional and local government, by delivering public services through contracting out to the private sector, and also by the privatisation of formerly state-run industries. This model of the state sees the state as 'steering' rather than 'rowing'. The objective is to improve the efficiency of delivery of such services to the citizen by its exposure to market forces (Harden, 1992). The result of these initiatives is that the business sector is increasingly drawn into the practice of government. The process of contract-making, through which private companies assume the task of service delivery, greatly expands the interface between the state and the private sector, blurring any public/private law distinction. Such developments also increase the potential for conflicts of interest to arise. In consequence, with increasingly complex overlapping of powers and functions, understanding the relationship between the state and the private sector becomes one of the great contemporary challenges of comparative constitutional law. Any such discussion may not only need to address evolving ideas of the state in developed nations, but also consider parallel issues of exposure to market forces in regard to processes of democratisation in developing and transitional states (see, eg Morison and Livingstone, 1995: 51, 54 *ff*; and Held, 1995).

In this part we have observed that a principal task of constitutions is to define and organise the various institutions of what is called 'the state'.

The Special Status of Constitutions

A constitution will normally also contain some statement as to the status of the constitution itself and the method or methods for amending it. In the majority of cases the constitution proclaims itself to be the supreme law and any law which is inconsistent with the constitution is invalid. The question of unconstitutionality of laws is almost universally given to the courts to determine, with the result that judicial review of legislation becomes a highly significant feature of the constitution. There are, however, cases where the provisions of the constitution are not intended to be legally enforceable in the courts. One might have expected that in this situation some other body such as the legislature would be given the right to determine the constitutional validity of laws. While this is, in effect, the position in constitutions that embody parliamentary, as opposed to constitutional, supremacy, in most cases of the 'unenforceable constitution' the provisions of the constitution remain merely statements of principle which are implemented, if at all, through the political process. It is common to regard constitutional provisions of this kind as 'nugatory' or even 'irrelevant'. In fact in many instances such statements of principle provide ground rules for organising the state in much the same way as 'enforceable' provisions, and are regarded as important political principles which may be countermanded only by overwhelming considerations.[17]

With regard to constitutional supremacy there is some variation amongst constitutions. Some operate this principle prospectively, prohibiting inconsistent legislation being passed after the constitution comes into force, while others also operate retrospectively, prohibiting all inconsistent legislation, even that passed prior to the constitution. Much may depend here on the circumstances in which the constitution was drafted and came into effect. If the constitution was designed to guarantee the maintenance of the *status quo*, or to provide for orderly development over a period of time, it will usually operate prospectively; but if it was designed to be *revolutionary* it will usually operate retrospectively as well as prospectively.

In addition some constitutions vest the power of judicial review of constitutionality in a special court—such as a 'constitutional court' (Ginsburg, 2003)—designed for the purpose, while others vest this power in the ordinary courts. Some consequences will follow from this: If there is a special court, it is to be expected that the ordinary courts will have power to refer to that court any constitutional issues which arise in the course of litigation. From this it will usually follow that the special court has power to determine the issues and return the matter to the court that referred it, which alone will have power to exercise jurisdiction over the case itself and award a remedy in accordance with the determination of the special court. Typically, there will be several other avenues whereby constitutional issues can be put before the special court, perhaps by members of the legislature or by specific office-holders such as the Prime Minister or the President.

Amending Constitutions: Rigid/Flexible

The power to amend the constitution is an extremely important power which determines the degree to which the constitution itself is entrenched. Most constitutions provide for some special method or methods of amendment. Indeed, those that do not display this characteristic cannot claim to embrace the principle of constitutional supremacy.[18] This special method is usually a requirement for a much greater majority (as opposed to a simple majority) in the legislature, which distinguishes the constitutional amendment procedure from the procedure for amending ordinary legislation, for example, a two-thirds majority of the members of each house, upper and lower, voting separately, as in India;[19] or a two-thirds majority in Parliament and six Provinces in the National Council of Provinces, in South Africa.[20] Some constitutions go further, requiring

---

[17] Eg in Vietnam considerable debate in 2000–01 centred on an unenforceable constitutional provision for free primary education: Sidel, 2002.

[18] The Privy Council has created a distinction between 'controlled' and 'uncontrolled' constitutions: *McCawley v The King* [1920] AC 691 (PC).

[19] Constitution of India, Art 368 (in the ordinary case).

[20] Constitution of the Republic of South Africa, s 74.

a referendum,[21] sometimes involving also a requirement that the amendment be supported by a special majority of electors or regions of the country, or a provision designed to ensure that there is a 'cooling-off' period between the introduction of an amendment bill and its passing, to avoid hasty amendments and create the opportunity for public debate.[22]

The terms 'rigid' and 'flexible' are often used to denote a constitution that is difficult or easy to amend (Bryce, 1905). However, the rigidity and flexibility of a constitution in practice involves much more than a consideration of the amendment procedure. A constitution such as that of the United Kingdom is in theory flexible, but has in practice proved somewhat rigid, evolving only slowly over time (although the flurry of reforms since 1997 seems to belie this tendency); whereas the Constitution of Brazil has been amended many times despite being, in theory at least, somewhat rigid.[23] The United States Constitution, on the other hand, is rigid both in theory and in practice. The operation of party politics (for example in a dominant-party system) or public opinion generally (for example, in referenda) will affect the extent of flexibility or rigidity. Whether a constitution should be rigid or flexible depends on how the constitution-building process is conceived by the constitution-makers. A new constitution can be regarded as absolutely fundamental and unchanging law, or it can be regarded as merely a work in progress, leaving much to be resolved by continuing debate. In a few cases[24] the constitution contains provisions which are expressed to be unalterable *in any circumstances*. It is also not unusual for a constitution to provide different methods of amendment according to the importance of the provision to be amended.[25] In India the Supreme Court has held that a bill for amending the constitution may not destroy the basic structure or essential features of the constitution.[26]

Apart from the amendment procedure, there are other less obvious ways in which constitutions may change. As indicated above, judicial decisions, conventions, constitutional or legislative practice and government policies may change over time and may affect significantly the nature of the constitutional order. The significance of these methods of effecting constitutional change may well be affected by the extent to which the formal amendment procedure is easily invoked. The complexity and the tight or open texture of the words used will also be a factor inviting or resisting change.

To summarise: a constitution also establishes the extent to which it may be changed, and its effect on prior or subsequent law-making.

---

[21] Eg, the Constitution of the Republic of Ireland, Art 46.

[22] Eg, the Constitution of Australia, at Art 128, requires a Bill amending the Constitution, after being passed by both houses of Parliament, to be submitted within 2–6 months to a referendum. The amendment is law only if supported by a majority of electors as well as a majority of electors in each State.

[23] Constitution of Brazil, Art 60, to which there were 33 amendments between 1992 and 2000. The Constitution of India had been amended 93 times since 1950 as at January 2006.

[24] Eg, Brazil, Germany, Italy, Namibia and Norway.

[25] The Federal Constitution of Malaysia specifies four different methods: Art 159.

[26] *Kesavananda Bharati v State of Kerala* (1973) 4 SCC 225.

III. COMPARATIVE CONSTITUTIONAL LAW

Having described constitutions and their functions, as the objects of comparative constitutional law, let us now ask what the subject itself is, how it differs from comparative politics and how it relates to comparative law in general.

Relationship to Comparative Politics

It is immediately apparent that the relationship between comparative politics and comparative constitutional law has been somewhat problematical because the latter differs from but overlaps with the former. Comparative constitutional law is the branch of comparative law that studies constitutions as *legal phenomena*. On the other hand, comparative politics compares political systems as *social phenomena*, and has to take account of constitutions to the extent that they define the space in which and the terms on which the political system operates. Further, comparative constitutional law has to take account of political science to the extent that it explains, in part at least, the context in which the constitution operates. The two disciplines are therefore different in terms of their main focus but each is very important for informing the work of the other (Finer, 1974; and Harding, 2002). Moreover, it is worth recognising that a centrally relevant question for constitutional lawyers concerns what might be termed 'fitness for purpose'. At one level the analyst will be inquiring into whether the constitution has been conceived so that it sets out an adequate institutional framework in any particular national context. At another level, the issue of 'fitness for purpose' involves an assessment of the effectiveness of the detailed provisions which have been included as part of a constitution. The focus will often be on evaluating institutional design in terms of the adequacy of accountability mechanisms and the degree of transparency that is present. In principle, there is an assumption that robust constitutional ground rules can at least contribute to containing or defining the political process. However, as we note in the discussion of constitutionalism that follows, constitutional design will not, in itself, guarantee good practice, good governance or adherence to a wider constitutional morality.

In summary, no sharp distinction can be made with comparative politics. However, it might be suggested that comparative constitutional law tends to focus on the conception of the legal and institutional framework of government and the evolution of the institutions of government rather than concentrating on the contestation of power and the actual exercise of power by politicians and other constitutional actors.

Constitutions and Constitutionalism

We have established then that comparative constitutional law is the branch of comparative law which studies constitutional law as a set of legal phenomena, in the sense that constitutional law is 'conceived as a structure of rules and principles which provides the foundation of the political order' (Loughlin, 2002: 193). Rather than merely looking at the political process itself, it deals with how law shapes and limits the conduct of politics. However, as we have set out above, this task is not simply a question of textual analysis, since there is invariably a gulf between the formal constitution and the manner in which government is actually conducted—in other words, between the constitution and what can be termed 'constitutionalism'. In general, it might be suggested that constitutions only seek to embed a given set of fundamental principles as part of the prevailing system of government. Constitutionalism, on the other hand, may be said to embody a normative dimension. Here, the constitution not only anchors and enforces certain principles, but also represents a clear set of values. Many constitutions will set out liberal democratic principles of some kind; others, like Eastern European constitutions of the past, may be based on principles of socialist ownership or, like that of Iran, seek to embody the religious nature of the state. Any commitment in the codified text towards general enfranchisement, democratisation and economic redistribution has to be assessed against the prevailing conditions of governance.[27] It has been recognised that

> when the idea that political power resides in the people is transformed into practice, it becomes a dynamic and liberating force, but also potentially dangerous and destructive (Loughlin, 2002: 111).

Achieving the objective of substantial conformity with the rules is the real challenge. Indeed, as one well known commentator, referring to developments in Western Europe, puts it:

> The fundamental notion of the *Rechtsstaat* or the rule of law was ... not conceived out of the blue and introduced without resistance. It was, in fact, the fruit of political conflict and scholarly disputes stretching over many centuries (Van Caenegem, 1995: 17).

In developing a response to such dangers, constitutionalism has been construed in a way that often suggests that any exercise of political power will be bounded by a system of higher order rules which will:

> determine the validity of legislative and executive action by prescribing the procedure according to which it must be performed or by delimiting its permissible content. The rules may be at one extreme (as in the UK) mere conventional norms and at the other, directions or prohibitions set down in a basic constitutional instrument, disregard of which may be pronounced ineffectual by a court of law. Constitutionalism becomes a living reality to the extent that these rules curb arbitrariness of discretion and are in fact observed by the wielders of political power, and to the extent that within the forbidden zones upon which authority may not trespass, there is significant room for the enjoyment of individual liberty (De Smith, 1962).

---

[27] 'Constitutional mechanism has no value or efficiency itself, independently of the moral and social forces which support it or put it in motion' (Boutmy, 1891: x).

The emphasis in the above statement explaining constitutionalism is not simply on procedure and rules, but on achieving conformity with the intention behind the rules. Apart from its positive aspects, namely dealing with the generation and organisation of power, a constitution may be taken to comprise a series of devices designed to curb discretionary or unlimited power. In many instances it seeks to establish different forms of accountability (Harlow, 2002: chapter one), not simply through a system of freely elected government, but by placing restrictions on the power of the majority. This accountability is reliant on transparency, and it is acted out in a number of familiar ways:[28] an obligation for the government to be responsible to the elected Parliament; legal limits established by the courts on the exercise of public power; formal financial accountability in public affairs; accountability through contractual agreement where public services are provided by private organisations; and, additionally, accountability through the intervention of specialist constitutional oversight bodies such as those designed as part of the recent constitutions in South Africa and Thailand (Hatchard, Ndulo and Slinn, 2004; and Leyland, 2006). Moreover, the constitution also results in further ground rules in the form of laws, codes of practice and conventions being adopted to ensure fair play at every level. But we would argue that an equally significant characteristic of constitutionalism is a degree of self-imposed restraint which operates beyond the text of the constitution and its attendant rules, especially on the part of political actors and state officials. The point to stress here is that all nations have a constitution of some kind, but constitutionalism is only established in the true sense where political behaviour is actually contained within certain boundaries. In addition, the rules need to embody a defensible constitutional morality which accords with principles of good governance[29]; but the constitution also represents a sufficiently widely accepted political settlement. Finally, in defining constitutionalism we have recognised that there must be a general adherence at all levels to the constitutional rules and the wider body of law and conventions associated with them.

The Relationship to Comparative Law Generally

Traditionally comparative law has been concerned with private law comparison and, at a more general level, with the comparison of legal traditions or legal families. Comparative constitutional law used to be considered an aspect of comparative politics or political theory, and incapable of being subjected to the doctrinal rigour of comparative law due to the great differences which existed in political systems (Kahn-Freund, 1974). Since the end of the cold war, however, there has

---

[28] For a discussion of the development of such mechanisms in the United Kingdom see Oliver, 2003: chs 9–12.
[29] For a discussion of 'good governance' from a global perspective see Botchway, 2001.

been an enormous increase in democratisation. Although there are still great differences in political systems and cultures, the main objectives of constitutional law have become more broadly similar than previously, due to the dominant international agendas of 'good governance', 'human rights', 'international trade', and 'sustainable development', all of which have had significant impacts on constitutions. In addition, the same process has tended to blur the distinction between the public and private sectors and therefore between constitutional and private law, as indicated above.

In truth, however, the amnesia of comparative law with regard to constitutional law was never justified. It was founded upon a number of things which are questionable. First, it assumed that comparison is only valid in the case of units of comparison that are similar, whereas in fact the relevance of similarity depends on the precise purpose of the comparison: sometimes we can learn more from difference than from similarity. Secondly, there were clearly many political systems and constitutions that were in fact significantly similar. Thirdly, it omitted to realise that many of the staple 'problems' of comparative law involve both public and private law questions, and therefore comparison involved moving smoothly in and out of constitutional and private law. Salient examples of this are labour law, environmental law, and industrial regulation. Fourthly, it failed to realise that even in the context of private law the political structure is highly significant. Consider, for example, contemporary 'constitutional' debates concerning same-sex marriage.

Despite what is said above about the recent rapprochement between comparative law and comparative constitutional law, it would be a mistake to think that the latter did not exist prior to the end of the cold war. Indeed, the recent reformation of comparative law has involved a merging of two, largely separate, traditions. Montesquieu, famously, engaged in comparative constitutional law in comparing the English and French constitutions (neither of which was at the time written). But one can find origins of the subject in Aristotle's *Politics* and *Constitution of Athens* (the latter, part of a grand survey of Greek city-states' constitutions). Another strand of intellectual history is the tendency of philosophers, from Plato through Cicero and Sir Thomas More to Thomas Paine and John Rawls, to theorise about the ideal republic or the ideal kingdom based on rational speculative inquiry, or reading the mind of God, or, in some cases, socio-legal inquiry. This tradition is relevant in that it sometimes involved assessing constitutional experience and imagining a better society. Undoubtedly the French and American revolutions had a galvanising effect on the subject, in that the promulgation of written documents embodying instruments of government or 'the rights of man' became an increasingly common phenomenon. Comparative constitutional law was undoubtedly relevant to the making of the United States Constitution, and without doubt the United States and French Constitutions informed constitutional reform processes over many parts of the world, notably in Latin America and Europe. The revolutions across Europe in 1848 created many opportunities for reconsideration of the 'good constitution' along comparative lines. These revolutions tried but generally failed to establish new, more democratic constitutions, but the experience provided a basis for future constitutional development through the 19th and 20th centuries. However, this trend was interrupted by the advent of communism and fascism, both of which believed in absolutist and highly authoritarian government. The comparative habit in constitution-making was thus established but a comparative constitutional law literature with its own classical texts and theoretical structure was distinctly lacking. Even now the practice of comparative constitutional law greatly exceeds in extent its theoretical literature. Nevertheless, since the early 1990s there has been a proliferation of comparative constitutional law literature, due to the creation of many reform projects, good governance programmes, teaching programmes, chairs and research centres devoted to the subject. All these have added significantly to the literature.[30] In summary, comparative constitutional lawyers have not yet (although there are some notable exceptions) provided us with a sophisticated and well-tried methodology, nor with a literature which examines in a comparative and analytical way the constitutions or constitutional systems of the world.[31] This is true not only of the newly established or reformed constitutions but even sometimes of well-established constitutions.

IV. THE PRACTICAL APPLICATION OF COMPARATIVE CONSTITUTIONAL LAW

We now proceed to examine the practical applications of comparative constitutional law. Here we identify constitution-making, constitutional reform, and constitutional adjudication.

Constitution-making

Over the span of modern history one can discern four waves of constitution-making.

The first wave occurred in the 18th century with the constitutions of the American states and the United States and French constitutions, together with the constitutions of those states that immediately followed these. These constitutions were very basic by modern standards and emphasised the 'rights of man' and popular assent to government.

The second wave occurred between the mid-19th and early 20th centuries, when the liberalisation and democratisation process commenced with the 1848 revolutions in Europe gradually worked itself out in modern constitutional forms. These constitutions were more concerned with the concepts of political representation, citizenship and equality before the law. They emphasised the legislature as the forum in which the exercise of power could be scrutinised, and the expansion of the franchise (Van Caenegem, 1995).

---

[30] See Bibliography and Further Reading.
[31] Hart Publishing is producing a series entitled 'Constitutional Systems of the World' from 2007: see eg Leyland (2007).

The third wave took place in the decades immediately following the Second World War, as colonial empires were disbanded and war-ravaged countries were occupied or recovered from occupation or instability. This process continued from the 1940s to the 1970s. The independence constitutions tended to copy the European and United States constitutions, depending on the identity of the colonial power, usually with some traditional elements. These constitutions were not often successful and many lasted for only a short period of time before being distorted beyond recognition by amendments or torn up by military or authoritarian leaders.

The fourth wave commenced in the mid-late 1980s, when increasing democratisation and globalisation, and the resolution of local conflicts, all assisted by the end of the cold war and the exercise of 'people-power',[32] propelled forward through the 1990s and 2000s the concept of a liberal and just state, based on free and fair elections, and operating with a sophisticated array of good-governance mechanisms. At the present time the process of constitution-making still goes on in some post-conflict states,[33] but by and large we are witnessing a period of implementation and consolidation as the detailed working of the new constitutions and their complex apparatus involving election commissions, constitutional courts and anti-corruption agencies—is being examined and adjusted. Unlike in previous generations, during this period the ordinary people have been prepared to protest unconstitutional actions and demand that the constitution operate fairly and transparently. 'People power' is a significant feature of fourth-wave constitutionalism. It is, however, at best a double-edged sword and not a substitute—except where there is no alternative—to constitutional government under the rule of law.

The development of constitutional experience has benefited considerably from the proliferation of models since the limited examples available to Indian, German, Italian and Japanese constitution-makers in the 1940s. Constitutions are no longer taken from the peg, but are tailored with some precision and consideration of global experience as well as local needs and practicalities. The constitution-making process has also been considerably democratised, which opens up both the careful consideration of diverse solutions and the accommodation of different views. The comparative dimension is now so ingrained that it is hard to imagine any constitution-building effort without it. Recent notable examples of states where comparative experience has proved significant are South Africa, Namibia, Cambodia, Thailand and Kenya.[34] The European Union is also an

---

[32] People-power was seen first in the Philippines in the 'EDSA' revolution, which led to the fall of President Marcos in 1986.

[33] Eg, Afghanistan, Cambodia, Iraq, Rwanda, East Timor, Somalia.

[34] To take one example, in devising a electoral system based on some form of proportional representation it may be desirable to exclude from the legislature very small Political parties with extreme and highly divisive views, which might also hold the balance of power. Here, the German electoral rule that excludes from the legislature those parties with less than 5% of the total votes cast has proved useful.

interesting but slightly different example, in that constitution-making has had to draw on the experience of member states rather than foreign states in an effort to meld together different constitutional experiences. In the cases of Kenya and the European Union the constitutional drafts have at the time of writing been rejected in referenda, but as with the 1848 constitutions this does not mean that the ideas they incorporate are dead. Comparative constitutional law can of course be equally instructive where constitutional reforms falling short of a new constitution are contemplated. International organisations concerned with issues of access to justice or sustainable development also use comparative constitutional law to construct international projects and draft international treaties. There is also increasing interest in the concept of 'world constitutionalism' embracing international organisations (Macdonald and Johnston, 2005).

Human Rights Adjudication

As signatories to the European Convention of Human Rights, which is an international treaty formulated in 1951 to prevent a repetition of the rights abuses of the Second World War, most European nations have incorporated the Convention into their domestic law.[35] However, more generally, in recent years increasing use has also been made of comparative constitutional law in constitutional litigation, particularly in human rights cases. This process involves judges looking at cases from a variety of jurisdictions that have considered the same question as that before the court. While previously this process was fairly common, it did not generally or necessarily result in the adoption of foreign case law: in fact it often resulted in its rejection. What is new is the extent to which courts look at cases from a wide variety of jurisdictions, not just those with the same constitutional tradition; the extent to which they are prepared to follow these cases; and the extent to which they are willing (or in the case of South Africa obliged[36]) to use international legal norms. Some comparative constitutional law scholars have even gone so far as to suggest that we are witnessing the emergence of a new common law or *ius commune* of human rights (McCrudden, 2002).[37]

We conclude this part with an assertion that comparative constitutional law has never been more important in practice than at the present time.

V. SPECIFIC ISSUES

In this part first we consider a question analogous to that relating to legal 'families' in the field of macro-comparison of legal traditions: Are there some general categories or families of constitutions, ie is there a taxonomy of constitutions? Can

---

[35] This was achieved recently in the United Kingdom by way of the Human Rights Act 1998.
[36] Constitution of the Republic of South Africa, s 38.
[37] See also ch 16 of this Handbook.

constitutions be further classified by developing the idea of 'ideal types'? Secondly, we mention some of the practical hurdles that need to be overcome in under-taking the task of in-depth comparative analysis and we propose a pragmatic approach to overcoming many of the challenges faced by researchers in the field.

Categorisation

In attempting to analyse a topic of enormous range and complexity there is a natural inclination to organise the subject-matter into more specific categories. For example, at least at a descriptive level, it is possible to identify obvious char-acteristics which can be selected and which may be indicative of broad types at a surface level. Kenneth Wheare divided constitutions into written/unwritten; flexible/rigid; unitary/federal; separated/fused powers; and republican/monarchi-cal (Wheare, 1964). One could also add presidential/parliamentary; controlled/ uncontrolled; one-party/multi-party; secular/religious; constitutional court/ legislative sovereignty; bicameral/unicameral; and justiciable/non-justiciable. This type of categorisation may be a useful way of identifying characteristics at a superficial level, and therefore of understanding something about the broad type of constitution being investigated, but it is of limited utility in that it does not look beneath the surface or provide anything approaching a comprehensive guide to a particular constitution.

Ideal Types

We might, moreover, consider whether the taxonomy of constitutions can be further refined. For example, Max Weber's conception of the 'ideal typical' has offered a widely tested method of analysis which could be applied to constitutions (Leyland, 2002: 221 *ff*; and Loughlin, 1992: 59). The first stage is the construction of certain elements of reality into logically precise, controlled and unambiguous conceptions, which are removed from historical reality (Gerth and Wright Mills, 1967: 59); and the second stage involves

> the synthesis of a great many diffuse, discrete, more or less present and occasionally absent concrete individual phenomena, which are arranged according to those one-sidedly emphasized viewpoints into a unified analytical construct (Cotterrell, 1984: 159, 166).

Although constitutions are usually complex formulations, it can be argued that certain features can be identified and stressed according to broad types. An approach which provides extreme and pure models will allow the analyst to con-sider that the 'real meat of history' falls somewhere between these extreme types. In other words, as will be apparent from the discussion below, after the analyst has been able to construct a given range of diverse examples, each exhibiting a series of clear characteristics, it is then possible to examine the actual cases (particular national constitutions) to see how closely they resemble the 'ideal' constitutional types that have been identified.

By way of example, viewed from the standpoint of their origins, a substantial number of constitutions are variations on what we might term the 'Westminster', 'Paris', 'Washington', or 'Socialist Party State' model (each of which might be developed into an 'ideal type'). On gaining independence from the United Kingdom the former colonies that became Commonwealth states usually retained a 'Westminster' parliamentary system which—as with the Westminster (UK) parliament itself—fuses the legislative and executive branches; has a permanent professional civil service; and operates within a legal system based on the common law. Many of these states, until relatively recently, relied on the Judicial Committee of the Privy Council in London as their final court of appeal, which had also the function of interpreting the constitution. Equally, some former French colonies have a colonial constitutional legacy which has influenced constitutional development in Africa.[38] French influence is discernible in other ways too. For example, the relatively brief period of Napoleonic conquest at the beginning of the 19th century left behind a legal code which was adopted with surprisingly little changes across much of Europe, and influenced legal development and hence public law in many states of Africa, Asia, and (via its Spanish and Portuguese offspring) Latin America. The United States Constitution has survived largely intact for over 200 years and many of its features have been widely disseminated, especially in 19th century Latin American states, which, inspired by American revolutionary ideals, wrested their independence from Spain. The United States Constitution has the attraction of being extremely concise but it was also 'state of the art' when it was conceived, as it was based on a clearly delineated separation of powers between the executive, legislative and judicial organs of the state. At the same time, it was symmetrical in conception and involved a uniform distribution of powers between the federal government and each state government. Not only is each State treated the same but also the state institutions of Governor, legislature and supreme court precisely mirror the President, Congress and Supreme Court at the level of the federal government. Finally, the enormous political influence of the Soviet Union on client states and other socialist regimes following the end of the Second World War resulted in single-party socialist dictatorships. These have disappeared from Europe following the collapse of the Soviet Union in 1990, but the residue of Soviet socialist models remains in the constitutions of North Korea, Vietnam, Cuba and the People's Republic of China (which have since been amended to reflect varying degrees of economic change from socialist ownership to a market economy). Apart from observing that a considerable number of constitutions incorporate religious features (eg Islam and shari'a law) it is difficult to propose additional distinct ideal types.

In the absence of a rigorous taxonomy for analysing constitutions, describing a constitution according to its conformity or lack of conformity with a classical

---

[38] Eg, in the Ivory Coast, Algeria and Togo.

model appears to have some utility, even if it leaves much detail to be explained or excepted.

Methodology

In approaching comparative constitutional analysis, while stopping well short of developing or advocating a particular methodology, it is possible to identify certain questions which nearly always need answering. For instance, it is interesting here to speculate whether there is a universal language of constitutional terminology, allowing for common assumptions to do with constitutional features. Even here we must maintain a degree of caution in how terms are used and what their implications might be. We have just noted that typologies are often useful. However, at all times it is crucial to deal with issues of terminology, ensuring that words have been correctly understood and avoiding simplistic translations which might lead to misunderstandings. In this regard it is necessary to remember that general and legal expressions, in any language, are often very, or just subtly, different,[39] and that we should look for actual, as opposed to linguistic, equivalents.

Moreover, the comparative dimension, consisting of references to foreign constitutional systems, is often prompted directly by the subject-matter under consideration.[40] The comparative task is mainly interpretive, but to interpret a constitution in a particular way is to explicitly or implicitly distinguish it from, or liken it to, other constitutions. Indeed, we have already explained above that it is not possible to understand the law, the constitution, and the institutions of any nation without understanding the context in which they come into being. Equally, it is important to grasp how institutions are perceived by a range of opinion within the nation under consideration, and also how these institutions operate or have operated in practice. In terms of an overall approach, it is recognised that a researcher might be loosely guided by a method that explicitly takes account of the aforementioned questions of terminology, language and context. However, we believe that such comparative work, particularly, if it is empirically based, will have to include a pragmatic dimension. The task of getting genuinely to grips with other constitutions will also be an active process involving discussion and debate with locally-based academic colleagues, legal practitioners, government officials and politicians.

To conclude, comparative constitutional law is, in our view, a wide-ranging discourse about constitutions and their interpretation which takes place at a different level to any purely national discourse. At the same time any academic discussion has to take account of the local constitutional context.

---

[39] Think of the ordinary and technical meanings of 'bill' in English; the difference between '*droit*' and '*loi*' in French; and the different meanings of 'cabinet' in English and French.

[40] For example, a discussion of administrative courts in Thailand, which were an important feature of the 1997 Constitution, reveals that the entire system was consciously modelled on the French Conseil D'Etat: Leyland, 2006.

VI. THE TEACHING AND THE STUDYING OF COMPARATIVE
CONSTITUTIONAL LAW

We now address briefly the teaching and the studying of comparative constitutional law.

Comparative constitutional law as a subject taught in universities has become much more common in recent years. Very many law schools world-wide now offer something resembling a course of this kind. Most of these are concerned with the comparison of major western constitutional traditions such as those of the United States, Britain, France, and Germany (see eg Cappelletti and Cohen, 1979). Those countries having a constitution influenced by one or more of these traditions will naturally emphasise it in comparative teaching. In recent years the scope of comparison in such courses has become manifestly wider, and constitutions other than those of Europe and North America are often addressed, notably those of India, South Africa and Japan. Apart from considerations of prestige of the constitutions studied, the accessibility of materials is a major factor in the choice of countries. The fact that all constitutions (and even historic texts) are now available on the Internet provides for ease of comparison of texts. What is much more difficult to find is thematic analyses of constitutional systems which explain and evaluate such texts.

Given the complexity of constitutional systems and the time constraints faced in organising courses, it may not prove practical to compare entire constitutional systems. However, comparative discussion can be very illuminating in regard to particular constitutional features. For example, it may be useful to consider to what degree specified constitutions display the characteristics of a federal system by comparing the respective provisions relating to the distribution of competences, law-making capacity, and tax-raising powers. The constitutional role of the courts in relation to constitutional review is another specific aspect which might be compared.

For teachers and students of such courses the purposes of comparative constitutional law are fairly clear, and reflect the purposes of any comparative law course. These include gaining insight into other constitutional systems and the nature of the societies in question, and also reflecting on one's own constitution in light of comparative experience.

> Comparative law offers the law student a whole new dimension: from it he can learn to respect the special legal cultures of other people, he will understand his own law better, he can develop critical standards which might lead to its improvement, and he will learn how rules of law are conditioned by social facts and what different forms they can take (Zweigert and Kötz, 1998: 21).

VII. CONCLUDING REMARKS

This collection of essays might be regarded as a response to the paucity of academic texts which systematically address comparative law issues. The barriers to teaching a demanding subject have included limitations on the availability of comparative expertise and lack of appropriate publications. At one level the availability of web-based sources, books such as this one, and books which address national constitutions, coupled with the launch of new journals, are essential to support the wider dissemination of the subject.

In this discussion many important characteristics of comparative constitutional law have been identified. Indeed, the classic purpose of studying constitutions from a comparative perspective is to define by comparative examination what is meant by the term 'constitution' in more than one nation and to explore the role of the constitution in the political process, but the task only partly involves the identification and understanding of structural characteristics as part of constitutional design. At some level functional parallels will inevitably be encountered between constitutions. That is because there is a common set of tasks that have to be performed by all constitutions. At the same time, there has been much cross-fertilisation and borrowing between constitutions, but the comparatist needs to interpret any set of national rules in a particular national context. Moreover, in explaining the task before us we have drawn a crucial distinction between constitutions as texts and constitutionalism, which seeks to gaze beyond the text to the evaluation of practice according to a range of criteria.

We wish to end the discussion by highlighting an important issue which comparative constitutional law will have to address in future—sometimes referred to as the 'convergence/divergence' debate. As with some other areas of comparative legal study, especially commercial and business law, many of those who study and write about comparative constitutional law appear to think, or perhaps just assume, that constitutional law is converging towards certain liberal-democratic principles, and that this is an inevitable consequence of the globalisation of democracy and human rights. One can also imagine a system of 'world constitutionalism' (indeed some might argue this already exists) based on the same principles. For example, it is possible to point at one level to cross-currents in academic thought, particularly as mentioned in the field of the constitutional 'oughts' relating to the protection of human rights, encouraged by mass communications and travel, but also, at another political level by the influence of the United Nations, the Word Bank, and the United States, where there has been more emphasis on the rather nebulous concept of 'good governance' (referred to above). Our own view is that while certain contemporary global trends do in fact encourage elements of convergence, and there is plenty of evidence of this taking place, it does not follow that constitutions will all eventually look the same or that they should look the same. And of course, when it comes to constitutional practice strong divergences do remain in the implementation of human rights principles and other constitutional features. Moreover, globalisation has within it tendencies which are both conducive and non-conducive to the promotion of constitutional government. While good governance, the rule of law and judicialisation have become highly prominent objectives of the international community, participative democracy and social justice, which are also crucial elements of relatively successful constitutions, are often contradicted by these limited objectives. In addition, political cultures and public law traditions are still very diverse, and a measure of what Patrick Glenn, in relation to legal traditions generally, calls 'sustainable diversity' (Glenn, 2003) may well be preferable to a bland one-size-fits-all constitution. This, however, is a problem which hopefully will be addressed, amongst others, by the readers of this chapter.

QUESTIONS FOR DISCUSSION

The following questions are intended to provide guidance in the use of this chapter in comparative law teaching.

1. How might the distinction between 'the text' and 'the constitution' be best expressed?
2. Is it possible to provide in a constitutional text a definition of the state, and what purposes might such a definition serve?
3. Consider examples of 'cross-over' between public law and private law, and whether crossing this line involves a different approach being taken to comparison.
4. With regard to the 'separation of powers', are there other 'powers' that should be provided for and included in the 'counter-balancing' of powers?
5. You are asked to design a project to consider the creation of a Constitutional Court for the (fictitious) Central Asian Republic of Burkhistan. What would be the main problems you would address in considering this question? How would comparative constitutional law impact on them?

APPENDIX I: PROJECT

This exercise is intended to give students first hand experience of studying constitutions comparatively. It requires students to look at constitutions in their original form and interpret the information contained therein in the light of their knowledge of constitutional principles.

Two contrasting constitutions are selected (see Bibliography and further reading section for relevant websites):

One from List A: India, Pakistan, People's Republic of China, Thailand, Malaysia, Indonesia, South Africa, Nigeria, Brazil.

One from List B: Australia, Canada, France, Italy, Germany, Norway, Sweden.

Cross-references to the constitution of the country in which the subject is being studied are welcomed, but the two selected constitutions should be the main focus of the exercise.

There are two tasks:

(1) Decide to what extent each of the chosen constitutions includes a separation of powers between the executive branch and the judicial branch.

To respond, students will need first to define the 'separation of powers' and then consider the way in which this principle operates within the context of the selected constitution, with particular emphasis on the safeguards that have been incorporated. It may be best to concentrate on analysing certain specific aspects to illustrate the point.

(2) Contrast and evaluate the procedures by which the selected constitutions can be amended.

BIBLIOGRAPHY AND FURTHER READING

Akiba, O (2004) *Constitutionalism and Society in Africa* (Aldershot, Ashgate).

Allison, JWF (1996) *A Continental Distinction in the Common Law* (Oxford, Oxford University Press).

Alston, P (1999) *Promoting Human Rights Through Bills of Rights: Comparative Perspectives* (Oxford, Oxford University Press).

Andenas, M (ed) (2000) *The Creation and Amendment of Constitutional Norms* (London, British Institute of International and Comparative Law).

Beer, LW (1992) *Constitutional Systems in Late Twentieth Century Asia* (Seattle, University of Washington Press).

Bell, J (2002) 'Comparing Public Law' in A Harding, and E Örücü (eds), *Comparative Law in the 21st Century* (The Hague, Kluwer).

Berggren, N, Karlson, N and Nergelius, J (2000) *Why Constitutions Matter* (Stockholm, City University Press).

Botchway, FN (2001) 'Good Governance: The Old, the New, the Principle and the Elements' 13 *Florida Journal of International Law* 159.

Boutmy, E (1891) *Studies in Constitutional Law: France - England - United States* (trans) EM Dicey, with intro by AV Dicey (London and New York, Macmillan).

Brown, NJ (2002) *Constitutions in a Non-constitutional World: Arab Basic Laws and the Prospects for Accountable Government* (New York, State University of New York Press).

Cappelletti, M and Cohen, W (1979) *Comparative Constitutional Law: Cases and Materials* (Indianapolis, Bobbs-Merrill).

Cotterrell, R (1984) *The Sociology of Law: An Introduction* (Butterworths, London).

Duchacek, ID (1973) *Power Maps: Comparative Politics of Constitutions* (Santa Barbara, ABC-Clio).

Duguit, L (1970) *Law in the Modern State* (New York, Fertig).

Ewelukwa, D (1993) *A Historical Introduction to the Nigerian Constitution* (Awka, Mekslink).

Fallon, R (2004) *The Dynamic Constitution: An Introduction to American Constitutional Law* (Cambridge, Cambridge University Press).

Finer, SE (1974) *Comparative Government* (Penguin, London).

—— (ed) (1979) *Five Constitutions* (Brighton, Harvester).

Franklin, DP and Baun, MJ (1994) *Political Culture and Constitutionalism: a Comparative Approach* (New York, ME Sharpe).

Gerth, HH and Wright Mills, C (1967) *From Max Weber*, 6th edn (London, Routledge and Kegan Paul).

Ginsburg, T (2003) *Judicial Review in New Democracies: Constitutional Courts in Asian Cases* (New York, Cambridge University Press).

Glenn, HP (2004) *Legal Traditions of the World*, 2nd edn (Oxford, Oxford University Press).

Harden, I (1992) *The Contracting State* (Buckiingham, Open University Press).

Harding, AJ (2000) 'Comparative Public Law: a Neglected Discipline?'in ID Edge (ed), *Comparative Law in Global Perspective* (New York, Transnational).

—— (2002) 'Comparative Public Law: Some Lessons from South East Asia'in A Harding and E Örücü (eds), *Comparative Law in the 21st Century* (The Hague, London, Kluwer).

—— (2004) 'The Westminster Model Constitution Overseas: Transplantation, Adaptation and Development in Commonwealth States' 4:2 *Oxford University Commonwealth Law Journal* 137.

Harlow, C (2002) *Accountability in the European Union* (Oxford, Oxford University Press).

Harlow, C and Rawlings, R (1997) *Law and Administration* 2nd edn (London, Butterworths).

Harvey, J, Morison J, and Shaw, J (2000) 'Voices, Spaces and Processes in Constitutionalism' 27 *Journal of Law and Society* 3.

Hassall, G and Saunders, C (2002) *Asia-Pacific Constitutional Systems* (Cambridge University Press, Cambridge).

Hatchard, J, Ndulo, M and Slinn, P (2004) *Comparative Constitutionalism and Good Governance in the Commonwealth: an Eastern and Southern African Perspective* (Cambridge, Cambridge University Press).

Held, D (1995) *Democracy and the Global Order: From the Modern State to Cosmopolitan Governance* (Cambridge, Polity Press).

Henkin, L and Rosenthal, L (eds) (1990) *Constitutionalism and Rights: The Influence of the United States Constitution Abroad* (New York, Columbia University Press).

Jackson, VC and Tushnet, MV (1999) *Comparative Constitutional Law* (New York, Foundation Press).

—— (eds) (2002) *Defining the Field of Comparative Constitutional Law* (Westport, CT, Praeger).

Kahn-Freund, O (1974) 'Uses and Misuses of Comparative Law' *Modern Law Review* 1.

Kelsen, H (1961) *General Theory of Law and State* (New York, Russell and Russell).

Leyland, P (2002) 'Oppositions and Fragmentations: In Search of a Formula for Comparative Analysis' in A Harding and E Örücü (eds), *Comparative Law in the 21st Century* (The Hague, London, Kluwer).

—— (2006) 'Droit Administratif Thai-Style' *Australian Journal of Asian Law* (forthcoming).

Loughlin, M (2002) *Sword and Scales: An Examination of the Relationship between Law and Politics* (Oxford, Hart Publishing).

—— (2007) *The Constitution of the United Kingdom: A Critical Analysis* (Oxford, Hart).

Loughlin, RM (1992) *Public Law and Political Theory* (Oxford, Oxford University Press).

—— (2000) *Sword and Scales: An Examination of the Relationship Between Law and Politics* (Oxford, Hart Publishing).

Macdonald, RS and Johnston, DM (comp and ed) (2005) *Towards World Constitutionalism* (Leiden, Martinus Nijhoff).

Mattei, U (1998) 'An Opportunity Not to Be Missed: The Future of Comparative Law in the United States' 46 *American Journal of Comparative Law* 715.

McHugh, JT (2002) *Comparative Constitutional Traditions* (New York, Peter Lang).

Morison, J and Livingstone, S (1995) *Reshaping Public Power: Northern Ireland and the British Constitutional Crisis* (London, Sweet and Maxwell).

Oliver, D (2003) *Constitutional Reform in the UK* (Oxford, Oxford University Press).

Oloka-Onyango, J (2001) *Constitutionalism in Africa: Creating Opportunities, Facing Challenges* (Kampala, Fountain Publishers).

Örücü, E (ed) (2003) *Judicial Comparativism in Human Rights Cases* (London, UK National Committee for Comparative Law).

Palmer, G (2002) 'The Hazards of Making Constitutions: Some Reflections on Comparative Constitutional Law' 33 *Victoria University Of Wellington Law Review* 631.

Pegoraro, L (2001) 'The Comparative Method and Constitutional Legal Science: New Trends' in A Rabello and A Zanotti (eds), *Developments in European, Italian and Israeli Law* (Milan, Giuffrè Editore).

Pegoraro, L (1997) 'Forme di governo, definizioni, classificazioni' in L Pegoraro and A Rinella (eds), *Semipresidenzialismi*, Quarderni Giuridici (Trieste)(Milan, CEDAM).

Pribán, J and Young, J (1999) *The Rule of Law in Central Europe: the Reconstruction of Legality, Constitutionalism and Civil Society in the Post-Communist Countries* (Aldershot, Ashgate).

Sartori, G (1996) *Comparative Constitutional Engineering: an Inquiry into Structures, Incentives and Outcomes*, 2nd edn (Basingstoke, Macmillan).

Sidel, M (2002) 'Analytical Models for Understanding Constitutions and Constitutional Dialogue in Socialist Transitional States: Re-interpreting Constitutional Dialogue in Vietnam' 6:1 *Singapore Journal of International and Comparative Law* 42.

Sunstein, CR (2001) *Designing Democracy: What Constitutions Do* (Oxford, Oxford University Press).

Teitel, R (2004) 'Comparative Constitutional Law in a Global Age' 117 *Harvard Law Review* 2570.

Tushnet, M (1999) 'The Possibilities of Comparative Constitutional Law' 108 *Yale Law Journal* 1225.

Van Caenegem, W (1995) *An Historical Introduction to Western Constitutional Law*, (Cambridge, Cambridge University Press).

Venter, F (2000) *Constitutional Comparison: Japan, Germany, Canada and South Africa as Constitutional States* (Juta, Kluwer).

Vile, M (1976) *Politics in the USA* (London, Hutchinson).

Walker, N (1996) 'European Constitutionalism and European Integration' *Public Law* 266.

Wheare, KC (1964) *Modern Constitutions* (Oxford, Oxford University Press).

Wolf-Phillips, LA (1968) *Constitutions of Modern States: Selected Texts and Commentary* (London, Praeger).

Websites

Centre for Comparative Constitutional Studies, University of Melbourne
http://www.law.unimelb.edu.au/cccs/

Centre for Comparative Constitutionalism, University of Chicago
http://ccc.uchicago.edu/

Centre for Constitutional Studies and Democratic Development, University of Bologna
http://www.ccsdd.org/

Centre of Democratic Governance, University of Illinois
http://www.csdg.uiuc.edu/

Centre on Democracy, Development and the Rule of Law, Stanford University
http://cddrl.stanford.edu/publications/

International Journal of Constitutional Law
http://icon.oxfordjournals.org/

Journal of Comparative Law
www.thejcl.org/

European Journal of Constitutional Law
http://journals.cambridge.org/action/displayJournal?jid=ECL

International Association of Constitutional Law
http://www.iacl-aidc.org/

Constitutions of the World (and Research Guides)
http://www.ll.georgetown.edu/intl/guides/compcon/print.html
http://www.constitution.org/cons/natlcons.htm
http://www.georgetown.edu/pdba/english.html
http://kclibrary.nhmccd.edu/constitutions-subject.html#t-v\
http://www.findlaw.com/01topics/06constitutional/03forconst/
http://www.uni-wuerzburg.de/law/home.html)
http://www.charter88.org.uk/politics/links/link_cons.html
http://confinder.richmond.edu
http://www.constitution.org/cons/natlcons.htm
http://kclibrary.nhmccd.edu/constitutions-subject.html;
http://www.washlaw.edu/forint/alpha/c/constitutionallaw.htm.
http://www.oceanalaw.com/gateway/main_Catalog.asp.
https://netfiles.uiuc.edu/zelkins/constitutions/links.htm
http://www.venice.coe.int/site/dynamics/N_court_links_ef.asp?L=E
http://www.concourts.net/index.php

15

Comparative Law for International Criminal Justice

PAUL ROBERTS[*]

KEY CONCEPTS

International criminal justice, International criminal law, Disciplinary taxonomy and conceptual analysis, Comparative legal method, International criminal courts, Institutional design, Legislation and adjudication, Transnational co-operation in policing and mutual judicial assistance, Legal harmonisation, The 'eternal triangle' of intellectual inquiry

I. INTRODUCTION

T HIS CHAPTER'S PRINCIPAL argument can be summarised succinctly. Comparative law, it will be argued, is capable of making unique and indispensable contributions to the realisation of international criminal justice. Expressed in such deceptively simple terms, however, neither the significance nor the complexity of this contention is readily apparent.

Scholars express divergent opinions on the meaning, merits and distinctive methods of 'Comparative Law' as a discipline (see, eg Zweigert and Kötz, 1998; Ewald, 1995; Legrand, 1996; and Frankenberg, 1985). Perceptions of the value of Comparative Law for international criminal justice will necessarily be conditioned by the stringency of one's aspirations for comparative scholarship, and also (it must follow) by the capacity of Comparative Law's disciplinary resources— theoretical, methodological and empirical—to satisfy the expectations placed upon it. Anybody willing to contemplate a relatively inclusive concept of Comparative Law will almost inevitably discover more extensive uses for comparative legal method in the theory and practice of international criminal justice than those who insist on more restrictive definitions.

Part I of this chapter investigates the concept and substantive content of international criminal justice. A flexible approach to disciplinary taxonomy is

[*] I am grateful to Rob Cryer and to the editors for helpful feedback on previous drafts.

maintained, in preference to stipulative definitions, by conceptualising a sequence of 'concentric circles' of international criminal justice. The significance of the events, institutions and practices in question will hopefully become self-evident as the discussion proceeds. Part II then takes up the chapter's central proposition, by exploring six different ways in which Comparative Law's contributions to international criminal justice should be regarded, in the aggregate, as both unique and indispensable. The discussion's overriding objective is to promote more explicit, systematic, and methodologically astute recourse to comparative legal method in the theory and practice of international criminal justice.

II. SEVEN CONCENTRIC CIRCLES OF INTERNATIONAL CRIMINAL JUSTICE

The very idea of international criminal justice is controversial to its core. Georg Schwarzenberger's mid-century evaluation is emblematic of the sceptical tradition:

> [I]n the present state of world society international criminal law in any true sense does not exist ... [T]he real swords of war and justice are still 'annexed to the Sovereign Power'. In such a situation an international criminal law that is meant to be applied to the world powers is a contradiction in terms (Schwarzenberger, 1950: 263 at 295).

Theorists of a Realist persuasion insist that Superpowers, if not all sovereign states, are *de facto* above the law. What hope, then, for legality—to say nothing of *justice*—within the anarchical world of power politics? Thinkers in the benign tradition of Immanuel Kant (1970 [1795]) who speak of international justice and perpetual peace are dismissed as idealistic dreamers. 'In the real world' (an appropriation of the concept of reality that can only be admired for its audacity), international diplomacy essentially involves outwitting foreigners in the single-minded pursuit of the national interest. This is best achieved by mutually-advantageous compromise, but ultimately rests on coercion, including, for the recalcitrant, resort to armed force—that is, less euphemistically, to guns and bombs. The 'law' of these relations is the law of the jungle. And if one still wishes to speak of justice in such environments, it is the 'justice' of Socrates' interlocutor Thrasymachus[1] or the lesson of the Peloponnesian War transmitted to posterity by Thucydides:

> right, as the world goes, is only in question between equals in power, while the strong do what they can and the weak suffer what they must (quoted in Reichberg, Syse and Begby, 2006: 13).

---

[1] In Plato's dialogue, Thrasymachus bluntly informs Socrates,

in all cities the same thing is just, namely what is good for the ruling authority. This, I take it, is where the power lies, and the result is, for anyone who looks at it in the right way, that the same thing is just everywhere—what is good for the stronger (Plato, 2000: 16).

Two-and-a-half thousand years later, the Realist school of law and international relations remains hale and hearty (see Dunne and Schmidt, 2005), predicting a looming 'clash of civilizations' (Huntington, 1996). But developments since the Berlin Wall came down in 1989 have made it much harder to maintain an unremittingly Schwarzenbergerian scepticism about international penal regulation. To establish the institutional reality of modern international criminal law, it is only necessary to point to the remarkable innovations which have occurred over the last decade-and-a-half in international criminal adjudication. This section will describe and critically evaluate these unprecedented institutional developments, having first reviewed some basic conceptual distinctions.

International criminal *law* is not to be equated with international criminal *justice*. This is merely an extrapolation to the international context of a familiar dichotomy. Institutionally valid (positive) law is patently capable of perpetrating injustice, sometimes extravagantly. Nazi racial purity laws, depriving Jews of their property, homes, livelihoods, liberty and ultimately their lives, were in this sense only an extreme example of a perfectly general phenomenon (Fraser, 2005). Conversely, however, justice is impossible without law—at least in complex modern societies in which legal duties are far from exhausted by simple, morally-intuitive prohibitions ('thou shall not kill'; 'thou shall not steal', etc). One can fairly be held responsible (that is, *answerable* morally or legally) only for deliberate rule-breaking or culpable neglect of duty through recklessness or ignorance. For morally-justifiable legal liability, these criteria presuppose general, prospective, publicised, clear, accessible and determinate criminal prohibitions, allowing citizens to order their conduct and affairs without fear of arbitrary penalisation. This is the kernel of the demand for justice under the rule of law.

Taken at its narrowest, 'international criminal law' might refer to the corpus of legal rules defining international crimes and procedures. Understood more broadly, 'international criminal law' might encompass, in addition to positive legal norms, the institutions—courts, tribunals, treaty regimes, international organisations, etc—created to implement, apply and develop international criminal laws. This rules-plus-institutions conception of international criminal law is frequently encountered in a rapidly expanding scholarly literature (eg Cassese, 2003; and Bantekas and Nash, 2003). A third, very different possibility is to regard international criminal law—or International Criminal Law (ICrimL)—as a fledgling academic discipline constituted by a distinctive set of norms, institutions, concepts, ideals, questions, issues, problems and challenges for further scholarly examination through research, teaching, analysis and critical commentary, and theoretical reflection. In a similar vein, International Criminal Justice (ICrimJ) might be regarded as a still broader academic discipline, integrating ICrimL within an overarching interdisciplinary enterprise also incorporating philosophical, historical, political and international relations, sociological, anthropological and criminological perspectives. ICrimJ, in this conception, is more methodologically diverse and correspondingly less preoccupied with the institutional features of international criminal law (in either its first or second senses), than ICrimL. These contrasting approaches in reality overlap and intersect in various complex and significant ways.[2]

Beyond these basic conceptual clarifications, there is no settled or agreed definition of international criminal law, still less of the more emphatically normative concept of international criminal justice. The following survey begins with the incontestable core of international criminal justice institutions and works out, through a sequence of concentric and interactive jurisdictional circles, to the progressively more debateable periphery.

The initial point of departure for any contemporary discussion of international criminal law must be the International Criminal Court (ICC),[3] created by a multilateral treaty agreed at Rome in 1998 (see Cassese, Gaeta and Jones, 2002). The ICC became fully operational on 1 July 2002, having secured the requisite 60 ratifications.[4] By November 2005 there were 100 fully-ratified States Parties, although significant absentees still include China, Russia and the United States—all of which, of course, enjoy permanent vetoes on the United Nations Security Council, underwritten by irresistible economic leverage, diplomatic influence, and military might. The ICC is invested with, exclusively prospective,[5] jurisdiction over four groups of substantive crimes: genocide, crimes against humanity, war crimes and the 'crime of aggression' (unjustified resort to armed conflict).[6] Under Article 12 of its Rome Statute, the ICC's jurisdiction is essentially[7] limited to international crimes committed on the territory of a State Party or by one of its nationals. In conjunction with Article 98, this limitation allows countries which remain opposed to the ICC—notably the United States (see Dietz, 2004; and Wedgwood, 2001)—to extort agreements from individual ICC members promising never to surrender the non-signatory's nationals to the ICC. Though it is sometimes referred to colloquially as the 'World Court', the scope of the ICC's jurisdiction is therefore plainly less than globally comprehensive.

At the heart of the ICC's institutional structure is the 'principle of complementarity'. It is not envisaged that every jurisdictionally competent allegation of international criminality, including even genocide, will automatically be referred to the ICC after July 2002. Instead, the ICC is intended to assert jurisdiction 'over the most serious crimes of concern to the international community as a whole' in a

---

[2] One form of intersection worth emphasising is the potential for ICrimL and ICrimJ, *qua* academic disciplines, to influence the design, implementation and future prospects of international criminal law and justice in their normative and institutional manifestations. That is to say, scholarly discourse already permeates the theory and practice of international criminal justice.

[3] See www.icc-cpi.int/.

[4] ICC Statute, Art 126.

[5] ICC Statute, Art 11.

[6] ICC Statute, Arts 5–8.

[7] In addition, the United Nations Security Council may refer situations to the ICC involving non-Party States: ICC Statute Arts 12(2) and 13(b).

manner which is 'complementary to national criminal jurisdictions'.[8] In practice, this means that the ICC will normally allow national criminal processes to take their course, unless the ICC Prosecutor judges that the relevant state 'is unwilling or unable genuinely to carry out the ... prosecution'.[9] In accordance with the principle of complementarity, therefore, domestic criminal courts are intended to be the primary agents of international criminal justice, with the ICC as supervisor and ultimate failsafe.

Although the ICC has yet to complete its first fully-fledged criminal trial, substantial preliminary steps have been taken to make inquiries, gather evidence, and execute arrest warrants.[10] Article 13 of the ICC Statute provides that 'a situation' suspected of involving crimes within the ICC's jurisdiction may be referred to the Prosecutor by a State Party or by the United Nations Security Council, or alternatively, may be investigated on the Prosecutor's own initiative. Four investigations of suspicious 'situations' are currently on-going, concerning civil war in the Democratic Republic of the Congo (DRC), the guerrilla activities of the 'Lord's Resistance Army' in Uganda, allegations of genocide in the Darfur region of Sudan, and war crimes in the Central African Republic.

The ICC is the focus of future hopes and aspirations for international criminal justice. A second circle of institutional activity, with a more tangible record of on-going achievement, comprises two ad hoc criminal tribunals created by the United Nations Security Council. Having previously been employed to authorise military intervention in Korea, Kuwait/Iraq and Somalia, the Security Council's Chapter VII enforcement powers were applied to the novel task of establishing judicial organs.[11] The International Tribunal for the Prosecution of Persons Responsible for Serious Violations of International Humanitarian Law Committed in the Territory of the Former Yugoslavia Since 1999—normally abbreviated to the International Criminal Tribunal for the Former Yugoslavia (ICTY)[12]—was created in 1993 to deal with allegations of war crimes and crimes against humanity (including 'ethnic cleansing') arising from the break-up of Yugoslavia and the descent of the Balkans into a series of vicious civil wars in the early 1990s (see Bass, 2000: chapter 6). With this precedent established, the Security Council's second juridical experiment followed promptly in 1994. The International Criminal Tribunal for Rwanda (ICTR),[13] situated in Arusha, Tanzania, was the United Nations' belated response to genocide in the Great Lakes region of Africa. Certainly 800,000 people, perhaps a million or more, were systematically slaughtered in just 100 days following the premeditated assassination of Rwandan President Juvenal Habyarimana in April 1994. Civil strife in Rwanda has a long,

---

[8] ICC Statute, Preamble.

[9] ICC Statute, Art 17.

[10] *Report on the Activities of the Court* ICC-ASP/4/16.

[11] Ch VII concerns 'action with respect to threats to the peace, breaches of the peace, and acts of aggression'.

[12] See www.un.org/icty/.

[13] See www.ictr.org/.

colonial and post-colonial history, but the immediate conflagration targeted members of the minority Tutsi population, who were hunted out and brutally massacred (along with moderate Hutu sympathisers) by members of the Hutu majority. Unarmed Tutsi civilians—men, women, children and babies—were murdered on sight in bestial orgies of violence by machete-wielding gangs of their erstwhile Hutu neighbours. Lieutenant-General Roméo Dallaire, the commander of the small UN peacekeeping force stationed in Kigali during 1993–94, declared that in the midst of the Rwandan genocide,

> I shook hands with the devil. I have seen him, I have smelled him and I have touched him. I know the devil exists ... We were not in a war of victors and vanquished. We were in the middle of a slaughterhouse (Dallaire, 2004: xviii, 281).

Both the ICTY and the ICTR were tasked with exacting mandates. The immediate objective of bringing to justice those responsible for genocide, war crimes and crimes against humanity was conceived as part of an all-encompassing international agenda, extending to: establishing an unassailable historical record of events; satisfying victims' grievances (which if left to fester unattended might easily precipitate self-help revenge-taking and further cycles of inter-ethnic conflict); deterring future international criminality by clearly signalling an end to the 'culture of impunity' (*cf* Bassiouni, 2000) by which the worst international criminals—especially deposed heads of state and other political and military leaders—have generally eluded legal accountability without having to answer for their crimes; promoting reconciliation between former adversaries; facilitating national political, social and economic reconstruction in war-torn regions; instilling respect for human rights and the rule of law; and helping to create the conditions for stable democratic government—all with the (additional) ulterior purpose of contributing to the restoration and maintenance of international peace and security. The extent to which such broadly-drawn, ambitious and potentially conflicting objectives have been, or ever could be, accomplished by international criminal trials of any description seems destined to be a topic of interminable debate and controversy.

More tangible achievements can be registered in the shorter-term. By 31 July 2005,[14] the ICTY had completed 20 trials involving 39 accused, 36 of whom were convicted on at least some counts whilst the remaining three were acquitted. A further 18 accused had pleaded guilty. Thirty four trials, many of them involving multiple defendants, remained on foot, and a further 50 indicted accused were awaiting trial. The ICTY now has three separate Trial Chambers, allowing six trials to be conducted simultaneously (each Chamber running two trials apiece, alternating between morning and afternoon sessions). The scale of these judicial operations, which are without precedent in the history of international criminal adjudication, helps to contextualise in a more favourable light the ICTY's well-publicised embarrassment of presiding over the abortive prosecution of former

---

[14] See the ICTY's *Twelfth Annual Report* to the United Nations General Assembly and Security Council, A/60/267—S/2005/532, 17 August 2005.

Yugoslavian president Slobodan Milosevic.[15] Insisting on representing himself in court, Milosevic took every opportunity to disrupt proceedings by denouncing his prosecution as a show trial and attempting to *subpoena* Western politicians—Bill Clinton[16] and Tony Blair[17] amongst them—as witnesses for the defence. The trial dragged on for over four years and ran to almost 50,000 pages of transcript, until, in progressively failing health, Milosevic's heart finally gave out and (according to preferred penal theology) he either prematurely reaped his just reward or *in extremis* frustrated justice.[18] It speaks volumes for the international community's sincerity of purpose that Milosevic, as a former head of state, was put on trial at all, but neither advocates nor critics of international criminal trials can be satisfied with what ultimately transpired. Another long-standing bone of contention concerns the obstructive attitude of certain successor Balkan states towards tracking down and surrendering to the Tribunal fugitives believed to be located in their territories. Although co-operation with the ICTY has, generally speaking, improved over time, several notorious indictees remain at large, apparently with the connivance of governmental authorities. As Judge Theodor Meron, former President of the ICTY, summarised the position in his 2005 *Annual Report*:

> The failure to arrest high-level accused, such as [former Republika Srpska President] Radovan Karadžic, [Bosnian Serb General] Ratko Mladic and [Croatian Commander] Ante Gotovina, despite several resolutions of the Security Council, is of grave concern for the proper administration of justice. Repeated appeals to the Governments and entities in the region and the international community to pursue and arrest them have so far not borne results ... To achieve the Tribunal's mandate of contributing to the maintenance of peace and stability in the region it is imperative that those fugitives are given their day in court in The Hague ... Ten years after the genocide in Srebrenica, the Tribunal is continuing in its quest for justice, truth, peace and reconciliation.[19]

The ICTR, meanwhile, began its first trial in January 1997, and by June 2006 had rendered 22 judgments relating to 28 accused. These proceedings produced 25 convictions and three acquittals. Jean Kambanda, former Prime Minister of Rwanda, claims the dubious distinction of being the first statesman ever to be convicted (he pleaded guilty to genocide)[20] of the ultimate international crime

---

[15] Prosecutor v Slobodan Milosevic (IT–02–54).

[16] "'If someone commits a horrific murder in Britain, do you attribute it to Tony Blair?" Slobodan Milosevic shamelessly used his war crimes tribunal this week to blame everyone but himself': P Sherwell, *Sunday Telegraph*, 17 February 2002.

[17] See *Decision on Assigned Counsel Application for Interview and Testimony of Tony Blair and Gerhard Schröder*, ICTY Trial Chamber, 9 December 2005.

[18] Judge Robinson's summation is exquisitely laconic:

'The Chamber has been advised of the death of the accused, Slobodan Milosevic. We express our regret at his passing. We also regret that his untimely death has deprived not only him but indeed all interested parties of a judgement upon the allegations in the indictment. His death terminates these proceedings' (Transcript p 49191, 14 March 2006).

[19] See the ICTY's *Twelfth Annual Report* to the United Nations General Assembly and Security Council, A/60/267—S/2005/532, 17 August 2005, paras 182, 257, 258.

[20] V Brittain, 'Rwanda's former PM admits role in Genocide', *The Guardian*, 2 May 1998.

(*cf* Friedrichs, 2000). In June 2006 the ICTR was conducting a further 11 on-going trials involving 27 defendants. Another 14 accused were awaiting trial in the Tribunal's detention facility in Arusha, and a further 18 indictees remained at large. This modest total of indicted individuals pales in comparison, however, to the overall numbers of perpetrators and collaborators in the Rwandan genocide. Over 130,000 suspects were initially detained, and many more—perhaps as many as a million people—were directly implicated in one way or another. Genocide in Rwanda was experienced alike by victims, perpetrators and bystanders as a virulent cultural virus which saturated the entire social fabric and infected every pore of the body politic. The sheer impossibility of prosecuting every perpetrator, at the ICTR or anywhere else (Rwanda's own depleted criminal justice infrastructure was manifestly unequal to the task), posed acute problems of selection. Jurists and administrators were forced to improvise imaginative alternatives to traditional penal process in their endeavour to promote justice, peace, security and reconciliation without backsliding into impunity (Drumbl, 2000a).[21]

The ICTR's general strategy has been to 'concentrate on the prosecution of those persons who bear the greatest responsibility for the tragic events which occurred in Rwanda',[22] whilst diverting lesser offenders to national prosecutions or indigenous '*gacaca*' mediation processes. This bifurcated approach, reserving international prosecution for the very worst or most high-profile offenders, has become a familiar pattern in international criminal adjudication.

The ad hoc Tribunals were never intended to be permanent institutions. Both the ICTY and the ICTR have formulated 'completion strategies', according to which all trials should be finalised by 2008, and appeal hearings (which are plentiful in these cases) concluded by 2010. By this time, outstanding work should have been transferred to local courts and prosecutors, and the ICC will henceforth be on-hand to assert jurisdiction if fresh atrocities should occur. A prominent place in the unfolding history of international criminal justice is already assured to the ad hoc Tribunals. Confounding Schwarzenbergerian sceptics, they have broken the spell of perpetrator-impunity in the most emphatic terms, by demonstrating that *there is something that can be done* by the international community in response to genocide, crimes against humanity and other massive, state-sponsored violations of fundamental human rights during civil wars or by tyrannical governments abusing their own people. Almost irrespective of the local merits and scope for replication of the Tribunals' activities, the practical enforcement of international criminal law can no longer be dismissed peremptorily, as the fantasy of idealists or logical self-contradiction.

As a template for the ICC, bequeathing personnel and experience as well as doctrinal innovation, the legacy of the ad hoc Tribunals will be subsumed into the core of international criminal justice. In the meantime, the ICTY and the ICTR have

---

[21]   *Cf* D Gough, 'Mass jail release haunts Rwanda', *The Guardian*, 19 October 1998.
[22]   ICTR *The Tribunal at a Glance—Fact Sheet No 1*, para 15. See www.ictr.org/.

stimulated the proliferation of a third concentric circle of international criminal tribunals, known as 'internationalised' or 'hybrid' courts (Romano, Nollkaemper and Kleffner, 2004). Whilst precise legal arrangements differ, these tribunals share the characteristic of being neither fully international, like the ICC and the ad hoc Tribunals, nor exclusively domestic in character. Instead, they blend features of municipal and international criminal proceedings in more or less unique combinations, tailored to particular circumstances. At one end of the spectrum, lobbying by international organisations might have been instrumental in creating a tribunal, whilst on-going international support—financial, administrative, legal, political and military—may condition its institutional design, operational protocols and future prospects. The Special Court for Sierra Leone, fashioned by treaty between the government of Sierra Leone and the United Nations, fits this pattern of major international sponsorship (see Cryer, 2001). Similar partnerships between post-conflict states and the international community have precipitated internationalised criminal tribunals in East Timor, Kosovo and Cambodia as an integral part of national processes of victim reparation, social reconciliation and political reconstruction. Towards the other end of the spectrum are predominantly national legal proceedings underpinned by international support and good will. For example, the Iraqi High Tribunal, established in the wake of the 2003 Gulf War to try Saddam Hussein and his henchmen for atrocities perpetrated against the Iraqi people, is, strictly speaking, a creature of Iraqi domestic law, but clearly would never have existed without United States-led military intervention to topple Saddam's Ba'athist regime and subsequent facilitation by the occupation Iraqi Provisional Authority. Indeed, it has been said that the

> Tribunal's origins doom its legitimacy, not merely because it appears to be yet another instance of the Hegemon applying to others what it refuses to apply to itself ... but because it suits US policy goals—including to undermine the ICC (Alvarez, 2004: 319 at 326–7).

The Scottish criminal court temporarily convened in the Netherlands to try two Libyan nationals suspected of having planted the terrorist bomb which brought down Pam Am Flight 103 over Lockerbie in 1988 (Murphy, 2001), is another illustration of the exotic legal combinations to be found at the domestic end of modern 'internationalised' criminal tribunals.[23]

A fourth 'concentric circle' of international criminal justice strains the geometric metaphor, because it takes us back in time as well as further from the core. The International Military Tribunal (IMT) 'for the just and prompt trial and punishment of the major war criminals of the European Axis',[24] located in Nuremberg during 1945–46, is often regarded as the *fons et origo* of modern international

---

[23] For international interest in the Lockerbie trial, see eg Security Council Res 1192/98, welcoming the initiative and calling on all United Nations members to co-operate with it.
[24] IMT (London) Charter, Art 1. Materials relating to the IMT, including a full trial transcript, can be found on Yale Law School's excellent *Avalon Project* website: www.yale.edu/lawweb/avalon/imt/imt.htm.

criminal proceedings.[25] It set a remarkable historical precedent, in subjecting to formal trial and judicial punishment—rather than summary execution, as many contemporaries would have preferred—the most prominent politicians, military leaders, ideologues and civil administrators in Hitler's Nazi government, including *Reichsmarschall* Hermann Goering. The Nuremberg trial in total produced 18 convictions of individuals,[26] three acquittals and 12 sentences of death (which Goering sensationally pre-empted by committing suicide hours before his planned execution: see Persico, 1994). The iconic significance of the 'legacy of Nuremberg' is still hotly debated (for contrasting views, see eg Taylor, 1992; Eckhardt, 1996; Falk, 1999; King, 1998; and Washington, 2003). Passing over more detailed criticisms and objections, there is broad agreement that the IMT did not conduct a truly international criminal process. As a joint-venture of the four principal victorious powers (Britain, France, Russia and the United States), it was more in the nature of military justice imposed by the Allies as the *de facto* government of occupied Germany (see Cassese, 2003: 332–3). The 'Nuremberg Principles', which were subsequently endorsed by a fledgling United Nations,[27] have nonetheless continued to exert a major influence on the development of international criminal law. Nuremberg pioneered the notion of individual criminal responsibility for international crimes which has subsequently been consolidated by the ad hoc Tribunals and the ICC.

Our fifth concentric circle might be termed 'transnational criminal law' (*cf* Boister, 2003). It embraces various forms of international co-operation, co-ordination and mutual judicial assistance in penal affairs, sometimes involving relatively modest bilateral agreements between two or more states but often founded upon major multilateral treaties or 'conventions' under the sponsorship of the United Nations or some other competent international organisation such as the Council of Europe (CoE).[28] Paradigmatic are the so-called 'suppression conventions': international agreements by which signatory states promise to enact national criminal laws to combat particular conduct of international concern. Suppression conventions have addressed, amongst other topics, torture, apartheid, drug-trafficking, environmental degradation, and international terrorism (see Bantekas and Nash, 2003: chapters 3–5; and Sunga, 1997: chapters 2–3). Transnational criminal law, broadly conceived, also includes extradition agreements, transborder mutual assistance in criminal investigations and prosecutions, and even state-sponsored abductions of suspects on foreign soil and other, more prosaic types of informal co-operation between national police forces,

---

[25] Much less is said, or even remembered, about the International Military Tribunal for the Far East, established in Tokyo between 1946 and 1948 to try alleged Japanese war criminals (Clark, 1997). For various legal and political reasons, the Tokyo Tribunal is not regarded as a particularly happy precedent for international criminal proceedings.

[26] Several corporate entities were also prosecuted, including, the SS, the Gestapo and the Leadership Corps of the Nazi Party, in order to facilitate subsequent prosecutions of their members.

[27] United Nations General Assembly Res 95(I), 11 December 1946.

[28] See www.coe.int/.

prosecutors and judiciaries. These arrangements do not, by and large, impose legal duties directly on ordinary citizens or public officials, and for this reason some commentators would exclude them from the core concept of international criminal law (eg Broomhall, 2004: chapter 1). It can be objected that transnational criminal law is not genuinely supra-national in conception or effect. We may grant that suppression conventions technically specify 'crimes under international law' rather than international crimes *stricto sensu*. However, this is no reason to downplay the obvious affinities between transnational criminal law and other norms of international criminal justice in constructing a reasonably comprehensive and inclusive disciplinary taxonomy.

Until recent times, the application of international criminal law was virtually the exclusive preserve of *national* criminal courts and military tribunals. This is a sixth concentric circle of international criminal process. Post-Second World War trials of Nazis and traitorous collaborators were mostly conducted by national courts (Marschik, 1997), and with some notable milestones along the way— including the trial of the Holocaust's senior bureaucrat Adolf Eichmann by the Israeli courts in 1961 (Douglas, 2001: Part 2; and Arendt, 1994 [1963])—national prosecutions have continued right up to the present day (Hirsch, 2001).[29] Erstwhile Latin American premiers, such as ex-Chilean dictator Pinochet (Webber, 1999), have also found themselves arraigned before national courts on charges of torture, murder, 'disappearances' and other systematic human rights violations. Moreover, even where fully international or hybridised criminal tribunals are established to prosecute the worst offenders, the bulk of the relevant caseload is always carried by domestic criminal courts and military courts martial. This was the experience in post-war Germany, in the Balkans and in Rwanda, and it will continue to be the pattern under the ICC's jurisdictional regime of complementarity. Treating national criminal proceedings as the sixth 'concentric circle' of international criminal justice might therefore be regarded as inappropriately marginalising, since national courts arguably populate the core.

The seventh, and final, 'concentric circle' of international criminal justice is more aptly conceptualised as a chord running through the entire enterprise. For it comprises scholars' and researchers' contributions to the broader 'ICrimJ' project, conceived programmatically as an emerging new academic discipline. In a nutshell, ICrimJ epitomises interdisciplinarity. Some of its specifically legal and jurisprudential complexities have already been touched upon, and will be elaborated further in Part II, where the significance of socio-legal and criminological contributions to ICrimJ will also become apparent. There is enormous scope for Criminology to enrich the theory and practice of ICrimJ (Roberts and McMillan, 2003; and Drumbl, 2003). Criminology has developed the methodological tools for investigating both the nature of international 'crime' and the variety of

---

[29] See also D Fuchs: 'Nazi war criminal escapes Costa Brava police search', *The Guardian* 17 October 2005; and I Traynor, 'Nazi sentenced to 10 years in Germany's "Last war crimes trial"', *The Guardian* 21 May 1999.

informal and official responses it provokes. Formal trial and punishment on the traditional model is only one amongst several potential responses to international criminality, which may also include—for example—'restorative justice' processes and indigenous dispute resolution (Drumbl, 2000b; and Alvarez, 1999).

The overlapping disciplines of Politics and International Relations (IR) frame the immediate geo-political and strategic context for concrete developments in international criminal justice, and thus also naturally figured in the preceding discussion. Since armed conflict has typically been the precursor, as well as the subject-matter, of international criminal trials, a role for sociologies of the military, and of waging war and making peace, is also implied by this disciplinary taxonomy. History (for these purposes incorporating Holocaust Studies) must inevitably infuse a subject on which the Second World War and the bloodstained annals of aggressive war, genocide and state-sponsored atrocity cast a long shadow.

Last but not least, Philosophy is always indispensable to serious theoretical enquiry, importing refined generic skills of logical reasoning, taxonomy and conceptual analysis, supplemented by more substantive ethical reflections on justice, authority, government, retribution, the nature of evil, wrongdoing, rights, human dignity, personal autonomy, punishment, responsibility, and moral culpability. These topics figure prominently amongst other pressing issues and questions demanding practical answers from the advocates, architects and practitioners of international criminal justice.

III. COMPARATIVE LAW'S UNIQUE AND INDISPENSABLE CONTRIBUTIONS

Having developed a sophisticated conceptualisation of international criminal justice, we may now explore Comparative Law's distinctive contributions, organised under six broad headings: institutional design; legislation; jurisprudence; operational policy-making and mutual judicial assistance; legal harmonisation; and research, analysis and critical evaluation. Since conceptual definition is paramount, not every example will be regarded by every reader as legitimate. Different examples might have been substituted, and those actually chosen could have been developed at much greater length. This flexible approach is calculated to persuade even conceptual sticklers that Comparative Law, however conservatively conceived, is capable of making *some* unique and essential contributions to international criminal justice, however narrowly defined. Readers who share my own preference for more inclusive conceptualisations should find that Comparative Law has much more to offer than conceptual minimalists perceive.

Designing the Institutional Frameworks of International Criminal Law

Modern domestic legal systems are grown, rather than deliberately made, normative orders (Allen, 1996: Part I), that is, slowly sedimented products of history, politics, jurisprudence and culture. International criminal tribunals, by contrast, have no institutional history, politics, culture or legal tradition to call their own, at least until they become fully operational. International legal orders are made, not grown. Everything about them is either borrowed or tailor-made. For their planners and architects, international criminal tribunals present the unique challenge that their institutions and foundational legal instruments must be designed essentially from scratch. This, however, does not necessarily imply that the drawing board is completely blank. We have already seen that the United Nations ad hoc Tribunals supplied an institutional model which was promptly adopted and adapted by various internationalised tribunals, and by the ICC. Historically, however, the primary source of ideas and inspiration for institutional and procedural models has been national criminal justice systems. In an ideal world, the architects of international criminal tribunals would draw upon the best examples of domestic institutional design from around the globe, suitably modified for the specialist task in hand. And this, of course, is where Comparative Law should make its mark, not as the fountain of all wisdom, but as an indispensable contributor to an interdisciplinary conversation (also see Delmas-Marty, 2003).

At least since Nuremberg, questions of basic institutional design have been conceptualised in terms of the distinction between 'adversarial' and 'inquisitorial' procedures. Notwithstanding the problematic nature of that dichotomy (see Jackson, 2005; and Nijboer, 1993), it remains a useful starting point for analysis. Describing negotiations over the drafting of the IMT's Charter, Telford Taylor remarks that

> [p]erhaps the most intractable problem was the technical one of stating the respective functions and responsibilities of the Tribunal and the prosecution—a problem caused by the differences between Continental and Anglo-American criminal procedures (Taylor, 1992: 63).

Chief Prosecutor Robert H. Jackson apparently shared this assessment:

> From the very beginning it has been apparent that our greatest problem is how to reconcile two very different systems of procedure (quoted *ibid*: 64).

In the event, the Russians and the French were willing to let adversarial preferences prevail in order to placate the Americans, and 'differences were resolved by compromises which were crude but proved workable' (Taylor, *ibid*). Yet there was plainly much ignorance and suspicion of unfamiliar trial procedures on all sides. Even Taylor's authoritative memoir, which is careful to acknowledge differences *within* as well as between the two procedural families, makes generalisations about 'Anglo-American practice', which look suspect through English eyes.[30] Greater

---

[30] According to Taylor, for example, it was 'contrary to Anglo-American practice' that defendants before the IMT 'could also make an unsworn statement at the end of the trial'. However, criminal defendants in England and Wales did not generally become competent witnesses in their own defence until 1898, and the accused's right to make an unsworn statement from the dock was maintained throughout most of the 20th century, until it was finally abolished by the Criminal Justice Act 1988 (primarily to stop bombers and assassins of the Irish Republican Army (IRA) from using their criminal trial as a platform for making political speeches and denouncing the authority of British courts).

comparative insight would help to distinguish those features of national criminal proceedings which are regarded as essential and more or less non-negotiable, from relatively ephemeral details attributable largely to historical accident or whimsical cultural preference. This exercise, if undertaken in a spirit of candour and co-operation, might ease the path to more acceptable compromises in the design of international criminal procedures.

In more recent history, the ICTY, ICTR and ICC have all combined characteristic features of adversarial and inquisitorial process in novel and imaginative ways. Very roughly speaking, United Nations-sponsored international criminal *trials* have been modelled on common law adversarial proceedings (Cassese, 2003: chapter 20), whereas the *pre-trial* phases of international criminal investigations and prosecutions have drawn substantially on the continental inquisitorial tradition. Comparative understanding of how these processes work in their native settings, and their capacity to withstand extrapolation to the international context, is surely no less important for successful institutional design than expertise in international law, diplomacy or international relations.

The inquisitorial caste of pre-trial international criminal process is personified in the figure of the prosecutor. In the ICC system, the Prosecutor 'may initiate investigations *proprio motu* on the basis of information on crimes within the jurisdiction of the Court', and to this end,

> may seek additional information from States, organs of the United Nations, intergovernmental or non-governmental organizations, or other reliable sources ... and may receive written or oral testimony at the seat of the Court.[31]

The ICC Prosecutor must, however, obtain the authorisation of the Court's Pre-Trial Chamber in order to proceed with an investigation and prosecution.[32] This institutional arrangement is modelled directly on continental criminal procedure codes. It is in marked contrast to the rigid separation between English police and prosecutors enshrined in the Prosecution of Offences Act 1985, which has dictated a somewhat estranged relationship between police investigators and the Crown Prosecution Service in England and Wales.[33] At the ICTY and ICTR, a succession of talented, energetic and personally well-respected prosecutors (Arbour, 1997; and Goldstone, 2000) has been instrumental in implementing the Tribunals' mandate (to the extent that it has been implemented) by doggedly pursuing fugitive indictees, amassing evidence of international crimes, preparing cases for trial, and cajoling or embarrassing reluctant national governments to fulfil their international obligations by complying with the Tribunal's requests for assistance.

---

[31] ICC Statute, Art 15(1)–(2).

[32] ICC Statute, Art 15(3).

[33] Recent developments, culminating in a transfer of the initial power to charge suspects form police to prosecutors under the Criminal Justice Act 2003, are in the process of reducing this institutional distance (Brownlee, 2004). Whether closer contact will facilitate effective prosecution, or damage Crown prosecutors' vaunted 'independence', remains to be seen.

The tendency of international criminal trial proceedings to conform to a broadly adversarial format, with party-orchestrated presentation of evidence and oral examination of witnesses, is attributable to several factors. Looking beyond the United States' disproportionate influence in all of these initiatives, the global human rights movement has left its mark. International human rights instruments like the United Nations' Universal Declaration of Human Rights (UDHR) 1948 and the International Covenant on Civil and Political Rights (ICCPR) 1966 contain various criminal process-related provisions—including the 'right to a fair trial', which is elaborated in considerable detail.[34] Global human rights instruments have been reinforced by regional organisations and treaties, such as the European Convention on Human Rights (ECHR). In extending its activities into the sponsorship of international criminal trials, the United Nations has naturally been at pains to preserve its long-standing commitment to human rights.[35] The ICTY, ICTR and ICC all consequently reproduce within their respective statutes a full suite of rights for suspects and the accused, including faithful translations of the ICCPR's Article 14 right to a fair trial.[36] Thus, every person facing criminal charges must be allowed to conduct their own defence, with the assistance of counsel if they prefer, and their entitlements shall include the right

> to examine, or have examined, the witnesses against him and to obtain the attendance and examination of witnesses on his behalf under the same conditions as witnesses against him.[37]

Anglo-American style examination-in-chief and cross-examination of party-summoned witnesses are clearly contemplated, in preference to the *dossier*-based, judicially-directed factual inquiry characteristic of continental criminal trials. Yet these generalisations barely scratch the surface of some complex and imperfectly digested legal issues. Comparative investigation would reveal that oral examination of witnesses by the parties has been embraced enthusiastically (albeit not always entirely successfully) in several historically 'inquisitorial' legal systems (see Weigend, 2003; Siegel, 2006; and Vogler, 2005), at the same time as classically adversarial exclusionary rules of evidence have been relaxed (Roberts, 2006) and judges have assumed more directive case-management functions in common law jurisdictions (Duff, 2004). Traditional procedural dichotomies have shifted and blurred. Nor is JH Wigmore's notorious boosterism for cross-examination as 'the greatest legal engine ever invented for the discovery of truth' (Wigmore, 1974: vol 5, para 1367) today unequivocally endorsed in the common law's heartlands. Even if cross-examination worked flawlessly in England and Wales or New York, which many critics vehemently dispute (see Roberts and Zuckerman, 2004: 215–21), it would be foolhardy to assume that it can be replicated with equal success in

---

[34] UDHR, Arts 10 and 11; ICCPR, Art 14. For general discussion, see Bassiouni (1993).

[35] The Preamble to the UN Charter reaffirms 'faith in fundamental human rights, in the dignity and worth of the human person, in the equal rights of men and women and of nations large and small'.

[36] ICTY Statute, Art 21; ICTR Statute, Art 20; and ICC Statute, Arts 66 and 67.

[37] ICCPR, Art 14(3)(e).

the multi-lingual, culturally diverse international courtrooms of The Hague or Arusha.[38] Microscopic examination of proof-taking and evidence-testing at the domestic level is required to identify the comparative strengths and weaknesses of procedural mechanisms, and to assess their capacity for extrapolation to the international context.

Comparative Law generates both 'negative' and 'positive' contributions to the basic design of international criminal justice institutions and procedures, potentially building into an indispensable reference-library of 'do's and don't's'. On the negative side, comparative analysis should help to dispel all-too-familiar caricatures of domestic legal systems as inflexibly static, exclusively parochial, ciphers of national mores. Ignorance of this kind is a crutch for nationalistic prejudice and an obstacle to successful international co-operation in penal affairs. Viewed more positively, Comparative Law supplies invaluable models, experience and juridical resources for robust institution-building at the international level.

Legislating Substantive International Criminal Law

International criminal law is *sui generis*, and one must avoid facile analogies to domestic criminal litigation (*cf* Tallgren, 2002: 561 at 572). This unique supranational enterprise should nonetheless be informed and enriched by comparative studies of municipal criminal law and process. The task of legislating substantive international criminal law exemplifies this duality.

Consider the four 'core international crimes', as specified by the ICC Statute. They comprise, first, genocide, which means (in summary) killing, seriously harming or interfering with human reproduction or childrearing 'committed with intent to destroy, in whole or in part, a national, ethnical, racial or religious group, as such'.[39] Secondly, 'crimes against humanity' involve murder, extermination, enslavement, deportation, unlawful imprisonment, torture, rape, sexual slavery, discriminatory persecution, enforced disappearances, apartheid, or 'other inhumane acts of a similar character' when 'committed as part of a widespread or systematic attack directed against any civilian population, with knowledge of the attack'.[40] Thirdly, 'war crimes' are specified in elaborate detail. They include generic criminal violations such as murder, rape and assault; breaches of military ethics like hostage-taking, mistreating surrendered combatants or POWs, or declaring 'no quarter'; and discrete prohibitions of illegal weaponry (eg poison gas or dumdum bullets) and forbidden tactics (eg bombardment of non-military targets or deployment of 'human shields'). Finally, fourth, the 'crime of aggression' concerns unjustified resort to warfare, in unprovoked armed attack or military conquest,

---

[38] Cross-examination of Goering at the Nuremberg IMT backfired for somewhat different reasons: Jackson's preparation was flawed and the former *Reichsmarschall* was adept at political point-scoring (Johnson and Hinderaker, 2002).

[39] ICC Statute, Art 6.

[40] ICC Statute, Art 7.

for example. Aggression violates the cardinal principle of state sovereignty, which is the legal and political foundation-stone of modern international relations. The ICC cannot assume jurisdiction over crimes of aggression unless and until the Assembly of States Parties reaches agreement on the meaning of 'aggression',[41] however, and this could be a long time coming.

The core crimes derive predominantly from International Humanitarian Law (IHL). Much of their substance is plainly far removed from the everyday concerns of criminal lawyers in domestic practice. To this extent, 'ICrimL' appears to be exactly what most of its exponents take it to be, a specialised branch of public international law (PIL). Yet two further considerations bring Comparative Law firmly back into focus.

First, ICrimL *does* draw directly on domestic criminal laws, both in its definitions of generic crimes like murder, rape and assault, and also in its general principles of criminal liability. Article 30 of the ICC's Rome Statute, for example, specifies that

> a person shall be criminally responsible and liable for punishment for a crime within the jurisdiction of the Court only if the material elements are committed with intent and knowledge

and the meaning of 'intent' is further defined. Articles 31 and 32 address such familiar topics as insanity, intoxication, self-defence, duress, and mistake of fact or law. Article 25 deals with accomplices, incitement and criminal attempts. Each of these definitional elements raises points of legislative drafting and underlying moral rationales on which domestic criminal legislation could shed important light. Comparative inquiry might ascertain not only points of convergence in national criminal laws—suggestive of international 'best practice' in criminalisation—but also distinctive domestic innovations potentially worthy of emulation at the international level. English criminal law, for example, has generated acres of judgments and commentary on the meaning of mens rea terms such as 'intention' (Ashworth, 2006: 174–81; and Simester and Sullivan, 2003: 126–36, 334–8) and 'knowledge' (Shute, 2002) which might inform drafting choices in international criminal legislation. To cap it all, Article 21 of the ICC Statute expressly qualifies 'general principles of law derived by the Court from national laws of legal systems of the world' as a formal, albeit tertiary,[42] source of legal authority in proceedings before the ICC.

Moreover, traffic between international and domestic criminal legislation is a two-way street. Many States Parties to international treaties are obliged by their national constitutions to enact enabling legislation to give effect to international agreements in domestic law.[43] Authentic interpretation is obviously essential for

---

[41] ICC Statute, Art 5(2).

[42] The ICC's primary law is the ICC Statute itself (plus ancillary materials), followed by applicable treaties and custom binding in public international law 'including the established principles of the international law of armed conflict'.

[43] See, eg the International Criminal Court Act 2001, giving effect in English law to the ICC Statute.

faithful transposition. But if international norms are partly derived from the legislation, jurisprudence and legal commentary produced by a diversity of national legal cultures and traditions, working knowledge of these domestic origins must surely be advantageous for any government lawyer or judge attempting to interpret international legal instruments. The challenge of transposition therefore implies a second reason why ICrimL cannot be relegated to a mere out-post of PIL, and another schedule of major works for comparative legal studies. For the reception of international criminal law into domestic legislation is only the first strand in a seamless web of normative migration, adaptation and reinvention in which comparative methodology assumes a central role. Straightforward enough, in conception if not in practice, at the macro level of legislation, these processes become infinitely more complex and variegated in the micro-dynamics of judicial practice.

Judicial Development of International Criminal Jurisprudence

National legal systems differ in the extent to which judicial law-making is formally acknowledged. Whether or not they embrace a formal system of precedent on the common law model, however, all appellate tribunals in mature legal systems contribute to the development of domestic law through their judgments in contested cases. This quasi-legislative side of legal adjudication bears profound significance for international criminal justice, and for the role of Comparative Law as its handmaiden.

It is impossible for a criminal code of any description to anticipate and legislate comprehensively for every conceivable contingency. Legislators therefore sensibly confine themselves to enacting general normative frameworks, leaving finer details to be supplied through judicial interpretation. Judicial contributions to international criminal law and procedure have been immense, not least because legislative materials prior to the enactment of the ICC Statute were remarkably sparse. The Nuremberg IMT's London Charter contained just 30 succinct Articles, briefly elaborating the Tribunal's jurisdiction, powers and procedure. Substantive legal doctrine and process had to be improvised by the judges, with the assistance of counsel, as the proceedings unfolded. The Statutes of the ICTY and ICTR are noticeably more detailed in specifying the form of trial,[44] suspects' procedural rights[45] and protections for victims and witnesses.[46] But they inevitably remain silent on the technical minutiae of criminal law and process (see May and Wierda, 1999). Indeed, there is a formal mechanism for the judges of the ICTY and ICTR to draft and update their own Rules of Procedure and Evidence.[47] This is a

---

[44] ICTY Statute, Art 20; ICTR Statute, Art 19.
[45] ICTY Statute, Art 21; ICTR Statute, Art 20.
[46] ICTY Statute, Art 22; ICTR Statute, Art 21.
[47] ICTY Statute, Art 15; ICTR Statute, Art 14. The ICTY's *Rules of Procedure and Evidence* are in their 37th revision: IT/32/Rev 37 (April 2006); and the ICTR's *Rules of Procedure and Evidence* had been amended 14 times to June 2005.

delegated legislative function. In their more familiar adjudicative role, the judges of the ICTY and ICTR are credited with having contributed substantially to the doctrinal development of international criminal law and procedure through evidentiary rulings and judgments in trials and appeals (see Cassese, 2003: Part II).

The centrality of comparative legal analysis to international criminal adjudication is guaranteed by multinational judiciaries. At Nuremberg, the IMT's judges represented four different legal traditions, though the Anglophones were common law cousins and the Russians and French shared an 'inquisitorial' legal heritage. Fast-forward half a century, and the ICC's 18 judges are drawn from 100 States Parties.[48] Consciously or otherwise, individual judges bring their national legal and cultural expectations, assumptions, preferences and prejudices (*cf* Merryman, 1988) into international courtrooms. A comparative approach is necessitated by the impetus in adjudication to debate national legal traditions. To be an effective member of a collegiate multinational bench, the international judge must gauge where his or her judicial colleagues are 'coming from', in terms of their legal background, training and professional cultural assumptions. How else can nationally-trained judges serving on international criminal tribunals hope to engineer appropriate compromises on points of disagreement, or garner support for their own preferred legal solution, or even just arrive at authentic and sustainable interpretations of international criminal law?

In a fundamentally devolved system of law, the comparativism integral to the work of international criminal courts is magnified at the regional and domestic levels. Both the ICTY and the ICTR are currently transferring selected defendants for trial before national courts and building up local judicial capacity as part of their respective 'completion strategies'. The 'internationalised' criminal tribunals are distinguished—from other forms of judicial process as well as from each other—precisely by their unique conjunctions of international and local laws. Referring generally to hybrid tribunals, Cassese observes:

> Both the prosecution and the bench are of mixed composition and there you have this huge problem—to make sure that the local component, and the international component, do cooperate, do understand each other, do work effectively in their pursuit of the common and shared goal of rendering justice (Cassese, 2004: 7).

And looking ahead, domestic courts in transitional or post-conflict societies will need to ensure that local prosecutions of international crimes are conducted in accordance with international due process, or risk intervention by the ICC Prosecutor asserting residual jurisdiction.[49] At each of these junction-points where international and domestic laws converge, the quality of legal analysis and decision-making can only be enhanced by expertise in Comparative Law. To qualify as the international community's agents in enforcing international

---

[48] The Court is currently comprised of judges from Brazil, Bolivia, Bulgaria, Canada, Costa Rica, Cyprus, Finland, France, Germany, Ghana, Ireland, Italy, Republic of Korea, Latvia, Mali, South Africa, Trinidad and Tobago, and the United Kingdom.

[49] ICC Statute, Art 17.

penal law, domestic courts must strive for a co-ordinated, culturally-sensitive, 'cosmopolitan' approach which is capable of being endorsed by the reasonable[50] majority of states, international organisations, NGOs, activists, and a 24-hour-global-news-led international public opinion.

The synthetic integration of comparative legal method within international criminal adjudication is reinforced by the salience of international human rights law (IHRL) for international criminal justice. Although human rights courts do not directly receive appeals from domestic criminal convictions, they *are* empowered to rule that a particular domestic criminal law or procedure, as applied to the accused in the instant case, is incompatible with respect for fundamental human rights. In this indirect fashion, international human rights courts exert tangible influence over the development and application of domestic criminal law and procedure—another facet of the contemporary internationalisation of municipal state law. Via the burgeoning jurisprudence of the Strasbourg-based European Court of Human Rights,[51] for example, IHRL indirectly informs interpretations of ICrimL at the domestic level (reinforcing IHRL's more overt presence in international treaties and their interpretational jurisprudence). Since comparative methodologies are already built-into European human rights adjudication (*cf* Carozza, 1998), this integral comparativism is automatically extended when human rights standards are subsumed within international criminal law. The interweaving circuits of jurisprudential influence and authority continue to expand, consolidate, and diversify exponentially and self-reflexively, as courts and tribunals with overlapping jurisdiction constantly revisit and rework their own and each other's previous decisions into novel legal arguments.

Operational Policy-Making and Mutual Judicial Assistance

Lawyers have a tendency to focus on formal treaties, constitutions, statutes and precedent cases, and specialists in PIL are far from immune from this fascination with positive sources of law. At least since the 1970s, however, socio-legal scholars have insisted that law must be conceptualised as an interlocking set of institutionalised 'social ordering practices' (Lacey, 1994: 28) which simultaneously shape and are shaped by their juridical, cultural, social, political, economic and historical environments. The 'law in the books' must be augmented by investigations of the 'law in action'. Having traditionally concentrated on national law and legal process, socio-legal scholars and criminologists have more recently branched out into the study of international crime and criminal justice (eg Morrison, 2006; Ruggiero, 2005; and Day and Vandiver, 2000).

---

[50] This equivocation implies something approximating Rawls's idea of an 'overlapping consensus' around 'reasonable pluralism' (Rawls, 1996: see especially Lecture IV). International criminal justice could never be founded on universal consensus, if only because international criminals will rarely assent to their own punishment.

[51] See www.echr.coe.int/echr.

Socio-legal research has repeatedly demonstrated that officials' conduct and decision-making are strongly influenced by a variety of 'soft' legal instruments and informal occupational routines or 'working rules', which tend to mediate— where they do not eclipse entirely—the strict letter of the law (see, eg Hawkins, 2002; Dixon, 1997; and McConville, Sanders and Leng, 1991). 'Soft law' sources and informal operational policy-making are no less significant for international criminal law and its enforcement than for domestic criminal process. PIL is awash with non-binding legal instruments and materials, such as United Nations General Assembly resolutions, International Law Commission (ILC) reports and working papers, multilateral draft conventions, accords, codes, guidelines and other indicia of 'state practice', a great many of which concern criminal justice issues (Bassiouni, 1994). The European Union's expanding portfolio of activities in the field of Justice and Home Affairs is another energetic contributor of soft law instruments bearing on the formation and implementation of criminal justice policy in the 27 EU Member States, and beyond via the European Union's 'external relations' (foreign policy) agenda. The European Union, for example, is a major sponsor of the ICTY, and the Tribunal dangles the carrot of potential European Union membership to coax reluctant governments in Belgrade and Zagreb to comply with its requests for indictees to be arrested and transferred to The Hague.

Frontline professionals' decision-making and conduct is typically motivated by 'third-tier' directives, such as police force orders, prosecutorial codes or military training manuals (which are not necessarily publicly available), rather than by primary legal rules or secondary delegated legislation. Sometimes 'policy' is not even written down; occasionally it is not written down *on purpose*. Unwritten operational policies occupy the shadow-lands of informal agreements, institutionalised routines, shared professional understandings, and taken-for-granted cultural assumptions. A striking recent example is the highly controversial policy of 'extraordinary rendition' (Weissbrodt and Bergquist, 2006),[52] whereby suspected terrorists have allegedly been handed over by Western powers to friendly jurisdictions with brutal policing methods, in order to circumvent domestic legal restrictions on torture—a backhanded compliment to American civil liberties and European human rights law, which simultaneously exposes the inadequacies of regionally discrepant approaches to human rights protection.

Comparative Law is an essential practical resource at all levels and in all phases of formal and informal operational policy-making and mutual judicial assistance. Towards the more formal end of international judicial co-operation, for example, extradition proceedings require judges to undertake comparative assessments of the compatibility of criminal laws in the requesting and requested states. This is not necessarily a straightforward textual exercise: concepts, terminology, rules and doctrines encountered in domestic criminal legislation must be interpreted

---

[52]   R Verkaik: 'The Big Question: What is Extraordinary Rendition, and What is Britain's Role in it?', *The Independent*, 8 June 2006.

holistically against the background of a distinctive national legal culture and tradition, itself dynamically responsive to social pressures and political events and increasingly moulded by extra-territorial normative influences, prominently including IHRL. Proceedings to extradite Senator Pinochet from the United Kingdom,[53] for example, turned in part on a somewhat convoluted legal analysis to ascertain whether internationally-proscribed torture had been a crime in English law at the material time (see Boister and Burchill, 1999). Likewise, transborder co-operation in police investigations must be informed by an appreciation of comparative criminal procedure, in order to satisfy proof-taking requirements and comply with evidentiary standards observed by the requesting state or tribunal. Despite a notable modern trend towards convergence (Safferling, 2001; and Bradley, 1993), rules of criminal procedure and evidence still differ markedly across legal jurisdictions, both national and international. The English courts, for example, have deprecated informal collaboration between national police forces designed to circumvent the inadequacies of existing extradition arrangements by deceit.[54] Israeli courts[55] and the United States Supreme Court,[56] on the other hand, do not regard even outright kidnapping as fatal to the successful prosecution and conviction of suspects identified and apprehended extra-judicially. Police officers of all ranks involved in international mutual judicial assistance need to be alive to these comparative legal distinctions.

Socio-legal studies of national criminal justice processes have frequently emphasised the ubiquity of *operational discretion*. From the informal 'working rules' of their occupational culture, police officers learn where to patrol or watch, the cues constituting 'suspicious' behaviour, which vehicles to stop and search, when to effect an arrest or, alternatively, settle for 'having a quiet word', when to interview a witness or suspect, how to handle informants, etc. Local variations in occupational culture virtually guarantee that comparative understanding will be a significant operational asset in co-ordinating transborder co-operation and international policing networks. Similar considerations apply to international co-operation between prosecutors, defence lawyers, judges, penal administrators, and military personnel, and in every sphere of informal operational policy-making and mutual judicial assistance. For as President George W. Bush recently reflected: 'Not everybody thinks the exact same way we think. Different words mean different things to different people'.[57]

---

[53] *R v Bow Street Metropolitan Stipendiary Magistrate, ex parte Pinochet Ugarte (Amnesty International and others intervening) (No 3)* [2000] 1 AC 147 (HL).

[54] See *R v Horseferry Road Magistrates' Court, ex parte Bennett* [1994] 1 AC 42 (HL); see also *R v Mullen (Nicholas Robert) (No 2)* [2000] QB 520 (CA).

[55] *Attorney General of Israel v Eichmann* (1961) 36 ILR 5 (Isr DC, Jerusalem); aff'd, (1962) 36 ILR 277 (Isr Sup Ct).

[56] In *US v Alvarez-Machain* (1992) 504 US 655 112 S Ct 2188 a 6-3 majority of the United States Supreme Court held (*per* Rehnquist, CJ) that although it might be true that the

    respondent's abduction was 'shocking'... and ... in violation of ... international law ... The fact of respondent's forcible abduction does not therefore prohibit his trial in a court in the United States.

[57] S Blumenthal: 'A Pantomime President', *The Guardian*, 18 July 2006.

Harmonising National Criminal Laws

Legal harmonisation lies at the more ambitious pole of international co-operation in criminal justice and penal affairs. Experience suggests that progress is best achieved by facilitating incremental assimilation of domestic criminal laws rather than by sweeping legislative schemes. Criminal law, in contrast to the law of commerce, property entitlements or even civil wrongs, tends to encapsulate a nation's fundamental political, social, moral and religious commitments, which states will not readily compromise for the sake of international uniformity. Nonetheless, through a series of United Nations-sponsored 'suppression conventions', and in softer legal instruments such as minimum standards for the treatment of detainees and indicative codes of professional conduct for police, prosecutors and judges,[58] a measure of convergence in domestic criminal law and practice has been promoted.

Gradual, piecemeal assimilation respects national sovereignty and acknowledges the reality of international law as a devolved and potentially dysfunctional system. Even the ICC Statute, the most unified and comprehensive system of international criminal law ever implemented, still defers to national variation within the loose parameters of complementarity. On a broader view of ICrimL, it is possible to find further examples of harmonisation of national laws through vertical legal integration within the European Union (generally, see Baker, 1998; and Peers, 2000). First pillar EC law, including competition law enforced by penal fines, is binding in Member States and takes precedence over conflicting national law.[59] Domestic criminal legislation infringing European Community rights may incur public liability to compensate affected parties.[60] And the exercise of discretionary powers by officials, including operational policy-making by senior police officers (Baker, 2000), must a fortiori be consistent with European Community prescriptions.

Other developments are more ad hoc and uneven in their impact. The *Corpus Juris* (Delmas-Marty and Vervaele, 2000) was an ambitious attempt to design a European-style criminal 'code', comprising both substantive offence definitions and procedural rules, to regulate European Union fraud (see Kuhl, 1998). Like the ill-starred European Union Constitution (which also contains provisions affecting criminal law and process), efforts to implement the *Corpus Juris* currently appear to have stalled. However, related initiatives have been taken forward, notably the adoption of a pan-European Arrest Warrant.[61] With mounting pressures for closer legal cooperation between Member States to combat fraud, illegal immigration, people trafficking, drug-smuggling, cross-border arms running, and—above

---

[58] See, eg http://www.uncjin.org/Standards/standards.html.
[59] *Costa v ENEL* [1964] CMLR 425 (ECJ).
[60] *R v Secretary of State for Transport, ex parte Factortame Ltd (No 5)* [2000] 1 AC 524 (HL).
[61] EC Framework Decision 2002/584/JHA on the *European Arrest Warrant and the Surrender Procedures between Member States* came into force on 1 January 2004 in those eight Member States (including the United Kingdom) which had satisfied the agreed implementation criteria.

all—international terrorism, the impetus towards integration and harmonisation of Member States' domestic laws is bound to intensify. Although regional examples of harmonisation in ICrimL are by definition geographically restricted, the extent of legal integration in criminal justice and penal affairs already achieved by Western European powers is unparalleled around the globe.

Comparative Law and legal method are indispensable resources for projects of legal harmonisation (Delmas-Marty, 2003). Pre-existing national laws must be surveyed, collated and subjected to critical examination as essential preliminaries. The tantalising prospect of harmonisation has inspired Comparative Law since its formative years (Clark, 2001: Part VI), and contemporary developments in international criminal law, including the European Union initiatives just mentioned, retain a strong comparative ethos (see, eg van den Wyngaert, 2001). The uncertain fate of the *Corpus Juris* testifies to the political obstacles standing in the way of fully-fledged supra-national vertical integration in domestic criminal legislation, even amongst broadly similar, economically developed, geographically proximate, secularised western democracies. One size invariably does *not* fit all. Successful programmes of legal harmonisation need to work with the grain of national legal traditions, and even sometimes to accommodate their foibles—so long as local variations are substantially consistent with the overall scheme. Without rigorous planning incorporating comparative legal analysis, however, projects of legal harmonisation are almost guaranteed to fail, even with committed political sponsorship.

Research, Analysis and Critical Evaluation

We have been exploring Comparative Law's contributions to international criminal justice predominantly from the perspectives of policymakers and practitioners (and policy-maker practitioners): legislators, government ministers, diplomats, civil servants, judges, lawyers, police, military commanders, armed services personnel, and the rest. Here we emphasise the scholarly component of ICrimJ, its seventh 'concentric circle'. ICrimJ needs to develop a systematic research base underpinned by mature theoretical inquiries, and Comparative Law and legal studies should be in the vanguard of this trail-blazing intellectual endeavour.

Comparative legal studies contribute to ICrimJ on every (inter)disciplinary front. Comparative lawyers have applied their research methods and data to illuminate the fundamental character of law and legality (Twining, 2000; and Glenn, 2004). A growing body of impressive work in the overlapping fields of comparative criminology and comparative criminal justice studies is making a determined effort to push Criminology beyond its traditional state-based comfort-zone (eg Sheptycki and Wardak, 2005; and Nelken, 2000). Comparative analyses of legal institutions today figure in Politics and IR textbooks (eg Christiansen, 2005) and curricula. Comparative histories of criminal justice have been written (Godfrey, Emsley and Dunstall, 2003). The philosophy of punishment has been enriched by comparative studies of criminal justice policy-making (Rutherford, 1996; and Garland, 2001; but *cf* Zedner, 2002), distinctive cultures of penality (Whitman, 2003), and the legal regulation and practical realities of penal treatment (Lazarus, 2004).

Conventional disciplinary taxonomies are stretched beyond breaking point by these novel conjunctions. Is a comparative study of the evolution of criminal procedure (*cf* Vogler, 2005) 'really' Comparative Law, Legal History, Criminology, Criminal Justice, all of the foregoing, or none of the above? Does it matter? Howsoever characterised, comparative legal theory, method, and research are manifestly integral to theorising, researching, advocating and institutionalising international criminal justice. When Comparative Law's contributions are not strictly unique, in the way of original empirical data or *bona fide* jurisprudential innovation, they nonetheless reinforce the multiple strands of ICrimJ's incomparably interdisciplinary constitution.

IV. SUMMARY AND CONCLUSIONS

Any research project can usefully be broken down into three foundational questions, which may be conceptualised, meta-methodologically (ie specifying the method of method), as an 'eternal triangle' of intimately interrelated, mutually conditioning considerations. First, the 'Question of Subject-Matter' concerns issues of taxonomy and conceptual definition. Secondly, the 'Question of Motivation' asks why the inquiry is worth undertaking and what one hopes to gain from it. Thirdly, the 'Question of Method' raises issues of methodological perspective and technique. The eternal triangle, in short, specifies the What?, Why? and How? of intellectual inquiry. To recap and conclude, let us apply this explanatory framework to the argument developed in this chapter.

To claim that Comparative Law is capable of making unique and indispensable contributions to international criminal justice might be regarded as puzzling on many levels. Most profoundly, neither 'Comparative Law' nor—still less—'international criminal justice' are terms with settled or transparent conventional meanings. Much of this chapter was consequently given over to taxonomy and conceptual definition in an effort to clarify the 'Question of Subject-Matter'. Comparative Law is plainly something to do with comparison and something to do with law, but it is not particularly illuminating to extend the label to all juridical comparisons of any description. Cross-jurisdictional comparisons between domestic national laws are the paradigm case. Yet the simple 'compare and contrast' model, conceptualising national legal systems as two discrete units of analysis, has been vastly complicated by modern law's promiscuously cosmopolitan tendencies, facilitated and reinforced by growing experimentation in supra-national legal regulation.

International criminal justice is controversial to its core. Many have denied its existence, and even scoffed at the suggestion. Rather than trying to formulate and defend a particular stipulative definition, this chapter explored the notion of 'international criminal justice' through a series of seven 'concentric circles', starting with the core activities of international criminal tribunals and fanning out into the hinterlands of transnational legal co-operation, national trials of international criminality, and related—both visionary and parasitic—scholarly commentaries and research. Sceptics might say that appeals to international criminal justice are really just the latest disingenuous apologetics for national self-interest, international finance capital, neo-colonialism or Western cultural imperialism. What can no longer be claimed, however, is that international criminal trials are a logical impossibility, or that political and military leaders can bank on impunity for atrocities, or that nobody will ever be convicted of genocide, or that rape will never be taken seriously as a war crime, or that the international community will forever sit on the sidelines wringing its hands. The very existence of the ICC, building on the unprecedented achievements of the ICTY and ICTR, demonstrates that (for all their admitted weaknesses and deficiencies) recent institutional and normative developments in international criminal justice have major significance for legality, for justice, for world peace, and—it is no exaggeration—for the future of humanity on this earth.

The 'Question of Motivation' barely requires extended examination in the light of these remarks, and this chapter's content. Why should one take an interest in the Holocaust and post-Second World War trials of Nazi war criminals, or in endeavours to resolve ethnic conflict in the Balkans, or in internationally-co-ordinated efforts to rescue the Great Lakes region of Africa from the fires of the Rwandan genocide—'one of the defining events of the twentieth century'[62]? Why be concerned about the ICC Prosecutor's investigations in northern Uganda and the Darfur region of Sudan, or the fate of child soldiers in Sierra Leone, or the outcome of the trial of Saddam by the Iraqi High Tribunal? To readers who already care passionately about promoting law, justice, human rights and human dignity at home and abroad, the answer will be all-too-painfully obvious. Those less secure in their convictions might profitably meditate on this epistemological and existential conundrum: what else could possibly matter, if these things don't? Once upon a time, it might have been possible for governments virtually to ignore foreign affairs whilst concentrating on improving national well-being within secure frontiers. But those days of Splendid Isolationism are gone. Drugs barons, people-smugglers, white-slavers, black-market arms traders, political insurgents and suicide bombers testify with one voice to this implication of globalisation: there is no rigid distinction between national and international criminal justice, just as there can be no 'domestic policy' hermetically sealed off from 'foreign policy'. There is only justice, and policy, in a global context, just as there is only a single human family to make this one world our home.

---

[62] Human Rights Watch (2004) *Leave None to Tell the Story: Genocide in Rwanda.* www.hrw.org/reports/1999/rwanda/index.htm.

If international criminal justice matters profoundly, and if Comparative Law might potentially make unique and indispensable contributions to its ultimate realisation, then this virtuous conjunction should be explored and explained, and its significance widely advertised. The strength of Comparative Law and legal scholarship lies in its distinctive methodologies, which brings us to the third point on the eternal triangle. *How* does Comparative Law contribute to international criminal justice? By extending comparative method, perspectives and insight into every phase and corner of international criminal justice policy-making and practice, including institutional design, legislation, adjudication, operational policy-making and transborder co-operation in policing, mutual judicial assistance, legal harmonisation, and scholarly theorising, commentary and research.

The precise nature and extent of Comparative Law's overall contribution to international criminal justice turns on questions of conceptual definition. My own preference for broadly inclusive conceptualisations has the congenial implication of maximising Comparative Law's potential in this respect. But those who prefer more orthodox conceptions of Comparative Law, or are disinclined to venture beyond the inner circles of international criminal law and practice, should still conclude, on the evidence of this chapter, that Comparative Law's contributions to international criminal justice are potentially both indispensable and unique.

QUESTIONS FOR DISCUSSION

1. What distinguishes 'international criminal law' from 'international criminal justice'? When, and why, are the differences important?
2. What, if anything, distinguishes international criminal justice from International Criminal Justice? Or international criminal law from International Criminal Law?
3. In what ways, and to what extent, can Comparative Law contribute to international criminal justice? (How are you defining 'Comparative Law'? How does your definition of 'Comparative Law' affect your answer to the original question? Would you like to reconsider your definition of 'Comparative Law' in the light of its implications for the relationship between Comparative Law and international criminal justice? Why (not)?)
4. Is there any (interesting, non-trivial) sense in which international criminal law is *not* comparative?
5. Are there any significant aspects of international criminal justice that comparative legal method cannot explain, or important questions it cannot answer?
6. Is disciplinary taxonomy completely arbitrary? Is conceptual analysis just sterile logic-chopping? Why (not)?
7. What is the 'eternal triangle' of intellectual inquiry? Can you apply it to illuminate any other research topic or question mentioned in this book? Or any other research topic or question you can think of?

BIBLIOGRAPHY AND FURTHER READING

Allen, RJ (1996) 'The Simpson Affair, Reform of the Criminal Justice Process, and Magic Bullets' 67 *University of Colorado Law Review* 989.

Alvarez, JE (1999) 'Crimes of States/Crimes of Hate: Lessons from Rwanda' 24 *Yale Journal of International Law* 365.

—— (2004) 'Trying Hussein: Between Hubris and Hegemony' 2 *Journal of International Criminal Justice* 319.

Arbour, L (1997) 'Progress and Challenges in International Criminal Justice' 21 *Fordham International Law Journal* 531.

Arendt, H (1994 [1963]) *Eichmann in Jerusalem: A Report on the Banality of Evil* (Harmondsworth, Middlesex, Penguin).

Ashworth, A (2006) *Principles of Criminal Law*, 5th edn (Oxford, Oxford University Press).

Baker, E (1998) 'Taking European Criminal Law Seriously' *Criminal Law Review* 361.

—— (2000) 'Policing, Protest and Free Trade: Challenging Police Discretion Under Community Law' *Criminal Law Review* 95.

Bantekas, I and Nash S (2003) *International Criminal Law*, 2nd edn (London, Cavendish).

Bass, GJ (2000) *Stay the Hand of Vengeance: The Politics of War Crimes Tribunals* (Princeton, NJ, Princeton University Press).

Bassiouni, MC (1993) 'Human Rights in the Context of Criminal Justice: Identifying International Procedural Protections and Equivalent Protections in National Constitutions' 3 *Duke Journal of Comparative and International Law* 235.

—— (ed) (1994) *The Protection of Human Rights in the Administration of Criminal Justice: A Compendium of United Nations Norms and Standards* (New York, Transnational Publishers).

—— (2000) 'Combating Impunity for International Crimes' 71 *University of Colorado Law Review* 409.

Boister, N (2003) '"Transnational Criminal Law"?' 14 *European Journal of International Law* 953.

Boister, N, and Burchill R (1999) 'The *Pinochet* Precedent: Don't Leave Home Without It' 10 *Criminal Law Forum* 405.

Bradley, CM (1993) 'The Emerging International Consensus as to Criminal Procedure Rules' 14 *Michigan Journal of International Law* 171.

Broomhall, B (2004) *International Justice and the International Criminal Court: Between Sovereignty and the Rule of Law* (Oxford, Oxford University Press).

Brownlee, ID (2004) 'The Statutory Charging Scheme in England and Wales: Towards a Unified Prosecution System?' *Criminal Law Review* 896.

Carozza, PG (1998) 'Uses and Misuses of Comparative Law in International Human Rights: Some Reflections on the Jurisprudence of the European Court of Human Rights' 73 *Notre Dame Law Review* 1217.

Cassese, A (2003) *International Criminal Law* (Oxford, Oxford University Press).

—— (2004) 'The Role of Internationalized Court and Tribunals in the Fight Against International Criminality' in CPR Romano, A Nollkaemper and JK Kleffner, (eds), *Internationalized Criminal Courts: Sierra Leone, East Timor, Kosovo and Cambodia* (Oxford, Oxford University Press).

Cassese, A, Gaeta, P and Jones, JRWD (eds) (2002) *The Rome Statute of the International Criminal Court: A Commentary* (Oxford, Oxford University Press).

Christiansen, T (2005) 'European Integration and Regional Cooperation' in J Baylis and S Smith (eds), *The Globalization of World Politics,* 3rd edn (Oxford, Oxford University Press).

Clark, DS (2001) 'Nothing New in 2000? Comparative Law in 1900 and Today' 75 *Tulane Law Review* 871.

Clark, RS (1997) 'Nuremberg and Tokyo in Contemporary Perspective' in TLH McCormack and GJ Simpson (eds), *The Law of War Crimes: National and International Approaches* (The Hague, Kluwer Law International).

Cryer, R (2001) 'A "Special Court" for Sierra Leone?' 50 *International and Comparative Law Quarterly* 435.

Dallaire, R (2004) *Shake Hands with the Devil: The Failure of Humanity in Rwanda* (London, Arrow Books).

Day, LE and Vandiver, M (2000) 'Criminology and Genocide Studies: Notes on What Might Have Been and What Still Could Be' 34 *Crime, Law and Social Change* 43.

Delmas-Marty, M (2003) 'The Contribution of Comparative Law to a Pluralist Conception of International Criminal Law' 1 *Journal of International Criminal Justice* 13.

Delmas-Marty, M, and Vervaele, JAE (eds) (2000), *The Implementation of the Corpus Juris in the Member States* (Utrecht, Intersentia).

Dietz, JS (2004) 'Protecting the Protectors: Can the United States Successfully Exempt US Persons from the International Criminal Court with US Article 98 Agreements?' 27 *Houston Journal of International Law* 137.

Dixon, D (1997) *Law in Policing: Legal Regulation and Police Practices* (Oxford, Oxford University Press).

Douglas, L (2001) *The Memory of Judgment: Making Law and History in the Trials of the Holocaust* (New Haven, Yale University Press).

Drumbl, MA (2000a) 'Sclerosis: Retributive Justice and the Rwandan Genocide' 2 *Punishment & Society* 287.

—— (2000b) 'Punishment, Postgenocide: From Guilt to Shame to *Civis* in Rwanda' 75 *New York University Law Review* 1221.

—— (2003) 'Toward a Criminology of International Crime' 19 *Ohio State Journal on Dispute Resolution* 263.

Duff, P (2004) 'Changing Conceptions of the Scottish Criminal Trial: The Duty to Agree Uncontroversial Evidence' in A Duff, L Farmer, S Marshall and V Tadros (eds), *The Trial on Trial Volume One: Truth and Due Process* (Oxford, Hart Publishing).

Dunne, T and Schmidt BC (2005) 'Realism' in J Baylis and S Smith (eds) *The Globalization of World Politics,* 3rd edn (Oxford, Oxford University Press).

Eckhardt, WG (1996) 'Nuremberg—Fifty Years: Accountability and Responsibility' 63 *University of Missouri-Kansas City* Law Review 1.

Ewald, W (1995) 'Comparative Jurisprudence (I): What Was it Like to Try a Rat?' 143 *University of Pennsylvania Law Review* 1898.

Falk, R (1999) 'Telford Taylor and the Legacy of Nuremberg' 37 *Columbia Journal of Transnational Law* 693.

Finnis, J (1980) *Natural Law and Natural Rights* (Oxford, Oxford University Press).

Frankenberg, G (1985) 'Critical Comparisons: Re-thinking Comparative Law' 26 *Harvard International Law Journal* 411.

Fraser, D (2005) *Law After Auschwitz: Towards a Jurisprudence of the Holocaust* (Durham, NC, Carolina Academic Press).

Friedrichs, D (2000) 'The Crime of the Century? The Case for the Holocaust' 34 *Crime, Law and Social Change* 21.

Garland, D (2001) *The Culture of Control: Crime and Social Order in Contemporary Society* (Oxford, Oxford University Press).

Glenn, HP (2004) *Legal Traditions of the World*, 2nd edn (Oxford, Oxford University Press).

Godfrey, B, Emsley, C and Dunstall, G (eds) (2003) *Comparative Histories of Crime* (Cullompton, Devon, Willan).

Goldstone, RJ (2000) *For Humanity: Reflections of a War Crimes Investigator* (New Haven, Yale University Press).

Hart, HLA (1968) *Punishment and Responsibility: Essays in the Philosophy of Law* (Oxford, Oxford University Press).

Hawkins, K (2002) *Law as Last Resort: Prosecution Decision-Making in a Regulatory Agency* (Oxford, Oxford University Press).

Hirsch, D (2001) 'The Trial of Andrei Sawoniuk: Holocaust Testimony under Cross-Examination' 10 *Social and Legal Studies* 529.

Huntington, SP (1996) *The Clash of Civilizations and the Remaking of World Order* (London, Free Press).

Jackson, JD (2005) 'The Effect of Human Rights on Criminal Evidentiary Processes: Towards Convergence, Divergence or Realignment?' 68 *Modern Law Review* 737.

Johnson, SW and Hinderaker, JH (2002) 'Guidelines for Cross-Examination: Lessons from the Cross-Examination of Hermann Goering' 59(Oct) *Bench and Bar of Minnesota* 22.

Kant, I (1970 [1795]) 'Perpetual Peace—A Philosophical Sketch' in *Kant: Political Writings*. H Reiss (ed), (trans) HB Nisbet (Cambridge, Cambridge University Press).

King, HT Jr (1998) 'The Meaning of Nuremberg' 30 *Case Western Reserve Journal of International Law* 143.

Kuhl, L (1998) 'The Criminal Law Protection of the Communities' Financial Interests Against Fraud—Parts I & II' *Criminal Law Review* 259 and 323.

Lacey, N (1994) 'Introduction: Making Sense of Criminal Justice' in N Lacey (ed), *A Reader on Criminal Justice* (Oxford, Oxford University Press).

Lazarus, L (2004) *Contrasting Prisoners' Rights: A Comparative Examination of Germany and England* (Oxford, Oxford University Press).

Legrand, P (1996) 'How to Compare Now' 16 *Legal Studies* 232.

Marschik, A (1997) 'The Politics of Prosecution: European National Approaches to War Crimes' in TLH McCormack and GJ Simpson (eds), *The Law of War Crimes: National and International Approaches* (The Hague, Kluwer Law International).

May, R and Wierda, M (1999) 'Trends in International Criminal Evidence: Nuremberg, Tokyo, The Hague and Arusha' 37 *Columbia Journal of Transnational Law* 725.

McConville, M, Sanders, A and Leng, R (1991) *The Case for the Prosecution: Police Suspects and the Construction of Criminality* (London, Routledge).

Merryman, JH (1988) 'How Others Do It: the French and German Judiciaries' 61 *Southern California Law Review* 1865.

Morrison, W (2006) *Criminology, Civilisation and the New World Order* (Abingdon, Routledge-Cavendish).

Murphy, SD (2001) 'Verdict in the Trial of the Lockerbie Bombing Suspects' 95 *American Journal of International Law* 405.

Nelken, D (ed) (2000) *Contrasting Criminal Justice: Getting From Here to There* (Aldershot, Ashgate).

Nijboer, JF (1993) 'Common Law Tradition in Evidence Scholarship Observed from a Continental Perspective' 41 *American Journal of Comparative Law* 299.

Peers, S (2000) *EU Justice and Home Affairs Law* (Harlow, Essex, Longman).

Persico, JE (1994) *Nuremberg: Infamy on Trial* (Harmondsworth, Penguin).

Plato (2000 [c.4th BC]) *The Republic* GRF Ferrari (ed), (trans) T Griffith (Cambridge, Cambridge University Press).

Rawls, J (1996) *Political Liberalism* (New York, Columbia University Press).

Reichberg, GM, Syse, H and Begby, E (eds) (2006) *The Ethics of War* (Oxford, Blackwell).

Roberts, P (2006) 'Theorising Procedural Tradition: Subjects, Objects and Values in Criminal Adjudication' in A Duff, L Farmer, S Marshall and V Tadros (eds), *The Trial on Trial Volume Two: Judgment and Calling to Account* (Oxford, Hart Publishing).

Roberts, P and McMillan, N (2003) 'For Criminology in International Criminal Justice' 1 *Journal of International Criminal Justice* 315.

Roberts, P and Zuckerman, A (2004) *Criminal Evidence* (Oxford, Oxford University Press).

Romano, CPR, Nollkaemper, A and Kleffner JK (eds) (2004) *Internationalized Criminal Courts: Sierra Leone, East Timor, Kosovo and Cambodia* (Oxford, Oxford University Press).

Ruggiero, V (2005) 'Criminalizing War: Criminology as Ceasefire' 14 *Social and Legal Studies* 239.

Rutherford, A (1996) *Transforming Criminal Policy: Spheres of Influence in the United States, the Netherlands and England and Wales During the 1980s* (Winchester, Waterside Press).

Safferling, CJM (2001) *Towards an International Criminal Procedure* (Oxford, Oxford University Press).

Schwarzenberger, G (1950) 'The Problem of an International Criminal Law' *Current Legal Problems* 263.

Sheptycki, J and Wardak, A (eds) (2005) *Transnational and Comparative Criminology* (London, Glasshouse).

Shute, S (2002) 'Knowledge and Belief in the Criminal Law' in S Shute and AP Simester (eds), *Criminal Law Theory: Doctrines of the General Part* (Oxford, Oxford University Press).

Siegel, DM (2006) 'Training the Hybrid Lawyer and Implementing the Hybrid System: Two Tasks for Italian Legal Education' 33 *Syracuse Journal of International Law and Commerce* 445.

Simester, AP and Sullivan, GR (2003; revised 2004) *Criminal Law: Theory and Doctrine* (Oxford, Hart Publishing).

Sunga, LS (1997) *The Emerging System of International Criminal Law: Developments in Codification and Implementation* (The Hague, Kluwer).

Tallgren, I (2002) 'The Sensibility and Sense of International Criminal Law' 13 *European Journal of International Law* 561.

Taylor, T (1992) *The Anatomy of the Nuremberg Trials* (Boston, Little, Brown & Co.).

Twining, W (2000) *Globalization and Legal Theory* (London, Butterworths).

Van den Wyngaert, C (2001) *Penal and Administrative Sanctions, Settlement, Whistleblowing and Corpus Juris in the Candidate Countries* (Brussels, Academy of European Law).

Vogler, R (2005) *A World View of Criminal Justice* (Aldershot, Ashgate).

Washington, E (2003) 'The Nuremberg Trials: The Death of the Rule of Law (in International Law)' 49 *Loyola Law Review* 471.

Webber, F (1999) 'The Pinochet Case: The Struggle for the Realization of Human Rights' 26 *Journal of Law and Society* 523.

Wedgwood, R (2001) 'The Irresolution of Rome' 64 *Law and Contemporary Problems* 193.

Weigend, T (2003) 'Is the Criminal Process about Truth? A German Perspective' 26 *Harvard Journal of Law and Public Policy* 157.

Weissbrodt, D and Bergquist, A (2006) 'Extraordinary Rendition: A Human Rights Analysis' 19 *Harvard Human Rights Journal* 123.

Whitman, JQ (2003) *Harsh Justice: Criminal Punishment and the Widening Divide between America and Europe* (New York, Oxford University Press).

Wigmore, JH (1974) *A Treatise on the Anglo-American System of Evidence in Trials at Common Law*, 3rd edn (1940) revised JH Chadbourn (Boston, Little, Brown & Co.).

Zedner, L (2002) 'Dangers of Dystopias in Penal Theory' 22 *Oxford Journal of Legal Studies* 341.

Zweigert, K, and Kötz, H (1998) *An Introduction to Comparative Law*, 3rd edn (trans) T Weir (Oxford, Oxford University Press).

16

Judicial Comparativism and Human Rights

CHRISTOPHER MCCRUDDEN[*]

KEY CONCEPTS

Human rights; Constitutional rights; Natural law; Positivism; Pluralism; Dialogic method; Functionalism; Judicial review; Counter-majoritarian difficulty; Judicial comparativism.

I. INTRODUCTION AND SUMMARY OF ARGUMENTS

DEBATES CONCERNING THE appropriate relationship between human rights interpretation and comparative legal methods have increased significantly in the past decade, and are by no means exhausted. This has occurred in part because of the increased citation by judges of 'foreign' legal materials, in particular judicial opinions, from jurisdictions that have no legal authority in the 'receiving' jurisdiction. Courts are playing an impressive role in the creation of what some see as a 'common law of human rights' or, in the context of Europe, 'a *ius commune* of human rights'. How human rights interpretation develops by making extensive use of comparative law is an intriguing example of the utilisation of comparative law by courts. Debates about the appropriateness of this have proven useful in illuminating aspects of both comparative law and human rights interpretation.

There are several aspects of this development that mark it out from some earlier debates about the role of comparative methods in law. First, the issues in this chapter involve issues of high political controversy, particularly at a time when human rights issues are of considerable salience for political debates, such as how to cope with changing sexual mores and dealing with terrorism. In the past, comparative legal methods were more often used to

[*] I am grateful to Rosalind Dixon, Veronika Fikfak, and Brian Flanagan for their comments on this chapter.

deal with essentially private and commercial law issues; in the human rights context, the issues are public, often constitutional, law. Secondly, the debate about the appropriate use of the comparative method is often a reaction to judicially-driven use of comparisons, rather than academically-driven advocacy of comparisons. We thus see human rights theory and comparative law theory struggling to make sense of relatively fast-moving judicial practice, rather than such theories giving rise to legal practice.

This chapter begins by sketching out several of the key concepts that these debates have involved. There are three sets of concepts that arise in the debate: one set arising in discussions of how we analyse human rights, another in how we think about the role and function of the comparative method, and a third in how the continuing debate about the legitimacy of judicial decision-making in human rights is conducted. We then turn to consider in more detail the issues that have arisen in the use by judges of comparisons in human rights interpretation.

Human Rights Concepts

The very concept of 'human rights' is contested. Sometimes a distinction is drawn between '*human rights*' and '*constitutional rights*', with the former referring to those rights that are legally required because of international legal obligations arising from treaties or custom, and the latter referring to rights that arise from national texts, such as Constitutions. For some, this distinction is crucial. The latter may accord rights to a smaller group of people than the former, for example the latter may accord rights only to citizens, whereas the former are unlikely to be so confined. Or international law may supply a basic standard that constitutional rights improve upon.

Whether this distinction is important points to another aspect of 'human rights' that is important for the purposes of this chapter. We need to distinguish between theories supporting human rights—including the *general principles* included in human rights—and their *application* in specific situations. There is much apparent agreement on the general principles of human and constitutional rights (such as the need to protect people from torture, or discrimination). Most charters of rights, whether national or international, contain much the same list of rights. Does this suggest agreement also on theories supporting human rights? Not necessarily. There is little agreement on *why* individuals should be protected in these ways. (Several conflicting general theories are often put forward: Because to treat people in this way is contrary to their 'dignity' or their 'autonomy'. Or because everyone is made in the image of God.) This lack of agreement on what theory or theories support human rights has some important implications, particularly because the way in which particular human rights are phrased in legal texts is often extremely general and thus subject to considerable interpretation when it comes to applying them in practice. What, exactly, do we mean by 'torture'? When, exactly, is 'discrimination' invidious?

There are several issues that arise from this need for interpretation of the general principles. One debate that arises is whether these various national and international texts, containing apparently common human rights principles, state a universal standard that is true across time and space. The universality of human rights is often thought to be central to conceptions of human rights. As Vicki Jackson has argued, referring to the United States,

> [m]any of our constitutional rights and values—liberty, equal protection of the law, due process, freedom of expression—reflect not only specific decisions made in the United States, but also widely shared commitments of many Western democracies (Jackson, 2004a; see also Jackson, 2004b).

Yet such claims have proven deeply controversial, with some arguing that the inclusion of common principles in these texts camouflages profound disagreement on their application as well the theory supporting them. Lord Hoffmann, for example, has stated:

> [O]f course we share a common humanity ... Nevertheless ... the specific answers, the degree to which weight is given to one desirable objective rather than another, will be culturally determined. Different communities will, through their legislature and judges, adopt the answers which they think suit them. (Hoffman, 1999: 159).

All that is left is an empty shell of principle and when the principle comes to be applied, the appearance of commonality disappears, and human rights are exposed as culturally relative, deeply contingent on local politics and values.

Despite claims to the contrary, the debate between *universalism* and *cultural relativism* refuses to go away, and it has considerable implications for the exercise of judicial comparativism. For those who support universalism, use of comparisons appears obvious—after all, it is the same principle that is being applied. For those who support cultural relativism, use of comparisons is pointless except to expose these differences—after all, it is a different principle that is being applied. The growth of regional legal systems complicates this debate somewhat, as one of their attractive aspects is that states that appear to share more common cultural and ethical roots can come together to establish human rights regimes that go beyond the state, but stop short of the global. This gives rise to the question as to whether *regionally shared conceptions of human rights* are emerging, for example, a European *ius commune*.

The debate between universalism and cultural relativism is related to, but different from, another debate that arises in the human rights context that is relevant to the use of comparisons. This is the issue of whether the obligations that human rights impose depend on the state for their existence or exist irrespective of state recognition. The issue is one of profound significance. Does an individual, who lives in a state that does not recognise human rights internationally or implement them in national law, still have such rights? Another way of putting the issue is in terms of the larger debate between *natural law* and *positivism*. This is, of course, an immensely complex jurisprudential debate, and any brief summary will fail to deal adequately with its complexity. Put briefly, however, we can pose the issue as follows: Are human rights *legal* rights because they are incorporated into positive law, or are they legal rights irrespective of whether they have been incorporated into any particular legal system, because they are already included in what we consider foundational to any legal system?

Leaving these debates aside for the moment, we can identify another issue that arises. A principled interpretation of these grand principles often seems to call for agreement on why we are against torture, or discrimination, but this type of theoretical agreement is often absent. Judges deciding these cases are, therefore, faced with a difficulty. Yet they do, of course, make decisions on the basis of specific facts. Cass Sunstein has described the process of deciding cases on their facts without necessarily agreeing on any particular theory supporting the decision as giving rise to 'incompletely theorised' agreements. Such agreements exist where individuals can agree on a specific result, even if they do not agree on the specific theory justifying that result (Sunstein, 1996). Some judges use comparative reasoning as part of the process of attempting to generate reasons justifying a particular result. Comparativism thus becomes a part of the process of reaching a more fully theorised (although still incomplete) agreement.

Concepts in Comparative Law Methodology

These key issues and concepts in human rights have some similarities with debates in comparative law. Thus, for example, there is a debate in comparative law theory between *univeralism* and *pluralism*. In the former camp are those who see the function of comparative law as being to explore what is common between legal jurisdictions; even sometimes going so far as to view comparative law as the basis for identifying the 'best' approach with the ultimate aim of securing its universal adoption. In the pluralist camp are those who see the function of the comparative method as being the identification of what is different between jurisdictions, stressing the need for an understanding of local context and emphasising the truth that even when similar concepts are being used across jurisdictions, they may not necessarily play the same role in each. These debates in comparative law echo the debates in human rights between universalism and cultural relativism. The more 'political' and 'constitutional' the issue, the more comparative lawyers tended to move to the cultural relativist end of the spectrum.

In addition, however, there is a somewhat more recent debate within comparative law scholarship that is of considerable importance to our understanding of judicial comparativism in human rights interpretation. This is the debate between *functionalism* and the *dialogic method*. Ruti Teitel has helpfully described functionalism in comparative law scholarship as an approach that

> treats comparative law as a technique of problem solving. The subject of comparative analysis is the legal problem, excised from its context (Teitel, 2004: 2570 at 2574).

She goes on to characterise functionalism as considering 'the relevant unit of analysis' not as 'a geographic entity, such as a country or region, but ... rather the problem and its legal solution' (*ibid*). She identifies Rudolph von Jhering as clearly representing this functionalist approach when he wrote:

> The reception of foreign legal institutions is not a matter of nationality, but of usefulness and need. No one bothers to fetch a thing from afar when he has one as good or better at home, but only a fool would refuse quinine just because it didn't grow in his back garden (von Jhering, quoted in Zweigert and Kötz, 1998: 17).

Functionalism was the dominant approach to comparative law scholarship during the second half of the twentieth century and still retains an important influence in comparative law circles. It has been challenged in recent years, if not before, by those who see functionalism as too divorced from context. One response to this has been the development of a pluralist critique of functionalism, often from a critical perspective.

Another response, however, has been to attempt to develop an approach that is an alternative to both functionalism and pluralism. Teitel, among others,[1] contrasts a functionalist approach with a 'dialogic' method, which she sees as both more recent and responding to 'the present context of a globalizing politics' (Teitel, 2004: 2570 at 2584). This theorises the comparative method 'as a dynamic interpretive and discursive practice' (*ibid*: at 2584–5). In the context of comparative constitutionalism in particular,

> the dialogical approach focuses on the processes of constitutional interpretation ... Comparative exchange is not bound in path-dependent or hierarchic ways. Rather, it poses a comity-based 'transjudicial' enterprise—a decentered view of constitutional practices deriving from pluralist sources, with the possibility of 'cross fertilization' (*ibid*: at 2586).

Controversies Concerning 'Judicial Review'

There is a third set of concepts that tend to arise in discussion of the phenomenon of judicial comparativism in human rights adjudication; those that are used in continuing debates concerning the legitimacy of '*judicial review*'. Since the Second World War, courts have increasingly been given (or taken on) a role in interpreting and applying constitutional rights, sometimes in specially created constitutional courts, sometimes in courts of general jurisdiction, and sometimes in administrative courts. Such adjudication usually involves the judiciary being

---

[1] Choudry, 1999: 819 at 838–9, contrasting dialogical comparison with universalistic and genealogical modes of comparison; Choudry, 2004: 50–52, contrasting dialogical with universalist and functionalist modes of comparison; L'Heureux-Dubé, 1998: 17, contrasting dialogical influence with 'reception' of foreign law; Slaughter, 2003, describing dialogical modes of transnational influence. I am grateful to Rosalind Dixon for these references; see further Dixon, to be published 2007.

asked to adjudicate on disputes that involve an allegation of a breach of a claimed right by the actions of a public body such as a Department of government, or by the legislature itself. This jurisdiction is frequently called 'judicial review' of administrative acts or of legislation. It is controversial because it runs the risk of creating tension with other constitutional principles, such as the separation of powers. Where judicial review involves judges striking down legislation on the ground that it breaches constitutional rights, it is particularly controversial because it also involves a body of unelected judges calling into question the decision of a democratically elected body, leading to the so-called '*counter-majoritarian difficulty*'. This has led to a continuing debate about the legitimacy of judicial review, particularly of this strong type, and how far it is compatible with notions of *democratic self-government*. Part of that debate involves close scrutiny of what *sources* judges derive their conclusions from.

II. RELATIONSHIP BETWEEN COMPARATIVE LAW AND HUMAN RIGHTS GENERALLY

Depending on which approaches are taken to human rights, and which comparative method is used, tensions may arise between comparative theorists and human rights practitioners. An emphasis on differences, in part to underscore diversity, gives rise to tensions with those human rights lawyers with universalist aspirations for human rights.

Human rights practice is often driven by a strong moral or ethical dimension, and consequently a further potential for considerable tension between the two disciplines arises. For the human rights advocate the role of comparison is that of *persuasion* to an essentially moral position. Lawyers in the human rights context often use comparison to legitimate their argument that a particular interpretation of an existing human rights norm should be adopted, or as part of the process of generating further norms. The use of comparison as part of the process of persuasion not infrequently gives rise to highly selective, often rather simplistic comparative arguments. For some modern comparatists, this must be intensely frustrating, as they attempt to generate increasingly sophisticated methodologies of comparison. Not only is the methodology of what might be called 'persuasive comparativism' apparently weak (cherry picking, weak evidence, overly formalistic assessment of what the law is), but several of these functions of comparison tend towards the older, universalist tendencies of comparative law scholarship that are now viewed critically by many modern comparative law scholars.

Judicial Comparativism: Contrasts between Jurisdictions

We turn now to consider the more particular issue of the use of comparative methods by *judges* in human rights interpretation. The first point to note is that judicial comparativism in human rights adjudication is immensely variable

between jurisdictions, not least in so far as the citation of cases from other jurisdictions is concerned. (It is likely that some jurisdictions that do not cite foreign
judgments nevertheless refer to them in private research.) Thus, for example,
there is a significant difference between the use of judicial comparativism in the
United Kingdom (relatively high) and France (very low), and between the United
States (relatively low) and South Africa (high). Secondly, the use of such material
differs within jurisdictions across time, so we see a relative increase in the use of
such material in recent years in several jurisdictions. (We might also see in the
future a decline in the use of such material, for example in South Africa, depending on why such material is being used there, of course.) Thirdly, even in those
jurisdictions in which the use of comparative material by judges is noticeable,
such use is often greater with regard to some types of human rights claims, and
less frequent with regard to other types of human rights claims. So, for example,
in the United States, judicial comparativism has been particularly prominent in
judging the constitutionality of the death penalty, but relatively little used in the
context of equal protection claims.

There is some controversy about what determines the degree of use of comparative material by judges in human rights adjudication, and little consensus. Few
jurisdictions have explored systematically the use of such material in their own
jurisdiction, and little empirical work has been completed that attempts to explain
the differences between jurisdictions or within jurisdictions in this respect. Nor
has sustained empirical work been conducted that would explain why the use
of such material is more politically and jurisprudentially controversial in some
jurisdictions and not others.

Judicial Comparativism and Human Rights Interpretation: Some Further Distinctions

In those jurisdictions that do explicitly engage with 'foreign' legal material, we
need to distinguish between different uses of such material, since only some of
these uses are controversial. Judges use 'foreign' judicial decisions to determine
the meaning of binding international law in their jurisdiction. Judges use 'foreign'
judicial decisions to determine the meaning of terms in contracts that are to be
interpreted according to the law of that other jurisdiction. Judges use 'foreign'
judicial material to determine the law of other jurisdictions in conflicts of law
disputes. None of these uses of foreign material is particularly controversial in
theory.

Judges also use decisions of courts outside their jurisdiction when there is some
relationship of authority between the two. So, for example, United Kingdom
courts constantly refer to decisions of the European Court of Justice in interpreting provisions of domestic law that implement European Community law. Even
prior to the Human Rights Act 1998, which now requires judges to have regard
to decisions of the European Court of Human Rights, English judges had regard

to decisions of the European Court of Human Rights in deciding what rights to accord under English law, in part because they knew that disappointed applicants could apply to have their complaints adjudicated under the European Convention on Human Rights, which the United Kingdom had ratified. Judges also frequently have regard to decisions of courts that they regard as sharing aspects of a common legal system, even where there is no issue of hierarchical authority in issue between them. So, courts in common law countries frequently have regard to decisions of 'foreign' courts in the interpretation of tort and contract. Again, none of these uses of foreign material is particularly controversial.

We are not primarily concerned with these uses of foreign material. Most controversy has arisen where other uses of 'foreign' material are involved, and it is with these that we shall be primarily concerned. But not even all these uses are controversial. There are four uses of this type that are frequently not sufficiently distinguished. The first is where a court in jurisdiction 'X' quotes from a court in jurisdiction 'Y' a particular phrase or way of describing an issue that appears to the judge particularly apposite or elegant. Some judges in some jurisdictions have had a way with words that is deemed by other judges to be particularly worth quoting. This can be termed the 'rhetorical' use of 'foreign' material and is akin to using quotations from Shakespeare or the Bible. The second is where a court in jurisdiction 'X' cites 'foreign' material such as a judicial decision in jurisdiction 'Y' as part of the evidence to support an empirical conclusion that a particular approach is or is not workable in practice, or has particular unintended effects.[2] The fact that it is a judicial opinion that is part of the evidence is, essentially, neither here nor there; it is merely a convenient source of the empirical information.

For Judge Posner, however, the problem with using 'foreign' judicial opinions arises in a somewhat different class of case. He writes:

> Problems arise only when the foreign decision is believed to have some (even if quite attenuated) persuasive force in an American court merely by virtue of being the decision of a recognised legal tribunal. This occurs, in short, when it is treated as an *authority*, albeit not a controlling one ... even though the issue is purely local, such as whether abortion should be forbidden, or the execution of retarded murderers forbidden, or gay marriage allowed. (Posner, 2004)

It is for this reason that the third and fourth uses are the most controversial. Both involve the use of a judicial decision in jurisdiction 'Y', or some other legal norm, that is not legally binding in jurisdiction 'X' (such as an unratified human rights convention), as part of a judicial decision regarding what is the legal position in jurisdiction 'X'. In both, the 'foreign' material is part of a normative argument, in a judicial context that is, in any event, often controversial. But there are significant differences within that general category. One use (our third approach) involves the citation of a 'foreign' material as establishing a reason (however attenuated)

---

[2] Compare the use of foreign material in *Washington v Glucksberg*, 521 US 702 at 730, 734 (1997) (Rehnquist, CJ).

why a human rights claim against a governmental entity should *not* succeed. Another (our fourth approach), and probably the most controversial, involves the use of 'foreign' material in a similar context where it establishes a reason (however attenuated) why a rights claim *should succeed.*

There are two critical aspects to the description of the problematic uses of foreign material in the previous paragraph. The first relates to the inclusion of non-binding international legal material as well as 'foreign' material such as a judgment of a foreign court. The important distinction that is drawn is between international law that is binding in the jurisdiction concerned, and international norms that are not binding in the jurisdiction concerned. Sometimes this distinction is not sufficiently recognised in discussions of the use of judicial comparativism, and the use of *all* international norms, whether binding in the jurisdiction or not, are treated as raising the same issues. This is unhelpful. Legally, there is a clear difference between the use of international legal material by the House of Lords in the *A* case,[3] and the use of legal material by the plurality of the United States Supreme Court in *Roper v Simmons*.[4] In the former case, the Lords disallowed the use of foreign torture evidence in administrative proceedings. The international material was used to establish what international law was binding on the United Kingdom, in order to ensure that the common law was interpreted in conformity with the United Kingdom's international commitments. In the latter, as we shall see subsequently, the plurality of the United States Supreme Court used international legal norms, which it explicitly accepted as *non*-binding, as part of a discussion about the current meaning of the Eighth Amendment.

The second point worth noting is that the distinction between the third and fourth types of judicial comparativism has attracted judicial attention. Scalia, J, dissenting in *Roper* draws attention to the distinction:

> Foreign sources are cited today, *not* to underscore our 'fidelity' to the Constitution, our 'pride in its origins', and 'our own [American] heritage'. To the contrary, they are cited *to set aside* the centuries-old American practice'.[5]

The two types are worth separating, as Mary Anne Glendon has argued, because there is a

> crucial difference between the legitimate use of foreign material as mere empirical evidence that legislation has a rational basis, and its use to buttress the court's own decision to override legislation (Glendon, 2005).

She views the distinction as important because of the unhealthy effects of 'judicial adventurism'. Where foreign material is used to uphold the democratic decision, those who believe the legislature got it wrong 'can work to change the law through the ordinary democratic processes of persuasion and voting'(*ibid*). But where

---

[3] *A (FC) v Secretary of State for the Home Department* [2005] UKHL 71, especially [27], [30], [33]–[35] (Lord Bingham).
[4] *Roper v Simmons* 125 S Ct 1183 (2005).
[5] *Ibid*, at 1229 (Scalia, J).

constitutions are difficult to amend, the effect of a court upholding a rights claim against the democratic decision-maker is dramatic:

> [T]he court's constitutional mistakes are exceedingly hard to correct. The unhealthy ripple effects of judicial adventurism are many: Legislatures are encouraged to punt controversial issues into the courts; political energy, lacking more constructive outlets, flows into litigation and the judicial selection process (*ibid*).

All this should lead courts to be more hesitant in using 'foreign' material to strike down legislation than to uphold it.

III. EXAMPLES OF JUDICIAL COMPARATIVISM IN HUMAN RIGHTS INTERPRETATION

There is now an extensive academic literature analysing the use of judicial comparativism in several jurisdictions, and no attempt will be made here to try to give a comprehensive survey. Instead, four examples drawn from recent decisions of the United States Supreme Court will be used to illustrate several of the points made above. These recent examples are particularly interesting because they provide, in a specific interpretative context, an extensive exploration by the judges of what judicial comparativism involves, and its potential problems, in a way that few other jurisdictions have yet engaged in. Three of the cases involve the constitutionality of aspects of the death penalty (the acceptability of delays in carrying out the sentence, the use of capital punishment against juveniles, and its use against the 'mentally retarded'). The fourth involves perhaps the most controversial recent example of judicial comparativism; its use in a case striking down the criminalisation of sodomy between consenting adults.

In *Knight v Florida*,[6] the court refused to stop an execution, rejecting an argument that delays in carrying out the sentence should be held to render the execution contrary to the Eighth Amendment's prohibition on cruel and unusual punishment. Breyer, J dissented, drawing on judicial decisions from foreign jurisdictions, which were extensively considered. The structure of his argument is of importance. First, he stressed that he was only concerned with 'courts that accept or assume the lawfulness of the death penalty',[7] thereby excluding courts in countries where the death penalty is not carried out. Taking this as the relevant set of comparators, he found that 'a growing number' of these courts 'have held that lengthy delay in administering a *lawful* death penalty renders ultimate execution inhuman, degrading, or unusually cruel'.[8] The Judicial Committee of the Privy Council's cases dealing with Jamaica were cited, as were decisions of the Supreme Court of India, the Supreme Court of Zimbabwe, and the European Court of

---

[6] *Knight v Florida* 120 S Ct 459 (1999).
[7] *Ibid*, at 462 (Breyer, J).
[8] *Ibid*. [TS close gap]

Human Rights in *Soering v United Kingdom*,[9] in which the court interpreted the European Convention on Human Rights as prohibiting the United Kingdom from extraditing a potential defendant to the Commonwealth of Virginia, in part because the delay that typically accompanied a death sentence there amounted to 'cruel, inhuman, [or] degrading treatment or punishment'[10] forbidden by the Convention. Secondly, Breyer, J acknowledged that '[n]ot all foreign authority reaches the same conclusion',[11] citing opinions from the Supreme Court of Canada and the United Nations Human Rights Committee that tended to go against the proposition he was supporting. Thirdly, the interpretation he advanced was not based on any supposed United States obligation in international law. Indeed, he noted how, after *Soering*, the United States Senate had insisted on reservations to various other human rights treaties to ensure that language similar to that of the European Convention on Human Rights did not

> restrict or prohibit the United States from applying the death penalty consistent with the … Constitution, including any constitutional period of confinement prior to the imposition of the death penalty.[12]

Fourthly, Breyer, J recognised that '*[o]bviously*, this foreign authority does not bind us'.[13] Quoting Scalia, J in an earlier case, he said '[a]fter all, we are interpreting a "Constitution for the United States of America"'.[14] In the context of this domestic constitutional interpretation, however,

> [T]his Court has long considered as relevant and informative the way in which foreign courts have applied standards roughly comparable to our own constitutional standards in roughly comparable circumstances. In doing so, the Court has found particularly instructive opinions of former Commonwealth nations insofar as those opinions reflect a legal tradition that also underlies our own Eighth Amendment.[15]

This, presumably, explains the choice of jurisdictions cited. In conclusion, then, Breyer, J's position justifying this exercise of judicial comparativism was that

> the foreign courts I have mentioned have considered roughly comparable questions under roughly comparable legal standards. Each court has held or assumed that those standards permit application of the death penalty itself. Consequently, I believe their views are useful even though not binding.[16]

---

[9] *Soering v United Kingdom*—(1989) 11 EHRR 439.
[10] *Knight v Florida* 120 S Ct 459 at 463 (Breyer, J).
[11] *Ibid.*
[12] *Ibid.*
[13] *Ibid.*
[14] *Thompson v Oklahoma* 487 US 815, n4, 101 L Ed 2d 702, 108 S Ct 2687 (1988) (Scalia, J, dissenting).
[15] *Knight v Florida* 120 S Ct 459 at 463—4 (Breyer, J).
[16] *Ibid*, at 464.

In *Atkins v Virginia*,[17] the court decided that the imposition of the death penalty for crimes committed by 'mentally retarded offenders' was unconstitutional. Stevens, J's opinion for the court drew on 'foreign' material to help reach a conclusion that

> within the world community, the imposition of the death penalty for crimes committed by mentally retarded offenders is overwhelmingly disapproved.[18]

Along with other information, Stevens, J concluded that the degree of consistency of this trend together with evidence of what was occurring in legislatures in the United States

> lends further support to our conclusion that there is a consensus [against imposition of the death penalty in such cases] among those who have addressed the issue.[19]

There are several differences to the approach that Breyer, J took in *Knight v Florida*. First, the foreign material was displayed much less prominently in *Atkins v Virginia* (it was confined to a footnote); it was dealt with much less extensively (it referred only to an amicus curiae brief containing the information); and it was much less specific, referring to the 'world community', rather than particular countries. In common with Breyer, J in *Knight v Florida*, however, Stevens, J also stressed that 'these factors are by no means dispositive'.[20]

In the later case of *Roper v Simmons*,[21] the Supreme Court held that the imposition of the death penalty on offenders under 18 was unconstitutional under the Eighth Amendment. In his opinion for the court, Kennedy, J drew on 'foreign' material. As with Breyer, J in *Knight v Florida* and Stevens, J in *Atkins v Virginia*, he stressed that this material, apparently demonstrating

> that the United States is the only country in the world that continues to give official sanction to the juvenile death penalty,[22]

was used only to *support a* determination that such uses of capital punishment are unconstitutional under the United States Constitution, and that this information 'does not become controlling, for the task of interpreting the Eighth Amendment remains our responsibility'. He stressed, too, that such information has relatively frequently been used by the court 'as instructive for its interpretation of the Eighth Amendment's prohibition of "cruel and unusual punishments"'.

Unlike in previous cases, however, Kennedy, J then referred to the provisions of the United Nations Convention on the Rights of the Child.[23] As he pointed

---

[17] *Atkins v Virginia* 563 US 304 (2002).
[18] *Ibid*, at 316, n 21(Stevens, J).
[19] *Ibid*.
[20] *Ibid*.
[21] *Roper v Simmons* 125 S Ct 1183 (2005). [TS close space]
[22] *Ibid*, at 1198 (Kennedy, J).
[23] United Nations Convention on the Rights of the Child, 20 November, 1989, 1577 UNTS 3, 28 ILM 1448 (entered into force 2 September, 1990).

out, the Convention, 'contains an express prohibition on capital punishment for crimes committed by juveniles under 18'.[24] The Convention had been ratified by 'every country in the world ... save for the United States and Somalia'.[25] No ratifying country had entered a reservation to the provision prohibiting the execution of juvenile offenders. There were 'parallel prohibitions'[26] contained in other significant international covenants some of which the United States had ratified, but with reservations protecting the use of the death penalty for juveniles:

> [O]nly seven countries other than the United States have executed juvenile offenders since 1990: Iran, Pakistan, Saudi Arabia, Yemen, Nigeria, the Democratic Republic of Congo, and China. Since then each of these countries has either abolished capital punishment for juveniles or made public disavowal of the practice.[27]

He concluded, on the basis of this information, that

> it is fair to say that the United States now stands alone in a world that has turned its face against the juvenile death penalty.[28]

This use of human rights conventions to demonstrate an international consensus against the juvenile death penalty is particularly noteworthy, given that some had not been ratified by the United States (the Convention on the Rights of the Child), and others which had been ratified had US reservations on the specific issue before the court. Kennedy, J also paid particular attention to the United Kingdom, whose experience was 'instructive' and of

> particular relevance ... in light of the historic ties between our countries and in light of the Eighth Amendment's own origins,

which he noted had been 'modeled on a parallel provision' in the English Declaration of Rights of 1689.[29] Decades before it had abolished the death penalty entirely, 'it recognized the disproportionate nature of the juvenile death penalty; and it abolished that penalty as a separate matter'.[30]

No doubt anticipating an attack on his use of these sources, the relevant section of his opinion ended with his reflection on the question whether the use of 'foreign' material in some way undermined the independent role of the Court in interpreting the Constitution. He sought to dampen down concerns that it might. The 'overwhelming weight of international opinion' against the juvenile death penalty, 'while not controlling our outcome, does provide respected and significant confirmation for our own conclusions'.[31] The guarantees in the Constitution

---

[24] Art 37.
[25] *Roper v Simmons* 125 S Ct 1183 at 1199 (Kennedy, J).
[26] *Ibid.*
[27] *Ibid.*
[28] *Ibid.*
[29] Declaration of Rights, 1 W & M, ch 2, para 10, in 3 English Statutes at Large 441 (1770).
[30] *Roper v Simmons* 125 S Ct 1183 at 1199 (Kennedy, J).
[31] *Ibid*, at 1200.

are 'original to the American experience', 'central to the American experience', and 'essential to our present-day self-definition and national identity'.[32] It did not lessen

> our fidelity to the Constitution or our pride in its origins to acknowledge that the express affirmation of certain fundamental rights by other nations and peoples simply underscores the centrality of *those same rights* within our own heritage of freedom.[33]

As we shall see subsequently, there was a strong dissent in *Roper v Simmons* concerning the use of 'foreign' material, as well as the substantive finding of unconstitutionality. Although O'Connor, J also dissented on the issue of constitutionality, she made clear her general support for the use of 'foreign' material, although not the conclusions the majority drew from it. She disagreed with the contention, advanced by Scalia, J in dissent, that foreign and international law 'have no place in our Eighth Amendment jurisprudence'.[34] In some areas of constitutional interpretation, on the other hand, she agreed with Scalia, J that

> American law is distinctive in many respects, not least where the specific provisions of our Constitution and the history of its exposition so dictate,

mentioning 'distinctively American rules of law related to the Fourth Amendment and the Establishment Clause'.[35] Over the course of nearly half a century, the court had, she said, 'consistently referred to foreign and international law as relevant to its assessment of evolving standards of decency'.[36] Unlike the majority, however, she saw the use of comparative material in the interpretation of the Eighth Amendment as particularly appropriate, 'reflect[ing its] special character' which 'draws its meaning directly from the maturing values of civilized society'.[37] The United States'

> evolving understanding of human dignity certainly is neither wholly isolated from, nor inherently at odds with, the values prevailing in other countries. On the contrary, we should not be surprised to find congruence between domestic and international values, especially where the international community has reached clear agreement ... that a particular form of punishment is inconsistent with fundamental human rights.[38]

The results of such an inquiry into these international values—and here she agrees with the majority—'do not dictate the outcome of our Eighth Amendment inquiry', but where 'an international consensus of this nature' exists, this 'can serve to confirm the reasonableness of a consonant and genuine American consensus'.[39]

---

[32] *Ibid.*
[33] *Ibid* (emphasis added).
[34] *Roper v Simmons*, 125 S Ct 1183 at 1215 (O'Connor, J).
[35] *Ibid.*
[36] *Ibid.*
[37] *Ibid.*
[38] *Ibid*, at 1215–16.
[39] *Ibid*, at 1216.

That is not the only role that she seems to envisage an inquiry into international consensus playing, since she also considered whether the international consensus would 'confirm' other arguments of principle that the majority advances. She concluded, however, that while such uses of international consensus would be appropriate, they were unconvincing in this particular case:

> Because I do not believe that a genuine *national* consensus against the juvenile death penalty has yet developed, and because I do not believe the Court's moral proportionality argument justifies a categorical, age-based constitutional rule, I can assign no such *confirmatory* role to the international consensus described by the Court.[40]

Scalia, J in dissent asked, perhaps somewhat mischievously, 'Why would foreign law not be relevant' to *the moral proportionality* judgment?

> If foreign law is powerful enough to supplant the judgment of the American people, surely it is powerful enough to change a personal assessment of moral proportionality.[41]

The (probably) most controversial use of 'foreign' material by the United States Supreme Court arose in *Lawrence v Texas*,[42] in which the court held to be unconstitutional under the Due Process Clause a state law that criminalised sodomy between consenting adults. There were two main uses of foreign material in this case. The material was used, first, to rebut an historical argument advanced in the earlier *Bowers v Hardwick* case,[43] in which the Court had upheld similar laws. In *Bowers*, Chief Justice Burger (as he then was) had adopted the argument that the history of Western civilisation and Judeo-Christian moral and ethical standards was consistent with the use of such legal restrictions. However, Kennedy, J's opinion for the majority in *Lawrence v Texas* argued that the

> sweeping references ... to the history of Western civilization and to Judeo-Christian moral and ethical standards did not take account of other authorities pointing in an opposite direction.[44]

Two particular pieces of evidence pointing in that opposite direction were cited, the first being the report of the influential Wolfenden Committee in Britain, which recommended the repeal of laws punishing homosexual conduct in 1957.[45] The United Kingdom Parliament enacted the substance of those recommendations 10 years later (except with regard to Northern Ireland).[46] The second piece of evidence used to rebut Burger, CJ's historical argument was the jurisprudence of

---

[40] *Ibid.*

[41] *Ibid,* at 1228 (Scalia, J).

[42] *Lawrence v Texas,* 123 S Ct 2472 (2003).

[43] *Bowers v Hardwick,* 478 US 186, 92 L Ed 2d 140, 106 S Ct 2841 (1986).

[44] *Lawrence v Texas,* 123 S Ct 2472 at 2481 (Kennedy, J).

[45] The Wolfenden Report: Report of the Committee on Homosexual Offences and Prostitution (London, HMSO, 1957).

[46] Sexual Offences Act 1967.

the European Court of Human Rights. In *Dudgeon v United Kingdom*,[47] an adult male resident in Northern Ireland stated that he was a practising homosexual who desired to engage in consensual homosexual conduct. The laws of Northern Ireland forbade him that right. He alleged that he had been questioned, his home had been searched, and he feared criminal prosecution. The European Court of Human Rights held that the laws proscribing the conduct were invalid under the European Convention on Human Rights. Referring specifically to *Dudgeon*, Kennedy, J said:

> Of even more importance, almost five years before *Bowers* was decided the European Court of Human Rights considered a case with parallels to *Bowers* and to today's case ... Authoritative in all countries that are members of the Council of Europe (21 nations then, 45 nations now), the decision is at odds with the premise in *Bowers* that the claim put forward was insubstantial in our Western civilization.[48]

The second use of 'foreign' materials in *Lawrence v Texas* was even more controversial because it sought to ascribe to these materials an additional function. Kennedy, J clearly considered that the values that were relevant to interpreting the Due Process Clause in this case were values held in common with at least some other countries. To the extent that this was true, then, how other countries interpreted and applied those common values was relevant to the interpretation of the United States Constitution. In particular, it was relevant to ask whether the approach put forward in *Bowers* had gained acceptance among those holding these values in common. Citing two more named decisions of the European Court of Human Rights that were decided after *Bowers*,[49] Kennedy, J concluded:

> To the extent *Bowers* relied on values we share with a wider civilization, it should be noted that the reasoning and holding in *Bowers* have been rejected elsewhere. The European Court of Human Rights has followed not *Bowers* but its own decision in *Dudgeon* v. *United Kingdom*.[50]

Citing an amicus curiae brief submitted to the court in *Lawrence v Texas* by Mary Robinson, the then United Nations High Commissioner for Human Rights, he noted that

> [o]ther nations, too, have taken action consistent with an affirmation of the protected right of homosexual adults to engage in intimate, consensual conduct.[51]

What use would be made of this evidence? Effectively, the use made was to raise a serious question as to whether the interest put forward by the government in this case to support the continued criminalisation of sodomy was convincing

---

[47] *Dudgeon v United Kingdom* (1981) 4 EHRR 149.
[48] *Lawrence v Texas*, 123 S Ct 2472 at 2481 (Kennedy, J).
[49] *PG & JH v United Kingdom*, App No 44787/98, (2001) 56 ECtHR 546, 25 September, 2001); *Modinos v Cyprus*, (1993) 16 EHRR 485; *Norris v Ireland* (1991) 13 EHRR 186.
[50] *Lawrence v Texas*, 123 S Ct 2472 at 2483 (Kennedy, J).
[51] *Ibid.*

enough to warrant upholding these criminal restrictions, given the strength of the competing right.

> The right the petitioners seek in this case has been accepted as an integral part of human freedom in many other countries. There has been no showing that in this country the governmental interest in circumscribing personal choice is somehow more legitimate or urgent.[52]

IV. JUDICIAL AND POLITICAL CRITIQUES OF JUDICIAL COMPARATIVISM

There are several current arguments that have been used to support a conclusion that using foreign sources is problematic. First, such use is thought to alter the balance between constraint and discretion that judges exercise in constitutional rights interpretation. Judges in all jurisdictions are both empowered and constrained at the same time by a set of rules and accepted practices. The use of foreign legal material, it is said, alters that balance by giving more discretion to the judge than hitherto. John Roberts, currently the Chief Justice of the United States, said in his confirmation hearings before the United States Senate that,

> relying on foreign precedent doesn't confine judges. It doesn't limit their discretion the way relying on domestic precedent does. Domestic precedent can confine and shape the discretion of the judges. Foreign law, you can find anything you want. If you don't find it in the decisions of France or Italy, it's in the decisions of Somalia or Japan or Indonesia or wherever.[53]

The assumption is, of course, that increased judicial discretion in exercising judicial review is problematic, and this reflects, perhaps, a latent unease with judicial review as currently practised and a judgement that it should not be expanded.

A second argument also arises from general scepticism and unease with judicial review and the counter-majoritarian difficulty that it gives rise to. There has been persistent criticism from sceptics that judicial review in some jurisdictions is 'results driven', meaning that judges decide the result they want to achieve and draw up reasons to support that conclusion, rather than letting the legal reasoning dictate the result, which is assumed to be the way proper judges behave. Some have seen legitimising judicial recourse to foreign material as giving yet another way that judges will be able to support the political choices that judges anyway wish to make. Thomas, J concurring in *Knight v Florida*, and arguing against Breyer, J's references to foreign material on the effect of delays on the legitimacy of carrying out the death penalty, suggested that

> the only reason why this material was resorted to was there was no support in the American constitutional tradition or in this Court's precedent for the proposition that

---

[52] *Ibid.*
[53] Confirmation hearing for United States Supreme Court of John Roberts as Chief Justice, September 2005.

a defendant can avail himself of the panoply of appellate and collateral procedures and then complain when his execution is delayed.[54]

Had there been

any such support in our own jurisprudence, it would be unnecessary for proponents of the claim to rely on the European Court of Human Rights, the Supreme Court of Zimbabwe, the Supreme Court of India, or the Privy Council.[55]

Scalia, J dissenting in *Roper v Simmons* reiterated this view:

What these foreign sources 'affirm' rather than repudiate, is the Justices' own notion of how the world ought to be, and their diktat that it shall be so henceforth in America.[56]

Judge Posner has argued extra-judicially that

[j]udges are likely to cite foreign decisions for the same reason that they prefer quoting from a previous decision to stating a position anew: They are timid about speaking in their own voices lest they make legal justice seem too personal and discontinuous ... Citing foreign decisions is probably best understood as an effort, whether or not conscious, to further mystify the adjudicative process and disguise the political decisions that are the core, though not the entirety, of the Supreme Court's output (Posner, 2004).

This intuition is also reflected in the criticism of the way that judges choose which jurisdictions to have regard to as involving 'cherry-picking'. Justice Scalia's criticism of a court using foreign judicial opinions is of this type when he accuses it of simply 'looking over the heads of the crowd and picking out its friends'.[57] Dissenting in *Lawrence v Texas*, he pointedly remarked on how the court's discussion of 'these foreign views ... ignor[es], of course, the many countries that have *retained* criminal prohibitions on sodomy'.[58] A somewhat different aspect of the charge of cherry-picking relates to the substantive issues concerning which the court is willing to look at comparative material. Dissenting in *Roper v Simmons*, Scalia, J pointed to the court's willingness to invoke 'foreign' material in the death penalty context, but not in other areas such as abortion, or separation of church and state.

The Court should either profess its willingness to reconsider all these matters in light of the views of foreigners, or else it should cease putting forth foreigners' views as part of the *reasoned basis* of its decisions. To invoke alien law when it agrees with one's own thinking, and ignore it otherwise, is not reasoned decisionmaking, but sophistry.[59]

---

[54] *Knight v Florida*, 120 S Ct 459 at 460 (Thomas, J).
[55] *Ibid.*
[56] *Roper v Simmons*, 125 S Ct 1183 at 1229 (Scalia, J).
[57] *Roper v Simmons*, 125 S Ct 1183 at 1223 (Scalia, J, dissenting).
[58] *Lawrence v Texas*, 123 S Ct 2472 at 2495 (Scalia, J) (emphasis added).
[59] *Roper v Simmons*, 125 S Ct 1183 at 1228 (Scalia, J).

A third criticism arises more from scepticism about the idea of universal human rights generally than from scepticism about the use of judicial forums for interpreting them. This objection has several elements. The first is that any *apparent* agreement that exists at the international level camouflages massive variations in actual practice. So, for example, Scalia, J, dissenting in *Roper v Simmons*, criticised the majority as,

> quite willing to believe that every foreign nation—of whatever tyrannical political makeup and with however subservient or incompetent a court system—in fact *adheres* to a rule of no death penalty for offenders under 18.[60]

A second aspect of this general scepticism is somewhat more sophisticated. It is that the way in which particular practices operate in particular countries is so tied in with other practices, that attempting to transplant the one without the others is to engage in bad comparative law. For Judge Posner, a significant problem with using foreign opinions,

> is that they emerge from a complex socio-historico-politico-institutional background of which our judges, I respectfully suggest, are almost entirely ignorant (Posner, 2004).

This position is not far from viewing the rights protected in each nation as so context-specific, so culturally contingent as to render interpreting one's nations set of constitutional rights in light of another's fatuous. Not surprisingly, we find just such a view being expressed by Judge Posner. 'To cite foreign law as authority', he argues,

> is to flirt with the discredited (I had thought) idea of a universal natural law; or to suppose fantastically that the world's judges constitute a single, elite community of wisdom and conscience(Posner, 2004).

Scalia, J, dissenting, in *Atkins v Virginia*, refers to the 'practices of the "world community", *whose notions of justice are (thankfully) not always those of our people*'.[61]

The fourth criticism of the use of judicial comparativism relates to its effect in circumventing national democratic controls on the creation of law. Domestic judges in most jurisdictions are appointed by bodies that are legitimated by domestic legislation or by a domestic constitution, thus allowing for democratic input directly or indirectly into their appointment. For John Roberts, in his confirmation hearings, this raised a significant problem for the use of foreign judgments. 'If we're relying on a decision from a German judge about what our Constitution means', he said,

> no President accountable to the people appointed that judge and no Senate accountable to the people confirmed that judge. And yet he's playing a role in shaping the law that binds the people in this country. I think that's a concern that has to be addressed.[62]

---

[60] *Ibid*, at 1226.
[61] *Atkins v Virginia*, 563 US 304 at 348 (Scalia, J) (emphasis added).
[62] See above n 55.

A similar concern arises in the context of references to world opinion more generally, or Resolutions of the United Nations General Assembly, or human rights treaties that have not been ratified. Here the problem is similar, that the constitutional mechanism that requires a democratic mechanism before domestic law is created is circumvented by judicial fiat. Scalia, J criticised the plurality's use of foreign sources in *Roper v Simmons* as based on the premise 'that American law should conform to the laws of the rest of the world'.[63] He was particularly scathing about the reference to unratified conventions or conventions which, though ratified, had relevant United States reservations.

> Unless the Court has added to its arsenal the power to join and ratify treaties on behalf of the United States, I cannot see how this evidence favors, rather than refutes, its position. That the Senate and the President ... have declined to join and ratify treaties prohibiting execution of under-18 offenders can only suggest that *our country* has either not reached a national consensus on the question, or has reached a consensus contrary to what the Court announces.[64]

In *Atkins v Virginia*, Rehnquist, CJ regarded the 'uncritical acceptance' of foreign sources as 'anti-democratic'[65]:

> The Court's suggestion that these sources are relevant to the constitutional question ... in my view, is antithetical to considerations of federalism, which instruct that 'any permanent prohibition upon all units of democratic government must [be apparent] in the operative acts (laws and the application of laws) that the people have approved'.[66]

Scalia, J's criticism of the use of 'foreign' sources in *Atkins* also reflects this view when he argues that

> where there is not first a settled consensus among our own people, the views of other nations, however enlightened the Justices of this Court may think them to be cannot be imposed upon Americans through the Constitution.[67]

It is this concern that also appears to be a significant part of the motivation behind the (so far unsuccessful) proposal in the United States Congress to enact a Constitutional Restoration Act, providing that,

> [i]n interpreting and applying the Constitution of the United States, a court of the United States may not rely upon any constitution, law, administrative rule, Executive order, directive, policy, judicial decision, or any other action of any foreign state or international organization or agency, other than the constitutional law and English common law.[68]

---

[63] *Roper v Simmons*, 125 S Ct 1183 (Scalia, J, dissenting).

[64] *Ibid*, at 1226 (Scalia, J).

[65] *Atkins v Virginia*, 563 US 304 at 322 (Rehnquist, CJ dissenting).

[66] *Ibid*.

[67] *Atkins v Virginia* 563 US 304 at n 4 (Scalia, J).

[68] HR 3799, 108th Congress § 201 (2004). See also HR Res 568, 108th Congress (2004); HR Res 468, 108th Congress (2003); Constitutional Preservation Resolution, HR Res 446, 108th Congress (2003).

Finally, the critics of the use of such foreign material argue that the distinction that is made between judges using such 'foreign' material as helping to determine the case (which advocates of the use of foreign judgments say is not the case), and merely using such foreign material as relevant, and informative (which is how its use is often characterised, for example, by the majority in *Roper v Simmons*), is untenable. Scalia, J, dissenting in *Roper*, argued:

> The Court's parting attempt to downplay the significance of its extensive discussion of foreign law is unconvincing. 'Acknowledgment' of foreign approval has no place in the legal opinion of this Court *unless it is part of the basis for the Court's judgment* which is surely what it parades as today.[69]

In other words, supporters of the use of such material cannot have it both ways: either the material is determinative (which few would accept), or the material is irrelevant, in which case it should not be discussed.

V. FUNCTIONALISM, NATURAL LAW, AND THE DIALOGIC METHOD

How do these examples of the phenomenon relate to the different approaches to comparativism discussed earlier? For Ruti Teitel,

> [a] consensus appears to be forming regarding the relevance of foreign sources, at least within circumscribed parameters. The justification for comparativist analysis is couched largely in functionalist terms: as a basis for the resolution of specific constitutional issues, particularly in areas of unsettled law (Teitel, 2004: 2570 at 2589).

Indeed, much of the debate between supporters and opponents of the use of judicial comparativism, as discussed above, is couched in functionalist terms, with supporters arguing that 'foreign' legal material helps them find solutions to legal problems that are similar to, or can be illuminated by, approaches taken elsewhere. Opponents often contest the idea that such comparisons can be of use, in part because they contest the idea that the issues faced elsewhere are sufficiently similar that comparisons can ever be useful. Mary Ann Glendon has neatly summed up the debate on this issue:

> As the issue was framed recently in a debate between Justices Stephen Breyer and Antonin Scalia, it comes down to this: The former says that if a judge abroad has dealt with a similar problem, 'Why don't I read what he says if it's similar enough? Maybe I'll learn something.' Yet the latter would exclude such material as wholly without bearing on the meaning of the Constitution; and quite apart from originalism, the different political, constitutional, procedural and cultural contexts in other nations drastically limit its relevance. Justice Breyer counters that the experience of others 'may nonetheless cast an empirical light on the consequences of different solutions to a common legal problem' (Glendon, 2005).

Others, however, want to break out of the limits of a functionalist explanation for judicial comparativism in human rights adjudication. In an article published some time ago, I asked,

---

[69] *Roper v Simmons*, 125 S Ct 1183 at 1229 (Scalia, J).

Is there something specific to human rights that explains the apparently greater use of foreign case law in human rights cases?

I suggested (following Anne-Marie Slaughter (Slaughter, 1994) that judges may consider themselves to be engaging in a common enterprise worldwide and that to those who thought that, it would seem natural to engage in a judicial conversation with colleagues in other jurisdictions. The use of foreign judgments is one way in which conversation is continued. I rejected, however, the idea that these judges were engaged in 'some form of new natural law' enterprise (McCrudden, 2000).

Paolo Carozza, in commenting on my article in the course of his own discussion of the phenomenon in the context of United States capital punishment adjudication, agreed with the question I asked, but not my answer (Carozza, 2003). Carozza identified the extensive use of the concept of 'human dignity' alongside the use of comparative judicial opinions. He agreed with my view that identified the judges' 'sense of sharing a common enterprise with judges in other jurisdictions' as one principal explanation for the use of comparative material. He identified my explanation as 'essentially functionalist, based in the shared task of seeking solutions to common problems' but regarded such functionalist explanations as impoverished, since

> there is more than functionalism present in the ethical premise of the value of human dignity so widely shared among the different courts involved in the transnational jurisprudence of capital punishment (Carozza, 2003: 1031 at 1081).

He supported this argument with evidence that,

> on many occasions we see judges specifically abstracting from and eschewing comparisons in the functional terms of 'common solutions to common problems' and speaking much more in terms of 'common principles for a common humanity'. It is, more often than not, the judge who wants to avoid foreign influences who takes a functionalist approach focusing on the unique, pragmatic aspects of the problem at home (*ibid*).

Leaving aside whether my explanation was 'functionalist', Carozza's critique is important in opening up a debate as to whether non-functionalist explanations of the phenomenon are more convincing. For Carozza, my 'mistake' was in too easily rejecting what I referred to as 'some form of new natural law'. For Carozza, natural law involves accepting that,

> moving from universal principles of justice (like basic human rights norms) to positive law involves the exercise of human reason in the contingent contexts of practical possibility, culture, history, and so forth. The concrete specification of the principles of natural law, therefore, necessarily admits a variety of reasonable solutions to most problems (*ibid*).

Viewed from this perspective, my contentions regarding what judges are actually saying that they do does not at all contradict the idea that there are some implicit natural law premises operative in the phenomenon of cross-judicial discourse on human rights (as distinct from other substantive areas of law) (Carozza: 1031 at 1082).

In the capital punishment cases,

> the tendency of courts ... to consistently place their appeal to foreign sources on the level of the shared premise of the fundamental value of human dignity is a paradigmatic example of naturalist foundations at work. Despite differences in positive law, in historical and political context, in religious and cultural heritage, there is the common recognition of the worth of the human person as a fundamental principle to which the positive law should be accountable (*ibid*).

For Carozza, the 'common enterprise' that I identified is,

> first and foremost, the working out of the practical implications, in differing concrete contexts, of human dignity for the rights to life and physical integrity (*ibid*: 1031 at 1081–2).

However, there is a third alternative that is neither functionalist nor based in natural law. We have seen that judges not infrequently seek to distinguish judgments from other jurisdictions, explaining why they are *not* persuasive. Why? A possible explanation of this particular aspect of the phenomenon, and perhaps of the phenomenon as a whole, is provided by the dialogical method of comparativism discussed earlier. Anne-Marie Slaughter speaks of the emergence of a 'global jurisprudence', referring to

> the existence of active dialogue among the world's judges in the language of a common set of precedents on any particular issue. No one answer is the right one; the principles of pluralism and legitimate difference again prevail (Slaughter, 2003: 203).

She has noted a trend to 'dialogue rather than monologue, and deliberation rather than gap-filling'. (*ibid*: 196) Claire L'Heureux-Dubé, a former member of the Canadian Supreme Court, has argued that 'the process of international influence has changed from reception to dialogue' (L'Heureux-Dubé, 1998: 17). Justice Ginsburg, of the United States Supreme Court has referred to the 'value of comparative dialogue' (Ginsburg, 2005: 578). Sujit Choudry has also set his discussion of the phenomenon within a model of dialogical interpretation (Choudry, 1999: 851–75).

There appears to be an identifiable move to use comparative approaches as one of the techniques of trying to reach 'solutions' to issues of human rights interpretation that are not the same in each jurisdiction, that are not imposed on a jurisdiction simply because another has adopted it, and that are not necessarily considered to be examples of emerging universal norms. The comparative method in this context often involves judges considering what occurs in other jurisdictions as well as their own in order to appreciate dimensions of the issue that might not otherwise have been as apparent. It is 'dialogic' because it involves each jurisdiction not only contributing to the bank of experience that each other jurisdiction draws on, but also discussing this with those in other jurisdictions who are regarded as carrying out a similar interpretative role. It is in the development of this dialogic method applied to the problem of incompletely theorised agreements in human rights that the most fruitful role for judicial comparativism may lie.

VI. CONCLUSION

A more complete study of the complex phenomenon discussed in this chapter should examine particular issues I have identified more systematically. Essentially, I have identified some empirical questions (How far does it happen, and where?); a jurisprudential question (Can we identify criteria which help explain why it does or does not happen?); and a normative question (Is it legitimate?). None of these basic questions has yet been adequately answered. The empirical question requires more consistently gathered evidence than the somewhat anecdotal evidence drawn from the one jurisdiction presented here. The jurisprudential question requires a more thorough examination of how the phenomenon is illuminated by current debates on the theory of judicial interpretation, and emerging theories of comparative law. The normative question requires a closer study of the relationship between the phenomenon and the universality of human rights.

QUESTIONS FOR DISCUSSION

1. Do you agree with Justice Scalia's criticism of a court using foreign judicial opinions when he accuses it of 'looking over the heads of the crowd and picking out its friends'?

2. Do you agree with Mary Ann Glendon that there is a 'crucial difference between the legitimate use of foreign material as mere empirical evidence that legislation has a rational basis, and its use to buttress the court's own decision to override legislation', when she contrasts the (inappropriate) use of foreign law by Justice Breyer in *Lawrence v Texas*, with the (appropriate) use of such law by Chief Justice Rehnquist in *Washington v Glucksberg*?

3. Do you agree with Judge Posner's argument that: 'citing foreign decisions is probably best understood as an effort, whether or not conscious, to further mystify the adjudicative process and disguise the political decisions that are the core, though not the entirety, of the Supreme Court's output.'?

4. Do you agree with John Roberts in his confirmation hearings that 'relying on foreign precedent doesn't confine judges. It doesn't limit their discretion the way relying on domestic precedent does. Domestic precedent can confine and shape the discretion of the judges. Foreign law, you can find anything you want'.

5. Is the use of foreign judicial opinions 'undemocratic'?

6. Do you consider, with Judge Posner, that a significant problem with using foreign opinions, 'is that they emerge from a complex socio-historico-politico-institutional background of which our judges, I respectfully suggest, are almost entirely ignorant'?

BIBLIOGRAPHY AND FURTHER READING

Allan, J and Huscroft, G (2006) 'Constitutional Rights Coming Home to Roost? Rights Internationalism in American Courts' 43 *San Diego Law Review* 1.

Barak, A (2005) 'Response to The Judge as Comparatist: Comparison in Public Law' 80 *Tulane Law Review* 195.

Carozza, PG (2003) '"My Friend is a Stranger": The Death Penalty and the Global Ius Commune of Human Rights' 81 *Texas Law Review* 1031.

Choudhry, S (1999) 'Globalization in Search of Justification: Toward a Theory of Comparative Constitutional Interpretation' 74 *Indiana Law Journal* 819.

—— (2004) 'The Lochner Era and Comparative Constitutionalism' 2 *International Journal of Constitutional Law* 1.

Cleveland, SH (2006), 'Our International Constitution' 31 *Yale Journal of International Law* 1.

Dixon, R (to be published) 'Co-operative Constitutionalism and Constitutional Comparison: Traces of Dialogue?'.

Ginsburg, RB (2005) '"A Decent Respect to the Opinions of [Human]kind": The Value of a Comparative Perspective in Constitutional Adjudication' 64 *Cambridge Law Journal* 575.

Ginsburg, RB (2006) '"A Decent Respect to the Opinions of [Human]kind": The Value of a Comparative Perspective in Constitutional Adjudication, Constitutional Court of South Africa', February 7, 2006, http://www.supremecourtus.gov/publicinfo/speeches/sp_02-07b-06.html

Glendon, M-A (2005) 'Judicial Tourism: What's wrong with the US Supreme Court citing foreign law' *The Wall Street Journal*, September 16, 2005 http://www.opinionjournal.com/editorial/feature.html?id=110007265

Harding, SK (2003) 'Comparative Reasoning and Judicial Review' 28 *Yale International Law Journal* 409.

Henkin, L (2001) 'The International Judicial Dialogue: When Domestic Constitutional Courts Join the Conversation' 114 *Harvard Law Review* 2049.

L'Heureux-Dubé, C (1998) 'The Importance of Dialogue: Globalization and the International Impact of the Rehnquist Court' 34 *Tulsa Law Journal* 15.

Hoffmann, Lord (1999), 'Human Rights and the House of Lords' 62(2) *Modern Law Review* 159.

Jackson, VC (2002) 'Narratives of Federalism: Of Continuities and Comparative Constitutional Experience' 51 *Duke Law Journal* 223.

—— (2004a) 'Comparative Constitutional Federalism and Transnational Judicial Discourse' 2 International Journal of Constitutional Law 91.

—— (2004b) 'Yes please, I'd love to talk with you: The court has learned from the rest of the world before. It should continue to do so', *Legal Affairs*, July/August 2004. http://www.legalaffairs.org/issues/July-August-2004/feature_jackson_julaug04.msp--

—— (2005) 'Foreword—Comment: Constitutional Comparisons, Convergence, Resistance, Engagement' 119 *Harvard Law Review* 109.

Jackson, VC and Tushnet, M (2002) *Defining the Field of Comparative Constitutional Law* (Westport, CT, Praeger Publishers).

—— (2006) *Comparative Constitutional Law* 2nd edn (New York, Foundation Press).

Jacobs, FG (2003)'Judicial Dialogue and the Cross-Fertilization of Legal Systems: The European Court of Justice' 38 *Texas International Law Journal* 547.

von Jhering, R (1955) *Geist des römischen Rechs auf den Verschiedenen Stufen Seiner Entwicklung* (Schwabe, 9th ed).

Jacobson, G (2003) 'The Permeability of Constitutional Borders' 82 *Texas Law Review* 1763.

Kentridge, S (2005) 'Comparative Law in Constitutional Adjudication: The South African Experience' 80 *Tulane Law Review* 245.

Kreimer, SF (1999) 'Invidious Comparisons: Some Cautionary Remarks on the Process of Constitutional Borrowing' 1 *University of Pennsylvania Journal of Constitutional Law* 640.

Larson, JL (2004) 'Importing Constitutional Norms from a 'Wider Civilization': Lawrence and the Rehnquist Court's Use of Foreign and International Law in Domestic Constitutional Interpretation' 65 *Ohio St Law Journal* 1283.

Levinson, S (2004) 'Looking Abroad When Interpreting the US Constitution: Some Reflections' 39 *Texas International Law Journal* 353.

McCrudden, C (2000) 'A Common Law of Human Rights?: Transnational Judicial Conversations on Constitutional Rights' 20 *Oxford Journal of Legal Studies* 499.

—— (2003) 'Human Rights and Judicial Use of Comparative Law' in E Örücü (ed), *Judicial Comparativism in Human Rights Cases* (London, UK National Committee of Comparative Law).

Markesinis, B and Fedtke, J (2005) 'The Judge as Comparatist' 80 *Tulane Law Review* 11.

Örücü, E (ed) (2003) *Judicial Comparativism in Human Rights Cases* (London, UK National Committee of Comparative Law).

Posner, R (2004) 'No thanks, we already have our own laws: The court should never view a foreign legal decision as a precedent in any way', *Legal Affairs*, July/August 2004. http://www.legalaffairs.org/issues/July-August-2004/feature_posner_julaug04.msp

Rosenfeld, M, Sajo, A, Baer, S and Dorsen, N (eds) (2003) *Comparative Constitutionalism: Cases and Materials* (New York, West Publishing Company).

Saunders, C (2006) 'The George P. Smith Lecture in International Law: The Use and Misuse of Comparative Constitutional Law', 13 *Indiana Journal of Global Legal Studies* 37.

Slaughter, A-M (1994) 'A Typology of Transjudicial Communication' 29 *University of Richmond Law Review* 99.

—— (2003) 'A Global Community of Courts' 44 *Harvard International Law Journal* 191.

Sunstein, CR (1996) *Legal Reasoning and Political Conflict* (New York, Oxford University Press).

Teitel, R (2004) 'Book Review: Comparative Constitutional Law in a Global Age' 117 *Harvard Law Review* 2570.

Tushnet, M (1999) 'The Possibilities of Comparative Constitutional Law' 108 *Yale Law Journal* 1225.

Waldron, J (2005) 'Foreword—Comment: Foreign Law and the Modern Ius Gentium' 119 *Harvard Law Review* 129.

Young, EA (2005) 'Foreword—Comment: Foreign Law and the Denominator Problem' 110 *Harvard Law Review* 148.

Zweigert, K and Kötz, H (1998) *Introduction to Comparative Law*, 3rd edn (trans) T Weir (Oxford, Oxford University Press).

Website connections:

Video archive and transcript of discussion on the constitutional relevance of foreign court decisions, between US Supreme Court Justices Antonin Scalia and Stephen Breyer, American University Washington College of Law, 13 January, 2005 http://www.wcl. american.edu/secle/founders/2005/050113.cfm

Confirmation hearings for US Supreme Court of John Roberts as Chief Justice, September 2005 http://www.c-span.org/VideoArchives.asp?CatCodePairs=Current_Event,SCourt&Arc hiveDays=365&Page=14 http://www.nytimes.com/2005/09/13/politics/politicsspecial1/ roberts_textindex.html?ex=1152936000&en=c622ad6bd5a1f97f&ei=5070

Confirmation hearings for US Supreme Court of Judge Samuel Alito, January 2006 http:// www.c-span.org/homepage.asp?Cat=Current_Event&Code=SCourt&ShowVidNum=5 1&Rot_Cat_CD=SCourt&Rot_HT=&Rot_WD=&ShowVidDays=365&ShowVidDesc= &ArchiveDays=365

17

Comparative Private Law in Practice:
The Process of Law Reform

SJEF VAN ERP*

KEY CONCEPTS

Law reform projects; Economic regional and global integration; Project advising; Experts; Project preparation; Donor country; Receiver country; Legal transplants; Expert preparation; Consultation process; The role of interpreters; The training of judges; Legal traditions; A pragmatic approach to comparative law; 'The adequate approach to comparative law'

I. INTRODUCTION

UNTIL SOME 20 or 30 years ago, comparative law was seen as a rather exotic branch of the law. It was a subject that could be chosen at the end of one's legal studies to learn of the remarkable ways in which foreign lawyers were educated and trained to think. Frequently, it also meant that one had to read legal materials in a foreign language. Comparative law was meant for those who were curious of mind. Perhaps a visiting foreign law professor might give a guest lecture in a foreign language on a topic one did not really understand, but, as a curious student, one still listened with great attention.

How the world has changed in such a short period! Comparative law, at least in Europe, has become one of the core subjects in the curricula of law faculties. In some law faculties comparative law is even at the heart of the law programme. The reasons behind this are the changing role and practical importance of knowledge in foreign legal systems. It is realised more and more that foreign law is not really so 'foreign' anymore. Within the European Union, to give but one example, growing intra-European trade has led to an increasing number of cases in which at least one of the parties is confronted with a different legal system to his/her own.

* I would like to thank Mel Kenny and Patrick O'Callaghan, researchers at the Centre of European Law and Politics at the University of Bremen, for their critical comments on this chapter.

Although in such a case the assistance of a lawyer from that foreign legal system will be necessary, that party (or his/her lawyer) still has to be able to understand at least the basics of what the foreign lawyer explains. Having studied comparative law facilitates the communication process.

This growing number of contacts with foreign law, provoked by economic regional and global integration, gives rise to an increasing need to harmonise or even unify certain legal areas to promote even more intensive trade. Legal diversity is often seen as a source of unnecessary 'transaction costs', which should be avoided. More often than not, these harmonisation or unification attempts are being prepared by comparative legal studies to examine the various solutions to be found in relevant legal systems and evaluate these solutions in order to decide what would be the best approach.

Next to the practical use of comparative law in such harmonisation and unification projects, comparative law became highly relevant when, after the fall of communism, countries that had so-called 'socialist' legal systems wanted fundamentally to change their economies. State-planned economies were to become free market economies. This meant that the law also had to change drastically. If the law had previously only allowed private ownership to a very limited degree and had declared that the means of production were in the hands of the state, the law had now to allow private ownership as a matter of principle. If trade had previously been in the hands of state-owned enterprises, which concluded administrative contracts between themselves within the framework of a central five-year plan, private companies now had to be allowed to contract freely on the basis of market conditions. It meant that the means of production and state enterprises had to be privatised. This had all to be done within a fairly short period, as the economies of most communist states at that time were close to bankruptcy. If, furthermore, a state had started negotiations with the European Union to become a new member, that state, as part of the accession process, had to adopt the European '*acquis communautaire*', which is already an enormous endeavour in itself, even without the need to reform the national legal system drastically. In order to accelerate the law reform process accompanying the economic transition, foreign lawyers were asked to give advice as to how to change the law and how to adopt the '*acquis communautaire*'. This chapter discusses what role these lawyers played in the reform process and how comparative law was used as a practical tool.

Not only the law had to be changed, but also the way the law had to be administered and the way courts decided cases. First of all, the independence of the judiciary had to be secured. Under communism, judges were not really independent. More than once I have heard from judges that a local secretary of the Communist Party called that judge to inform him/her that the Party would very much favour a particular outcome. Such 'telephone justice' was, of course, to be absolutely forbidden in a legal system firmly based on the rule of law. This meant that a fundamental change of mind and legal culture had to be achieved, otherwise the changes with regard to substantive law would not have the desired result. Here, again, foreign lawyers, especially judges, were asked to give advice and organise training sessions.

In the following paragraphs I will discuss how, generally speaking, a law reform project proceeds. Topics to be discussed will include how lawyers get involved in these projects as advisors (frequently called 'experts'), how they prepare themselves, how they give advice (written advice, oral presentations, discussions, comments on legislative drafts) and how judges are trained to work as independent officials applying the law in a non-bureaucratic way.

II. PROJECT PREPARATION: CHOICE OF EXPERTS

The initiative for a law reform project can be taken by either a particular country or by an organisation that is in need of advice—I will call such a country or organisation the 'receiving country' and 'receiving organisation'—or it can be taken by a 'donor' country or organisation that feels it can be of assistance. Donors can be international organisations such as the European Bank for Reconstruction and Development, the Asian Development Bank, the World Bank and the United Nations Development Programme.[1] Although the first three of these institutions are banks, they have been very much involved in law reform in order to create a legal environment in which a market economy can develop. A donor could also be a particular country (usually acting via its Ministry of Justice) or a national organisation from that country aiming to assist foreign law reform projects. Examples of the latter are the *Deutsche Gesellschaft für Technische Zusammenarbeit* (GTZ), the Dutch Center for International Legal Co-operation (CILC) and the United States Agency for International Development (USAID).[2]

Gradually, after contacts at the level of academics and civil servants have been restored, a development can be seen towards more direct cross-border contacts between lawyers. Once networks between lawyers have been created, it is easier for lawyers in the receiving country to approach a foreign colleague abroad more directly. However, when funding is required, the above-mentioned organisations will often be directly or indirectly involved.

As far as I know, most—not to say all—Central and Eastern European countries that have gone through a transition process from a planned to a market economy have requested at least some assistance during their processes of law reform. However, law reform projects are undertaken in various parts of the world and I would like to avoid the impression that what I am writing is limited to law reform in Europe. These law reform projects are certainly not always related to a

---

[1] For more information, see the respective websites of these financial institutions. European Bank for Reconstruction and Development: http://www.ebrd.com/; Asian Development Bank: http://www.adb.org/About/default.asp; World Bank: http://www.worldbank.org/; United Nations Development Programme: http://www.undp.org/.

[2] GTZ: http://www.gtz.de/en/index.htm; CILC: http://www.cilc.nl/; and USAID: http://www.usaid.gov/.

change of economic system. To give but one example: a country that wants to set up a land registry might seek the help of a state in which a well-functioning land registry system already exists.[3] This chapter, however, will take as a starting point law reform within Europe as a result of the fall of communism.

Depending upon the donor, either a tender procedure is followed, according to which organisations that intend to be involved in the project make an offer at a given price, or organisations are contacted directly. In both cases the organisations approach experts, either because the donor needs to be informed about the experts as part of the bidding process or because the organisation wants to be certain beforehand that it can fulfil its promises to give the required assistance. Experts are chosen basically on one ground: the person concerned must truly be an expert in his/her field of law. Although a national organisation generally prefers experts from its own country, sometimes experts from other countries are approached as well. This happens for example if an organisation in a common law jurisdiction, is asked to give advice to a country that belongs to the civil law. Furthermore, experts are preferred who have some basic knowledge of the legal system as it existed before the fall of communism. Especially during the first years after the fall of communism, knowledge about the old socialist legal systems was of great importance. In order to understand what had to be changed and how, the existing law had to be understood. Otherwise, a useful exchange of ideas with lawyers from the receiving country would be difficult.

Let me give an example from private law. In socialist legal systems, private ownership was only allowed to a very limited degree. Ownership of houses or farm estates was curtailed to prevent accumulation of wealth in the hands of a few private parties ('capitalists'). What was allowed depended upon the country. Consumer goods for private purposes were still recognised as private property, once they had been acquired (frequently after queuing). Trading in goods could only be done by state-owned enterprises, as the means of production and the goods produced were in the hands of the state. The various factories (numbered, such as: shoe factory 1) concluded administrative agreements among themselves in order to implement the economic five-year plan. Depending upon the country and upon the period, hardly any (or, sometimes, a measure of) freedom was allowed to the managers of these factories to implement the plan. In a market economy this had to change drastically. Markets had to be created, and this presupposed the existence of private ownership and freedom of contract. Foreign experts had to be aware of the existing situation in order to understand lawyers who had been working in a socialist legal system, sometimes for their whole lives. Creating a market economy means the creation of choice and freedom, but it also means less protection provided by the state. This required a radical change of mentality, and the foreign expert had to understand this. Debates on draft civil

---

[3] See, eg the information on international projects on the website of the Dutch Land Registry: http://www.kadaster.nl/international-english/default.html.

codes are, in such a situation, never purely technical discussions, as the new rules are the expression of a new economic model and a new, sometimes experienced as alien, mentality. For lawyers from the receiving state it was sometimes difficult to accept that foreign lawyers from the West could change from representations of the capitalist threat to colleagues in the search for legal solutions. Communism was still seen by some lawyers as the ideal society, in which everything would be shared by all, and where one worked according to one's abilities and received according to one's needs. From an outsider's viewpoint this may sound unrealistic and it may be clear that the ideal was never reached, but the force of believing in ideals should not be underestimated. I need only remind the reader of the inspiration which some still derive from the 'American dream' that you can start your life as a newspaper boy and end as the owner of a newspaper conglomerate.

Not only does the expert need to understand the pre-existing law, or at least be willing to learn more about it, but the expert must also be able to at least understand and speak English, preferably also German and/or French. In my experience English is the language most frequently used, followed by German. French is only used occasionally. It might seem that this gives an advantage to lawyers educated in, for example, the United Kingdom or the United States, but this need not necessarily have to be the case. The English legal language is intimately linked to the English common law and this might be highly problematic when discussing law reform in a civil law system. Law reform in civil law systems can be far more adequately discussed in a civil law language, such as French or German. That is why sometimes, although English is the main language, experts and lawyers from the receiving country discuss certain problems in German or French.

III. EXPERT PREPARATION

After agreement has been reached between the donor and the organisation in charge of performing the contract, the experts are informed that they are, in turn, expected to perform their (in most cases informal) contracts with the organisation through whom they will offer their services to the receiving country. Generally the so-called 'TOR' (Terms of Reference) are agreed upon, in which the purpose of the project is laid down and the various work packages are defined, such as the number of expert meetings or seminars. The responsible project manager then organises a first meeting with the experts and is also in touch with the receiving country.

It is at this stage that the experts receive more information on the receiving country's legal system. Legislation, if available in translation, is provided and it is discussed which additional legal texts should be translated to enable the experts to prepare themselves. All legal documents to be discussed (eg draft civil code, draft legislation) will have to translated into a language which the experts understand. If the lawyers of the receiving country do not speak English, German or French the meetings cannot take place without an interpreter. Two forms of interpretation can be used: consecutive or simultaneous interpretation. Consecutive translation means that after someone puts forward what he/she wants to say, that person then waits to allow the interpreter to translate into the language required. In case of simultaneous translation the interpreter translates what was said immediately. It will be clear that with consecutive translation much time is lost. If a presentation is scheduled for one hour, it in effect means half an hour. The translator can be someone from the country of the expert, who speaks his/her language, but frequently the interpreter comes from the receiving country and only speaks one foreign language, usually English. It can happen that the (draft) legal text to be discussed has been translated into a language that is understood by the expert (eg into German), whereas the interpreter can only translate between his/her national language and English or the other way around. This creates a situation which can be highly demanding for all the lawyers involved. It may even become more complicated when the experts want to discuss a particular point among themselves quickly and they choose to do this in their own language. The same happens when lawyers from the receiving country want to discuss a particular point among themselves in their own language. The linguistic process then becomes highly hazardous and so, consequently, the process of giving legal advice. It could mean—and this is an example from a situation I once found myself in— that after a discussion by Dutch experts in Dutch on a draft civil code translated from the original language into German, the outcome of that discussion had to be explained to the interpreter in English, who would then have to translate this into the national language of the lawyers from the receiving country. When several legal languages are involved (in my example, four) varying concepts are also involved and both the experts as well as lawyers from the receiving country (and, not to be forgotten, the interpreters!) must be aware of the pitfalls.

IV. THE PROCESS OF GIVING ADVICE

The actual consultation process can take place in several ways. It can be done in the form of conferences and seminars, with participants from legal practice, the academic legal world and the civil service involved. These conferences and seminars are usually held in the receiving country, but sometimes in the donor country to allow lawyers from the receiving country to visit, for example, a Ministry of Justice or the Supreme Court. During these conferences and seminars presentations are made, followed by discussion. A different form, frequently used when the topic is to discuss legislative drafts (such as a civil code), is an expert meeting. During such a meeting a limited number of people attend—from the receiving country only those who are directly involved in the legislative process. The discussions generally take place on the basis of a presentation by both the lawyers from the receiving country and the experts. This is then followed by a detailed discussion of legislative texts. After the session, sometimes the discussion continues by e-mail. This can be done on the basis of a supplementary questionnaire or by answering individual questions.

A difficult aspect of these meetings is the actual preparation, ie choice of topics and access to documents. If, for example, a draft civil code is to be discussed the text should be available in translation long before the meeting. This is not always done. It may also be useful to have a translation of existing legislation. Furthermore, anyone who takes part in these meetings knows that black letter rules do not present the whole picture of the law. This means that questions have to be prepared on the impact of case law as well as legal and commercial practice. This has to be done by both the lawyers from the receiving country, and the experts. Particularly the experts, but frequently also the lawyers from the receiving country, are well-experienced comparative lawyers who understand the risks of misunderstanding and know how to avoid these risks as far as possible.

V. THE TRAINING OF JUDGES

After the law has been changed, a mentality change has to take place. Everyone involved in the law reform process realises this. A mentality change, however, does not happen overnight and it has to include all legal actors, particularly the judiciary. During the communist era courts were not independent in the way that they are considered to be independent in, for example, Western Europe and the United States. Courts were bureaucratic institutions under the control of the government. Reference can be made to the Russian '*Prokuratura*' which controlled the courts. Once I was told that a government had exercised indirect pressure on a court by limiting the supply of coal to the courthouse during a winter period, thus creating an unworkable atmosphere. Under the rule of law, judges make up their own minds and they are no longer dependent upon circular letters or instructions from the government or the Communist Party. Freedom, however, brings with it responsibility. How should open-ended norms, such as 'good faith', be interpreted?

In order to support judges in their endeavours to form a truly independent judiciary, training sessions are organised to discuss the role of courts under the rule of law. Independence in this respect means that the judiciary dares to be creative and, if necessary, shape events, albeit within the limits set by the constitutional separation of powers and a system of checks and balances. The experts in these sessions are, of course, usually experienced judges from, eg, a donor country.

The problems such as translation and preparation, discussed above, can also be seen here. Generally speaking, it can be said that the experts/judges involved either already have a strong comparative law interest or come with an open mind and are willing to understand their colleagues. What is interesting to note is that judges seem to be able to understand one another fairly quickly. Reading claims and defences, listening to oral argument, discussing a case in chambers, deciding a case and writing a judgment seems to provoke the same problems, but more importantly, the same attitude everywhere.

VI. CRITICAL EVALUATION

It will have become clear that the process of giving advice in a law reform project demands a high level of awareness of possible misunderstandings. Lawyers involved in such projects generally develop an attitude that enables them to avoid problems as much as possible, although misunderstanding can never be excluded. Misunderstanding is not, however, characteristic only of law reform projects, but of human communication generally. What if, to avoid any misunderstanding, these projects did not take place? An opportunity would have been missed to try to help lawyers from another legal system who had requested assistance. If all those involved realise the difficulties and also realise that misunderstandings might occur, the risks involved are brought back within acceptable limits. In my inaugural lecture I have called this the adequate approach to comparative law (van Erp, 1998).

What I consider to be of utmost importance is the expert's knowledge (the person should be a real 'expert' and not simply be called such because of his/her being a lawyer from the West), his/her legal, socio-cultural, economic and political awareness and his/her integrity. As to integrity, funding could be a problem, although usually it is not. Funding can, of course, influence the aim of the law reform project. If, to give but one example, a particular organisation deems it inevitable for future economic development that a particular legal model is adopted, this might be the explicit or implicit aim of the project. It is particularly this latter issue of implicit aims, which might be problematic for independent experts. In the case of explicit aims, an expert can decide to take part or not, depending upon whether he/she agrees with such an aim. It is, of course, completely different with regard to implicit aims. In the latter case, it might only become clear during the consultation process what the donor expects, and this might then create problems if the expert disagrees or if the lawyers from the receiving country are not prepared to follow the path chosen by the donor. Sometimes not even the donor realises that it had set its own implicit aims. It could, for example, very well be the case that the funding organisation is so convinced of the rationality and reasonableness of the solutions it favours that deviating opinions by experts—particularly if they come from the same country as the donor—come as an unexpected and unwelcome surprise. In my experience, the chance that this may happen arises especially when the donor organisation is established in a common law jurisdiction and the expert is a civil lawyer.

This aspect of law reform brings us to the economic and political side of the process. If a country adopts a model developed in another country, that is, a 'legal transplant', the donor country gains an advantage over the receiving country, as its own lawyers will then have better insight into the law of the receiving country than lawyers from the receiving country itself (see Watson, 1993). It would make doing business by eg companies from the donor country easier, as the law will be familiar and this might also be of advantage vis-à-vis competitors from other countries for whom that particular part of the law might not be so familiar. A receiving country might experience this as a 'take-over' and for that reason reject the foreign solution. At the end of the day, it is the receiving country that decides what the new law will be. However, with regard to the adoption of the European '*acquis communautaire*', the European Commission in Brussels can exercise decisive influence as to countries that intend to become Member States of the European Union. It is a condition for membership that the existing *acquis* is adopted.

A foreign expert must therefore realise what the aims of the law reform project are, what his/her expertise is and what one's role is expected to be. In my experience, experts are especially highly valued who know their national legal system inside out both from a theoretical as well as a practical viewpoint, who have sufficient comparative expertise to be able to explain different solutions chosen in different legal systems, and who know when to step back and accept that the final decision as to the new law is part of the political process in the receiving country. Comparative legal analysis is a way to counterbalance an expert's own prejudices (in the sense of what in German is called '*Vorverständnis*'('preconception')), meaning that one realises and becomes aware of one's own cultural, social, economic, political and even personal background and how it affects legal thinking. All these aspects of personality are an integral part of the way a person thinks and argues and are therefore relevant for one's self-perception also as a lawyer. In my view, which I expressed in my inaugural lecture at the University of Maastricht in 1998, comparative law is only possible in practice if it follows, what I called, the adequate method of comparative law. The comparative lawyer must constantly reflect upon his/her work within the context of the project in which he/she is involved. A law reform project demands a different approach than an in-depth academic article. If this pragmatic approach is used, useful results can be reached in practice. The possible post-modern death of comparative law, as would follow from Pierre Legrand's views on comparative law, is not likely to happen (*cf* Legrand, 1999; and Watson, 2000). Post-modern theory is trumped by practice.

As to the results of law reform projects, one has to be realistic and not idealistic. Sometimes the direct influence of the advice given can be detected, but that does not mean that the new law in the receiving country really functions well or is applied at all. Introduction of the English-American trust in a civil law system might be the outcome of pressure from advisers inspired by a common law approach, but that does not mean that the legal system is able to incorporate a concept which is alien to that system. What happens is the same as can be seen with the transplant of an organ: it is rejected. What are the factors which favour the adoption of a foreign solution? First of all, if the solution comes from the same tradition (in Central and Eastern Europe, the civil law) it is easier to follow such a solution than one from a different tradition. Secondly, if the advice given is seen as objective information, based upon arguments pro and contra and presented from a comparative perspective without arguing from a purely nationalist perspective, the advice is more likely to be considered seriously or to be followed. This means that only making references to a particular national civil code, without referring also to other solutions and discussing developments at a European level—such as the Lando Principles (Principles on European Contract Law) or the work concerning the European Common Frame of Reference aimed at giving a systematic overview of large parts of European private law—is counter-productive.[4] Thirdly, it should always be made clear that the expert is there to give advice and not to decide the matter. Fourthly, it is important that the receiving country takes the initiative for asking advice itself. Fifthly, advisers from a smaller jurisdiction have a certain advantage, because, if the donor organisation is also from that same country, it is less likely that the donor may have a hidden agenda with implicit (eg political) aims.

To conclude, it can be said that giving advice in a law reform project shows the strength of comparative law as a method, a way of thinking, and as a source of knowledge. Its influence is, first of all, intellectual, as it leads to reflection on legal solutions that might otherwise be considered to be self-evident. Comparative legal analysis can also influence judicial decision-making and the work of the legislature, but this influence is sometimes somewhat invisible, as it might be hidden in preparatory documents. As we have seen, comparative law can also contribute to the success of a law reform project. Nevertheless, also here the results of comparative legal analysis may be less clear and difficult to define.

QUESTIONS FOR DISCUSSION

1. What examples do you know of the practical use of comparative law?
2. Give a description of a law reform project, discussing aims and results.
3. Give examples of legal transplants and evaluate whether these transplants have been successful.
4. What are the essential characteristics of the socialist legal systems?
5. Why could it be said that the legal system of China is becoming a 'mixed' legal system?
6. The approach advocated in this chapter is a pragmatic approach to comparative law, limited by continuous self-reflection within the context of law reform projects. What do you think of this approach?
7. How would you evaluate the role of 'experts' in law reform projects?

BIBLIOGRAPHY AND FURTHER READING

Channell, W (2006) 'Lessons not Learned: Problems with Western Aid for Law Reform in Post-communist Countries' 1:2 *Journal of Comparative Law* 321.

Legrand, P (1999) *Le droit compare* (Paris, Presses Universitaires de France).

Mistelis, LA (2000) 'Regulatory Aspects: Globalization, Harmonization, Legal Transplants and Law Reform—Some Fundamental Observations' 34 *The International Lawyer* 1055.

---

[4] The Lando Principles can be found at: http://www.jus.uio.no/lm/. More information on the European Common Frame of Reference can be found at: http://ec.europa.eu/consumers/index_en.htm.

Seidman, A and Seidman, RB (1995) 'Drafting Legislation for Development: Lessons from a Chinese Project' 44 *American Journal of Comparative Law* 1.

van Erp, JHM (1998) 'European private law: Postmodern dilemmas and choices. Towards a method of adequate comparative legal analysis' inaugural lecture Maastricht, 1998 (trans) 3.1 *Electronic Journal of Comparative Law* (August 1999) <http://www.ejcl.org/31/art31-1.html>.

Watson, A (1993) *Legal transplants: an approach to comparative law* (London, University of Georgia Press).

—— (2000) 'Legal transplants and European private law' 4.4 *Electronic Journal of Comparative Law* <http://www.ejcl.org/44/art44-2.html>.

18

Comparative Law in Practice: The Courts and the Legislator

ESİN ÖRÜCÜ

KEY CONCEPTS

Comparative law as a tool for law reform and legislation; For interpretation and construction by the courts; 'Decorative' use of; 'Functional' use of; As an 'auxiliary source of law'.

I. INTRODUCTION

Developments of the law in this country cannot of course depend on a head-count of decisions and codes adopted in other countries around the world, often against a background of different rules and traditions. The law must be developed coherently, in accordance with principle, so as to serve, even-handedly, the ends of justice. If, however, a decision is given in this country which offends one's basic sense of justice, and if consideration of international sources suggests that a different and more acceptable decision would be given in most other jurisdictions, whatever their legal tradition, this must prompt anxious review of the decision in question. In a shrinking world … there must be *some virtue in uniformity of outcome whatever the diversity of approach in reaching that outcome.*[1]

Strongly though I support the study of comparative law, I hesitate to embark in an opinion such as this upon a comparison, however brief, with a civil law system, because experience has taught me how very difficult, and indeed potentially misleading, such an exercise can be. Exceptionally however, in the present case, thanks to material published in our language by distinguished comparatists, German as well as English, we have direct access to publications which should sufficiently dispel our ignorance of German law and so *by comparison illuminate our understanding of our own.*[2]

---

[1] *Fairchild v Glenhaven Funeral Services Ltd* [2002] 3 All ER 305 (HL) at 334 (Lord Bingham).
[2] *White v Jones* [1995] 1 All ER 691 (HL) at 705 (Lord Goff of Chieveley).

I have not been referred to the law of any continental jurisdiction except Switzerland. It seems to me unlikely that in any system derived from the civil code, the law will differ in this respect from the position under Swiss law. It seems ... that under Scottish law a creditor can contract out of or waive his right to set-off and if so, he can presumably validly agree that his debt be subordinated. I have set out the leading authorities in South Africa, The United States and Australia. It would, I think, be a matter of *grave concern if, at a time when insolvency increasingly has international ramifications, it were to be found that English law alone refused* to give effect to contractual subordination.[3]

The discipline of comparative law does not aim at a poll of solutions adopted in different countries. It has the different and inestimable value of sharpening our focus on the weight of competing considerations.[4]

Does the above indicate that comparative law merely facilitates the incorporation by judges of 'holus bolus from some other system of law',[5] or does it indicate the way forward?

The first aim of this chapter is to look at the 'practical' and 'functional' use of comparative law by courts and to throw light on some of the following questions in detail: How far is foreign law referred to by courts? Are there more references to some particular jurisdictions and why? Do some courts present a different picture to others and why? In which areas are most of such references made? Do the courts resort to foreign law to correct and improve domestic law, to help the development of domestic law, to fill gaps in domestic law, clarify the law, seek support and guidance or bring about harmonisation? Apart from cases when there has to be a reference for reasons of conflict of laws or because a foreign law is applicable to the case, why are references made? Have membership of the European Community, the growing importance of international conventions and the growth of international commercial practice made any difference in this field? What are the limits of such use of comparisons? There is talk of the changing climate and a greater internationalisation in the approach of national courts (Bingham, 1992; and Koopmans, 1996). Is this the case?

The second aim is to consider briefly the role of comparative law in legislative law reform.

Comparative law has been in use for centuries in efforts to develop the law in many areas and help ideas cross borders. One practical aspect of comparative law is its use as a tool of interpretation, another is as a tool of law reform. It now seems natural in the development of globalising law, to borrow from the international for the national, and from one national for another national. Therefore the debate on the use or non-use of comparative experience remains theoretical when

---

[3] *Re Maxwell Communications Corporation plc (NZ)* [1994] 1 All ER 737 (Ch) at 754, 755 (Vinelott, J).
[4] *McFarlane v Tayside Health Board* 2000 SC 1 (HL) at 15 where the *ius commune* case book on tort law was also considered (Lord Steyn).
[5] *McShannon v Rockware Glass Ltd* [1978] AC 795 (HL) at 811 (Lord Diplock).

viewed from the ground of what is actually taking place. However, the degree of, and the reasons for, the borrowing differ. In addition, the attitudes of legislators, academics, practising lawyers and judges to the use of foreign material also differ, all making use of this tool in their own ways.

The term 'comparative law' is used in this chapter in its widest sense, to cover even passing reference to foreign law by a legislator, a court or a practising lawyer, and the use of a foreign solution or argument by a domestic judge as a guide to interpretation (see Örücü, 1999: 253).

II. COMPARATIVE LAW IN COURTS

Comparative law method is among the tools used by courts for the interpretation of national rules in conjunction with the usual methods of interpretation and construction. Although when there is unequivocal national law, foreign material cannot be used to by-pass these rules, where the construction is doubtful or there is a gap, the judge acts as the legislator, and like a modern legislator, looks to comparative law for solutions. Comparative law can serve to confirm and support a result reached by a traditional route. The aim of any reference to foreign law by courts may be to promote a change at home, fill in a gap or discard an unsatisfactory domestic solution—that is, the 'functional use' of foreign law. The aim may also be a 'decorative use' of foreign law in that an opinion in a developing area of law might appear to be out of date, unless reference were made to some recent progressive development elsewhere. There are also cases where a court, comparing different rules of foreign and domestic systems thoroughly, opts for one of these as the 'better' answer to the problem under consideration. However, a judge tries to avoid any suspicion that he has borrowed the law from a foreign system to fill in a gap. Of course, a judge may also be intellectually arrogant, nationalistic or genuinely believe that a foreign solution will not be of practical use.

Judges and counsel go through three phases in the process of using foreign law: discovering, understanding and applying. However, of what is found, what is to be used: the result or the reasoning? How far does this activity of borrowing go? Why are some judges in some jurisdictions more ready to use comparative law than others?[6] What is the measure of success? If a sign of success is uniformity of treatment and values, does this lead to the creation of uniform socio-economic and cultural conditions?

Comparative Law in British Courts

Courts in Britain make extensive use of cases from other common law jurisdictions. The question is: Has membership of the European Union affected the number of cases in the UK where reference is made to a continental legal system

---

[6] For the use of comparative law by courts in general in 17 jurisdictions see the General Report submitted by Drobnig, 1999: 3–21. Also see contributions to Canivet, Andenas and Fairgrieve, 2004.

or a rule of such when new areas of law are being built up or in cases where Common Law is not clear? Is there a trend in this direction as suggested by Bingham (Bingham, 1992)?

To this end decisions rendered in 1972, 1982, 1992 were looked at in earlier research (Örücü, 1999) and in this chapter, 2002 has been added to that survey. This would be one way of approaching the topic. Another approach could be to investigate various areas of law. Are there more references to foreign law in negligence, contract and competition law for example, than in tax, divorce or adoption?

Looking intensively at the period 2003–06 could also help to test the findings of the 10-yearly search, discover tendencies (if any) and make predictions, using both statistical and substantive information. One might also find the answer to the question: Have things changed in the last decade?

There are certain practical considerations in the use of comparative law that must be stressed at the outset: Language skills; national insularity and/or pride; the enormous pressures under which judges and counsel work because of lack of time and volume of work; and an increasing awareness of expenditure on the part of clients. Of these, four distinct elements pertaining to the United Kingdom position must be separately considered.

One is language skills. English is a world language. There is rather little incentive to learn foreign languages in the United Kingdom. It is easier and more natural for a person unfamiliar with foreign languages to have access to common law materials (see Gutteridge, 1949: 44–5).

The second element is the difficulties created by the rules on proof of foreign law, which is a question of fact, and must be pleaded and proved by expert evidence. The court cannot take judicial notice of foreign law, though the judge may be perfectly aware of the existence of the foreign rule. In addition, in the absence of evidence, foreign law is presumed to be the same as domestic law.[7] For example, in *Morrison v Panic Link Ltd* it was held:

> If it was suggested that there was any difference between English law and Scots law in relation to the construction of this contract, it would be necessary for the defenders to aver what that difference was in the present action. They have made no such averments and accordingly it must be assumed that the English law is the same as Scots law as far as the construction of the contract is concerned.[8]

This means that an awareness and the use of foreign cases and foreign material by counsel are more important than a judge's knowledge of them in reference to foreign law in a particular case. As Lord Mustill stated in *Channel Tunnel Ltd v Balfour Beatty Construction Ltd:*

> It is perhaps just permissible to take notice that the contemporary Belgian Law of arbitration differs from the law of other European countries, but beyond this I would

---

[7] *El Ajou v Dollar Land Holdings plc* [1993] 3 All ER 717(Ch) at 739 (Millet, J). However, in appeals before the House of Lords all questions of Scots, English and Northern Irish law are treated as matters of law within the judicial knowledge of their Lordships.

[8] *Morrison v Panic Link Ltd* 1993 SLT 602 (OH) at 604.

certainly not be willing to go since, most remarkably, no evidence of Belgian law is before the court.[9]

The rules of foreign law are to be proved by the testimony of experts giving evidence. When there is a conflict in the evidence of the experts, the judge has to decide between them, so he may pursue his own inquiries into the sources of foreign law if he is equipped to do so, and draw his own conclusions.

The third element has been summarised as: 'Why bother with foreign cases when we have so much material of our own' (Markesinis, 1990). This may not be solely a British attitude but as Lord Justice Bingham says of the period when he started practice,

> it was an almost universal article of faith that English law and legal institutions were without peer in the world with very little to be usefully learned from others (save, on occasion, the High Court of Australia) (Bingham, 1992: 514).

This he characterises as the proud, confident and self-reliant spirit. Thus a judge's mentality and his unwillingness to be guided by foreign experience may be an obstacle.

The fourth is an element more particular to the common law family than to others. It is the consciousness that common law is a whole. The unity of common law is a very real tie between the jurisdictions within the common law family, and the citing of decisions from another common law jurisdiction as authority is very frequent, though usually for the purpose of 'help' or 'comfort'. When the aim is to improve national law, British courts often cite Canadian, Australian and New Zealand judgments, almost as if they were domestic judgments. Indeed, 'It is manifestly desirable that the law on this subject should be the same in all common law jurisdictions',[10] and also that the law north and the south of the border should be the same or similar as far as possible. For example Lord Clyde opined in *Smith v Bank of Scotland* that

> [i]n the present case we are dealing with an area of law whose development has for a long time been influenced by decisions on the other side of the border. I am not persuaded that there are any social or economic considerations which would justify a difference in the law between the two jurisdictions in the particular point.[11]

This element is also tied to the shared language, culture and appreciation of mental constructs and consideration of uniformity of these jurisdictions. Lord Bridge stated in *Bennett v Horseferry Road Magistrates' Court*:

> Whatever differences there may be between the legal systems of South Africa, the United States, New Zealand and this country, many of the basic principles to which they seek to give effect stem from common roots.[12]

---

[9] *Channel Tunnel Ltd v Balfour Beatty Construction Ltd* [1993] 1 All ER 683 (HL) at 691.
[10] *Cheah v Equiticorp Finance Group Ltd* [1991] 4 All ER 989 (PC) at 992 (Lord Browne-Wilkinson).
[11] *Smith v Bank of Scotland* 1997 SC 111 (HL) at 120 (Lord Clyde).
[12] *Bennett v Horseferry Road Magistrates' Court* [1993] 3 All ER 138 (HL) at 155 (Lord Bridge).

Again, when there is no domestic authority to help them, courts do not hesitate to rely on other Commonwealth and common law authorities, for example by saying:

> In the absence of any countervailing authority in English courts, I am of opinion that the principles to be derived from the foregoing sources should be accepted as valid in English law.[13]

Even when there are domestic solutions but these prove to be unsatisfactory in dealing with contemporary problems, courts will refer to these same foreign Commonwealth and common law jurisdictions.[14] In the last decade however, there have been a few significant cases where laws of legal systems from the civilian tradition have been resorted to.

One question is: Would the judge as interpreter be able to, or be entitled to, invoke a superior foreign solution? In fact, in the face of an unequivocal national enactment, foreign material cannot be used to by-pass those rules. However, when the construction is doubtful or there is a lacuna, the judge, as does the legislator, sometimes takes his solutions from comparative law. Then the question is: 'How far can, or should, this go?' Comparative law helps the courts to clarify and amplify the law, to throw light on domestic law and—used in conjunction with usual methods—to confirm and support a result reached by a traditional route. But merely to juxtapose the laws of various jurisdictions without comment is not comparative law, and to compare only parts of a solution could be not only unprofitable, but misleading.

It is interesting however, to note that Lord Diplock, whose many judgments contain references to continental, especially French and German law, and American positions, did not seem to adhere to the 'pious fiction' that 'the judge must avoid any suspicion that he has borrowed his law from a foreign system', when he openly used Evans's translation of Pothier in developing 'primary and secondary obligations' and 'synallagmatic and unilateral' contracts, saying, 'I have borrowed it from French law and the Civil Code arts.1102—1103'.[15]

Roman law has also been frequently resorted to by judges of the Chancery Courts, and English commercial law is largely derived from foreign sources, partly by its descent from the *lex mercatoria* of the Middle Ages (see Gutteridge, 1949: 38).[16]

When judges use foreign judgments, this is more by way of testing the soundness of their conclusions than in reliance on those decisions. Indeed, all judges cannot be expected to be comparatists, but it is their duty to consult those who are

---

[13] *Martin v Watson* [1995] 3 All ER 559 (HL) at 562, 566 (Lord Keith).

[14] See eg, *Mercedes-Benz AG v Leiduck* [1996] 3 All ER 929 (PC); and, *Attorney General for Hong Kong v Reid* [1994] 1 All ER 1 (PC).

[15] *United Dominion Trust (Commercial) Ltd v Eagle Aircraft Services Ltd* [1968] 1 WLR (HL).

[16] Note that in Scotland though from time to time there is reference directly to Roman law or institutional writers, this falls into 'historical interpretation' and not the 'comparative'. See eg, *Sharp v Thomson* 1997 SLT (HL), where Lord Hope said: 'Scots law, following Roman law, is unititular'.

in a position to supply the information needed, which indicates the importance of partnership with the academic profession.

Let us now throw some empirical light on the above views related to this topic.

Empirical Evidence

As far as the United Kingdom is concerned, judicial practice at the 10-yearly intervals since the United Kingdom joined the European Union, shows us that in 1972, there were 26 cases where foreign law was referred to. Of these, three were conflict cases, and three dealt with international conventions. There were 12 references to continental law/civilian and 30 to common law/Commonwealth jurisdictions (USA–10; Australia–seven; Canada–two, New Zealand–three, and Scotland–three).

In 1982, 29 cases referred to foreign law. Of these, there were two conflict cases, three references to the European Court of Justice or European Commission, four to international conventions, four to continental or civilian systems, and 42 to common law/Commonwealth jurisdictions (United States–nine; Australia–six; Canada–seven; New Zealand–five; Scotland–none).

In 1992, there were 25 cases with references to foreign law: six were conflict cases, there were seven references to the ECJ or EC, four to international conventions, seven to continental or civilian jurisdictions and 33 to common law/Commonwealth jurisdictions (United States–nine; Australia–seven; Canada–seven; New Zealand–two; Scotland–two).

In 2002, however, 121 cases referred to foreign law: five were conflict cases, 16 references were to the ECJ or European Commission, 76 were to international conventions, mostly the European Convention on Human Rights and, seven to continental or civilian jurisdictions and 57 to common law/Commonwealth jurisdictions (United States–18, Australia–22, Canada–14, New Zealand–22, Scotland–16, South Africa–two, Ireland–three and India–one). This picture shows the changing balance of references.

When we look at the fields into which the above statistically analysed cases fall, we see a very wide and varied picture such as: Substitution, mergers; Company; Proper law of contract; Wills; Occupier, duty owed by occupier to trespasser; Causation, duty to take care, breach of duty; Duty to share holders; Vicarious liability; Gaming, lottery; Libel; Slander; Divorce, living apart, maintenance order; Marriage, validity; Division of matrimonial property; Income tax, double taxation; Stay of proceedings; Currency control, debt in foreign money; Contempt of court; Criminal evidence, hearsay; Carriers, loss or damage to goods; Trial, evidence in the absence of the jury; Extradition, committal; EC law, competition; Employment, equal pay, equal work; Constitutional law, long delay in executing of sentence; Sale of land, fraud; Limitation of action, public authorities; Shipping, carriage by sea; Gift, *donatio mortis causa*; Title to foreign copyright; Compulsory purchase; Right not to be hindered in the enjoyment of freedom of expression;

Minor, abduction; Custody; husband and wife, Divorce; Carriage of goods by air; Pre-trial, post judgment relief; Copyright, infringement; *Forum non conveniens;* Mental health, patient, recall to hospital; Refusal of medical treatment; Medical treatment, withdrawal of consent; Malicious falsehood, negligence; False imprisonment, residual liberty; Blasphemy; Conspiracy; Abortion, medical negligence; Rape, marital exemption; Easement, right of way; Sunday trading, proportionality; Judicial review; Drug trafficking; Insurance; Abuse of process; Solicitor, professional negligence; Tort, harassment; Arbitration; Fraud, will, succession, reduction; Loss of earnings, capacity; public interest, pyramid selling; Landlord and tenant, lease, irritancy; Employment, unfair dismissal, racial discrimination; Copyright, statutory interpretation; Administrative law, natural justice, unjustified enrichment; Bankruptcy, sequestration, evidence, sale of goods; Implied terms, agent and principal, Warsaw Convention; The Hague Convention; Brussels Convention.

When and How is Foreign Law Used?

Foreign law is used in cases where it is indicated. The first type of case here is conflict of laws. When conflict of laws points to foreign law or when the case has a foreign element such as recognition of a foreign divorce, any relevant foreign law will be referred to. As observed above, in such cases domestic law will preferably be used and foreign law will be assumed to be the same as domestic law unless evidence is brought to show otherwise,[17] (as there is a presumption that law of another jurisdiction is the same as that of the forum where no proof or insufficient proof to the contrary is presented). In addition, often natural justice and public policy grounds may show that foreign judgments cannot be enforced,[18] as the existence of prior orders from foreign courts is not significant; the principles should be acceptable to British courts.[19] The courts also ask whether there are considerations of European law or comity. In many such cases European Court of Justice rulings serve as a guide.[20] Usually the determination of applicable law depends on the public interest of the forum in dispute, the parties' access to foreign law materials, the clarity of choice of law rules and the nature of the foreign legal system involved.

However, British courts do have an internationalist attitude, nurtured by the doctrine of international comity, because of which they are reluctant to invoke public policy against the normally applicable foreign law.

---

[17] For instance, this was stated clearly in *Bumper Development Corp Ltd v Commissioner of Police of the Metropolis*[1991] 4 All ER 638 (CA). For a similar statement see *El Ajou v Dollar Land Holdings plc* [1993] 3 All ER 717 (Ch).

[18] This was the case in *Adam v Cape Industries plc* [1991] 1 All ER 929 (Ch).

[19] *Re F (minor)* [1990] 3 All ER 97 (CA).

[20] Good examples are *Webb v Webb* [1992] 1 All ER 17 (Ch); *Union Transport Group plc v Continental Lines SA* [1992] 1 All ER 161 (HL); *Dresser UK Ltd v Falcongate Freight Management Ltd The Duke of Yare* [1992] 2 All ER 450 (HL); and *Johnson v Coventry Churchill International Ltd* [1992] 3 All ER 14 (QBD).

The second type of case is where courts look at foreign law and an international convention concerned, to understand its application or for the sake of comity.[21] For instance, in *Michael Galley Footwear Ltd (in liq) v Iaboni*,[22] Belgian, Dutch and German cases were looked at in order to understand the application of the Contract for the International Carriage of Goods by Road, in view of comity. In *T v Secretary of State for the Home Department*, Lord Lloyd said:

> In a case concerning an international convention it is obviously desirable that decisions in different jurisdictions should, so far possible, be kept in line with each other.[23]

In *Re A and another (minors)* for example, Balcombe, J said:

> Since French and English are both official languages of the Hague Convention, we were referred also to the French version of art 13(a) … Since we are here concerned with the meaning of 'acquiesced' in an international convention to which many countries, not only those with a common law background, have adhered, it cannot be right to attempt to construe 'acquiesced' by reference only to its possible meaning at common law or equity.[24]

However, we should note the observation by Lord Hope in *Herd v Clyde Helicopters Ltd*, when he said:

> [T]he fact that the jurisprudence in one country has adopted an interpretation of the Convention which supports counsel's argument is not in itself a compelling reason for holding that we should follow the same approach in our interpretation.[25]

Before the Human Rights Act 1998, the use of the European Convention of Human Rights could be deployed for the purpose of the resolution of an ambiguity in domestic primary or subordinate legislation.[26] It was accepted that domestic law should develop alongside the European Convention on Human Rights, as stated by Lord Scarman in *Home Office v Harman*:

> We believe the true path forward is to ensure that our law develops in a way which is consistent with the obligations accepted by the UK in the European Convention and with the developments of the common law achieved in America … Of course, neither American law nor the convention can be decisive of this appeal. But both are powerfully persuasive, the convention because its observance is an obligation of the United Kingdom, and American law because of its common law character. Each reinforces conclusions which we draw independently from our own legal principles.[27]

---

[21] See, eg *Hewitson v Hewitson* [1995] 1 All ER 472 (CA).

[22] *Michael Galley Footwear Ltd (in liq) v Iaboni* [1982] 2 All ER 200 (QBD).

[23] *T v Secretary of State for the Home Department* [1996] 2 All ER 865 (HL) at 889 This was the Convention relating to the Status of Refugees, 1951. Phillip, J said in *Kinnear v Falconfilms NV*:

> 'In a convention case it would not be proper for the court to apply domestic rules to decline jurisdiction under 6(2) simply because the third party was domiciled abroad' ([1994] 3 All ER 42 (QBD) at 50).

[24] *Re A and another (minors)* [1992] 1 All ER 929 (CA).

[25] *Herd v Clyde Helicopters Ltd* 1997 SC 86 (HL) at 102 (Lord Hope).

[26] *Rantzen v Mirror Group Newspapers (1986)* [1993] 4 All ER 975 (CA) at 993 (Neill, J).

[27] *Home Office v Harman* [1982] 1 All ER 532 (HL). For another such case see *Re D and another (minors)* [1995] 4 All ER 385 (HL) at 397. See also *R v Secretary of State for the Home Department, ex parte Wynne* [1992] 2 All ER 315 (CA).

In *R v Secretary of State for the Home Department, ex parte McQuillan*, Sedley, J looked at the Convention through the jurisprudence of the Court of Justice of the European Community and said:

> Once it is accepted that the standards articulated in the convention are standards which both march with those of the common law and inform the jurisprudence of the European Union, it becomes unreal and potentially unjust to continue to develop English public law without reference to them.[28]

The third type is when there is an involvement of European Community law. British courts look at cases in the European Court of Justice and via these to cases involving foreign systems of law, this being done within the scope of ECJ decisions. The courts are keen to keep to meanings as defined by the ECJ, especially if the matter is not covered by domestic authority. ECJ decisions give guidance, and a judgment obtained in a Member State on a matter of European Community law has a special weight. For instance, Lord Goff remarked in *Woolwich Building Society v Inland Revenue Commissioners (No 2)*[29]:

> I only comment that, at a time when Community law is becoming increasingly important, it would be strange if the right of the citizen to recover overpaid charges were to be more restricted under domestic law than it is under Community law.

Foreign law is also used in developing English law when there is no statutory law. When the area under scrutiny is one of common law, counsel introduces decisions from other common law or Commonwealth jurisdictions. *In United City Merchants (Investments) Ltd v Royal Bank of Canada*,[30] for instance, it was pointed out that,

> although there does not appear among English authorities any case in which this exception has been applied, it is well established in the American cases.

Judges use these decisions for 'support', 'aid' and 'guidance' or because they give 'comfort'. The decisions are referred to 'with great respect' as 'powerful', 'persuasive', 'helpful', 'illuminating' or 'applicable'. This respect arises sometimes because the principle was first developed in the jurisdiction referred to. These decisions are sometimes preferred over domestic law,[31] sometimes 'accepted unreservedly',[32]

---

[28] *R v Secretary of State for the Home Department, ex parte McQuillan* [1995] 4 All ER 400 (QBD) at 422.

[29] *Woolwich Building Society v Inland Revenue Commissioners (No 2)* [1992] 3 All ER 737 (HL) at 764 (Lord Goff).

[30] *United City Merchants (Investments) Ltd v Royal Bank of Canada* [1982] 2 All ER, 720 (HL).

[31] For example, in interpreting the Copyright Act 1982, the view expressed by the High Court of Australia was preferred in *Express Newspapers plc v News (UK) Ltd* [1990] 3 All ER 376 (Ch). For another case, see *Galoo Ltd (in liq) v Bright Grahame Murry (a firm)* [1995] 1 All ER 16 (CA) at 26 where Glidewell LJ says:

> 'The answer in my judgment is supplied by the Australian decisions to which I was referred, which I hold to represent the law of England as well as of Australia, in relation to a breach of duty imposed on the defendant whether by contract or in tort'.

[32] *C v S (minor)* [1990] 2 All ER 449 (CA).

sometimes used to 'clarify definitions' and almost always for the furtherance of common law. In all cases, the courts tend to look at and extensively discuss developed Commonwealth jurisdictions such as Australia, Canada and New Zealand, and the common law jurisdiction of the United States of America as 'authority' and use them for 'assistance'.[33]

This being the area in which comparative method is most extensively used, it will be considered in further detail for the sake of clarity.

Common law jurisdictions provide unity and uniformity of common law. In one case the court followed American solutions to provide uniformity in the whole common law world as seen in *Cheah v Equiticorp Finance Group Ltd.*[34] In another case,[35] in the name of comity in common law, the Australian position was followed.

When there is no modern decided English case[36] *as in Woolwich Building Society v Inland Revenue Commissioners (No 2)*[37] and *Airedale NHS Trust v Bland*,[38] or English law has not moved on since, for instance, 1861, as in *White v Jones*,[39] the courts search for a general principle by looking at other developed common law jurisdictions.

When there is no direct English authority, other common law authorities are helpful and persuasive. For instance, in *Martin v Watson*, McCowan, LJ said:

> I have found no English authority which is directly in point in the present case … In the Commonwealth: however, there have been a number of cases which posed similar problems … I find myself in complete agreement with these views (Australian, Canadian, New Zealand and American cases were looked at).[40]

Again in *Mulcahy v Ministry of Defence*, while looking into negligence and duty of care, Neill, LJ said:

> It was accepted on behalf of the defendants that there was no direct English authority to support the proposition that no duty of care in tort is owed by one soldier to another when engaging the enemy in battle conditions … I consider that an English court should approach this claim in the same way as the High Court of Australia in the *Shaw Savill* case.[41]

[33] *Murphy v Brentwood District Council* [1990] 2 All ER 908 (HL).

[34] [1991] 4 All ER 989 (PC).

[35] *Attorney General v Sport Newspapers Ltd*, [1992] 1 All ER 503 (QBD).

[36] For more such cases see: *Ancell v McDermott* [1993] 4 All ER 355 (CA); *R v Secretary of State for the Home Department, ex parte Bentley* [1993] 4 All ER 442 (QBD); *Coppee-Lavalin SA/NV v Ken-Ren Chemicals and Fertilizers Ltd (in liq); Voest-Alpine AG v Ken-Ren Chemicals and Fertilisers Ltd* [1994] 2 All ER 449 (HL); *Connaught Restaurants Ltd v Indoor Leisure Ltd* [1994] 4 All ER 834 (CA); and *T v Secretary of State for the Home Department* [1996] 2 All ER 865 (HL).

[37] *Woolwich Building Society v Inland Revenue Commissioners (No 2)* [1991] 4 All ER 577 (CA) and [1992] 3 All ER 737 (HL).

[38] *Airedale NHS Trust v Bland* [1993] 1 All ER 821 (HL). This case illustrates all the types of references and relationships that exist between the legal systems in the common law world and therefore, is an all-rounded excellent example to study.

[39] *White v Jones* [1993] 3 All ER 481 (CA).

[40] *Martin v Watson* [1994] 2 All ER(CA) 606 at 627.

[41] *Mulcahy v Ministry of Defence* [1996] 2 All ER 758 (CA) at 766, 770.

When English common law is inadequate such as in *Simmonds v Dobson*,[42] *Derbyshire County Council v Times Newspapers Ltd*[43] and *Khorasandjian v Bush*,[44] again reference is made to other common law jurisdictions.[45]

To extend the law as in *Bennett v Horseferry Road Magistrate's Court*,[46] or to move the law on, as in *White v Jones*,[47] or in furtherance of common law in novel cases of negligence and damages, great weight is given to Australian, Irish, Canadian and United States cases such as in *Burton v Islington Health Authority*[48] and *Jones v Wright*.[49]

When there is much to learn from imaginative legal developments from, for example, Australia, New Zealand, Canada and the United States as in the case of *White v Jones*,[50] English courts refer to such other common law jurisdictions. In this case, German, French and Dutch positions were also considered.

When seeking to soften the impact of an English rule as in *British Railways Board v Herrinton*,[51] it was pointed out that

> there is a growing tendency of courts both in England and Scotland to try to soften the impact of the rule in *Addie's case*. Australian authorities are even more persuasive and far reaching that those in this country.

When seeking support for the position of the English court developing the law and helping the judge to make up his mind, such as in the area of negligence and duty of care, Australia provided 'inspiration' as in *Caparo Industries plc v Dickman*.[52] Lord Jauncey, in a case involving personal injury and nervous shock, looked at Scotland, Australia and the United States and said:

> My Lords, as is so often the case, in the field of negligence valuable contributions to the discussion are to be found in judgments of the High Court of Australia.[53]

In Stoke-on-Trent City Council v B & Q plc; Norwich City Council v B & Q plc,[54] dealing with proportionality, Canadian judgments were referred to in addition to the jurisprudence of the European Court of Justice, to confirm the views of the judge.

When we consider the Privy Council decisions, we see that on the whole the Privy Council prefers the English law's understanding of rules. However, the Privy

---

[42] *Simmonds v Dobson* [1991] 4 All ER 25 (CA).
[43] *Derbyshire County Council v Times Newspapers Ltd* [1992] 3 All ER 65 (CA).
[44] *Khorasandjian v Bush* [1993] 3 All ER 669 (CA).
[45] Other cases of interest are: *Giles v Thompson* [1993] 3 All ER 321 (HL); and *Tinsley v Milligan* [1993] 3 All ER 65 (HL).
[46] *Bennett v Horseferry Road Magistrate's Court* [1993] 3 All ER 138 (HL).
[47] *White v Jones* [1993] 3 All ER 481 (CA); [1995] 1 All ER, 691 (HL).
[48] *Burton v Islington Health Authority* [1992] 3 All ER 833 (CA).
[49] *Jones v Wright* [1991] 1 All ER 353 (QBD).
[50] *White v Jones* [1993] 3 All ER 481 (CA); [1995] 1 All ER 691 (HL).
[51] *British Railways Board v Herrinton* [1972] 1 All ER 749 (HL).
[52] *Caparo Industries plc v Dickman* [1990] 1 All ER 568 (HL).
[53] *Page v Smith* [1995] 2 All ER 736 (HL) at 745.
[54] *Stoke-on-Trent City Council v B & Q plc, Norwich City Council v B & Q plc* [1991] 4 All ER 221. (Ch).

Council gives special weight to the views of judges in the lower courts in those Commonwealth systems under its jurisdiction in so far as they reflect the advantage of familiarity with prevailing local conditions. This is done with the proviso that the courts have used that advantage, as seen in *Hector v Attorney General of Antigua and Barbuda*.[55] The Privy Council plays a crucial role in maintaining the harmony of the common law within the Commonwealth world, laying down paths for cross-fertilisation.[56]

As noted, British courts at times make use of continental law and the civil law tradition. Though continental law is usually mentioned only in passing by British courts when brought to their attention and is not normally used for support or guidance, in *Antwerp United Diamonds BVBA v Air Europe* for example, a Dutch and a Belgian case were presented to the Court of Appeal together with a case from the United States and another from British Columbia as foreign authority. There was no English decision on the question prior to the decision of the lower court in the present case. Hirst, LJ said:

> Of these by far the most significant decision, both by virtue of its high authority and by virtue of its close reasoning and analysis, is in my judgment *Insurance Co of North America v Royal Dutch Airlines* in the Supreme Court of the Netherlands … I find (this decision) very strongly persuasive … even though it is not of course binding upon us or conclusive.[57]

Again, in *Barclays Bank plc v Glasgow City Council* and *Kleinwort Benson plc v Glasgow City Council*, where a question arose as to the meaning of a term taken from the Common Customs Tariff and used as part of German tax law, Lloyd, LJ said: 'But there is precedent for the course we propose to take, provided by the German courts (case cited in—C–231/89)'.[58]

Woolwich Building Society v Inland Revenue Commissioners (No 2), is more typical where Lord Goff pointed out in his judgment:

> An instructive example of this approach is to be found in German law, in which we find a general right of recovery … Such draconian time limits as these may be too strong a medicine for our taste; but the example of a general right of recovery subject to strict time limits imposed as a matter of policy is instructive for us [59]

Another important example is the case of *White v Jones*, where the House of Lords dealt with negligence and duty of care in relation to solicitors. Lord Goff looked at the experiences in other countries in this developing area and stated that the question was

---

[55] *Hector v Attorney General of Antigua and Barbuda* [1990] 2 All ER 103 (PC).

[56] See eg, *Invercargill City Council v Hamlin* [1996] 2 WLR 367, where the Privy Council not only recognises but values difference: 'a monolithic uniformity might be destructive of the individual development of a distinct common law system', at 367 (Lord Lloyd Berwick).

[57] *Diamonds BVBA v Air Europe* [1995] 3 All ER 424 (CA) at 428 (Hirst, LJ).

[58] *Barclays Bank plc v Glasgow City Council; Kleinwort Benson plc v Glasgow City Council* [1994] 4 All ER 865 (CA) at 889 (Lloyd, LJ).

[59] *Woolwich Building Society v Inland Revenue Commissioners (No 2)* [1992] 3 All ER 737 (HL) at 761 (Lord Goff).

much discussed, not only in this country and other common law countries, but also in some civil law countries, notably Germany.[60]

Pointing out also similar conclusions reached by French and Dutch courts, he extensively discussed all cases, civilian and common law, reserving extensive treatment to German law, though his solution was based on tort and English authority. Again, in a case in relation to psychiatric damage, *Greatorex v Greatorex*,[61] the High Court considered arguments derived from a German case.

More recently, in the *Fairchild v Glenhaven Funeral Services Ltd* case, not only decisions and doctrine from the traditional sources such as Australia, Canada, the United States and Scotland were considered, but decisions and doctrine from Germany, France, the Netherlands, Austria, Spain and, Norway, and Roman Law were also extensively discussed, though again the end result relied on a common law case.[62]

However, most of the references to a continental system occur in cases where that foreign law is indicated in the dispute. Cases related to child abduction, extradition, recognition and enforcement of judicial decisions, and double taxation are the types of cases where we see such references. For example, in *G and H Montage GmbH v Irvani*,[63] English, German and Iranian laws were compared in relation to a signature placed on a bill.

Yet, here there are problems. For example in *Webb v Webb*,[64] Judge Paul Baker, QC, after stating that under the law of the European Community the French courts seem to have exclusive jurisdiction in the case, said that the conferment of exclusive jurisdiction could lead to great inconvenience for the parties and therefore there was sound reason for limiting it as far as possible. He even complained,

> Article 16 is couched in the concepts of the civil law systems of the original member states. It does not readily fit in with the system of legal and equitable interests in property obtaining in England and Wales and in both parts of Ireland.

However, in *Dresser UK Ltd v Falcongate Freight Management Ltd, The Duke of Yare*, Bingham, LJ opined:

> But procedural idiosyncrasy is not (like national costume or regional cuisine) to be nurtured for its own sake and in answering the question before us we must have regard to the realities of litigation in this country and the purpose of the convention, not to tradition, nomenclature or rules developed for other purposes. [65]

In a few cases brief comments are made in general reference to continental or civilian tradition, to indicate the background and the origin of legal rules.[66] Even Roman law and Justinian are occasionally mentioned when indicating sources of

---

[60] *White v Jones* [1995] 1 All ER 691 (HL) at 697 (Lord Goff).
[61] *Greatorex v Greatorex* [2000] 1 WLR 1970 (QBD).
[62] *Fairchild v Glenhaven Funeral Services Ltd* [2002] 3 All ER 305 (HL).
[63] *G and H Montage GmbH v Irvani* [1990] 2 All ER 225 (CA).
[64] *Webb v Webb* [1992] 1 All ER 17 (Ch) at 25 (Baker, J).
[65] [1992] 2 All ER 450 (CA) at 467 (Bingham, LJ).
[66] See *El Ajou v Dollar Holdings plc* [1994] 2 All ER 705 where English law and German law are compared in the use of the term 'directing mind' derived originally from German law.

laws, but not for help, such as in *Sen v Headley*, discussing gifts and *donatio mortis causa*, where Roman law was only cited as the origin of the concept:

> Although *donationes mortis causa* were taken from Roman law, it is only the first two requirements which now bear evidence of that ancestry. They are embodied in the definition given in Justinian's Institutes (2 Just Inst,tit vii) which was adopted by Lord Loughborough LC in *Tate v Hilbert* (1793) 2 Ves III at 119 ... We can therefore turn away from Roman law and give our whole attention to the English authorities.[67]

In *The Funabaski Sycamore Steamship Co Ltd v Owners of the Steamship White Mountain*[68] Dunn, J said that the Admiralty Court always awarded interest on a limitation fund and then quoted from Lord Denning:

> Court of Admiralty did not apply common law. It followed the civil law and gave interest on damages whenever the non-payment was due to the wrongful delay of the defendant. Ex mora the obligor; ex mora means 'on account of the delay'. It is so stated in the Digest 21.1.32(2).

How Far Can, and Do, Courts Go?

We see the following clauses used by judges when referring to foreign cases: 'ample support', 'particularly useful', 'helpful', 'compatible with values of democratic societies', 'instructive', 'persuasive but not binding', 'of assistance', 'of interest' and 'gives comfort'. We also see that judges often turn to foreign jurisdictions in developing the law, in cases when the existing law is inadequate, or in extending the law, to achieve some uniformity within the 'civilised' world. This may also be done in order to soften the impact of a domestic rule. Judges may be confronted with novel issues. They may wish to depart from domestic understandings. Concepts of equality, morality and justice may demand new approaches. There may be insufficient domestic guidance on a matter. In such cases, comparative law is a valuable tool of interpretation.

To achieve improvement in the law and to create unity in all common law jurisdictions courts may depart from domestic law.[69] In keeping with this, Commonwealth cases are sometimes treated as if they are English cases and cited as authority, as seen in *R v Lord Chancellor's Department*[70] and in *Airedale NHS Trust v Bland*.[71]

However, when domestic law is well established and satisfactory, the courts do not depart from it. When an area of English or Scottish law is covered by statute not by common law, a domestic judge cannot benefit directly from

---

[67] *Sen v Headley* [1991] 2 All ER 636 (CA) at 640. See also *Fairchild* (2002) 3 All ER 305 at 378.

[68] *The Funabaski Sycamore Steamship Co Ltd v Owners of the Steamship White Mountain* [1972] 2 All ER 181 (Adm) at 183 (Dunn, J).

[69] See *Cheah v Equiticorp Finance Group Ltd* [1991] 4 All ER 989 (PC); and *Behzadi v Shafterbury Hotels Ltd* [1991] 2 All ER 477 (CA); [1993] 3 All ER, 669 (CA).

[70] *R v Lord Chancellor's Department* [1992] 1 All ER 897 (QBD).

[71] *Airedale NHS Trust v Bland* [1993] 1 All ER 821 (HL).

foreign law, common law or otherwise. For instance, in *Luc Thiet Thuan v R*,
Lord Goff said:

> It must be unwise to impose uncritically upon an English statute an interpretation
> placed upon a statute from another jurisdictions, which is not expressed in the same
> words. Of course, there is a strong affinity between England and New Zealand law
> on this subject, reflecting their common origin; and anything which has fallen from
> North, J is regarded with great respect in this country, as it is in New Zealand. But their
> Lordships feel compelled to say that the wholesale adoption, without analysis of a sub-
> stantial part of this obiter dictum, which covers a whole range of points on a notoriously
> difficult subject with particular reference to the New Zealand statute, is not a satisfactory
> approach to the interpretation of the objective test in provocation as recognised in the
> English statute. Each point must, in Hong Kong as in England, fall to be considered by
> reference to the words of the statute, their historical derivation from the common law,
> and the legislative setting (where relevant) at the time of enactment.[72]

However, when it is a matter of interpretation of a statutory obligation,
judge-made law is important. Support and guidance is then sought from other
common law jurisdictions.

In Courts 'Elsewhere'

According to Koopmans, national courts in many jurisdictions have been more
interested in using the comparative method over the last 15 years or so than previously and the climate is changing especially when there is a lack of suitable precedents (Koopmans, 1996). As well as the ties to cultural and historical influences
and current role models and knowledge of the specific language of the models,
there are further reasons why comparative law is used, such as: for prestige or
for the quality of the legal rules to be exported and imported; efficiency; the role
of the national elite; practical utility; cultural forces; imposition; and chance.
Increased inter-system contact creates a receptive atmosphere whereby ideas cross
borders and lead to convergence. In addition, reference to other jurisdictions may
give broader legitimacy to judicial decisions.

In the civilian tradition, we cannot easily detect comparative law at work in
courts, where it is the advocate-general who writes the advisory opinion, carries
out comparisons and makes a thorough analysis of foreign laws. Courts rarely
discuss or refer to such material. In many cases, comparative work may have had
an effect on the preliminary investigation but does not find an explicit place in
the decision, although it may have inspired that decision. It can only be traced by
the inductive reasoning of the researcher.

The universal rule is that national courts apply national law unless they are
required to do otherwise. However, in difficult cases, controversial new cases, in
cases where no solution is available in national law, or where the applicable rule

---

[72] *Luc Thiet Thuan v R* [1996] 2 All ER 1033 (PC) at 1042–3 (Lord Goff).

is not clear, courts resort to comparative reasoning. Increased contact leading to convergence in many areas of law has made it easier, more palatable and justifiable for courts to look at foreign law, whether it be to foreign court decisions or foreign doctrine. In some jurisdictions in the civilian tradition, such as the German and the Dutch, this trend is more easily traceable than in others, such as the French. In the United States courts seldom look at foreign law, though comparison between State laws is common practice.

It is worth noting that South Africa has the first Constitution setting out an explicit mandate for the courts to use comparative and international law in their human rights reasoning. In its interpretation section 39(1)(b) and (c), the 1996 Constitution provides that a court, tribunal or forum 'must consider International law' and 'may consider foreign law' in interpreting the Bill of Rights, which is a tacit invitation to the judiciary to apply comparative law. In this context, extensive use is made of American, Australian, Canadian, Indian and German cases. The basic question to be asked is whether European and North American models are appropriate in areas of law where the aim is to correct past failures and respond to specific or unique home concerns. In such cases it is more appropriate to prefer cultural exceptionalism rather than comparativism. According to David Carey-Miller, comparative law as used in human rights cases by South African courts can be classified as 'illustrative', 'supplementary', 'elucidatory' or 'going to core substance' (Carey-Miller, 2003).

It is interesting to note that the European Court of Human Rights also makes 'reverse' reference to national laws, establishing two-way traffic between international law and national laws in a comparative context. In fact, the European Convention itself derives from principles already recognised under the domestic laws of all democratic countries. We also see the European Court of Justice, as an active court in the use of comparative material, borrowing both from the laws of the Member States and international conventions and the decisions of the European Court of Human Rights.

III. COMPARATIVE LAW AND THE LEGISLATOR

The first interest in foreign law was in the area of legislation, and 'comparative legislation' was encouraged by the French-based *Société de Législation Comparée*, founded in 1869, although one could even go back to Roman times, as far back as the Twelve Tables (450 B.C.). All the continental codes drew inspiration from foreign law in their preparation. National legislatures have always used comparative law in creating and reforming the law. This is usually done in the search for a better solution to the problem at hand. In fact, interest in using comparative law and looking 'sideways' to other legal systems in the process of law reform is an activity used earlier by legislatures than by courts.

Although in drafting statutes comparative reasoning plays a vital role, it is never possible to exactly measure the extent of the influence of comparative law in the final statute, despite abundant reference to foreign law in the explanatory memoranda. For instance, in the United Kingdom, both the Law Commissions for England and Wales and for Scotland are under an obligation to look at foreign law in the preparation of new legislation. Section 3(1)(f) of the Law Commissions Act 1965 states that the Law Commissions must

> obtain such information as to the legal systems of other countries as appears to the Commissioners likely to facilitate the performance of any of their functions.

Laws of other common law jurisdictions and civilian countries are surveyed in reports and preliminary memoranda. However, it is not always possible to trace the outcome of this research in the Acts that follow. In the United States, in drafting the Restatements of Law, the American Law Institute uses information gleaned from comparative law surveys, mostly inter-State, but inspiration is sometimes drawn even from European experience.

Today in many areas of law similar laws are being produced by European legislatures, mostly fulfilling the requirements of the European Directives. Little new legislation is enacted that does not involve some comparative research, as there are very few, if any, unique areas of law left to the creative forces of a single state. For instance, we see similar developments in the areas of social security law, environmental law and environmental liability, company law, anti-terrorist legislation, same-sex relationships, adoption and euthanasia.

There are, of course, wholesale imports such as the taking over of an entire civil code. This was the case in the earlier part of the last century for countries such as Turkey and Japan and later for East and Central European states entering the socialist sphere.

IV. JUSTIFICATION OF COMPARATIVISM AND THE VERDICT

In Britain, the main judicial comparisons are between the members of the common law family, with courts making frequent reference to Commonwealth jurisdictions and the United States. As new areas are being developed and as domestic law needs modernisation, there is a general increase in reference to foreign law. The major justification for reference to Australia, the United States and New Zealand, is the perceived unity of common law, which allows the use of decisions from other common law jurisdictions as if they are domestic authority. This usage and reference does not extend however, to statutory laws.

In theory, there is ample justification for referring to laws of the other Member States of the European Union, especially in comparing their attitudes to the interpretation of European Community law. However, British cases do not reflect an 'integrationist' approach with other Member States of the European Union except when the specificities of a case so demand. There does not seem to be the kind of cross-fertilisation between the Member States of the European Union as there is between the jurisdictions of the common law. This applies as much to Britain as it does to the legal systems of the civilian tradition.

When comparisons are made between British law and other common law jurisdictions, this is essentially a 'functional use' of comparative law, whereas when civilian systems are considered, it reflects a 'decorative use' of comparative law. In the first group, the British cases deal mostly with domestic law and domestic problems. In the second group, the cases fall mostly within a wider ambit, usually of European law or an international convention. Again, in the first group, foreign cases are either directly used or used to give guidance and support, reflecting the 'integrationist' approach in the common law world. In the second group, the moral and political considerations necessitate looking into the laws of the civilian states, especially if the case is related to European Community law or a convention, at which point we even see that

> [t]here seems no doubt that, while national laws of contract differ, there is a general sense in which the word contract is understood by the signatories to the convention. English notions of consideration and privity must be discarded.[73]

Here certainly the 'internationalism' is manifest. As for seeking guidance or support from, or direct use of, civilian cases in preference to United Kingdom law or other common laws, the same cannot be said. As foreign law is a question of fact in common law, it is worth repeating once more that it is the counsel who must be convinced of the value and relevance of comparisons, and, since the judges rely on counsel, the concept of 'in practice' used in the title of this chapter must be taken to cover all actors of the law.

The crucial issue is whether comparativism is used for inspiration and as an interpretative tool, or to seek the legitimation of a foregone conclusion. Sometimes there is a real effort at a 'common enterprise' and sometimes a search for justification for a domestic decision. For example, in discussing 'compatibility' with the European Convention on Human Rights as embodied in the 1998 Human Rights Act in the United Kingdom, judges are rapidly becoming conversant with human rights issues, and in this area comparativism is gaining weight, becoming second nature to judges and providing a valuable interpretative tool. As we assess this 'transjudicial communication' (see Slaughter, 1994), the present chapter claims that the starting point should be a positive, welcoming approach.

Judges are 'tuners' of the law. While they adapt the law to the evolution of society and create bridges between the law and the values of the society in which they live, they also build bridges between that society and other societies and universal values by means of comparativism. The basic values used are those of the judge's own society but as integrated into a wider universe. This also provides a certain anchorage for domestic decisions. Obviously there is the added assumption in the Western world, that the basic values underpinning democratic societies are shared values. Comparisons reveal these shared values and therefore it is appropriate to use comparativism as an interpretative tool. However, it is not the technical aspects of the foreign solution that should be studied, but the legal, economic

---

[73] *Kleinwort Benson Ltd v Glasgow City Council* [1996] 2 All ER 257 (CA) at 273.

and cultural contexts within which similar cases are decided by judges of foreign jurisdictions. Here, integration can be created by comparative analysis, since looking at things comparatively brings an incremental common perspective. This gives rise to a gradual 'internalisation of common values' by the courts of national legal systems. Practising lawyers should also take part in this process.

Comparativism feeds cross-fertilisation and cross-fertilisation encourages instrumentalisation and transposition of the received. In this way commonality is developed, albeit at a more abstract and higher level of principle than at the level of rules. Comparativism certainly broadens the spectrum of choice and provides inspiration to an activist judge.

Comparative law is often treated today by courts and practitioners as 'an auxiliary source of law', 'a subsidiary method of interpretation'. In addition, the courts of developing countries and newly-emerging democracies are looking to other legal systems considered 'Western' or 'developed' (see, eg Dupré, 2003).

The most problematic and most important area of concern is related to legal rules of a purely domestic character. Here, references to foreign solutions are few, and their use is difficult to justify. The courts tend to look only at the content of the foreign rules rather than their context or effects—such references being rather short—with attention paid only to results and rarely to reasoning, and the courts proceed pragmatically. References are often over-simplistic. The selection of countries also seems random. Sometimes only certain groupings are used, problems of language and documentary access being the main obstacles.

For lawyers, it is only necessary to bring foreign law to the attention of the courts, and for the courts to have sufficient knowledge to ask the foreign law expert the pertinent questions. Foreign law could only concern a lawyer if, for example, her client had a traffic accident in a foreign country, or the company she represents established a new branch in a foreign jurisdiction. Then, she could use the services of appropriate foreign lawyers in her international network. All she needs to do is to give the foreign expert the right instructions and ask the right questions.

In the common law world the practising lawyer is, in essence, looking for foreign cases in order to ask the court to depart from an established precedent, and therefore is searching for solutions that are different from the domestic to further her cause. However, in many cases, a court uses foreign decisions to strengthen its hand in reaching what is in fact a foregone conclusion. So the practising lawyer and the judge will not always be working towards the same end and what aspect of the foreign law each will stress will not be the same.

What do we detect overall? The use of foreign law and foreign cases is selective and there is no logical approach to the choice. Neither is a specific methodology applied. In addition, the decision to use foreign judicial judgments remains largely in the realm of judicial discretion, and the exercise of this discretion may be due to many factors. We should also ask whether courts are properly equipped to carry out detailed comparative law surveys in every suitable case. Courts may make decisions on the basis of superficial or even misleading comparisons. Picking and choosing is a grave danger. In any event, very often, the exact nature of foreign law influence may not be obvious from reading a case, and this not only in the civilian tradition either.

It must also be admitted that comparativism may be used solely to further a particular cause, with the aim of having a particular 'effect' on a target audience. Judges would have reached the same conclusion without comparativism. It is also natural that courts want to claim full decisional autonomy.

The choices made by judges can be tied to cultural and historical influences, historical ties, a current role model, a legal system being fashionable at that particular time, or knowledge of a specific language by a group of lawyers. Choices may also be made because of the influence of European Community law or the European Convention on Human Rights, because there are similar circumstances to the case at hand and there is no applicable domestic law, or because the changing culture of judges through education and new technical developments makes access to foreign judgements easier. Obviously, there may also be misunderstandings, errors—even deliberate errors.

In Europe, cross-breeding comes through the direct and indirect influence of the European Union, through the 'better law' filter applied by Community judges and the judges of the European Court of Human Rights; through the spreading of knowledge by academic writers; or through following a transplant deriving from an autonomous action by the courts. The cultural gap in the training of judges and lawyers and their use of foreign law remains, but a corpus of fundamental principles common to European orders is identifiable today.

In the area of human rights, for instance, comparativism can provide the basis for an a historical development not specific to any one nation state's history but to universal history. When established understandings are challenged in the name of this universalism, what should judges do? It has been said that 'courts are talking to one another all over the world' (Slaughter, 1994) as judges are involved in active international traffic. Research shows that courts of some jurisdictions are in constant conversation, while others are not. So, apart from the matter of why this is the case, an additional matter arises as to what are the frontiers of judicial comparison. It is possible to say that human rights case law is more likely to flourish if it is supported by the legitimacy of virtual unanimity amongst the judges.[74]

When the law is well established and satisfactory, judges may see no need to look abroad. Where there is a legislative framework in an area under consideration, judges may feel bound to follow the direction laid down for them by the legislature, even though they may know that there are other, and possible better, answers elsewhere. Many laws deal with problems of a national past and therefore, there may be no full correspondence between these and universal rules and standards.

Our century will certainly witness new reciprocal influences and cross-fertilisation between legal systems within the Western legal tradition. These

---

[74] See ch 16 in this Handbook.

reciprocal influences may prove extremely beneficial for the development of the law to meet the changing needs and demands of the people the law serves. For this we need imaginative and pro-active judges, informed and active counsel, creative academics, a flexible legal education, an enlightened legislature, a daring executive, Law Commissions with insight, and a good and fruitful balance between these. It is time to change the general belief that 'other systems of jurisprudence are relevant only so far as they throw light on our law' (Gutteridge, 1949: 39 *ff*), though this in itself is a valuable starting point.

Domestic courts must look forward, sideways, at each other and beyond. Comparativism must be at the heart of all judicial activity if law is to embody principles that are 'universal' rather than purely domestic or even 'European'. When actors of the law, that is academics, legislators, judges and lawyers, adopt a pragmatic and progressive approach, then comparativism can provide the most effective tool for interlocking legal systems.

QUESTIONS FOR DISCUSSION

1. What do you regard as the 'proper object' of comparative law efforts by courts?
2. Comment on comparative law in courts as part of 'necessary comparison', in 'legal rules with an international element' and in 'legal rules with a purely domestic character'.
3. Comment on the use of comparative law by courts for the purposes of abrogating existing national rules, of filling gaps and for decorative or ornamental purposes.
4. How can the use of cases and doctrine from foreign jurisdictions by domestic courts be justified?
5. Is it appropriate to use foreign solutions for domestic problems?
6. Do you think that the *Fairchild* case is an indication that the common law and civil law worlds are converging?
7. Comment on the use of comparative law by the legislators.

BIBLIOGRAPHY AND FURTHER READING

Bingham, J (1992) 'There is a World Elsewhere: The Changing Perspectives of English Law' 41 *International Comparative Law Quarterly* 513.

Canivet, G, Andenas, M and Fairgrieve, D (eds) (2004) *Comparative Law Before the Courts* (London, British Institute of International Comparative Law).

Canivet, G and Palmer, VV (2006) 'The Practice of Comparative Law by the Supreme Courts: Brief Reflections on the Dialogue between the Judges in French and European Experience' 80 *Tulane Law Review* 1377.

Carey-Miller, DL (2003) 'The Great Trek to Human Rights: The Role of Comparative Law in the development of Human Rights in Post-reform South Africa', in E Örücü (ed), *Judicial Comparativism in Human Rights Cases* vol 22 United Kingdom Comparative

Law Series (London, UK National Committee for Comparative Law/British Institute of International Comparative Law).

Drobnig, E (1999) 'The Use of Comparative Law by Courts' in U Drobnig and S van Erp (eds), *The Use of Comparative Law by Courts* (The Hague, Kluwer Law International).

Dupré, C (2003) *Importing the Law in Post-Communist Transitions: The Hungarian Constitutional Court and the Right to Human Dignity* (Oxford, Hart Publishing).

Gutteridge, H (1949) *Comparative Law* (Cambridge, Cambridge University Press).

Kaminski, IC (2000) 'The Power of Aspiration: The Impact of European Law on a non-EU Country' in M van Hoecke and F Ost (eds) *The Harmonisation of European Private Law* (Oxford, Hart Publishing).

Koopmans, T (1996) 'Comparative Law and the Courts' 45 *International Comparative Law Quarterly* 544.

Markesinis, B (1990) 'Comparative Law—A Subject in Search of an Audience' 53 *Modern Law Review* 4.

—— (2003) *Comparative Law in the Courtroom and Classroom: The Story of the Last Thirty-five Years* (Oxford, Hart Publishing).

—— (2006) 'Judicial Mentality: Mental Disposition or Outlook as a Factor Impeding Recourse to Foreign Law' 80 *Tulane Law Review* 1325.

Markesinis, B and Fedtke, J (2005) 'The Judge as Comparatist' 80 *Tulane Law Review* 11.

Örücü, E (1999) 'Comparative Law in British Courts' in U Drobnig and S van Erp (eds), *The Use of Comparative Law by Courts* (The Hague, Kluwer Law International).

—— (2000) 'Comparative Law as a Tool of Construction in Scottish Courts' Part I *Juridical Review* 27.

—— (2003) 'Whither Comparativism in Human Rights Cases?' in E Örücü (ed), *Judicial Comparativism in Human Rights Cases*, vol 22 United Kingdom Comparative Law Series (London, UK National Committe for Comparative Law/British Institute of International and Comparative Law).

Rozakis, CL (2005) 'The European Judge as Comparatist' 80 *Tulane Law Review* 257.

Slaughter, A-M (1994) 'A Typology of Transjudicial Communication' *University of Richmond Law Review* 99.

Zaring, D (2006) 'The Use of Foreign Decisions by Federal Courts: An Empirical Analysis' 3 *Journal of Empirical Legal Studies* 297.

Zweigert, K and Kötz, H (1998), *An Introduction to Comparative Law*, 3rd edn (Oxford, Oxford University Press).

19

A Project: Comparative Law in Action

ESİN ÖRÜCÜ

I. INTRODUCTION

MANY COMPARATISTS IN Europe today are involved in harmonisation projects looking for 'common cores' or the 'better law'.[1] These projects are geared towards either harmonisation of a particular area of law, such as contract law, family law or tort (delict) law, or unification of law by drawing up European codes in, for example, criminal law or contract law. Other comparatists are occupied in assisting the European Union to draw up Directives, Regulations or treaties.

An overview of ongoing projects related to a number of fields of private law, for instance, shows us that most projects begin with questionnaires, though the questionnaires themselves are not standardised (see Hondius, 2003: 118-39). Some projects present the contributors, usually National Rapporteurs, with factual questions, while some create hypothetical cases and ask for solutions from the different legal systems involved in the project. Others present specific problems and try to find out how different systems would resolve them.

For example, the Trento-Project, which seeks to broaden the scope of the Cornell Project (see Schlesinger, 1961) beyond contract law, has put the emphasis on contract, property and tort, with a number of sub-topics such as commercial trusts, mistake and fraud in contract law; security rights in moveable property; pure economic loss, enforceability of promises, good faith, and strict liability in tort law. This project relies on the factual approach, that is, 'fact-based, in-depth research' methodology, or a 'question and answer' methodology, presenting a number of cases to national reporters and asking for solutions offered by their legal systems (see Bussani, 1998). Information is requested on all the relevant elements that affect the legal solutions to a given case, including policy

[1] Most of these projects are in a number of fields of private law and include the Lando Commission on European Contract Law that prepared the Principles of European Contract Law; UNIDROIT on a very similar project, the Principles for International Commercial Contracts; the Von Bar Study Group on the European Civil Code; Gandolfi's Code of Contract Law; the Trento Common Core of European Private Law; the Spier and Koziol group dealing with causation among other things; the *acquis communautaire* Group and the SECOLA, and the Commission on European Family Law.

considerations, economic and social factors, social context and values, and the structure of the process.

Another example is the Commission on European Family Law, which has undertaken the academic activity of harmonising a number of areas of family law such as divorce, maintenance, custody and parental responsibility. This Commission uses what it calls the 'comparative research-based drafting of principles' as the process, having been inspired by the American Restatements. A team of specialists from 26 jurisdictions targets legislators who may be in the process of modernising their national family laws, the hope being to create a source of inspiration. In concert with this hope, both the 'common core' and the 'better law' approaches are adopted. They draft questionnaires employing the functional approach, draw up national reports reflecting both the law in the books and law in action, draft the Principles having chosen between the 'common core' and 'better law' approaches and then publish these Principles. The drafters choose 'the best', 'the more functional' and the 'most efficient' rules, the touchstone being the modernisation of the law. The overall justification lies in the shared notions of human rights in Europe, with the additional emphasis on 'increasing choice'. Thus the options are: the common core is found and selected as the best solution; the common core is found, but a better solution is selected; the common core is found, but the selection is left to national law; no common core is found and 'a best solution' is selected; and finally, no common core is found and the solution is left to national law.

Comparatists involved in the above processes employ a comparative law methodology, albeit based on the factual problem-oriented approach or the functional/institutional approach, widely discussed in various chapters of this Handbook both at the theoretical and the practical levels.[2] Most projects rely mainly on functional equivalence. Projects comparing cases that have been decided on similar facts also compare solutions. A substantial number of projects do not consider general doctrine, different techniques, historical processes or different *mentalité*. The context of the rules is rarely analysed. The search is frequently for the 'common core', with similarities being treated as more important than differences. These projects may have specific short-term aims, but in the long run they are all trying to lay down a foundation for a common European law.

Comparing cases, comparing problems, comparing solutions, seeking answers to hypothetical fact situations in an effort to discover similarities, working through functional equivalence—and where none can be found, suggesting a better law—are among the shared characteristics of these projects, though the paths followed, the techniques used and the end products may look quite different.[3]

Yet other comparatists are involved in assisting legal systems in their law reform efforts by providing advice on which model would best suit their situation

---

[2] See chs 2, 3, 10 and 11 in this Handbook for more information and especially a discussion on functional equivalence.
[3] See, eg chs 10 and 11 in this Handbook.

and system.[4] These comparatists are working as advisers to foreign working groups or governments, aiding their efforts to import 'modern' or 'efficient' or 'European law-friendly' changes into their substantive and procedural laws.

On the 10th anniversary of the United Kingdom's membership of the European Community, a research project was initiated to study the impact of membership of the European Community (now European Union) on practising lawyers in Scotland and The Netherlands, as a contribution to the study of the role of lawyers in the process of European integration. This was not a grand scale project such as those mentioned above. It was not ambitious. It did not aim to harmonise the law or produce general principles in a specific area of law. It was born out of the curious minds and experiences of a small group of academics. It illustrates therefore, a middle-sized piece of empirical research, which also involved testing the hypotheses which the members of the research team individually wanted to test.[5] The way the project was set up and carried out is presented here as an example of the use of comparative law methodology. It can be an initiation exercise for novices wanting to undertake comparative law research.[6]

II. THE SETTING UP OF THE PROJECT

Composition of the Team

The project was undertaken by five people: a social psychologist, a lecturer in European Law, a legal practitioner and senior lecturer in European Law, a lecturer in Comparative Law, and a Professor of Comparative Law.[7] Convenience, existing links of friendship and scholarship, and the nature of the project itself—which, by definition, was multi-disciplinary and multi-national—dictated the composition of the research team. The project demanded the knowledge and skills of a group of people drawn from diverse academic backgrounds. In addition to the involvement of legally-trained researchers with experience in the relevant legal systems, in European law and comparative law, it required the contribution of a methodologist with expertise in the gathering and analysis of empirical data—skills that are lacking in present-day legal training. All the members of the team were working outside their traditional boundaries.

[4] See, eg ch 17 in this Handbook.
[5] The following sections of this chapter rely on excerpts from the published findings of the project. See Aitkenhead, Burrows, Jagtenberg and Örücü, 1988.
[6] The project started in 1982 and the results were published in book form in 1988. Obviously it is not a recent work. It is presented here as a successful project using certain methods and strategies of comparative law. It should not be taken to imply that doing empirical research does not change over time and that its methods have not been refined in the intervening period.
[7] Marilyn Aitkenhead—social psychologist lecturer at Loughborough University of Technology in Management Studies, Noreen Burrows—lecturer in European Law at the University of Glasgow, Douwe Gijlstra—legal practitioner in Amsterdam and senior lecturer in European Law at the Europa Institute of the University of Amsterdam, Rob Jagtenberg—lecturer in Comparative Law at Erasmus Universiteit, Rotterdam, and Esin Örücü—senior lecturer in Comparative Law at the University of Glasgow and Professor of Comparative Law at Erasmus Universiteit, Rotterdam.

The Subject: The Personnel of the Law

The project centred on lawyers, an 'umbrella' term, which was taken to mean advocates and solicitors in Scotland and *advocaten* and *notarissen* in The Netherlands. It was felt that the role of members of the legal profession, other than the judiciary, was also crucial in the operation of a European legal system, as cases arrive at courts via the intermediary of lawyers. Their role and the importance of their active participation in furthering the process of European integration had so far been ignored. Therefore, the study was meant to examine how European law was put into operation in the municipal sphere by lawyers in private practice. Were they, for instance, 'European minded'? Did they discount or misapply the rules made by the European Court of Justice? Did they contribute to the functioning of the Community?

The assumption was that the legal profession exerts great influence on the legal and the political system. Another assumption underlying the study was that European integration could not advance significantly without the active participation of the legal profession as a whole.[8]

The Hypotheses to be Tested

It was decided to use a comparative approach so that similarities and differences could be assessed and their implications for European integration elucidated. Though the best strategy would have been to investigate in detail the legal practitioners in each European Community Member State, limited resources precluded this, so two jurisdictions were opted for. Scotland and The Netherlands were chosen for a variety of practical and theoretical reasons. The research team had good academic and professional contacts in both jurisdictions. This practical consideration, which is always a good starting point, would not in itself justify the choice made however. The theoretical underpinnings were that the United Kingdom was a relatively new member of the European Community at the time of the research, whereas The Netherlands was a founding member. Therefore, lawyers in The Netherlands would have had longer experience and this might have impacted their attitudes, approaches, familiarity and use of European law. In addition, geographic and economic differences could also be factors contributing to any differences in the attitudes and behaviour of lawyers in the two jurisdictions. For instance, Scotland is on the periphery of Europe, trading to a large extent with England, whereas The Netherlands is more central and therefore in closer contact

---

[8] In this chapter the reader will find the bare bones of the research project, as the aim is to show how a project is conceived and set up, how a questionnaire is drawn up, what conceptual problems are encountered and what kind of hypotheses can be tested by questionnaires alone. The aim of this chapter is not to highlight socio-legal studies, discussions and the wide-ranging research on the legal profession. However, for the relationship of the legal profession to society at large and to their clients, their legal culture and factors influencing these issues see Aitkenhead, Burrows, Jagtenberg and Örücü, 1988: chs 1, 3, 5, 6 and 7.

with other Member States. Moreover, The Netherlands is a civilian jurisdiction and Scotland, though a mixed jurisdiction, more akin to the common law. These hypotheses had to be tested. The survey would throw light on such issues via a carefully constructed questionnaire. Conversely, there were similarities too, such as historical links and similar geographical size.

The research project started with hypotheses. The underlying anticipated outcomes were: (i) Dutch lawyers would perceive greater relevance of European Community law for their practices than their Scottish counterparts; (ii) as a consequence, legal education received by lawyers in The Netherlands would place greater emphasis on European law than did legal education in Scotland; (iii) as a further consequence, Dutch lawyers would be more aware of areas of law where Community law would arise; (iv) the Dutch lawyers would come across problems relating to Community law more often; and (v) therefore, they would find ways of keeping up to date with developments in European law and adopt strategies for dealing with issues as they arose. Taking all these factors into account, it was expected that the Dutch lawyers would have more positive attitudes to European law and towards the Community in general (Aitkenhead, Burrows, Jagtenberg and Örücü, 1988: 16–17). In addition it was felt desirable to find the reason why a rather limited number of cases were referred from Scottish courts to the European Court of Justice for a preliminary hearing. Did issues related to the European Community law not arise? Or did the lawyers in Scotland fail to use European procedures for other reasons? For instance, in 1982 Dutch courts referred 21 cases, but the Scottish courts none.

It was obvious that only a crude assessment could be made, that the cause-effect linkages could not be readily determined, and therefore the results of the survey should not be read in isolation. Explanations from other sources were therefore sought when discussing the empirical results.

The Method

In this piece of research the comparative approach combined sociological analysis (through empirical observation of 'how things are' viewed within the frame of the survey) with comparative jurisprudence, or 'how things ought to be' according to the desired end—that is European integration. Comparative law was regarded both as an aspect of sociology of law and as a method of approaching the problem in hand. The study relied on expert knowledge in the areas of social science methodology, comparative law and European law; a vast amount of discussion and determination of hypotheses to be tested; a questionnaire reflecting the hypotheses; and finally, analysis of the findings.

Schlesinger asked:

> Should the classificatory scheme of one or the other national system be adopted? Or should one try to create a new system of classification by merging or compromising between some of the divergent categories found in the various systems? Or is it preferable to create a brand new set of categories for comparative purposes? (Schlesinger, 1961: 76).

At the macro-level, neither the Scottish nor the Dutch legal system had any difficulty in meeting the requirements of a number of definitions of a legal system used. This was so despite the fact that Scotland is a sub-system within a politically unitary state. A link to independent statehood has never been a prerequisite for the existence of a legal system. Moreover, the independence of the Scottish legal system is guaranteed by the 1707 Act of Union.

Therefore, it could confidently be said that the systems were comparable, and there was no need to resort to any of the paths suggested by Schlesinger in the quotation above, although there were a number of differences and a number of similarities between the legal systems, and obviously each system also had its own distinct features.

At the micro-level, the first and crucial problem was to decide on the functional comparability of advocates and *advocaten*. These are homonymous expressions but are not precisely equivalent. The equivalence materialised only when advocates and solicitors together and *advocaten* and *notarissen* together, were taken as the unit under survey. Here, the third path suggested in the above quotation by Schlesinger had to be followed. Thus, an 'umbrella' concept was to be created to cover both groups of actors, since synonyms and taxonomies were not suitable. Although the profession of a practising lawyer covers a wide spectrum of basic legal activities—ranging from litigation to non-contentious affairs, from court work to out of court assistance, from preparing documents to appearing in court, from training other professionals to giving moral advice—there is a difference in the way in which these activities are distributed between the specific professional groups. After studying what the existing institutions entailed, an umbrella concept had to be created on the basis of aggregate functions of all groups, for use as a problem-solving technique, and a definition elaborated that did not involve concepts exclusive to one of the jurisdiction. This is still a functional definition but wider than the existing individual concepts. An assessment of overall comparability was made of the four individual professions and since all institutions were sufficiently comparable, a meaningful umbrella concept 'the lawyers in private practice' could be ascertained to cover all.[9]

At the start each group was analysed by looking into educational requirements; in-service training; professional organisation, conduct and discipline; partnerships; size of firm; function and scope of practice; relationship with the client; and relationship with the other branch of the profession. Certain factors such as the relative size of each distinct group, the size of practice and the case-loads created quantitative problems despite the overall functional equivalence. These are inevitable differences and they were taken into account in analysing the results. For instance, advocates always deal with cases which have a counterpart in the

---

[9] This activity should also remind us of Zweigert and Kötz who advocate developing a special syntax and vocabulary, with concepts large enough to embrace the quite heterogeneous institutions which are functionally comparable—the higher concept being related to the function common to all (Zweigert and Kötz, 1998: 37–8).

case-loads of solicitors: these cases had to be counted twice when the case-loads of advocates and solicitors were added together. A similar relationship does not exist between *advocaten* and *notarissen*.

On the subject of areas of law to be covered in the questionnaire, that is, in the choice of concepts and categories or topics of law, again, functional equivalence was resorted to. Problems arose when it was realised that certain areas of law, such as law relating to transport or competition, had a narrower scope in Scottish law than in the Dutch. Therefore, direct translations or synonyms did not suffice. Here, the chosen path was the second one suggested by Schlesinger. This entailed a definitional effort from the outset of either redefining or delineating existing concepts in order to communicate across the barriers. Functional equivalents were sought. The questionnaires in two languages, English and Dutch, were directed to two different groups. Hence there would be no advantage in creating universal concepts, which, for the purposes of the questionnaire, would add new problems rather than solving existing ones. Areas of law that performed the same tasks, that is, institutions that served the same function, were looked at. Care was taken to identify functions in terms of system-relevance.

The Design of the Survey

It was decided that a large and representative group of lawyers should be approached in order to be reasonably certain that the results would reflect the characteristics of lawyers in both countries. Of all lawyers in private practice in the selected cities, a commercial centre, an industrial centre, a third major city and a rural area (Edinburgh, Glasgow, Aberdeen and Perth in Scotland; and Amsterdam, Rotterdam, the Hague and Leeuwarden in The Netherlands respectively) one in four were chosen at random. These were taken from a carefully defined population—the law society or bar list of members—excluding those not in private practice. This is a fairly large sample, so a high degree of confidence in the results was achieved.

The survey method was to send questionnaires to this randomly-chosen sample of lawyers. A high response rate was also needed.[10] Various precautions were taken to achieve this. The questionnaire was prepared so as to include questions that would throw light mainly on the frequency with which European Community law was encountered by lawyers; their education in European Community law; their knowledge of European Community law; and the attitude they had towards European Community law and the European Community. Additional issues such as whether they had studied comparative law during their degree course, the level to which they specialised in European Community law, and background information as to their qualifications and experience were also sought. Furthermore,

---

[10] For the details of the survey methodology employed and the theoretical discussion related to hypothesis-testing and the choices, see Aitkenhead, Burrows, Jagtenberg and Örücü, 1988: 65–95.

information was gathered as to the sex of the respondents, number of years in practice, and the size of their firms.[11]

The overall hypothesis that lawyers in The Netherlands are more involved with Community law was to be tested by posing appropriate questions. All the questions proposed by the members of the team had to be corrected or approved by the social scientist member of the team, to ensure that they were not leading questions. The strands of evidence obtained were not, however, directly concerned with the day-to-day activities of the lawyers. Additional hypotheses were related to issues surrounding the education of the lawyers and their attitude towards this education: Scottish lawyers were less well educated in European Community law than their Dutch counterparts. They therefore had more negative attitudes, and read fewer journals to keep themselves informed.

The Questionnaire

The Construction

Since mail surveys are regarded as inferior to interviews, Dillman's Total Design Method (TDM), a classic work on survey design and implementation (Dillman: 1978), was followed step-by step in order to maximise the response rate. One of the assumptions of this procedure is that people's behaviour is motivated by the benefits they expect to achieve from behaving in particular ways. The costs such as effort, time, incurring negative feelings of social disapproval and so on, have to be counterbalanced (exchange theory). The sample is more likely to respond to a mail survey, for instance, if they perceive the benefits of doing so. Therefore, the cost of responding was minimised by including self-addressed envelopes. The rewards of responding were maximised by making the answering process easy, allowing them also to make comments and promising them that they would receive the results of the research, establishing trust that the reward would be delivered.[12] Follow-up letters were also sent after one, four and seven weeks. A 70 per cent response rate was achieved in The Netherlands and an 80 per cent response rate in Scotland. A third of the respondents wanted the results to be posted to them.

The Content

The questions from the Scottish version of the questionnaire are provided below. There were 23 questions, some with three optional answers to be circled, such as 'unimportant', 'important' and 'extremely important'; 'not at all useful', 'useful' and 'extremely useful'; or 'are sufficiently knowledgeable', 'are not sufficiently knowledgeable' and 'don't know'.

---

[11] It was clear that the sample, like the legal profession at large, was predominantly male. Most had had several years in practice and very few had a post-graduate degree in law.

[12] See for details of the aspects, recommendations and the rationale of our questionnaire construction and implementation Table 4.2, Aitkenhead, Burrows, Jagtenberg and Örücü, 1988: 73–6.

Questions 1–4 were designed to ascertain the views of the respondents concerning the teaching of European Community Law (ECL).

1. How important do you feel it is for the legal profession that ECL is taught in Scottish Universities?
2. How useful do you feel it is for lawyers practising in Scotland today to have a good knowledge of ECL?
3. On the whole, do you think that lawyers practising in Scotland today are, or are not, sufficiently knowledgeable about ECL to recognise the legal implications raised by United Kingdom membership of the EC?
4. On the whole, do you think that members of the judiciary in Scotland today are, or are not, sufficiently knowledgeable about ECL to cope with the issues raised by United Kingdom membership of the EC?

Questions 5–8 concerned their education in law.

5. When you were studying for your university degree(s) and for your professional qualification(s), which of the areas listed below did you study? How much consideration was given to EC aspects of each area? (The areas cited were agricultural law; taxation; criminal law; monopolies and mergers; company law; family law; immigration law; consumer protection/product liability; employee/employer relations; social security law; conveyancing; copyright, patents and trademarks; law relating to customs and excise; law relating to transport; wills; and evidence and procedure).
6. Have you studied any of the following aspects of ECL? (Institutional law; Judicial remedies; Substantive law; other).
7. Which of the following, if any, would you like to see made available to lawyers practising in Scotland today? (A basic course in ECL; A refresher course in ECL; Seminars in practical topics of ECL; other).
8. When you were studying to qualify as a lawyer, was consideration given to comparative law? (In no course; In some courses; In all courses; If in some courses, please specify).

The next six questions relate to finding out the effect of ECL on the working lives of lawyers.

9. In the course of your practice, in the last five years, have you had occasion to visit another country for professional reasons connected with ECL? For the purposes of this question, assume that Scotland and England are separate countries (Yes/No. If yes, specify the country and approximate number of visits).
10. In which of the following areas might you expect there to be an aspect of ECL? (The list produced is the same as in question 5).
11. For the year 1 January, 1982 to 1 January, 1983, please indicate in the columns below the approximate number of cases you dealt with involving each of the areas of law listed; the approximate number of cases in each

area where an aspect of ECL was raised. (The list produced is again the same as in question 5).

12. In the year 1 January, 1982 to 1 January, 1983 which, if any, of the following journals have you consulted: to keep yourself generally informed on ECL and/or, to obtain information relevant to specific cases you have dealt with where an aspect of ECL was involved? (11 journals were given and five additional slots were provided for others).

13. If a client were to come to you with a case in which you suspect ECL was involved, how would you deal with such as case? (The list of courses of action was: (1) Deal with it yourself. (2) Deal with it in consultation with a specialist. (3) Send it to a specialist in another firm in the same city. (4) Send it to another firm in Scotland. (5) Send it to another firm in London. (6) Other, please specify).

14. This question aims at finding the differences in working practices, if any, between cases where an aspect of ECL is raised and those where it is not. If you have never dealt with a case involving ECL, please go straight to question 15. In those cases you deal with yourself or in consultation with a specialist, in which an aspect of ECL is raised, do you find that: (1) You have to do more research. (2) You need more consultations with clients. (3) You need to travel outside Scotland. (4) You encounter language problems. (5) You have increased financial outlay. (6) None of these. (7) Other, please specify.

The next few questions are to ascertain the respondent's opinion on ECL.

15. Please indicate whether you agree or disagree with each of the following nine statements (Agree/disagree/no opinion are the options): (1) I would welcome moves to harmonise laws within the European Community. (2) I think it is easy to keep pace with developments in ECL. (3) In my view it is difficult to gain access to information regarding ECL. (4) In my opinion the relationship between ECL and domestic law is too complex. (5) I find it difficult to appreciate the merits of ECL because it is so different from my own domestic system. (6) I believe that European integration is a good thing for Scotland. (7) I would welcome moves to encourage free movement of lawyers within the EC. (8) I fear that the influence of ECL will adversely affect the integrity of the Scottish legal system. (9) In my opinion ECL is more relevant to the legal profession in other EC countries than it is to the legal profession in Scotland.

16. In proceedings in which an aspect of ECL is raised, the case is not always referred to the European Court of Justice. Why do you think this is so? (The options were: (1) Unacceptable additional delays may arise. (2) Unacceptable additional costs may be incurred. (3) Judges and tribunal chairmen prefer to decide issues on the basis of domestic law. (4) Don't know. (5) Other.)

17. Fewer cases have gone to the European Court of Justice from Scotland than from The Netherlands. Why do you think this is so? (More than one option can be circled: (1) Scotland joined the EC later than the Netherlands. (2) ECL issues arise less often. (3) The bench is conservative. (4) There are anti-European feelings amongst the legal profession. (5) The legal profession is not sufficiently knowledgeable about ECL. (6) There is no tradition of uniformity of interpretation in the UK. (7) Don't know. (8) Other.)

Finally, some questions were about the respondents to help interpret the results of the survey:

18. How long have you been practising as a lawyer?
19. How many partners are there in your firm?
20. How many assistants are there in your firm?
21. How many trainees are there in your firm?
22. Of which of the following are you a member? (The Scottish Lawyers European Group; The Solicitors European Group; The Young Lawyers European Group; The International Bar Association).
23. Please specify your academic and professional qualification(s) with date(s). (Options were Degree(s), diploma(s), professional qualification(s)).

Are there any further comments you wish to make on the matters dealt with in this questionnaire? If so, please use this space for that purpose (a full page was left).

III. THE RESULTS

There were three clear aims behind the project. The first was to examine the impact of membership of the European Community on the legal professions of the two jurisdictions. The second aim was educational. It was hoped that the distribution of questionnaires to a large sample of the legal profession would generate or stimulate their interest in European Community law (ECL), make them more aware of the possibilities it afforded, act as a gentle reminder that membership of the Community has implications for them, and lead them to examine the gaps in their own knowledge. The third aim, also educational, was related to work done in the universities. Was legal education preparing prospective lawyers for practice and the needs of the day?

Considering these overall aims, it can be said that a great deal of information was obtained about the education of the lawyers sampled, their attitude to ECL, the frequency and nature of their work in ECL and any tendency to specialise in particular areas of law. In addition to increasing knowledge, the project had some success in improving university teaching, in that adjustments were made to teaching both European and Comparative Law in Glasgow University and in Erasmus Universiteit, Rotterdam. A joint study programme was initiated in 1986 between these two universities specifically on the topic of the legal profession in European integration. The course was funded by the European Community and entailed the exchange of students between the two countries, allowing them to work in legal practices in their host countries. The hope was that the results obtained from the survey would be useful in teaching future generations of students to see themselves as part of a wider legal environment and to show them how they could critically evaluate their own contribution to the development of their legal cultures.

However, some weaknesses of the questionnaire also became apparent, not least that it failed to address certain problems that were subsequently thought to be of importance. Furthermore, it is difficult to measure the degree of 'consciousness raising' that might have been achieved. Also, there is no guarantee that the results were read, although they were available for those interested.

As to the particular hypotheses: it was predicted that Scottish lawyers would deal with fewer ECL cases than their Dutch counterparts. This prediction was strongly upheld in every area of law. It was clear that there was much greater involvement with ECL cases in The Netherlands than there was in Scotland. This finding was so overwhelmingly powerful that it could confidently be said that this reflected a real difference in the workloads (Aitkenhead, Burrows, Jagtenberg and Örücü, 1988: 82–4).

Another hypothesis was that a smaller proportion of lawyers in Scotland had studied ECL than was the case in The Netherlands.[13] Here it was important to distinguish those who studied law before 1957 (the year the European Economic Community was founded) in The Netherlands and 1972 (the year the United Kingdom joined the European Economic Community) in Scotland. In addition, each area of law was examined separately. Once again the hypothesis was clearly supported. In every area of law except immigration law, a higher proportion studied its European Community aspects in The Netherlands than in Scotland. However, it was also discovered that the education in ECL did not meet the needs of practising lawyers in either jurisdiction (Aitkenhead, Burrows, Jagtenberg and Örücü, 1988: 84–6 and 96–110).

The hypothesis that the Dutch lawyers would be more knowledgeable in ECL was derived by the investigators from their knowledge of those areas where ECL was involved most fully and those where it was hardly involved. The strategy adopted for assessing knowledge was a fairly crude one and therefore the results here were regarded as a tentative exploratory step. Omissions (failing to include a 'relevant' category) and commissions (inclusion of 'irrelevant' areas into the 'relevant' category) were looked for. Less knowledgeable lawyers were expected to commit more such errors. This hypothesis was not successfully proven and here it was concluded that interviewing as a technique would be more useful, as possibly the questions asked were open to a number of interpretations. In the face of such difficulties, it was decided not to draw too many firm conclusions from the results gained (see Aitkenhead, Burrows, Jagtenberg and Örücü, 1988, 87–90).

---

[13] See Table 4.5 in Aitkenhead, Burrows, Jagtenberg and Örücü, 1988: 85; and see also Aitkenhead, Burrows, Jagtenberg and Örücü, 1986.

The most important hypothesis on trial was the one on attitudes. What was clear from the results was that, for every attitude statement, a higher proportion of the Dutch lawyers showed a positive attitude and for every statement except one (that relating to the difficulty of obtaining information about ECL) a lower proportion of Dutch lawyers showed a negative attitude. Thus the hypothesis was strongly supported (see Aitkenhead, Burrows, Jagtenberg and Örücü, 1988: 90–91 and 111–27).

In the analysis, the results obtained from each hypothesis were also pitched to the others. Then some deviations were noted. For example, when the hypothesis that education and attitudes are linked was examined, it was found that although the Dutch sample had much more positive attitudes and more education in ECL than the Scottish sample, a direct test of the hypothesis within each sample revealed no relationship between the two whatsoever. Some explanations could be offered: It could be that legal education does not influence the way lawyers think about ECL and European integration. There may also be a problem with the size of the sample, caused by having too few lawyers who had had extensive training in ECL. Thus, the true nature of the relationship between education and attitudes was difficult to reveal. It is also possible that lack of exposure to ECL in practice may have more to contribute to attitudes than education. It might also be that the Scottish lawyers feel that their legal system is more under threat from ECL because, ever since the 1707 Act of Union with England, the Scottish legal system is a source of pride related to a feeling of independence, and thus something to be preserved and protected from outside influences. The Dutch have already been involved in other integration processes, such as within the Benelux.

The implications of the findings gave some cause for alarm for the process of European integration. It was clear from the findings that lawyers felt somewhat distant from the European legal system, they had difficulties in gaining access to information, they believed that the inter-relationship between ECL and their domestic law was too complex, and they found it difficult to keep pace with developments. For example, nearly half the lawyers in both countries thought that the reason why there were few referrals to the European Court of Justice was because unacceptable delays might arise, and nearly half in Scotland, and around a quarter in The Netherlands, thought that unacceptable additional costs might be an inhibiting factor. In both countries around 40 percent felt that judges and tribunal chairmen have a preference for deciding cases on the basis of domestic law.

However, considering the conservatism of legal systems and lawyers who operate them, it might be argued that, given time, lawyers in all jurisdictions of the European Community would come to terms with the provisions of the ECL and eventually accept Brussels and Luxembourg as essential sources of law.

Two levels of problems were indicated by the study: those at an institutional level and those at a personal level. Problems at the institutional and personal levels are, of course, related and can to some extent be explained by examining the traditional patterns of the national legal systems. The study clearly demonstrated a certain lack of harmony between the aspirations of the European Community and rhetoric of European integration, and the experiences of lawyers in day-to-day practice. Many explanations can be offered for this but would involve a great deal of speculation and cannot be offered with any certainty. It was felt that they should, however, be explored further to provide the full picture of how law and lawyers can contribute to the process of European integration.

The subject has not lost its relevance today, and similar empirical and theoretical research should be carried out in the new Member States of the European Union. In this, the project discussed can be used as a starting point or as a template, with refinements reflecting more recent developments in research techniques and methods of in-context analysis. The problems are all the more acute since the European Union is enlarging with serious cultural implications and Community law is increasing in both importance and scope affecting major areas of domestic law today. In certain areas it is even taking the place of domestic law or is being superimposed on it or enmeshed with it.

QUESTIONS FOR DISCUSSION

1. Select a topic and set up a hypothetical research project. Justify your choice of the topic, the legal systems, the membership of your research team, your research design and methodology. Formulate at least three hypotheses you would like to test and the results you expect, with reasons.
2. If you were approached by your government to carry out a piece of comparative law research to facilitate harmonisation of family law especially related to the area of do-it-yourself-divorce in the European Union, but also looking at the problem in a culturally wider context, what kind of methodology would you use? What kind of problems would you expect to come across? And how would you propose to solve these?
3. 'There is no standard comparative law methodology: the method depends on the researcher's purpose'. Assess this statement with examples.

BIBLIOGRAPHY AND FURTHER READING

Aitkenhead, M, Burrows, N, Jagtenberg, R and Örücü, E (1985) 'Advocaat en Europees Recht: Kwantitatieve Praktijkgegevens, Specialisatie en Opleiding' 21 *Advocatenblad* 501.
—— (1985) 'European Law and the Practitioner' *Journal of the Law Society of Scotland* 270.
—— (1986) 'Education on Community Law in Scotland and the Netherlands' *The Law Teacher* 79.
—— (1988) *Law and Lawyers in European Integration: A Comparative analysis of the education, attitudes and specialisation of Scottish and Dutch lawyers* (Rotterdam, Mededelingen van her Juridisch Instituut van de Erasmus University Rotterdam No 43).
Boele-Woelki, K (2002) 'Comparative Research-Based Drafting of Principles of European Family Law' in M Faure, J Smits and H Schneider (eds), *Towards a European Ius Commune in Legal Education and Research* (Antwerp-Groningen, Intersentia).

Bussani, M (1998) 'Current Trends in European Comparative Law: The Common Core Approach' 21 *Hastings International and Comparative Law Review* 785.

Dillman, DA (1978) *Mail and Telephone Surveys* (New York, Wiley).

Hondius, E (2003) 'Towards a European Ius Commune: The Current Situation in Other Fields of Private Law' in K Boele-Woelki (ed), *Perspectives for the Unification and Harmonisation of Family Law in Europe* (Antwerp-Oxford-New York, Intersentia).

Schlesinger, RB (ed) (1968) *Formation of Contracts: a Study on the Common Core of Legal Systems* (Dobbs Ferry, Oceana Publications).

—— (1961) 'The Common Core of Legal Systems, An Emerging Subject of Comparative Study' in KH Nadelmann, AT Von Mehren, and JN Hazard, (eds), *XXth Century Comparative and Conflicts Law: Legal Essays in Honor of Hessel E. Yntema* (Leyden, AW Sijthoff).

Zweigert, K and Kötz, H (1998) *An Introduction to Comparative Law*, 3rd edn (trans) T Weir (Oxford, Clarendon Press).

Index

Lightning Source UK Ltd.
Milton Keynes UK
UKOW020021250112

185992UK00001B/9/P